■ THE STUDY OF PHILOSOPHY

■ THE STUDY

ROWMAN & LITTLEFIELD

OF PHILOSOPHY

A TEXT WITH READINGS

SEVENTH EDITION

Andrew Pessin and S. Morris Engel

Lanham • Boulder • New York • London

Published by Rowman & Littlefield
A wholly owned subsidiary of The Rowman & Littlefield Publishing Group, Inc.
4501 Forbes Boulevard, Suite 200, Lanham, Maryland 20706
www.rowman.com

Unit A, Whitacre Mews, 26-34 Stannary Street, London SE11 4AB

British Library Cataloguing in Publication Information Available

Library of Congress Cataloging-in-Publication Data
Pessin, Andrew, 1962– author.
  The study of philosophy: a text with readings / Andrew Pessin and S. Morris Engel. —7th Edition.
    pages cm
  Includes bibliographical references and index.
  ISBN 978-1-4422-4282-1 (pbk.)— ISBN 978-1-4422-4283-8 (electronic)
  1. Philosophy—Introductions. I. Engel, S. Morris, 1931– author. II. Title.
  BD21.E6 2015
  100—dc23   2014042261

■ PART III PHILOSOPHY'S MAIN QUESTIONS

CHAPTER SIX Ethics: What Are We Like, and What Should We Do?   135

CHAPTER SEVEN Religion: The Nature and Existence of God   173

CHAPTER EIGHT Epistemology and Metaphysics: The Rationalists   215

CHAPTER NINE Epistemology and Metaphysics: 257
The Empiricists and Kant

PART IV CONTEMPORARY DIRECTIONS

CHAPTER TEN Twentieth to Twenty-First Century Developments   307

MANY STUDENTS APPROACH their first introductory course in philosophy with eagerness and anticipation, assuming that philosophy deals with the big questions of existence. In fact it does, but (they soon learn) it also deals with medium and little questions too, all of which are ultimately *parts* of the big questions of existence. In this book we have aimed to get that point across in a manner that is both accessible yet not oversimplified. To achieve this it has seemed to us that the best way is simply to tell the story of philosophy.

This book thus begins with a discussion of the nature and scope of the discipline. Philosophy, this first chapter explains, is a critical examination of our basic values and beliefs. It attempts to discover, by means of careful reasoning and argument, what sort of life is best worth living and which ideals are most worth pursuing. It attempts to answer the following fundamental questions: What sort of world is it that we inhabit? Is it a world that is basically friendly or unfriendly to us?

> We do not go into this merely to be titillated by nice arguments or caught up in playing intellectual games. We are trying to find those things that will enhance our understanding of life, and even ennoble our minds and make our hearts better. It is really not too much to think that philosophy has this power.
>
> —**Richard Taylor** (1919–2003)

And what sorts of beings are we, and what should our purpose be? How do we know about our world and ourselves? And how much confidence can we have in this kind of knowledge?

But how did the discipline begin? And where? Who were the first philosophers, and what were some of their first questions? This is the subject of the second chapter. It tells the story of how the first philosophers, without any instruments or scientific traditions to aid them, came to ask the most fundamental question about the physical universe: What is the basic stuff that it is all made of? The chapter explores their struggles with this question, the difficulties that confronted them, their sometimes bold and brilliant resolutions of these difficulties, and the answer they arrived at—one that, in its essentials, is still accepted by science today.

But is reason's purpose only to discover the secrets of nature? Isn't humankind itself a secret? And reason, too, whose possession distinguishes humans from all other beings in the world—what is it for? The person who turned philosophy's attention to these questions—and who earned the title of "father of philosophy" as a result—was Socrates, a truly remarkable man. Chapter 3 gives an account of his life, his method of philosophizing, the nature of his teaching, and his tragic execution at the hands of the worried authorities. It also introduces us to one of the greatest philosophers of all time, his student Plato, whose dialogues about Socrates rank among the great literature of Western society.

But if philosophy attempts to use reason to gain an understanding of the world and of ourselves, what precisely can be said about reason itself? When can we know we have reasoned correctly and when not? What are the basic concepts and principles of good reasoning? These questions are taken up in part II of the text, concerned with the discipline of logic, one first founded by Plato's own great student, Aristotle.

Having sketched what philosophy is, where and how it began, who initially gave it direction, and what its main method is, we turn in part III to the more detailed study of some of its specific subject areas. We start in chapter 6 with ethics, concerned with questions such as How should we live? What is a good human life? Which sorts of actions are good or right to do, and which are bad or wrong? We survey answers to these questions from Aristotle, from the great eighteenth-century German philosopher Immanuel Kant, and the late nineteenth-century British thinkers Jeremy Bentham and John Stuart Mill. These thinkers have surprisingly different perspectives on these questions, perspectives which remain very much in play in the twenty-first century.

In chapter 7 we then turn to philosophical approaches to the nature and existence of God. We survey some of the famous proofs for God's existence, along with some possible objections to those proofs. We then explore what philosophers have had to say about God's nature, about some of His possible properties, such as omnipotence (power), omniscience (knowledge), and goodness. Does God's great power mean He can create contradictory things, like round squares and married bachelors? Does His knowing everything, including the future, conflict with our having free will? Most importantly, there's the problem of evil: Does the existence of so much evil in the world challenge God's goodness, or even His existence?

Chapters 8 and 9 bring us to the "early modern" period of philosophy, the seventeenth and eighteenth centuries. Here we learn how the famous French thinker René Descartes developed brand new theories of the nature of physical matter and of mind, dramatically influencing thinkers over the following two centuries and to this very day. We learn about the great rationalists, Benedict Spinoza and G. W. Leibniz, who stress the role of reason in generating knowledge, and about the very strange theories of the world they developed. We learn about the great empiricists, John Locke, George Berkeley, and David Hume, whose stress on sensory experience in generating knowledge led them to extremely *different* theories of the world both from the rationalists and from each other. The chapter concludes with the work of Immanuel Kant, said to have "synthesized" rationalism and empiricism with his own self-declared "revolution" in understanding the manner in which human minds come to know the world.

Part IV brings us up to date, with some twentieth- and twenty-first-century developments in philosophy. Chapter 10 presents the famous movement of existentialism, in which thinkers from very different orientations grappled with the question of the meaning (or better, meaninglessness) of life. We then examine some ways in which contemporary philosophers have continued the conversations started in our earlier chapters. In ethics, thinkers focus carefully on just what we mean when we call certain actions *good* or *bad*, arguing (you may be surprised to learn) that we literally mean *nothing* in our moral discourse. With respect to religion, we survey new developments in proofs of God's existence, and examine Alvin Plantinga's analysis of the proper relationship between science and religion. (Rather than see them in conflict, he argues that the success of science actually supports the truth of religion.) With respect to the theory of knowledge, one twentieth-century development reveals that despite twenty-five centuries of philosophical reflection, still no one really has a clear definition of what knowledge is. The chapter concludes with some contemporary efforts to understand the mind and its relation to matter, and suggests that the theories bequeathed to us by Descartes are still very much alive.

Chapter 11, finally, takes us through some contemporary moral problems. We live in a complicated world, with complicated moral questions about almost everything—matters of health and medicine, life and death, sexuality and gender, crime, justice, and punishment, the boundaries between public and private, between regulation and liberty, matters of the climate and environment, domestic and global inequalities, and so on. Many philosophical questions are abstract but these are quite concrete, and pressing, and you can't avoid getting your hands dirty here: you have to have opinions on them, since any behavior you choose in fact reflects an opinion. In this chapter, then, we survey some general questions in medical ethics, then look closely at the controversial work of Australian moral philosopher Peter Singer, who has galvanized debates with his work on animal rights, the sanctity of life, and global poverty.

Hopefully by the time you've completed the journey you will have a sense of how rich and deep philosophical questions are, of how much they matter whether they are abstract or concrete, and, despite philosophy's sometimes reputation, of how much you can gain by devoting some of your energy to studying them. For philosophy will help you develop your ability to think clearly and methodically, to reason rigorously, to distinguish between better and worse arguments; it will help you learn to think deeply and patiently, to go past the surfaces of issues and penetrate to their core, to cut through the sheen of emotion and find the truth beneath. Taking a few philosophy courses will also hone your writing skills, as you learn how to carefully present a line of thought, entertain problems or objections to it, and then deal with

> Philosophy is to be studied, not for the sake of any definite answers to its questions . . . but rather for the sake of the questions themselves; because these questions enlarge our conception of what is possible, enrich our intellectual imagination and . . . because, through the greatness of the universe which philosophy contemplates, the mind also is rendered great, and becomes capable of that union with the universe which constitutes its highest good.
>
> —**Bertrand Russell** (1872–1970)

them. These are skills that will serve you well no matter what you pursue in life, personally or professionally, whether in the arts, humanities, sciences, or business. Many surveys in fact show that employers are often keenly interested in hiring philosophy majors, for anyone capable of completing a major in the field must have demonstrated the abilities to think, reason, and write well.

But even aside from these practical benefits, philosophy can change the way you think about and interact with the world around you. You will grapple intelligently with such profound and important questions as what a good life should be, what society should look like, what and whom you can trust. Your horizons will expand as you realize that even the simplest things can provoke the deepest questions, once you start thinking about them. You will never take anything for granted again, but the world will, for you, be perpetually brand new.

And finally, hopefully, you will find that doing philosophy is simply just fun.

Andrew Pessin
S. Morris Engel
January 2015

PART I

PHILOSOPHY AND ITS BEGINNINGS

FINDING HIMSELF ONE DAY at the Olympic games, the ancient Greek thinker Pythagoras (570–490 B.C.E.) observed that three classes of people were present. First, many people had come to trade and barter. *Lovers of gain*, he called them. Then there were the people who had come to participate in the games in the hope of winning fame and fortune for themselves and their cities. Pythagoras called them the *lovers of honor*. Finally, there were those who had come simply to watch. Pythagoras called them the *lovers of the spectacle*.

It then occurred to Pythagoras, the story goes, that one can find these same three classes of people everywhere. There are, first, the vast majority of people, whose main object in life is to acquire as many material goods as possible. These are the lovers of gain. A second group, smaller than the first, contains those whose main goal is to achieve fame by distinguishing themselves in some pursuit. They are the lovers of honor. Finally, there is a third group, smaller even than the second, who do not care much for wealth or fame but whose main hope is to gain an understanding of this spectacle called life. Pythagoras thought a good name for these lovers of the spectacle was *philosophers*, a term literally meaning "lovers of wisdom." Including himself in this group, he went on to remark that it would not be appropriate to call them wise, for only God is wise, but they may at least call themselves lovers of wisdom. And thus the word **philosophy** was coined, or *love of wisdom*.

> The philosophy of one century is the common sense of the next.
>
> —Found in a fortune cookie

Although few since then have denied that philosophy is somehow connected with the love of and search for wisdom, philosophers have not found it easy to say exactly what "wisdom" is. Wisdom is not something achieved merely by discovering some new fact. In this respect philosophy is unlike science. The failure to solve a scientific problem lies, generally, in our inability to get at some missing piece of information. But this is not the reason that many philosophical problems have continued to elude us. It is not for the lack of some fact that philosophical problems escape solution. In many cases the trouble is that we already have too many facts.

It is like working at a massive jigsaw puzzle. Our difficulty assembling the puzzle does not normally lie in the fact that certain pieces are missing, but in the fact that we don't see how the (say) thousand little pieces we have all fit together. Adding another piece to the thousand would be of no help at all. What we need instead is a way of seeing the thing whole. Similarly, as the English philosopher John Wisdom (1904–1993) once put it, philosophy is not "knowledge of new fact" but "new knowledge of fact"—it is a deeper understanding of the facts we already have.

How do we go about getting at this deeper understanding of the facts? We do it by trying to see things not in isolation and separate but as they are connected and related in a larger whole of which they are merely parts. Seeing things whole in this way is to see them in proper perspective—

> Life can only be understood backwards; but it must be lived forwards.
>
> —**Søren Kierkegaard** (1813–1855)

and this is what wisdom is, both in philosophy and in life. That is why wisdom typically comes (if it does at all) only late in life, after much reflection and experience. For to see the true place and role of a thing requires that it be viewed from a distance and from different perspectives. And that takes time and maturity.

HOW PHILOSOPHY AND SCIENCE DIFFER

Ancient philosophical concerns laid the foundation for modern scientific inquiry, although at that time the political implications for investigating the natural order of things without appeal to the gods could be dire. The ancient Greek thinker Socrates (469–399 B.C.E.), for example, was sentenced to death for "impiety" because his society believed him to be a **natural philosopher**, that is, one who sought to understand how nature works in only natural (rather than supernatural) terms. A natural philosopher might conduct observations and extrapolate from them that (for example) lightning was a natural phenomenon with explainable origins that need not include invoking lightning-bolt-wielding Zeus. Such conclusions would increasingly erode the authority of the gods, slowly stealing from them one power after another. Consequently it was seen as a form of impiety.

From such beginnings grew the work of Aristotle (384–322 B.C.E.), the ancient Greek thinker whose systematic treatment of natural phenomena from flora and fauna to human-made political constitutions and languages is the ancestor of the empirical sciences. His categorization of natural objects (trees, birds, humans, rocks, etc.) bequeathed to the biological sciences the divisions of genus and species and the many subdivisions within those. His systematization of reasoning into syllogistic forms is invaluable to logic to this day. The Aristotelian categories of literary analysis are still among the fundamental forms of grammar, literary criticism, and dramatic review. And his analysis of different forms of political systems is no mere historical artifact but is taken into account even in the most current debates concerning political theory and practice.

Following Aristotle, philosophy slowly developed, fragmented, and gave birth to new disciplines. Thus, the physical sciences, the social sciences, and the political sciences all have their origin in the unified approach of philosophical inquiry. For this reason, philosophy is often seen as that discipline that is deeply interested in the interconnectedness of the several realms of scientific inquiry—in trying to "see things whole."

How do philosophers go about "seeing things whole"? They do so by enquiring not into the how or what of things but into their why. Let us, for example, take the question "Why are there natural evils in the world, such as earthquakes that devastate lives?" and note first how a scientist would answer it, then how a philosopher would do so.

An earth scientist might say to us, "Well, as far as earthquakes are concerned, the earth has a certain mantle around it and there are various breaks in it. People build cities over or near these breaks or 'faults,' and when the breaks widen, buildings collapse, kill their occupants, and bring death, misery, and suffering."

True as that may be, such an answer would scarcely satisfy the philosopher because we already understand well enough *how* that sort of evil comes about. In asking the question, we were not asking for the physical causes of those evils; we were asking the more general and basic question of why any such evils should exist at all, what their purpose is, how they might inform our understanding of the world.

It is in this respect that philosophy differs significantly from science. Philosophy tries to see things whole by asking questions that are more general than those of science, in the sense that their answers have far-reaching consequences for our understanding of ourselves and our world. A scientist, again, might be interested in the explanation of a certain phenomenon. He or she may spend a lifetime pursuing this problem and, if fortunate, may discover its cause, making an important contribution to our knowledge and perhaps our welfare. But while the philosopher would be interested in the discovery, he or she would ask a different set of questions, larger, more general questions. What counts as "explaining" a phenomenon? Must explanations always involve "causes"? Must causation always involve laws of nature? *Are* there even "laws" of nature, in the sense of necessary regularities?

Philosophy also tries to see things whole by asking questions that are concerned with how different sets of facts are related. Not only does the nature of the pieces of the puzzle pose a problem, but how they fit together does as well. The philosopher might thus ask, for example, whether if we indeed accept science's basic assumption that cause and effect govern all of nature, including human nature, we are truly justified in holding people legally and morally responsible for what they do. Like the problem of evil, this is a long-standing question in philosophy, one still largely unresolved. Because it exemplifies the general type of question (in contrast with the strictly factual type) so typical of philosophy, let us spend a few more moments on it.

Suppose that everything that happens in nature (of which we are a part) is governed by the law of cause and effect. Then it would seem that just as the stone Mike just threw cannot help hitting the window that it shatters (as a result of its being thrown) nor falling to the ground afterward (as the result of the force of gravity), so too Mike, given his particular background and nature, could similarly not help *throwing* the stone, shattering that window in the jeweler's store, and helping himself (say) to that enticing jewelry. Were our knowledge of human psychology as secure as our knowledge of physics, we could even have predicted the action in question. But then why should we hold him responsible for this action, when he was no more in control of it than the stone was for being thrown?

We are not looking for some further facts here, in asking this question. We are given the facts, about the causal laws governing nature. We're instead asking how the facts we already have impact various other beliefs we have, about human freedom and moral responsibility.

Philosophy's questions are nonfactual in a further way as well. Take, for example, the question "When does life begin?" which is central in the discussion of the issue of abortion. Although this looks like an ordinary empirical or scientific question, subject to "expert" opinion, it really is not. Perhaps a fertilized egg counts as alive, but what about the sperm and egg prior to conception? We think of single-celled amoebae as alive, so why not sperm cells, or other cells in the body? What about a virus: is it merely an inanimate machine that transfers its genetic material into living cells, or is it itself alive? What about strings of genetic material themselves, which seem quite focused on, and successful at, reproducing themselves? In cases like these we have all the biological facts before us; but left over is the philosophical question "What is it to be alive?," one whose answer depends on one's definition or understanding of "life," hence its difficulty. (We'll see in chapter 11 some discussion of the equally difficult question of just when "death" occurs.)

And such a question is difficult to resolve because unlike ordinary, empirical questions, which are answered either by observation or by experiment, this type of question often involves the weighing of values rather than merely facts. For example, we will probably be in no better position one hundred years from now than we are today in answering the vexing question "Should there be censorship in a free society?" And the reason again is that this is not simply an empirical or factual question. What is involved here are rights and values, which are very difficult to resolve. Where they are concerned, it is all too easy to go overboard, to adopt extremist views, to become blind to alternative perspectives—to give in to fanaticism. For, indeed, a fanatic is a person for whom one particular value ("life" or "free speech") is so precious, so all-important, that other values cease to matter. The philosophic approach is typically to resist such fanaticism, to try rather to see things in perspective and balance.

Our ordinary understanding of what philosophy is captures this accurately. When, for example, we say of someone that "He took his defeat philosophically," what we mean is that he did not allow himself to be destroyed by reversals of fortune, for he was able to keep it in the proper perspective. He did not allow that one incident (or that one value) to overshadow all the others, or the whole of his life.

HOW PHILOSOPHY AND RELIGION DIFFER

Having seen how science and philosophy differ in their approaches, let us see how philosophy and religion approach things differently by returning to the problem of evil (which we'll explore in more depth later). No one has expressed the problem more succinctly than the Greek philosopher Epicurus (341–270 B.C.E.), who put it as a dilemma: Is God willing to prevent evil but not able to do so? In that case He cannot be all powerful. Or is He is able but not willing to do so? In that case He is not benevolent but malevolent. But if He is both willing and able to prevent evil, whence comes evil? This problem is pressing, obviously, on anyone who wants to believe in the existence of a powerful and benevolent God.

Certainly, prior to the Middle Ages, philosophy and religion were often conjoined, so closely intertwined that they could not easily be separated. For early Catholic thinkers like St. Augustine (354–430 C.E.), the concepts and worldview inherited from the ancient Greek Plato (429–347 B.C.E.) provided the framework to systematize Catholic doctrines concerning God, humanity, sin, grace, and more.

During the medieval period, however, fissures began to appear between philosophy and religion. For St. Thomas Aquinas (1225–1274 C.E.), religion concerned the revelation of God as expressed in sacred texts and the careful study of that self-revelation, through the mediation of the Catholic Church. Thus, he conceived religion as a "top-down" field where God's revelation to humanity is the starting point. Philosophy for Aquinas, on the other hand, begins on the bottom and moves upward. It starts with the observation of natural phenomena, then proceeds, through reasoning, to extrapolate upward to knowledge of God. Thus, philosophy and religion are closely related but quite opposite in their approaches. One of Aquinas's concerns was whether, and in what ways, the two fields in fact could meet. Are all the truths of faith (or revelation) demonstrable, ultimately, from reasoning about the natural world? Or are there gaps, meaning that reasoning can only take us so far in our quest for personal salvation? (This question remains alive to this day in the alleged "conflict" between religion and science, to which we will turn in chapter 10.)

> A little philosophy makes a man an atheist; a great deal reconciles him to religion.
>
> —**Francis Bacon** (1561–1621)

If you separate religion and philosophy this way—relegating to religion the dictates of revelation and the faith required to believe them, and to philosophy the demand for rational explanation and demonstration before you believe anything—then the two fields will take very different approaches to matters involving God. Religion demands acceptance and belief, and philosophy demands explanation. Philosophy demands that God be *intelligible*, that He and His actions should make sense to us. To demand that is to demand that when things occur in the world, they *can* be made sense of—not merely by providing their causes but by providing an account of why the world in general was set up to arrive at those events. But lest you too quickly believe that philosophy is in the right, over religion, in making its demands here, be sure you ask, first, just why you think the world *must* be intelligible to us. Or if God exists, why He or His actions must be intelligible to us? Or is it perhaps the very height of presumption to demand that the world, or God, make sense—to *us*?

Philosophers interested in religion do make a strong go at making sense of the existence of evil in the world. In chapter 7 we'll explore a variety of philosophical approaches to the problem, allowing you to judge which, if any, succeed. If one does, then great. But if not, perhaps there is something to be said for the religious approach. If we cannot attain the illumination of knowledge perhaps we can acquire the consolation of belief.

Why *do* bad things happen to good people? Perhaps the most forceful response is still, after centuries, the one first enunciated in the Book of Job. Job, having lost all his possessions, his friends, and his wife and children and now afflicted with a painful disease, has removed himself from the city. Sitting on a refuse heap outside the city walls, he raises an accusing finger at God, demanding to know why this misery has been visited on him. In reply, God appears to Job and demands of him, "Where were you when I made all this?"—pointing to the stars, the earth, the heavens—the implication being that if He could do all that, then surely He could have prevented what has happened to Job; and if He did not prevent it, there was good reason for Him not to. Although this does not make Job's suffering any more intelligible to him, it perhaps makes it more acceptable. Indeed if God appeared to any one of us and gave us His personal assurance that everything was justified, and perhaps that everything would be all right, then we too might receive some needed consolation.

To accept such an answer, to believe it and trust in it, requires, of course, enormous faith. Perhaps very few of us have that much faith or are capable of it. No doubt most of us are like the man who fell over the edge of a cliff but was able to catch hold of a tree. He hollered, "Hey, can somebody up there help me?" A deep voice

Where Are We in the Universe?

We inhabit "a minor planet orbiting a very average star in the outer suburbs of a fairly typical spiral galaxy."

—**Stephen Hawking**, inaugural lecture: "Is the End in Sight for Theoretical Physics?"

answered, "This is God. I want you to follow My instructions. First, let go of the tree." At this the poor fellow's fear only increased, and he yelled back, "Is there anybody else up there?" That is not faith, certainly not the type religion says is necessary for understanding.

In summary, then, philosophy differs from religion in that it bases its conclusions primarily on reasoning and evidence and not, like religion, on appeal to revelation and sacred authority. Philosophy, unlike religion, wants to find out "what it's all about," using reason as its primary tool. This needn't mean that it must reach different conclusions than those offered in religion—as we'll see in chapter 7—just that it would reach them by different methods.

PHILOSOPHY'S THREE MAIN SUBJECT AREAS

We have seen that philosophy differs from science in asking questions that are more general, and its methods differ from those of religion in that they depend primarily on reason and evidence. We might then characterize philosophy, in its "love of wisdom," as the rational attempt to gain an overall understanding of ourselves and of the world we live in.

With those points in mind, it is traditional to divide philosophy into three main domains or subject areas. Along the way we will see that these domains are intimately related and sometimes overlap, but still these divisions are useful for a start.

Questions about the fundamental nature of the world as a whole fall into the domain called **metaphysics**. Here we explore such questions as What is the world like? What sorts of things exist, and what is their nature? Does God exist? Are minds or souls distinct from physical matter? Is the universe rational, purposive, evolving to some goal friendly to us and our needs? Or is it a nonrational, goalless thing, dead matter conforming to immutable law?

> According to Plato, man's life is a perpetual search for something he has not got, though without it he can never be at peace with himself. This something is "the good for man," "that which would make any man's life happy," if only he had the fruition of it. . . . Hence the need of "philosophy" for the direction of life; the whole object of philosophy is to lead us into a sure and abiding knowledge of good and evil, and so to make our judgment and the conduct which ensues from it, sound, and to restore the soul to health and unity with itself.
>
> —**A. E. Taylor** (1869–1945),
> *Platonism and Its Influence*

Of course your answers to metaphysical questions will often invite the response "And how do you *know* that?" Questions about knowledge constitute the domain called **epistemology**, from the Greek meaning "theory or study of knowledge." Here we explore such questions as What constitutes knowledge? Are there different kinds of knowledge? Is perception a reliable source of knowledge? What is the appropriate balance between perception and reasoning in obtaining knowledge? Are there limits to what can be known?

Finally there are questions about the sort of lives we should lead, which constitute the domain called **ethics**. What is a good life? How should we order our lives? What goals should we seek? Which actions are right or good, and which are wrong or bad?

These three areas, although representing the core of philosophy, do not exhaust the traditional interests of philosophy. For philosophers have also often been interested in exploring the foundations and concerns of other disciplines as well—of artists, scientists, historians, and so on. What is it that these people do, philosophers have asked, and what is its meaning? What are the methods, arguments, reasons, and presuppositions that lie at the foundations of their work, and how sound are they? These interdisciplinary interests you may well find reflected in the philosophy course offerings at larger universities, in courses such as Philosophy of Science, Philosophy of Art,

Philosophy of History, and so on. Indeed the highest degree you can earn in many fields of study is the Ph.D., or "Doctor of Philosophy": When you get a Ph.D. in physics or in history, you are thought to have mastered the deepest and hardest questions of the field in question—and are now a "philosopher" in that field!

This wide reach of philosophy sometimes makes the subject appear almost amorphous. But appearances can be deceiving, as philosophy itself will teach us in the course of this book. Everywhere, and ultimately, philosophy's concern is the same: To get at the deeper meaning of things, and to understand how they all fit together. And so Pythagoras was, perhaps, right: Philosophers are lovers of the spectacle—not there to profit from it, to participate in it, but simply to understand it.

PHILOSOPHY'S MAIN METHOD

Philosophy aims to understand, as we just remarked, but it also aims to do this in a particular manner: by the use of reason. While we will explore what this means throughout the whole book, and particularly in chapters 4 and 5, our introduction would not be complete without a few words here.

To proceed via reason is to proceed primarily via **argument**. As used in this sense, the word means not a quarrel (as when we "get into an argument") but a piece of reasoning in which one or more statements are offered as logical support for some other statement. By "logical support" we mean that the supporting statements provide reasons to believe that the supported statement is true. The statement being supported is called the **conclusion** of the argument. The reasons given in support of the conclusion are called **premises**. We may say, "This is so (conclusion) because that is so (premise)." Or, "This is so and this is so (premises), therefore that is so (conclusion)."

To make an argument, then, is to offer reasons to believe a particular conclusion. There are many styles and forms of argument, as we'll see, some of them very good, some of them fairly good, and some of them downright awful. What we aim for in making a good argument is that it should be **valid**, meaning that the conclusion in fact logically follows from the premises. And what *that* means, in turn, is this: that if the premises of the argument are true, the conclusion must be true. An **invalid argument** would be one where the premises may well be true and yet the conclusion turns out to be false.

Valid arguments can be hard to make, but invalid arguments are easy. The street is soaking wet, you offer as a premise; therefore it must have rained here recently. But the truth of the premise does not require the truth of the conclusion: the street may have been soaked by an opened fire hydrant, or a child playing with a hose.

One more important point. While *validity* refers to the correctness with which a conclusion is inferred from its premises, *truth* refers to whether those premises and conclusion accord *with the facts*. It is thus possible in logic to start with true premises but reach a false conclusion (because we reason badly with those premises, i.e., invalidly), *or* to reason correctly (validly) *without* reaching a true conclusion—because our premises are false. To put that differently, you can still make a valid argument starting from false premises. To say that the argument is valid is just to say that if the premises are (or *were*) true, the conclusion would have to be true; it is not to say that the premises in fact *are* true.

Here is a quick example: "Fred is the President of the Entire World, therefore Fred has the authority to tell everyone what to do." We may suppose this small argument is valid, for *were* Fred President of the World, he *would* have that authority: the conclusion follows from the premise. But of course, fortunately for us, Fred is not president, so the premise is false. So we have a valid argument despite its having a false premise.

The best, strongest arguments we aim for, then, are not merely valid ones, but valid ones with actually true premises. Such arguments are called **sound arguments**. What makes them so desirable is that the conclusion of a sound argument must be true, for it follows validly from its true premises.

When making arguments, or evaluating those of others, then, here are the questions to ask. First, are the premises of the argument in fact true? Premises are the foundation of an argument; if they are unreliable or shaky, the argument built on them will be no better. Second, does the conclusion logically follow from those true premises, that is, is the argument valid?

If the answers to both questions are yes, then the argument is sound—and a rational person must accept its conclusion.

SUMMARY

1. Philosophy literally means "love of wisdom." The word was coined by Pythagoras.

2. Philosophy differs from science in asking deeper, more general questions; in not seeking facts but in seeking how things all fit together; in exploring values and not just facts.

3. Philosophy differs from religion in demanding rational explanation and demonstration and not being satisfied with revelation and faith; in expecting that the world, and God, might be intelligible to us.

4. The three main subject areas of philosophy are metaphysics, epistemology, and ethics. In addition, philosophers explore some of the deeper questions in other disciplines, such as science, art, and history.

5. The main method of philosophy is to proceed by argument, preferably by valid argument, and even more preferably by sound argument.

KEY TERMS

argument
conclusion
epistemology
ethics
invalid argument
metaphysics

natural philosopher
philosophy
premise
sound argument
valid argument

REVIEW QUESTIONS

1. What is the origin of the term *philosophy*?
2. How does philosophical inquiry differ from scientific inquiry?
3. How are religion and philosophy different?
4. What are the three main subject areas of philosophy? What are some of the questions each area tries to answer?
5. What is the main method of philosophy?

■ Reading
"The Philosopher within You"

ANDREW PESSIN

From The 60-Second Philosopher *(Oxford, UK: Oneworld Publications, 2009), Chapter 1. Reprinted by permission.*

There's the legend of the fish who swam around asking every sea creature he'd meet, "Where is this great ocean I keep hearing about?" A pretty small legend, true—but one with a pretty big message.

We are very much like that fish.

For consider, it's hard to look at a newborn baby without thinking: what an incredible miracle. But when was the last time you looked at an adult and had the same thought? But why not? Every adult *was* a little baby; if the latter is a miracle then so is the former. But it never occurs to us to think this way for one simple reason: we're so used to seeing people that we stop reflecting on them.

Or you drop something, a spoon, and it falls to the floor. But why? Couldn't it, in theory, have remained floating in air or moved upwards? And *how* exactly does it fall to the floor, by "gravity"? There are no strings connecting the earth to the spoon. How can the earth pull on something from a distance, that it's not even attached to? Why don't we pause every time something drops and say: what an incredible miracle!

The most ordinary things contain a whole lifetime of questions, if only we are reminded to start asking them.

Children already know to ask these questions. Every answer you provide to one of their "Why?" questions just generates the next question. But we were all children once. What we need to do now is to let the child still within us—the philosopher within us—re-emerge. What we need now are a few seconds out of our ordinary conceptual habits. We need to take a cold wet plunge into the great deep ocean of thought.

It's time to start thinking.

The Pre-Socratics

PHILOSOPHY BEGAN in the coastal city of Miletus, near the Greek island of Samos, on the mainland of what is now Turkey. In the sixth century B.C.E., Miletus was a prosperous Greek city, founded two hundred years earlier by the Athenians. What strikes one about this and the many other famous centers of ancient Greek civilization is the way it was surrounded by water. Everywhere there was water, and water was everywhere.

The center of the world for the Greeks was a body of water—the Aegean Sea. On one side lay their European towns and cities; on the other side, their Asian settlements. In the middle were the many islands with their now famous names: Melos, Delos, Rhodes, Samos, Lesbos.

If the waters separated them within this great sea, the mountain ridges, carving the landscape into tiny, island-like plains, did the same for their inland centers. The paradox of diversity and unity, of isolation and community, that came to characterize these ancient Greeks was to no small degree a result of this curious geography.

Although the country was rugged and isolated, its climate was mild and hospitable, allowing its inhabitants to spend much of the year outdoors and in each other's company. In addition, the towns and cities on the coastal plains, although separated from each other, lay at the crossroads of the world, with Asia to the east, Europe to the west, and the ancient civilizations of the Near East to the south. The rational and skeptical spirit that came to characterize them was nourished by this exposure to these diverse cultures.

At first, life could not have been easy for the average person. The basic occupation was farming, and both the land and the primitive methods used to cultivate it produced small if any surpluses. Most people lived a short, dismal existence, the usual life span for men being thirty-five years. Because of the risks of childbearing, women's life expectancy was even shorter, and that of infants shorter still.

This harsh and uncertain life was reflected in their religion, dominated by gods whose decrees were as arbitrary and uncertain as the lives they were thought to control; gods whose bitter conflicts with each other spelled mostly trouble for those who worshipped them.

But with the development of industry and commerce, the situation of the people improved. By exporting such resources as marble, copper, iron, lead, and silver (and later such manufactured items as pottery, statuary, and textile goods), they were able to import what their own land could not produce. This commerce gave rise to an expanding population and for some a more prosperous existence. Prosperity gave birth to leisure, leisure to curiosity, and curiosity to science and philosophy.

Other peoples at different times and places had also achieved similar leisure; but science and philosophy only arose among these ancient Greeks. Why?

Aristotle tells us that it was the Greeks' "wonder" about their world that gave birth to science and philosophy. But surely that was not the whole answer. There were at least two other factors involved. First, the Greeks asked new questions, curious about new sorts of things. In the older civilizations the questions, of a religious kind, were concerned mainly with life in the hereafter. What others principally wanted to know was what that life was like and what they could do to make their journey to that other world a successful one. The Greeks, on the other hand, were interested in investigating *this* world and *this* life.

The Greeks also pursued this interest in a new way. They were the first people not merely to collect facts and knowledge but to attempt "systematizing" this knowledge. Take geometry, for example. Long before the Greeks, the ancient Egyptians knew many important facts about geometry. The construction of their pyramids and temples would have been impossible without them. But in the hands of the Egyptians, these facts remained merely scattered "observations" or "theorems." The Greeks were the first to try to *prove* these theorems, to try to find some basic and simple axioms from which all theorems could be deduced. The concept of proof, of achieving a system, of bringing separate theorems into a single framework, was what distinguished their approach from their predecessors'. Nor was there any immediate practical benefit to systematizing. As the first Greek historian Herodotus (484–425 B.C.E.) put it, the Greeks began to study these matters "for the sake of inquiry alone."

But despite their innovations, the early Greek thinkers were not able to start entirely afresh, with a completely clean slate. Although *generally* abandoning **supernaturalism** for **naturalism**—trying to explain events as arising not from the whim of the gods but from the workings of laws—they inherited several assumptions or "myths" from the past that continued to impact their thinking.

Four basic assumptions restricted their thinking. They believed, first, that the world was initially in a state of chaos but then that some god (or gods) brought order out of the chaos by fashioning the earth, the sun, the stars, and so forth. Second, they believed that the natural world, now so secured, was just and fair and would continue to be so as long as each god (who was given a different portion of the universe to rule over) refrained from upsetting the balance by impinging upon some other god's territory. Third, they believed that strife and tension were present, along with order. However, this tension (as between such opposing forces as Night and Day, Winter and Summer, Love and Hatred) never went too far, with one force permanently triumphing over the other. Were that to happen, chaos would again set in; but they were certain it wouldn't happen. They believed, finally, that the world, so fashioned and so sustained, was composed of four different kinds of stuff (or **elements**): earth, air, fire, and water.

Before considering the limits these assumptions imposed upon the first philosophers—known as the **pre-Socratics** because they came before the great philosopher Socrates—we should note a much more subtle limit or boundary, the linguistic boundary. It has become commonly accepted in our day that our language and its uses vastly affect thought and its possibilities. At the start of the pre-Socratic era, Greece was still largely an oral culture. This meant that information was not written and read but spoken and heard. A book can be placed on a shelf and retrieved later, but without the written word, memory must play an enormous role.

To facilitate better memorization, Greek works in this period were composed almost exclusively in poetry, not prose, with rhythm and rhyme. The basic units of the Greek language became not single words but groups of recurring words. Lastly, much of the vocabulary that is necessary for serious philosophical consideration was simply lacking. Thus, we must credit these early thinkers with fighting not only restrictive cultural frameworks but also restrictive linguistic frameworks.

THE PROBLEM OF BEING

Miletus was home to the first thinkers to be considered philosophers, known as the **Milesian school**, marked by their interest in discovering the fundamental nature of the matter of the world: Thales, Anaximander, and Anaximenes.

When they reproached Thales because of his poverty, as though philosophy were no use, it is said that, having observed through his study of the heavenly bodies that there would be a large olive crop, he raised a little capital while it was still winter, and paid deposits on all the olive presses in Miletus and Chios, hiring them cheaply because no one bid against him. When the appropriate time came there was a sudden rush of requests for the presses; he then hired them out on his own terms and so made a large profit, thus demonstrating that it is easy for philosophers to be rich, if they wish, but that it is not in this that they are interested.

—**Aristotle** (384–322 B.C.E.), *Politics*

Thales (c.624–c.546 B.C.E.)

The person credited with being the first philosopher was Thales (pronounced "Thay-leez"), who, as historians like to put it, "flourished" in Miletus around 585 B.C.E. This is not the year of his birth but rather the year in which he predicted that an eclipse of the sun would occur; he was apparently off by only some minutes. Although this was a remarkable feat, Thales is remembered not so much for this as for the question he was the first to raise and the answer he proposed to it.

If we look around us, what strikes us, as it must have struck Thales, is the enormous profusion and variety of things. Perhaps, Thales wondered, this infinite variety all around us is just different forms of the same basic and fundamental stuff? And if so, he asked, what is the nature of that stuff out of which all of this variety arose? Looking around him once more, the answer seemed almost inevitable: it all arose from water.

Why choose water as the prime element? It is not difficult to imagine what may have played a role in his choice. Water was, first, one of the elements singled out by tradition; second, there was a lot of it around; third, it was present in all living things and was essential to life; and fourth, it was capable of taking on the form of the other three traditional elements. Water freezes and so becomes a solid ("earth"), it evaporates into a mist and becomes "air," and it is used by the sun (which is a "fire") as a kind of fuel (when the

THALES

sun "draws water to itself" or "burns off the mist"). So perhaps water was the fundamental element out of which the other elements were composed.

Although still influenced by tradition, in choosing a physical element as his principle of explanation Thales was actually in the process of establishing a new naturalist tradition, one that was to profoundly affect Western civilization. We might also observe that he wasn't all that far from the truth in choosing water as the fundamental element underlying all things. According to our own present understanding, about 90 percent of the observable universe is hydrogen, with the remaining 10 percent consisting of helium, oxygen, and so on. Hydrogen and oxygen—or water—do indeed constitute a good portion of the universe.

> A witty and attractive Thracian servant-girl is said to have mocked Thales for falling into a well while he was observing the stars and gazing upwards, declaring that he was eager to know the things in the sky but that what was behind him and just by his feet escaped his notice.
>
> —**Plato** (429–347 B.C.E.), *Theaetetus*

Lest we grant Thales more credit than he may deserve, though, let us also observe that he did not yet succeed in entirely abandoning the mythology. In a fragment that has survived, he is quoted as having taught that "all things are full of the gods."

Anaximander (610–546 B.C.E.)

Thales was raising for the first time the problem, as it is referred to, of *Being*: here, the problem of just what *is* there in the world. The second early thinker to approach this problem was Thales's pupil, Anaximander.

Anaximander seems to have been much bolder in his speculations than Thales. In considering what that fundamental stuff might be, he decided it could not be any one of the four traditional elements. For had one of these been elevated above the others, this would have involved a kind of unfairness to the other three, with disastrous results. The basic element must have therefore been something more primitive than these four.

All this seems to be suggested in the single sentence of his that has been preserved. Things return to their origins, that sentence runs, "according to what must be; for they make reparation to one another for their injustice according to the ordinance of time."[1] The dominance of one thing over another, he seems to be saying, is a kind of cosmic injustice for which a penalty (death) is exacted, the penalty being assessed by Time. Though his work was widely discussed across the ancient world, one wishes more of his writings had survived.

If Anaximander seems still overly influenced by the ancient myths (in this case the idea of justice in nature), such belief led him to a much more promising notion of the basic stuff than the one propounded by Thales. Reasoning that whatever has definite qualities must in time lose them (die), and since the fundamental stuff from which everything else arose must be eternal and indestructible, it must have lacked all definite qualities. He came, therefore, to call that basic element the **apeiron**, the "boundless," meaning a kind of neutral, indeterminate stuff, unlimited in amount.

Recalling the idea of chaos in the old myths, initially there was, he speculated, nothing but this boundless, indeterminate matter. But as a result of a kind of shaking process, perhaps like that of a gigantic sieve (for it was not due to the gods), the four elements separated off. The first to do so was the solid element, earth, which fell to the center; second was water, which covered the earth; then followed air, which formed a sphere around the water; and finally there appeared a sphere of fire.

Although nothing remains of these speculations, the essential thing is that, in being naturalistic, they are of the same kind as modern science, appealing to the same sorts of explanatory principles. They represent an advance upon the earlier mythic or supernaturalistic approaches to the world.

Anaximander also hit on the modern idea of the evolution of human beings and animals from lower forms of life, using something like Darwinian natural selection to explain the extinction of some species and the survival of others. He suggested that life began in the warm, moist slime at the edge of the sea—not a bad guess!—and that the first forms of life were marine creatures. Then, he speculated, some of these early marine creatures began to live on land and gradually developed organs to enable them to survive outside water. Thus, land animals arose, and finally, the last to develop were humans. He further noted that during the course of evolution, very strange types of animals must have emerged; some were fitted to cope with their environment and survived, while other forms were not and thus died out.

Anaximander was also the first, as far as we know, to draw a map of the known world.

Anaximenes (585–524 B.C.E.)

The last member of this Milesian school, a generation younger than Anaximander and possibly his student, was Anaximenes. In his search for the fundamental stuff, Anaximenes reverted back to the four elements and chose air—a choice motivated, it seems, by his desire to balance the views of his predecessors and preserve what was best in each. First, air, although like water present and indispensable to all life, has the advantage that it does not have as specific a nature as water, and is therefore more capable of transforming itself into the great variety of objects around us. And, second, air is a more likely source of this variety than Anaximander's *apeiron*, for the "boundless" seems *too* indeterminate to play that role. Air, lacking the heaviness or solidity of water and being as infinite, as all-pervading, and as supple as the boundless, must have been the source of it all.

His efforts to explain how air could become any of the other elements led Anaximenes to the notions of condensation and rarefaction. He argued that when particles of air get packed together the result is a fluid, and when still more tightly packed the result is a solid. On the other hand, when the particles become increasingly rarefied and separated, the solid turns to a fluid, the fluid to a mist, and the mist (or air) to fire.

Seeing, apparently, that the thinner or "rarer" air is, the hotter it becomes, and that the thicker it is, the colder it becomes, Anaximenes conducted the first recorded experiment. Blow on your hand through compressed lips, he said, and you'll find the "thick" air feels cold. Now open your mouth wide and blow gently: the "thin" air is warm.

Although Anaximenes's physical explanation of the process whereby one substance gets transformed into another is superior to the moral explanation entailed in Anaximander's theory (the giving of satisfaction for some injustice), like

> Whether our brethren of the deep cherish equally delicate sentiments towards us is not recorded.
>
> —**Bertrand Russell** (1872–1970)

> No man knows or ever will know the truth about the gods and about everything I speak of: for even if one chanced to say the complete truth, yet oneself knows it not; but seeming is wrought over all things.
>
> Not from the beginning have the gods revealed all things to mortals, but by long seeking, men find what is better.
>
> —**Anaximenes** (585–524 B.C.E.)

Anaximander and Thales before him, his overall view was still not entirely free of **anthropo-morphism**, the assignment of human characteristics to nonhuman beings. Air, he thought, was the more fundamental element because "just as our soul (being air) controls us, so breath and air encompass the whole world-order":[2] air is the soul of the world.

With Anaximenes, the Milesian school came to an end. Its speculations, marking the beginning of science and with it the beginning of Western culture, were conducted in the shadows of the rise in the east of the great Persian Empire. Founded by Cyrus the Great in 550 B.C.E. with his conquest of the Near East, this empire eventually spread to the Greek cities on the east coast of the Aegean Sea. When, in 499 B.C.E., these Greek city-states revolted, the Persians put down the revolt and destroyed their greatest city, Miletus.

> The major advances of civilization are processes that all but wreck the societies in which they occur.
>
> **—Alfred North Whitehead** (1861–1947)

THE PROBLEM OF BECOMING

The question raised by the Milesian thinkers soon gave rise to a second, for the first question asked essentially, "What *is* it that is constantly changing?" and it was soon realized that change, or "becoming," was itself a puzzling thing.

There is indeed something curious about the idea of change. When something changes, it ceases to be what it was and becomes something else. But if this is so, what becomes of that original thing? Has it vanished from existence? If it hasn't, then it is permanent, but then what exactly has changed? But if it has vanished, where did it go? And what sort of reality or being could it have had, seeing how it could lose it so completely? Surely not real *Being*, which suggests a kind of permanence.

Parmenides (c.6th century B.C.E.)

Such thoughts about being and change led Parmenides, born in Elea, a city in southern Italy, to the very odd position of maintaining that change is really an impossibility. Things do *seem* to change, he admitted, but logic shows that in reality they do not. And his logic was simple and seemingly irrefutable. He started by laying down the following basic principle: what is, is (Being is); and what is not, is not (Non-Being—nothing—is not). Now consider, he reasoned, the possibilities:

(a) Being changing into Being.
(b) Non-Being changing into Non-Being.
(c) Being changing into Non-Being.
(d) Non-Being changing into Being.

Now, case (a) cannot occur, for this is not change at all. If we have the very same thing at the beginning and end, we do not have change. Case (b) cannot occur for the same reason. How about case (c)? Here we would have to suppose something is capable of becoming or being nothing, of disappearing into nothingness, but that too seems impossible. (Where would it go?) And, finally, case (d) is equally impossible, for here we would have to suppose that what is *not* becomes what *is*, that something comes into being from *nothing*! As later Western religious thinkers would agree, **creation *ex nihilo***—creation out of nothing—is unintelligible and could only be accepted as a complete miracle.

Similar reasoning demonstrated that motion, a particular kind of change (change of location), is impossible. Motion requires the existence of empty space, for there must be some room for the object moving to move *in* to. But empty space is impossible, Parmenides argued: empty space is nothingness, and nothingness is Non-Being, and Non-Being cannot *be*. In fact Non-Being cannot even be *thought* of, for to think of Non-Being is to think of nothing, and to think of nothing is not to think! So whatever we mean by *space* could not be *nothing*, but *something*; therefore, with no void between things, motion, as movement in or into empty space, must be impossible.

Similar reasoning also demonstrates the impossibility of multiplicity, that reality could not consist of multiple entities. For there to be two beings, there must be something to separate or distinguish them, there must be space between them; if there were no space between them, after all, they would be one single continuous thing. But space is nothingness, or nothing; to say there is space between two things is to say there is nothing between them. But if there is nothing between them, they are continuous, and are one thing! So there could not be more than one thing in the world!

Parmenides concluded, then, that although our senses tell us that multiple things exist, changing and moving, our reason demonstrates that

One way remains to be spoken of: the way how it is. Along this road there are very many indications that what is is unbegotten and imperishable; for it is whole and immovable and complete. Nor was it at any time, nor will it be, since it is now, all at once, one and continuous.

For what begetting of it would you search for? How and whence did it grow? I shall not let you say or think "from what is not"; for it is not possible either to say or to think how it is not. Again, what need would have driven it, if it began from nothing, to grow later rather than sooner? Thus it must exist fully or not at all. Nor will the force of conviction ever allow anything over and above itself to arise out of what is not; wherefore Justice does not loosen her fetters so as to allow it to come into being or pass away, but holds it fast.

Concerning these things the decision lies here: either it is, or it is not. But it has been decided, as was necessary, that the one way is unknowable and unnameable (for it is no true road) and that the other is real and true. How could what is perish? How could it have come to be? For if it came into being, it is not; nor is it if ever it is going to be. Thus coming into being is extinguished, and destruction unknown.[3]

—**Parmenides** (c.6th century B.C.E.)

multiplicity, change, and motion are impossible. Appearances are therefore deceiving, a most fundamental philosophical insight: logic overrides the sensory experience, and logic teaches that "Becoming" is impossible, so ultimate reality must be an unchanging, unitary Being. Nothing determinate, of course, could be said of this Being, which he spoke of simply as *It*.

Zeno (c.490 B.C.E.)

Parmenides's argument was reinforced by one of his followers, Zeno the Eleatic. Zeno developed several famous paradoxes, designed to support the contention that change or motion is impossible. All have to do with motion in space, with change of position.

Now, by a **paradox** we mean a situation where we have good reason to believe two opposing or contradictory things; this may include situations where a given statement appears to be self-contradictory, yet could be true nevertheless. One particularly well-known paradox comes from St. Paul. Writing to Titus (about 64 C.E.), who had been left on the island of Crete to spread the gospel, Paul said, "Be careful of the Cretans. They are liars—a Cretan himself said so." Now the trouble here is that if the Cretan was lying (in saying that "all Cretans are liars"), then he might have been telling the truth; and if he was telling the truth (that all Cretans are liars), then he was lying! So it seems impossible for a Cretan to assert that all Cretans are liars—even though it could well be true that all Cretans are liars (at least *logically* speaking; no offense intended against contemporary Cretans).

Let's turn, then, to Zeno's first paradox, of Achilles racing the tortoise. Since Achilles is the fastest being in the world and the tortoise the slowest, let us give the latter a head start of one hundred yards before they race. And now off they go! By the time Achilles reaches the hundred-yard point, the tortoise will have advanced, say, ten yards; by the time Achilles reaches this point, the tortoise will have advanced, say, another one yard; by the time Achilles gets to *this* point, the tortoise will have advanced another one-tenth of a yard, and so on. But then Achilles can never catch up to the tortoise, let alone pass him: every time Achilles reaches the tortoise's current location, the tortoise will have advanced. Now we all know that this is absurd: in real life Achilles would win the race, and, given their respective rates and locations, we can even compute where he would catch and pass the tortoise. Yet once we begin to think about it along the lines Zeno suggested, it simply isn't clear how that is possible. His reasoning gives us good reason to believe it's impossible for Achilles to win the race; but our senses give us good reason to believe it is possible.

> Aristotle's criticism: Zeno's argument involves a confusion of infinite length with infinite divisibility of length. The argument attempts to prove that the space that Achilles must cover before overtaking the tortoise is an infinite magnitude; it does not prove this but rather that the space in question is divisible ad infinitum. Hence, the argument commits a fallacy of irrelevance (see chapter 5).

Now consider Zeno's racetrack paradox. Before you cover the full distance of a race, you must first cover half the distance; before you cover the half, you must cover a quarter; before the quarter the eighth, and so on. Before you get *anywhere* you must first get to the halfway point, but before that you must first get to *its* halfway point, and so on. But since you'll never run out of numbers, out of halfway points, you're obviously never going to get to the end!

Or consider, finally, the flying arrow: at any given moment the allegedly moving arrow simply occupies a space equal to its length and is therefore at rest or motionless. But if at every moment of its alleged flight it is not moving, if at no instant is it ever moving, then how can it move at all? Parmenides was right: motion is impossible.

In each case we find the same pattern: some compelling reasoning shows that motion is impossible, while some perhaps equally compelling sensory experience suggests that motion occurs all the time. Parmenides and Zeno, with their emphasis on reason, conclude that where compelling reasoning contradicts sensory experience, the reasoning wins: our senses deceive us about motion. And we should note that the reasoning in these paradoxes *is* rather compelling: after twenty-five centuries these paradoxes are still being discussed by philosophers and mathematicians. And while most contemporary thinkers privilege our sensory experience over Parmenides's and Zeno's reasoning, there is no general consensus on just where their reasoning goes wrong.

Heraclitus (540–480 B.C.E.)

About the same time as Parmenides, a thinker named Heraclitus took a diametrically opposite view of reality. So impressed was Heraclitus by the universality of change that he compared reality to a river. You cannot step into the same river twice, Plato famously cited him as asserting—for both you and the river are constantly changing. Thus Heraclitus is widely associated with the view that the key feature of reality is flux, or change, or "Becoming."

Interestingly, however, what Heraclitus *actually* said was "Upon those who step into the same rivers flow other and yet other waters."[4] This allows the fascinating metaphysical idea that the river remains the "same" even as the waters composing it constantly change. But even if the "river" remains the same, the waters—the more fundamental level of reality, the *constituents* of reality in the analogy—*are* continuously changing.

With "change" foremost in mind Heraclitus thought of fire as the underlying nature of the world, as the thing that is constantly in flux. (Unlike earth, air, and water, if you think about it, fire is continuously in process.) In doing so, he was perhaps approaching more closely to our modern views than his predecessors. As the physicist Werner Heisenberg (1901–1976) wrote,

> modern physics is in some way extremely near to the doctrines of Heraclitus. If we replace the word "fire" by the word "energy" we can almost repeat his statements word for word from our modern point of view. Energy is in fact that substance from which all elementary particles, all atoms and therefore all things are made, and energy is that which moves. Energy is a substance, since its total amount does not change, and the elementary particles can actually be made from this substance as is seen from many experiments on the creation of elementary particles. Energy can be changed into motion, into heat, into light and into tension. (*Physics and Philosophy*)

Heraclitus's view that nothing is constant is clearly more in agreement with our sense experience than Parmenides's. Yet from the point of view of reason, we still have our difficulties. Could change truly be fundamental, if there were not some *thing* changing? But if there is a "thing," is there not something permanent? So change seems to involve permanence, but the difficulty is to see how they are related. Parmenides retained the permanent and ruled out the existence of change, despite our sensory experience; Heraclitus retained the change and attempted to reject the permanent. But perhaps the overall account of reality needs somehow to make room for both.

Sayings of Heraclitus[5]

The way up and the way down are the same.
Changing, it rests.
Life is a child moving pieces in a game.
  The kingship is in the hands of a child.

THE THEORY OF ATOMISM: A SYNTHESIS

During the next fifty years, attempts were made to understand change in the world without resorting to the extreme positions of either Heraclitus or Parmenides. Eventually an ingenious solution to the problem was developed, which is still in its essentials accepted by science today. This is the theory of **atomism**, propounded by Leucippus (490–430 B.C.E.) in *The Great World System* and developed by Democritus (c.460–c.370 B.C.E.) in *The Small World System*.

Leucippus began by rejecting Parmenides's claim that space, as Non-Being, could not *be* (and with it the basis of Parmenides's argument that motion is impossible). If we could indeed think of space as a kind of receptacle, full in some parts and empty in others, Parmenides's difficulties about change and motion would not arise, he thought. He next claimed that within this space, which he saw as extending infinitely, there moved an infinite number of tiny particles, which he called *atoms*—meaning, in the original Greek, "uncuttables."

How did he come to this notion? Matter, Leucippus reasoned, was clearly divisible into parts, and those parts into smaller parts. Such division, however, must lead eventually to particles so tiny that, because they would be absolutely solid and have no space within them, would resist further division. These would be the uncuttable atoms. Leucippus thought that there must be an infinite number of these particles, moving randomly about in infinite space.

These atoms, Leucippus and Democritus believed, were not regular in shape, like the tiny billiard balls in elementary descriptions of modern science. Rather, they had irregular surfaces, some even having little hooks. Originally the atoms flew in random directions through empty space, motion being natural to them. Often two would collide, only to bounce off and continue on their separate paths. Now and then, however, two atoms would get entangled. Now hooked together, they would soon be joined by another atom, with others following. As a large mass formed, a vortex was created that swept more and more matter into its orbit. Out of these larger masses there eventually arose our universe of stars, sun, moon, and planets.

> As [the atoms] move, they collide and become entangled in such a way as to cling in close contact to one another, but not so as to form one substance of them in reality of any kind whatever; for it is very simple-minded to suppose that two or more could ever become one. The reason he gives for atoms staying together for a while is the intertwining and mutual hold of the primary bodies; for some of them are angular, some hooked, some concave, some convex, and indeed with countless other differences; so he thinks they cling to each other and stay together until such time as some stronger necessity comes from the surrounding and shakes and scatters them apart.
>
> —**Aristotle** (384–322 B.C.E.) on Democritus

In this view, then, every physical body is simply a collection of atoms, all things of whatever kind being ultimately made of the same particles. But if so, why do things *appear* different, to our senses? Because, the atomists explained—invoking Anaximenes's theory of condensation and rarefaction—of the different ways in which the atoms are joined together. If they are tightly joined, they make a solid; more loosely joined, a liquid; more loosely still, a gas. Other differences (such as differences in color, or taste) were due to the different orderings of the same atoms. (In the reading for this chapter, a later atomist, the Roman philosopher Lucretius (c.99–c.55 B.C.E.), explains how the color differences in macroscopic bodies are due to different arrangements of the same colorless atoms.)

Without scientific instruments, armed with only their senses and reason, these first atomists managed to solve the two major problems bequeathed to them by their predecessors, of Being and Becoming. Parmenides, they showed, was right to maintain that what is truly real does not change, for atoms are what's ultimately real and they do not themselves change; and Heraclitus was right in insisting on the existence of change, for change, too, is real, but it occurs only to complex bodies, in the orderings of their atoms. Each, atomism indicated, had been correct in what he asserted but wrong in what he denied.

In a way foreshadowing early modern and contemporary debates about the relationship between science and religion, Democritus subsequently went on to develop the atomic theory's mechanistic-materialist implications for religious orthodoxy. The fears and superstitions religions create need no longer plague us, he insisted: all phenomena are explainable as being the product of the mechanical and ultimately random combinations and dissolutions of atoms. There is no place remaining in such a world for demonic forces and powers and the tortures and torments of hell.

An interesting story about Democritus illustrates his approach. Considerable interest had been aroused by the strange death of a prominent man. While the man was strolling along the beach, an eagle dropped a turtle on his head and killed him. It was recalled that an oracle had once predicted that the man would die by a "bolt from Zeus," and although this suggested he would die by lightning, it was nevertheless felt that the prediction had been fulfilled since the eagle was a bird sacred to Zeus. But this explanation did not satisfy Democritus, who went out to the beach to observe the eagles. He noticed that they would swoop down and seize a turtle with their talons and then fly up and drop it on a rock to crack the shell to get at the meat. When Democritus recalled that the deceased had been bald, his head looking from above like a rock, the solution unfolded itself. There was no need to appeal to the designs of unseen beings in order to solve the mystery; ordinary natural principles sufficed.

Democritus concluded that worlds come into being through the coming together of large collections of atoms isolated in large patches of void. There are probably, therefore, an infinite number of worlds such as ours, worlds in the process either of formation or of dissolution.

The achievements of these first philosophers and scientists must be measured not by the empirical validity of their specific findings (remarkable as these sometimes were) but rather by their choice of methods and assumptions. They tried to answer questions about nature without resorting to divine revelation but by speculating in a rational way about the natural world and its possible origins. They replaced the older concept of a world governed by gods with the concept of nature as obedient to law, one intelligible to reason and amenable

At the beginning of the [twentieth] century it was shown that matter was not continuous but was made up of atoms. Shortly thereafter it was discovered that these supposedly indivisible atoms were made up of electrons revolving about a nucleus. The nucleus in turn was found to be composed of so-called elementary particles, protons and neutrons. The latest episode in this story is that we have found that the proton and the neutron are made up of quarks.

—**Stephen Hawking**, "Is the End in Sight for Theoretical Physics?"

DEMOCRITUS

to its methods of investigation. That they achieved all this without the aid of scientific instruments and in the face of an opposing tradition is all the more remarkable.

But they were remarkable people living in a remarkable period of history. The sixth century B.C.E., when all this began, was a century unlike any other either before or after it. The last prophecies of the Biblical Jeremiah (c.645–580 B.C.E.) date from this period; it also marked the rise of the Buddha in India (563–483 B.C.E.), of Confucius in China (551–479 B.C.E.), and of Zarathustra or Zoroaster in Persia (627–551 B.C.E.), the founder and prophet of a religion that had an enormous impact on both Judaism and Christianity.

It would be the fate of these two great traditions, the religious and scientific, with their separate rallying calls of faith and reason, to run headlong into each other in subsequent centuries as each grew in strength and followers.

Democritus holds the same view as Leucippus about the elements, full and void . . . he spoke as if the things that are were in constant motion in the void; and there are innumerable worlds which differ in size. In some worlds there is no sun and moon, in others they are larger than in our world, and in others more numerous. The intervals between the worlds are unequal; in some parts there are more worlds, in others fewer; some are increasing, some at their height, some decreasing; in some parts they are arising, in other failing. They are destroyed by colliding with each other. There are some worlds without any living creatures, plants, or moisture.

—**Hyppolytus** (175 C.E.–235 C.E.)

SUMMARY

1. Philosophy and science arose in the sixth century B.C.E. in the ancient Greek city of Miletus.

2. Though they inherited a set of traditional mythic or religious beliefs about the role of gods in the origin and running of the world, their great innovation was to seek primarily naturalistic explanations of things.

3. The first philosopher and scientist of the Milesian school was Thales, who focused on the nature of "Being." He argued that the fundamental element out of which all things are made is water. His contemporary, Anaximander, thinking that that choice would upset the balance of nature, argued that the fundamental element must be even more primitive than any of the four traditional elements of earth, air, fire, and water. He identified it as *apeiron*, or the "boundless," some neutral, indeterminate stuff. Finally Anaximenes suggested that the fundamental stuff was air, not quite so definite as water and not so indefinite and empty as the "boundless."

4. Turning to the problem of "Becoming," or change, Parmenides argued that change, motion, and multiplicity were impossible, despite the testimony of our senses. His arguments were reinforced by his follower Zeno, who developed a set of famous paradoxes about motion.

5. A contemporary of Parmenides, Heraclitus, adopted the opposite view, that change is fundamental to reality, choosing fire (itself perpetually "in process") to be the basic thing constantly changing.

6. The atomists, Leucippus and Democritus, developed a position midway between Parmenides's stress on the permanent and Heraclitus's stress on change. The basic stuff of the world is atoms, or "uncuttables," tiny, indivisible, indestructible particles, infinite in number. Bodies, large and small, are collections of atoms, constantly assembling and dissolving.

Changes in the arrangements of atoms explained changes in the various properties of the larger bodies. Atoms were permanent, as Parmenides stressed, but were constantly in motion and changing in their arrangements, as Heraclitus stressed.

KEY TERMS

Anthropomorphism

apeiron

atomism

creation *ex nihilo*

elements

Milesian school

naturalism

paradox

pre-Socratics

supernaturalism

REVIEW QUESTIONS

1. Where did philosophy begin? Who is considered to be the "first" philosopher?

2. What were the four basic assumptions of "myths" that restricted early Greek thought?

3. What was the *apeiron*, who posited it, and why?

4. Who were the members of the Milesian school, and what did each consider to be the fundamental "stuff"?

5. In what sense are Parmenides and Heraclitus diametrically opposed to each other in their views?

6. Why does Parmenides think that motion and change are impossible?

7. Briefly summarize the three paradoxes of Zeno discussed in the text.

8. What is the theory of atomism? Which early Greek thinkers are most closely connected with this theory?

NOTES

1. In John Manley Robinson, *An Introduction to Early Greek Philosophy* (New York: Houghton Mifflin, 1968), 34.

2. In John Manley Robinson, *An Introduction to Early Greek Philosophy* (New York: Houghton Mifflin, 1968), 47.

3. In John Manley Robinson, *An Introduction to Early Greek Philosophy* (New York: Houghton Mifflin, 1968), 113.

4. In John Manley Robinson, *An Introduction to Early Greek Philosophy* (New York: Houghton Mifflin, 1968), 91.

5. In John Manley Robinson, *An Introduction to Early Greek Philosophy* (New York: Houghton Mifflin, 1968), 94, 96, 102.

■ Reading

"Ionian Science before Socrates"

F. M. CORNFORD

From Before and After Socrates *(Cambridge, UK: Cambridge University Press, 1932/1950), pp. 5–27. Reprinted with the permission of Cambridge University Press.*

In this reading, Cornford provides a general overview and analysis of pre-Socratic philosophy, with particular attention to the ancient doctrine of atomism.

[W]e must now consider the early Ionian science of Nature, its character, and how it arose.

This science is called "Ionian" because it was begun by Thales and his successors at Miletus, one of the Ionian colonies on the coast of Asia Minor. Thales lived at the beginning of the sixth century. The development of Ionian science culminated two centuries later in the Atomism of Democritus, a contemporary of Socrates and Plato.

All the histories of Greek philosophy, from Aristotle's time to this day, begin with Thales of Miletus. It is generally agreed that with him something new, that we call Western science, appeared in the world—science as commonly defined: the pursuit of knowledge for its own sake, not for any practical use it can be made to serve. Thales . . . found that the Egyptians possessed some rough rules of land measurement. Every year the inundation of the Nile obliterated the landmarks, and the peasants' fields had to be marked out afresh. The Egyptians had a method of calculating rectangular areas, and so solved their practical problem. The inquisitive Greek was not interested in marking out fields. He saw that the method could be detached from that particular purpose and generalized into a method of calculating areas of any shape. So the rules of land measurement were converted into the science of geometry. The problem—something to be done—gave place to the theorem—something to be contemplated. Reason found a fresh delight in knowing that the angles at the base of an isosceles triangle are always equal, and why they must be equal. The land surveyor still makes use of this truth in constructing maps; the philosopher is content to enjoy it because it is true.

In the same way the Greeks turned the art of astrology into the science of astronomy. For many centuries the Babylonian priests had recorded the movements of the planets, in order to predict human events, which the stars were believed to govern. The Greeks borrowed the results of observation, and Thales predicted an eclipse which occurred in Asia Minor in 585 B.C. But they ignored the whole fabric of astrological superstition which had hitherto provided the practical motive for observing the heavens. There is hardly a trace of astrology in Greek thought.

. . . Looking back across some 2,500 years, we see the cosmogonies of the Milesian School as the dawn or infancy of science. . . . [We should see pre-Socratic] speculation [not] as rudimentary and infantile, but as the crowning epoch in a development covering many more ages than history can record.

I have spoken of this epoch as the discovery of Nature—a phrase which calls for explanation. I mean the discovery that the whole of the surrounding world of which our senses give us any knowledge is natural, not partly natural and partly supernatural. Science begins when it is understood that the universe is a natural whole, with unchanging ways of its own—ways that may be ascertainable by human reason, but are beyond the control of human action. To reach that point of view was a great achievement. If we would measure its magnitude, we must take a backward glance at certain features of the pre-scientific age. These are (1) the detachment of the self from the external object—the discovery of the object; (2) the preoccupation of intelligence with the practical needs of action in dealing with the object; (3) the belief in unseen, supernatural powers, behind or within the object to be dealt with.

. . . [With regard to the third] then, the scope of [pre-scientific] thought was bounded by the imperious needs of action. External things were selected for notice in proportion as they entered into human activities. They were not interesting for what they are in themselves, but as things we can do something with, or that can act upon us. Let us now consider them in this second capacity, as agents.

To go back to [the primitive] ape, pausing in his thwarted desire to seize the banana. In the interval of suspended action, we may imagine him feeling that things are opposing his desire with some contrary will of their own—an experience familiar enough in his dealings with his brother apes. There are resistances to be overcome—powers to be circumvented by his own power. And when he perceives that the boxes will help him to gain his end, he will feel that the world is not all against him: there are also things with benevolent intentions that sympathize with and forward his wishes. These helpful or harmful intentions, these unseen forces that further or thwart action, are fragmentary elements of personality. They are the raw material from which man, when he began to reflect, constructed the supernatural world. In Roman religion we find countless *numina*—powers whose whole content is expressed in abstract nouns, *nomina*: Janus is not a fully personal god presiding over doorways, but simply the spirit of "doorness," conceived as a power present in all doors, that can help or harm one who passes through them. From such elementary *numina* there is a scale ranging through spirits of various kinds up to the completely anthropomorphic god, like the gods of Homer.

These fragmentary elements of personality at first simply reside in things. In a sense, they are projected from man's self into the object; but we must not think of them as the creations of any conscious theory. In a census return, primitive man would not have entered his religion as "Animist," or even as "Pre-animist." The assumption that helpful or harmful things have the will to help or harm is made as unreflectingly as by the child who kicks a door that has pinched his finger, or by the man who curses his golf club for slicing a stroke. If such a man were logical, he would pray to his golf clubs before beginning a match; or he would murmur some spell to charm them into hitting straight. For these projected elements of personality are the proper objects of magical art. They are "supernatural" in that their behavior is not regular and calculable; you cannot be sure which way they will act, as you can be sure that if you touch flame you will be burnt. Magic includes a whole collection of practices designed to bring these supernatural forces under some measure of control. And if they are to be controlled, the more we can know of their nature and habits the better. Mythology supplies this need by fabricating a history of the supernatural, with the effect of fixing the unseen powers in more definite shape and endowing them with more concrete substance. They become detached from the things in which at first they resided, and are filled out into complete persons. So magic and mythology occupy the immense outer region of the unknown, encompassing the small field of matter-of-fact ordinary knowledge. The supernatural lies everywhere within or beyond the natural; and the knowledge of the supernatural which man believes himself to possess, not being drawn from ordinary direct experience, seems to be knowledge of a different and higher order. It is a revelation, accessible only to the inspired or (as the Greeks said) "divine" man—the magician and the priest, the poet and the seer.

Now the birth of science in Greece is marked by the tacit denial of this distinction between two orders of knowledge, experience and revelation, and between the two corresponding orders of existence, the natural and the supernatural. The Ionian cosmogonists assume . . . that the whole universe is natural, and potentially within the reach of knowledge as ordinary and rational as our knowledge that fire burns and water drowns. That is what I meant by the discovery of Nature. The conception of Nature is extended to incorporate what had been the domain of the supernatural. The supernatural, as fashioned by mythology, simply disappears; all that really exists is natural.

Enough, perhaps, has been said to justify the statement that the discovery of Nature was one of the greatest achievements of the human mind. Like all other great achievements, it was the work of a very few individuals with exceptional gifts. Why were these individuals Ionian Greeks of the sixth century?

The Ionian cities in Asia Minor were then at the height of Western civilization. There were men in them who had outgrown the magical practices that were never to die out among the peasantry. They had also outgrown the Olympian religion of Homer. Thanks to the poets, the anthropomorphic tendency of myth had over-reached itself. The Greek imagination was, perhaps, unique in visual clarity, far surpassing the Roman in this respect. The supernatural powers had taken human shapes so concrete and well defined that a Greek could recognize any god by sight. When the tall and bearded Barnabas and the restless eloquent Paul came to Lystra, the inhabitants at once identified them as Zeus and Hermes. It was inevitable that, when the gods had become completely human persons, some skeptical mind should refuse to believe that a thunderstorm in Asia Minor was really due to the anger of a deity seated on the summit of Olympus. In the sixth century Xenophanes attacked anthropomorphic polytheism with devastating finality:

If horses or oxen had hands and could draw or make statues, horses would represent the forms of the gods like horses, oxen like oxen.

Henceforth natural science annexed to its province all that went on "aloft" in the sky or "under the earth." Thunder and lightning, Anaximander said, were caused by the blast of the wind. Shut up in a thick cloud, the wind bursts forth, and then the tearing of the cloud makes the noise, and the rift gives the appearance of a flash in contrast with the blackness of the cloud. This is a typically scientific "explanation." There is no longer a supernatural background, peopled with fragmentary or complete personalities accessible to prayer and sacrifice or amenable to magical compulsion. Intelligence is cut off from action. Thought is left confronting Nature, an impersonal world of things, indifferent to man's desires and existing in and for themselves. The detachment of self from the object is now complete.

To the few advanced intellects who had reached this point of view, it probably seemed that they had disposed of mythology, once for all, as simply false. It is important to bear in mind that they did not carry with them the rest of the Greek world. For a thousand years the smoke of sacrifice was still to rise from the altars of Zeus. . . . So myth was destined to survive the contempt of Ionian rationalism and to await reinterpretation.

But at the moment we are now considering science seems to have swept mythology away. The systems of the sixth century are cast in the form of cosmogony. Two principal questions are answered. First, how did the world we see come to be arranged as it is: at the center, the earth with the great masses of water in the hollow seas; round it the airy region of mist and cloud and rain;

and beyond that the heavenly fires? Secondly, how did life arise within this order? The answer is a history of the birth of a world order out of an initial state of things (a "beginning," *arché*).

Take for illustration the most complete and daring of these cosmogonies, the system of Thales's successor, Anaximander, which set the pattern for the Ionian tradition. At first there was an unbounded and unordered mass of indiscriminate stuff, containing the antagonistic powers of heat and cold. This mass had the living property of eternal motion. At some point a nucleus, pregnant with these warring powers, took shape—a rationalized equivalent of the world-egg of mythical cosmogony. Perhaps because the hostility of the hot and the cold drove them apart, the nucleus was differentiated. The cold became a watery mass of earth enveloped in cloud; the hot, a sphere of flame enwrapping the whole, like bark round a tree. Then the sphere of flame burst, and was torn off to form rings of fire enclosed and hidden in dark mist. Sun, moon, and stars, the points of light we see in the sky, are spouts of fire issuing from holes in these opaque rings, as the air issues from the nozzle of a bellows. The earth was then dried by the heat of the heavenly fires, and the seas shrank into their hollow beds. At last, life arose in the warm slime. The first animals were like sea urchins enclosed in prickly shells. From these sea creatures, land animals, including man, were evolved.

The significance of this cosmogony lies not so much in what it contains as in what it leaves out. Cosmogony has been detached from theogony. There is not a word about the gods or any supernatural agency. . . . It was an extraordinary feat of rational thinking, to dissipate this haze of myth from the origins of the world and of life. Anaximander's system pushes back to the very beginning the operation of ordinary forces such as we see at work in Nature every day. The formation of the world becomes a natural, not a supernatural, event.

Such were the Ionian cosmogonies of the sixth century: they told how an ordered world was evolved out of an undifferentiated initial state of things. In the fifth century, science takes a somewhat different line, which it has followed ever since. Retaining the form of cosmogony, it becomes more particularly an inquiry into the ultimate constitution of material substance—the uniform and permanent "nature of things." Let us consider, in conclusion, the outcome of this inquiry—the Atomism of Democritus.

Atomism is a theory of the nature of tangible bodily substance. The notion of substance is taken from common sense. The belief in substantial things outside ourselves goes back to the original detachment of self from the object. A substance is something that exists independently of my seeing or touching it—something that endures, as the same thing, whether I am there to see it or not. The problem for science is: What is this substance that endures when it has ceased to yield us sensations? I have under my eyes what I call a sheet of paper. What I actually see is a white area with black marks. When I touch it, I feel the resistance of a smooth surface, and I can trace with my finger its rectangular shape. These sensations are my only assurance that something is there, outside me. If I turn my eyes in another direction, the whiteness and the black marks disappear. I have only the tactile sensations of the resistance of the smooth rectangular surface. If I lift my finger, these sensations also disappear. Yet I am absolutely certain that something is still there—a substance which does not depend upon my having sensations derived from it. Which of these properties—white and black, resistance, smoothness, shape—really belong independently to the thing outside me, and continue to exist when I am not looking and touching?

The Atomists held that the tactile properties are the real ones; the visual properties are not substantial or objective. They are not there when I am not looking. In a dark room the sheet of paper would lose its color; I should see nothing. But I should still feel the shape and resistance of the surface. If I could not detect those properties, I should feel nothing and be sure the thing was not there. If I did detect them, I should be certain that, when I turned on the light, the visual properties would spring into existence again.

By this train of thought common sense can be led towards the fundamental doctrines of Atomism. The atoms of Democritus are hard bodies, too small to be seen, and deprived of all properties except shape and resistance—the tangible properties necessary and sufficient to convince us that something real is there. A larger body is not destroyed when it is broken up into atoms. All the pieces are still there, and they can be reassembled. Also they can move in space without suffering any change of quality. Atomism held that the real—the enduring and unchanging core of substance—is nothing but atoms, moving in empty space. Not only are these atoms real, but they are the whole of reality.

I do not mean to suggest that the Atomism of Democritus was actually reached by the train of thought I have outlined. In historical fact, it arose as a mathematical theory that matter consists of discrete units. But the result is the same. The atoms of Democritus are tiny bodies, into which larger bodies can be cut up, but which cannot themselves be cut into smaller pieces. They are absolutely solid, compact, impenetrable.

Where scientific Atomism went beyond common sense was in its demand that the atoms of body shall be absolutely indestructible and unchanging. This was a requirement of the reason. Common sense, untutored by science, would suppose that bodies can be, and constantly are being, destroyed. A thing will remain the same thing for a time, though some of its properties change; but then it may simply cease to exist and something else will come into being. But ancient science, holding to the principle that nothing can come out of nothing, demanded some permanent and indestructible "being" behind the screen of shifting appearances. This postulate met the same rational need that has prompted the assertion by modern science of the principle of conservation in various forms: the law of inertia, the conservation of mass, the conservation of energy. It has been observed that all these propositions were at first announced either without proof of any sort or as the result of a priori demonstration, although later they have often been regarded as purely empirical laws.[1] The something—whatever it may be—of which modern science has required the conservation corresponds to the permanent "being" or "nature of things" required by the ancients. For the Atomists it was impenetrable particles of material substance.

Ancient science, having deduced the indestructible atom, thought it had arrived at the real nature of things. The variable qualities which things seem to have, but atoms have not—colors, tastes, and so forth—were disposed of as mere sensations which fall inside our organs of perception. They are not "substantial," for they depend on us for their existence. Atoms alone are real, with the void in which they move and strike one another.

The essential feature of this Atomism is that it is a materialist doctrine. By that I do not mean merely that it is an account of the nature of material substance or body. It is materialist in the sense that it declares that material substance, tangible body, is not only real but the whole of reality. Everything that exists or happens is to be explained in terms of these bodily factors. The world is resolved into an invisible game of billiards. The table is empty space. The balls are atoms; they collide and pass on their motion from one to another. That is all: nothing else is real. There are no players in this game. If three balls happen to make a cannon, that is a mere stroke of luck—necessary, not designed. The game consists entirely of flukes; and there is no controlling intelligence behind.

Considered as a theory of the nature of material substance, Atomism was a brilliant hypothesis. Revived by modern science, it has led to the most important discoveries in chemistry and physics. But, as I have said, ancient Atomism went farther than this. It claimed to be an account of the whole of reality—not a mere scientific hypothesis, but a complete philosophy.

As such, it should include an account of the spiritual aspect of the world, as well as of the material. But when we consider the system from that standpoint, we find that anything we can recognize as spiritual has simply disappeared. When the Atomist is asked for an account of the soul, he replies that the soul (like everything else) consists of atoms. These soul-atoms are of the same impenetrable substance as all others; only they are spherical in shape, and so can move very easily and slip in between the angular and less mobile atoms of the body. Sensation is due to atoms from outside knocking up against the soul-atoms. The variety of qualities we perceive corresponds to the variety of atomic shapes. As late as 1675, a French chemist, whose treatise remained classical for half a century, wrote:

> The hidden nature of a thing cannot be better explained than by attributing to its parts shapes corresponding to all the effects it produces. No one will deny that the acidity of a liquid consists in pointed particles. All experience confirms this. You have only to taste it to feel a pricking of the tongue like that caused by some material cut into very fine points.[2]

That statement might have been written by [the Atomist] Lucretius, and (so far as it goes) it is a reasonable explanation of the mechanical cause of a certain sensation. But if I turn from the mechanical cause to the sensation itself, and then to the soul which has the sensation, and also has feelings, thoughts, and desires, I am not so easily convinced that the soul itself consists of round atoms, and that nothing really happens except collisions. It is much harder to believe that a process of thought or an emotion of anger is either totally unreal or else actually consists of a number of solid particles banging together. If man had begun by studying himself, rather than external Nature, he would never have reached so fantastic a conclusion.

Perhaps what I said earlier about the peculiar visual clarity of Greek mythology, may explain how science came at last to ignore or deny the spiritual, as distinct from the material. If the world has a spiritual aspect, man can only give an account of it in terms of his own spirit or mind. At first he projected elements of his own personality into external things. Then the Greek imagination developed these elements into the complete human personalities of anthropomorphic gods. Sooner or later the Greek intelligence was bound to discover that such gods do not exist. Thus mythology overreached itself and discredited the very existence of a spiritual world. Science drew the conclusion, not that the spiritual world had been misconceived, but that there was no such thing: nothing was real except the tangible body composed of atoms. The result was a doctrine that philosophers call materialism, and religious people call atheism.

REVIEW AND DISCUSSION QUESTIONS

1. What exactly is "animism," and in what way(s) did the Ionian thinkers reject it?

2. Must a materialistic account of the world entirely exclude the existence of the mind, or of spirit, or might they be compatible? Why?

3. Must a materialistic account of the world entirely exclude the existence of God or gods, or might they be compatible? Why?

NOTES

1. Cf. E. Meyerson, *De l'explication dans les sciences* (Paris: Payot, 1921), II, 327; Paul Tannery, *Pour l'histoire de la science hellne* (Paris, 1887), p. 264.

2. Lémery, Cours de Chymie, quoted by E. Meyerson, *De l'explication dans les sciences* (Paris: Payot, 1921), I, 285.

■ Reading

On the Nature of Things

Lucretius

From T. Lucreti Cari, De Rerum Natura, Libri Sex, *4th ed., transl., H. A. J. Munro (Cambridge, UK: Deighton Bell and Co, 1886), Book II, pp. 37–39, 40, 45–48.*

> In this reading, Lucretius sketches some of his atomist theory. Atoms—which he refers to as "seeds," or "first-beginnings"—come in different sizes and shapes, some smooth, some hooked, and these different properties result in their causing different sorts of sensations in us, including pleasant and unpleasant ones. In particular he offers several arguments that the colors we perceive bodies to have result from the different arrangements of the otherwise colorless atoms.

. . . Moreover the liquids honey and milk excite a pleasant sensation of tongue when held in the mouth; but on the other hand the nauseous nature of wormwood and of harsh centaury writhes the mouth with a noisome flavour; so that you may easily see that the things which are able to affect the senses pleasantly, consist of smooth and round elements; while all those on the other hand which are found to be bitter and harsh, are held in connexion by particles that are more hooked and for this reason are wont to tear open passages into our senses and in entering in to break through the body.

Line 408] All things in short which are agreeable to the senses and all which are unpleasant to the feeling are mutually repugnant, formed as they are out of an unlike first shape; lest haply you suppose that the harsh grating of the creaking saw consists of elements as smooth as those of tuneful melodies which musicians wake into life with nimble fingers and give shape to on strings; or suppose that the first-beginnings are of like shape which pass into the nostrils of men, when noisome carcases are burning, and when the stage is fresh sprinkled with Cilician saffron, while the altar close by exhales Panchaean odours; or decide that the pleasant colours of things which are able to feast the eyes are formed of a seed like to the seed of those which make the pupil smart and force it to shed tears or from their disgusting aspect look hideous and foul. For every shape which gratifies the senses has been formed not without a smoothness in its elements; but on the other hand whatever is painful and harsh, has been produced not without some roughness of matter. There are too some elements which are with justice thought to be neither smooth nor altogether hooked with barbed points, but rather to have minute angles slightly projecting, so that they can tickle rather than hurt the senses; of which class tartar of wine is formed and the flavours of elecampane. Again that hot fires and cold frost have fangs of a dissimilar kind wherewith to pierce the senses, is proved to us by the touch of each. For touch, touch, ye holy divinities of the gods, the body's feeling is, either when an extraneous thing makes its way in, or when a thing which is born in the body hurts it, or gives pleasure as it issues forth . . . or when from some collision the seeds are disordered within the body and distract the feeling by their mutual disturbance; as if haply you were yourself to strike with the hand any part of the body you please and so make trial. Wherefore the shapes of the first-beginnings must differ widely, since they are able to give birth to different feelings.

444] Again things which look to us hard and dense must consist of particles more hooked together, and be held in union because welded all through with branch-like elements. In this class first of all diamond stones stand in foremost line inured to despise blows, and stout blocks of basalt and the strength of hard iron and brass bolts which scream out as they hold fast to their staples. Those things which are liquid and of fluid body ought to consist more of smooth and round elements; for the several drops have no mutual cohesion and their onward course too has a ready flow downwards. All things lastly which you see disperse themselves in an instant, as smoke mists and flames, if they do not consist entirely of smooth and round, must yet not be held fast by closely tangled elements, so that they may be able to pierce the body and enter it with biting power, yet not stick together: thus you may easily know, that whatever we see the senses have been able to allay, consists not of tangled but of pointed elements. Do not however hold it to be wonderful that some things which are fluid you see to be likewise bitter, for instance the sea's moisture: because it is fluid, it consists of smooth and round particles, and many rough bodies mixed up with these produce pains; and yet they must not be hooked so as to hold together: you are to know that though rough, they are yet spherical, so that while they roll freely on, they may at the same time hurt the senses. And that you may more readily believe that with smooth are mixed rough first-beginnings from which Neptune's body is made bitter, there is a way of separating these, and of seeing how the fresh water, when it is often filtered through the earth, flows by itself into a trench and sweetens; for it leaves above the first-beginnings of the nauseous saltness, inasmuch as the rough particles can more readily stay behind in the earth.

478] And now that I have shown this, I will go on to link to it a truth which depends on this and from this draws its proof: the first-beginnings of things have different shapes, but the number of shapes is finite. . . .

522] And now that I have shown this, I will go on to link to it a truth which depends on this and from this draws its proof: the first-beginnings of things which have a like shape one with the other, are infinite in number. . . .

730] Now mark . . . lest haply you deem that those things which you see with your eyes to be bright, because white are formed of white principles, or that the things which are black are born from black seed; or that things which are steeped in any other colour, bear that colour because the bodies of matter are dyed with a colour like to it. For the bodies of matter have no colour at all either like to the things or unlike. But if haply it seems to you that no impression of the mind can throw itself into these bodies, you wander far astray. For since men born blind who have never beheld the light of the sun, yet recognize bodies by touch, though linked with no colour for them from their first birth, you are to know that bodies can fall under the ken of our mind too, though stained with no colour. . . . And since I prove that this is the case, I will now show that there are things [which are possessed of no colour]. Well, any colour without any exception changes into any other; and this first-beginnings ought in no wise to do: something unchangeable must remain over, that all things be not utterly reduced to nothing. For whenever a thing changes and quits its proper limits, at once this change of state is the death of that which was before. Therefore mind not to dye with colour the seeds of things, that you may not have all things altogether returning to nothing.

757] Moreover if no quality of colour is assigned to first-beginnings and they are yet possessed of varied shapes out of which they beget colours of every kind and change them about by reason that it makes a great difference with what other seeds and in what position the seed are severally held in union and what motions they mutually impart and receive, you can explain at once with the greatest ease why those things which just before were of a black colour, may become all at once of marble whiteness; as the sea, when mighty winds have stirred up its waters, is changed into white waves of the brightness of marble: you may say that when the matter of that which we often see to be black, has been mixed up anew and the arrangement of its first-beginnings has been changed and some have been added and some been taken away, the immediate result is that it appears bright and white. But if the waters of the sea consisted of azure seeds, they could in no wise become white; for however much you jumble together seeds which are azure, they can never pass into a marble colour. But if the seeds which make up the one unmixed brightness of the sea are dyed some with one, some with other colours, just as often out of different forms and varied shapes something square and of a uniform figure is made up, in that case it were natural that as we see unlike forms contained in the square, so we should see in the water of the sea or in any other one an unmixed brightness colours widely unlike and different to one another ... but the various colours of things are a let and hindrance to the whole thing being of a uniform brightness....

795] Moreover since colours cannot exist without light and first-beginnings of things do not come out into the light, you may be sure they are clothed with no colour. For what colour can there be in total darkness? Nay it changes in the light itself according as its brightness comes from a straight or slanting stroke of light. After this fashion the down which encircles and crowns the nape and throat of doves shows itself in the sun: at one time it is ruddy with the hue of bright pyropus; at another it appears by a certain way of looking at it to blend with coral-red green emeralds. The tail of the peacock when it is saturated with abundant light, changes in like fashion its colours as it turns about. And since these colours are begotten by a certain stroke of light, sure enough you must believe that they cannot be produced without it. And since the pupil receives into it a kind of blow, when it is said to perceive a white colour, and then another, when it perceives black or any other colour, and since it is of no moment with what colour the things which you touch are provided, but rather with what sort of shape they are furnished, you are to know that first-beginnings have no need of colours, but produce sensations of touch varying according to their various shapes....

826] Again the more minute the parts are into which any thing is rent, the more you may perceive the colour fade away by little and little and become extinct; as for instance if a piece of purple is torn into small shreds ... from which you may infer that the shreds part with all their colour before they come back to the seeds of things....

842] But lest haply you suppose that first bodies remain stripped of colour alone, they are also wholly devoid of warmth and cold and violent heat, and are judged to be barren of sound and drained of moisture, and emit from their body no scent of their own.

REVIEW AND DISCUSSION QUESTIONS

1. How does Lucretius explain the difference between pleasant and unpleasant sensations?

2. Identify at least three separate arguments that Lucretius makes to support his claim that atoms are themselves colorless.

CHAPTER THREE

■ Socrates and Plato

OCRATES (469–399 B.C.E.) wrote nothing, left not even a scrap for posterity, and is known only secondhand, primarily through the writings of his famous student, Plato (429–347 B.C.E.). Yet he was one of the most remarkable people who ever lived and was part of a culture whose profound effect on the Western world helped determine the form our civilization has taken.

In an absorbing series titled "The Miracle of Greece" that appeared in *Life* magazine, this age and this people were described in its opening lines:

> It was sudden. It was miraculous. Nobody knows why it happened. But on a small rock-bound Mediterranean peninsula 2,500 years ago a handful of people called Greeks roused the human race to a new ambition and sense of purpose and launched it into history. (January 4, 1963, p. 28)

On the surface, the article continued, these Greeks seem unlikely candidates for this mission:

> They were always fighting among themselves. They were garrulous and monstrously egocentric. They were often treacherous. They were so eager that they had to mount the slogan "Nothing to Excess" in big letters at Delphi to remind them to be less excessive. But they did have one idea, so novel and profound that a whole new age dawned in its light. It was simply that man's nature, even in its mortality, is the glory of creation, and that man has a noble purpose: to live at the highest possible pitch of human perfection—physically, morally and intellectually. (p. 29)

To Socrates, who understood that idea perhaps better than anyone else, it consisted in the belief that humans possess a **psyche**, a soul or mind, the part of them that is most truly the self. This was his single greatest discovery—and one that more than anything else accounts for the obsessive urgency with which he went about trying to reveal it to others.

Socrates was not the first to speak of the soul. Among the pre-Socratics, both Democritus and Heraclitus had plenty to say about it. Democritus, for example, maintained that the soul was composed of "finer" atoms, and Heraclitus believed that the most reasonable soul was the dry one, the one closest to that ultimate stuff, fire. Heraclitus added, as evidence, that imbibing liquor moistens the soul, with obvious results. Socrates's conception, however, went beyond these earlier materialistic notions to conceive of the soul as being more than mere atoms or matter. Moreover he focused on what was genuinely important: the excellence of the soul and how to attain it.

Indeed, this new conception of the soul and the use he made of it cost Socrates his life, as we'll see below. But first, it will be useful to consider a group of other thinkers circulating in Athens at the time with whom, unfortunately, Socrates tended to be confused.

THE SOPHISTS

It is ironic that Socrates, who believed that the human soul was the only thing worth caring about, should be confused with people whose main concern was not the soul but the secret of worldly success.

Who were these **Sophists**? They were itinerant teachers who began to gravitate to Athens around the fifth century B.C.E. The Greek term that referred to them, reflecting the respect in which they were initially held, meant "expert" or "wise one." They did not, however, succeed in retaining this good name for very long. Becoming masters of the arts of political success, they offered to teach these skills to anyone able to afford their fees. Athens was now a democracy, and such skills were important for anyone wishing to succeed in life. Understandably, the demand for their services increased, and the Sophists grew wealthy from their fees. The poor, who could not afford to pay, came to despise them.

Although confining themselves at first to teaching only practical subjects, the Sophists began to explore matters of wider implication, regarding the state and its justification, traditional religion, and orthodox morality. As they became more radical, their attacks on the established systems of political, social, and religious life became more severe. Might it not be the case, they began to ask, that our systems of law, conduct, and religion do not enjoy any objective truth or validity, but are merely a matter of custom and convention? If so, by what right can we say one way is better than another? And if we have indeed merely agreed to adopt certain ways of conducting and governing ourselves, what stops us, should we be so inclined, from abandoning these ways or overthrowing them?

The result of this Sophist line of thinking is perhaps best captured in the famous line of Protagoras (c.490–c.420 B.C.E.), that "Man is the measure of all things." There is no objective order dictating how we should live. We get to determine that ourselves.

From teaching how to win, by fair means or foul, the Sophists proceeded to inquire whether there even was such a thing as fair or foul, right or wrong, and then finally to wonder whether perhaps winning is all that matters. The public, scandalized by such views, came to regard them with increasing suspicion and alarm. In time, in fact, the word *sophist* has come to connote those who reason fallaciously, with the intent to deceive.

> How can man be the measure of all things when he is not the measure of himself?
>
> —**Richard Taylor** (1919–2003)

Opposed to the Sophists, although no less critical of the establishment than they, stood Socrates, who criticized both them and the state for neglecting what he believed should be their chief and proper concern: knowledge of oneself and of the right way to live. For he believed there *was* a right way to live and that it was not all simply relative or a matter of convention. Yet he was also certain it had not yet been found, at least in Athens.

The details of Socrates's life are unremarkable. He came from a middle-class Athenian family. His father was a bricklayer and his mother a midwife. Socrates himself seems to have been trained in his father's craft. Physically, he was by all accounts rather odd looking: short, ugly, pop-eyed, potbellied, pug-nosed, walking with a shambling gait. But he was also a man of bravery and vigor, well known for his courage in battle. Intellectually, needless to say, he was brilliant.

But he does not seem to have worked very hard, if at all, at his trade, nor does he seem to have spent much time with his family, preferring to spend it pursuing philosophy, which took the form of questioning his fellow Athenians concerning their beliefs and way of life. He believed they were occupied with mostly trivial pursuits and were neglecting the more important pursuit of virtue and knowledge. He thought it was not possible to acquire virtue, to act rightly, without knowledge. This was why clear thinking and the need to achieve exact definitions were of such importance to him, as necessary first steps.

SOCRATES

To this, however, he added a view that perhaps looks strange to us: that if you do have the knowledge, if you truly understand virtue and right conduct, you cannot fail to be good and act as a good person should, regardless of your circumstances.

In maintaining this, Socrates was addressing two different but related questions. The first concerned the role that learning plays in making a person good. Most of us would probably agree that learning does indeed contribute to good behavior. We believe, for instance, in trying to incorporate a "moral education" in our children's upbringing, to teach them what kinds of acts are right as well as what makes them right. Also, we tend to believe that by example of those around us, we can assimilate some good traits. So learning seems to be at least a necessary condition for developing a good character and acting as a good person.

Socrates was, however, also making a more ambitious claim: that the relevant learning was also a *sufficient* condition for becoming a good person. This means that once we acquire the correct knowledge of good and bad, right and wrong, we could not help becoming a virtuous person. It also means that morally undeveloped or bad people necessarily *lack* such knowledge, and are as they are *because* they lack it. This position is much harder to defend against empirical evidence. We hear of people daily committing heinous acts even while admitting that they knew they were wrong. We do not usually think of the murderer as one who merely lacks knowledge of right or wrong but rather as one who has that knowledge but perpetrates the crime anyway.

Be that as it may, Socrates believed that he himself still lacked this knowledge that would make him truly good, and was hoping to find it with the help of others who might be, as he would add (perhaps ironically) "more gifted than himself." Obviously he could not have run into many who were *actually* more gifted than he; equally obviously many were not too happy to be shown, by him, that they actually didn't have the knowledge they claimed to have. So there were reasons enough for his growing unpopularity with many of his fellow citizens.

Thus, it could not have been entirely unexpected that when he was brought to trial—for heresy and for "corrupting the minds of the young"—he took the opportunity to dwell again on their past mistakes and to explain to them the real source of their animosity toward him. This stemmed, he said, from his philosopher's mission of searching into the true self, from his having been a gadfly to the state, urging its citizens to self-improvement, and from his search for wisdom, which only exposed their own ignorance. His true enemies were not his present prosecutors but all those who opposed the life of reason and virtue and who shrank before his famous conviction that "the unexamined life is not worth living."

To understand why Socrates was brought to trial and eventually executed, we must understand the social and political events of the last thirty or so years of this fifth century B.C.E.

LIFE IN ATHENS AND CONQUEST BY SPARTA

Athens reached its peak under the great democratic statesman Pericles (495–429 B.C.E.). It was a great naval and military power, had built an empire of great wealth, and had advanced to a democratic form of government. If you will think of a small city of about 130,000 people producing in a short span of time buildings unsurpassed in beauty to this day, two of the greatest historians of all time, some of the greatest dramatists ever, to say nothing of their achievements in philosophy, sculpture, and music, you will have some idea of the splendor of the age.

Yet this high point of Athenian development was no sooner reached than its decline began. As is often the case, the cause was war, here the Peloponnesian War (431–404 B.C.E.). Socrates was thirty-eight when this long, exhausting war began, and it ended in the defeat of Athens by Sparta and its allies. The Spartans reduced the population to the condition of serfs. The serfs, called *helots*, were forced to work the land for their new masters. The helots bitterly resented their condition and, when they could, rebelled. The Spartans had secret police to deal with this danger. In addition, once a year they would declare war on the helots so that their young men could legally kill any helot who seemed insubordinate.

Freed from labor, which they regarded as degrading, the Spartans devoted themselves from birth to becoming invincible warriors. Sickly children would be killed by exposure, and only those judged vigorous were allowed to live. Those so selected were then, to the age of twenty, trained in one big school. The object of the training was to make them hardy, indifferent to pain, and submissive to authority.

At twenty, actual military service began. Although marriage was permitted to anyone over twenty, all men (including those who were married) had to live in the "men's house" until the age of thirty. Homosexuality was encouraged in the belief that fighting next to one's lover would make one braver and more heroic. It was also held that no Spartan should be poor or rich. No one was therefore allowed to own gold or silver. Spartan simplicity became proverbial.

Women were also treated differently in Sparta than anywhere else in Greece. They were given the same training as the boys, with the same design in mind—to turn them into devoted citizens of the state. They were not allowed to show grief if their newborn child was condemned to death or if their son was killed in battle. If childless, they were trained to raise no objection if the state ordered them to attempt reproduction with a man other than their husband. Children, once begotten, reared, trained, and sent off to battle, would be told by their mothers to come back either with their shields or on them.

It was these people, who sacrificed everything to success in war, who finally managed to defeat Athens in 404 B.C.E. Driving out the whole population, the Spartans forced the Athenians to tear down the wall surrounding their once proud city, marking the end of that great civilization.

But that Athenian greatness, as glorious as it might appear, had in fact been achieved at a high price. Greece's Golden Age began with the victories over Persian invaders in 490 and 480 B.C.E. After the Persians had been repulsed, the Greeks, led by Athens, formed a league to defend against further Persian attacks. In time the Athenians, by threat and deception, converted this voluntary league into an empire, one that exacted with growing ruthlessness huge sums of money from its subject states, money that it used to increase its military might, beautify the city, and finance the expensive projects on the Acropolis. The statue of Athena in the Parthenon alone cost the equivalent of millions of dollars. All this occurred while some twenty thousand slaves, many of them Greeks, were worked to death in Athens and its silver mines.

There was, then, much to criticize. Democracy with its achievements was financed by imperialism abroad and exploitation at home. Dreams of world conquest and the good life corrupted the Athenians, proving that the democracy they had achieved—for the elite—was only skin deep after all. On the stage, their dramatists portrayed and taught how a surplus of goods leads to pride, rashness, and ruin, and their audiences proved them right.

But however comforting it might be to believe that the Athenians recognized that they did not deserve to keep what they had so ignobly obtained, and took Socrates's life because of the guilt he aroused in their hearts, that's probably not how they saw it. They undoubtedly regarded those who, like Socrates, asked too many questions and raised doubts about worldly gain, as subversives undermining the loyalties of those on whom the city's prosperity depended, particularly the youth. And so in 399 B.C.E., after Athens had managed to overthrow Sparta and reinstall its own leaders, Socrates was indicted on the charge of "corrupting the minds of the young and introducing strange gods."

Why the "strange gods"? Socrates professed to being guided by a "voice," one he understood to be of divine origin and as such always correct. "I am subject," he said of it at his trial, "to a divine or supernatural experience, which Meletus [one of his accusers] saw fit to travesty in his indictment." Today we might call it his conscience, but his accusers understood him to be following his own personal god.

Socrates was obviously not unaware of the danger he was in, but at his trial he seemed less interested in defusing the accusations than in once more explaining to his fellow citizens what their mission in life should be. One wonders whether this was from his profound devotion to the truth, from bravery or foolhardiness, or from a desire for martyrdom—or all of the above.

SOCRATES'S CHRONICLER: PLATO

The person who immortalized Socrates was his student Plato. Born in 429 B.C.E., Plato was a young man when Athens was defeated by Sparta and may even have fought in the war. He belonged to one of the best and established families in Athens, one both wealthy and politically influential. The normal career for him would have been in politics, but the political life of Athens had degenerated greatly in the last thirty years of the century. The Peloponnesian War had exhausted the city's resources, and Plato, after his military service, steered clear of politics. He decided instead to develop a sound political philosophy, which remained a leading interest with him all his life. He began by writing dialogues to commemorate his teacher and mentor, Socrates, in whose company he had spent over ten years. He was twenty-eight years old when Socrates was executed.

> Plato has cast a spell on many generations, the sense of a quest on the verge of fulfillment, of wonderful things glimpsed, but never clearly seen, so that keeping company with him seems to carry a promise.
>
> —**F. J. E. Woodbridge**,
> *The Son of Apollo* (1929)

Plato's lifelong passion, partly motivated by the unjust death of his teacher, was to arrive at a conception of a state in which such an injustice could not be perpetrated. Justice, or the just state, is thus the subject of many of his works, including the best known of these, *Republic*. It is in this work that he arrived at the solution that the just state will be achieved only when either philosophers become kings or kings become philosophers.

It is interesting that Plato's conception of justice, which leads to this solution, is reminiscent of one of the early mythic beliefs we explored in the previous chapter. Justice is a kind of disposition existing in each member of the just society (rulers, soldiers, workers) to mind his or her own proper business and not meddle in others' affairs—affairs in which, by their nature, they lack competence. If your nature makes you a first-rate shoemaker, you should resist the temptation to accept promotion to some higher office for which you lack any competence (e.g., the management of the entire shoe factory). In Plato's view, a just society is one where everything has its proper place and everyone does what his nature prepares him best for. Crucial to this view, of course, is the very idea that we *have* a nature, that we are born with abilities and predispositions that suit us to one particular life rather than some other.

PLATON PHILOSOPHE GREC.
Chap. 29.

PLATO

Plato had an opportunity to put his theories into practice. About eleven years after Socrates's death, Plato was invited by the tyrant of Syracuse, Dionysius I, to visit his court. Plato disliked the dissolute life there, and Dionysius did not care much for Plato, either. The encounter ended, allegedly, in Plato being sold into slavery. Friends fortunately managed to ransom him. On his return to Athens, they refused his offer to repay the ransom, so Plato used his money to found his famous Academy. This school, of which he remained the leader until his death in 347 B.C.E., was the first university in the Western world. He gathered scholars and pupils, and the scholars soon made great contributions in such fields as mathematics and astronomy. The Academy continued for over nine hundred years before it was finally closed by the Roman emperor Justinian in 529 C.E.—a record for unbroken existence not yet exceeded by any other university.

Plato was the first philosopher whose literary output is largely (but not wholly) preserved. Most of his writings are in the form of dialogues, as a means of paying tribute to Socrates. Socrates is the main speaker in all but a few, and is represented as being present in all save one. Since Socrates did not leave any of his own writings, it isn't very clear which philosophical doctrines are his own and which in fact are Plato's put into Socrates's mouth. It is not uncommon, therefore, for scholars to treat Socrates's views as simply being Plato's.

With that in mind, Plato's work is traditionally distinguished into three periods.

The early, or Socratic, period includes a dozen or so dialogues, of which *Euthyphro* and *Apology* are good examples. These dialogues analyze the chief virtues and are characterized by Socratic irony, although the real answers to the questions raised are indicated rather clearly.

The middle period consists of longer works, and it is here that Plato reaches the height of his dramatic power. *Republic* and *Phaedo* are good examples.

Finally, there are the works of the late period. These are drier and more technical. Plato was getting into questions here that Socrates probably did not discuss. *Theaetetus* (a long dialogue about knowledge in which Plato attempted to demolish the view, ascribed to Protagoras, that knowledge is based on sense perception and is relative to the individual perceiver) and *Timaeus* (a similarly long work dealing with cosmology) are typical of this period. Finally there is *Laws*, Plato's last work, which is also concerned with the problem of constructing an ideal state. The deeply conservative view that Plato took here has led some to regard him as one of the major Western proponents of totalitarianism.

Gorgias's Advice to Socrates

Of course, Socrates, philosophy does have a certain charm if one engages with it in one's youth and in moderation; but if one dallies overlong, it's the ruin of a fellow. If a man . . . goes on philosophizing throughout his life, he will never come to taste the experiences which a man must have if he's going to be a gentleman and have the world look up to him. You know perfectly well that philosophers know nothing about state laws and regulations. They are equally ignorant of the conversational standards that we have to adopt in dealing with our fellow men at home and abroad. Why, they are inexperienced even in human pleasures and desires! In a word, they are totally innocent of all human character. So, when they come to take part in either a private or a public affair, they make themselves ridiculous—just as ridiculous, I dare say, as men of affairs may be when they get involved in your quibbles, your "debates."

But the best course, no doubt, is to be a participant in both. It's an excellent thing to grasp as much philosophy as one needs for an education, and it's no disgrace to play the philosopher while you're young; but if one grows up and becomes a man and still continues in the subject, why, the whole thing becomes ridiculous, Socrates. . . . When I perceive philosophical activity in a young lad, I am pleased; it suits him, I think, and shows that he has good breeding. . . . Whereas when I see an older man still at his philosophy and showing no sign of giving it up, that one seems to me, Socrates, to be asking for some hard knocks! . . . Such a fellow must spend the rest of his life skulking in corners, whispering with two or three little lads, never pronouncing any large, liberal, or meaningful utterance.

—**Plato** (429–347 B.C.E.), *Gorgias*

Although Plato was the greatest student of Socrates to write about him, he was not the only one. We have, in fact, two other sources of information regarding Socrates: Aristophanes (c.446–c.386 B.C.E.) and Xenophon (c.430–c.350 B.C.E.). Scholars don't attach much significance to Xenophon, of whose intellectual abilities they have reservations. Nor is it clear how to weigh the work of Aristophanes, despite his being the only one to write about Socrates while he was still alive, for his comic drama *The Clouds* was intended as a farce and Socrates was caricatured neither as a moral reformer nor as a political subversive but as a kind of crack-brained scientist, running a shabby establishment called a Thinkery. The play was first performed in 426 B.C.E., about twenty-five years before Socrates's trial. On the other hand, some twenty-five thousand spectators viewed it then, and it is difficult to say what role this depiction of Socrates as a type of Sophist may have played in some people's minds—even at that much later (and fatal) date of 399 B.C.E.

THE DIALOGUES: SOCRATES'S TRIAL AND DEATH

We will complete our account of the life and thought of Socrates by basing it on Plato's dialogues *Euthyphro*, *Apology*, *Crito*, and *Phaedo*, all of which form a single story written to perpetuate and vindicate Socrates's memory.

Although *Euthyphro* tells an earlier part of Socrates's story than *Apology* and *Crito*, it is thought to have been written after them. *Apology* is not really a dialogue: it is the series of speeches delivered by Socrates at his trial. There can be little doubt that it is a faithful record of what was said, for it was written soon after the event and meant to be read to and by people who had been at the trial.

The same may be said of *Crito*, which depicts Socrates in prison, although the conversations it contains may well be a dramatic summary of arguments with several friends on different occasions. The object of the dialogue is to explain Socrates's attitude toward escape for the benefit of those friends who felt that he was sacrificing himself too easily. It also aims to display Socrates's loyal obedience to constitutional authority. The guilt for his condemnation was attached not to the state or its laws but to those enemies of the state who had perverted justice. *Euthyphro*, then, is the prologue of this drama. It shows Socrates awaiting his trial and informs us of the charges against him. The story of Euthyphro prosecuting his father for manslaughter is probably fictional. The dialogue illustrates Socrates's methods and suggests some ground for his unpopularity. Finally, *Phaedo*, whose theme is the immortality of the soul (not inappropriate for the occasion!), carries the story to its conclusion by describing, through an eyewitness (Phaedo of Elis), the last day in Socrates's life and the manner of his death.

Let us turn now to the first of these four dialogues.

Euthyphro

Outside the courtyard where he is to stand trial, Socrates meets Euthyphro, a seer and religious expert who says that he is going to charge his own father with manslaughter. Socrates is startled and inquires how Euthyphro can be sure that such conduct is consistent with his religious duty. The result is a discussion of the true nature of piety or holiness, and the first raising of an important question for the long subsequent history of Western thought: what is the precise relationship between God and morality?

Euthyphro is obviously sympathetic to Socrates. But he is also the kind of person to whom Socrates likes to apply his curative treatment, for Euthyphro claims confidently to be an expert in his field. Socrates is going to clear the young man's mind of some of his false assumptions and thus enable it to receive real knowledge.

Euthyphro is surprised to find Socrates before the religious courthouse and asks him why he is there and not, as is usual with him, at the Lyceum, the recreation grounds.[1] Socrates tells Euthyphro that Meletus has brought serious charges against him. Unworried, Euthyphro assures Socrates that his case will go as well as his own. Socrates naturally enquires about the latter, and is quite surprised to learn that Euthyphro is prosecuting his own father for manslaughter. When Socrates gets over the shock, he says to Euthyphro, with his tongue in his cheek, "Of course, most people have no idea, Euthyphro, what the rights of such a case are. I imagine that it isn't everyone that may take such a course, but only one who is far advanced in wisdom." To this Euthyphro replies: "Far indeed, Socrates."

Euthyphro tells his story:

> We were farming in Naxos and the deceased was working for us there. Well, he got drunk, lost his temper with one of our servants, and knifed him. So my father bound him hand and foot and threw him into a ditch; and then sent a man over here to ask the proper authority what has to be done. In the meantime he . . . neglected [the prisoner] . . . , considering that he was a murderer, and it would not matter if he died. And that was just what happened; what with starvation and exposure and confinement, he died before the messenger came back. . . . That is why both my father and my other relatives are angry with me; because on the murderer's account I am prosecuting my father for manslaughter, whereas . . . he did not kill the man, and . . . even supposing that he did kill him, since the dead man was a murderer, one ought not to concern one's self in defense of such a person, because it is an act of impiety for a son to prosecute his father for manslaughter. They have a poor comprehension, Socrates, of how the divine law stands with regard to piety and impiety.

But this leads Socrates to ask, "But tell me, Euthyphro, do you really believe that you understand the . . . divine law, and what makes actions pious and impious, so accurately that in the circumstances that you describe you have no misgivings; aren't you afraid that in taking your father into court you may . . . be committing an act of impiety yourself?"

When Euthyphro assures Socrates that he knows what piety and impiety are, Socrates is ready to be instructed. Euthyphro's first definition of piety is that it is "prosecuting a wrong-doer, whether the offender happens to be your father or anybody else." He then supports his case by reminding Socrates that that is what the children of the gods do, so it would be absurd to criticize him for doing the same. In taking him to task, he concludes, his family contradict themselves "by laying down one rule for the gods and another for me."

(What Euthyphro has in mind here are such tales of the Greek gods as that of Uranus [Heaven], who imprisoned his children, the Titans, deep in the body of his consort Gaia [Earth]. She encouraged them to assert themselves, and Cronos, the youngest but most formidable, attacked Uranus and castrated him. To avoid such a fate for himself, Cronos swallowed his own children as they were born. But his wife Rhea smuggled the infant Zeus away to Crete and put his baby clothes on a stone, which Cronos also swallowed. The clothes acted as an emetic and made him vomit up the other children. Zeus later revolted against Cronos and put him in chains.)

Socrates is not satisfied with the definition of piety offered by Euthyphro. In fact, he points out, it is not really a *definition* of piety but merely an example of it. Surely, Socrates adds, there are other things that are pious in addition to bringing a wrongdoer to trial, and what is it that is common to all of them?

To this demand, Euthyphro offers this new definition: "Piety is what the gods love." But to this Socrates replies that while it is a definition, whether it is correct they will have to see. Isn't it true, Socrates asks, that the gods often disagree about such things as right and wrong, good and bad? But if they disagree over these, then what sort of authority are they on these matters? We cannot appeal to them. For if you ask Uranus, he might say, "Yes, it is right," but if you ask Cronos, he might say, "No, it is wrong." Piety can't be "what the gods love," if they do not "love" the same things!

Euthyphro hesitates, but then gets a brilliant idea. The gods may disagree sometimes, he admits, but surely they wouldn't disagree on this: that the guilty should be punished.

It's true, Socrates admits, that no one would dispute that the guilty should be punished. But what is in *dispute*, Socrates goes on to object, is when and whether particular individuals are guilty of something. Can Euthyphro actually prove that his father is "guilty"—namely, that all the gods regard what his father has done as being wrong?

But in fact Socrates does not want to push this point too far. On the contrary, he realizes that even if it could be proven that all the gods find what Euthyphro's father did to be wrong or right, the question of *what* piety is would still be left unanswered. Euthyphro's proof would only supply information about that particular action but would reveal nothing, in general, about the meaning of these terms. Indeed even if it turned out that gods were *unanimous* in everything they loved, that they all loved and despised the same actions, we still wouldn't know the essence of piety. Their unanimous approval of some action would be a sign or proof *that* the action is pious (good, right, just, etc.), but it wouldn't tell us just what it *means* for that action to be pious. We would still lack the ultimate definition or essence of piety.

To see why this is so, Socrates continues, let us ask this question: "Is what is pious loved by the gods because it is pious, or is it pious because it is loved by them?" It is this question that would occupy thinkers a great deal during the Middle Ages, as it explores the fundamental relationship between morality and the Western monotheist's God's creative will. It then took a slightly different form. Is a given action good because God wills for us to do it, or does God will for us to do it *because* it is (already) good?

This may seem to be a quibbling question, but our very conception of God rides on it.

If we choose the first answer, that the goodness of the action results from God willing us to do it, then we commit ourselves to the belief in the unlimited power of God. God not only creates the natural world but also the moral world: acts are right and wrong only because God makes them so. The down side of this view is that it seems to make God's will arbitrary: we have no insight into *why* God chooses certain actions to be right and others to be wrong. Moreover, He could just as well will differently than He does. He could will murder to be good and giving charity to be bad.

To avoid this conclusion we might choose the second answer: God wills us to do certain actions because they are already good. This avoids the arbitrariness, as God wills for us to give charity *because* charity is good, and, being good Himself, God wouldn't change his will. But the downside is that we now seem to have limited God's power. God does not Himself create morality but is constrained by it, as He is subject to moral standards that are prior to Him and govern His will. Moreover, we still have not been told just what goodness consists in, only that it exists independently of God's will.

The reply Euthyphro basically gives to his form of the question is that "the gods love the pious thing because it is pious; it is not pious merely because they love it." Hearing this, Socrates responds, "But if it is something else and not their *loving* it which makes it pious, then what is that something else about piety that makes the gods love it so? What then, indeed, is piety? Aren't we back where we began—now saying again that piety is what the gods love?" (And we are still in the dark, as before, as to why they love it; or as we just observed, we still don't know what goodness is and why it might be "lovable.")

Not surprisingly, the dialogue ends without resolution:

> SOCRATES: We shall then have to start our inquiry about piety all over again from the beginning; because I shall never give up of my own accord until I have learnt the answer. Only don't refuse to take me seriously, but do your best to give me your closest attention, and tell me the truth, because you know it if any man does. If you didn't know all about piety and impiety you would never have attempted to prosecute your aged father for manslaughter; you would have been too much afraid of the gods, and too much ashamed of what men might think, to run such a risk, in case you should be wrong in doing so. As it is, I am sure that you think you know all about what is pious and what is not. So tell me your opinion . . . worthy Euthyphro, and don't conceal it.
>
> EUTHYPHRO: Another time, Socrates; at the moment I have an urgent engagement somewhere, and it's time for me to be off.

And this is how this dialogue ends. It shows how people's actions, which often have serious and even tragic consequences, are all too often based on ignorance. Euthyphro is about to prosecute his own father for impiety, and when asked what impiety is, he becomes confused and must admit his ignorance. And similarly with Socrates: he is about to be prosecuted on the same charge by people who are probably as confused and ignorant as Euthyphro regarding this matter. But in Socrates's case, of course, it will lead to his condemnation and execution.

Apology

The title of our next dialogue comes from the Greek word **apologia**, which was the technical term for a defendant's speech. What the dialogue contains is not an apology in our sense of the word. It is, rather, Socrates's defense of himself.

The charges against Socrates were formally brought by three Athenians, Meletus, Anytus, and Lycon, though only Meletus appears in the dialogue. The charges were that he was guilty, first, of heresy or impiety and, second, of corrupting the minds of the young by his teaching. The procedure in court was for the litigants to state their own cases. The prosecution spoke first and the defendant replied. The jury, consisting of 501 citizens, would then give its verdict by a majority vote. If the prosecutor received less than one-fifth of the total number, he was fined. If the verdict was guilty and, as in the present case, there was no penalty fixed by law, the prosecutor proposed one, the defendant proposed another, and the jury voted between them.

Apology consists of three separate speeches: Socrates's defense, his counterproposal for the penalty, and a final address to the court. (The complete text serves as the reading of this chapter.) We do not have the prosecutor's speech, but Socrates's sarcastic opening remarks tell us much about its tone. The dialogue begins with Socrates:

> I do not know what effect my accusers have had upon you, gentlemen, but for my own part I was almost carried away by them; their arguments were so convincing. On the other

hand, scarcely a word of what they said was true. I was especially astonished . . . when they told you that you must be careful not to let me deceive you—the implication being that I am a skillful speaker. I thought that it was peculiarly brazen of them to tell you this . . . since they must know that they will soon be effectively confuted, when it becomes obvious that I have not the slightest skill as a speaker—unless, of course, by a skillful speaker they mean one who speaks the truth. If that is what they mean, I would agree that I am an orator, though not after their pattern.

Socrates goes on to deal with his earliest accusers, those not present but who have been spreading false rumors about him for many years. This is his big task—to rid his listeners of these ancient prejudices and charges against him, those often made against all philosophers. He pretends to read out the affidavit his ancient critics would have drawn up had they brought him to trial: "Socrates is guilty of criminal meddling in that he inquires into things below the earth and in the sky, and teaches people to disbelieve in the gods." The accusation is, in other words, that Socrates is a student of philosophy or science and as such must be an atheist. To this he replies,

I mean no disrespect for such knowledge . . . but the fact is, gentlemen, that I take no interest in it. What is more, I call upon the greater part of you as witnesses to my statement, and I appeal to all of you who have ever listened to me talking . . . to clear your neighbors' minds on this point. Tell one another whether anyone of you has ever heard me discuss such questions . . . and then you will realize that the other popular reports about me are equally unreliable. The fact is that there is nothing in any of these charges. But here perhaps one of you might . . . say, "But what is it that you do, Socrates? . . . Surely all this . . . gossip about you would never have arisen if you had confined yourself to ordinary activities, but only if your behavior was abnormal. Tell us the explanation, if you do not want us to invent it for ourselves." This seems to be a reasonable request, and I will try to explain to you what . . . has given me this false notoriety.

At this point he tells them of his friend's visit to the famous oracle at Delphi, where the oracle proclaimed Socrates to be the wisest of all. Here follows a long section that deserves to be quoted in full:

When I heard about the oracle's answer, I said to myself, "What does the god mean? . . . I am only too conscious that I have no claim to wisdom . . . so what can he mean by asserting that I am the wisest man in the world? . . ."

After puzzling about it for some time, I set myself at last with considerable reluctance to check the truth of it. . . . I went to interview a man with a high reputation for wisdom, because I felt that here if anywhere I should succeed in disproving the oracle and pointing out to my divine authority: "You said that I was the wisest of men, but here is a man who is wiser than I am."

Well, I gave a thorough examination to this person—one of our politicians—and in conversation with him I formed the impression that although in many people's opinions, and especially in his own, he appeared to be wise, in fact he was not. Then when I began to try to show him [this], my efforts were resented both by him and by many of the other people present. However, I reflected as I walked away: "Well, I am certainly wiser than this man. It is only too likely that neither of us has any knowledge to boast of; but he thinks that he knows something which he does not know, whereas I am quite conscious of my ignorance. At any rate it seems that I am wiser than he is to this small extent, that I do not think that I know what I do not know."

After this I went on to interview a man with an even greater reputation for wisdom, and I formed the same impression again; and here too I incurred the resentment of the man himself and a number of others.

From that time on I interviewed one person after another. I realized with distress and alarm that I was making myself unpopular, but I felt compelled to put my religious duty first. Since I was trying to find out the meaning of the oracle, I was bound to interview everyone who had a reputation for knowledge. And . . . my honest impression was this: it seemed to me . . . that the people with the greatest reputations were almost entirely deficient, while others who were supposed to be their inferiors were much better qualified in practical intelligence.

I want you to think of my adventures as a sort of pilgrimage undertaken to establish the truth of the oracle once and for all. After I had finished with the politicians I turned to the poets. . . . I used to . . . question them closely about the meaning of what they had written, in the hope of incidentally enlarging my own knowledge. Well, gentlemen[,] . . . [i]t is hardly an exaggeration to say that any of the bystanders could have explained those poems better than their actual authors. So I soon made up my mind about the poets too: I decided that it was not wisdom that enables them to write their poetry, but a kind of instinct or inspiration, such as you find in seers and prophets who deliver their sublime messages without knowing in the least what they mean. . . . So I left that line of inquiry too with the same sense of advantage that I had felt in the case of the politicians. Last of all I turned to the skilled craftsmen. I knew quite well that I had practically no technical qualifications myself, and I was sure that I should find them full of impressive knowledge. In this I was not disappointed. . . .

But, gentlemen, these professional experts seemed to share the same failing which I had noticed in the poets; I mean that on the strength of their technical proficiency they claimed a perfect understanding of every other subject . . . and I felt that this error more than outweighed their positive wisdom. So I made myself spokesman for the oracle, and asked myself whether I would rather be as I was—neither wise with their wisdom nor stupid with their stupidity—or possess both qualities as they did. I replied through myself to the oracle that it was best for me to be as I was.

The effect of these investigations of mine, gentlemen, has been to arouse against me a great deal of hostility . . . which has resulted in various malicious suggestions, including the description of me as a professor of wisdom. This is due to the fact that whenever I succeed in disproving another person's claim to wisdom in a given subject, the bystanders assume that I know everything about that subject myself. But the truth of the matter, gentlemen, is . . . that real wisdom is the property of God, and this oracle is his way of telling us that human wisdom has little or no value. It seems to me that he is not referring literally to Socrates, but has merely taken my name as an example, as if he would say to us "The wisest of you men is he who has realized, like Socrates, that in respect of wisdom he is really worthless."

And so I go about the world, obedient to the god, and search . . . into the wisdom of anyone, whether citizen or stranger, who appears to be wise; and if he is not wise, then in vindication of the oracle I show him that he is not wise.

Thus Socrates ends his defense against the charges brought by his earlier critics, and turns to his present prosecutors. He questions Meletus on the new charges and in a short time shows him to be as confused about these questions as Euthyphro was. Knowing that there are still many questions troubling the jury, he next addresses himself directly to them:

But perhaps someone will say, "Do you feel no compunction, Socrates, at having followed a line of action which puts you in danger of the death penalty?" I might fairly reply to him, "You are mistaken, my friend, if you think that a man who is worth anything ought to spend his time weighing up the prospects of life and death. He has only one thing to consider in performing any action; that is, whether he is acting rightly or wrongly, like a good man or a bad one. The truth of the matter is this, gentlemen. Where a man has once taken up his stand, either because it seems best to him or in obedience to his orders, there I believe he is bound to remain and face the danger, taking no account of death or anything else before dishonor."

This being so, Socrates will not make any concessions in order to save his own life, for he does not know whether death is a good or an evil. Then he goes on to raise, on their behalf, another question:

Suppose you said to me, "Socrates, on this occasion we shall . . . acquit you, but only on one condition, that you give up . . . philosophizing. If we catch you going on in the same way, you shall be put to death." . . . I should reply, "Gentlemen, I am your . . . devoted servant, but I owe a greater obedience to God than to you; and so long as I draw breath and have my faculties, I shall never stop practicing philosophy and exhorting you and elucidating the truth for everyone that I meet. I shall go on saying . . . 'My very good friend, you are an Athenian and belong to a city which is the greatest and most famous in the world for its wisdom and strength. Are you not ashamed that you give your attention to acquiring as much money as possible, and similarly with reputation and honor, and give no attention or thought to truth and understanding and the perfection of your soul?' . . . It is my belief that no greater good has ever befallen you in this city than my service to my God; for I spend all my time going about trying to persuade you . . . to make your first and chief concern not for your bodies nor for your possessions, but for the highest welfare of your souls. . ." And so, gentlemen, I would say: "You can please yourselves whether . . . you acquit me or not; you know that I am not going to alter my conduct, not even if I have to die a hundred deaths."

He throws out a challenge to them. If he has indeed corrupted anyone, then surely they will rise and say so. A good many of his listeners are there in court. And if they won't speak up, perhaps their family members will do so. These are the people Meletus should have produced as his witnesses. "If he forgot to do so then," Socrates says with sarcasm, "let him do it now." Socrates will not appeal to the pity of his judges or make a scene in court. The judge should not be influenced by his feelings but convinced by his reason.

A vote is taken and the verdict is "guilty": 281 against Socrates, 220 for. Since there is no penalty fixed by law, each side has the option of proposing one. The prosecution proposes the death penalty. Socrates argues that since he has really been a benefactor of the state, the only just penalty would be to pension him off, like the Olympic heroes, in one of the fancy "hotels" of Athens. His friends—Plato among them—become alarmed and urge him to propose a fine, which he does—first a ridiculously low one (arguing that he cannot afford more) and then, at the urging of Plato and others who will guarantee it, a larger one.

Another vote is taken, and Socrates is condemned to death, this time by an even larger majority: 301 against him, 200 for him.

The dialogue ends with a short address by Socrates in which he prophecies that they will be accused of killing a wise man. And why could they not wait a few more years? He is an old man and certainly has not much longer to live. They are about to kill him because he has been their accuser, but other accusers will rise up and denounce them even more vehemently. He believes that what is happening to him will be good because that inner voice of his, which always restrains him when he is about to do something that he should not, gives no sign of opposition. Death, he finally argues, is either good or is nothing; it is either a profound sleep or a prelude to another life. If the latter, then how wonderful it would be to rejoin and converse with Homer and Hesiod, to see the heroes of Troy, and to continue the search after knowledge in another world. He adds that nothing can harm a good man either in life or in death, and his fortunes are not a matter of indifference to the gods.

Crito

In Athens, a sentence of execution was normally carried out at once. But the day before Socrates's trial was also the first day of the annual mission to Delos, Apollo's birthplace. This was a state holiday, during which no executions were permitted. Because of bad weather, the mission to Delos in 399 B.C.E. took so long that Socrates remained in prison for a month. In *Crito*, the ship returning from Delos has now been sighted and is about to reach Athens.

Crito has come to tell Socrates the bad news. He is a wealthy Athenian, an old man, and Socrates's closest friend. He beseeches Socrates to let his friends save him. They are ready with money, and a refuge can easily be found. Crito knows people who will take Socrates out of the country where friends will take care of him. He mustn't worry about the risks involved. They are prepared to risk a large fine, loss of property, or other punishment. Socrates must act quickly, for time is running out.

By submitting to the Athenian sentence, Crito tells Socrates, he is playing into the hands of his enemies, deserting his children, and allowing the world to believe his friends lack courage:

> Your death means a double calamity for me. I shall not only lose a friend whom I can never possibly replace, but besides a great many people . . . will be sure to think that I let

In Xenophon's *Symposium*, Socrates declared that women are inferior to men only in physical strength and in the training given to them in Athens. "Therefore," he continued, "let any man teach his wife whatever he desires." "How is it then, Socrates," a fellow guest asked, "that you haven't trained Xanthippe? I think she is the hardest to get along with of all women who have ever lived—or ever will." Socrates smiled. "Very early in my life," he replied, "I determined to get along with everybody. I noticed that all who became fine horsemen chose the most spirited horses. So I chose Xanthippe."

49

you down, because I could have saved you if I had been willing to spend the money; and what could be more contemptible than to get a name for thinking more of money than of your friends? Most people will never believe that it was you who refused to leave this place although we tried our hardest to persuade you.

To this Socrates replies, "My dear Crito, I appreciate your warm feelings very much—that is, assuming that they have some justification. Very well, then, we must consider whether we ought to follow your advice or not."

Crito has argued that Socrates should consider the consequences of his staying, but what Socrates wants to consider are only the *principles* on which he has always acted, whatever the consequences. Socrates remarks,

> The principles which I have hitherto honored and revered I still honor, and unless we can at once find other and better principles, I am certain not to agree with you. Shall we be acting rightly in paying money and showing gratitude to these people who are going to rescue me, and in escaping or arranging the escape ourselves; or shall we really be acting wrongly in doing all this? If it becomes clear that such conduct is wrong, I cannot help thinking that the question whether we are sure to die, or to suffer any other ill effect for that matter, if we stand our ground and take no action, ought not to weigh with us at all in comparison with the risk of doing what is wrong.

For him to try to escape now, he explains, would be to reverse the whole conduct of his past life, to say nothing of making a hypocrisy of his statement at the trial that he would prefer death to exile. For although he has been a critic of the state, he recognizes the authority of law as well as of his own conscience. The trial may have been unjust and the charges false, but the sentence was pronounced by the law of Athens, and it is therefore his duty to submit. Indeed, in wrongly convicting Socrates of an offense he had not committed, the culprit was not the law itself but those who abused it. If Socrates were now to take Crito's advice and flee, *he* would be the culprit—not only by violating the law but also by weakening its very fabric and authority.

"Compared with your mother and father and all the rest of your ancestors," Socrates insists, "your country is something far more precious, more venerable, more sacred, and held in greater honor both among gods and among all reasonable [people]."

This remark has occasioned much discussion. It, and others like it elsewhere in Plato's writings, are why Plato is sometimes interpreted as a kind of totalitarian. For it embodies one side of a debate that has been carried on in political philosophy for centuries. Proponents of this view tend to revere the state itself as something holy and magnificent, as a creation separate from and higher than the individuals composing it. As such, it is more worthy than the citizens themselves, whose good must always be subordinate and sacrificed for the good of the state. (Perhaps the best known among those holding this view was the German philosopher, G. W. F. Hegel [1770–1831]. Nazi Germany was able to exploit this idea to the extreme, with well-known consequences.)

The opponents of this view take a much less romantic view, typified by historical and contemporary libertarian movements. For these, the state is nothing more than a human institution. It is an instrument designed to do the necessary jobs of offering services to a populace and protecting its citizens from each other. Indeed, this approach maintains that it might be better if there were no need for a state at all. But, as there is a need, we must do our best to see to it that it does not get out of hand. Under this view the state serves an important function, but to revere it, to elevate it above the interests of its citizens, is dangerous.

Socrates's further argument here, however, is that if he did not like the law of Athens, he was free to go to another city or state. By staying, he has entered into a pact with the laws that he is not free to break at his pleasure. If he does break this pact and escape, he will disgrace himself. He must think of justice first and of his life and family afterward, so that when he enters the next world he may have all this to plead in his defense before the authorities there.

"Socrates," Crito concedes sadly, "I have nothing to say."

And so, Socrates declines his offer to escape.

Phaedo

We come to the last hours of Socrates's life. Unlike *Crito*, *Phaedo* is long and difficult. It has two main themes, the death of Socrates and the immortality of the soul. Indeed it is Socrates's firm belief in the latter that enables him to meet his death so courageously and hopefully. The scene is Socrates's prison room on the day set for his death. His friends have come to say goodbye. Toward evening, the jailor brings in the cup of poison hemlock. All this is told by an eyewitness, Phaedo, to a group of fellow philosophers, only one of whom is named and speaks. Plato, we are told, was not present at the execution; he is at home, ill.

The friends gathered around Socrates in his final hours express surprise that he remains as calm and reasonable as ever in the face of approaching death, but he argues that the philosopher has nothing to fear. Philosophy, which is always trying to release the soul from the limitations of the body, is, in effect, the study of death. What Socrates means by this strange remark is that it is only at death, when the soul is freed from the body, that it is at long last able to see things as they really are. For so long as our soul is in the body, it must view reality through the distortions of our bodily organs.

The arguments in support of immortality that Socrates discusses in this dialogue are difficult. One involves the doctrine of **nativism**, which claims that at least some of our ideas, beliefs, or knowledge is or are **innate**, that is, that we are born with it even though we don't realize it initially. But if we are already born with it, we must have learned it at *some* time, in some earlier life, in which case the soul must survive the transition between bodies. Another argument invokes our ability to glimpse or grasp the *Forms* (which we'll discuss below): if the soul can perceive the Forms of Truth, Beauty, and Goodness, which are themselves eternal and immortal, then the soul must itself be eternal and immortal. And if human beings can know God, the Eternal, we must have something eternal in us that is God-like.

At death, Socrates goes on to argue, the soul retires into another world. In a pair of beautiful myths he attempts to describe the other world. These descriptions provide ground enough "for leaving nothing undone to attain during life some measure of goodness and wisdom; for the prize is glorious and the hope great."

It is typical of Plato that where he reaches a point in his thought at which he can only speculate, where he is no longer certain, he presents his account in the form of a story or a myth. It is as if he were saying that here is where philosophy ends and fiction begins. But, of course, it is not mere fiction for him. It may be a product of his imagination, but there may be, for all we know, much truth in the account.

The myths from *Phaedo* should be read together with the similar matters described in Plato's *Republic*, especially the "Myth of Er" toward the end of the work. Er, having died before

THE DEATH OF SOCRATES

his time was really up and having already seen part of what lies ahead, was sent back to tell his fellows what awaits them. After telling his tale, Plato adds these concluding words:

> And so Glaucon . . . if you will believe with me that the soul is immortal and able to endure all good and ill, we shall keep always to the upward way and in all things pursue justice with the help of wisdom. Then we shall be at peace with heaven and with ourselves, both during our sojourn here and when, like victors in the Games . . . we receive the prize of justice; and so, not here only, but in the journey of a thousand years of which I have told you, we shall fare well.

"[E]ither this or something very like it," Socrates asserts here in *Phaedo*, "is a true account of our souls and their future habitations—since we have clear evidence that the soul is immortal— this, I think, is both a reasonable contention and a belief worth risking; for the risk is a noble one. We should use such accounts to inspire ourselves with confidence."

The last few pages of *Phaedo*, describing Socrates's death, are among the most moving in Western literature:

> When he had finished speaking, Crito said, "Very well, Socrates. But have you no directions for the others or myself about your children or anything else? What can we do to please you best?"
>
> "Nothing new, Crito," said Socrates, "just what I am always telling you. Look after yourselves and follow the line of life as I have laid it down now and in the past."
>
> "We shall try our best to do as you say," said Crito. "But how shall we bury you?"

"Any way you like," replied Socrates, "that is, if you can catch me and I don't slip through your fingers." He laughed gently as he . . . went on: "I can't persuade Crito that I am this Socrates here who is talking to you now and marshalling all the arguments; he thinks that I am the one whom he will see presently lying dead; and he asks how he is to bury me! As for my . . . elaborate explanation that I shall depart to a state of heavenly happiness, this attempt to console both you and myself seems to be wasted on him. You must assure him that when I am dead I shall not stay, but depart and be gone. That will help Crito to bear it more easily . . . when he sees my body being burned or buried, as if something dreadful were happening to me; or from saying at the funeral that it is Socrates whom he is laying out or carrying to the grave or burying. No, you must keep up your spirits and say that it is only my body that you are burying; and you can bury it as you please."

. . . With these words he got up and went into another room to bathe; and Crito went after him, but told us to wait. So we waited . . . dwelling upon the greatness of the calamity which had befallen us; for we felt just as though we were losing a father and should be orphans for the rest of our lives. Meanwhile when Socrates had taken his bath, his children were brought to see him—he had two little sons and one big boy—and the women of his household. . . . He talked to them . . . and gave them directions about carrying out his wishes; then he told the women and children to go away, and came back himself to join us.

It was now nearly sunset. . . . He came and sat down, fresh from the bath; and he had only been talking for a few minutes when the prison officer came in. . . . "Socrates," he said, "at any rate I shall not have to find fault with you, as I do with others, for getting angry with me and cursing when I tell them to drink the poison—carrying out Government orders. I have come to know during this time that you are the noblest and the gentlest and the bravest of all the men that have ever come here. . . . So now—you know what I have come to say; try to bear what must be as easily as you can." As he spoke he burst into tears, and turning around, went away.

Socrates looked up at him and said, "We will do as you say." Then addressing us he went on "What a charming person! All the time I have been here he has visited me, and sometimes had discussions with me, and shown me the greatest kindness, and how generous of him now to shed tears for me at parting! But come, Crito, let us do as he says. Someone had better bring in the poison if it is ready prepared; if not, tell the man to prepare it."

"But surely, Socrates," said Crito, "the sun is still upon the mountains; it has not gone down yet. Besides, I know that in other cases people have dinner and enjoy their wine and sometimes the company of those whom they love, long after they receive the warning; and only drink the poison quite late at night. No need to hurry; there is still plenty of time."

"It is natural that these people . . . should act in that way, Crito," said Socrates, "because they think that they gain by it. And it is also natural that I should not; because I believe that I should gain nothing by drinking the poison a little later—I should only make myself ridiculous in my own eyes if I clung to life . . . when it has no more to offer. Come, do as I say and don't make difficulties."

At this Crito made a sign to his servant. The servant went out and . . . returned with the man who was to administer the poison; he was carrying it ready prepared in a cup. When Socrates saw him he said, "Well, my good fellow . . . what ought I to do?"

"Just drink it," he said, "and then walk about until you feel a weight in your legs, and then lie down. Then it will act of its own accord."

As he spoke he handed the cup to Socrates, who received it quite cheerfully, without a tremor, without any change of color or expression, and said, looking up under his brows with his usual steady gaze, "What do you say about pouring a libation from this drink? Is it permitted, or not?"

"We only prepare what we regard as the normal dose, Socrates," he replied.

"I see," said Socrates. "But I suppose I am allowed, or rather bound, to pray the gods that my removal from this world to the other may be prosperous. This is my prayer, then; and I hope that it may be granted." With these words, quite calmly and with no sign of distaste, he drained the cup in one breath.

Up till this time most of us had been fairly successful in keeping back our tears; but when we saw that he was drinking, that he had actually drunk it, we could do so no longer; in spite of myself the tears came pouring out, so that I covered my face and wept brokenheartedly—not for him, but for my own calamity in losing such a friend. Crito had given up even before me, and had gone out when he could not restrain his tears. But Apollodorus, who had never stopped crying even before, now broke out into such a storm of passionate weeping that he made everyone in the room break down, except Socrates himself, who said:

"Really, my friends, what a way to behave! Why, that was my main reason for sending away the women, to prevent this sort of disturbance; because I am told that one should make one's end in a tranquil frame of mind. Calm yourselves and try to be brave."

This made us feel ashamed, and we controlled our tears. Socrates walked about, and presently, saying that his legs were heavy, lay down on his back—that was what the man recommended. The man kept his hand upon Socrates, and after a little while examined his feet and legs; then pinched his foot hard and asked if he felt it. Socrates said no. Then he did the same to his legs; and moving gradually upwards in this way let us see that he was getting cold and numb. Presently he felt him again and said that when it reached the heart, Socrates would be gone.

The coldness was spreading about as far as his waist when Socrates uncovered his face—for he had covered it up—and said (they were his last words):

"Crito, we ought to offer a cock to Asclepius. See to it, and don't forget."

"No, it shall be done," said Crito. "Are you sure there is nothing else?"

Socrates made no reply to this question, but after a little while he stirred; and when the man uncovered him, his eyes were fixed. When Crito saw this, he closed the mouth and eyes.

Such was the end of our comrade, who was, we may fairly say, of all those whom we knew in our time, the bravest and also the wisest and most upright man.

Why, you might be wondering, did Socrates use his last words to insist upon making an offering to "Asclepius"? Because he was consistent to the very end. Asclepius was the god of healing. People who had recovered from a serious illness would offer a sacrifice to him in gratefulness. And so now that Socrates is, with his death, about to enter a greater life, he wants to thank the god of healing, as this life is like a serious illness from which he is now recovering. It is Socrates's final irony: he has been accused of impiety, and he is about to die because of it. Yet his last deed is one of deep piety.

Socrates may now be gone from our narrative, but Plato is still very much with us. We would be remiss were we to conclude our sketch of ancient Greek philosophy without saying a little about one of Plato's most famous and important doctrines. (Again, where Socrates leaves off and Plato begins it is not easy to say; so we shall just treat this as Plato's doctrine.)

What is the doctrine of Forms? Very briefly, it involves the claim that there's more to the world than what you see, or even *could* see. For in addition to the ordinary objects we perceive around us with our senses, there also exists a completely separate, non-physical realm in which there are eternal, uncreated, unchanging—and unperceivable—objects called *Forms*.

Our first task, then, is to get clearer on just what these are.

What Exactly Are Forms?

According to Plato's own great student, Aristotle (384–322 B.C.E.), Plato "separated universals from the particulars," and called them *Forms*.[3]

Forms are *separated* universals.

Separated from what? From the "sensible order," that is, from the world as we can sense it with our eyes, our ears, and so on. Since Forms are not part of the sensible order they must exist in some "separate" realm, distinct from that of the ordinary objects around us.

Moreover, they are separated *universals*.

Something is a **universal** insofar as it is or can be "repeatable," that is, occur in many different particular things (or just **particulars**). For example, suppose that some grass, an unripe banana, and a certain car are all the same shade of green; that is, the very same greenness appears in each of the different individual things. The different individuals are *particulars*, and the greenness is a *universal* (henceforth, we'll denote universals with capital letters, "Greenness"). Similarly, a ball, a boulder, and the sun may all be round: "Roundness" then refers to the universal occurring in each of the particular round things. Or there are many electrons in existence: each individual electron is a particular, while "Electron" or "Electronhood" refer to the universal "repeating" itself in each of the particulars.

In "separating Forms from the sensible order," then, Plato is suggesting that things such as Greenness, Roundness, and Electronhood are distinct from, or exist separately from, the individual things which *are* green, round, and electrons.

> The safest general characterization of the European philosophical tradition is that it consists in a series of footnotes to Plato.
>
> **—Alfred North Whitehead** (1861–1947)

Forms Are Neither Perceivable, Changeable, Nor Even Here

Once Forms are separated in this way, there are immediate implications.

For one, individual green things, round things, or electrons (i.e., particulars) typically are objects of our bodily senses: we can see them, or touch them, and so on. We can even observe particular electrons, with the help of fancy equipment. But if the Forms are separate from the particulars, then seeing the particular is not the same thing as seeing the Form: the Forms themselves cannot be "seen" in the same way or sense.

Second, while all the particulars around us are constantly in flux (coming into and going out of being, changing, etc.), the Forms, separate from them, may themselves be uncreated and unchanging. So when a banana ripens, a particular individual thing may change from green to yellow, but Greenness itself, what it is to *be* green, never changes. Similarly, Socrates the particular human being may change over time in many ways, he may become more or less virtuous, taller or shorter, and may even, on dying, lose his humanity altogether—but what Virtue itself is, and Height, and Humanity, do not change.

Finally, and most generally, while individual green things, round things, or electrons exist here in the world around us, if Greenness and the other Forms are separated from them then they must exist "elsewhere"—whatever that means exactly.

Separating Forms from the sensible order, in short, makes them into very different sorts of things than ordinary objects.

How Many Forms Are There?

The short answer is, a lot.

In his earlier dialogues Plato was primarily concerned with Forms related to ethical concerns, such as Justice, Piety, and Goodness. To investigate these is to ask a question such as, for example, "What is Goodness?" As we saw in *Euthyphro* above, an answer might begin by listing particular actions or things which *are* good, but that merely tells us where Goodness may be found, not what Goodness actually *is*. To determine *that* requires generating a *definition* of Goodness, a definition such that every thing which fits the definition is good and every thing which doesn't, isn't.

And this process, the formulating of a definition, involves something other than our senses. We don't merely "look and see" what Goodness is but we have to *think*, carefully, about what it is that all good things might share. As Plato writes,[4]

> Do we say that there is such a thing as the Just itself, or not? We do say so, by Zeus. And the Beautiful, and the Good? Of course. And have you ever seen any of these things with your eyes? In no way, he said. Or have you ever grasped them with any of your bodily senses? I am speaking of all things such as Bigness, Health, Strength and, in a word, the reality of all other things, that which each of them essentially is. Is what is most true in them contemplated through the [senses], or is this the position: . . . he will [know] this most perfectly who approaches the object with thought [intellect] alone. (*Phaedo* 65d–66a, 57)

Note here how this passage reflects the separateness of Forms from the particulars, for those latter we surely *do* detect via our senses. Note, too, Plato's view that the Forms are "the reality" of things, "that which each of them essentially is": the Form of Goodness is what goodness essentially *is*, while particular good things merely reflect Goodness without capturing it completely. Further, Plato adds elsewhere that the Forms are "perfect," and are what the particulars reflecting them strive to be (if not always successfully).

All these points are perhaps best illustrated by Plato's conception of mathematical Forms.

Consider the Form of the Triangle. The definition or essence of a triangle is to be a three-sided closed figure. But while every particular triangular thing we may encounter through our senses, everything triangular thing, will reflect this essence, none will reflect it perfectly. For the line segments composing the Triangle are both perfectly straight and purely one-dimensional, lacking all breadth; but the sides of every actual particular triangle will be neither *perfectly* straight nor *entirely* lacking in breadth. We might say that every particular triangle is an "approximation" of the perfect Triangle, while "the Triangle" is the real deal. The same goes for particular good things, beautiful things, and so on.

So far, then, Plato admits ethical Forms, mathematical Forms, and Forms such as Bigness, Health, Beauty, and Strength. But now that isn't all. In his late work, *Timaeus*, Plato examines the creation of the universe. Here he suggests that, prior to creating, the Creator models what he creates on the Forms, much as a craftsperson might have a certain model or idea of a bed (say) in his head before building it. But of course one cannot impose Forms on nothing, any more than one could build a bed with no materials: there must be some matter or material with or on which to work. So just as a human craftsperson might take some wood and fashion it into a bed, so Plato's Creator took the matter of the universe and imposed Forms on it. He made humans and horses and stones by imposing Humanity, Horsehood, and Stoniness on matter. This picture suggests that there are Forms corresponding to *every* natural kind of thing there is, and, possibly, to every kind of artifact as well.

The analogy also suggests one further question. If the Creator created all the particular things of the universe by imposing Forms on matter, then where did the Forms and matter *themselves* come from?

Answer: nowhere.

Unlike the particular things, which come and go and change, Forms and matter simply always have been around, eternal, unchanging, and uncreated. For Plato, the universe as a whole has, on the fundamental level, always existed.

One More Important Implication

Let's briefly note here how all this supports Plato's belief in the immortality of the soul, mentioned earlier. Forms are separated from this physical world, and thus not perceivable by our bodily senses. If we do "perceive" (or grasp) them, it is not by virtue of our senses but of our intellect (or "intellectual soul," as Plato might put it). Our intellectual soul must therefore itself be separate from our body, because it can engage with these non-physical Forms. If it is already separate from the body, then the death of the body no longer entails the death of the soul. Moreover, since the Forms are eternal and unchanging, our intellect, to engage with them, must be as well. So our intellectual souls are eternal and unchanging—in which case they surely do not expire with the body.

So some impressive things follow, if Plato is right about the existence of Forms.

But is he?

Why Should We Believe in the Existence of Forms?

Interestingly, Plato himself never sets down his arguments for the existence of Forms in any systematic way. But fortunately his attentive student Aristotle summarizes several such arguments which are at least Platonic in nature.[5]

(1) The Meanings of General Terms

Every human being may be called "human"; every animal may be called "animal." Yet in no case is the name for some particular individual synonymous with the name for the general property or kind. When we say "Fred is human," "Fred" applies only to that individual while "human" applies to many others. Similarly, the name "Rover" is not synonymous with the general term "animal" or even "dog." Words such as "human" and "animal," therefore, refer to something more general than any of the particulars around us, that is, to a Form. So there must exist Forms, to serve as the meanings for our general terms.

Now this argument may invite the following objection.

Sure, "Fred" only applies to this one guy while "human" applies to many others. But that doesn't mean that "human" refers to some general or universal thing, a Form. For perhaps "human" simply means "every human being," and while that meaning *is* more general than "Fred," that's not enough to make this "general thing" be a "Form." Rather, the general thing just is the collection of all the particulars, of all the human beings, a collection as changing, transient, and this-worldly as the particular human beings themselves in the collection. So Argument (1), the objection concludes, does not support belief in Plato's Forms.

The next three arguments are responses to this objection.

(2) Destruction of Particulars

The word "human," the response now goes, cannot merely mean "the collection of all human beings," because what "human" means remains fixed even while that collection changes. As we've seen, Socrates the human being may change but what it is to *be* a human being never does. More generally, particular humans may come and go (as they are born and die), but what it is to *be* human—what we mean by the general term "human"—does not. So there is more to the meaning of "human" than simply the collection of all particular human beings, and this additional thing is the Form, Humanity.

(3) Knowing What We Mean

To this point we may add another. We often know fully well what we mean when we use a general term even when we have no idea just which, and how many, particular individuals fit that term. In this case we know fully well what we mean by "human" even when we haven't the faintest notion just which and how many particular human beings there currently may be. Thus what we mean by "human" is not "the collection of all humans," again, but something more general in nature, a Form.

(4) Sameness or Similarity

And indeed, there's a good *reason* we apply the same general word to distinct individual particulars. There's a reason that "human" applies to the many individual humans: it's because they are the same with respect to whatever we mean by "human." Imagine, to illustrate, you are in the jungle looking for new species of animals. You come upon one individual animal and then another, and you determine that they belong to the same "species." How? Because they share certain features: they are both mammals, they both have four legs and a certain striped pattern, and so on. They are both called "tiger" (say) because they are both *tigers*: they are members of the same kind insofar as there is one thing they both are, namely *tiger*.

But that is to say that one thing, *Tigerhood*, is present in both of them. This particular tiger may be over here, that particular tiger may be over there, but Tigerhood is present in both places. Indeed Tigerhood is *fully* present in both places because each animal is fully, completely, a tiger.

But think about what this means.

Sometimes we explain why two things are similar by saying they "share" a property. This is red and that is red; they share the property of Redness. But what does it mean to share something? Two people may share a condo, or a name, or (if they are conjoined) even a kidney. In each case there is literally one thing to which both have access. So if this is a tiger and that is a tiger, there must be one thing—Tigerhood—to which both have access. But this one thing cannot literally be located in any one place. If it were located over *here*, the tiger over *there* couldn't access it; if it were over *there*, then the tiger over *here* couldn't access it. Indeed two tigers both have access to Tigerhood even if they are miles or continents or centuries apart. So whatever Tigerhood is, exactly, it is not literally located *anywhere*.

It is, in other words, a Form. And like all Forms, the Form of the Tiger is separate from all the individuals who are themselves tigers.

That's why you should believe in the existence of Forms.

PHILOSOPHERS AND CAVE PERSONS

So Forms are separate from the particulars of the world. Unlike particulars they are uncreated and eternal and unchanging, and particular things are modeled after them and strive to be like them. As such, Forms are more perfect, and ultimately more "real," than the particulars of this world.

This doctrine, Plato is well aware, seems deeply opposed to common sense. What's real, most people think, is what you can see and hear and touch. Anything else is just a fiction, a creation of the mind, an "idea." That's why ordinary people look strangely at the philosopher, who incomprehensibly speaks of mysterious realms of separate beings.

The painful irony, in Plato's view, is that common sense has things backward. It is the philosopher who grasps reality through reasoning and intellect who has things right, while the ordinary individual, relying on his senses, gets things wrong.

Plato illustrates the situation in *Republic*'s famous analogy:

> Imagine human beings living in an underground, cavelike dwelling, with an entrance a long way up. . . . They've been there since childhood, fixed in the same place, with their necks and legs fettered, able to see only in front of them. . . . Light is provided by a fire burning far above and behind them. Also behind them, but on higher ground, there is a path stretching between them and the fire. Imagine that along this path a low wall has been built, like the screen in front of puppeteers above which they show their puppets. . . . Then also imagine that there are people along the wall, carrying all kinds of artifacts that project above it—statues of people and other animals. . . . Do you suppose . . . that these prisoners see anything . . . besides the shadows that the fire casts on the wall in front of them? (*Republic* VII, 514a–515b, 1132–33)

The cave people see not themselves or each other, but only *shadows* of things projected on the wall in front of them, shadows of the things being carried by the people above and behind them. Since this is all they have ever seen, they believe that these shadows are what there is: reality consists in these "objects" and their motions.

But now consider

> what being released from their bonds and cured of their ignorance would naturally be like. . . . When one of them was freed and suddenly compelled to stand up, turn his head, walk, and look up toward the light, he'd be pained and dazzled and unable to see the things whose shadows he'd seen before. (*Republic* VII, 515c–d, 1133)

Being used to seeing only shadows in dim light, a freed individual would initially have trouble seeing the actual carved objects themselves in front of the fire; and if you were to tell him that the carved objects were "more real" than the shadows he'd been accustomed to seeing, he would be very perplexed!

But now imagine further,

> if someone dragged him away from there . . . up the rough, steep path . . . into the sunlight, wouldn't he be pained and irritated at being treated that way? And when he came into the light, with the sun filling his eyes, wouldn't he be unable to see a single one of the things now said to be true? (*Republic* VII, 515e–516a, 1133)

If seeing the carved objects before the fire was difficult, imagine how much more difficult to look at the real objects, after which those carved objects were modeled, in the real sunlight! The freed individual would be disoriented, perhaps inclined to run back to the "reality" he previously knew. But in time, with acclimation, he'd be able to see the trees, the animals, the objects here in the sunlight; and come to recognize that the carved objects were merely imitations of, imperfect copies of, those real objects; and then come to recognize that the shadows cast by those carved objects, which he initially took to be "reality," were about as far removed from true reality, outside the cave, as one could get.

The overall analogy is clear.

The particular objects around us are like the shadows in the cave, while the Forms are the "real" objects outside the cave. Ordinary people who, by common sense, take the objects we perceive around us to be real are like the cave people who see only shadows, and take these shadows for reality. The philosopher is the one who has escaped from the cave, and come into the sunlight, and truly perceives reality—the Forms.

And now it is the philosopher who has the perhaps unenviable task of convincing those remaining in the cave, who have never seen the fire or the sunlight, that what they have been perceiving their entire lives is in fact far removed from what is truly, ultimately real.

And doing so without, hopefully, getting himself forced to drink the Hemlock that Plato's predecessor Socrates was forced to drink, for the same reason: showing people that what they thought was real and true in fact was nothing but shadows.

SUMMARY

1. Socrates differed from previous Greek philosophers in being concerned not with the external world but far more with the inner world of human beings and our nature, our *psyche*. He tried to persuade others that wealth and glory are far less valuable than knowledge and glory. He was sometimes confused with the Sophists, who over time lost their good name as a result of their increasingly severe attacks on the established system of law, ethics, and religion.

2. Socrates created great resentment in challenging the self-proclaimed experts and wise individuals of his time, eventually being arrested and brought to trial for impiety and corruption of youth.

3. The person who immortalized Socrates was his student Plato, in a series of dialogues mostly featuring Socrates. Of these, *Euthyphro, Apology, Crito,* and *Phaedo* form a unit describing Socrates's thought, trial, and death.

4. *Euthyphro* examines the relationship between the divine and morality. After Euthyphro eventually defines piety (or goodness) as "what all the gods love," the question emerges whether the pious (the good) is loved by the gods because it is pious (good), or whether it is pious (good) because it is loved by the gods. Euthyphro opts for the former, but Socrates points out that that leaves us not knowing just what piousness (or goodness) actually is.

5. In *Apology* Socrates responds to the charges against him, that he has been spreading heresy or impiety and that he has been corrupting the minds of the young. He describes his effort to disprove the Delphic oracle's claim that he was the wisest person in the world, by interviewing those with great reputations for wisdom. Socrates discovers that these individuals in fact know nothing, and that his own wisdom consists in his at least recognizing that he knows nothing. The jury finds him guilty, and sentences him to death.

6. In *Crito*, Socrates is in prison awaiting execution and rejects Crito's pleas to help him escape. Despite his wrongful conviction, he explains, the wrong has been inflicted not by the state or law itself but by those individuals who have misused the law. Were he to escape he would challenge the whole institution of law, which is greater than any of the individuals who misuse it. Besides, by having voluntarily stayed in Athens his whole life and enjoyed its benefits, he had entered into a pact to comply with the law that he is not free to break at his pleasure.

7. *Phaedo* tells of the final hours of Socrates's life. Surrounded by friends, Socrates explains why the philosopher does not fear death, offering arguments for the immortality of the soul. One of these invokes nativism, another our ability to grasp the eternal Forms. The dialogue ends with a moving account of Socrates's last moments and death.

8. One of Plato's most famous doctrines is his belief in the existence of Forms. These are "separated universals": separated from the world that we can perceive, and universal in that they are "repeatable." Forms are neither perceivable, nor changeable, nor even literally present in the world we inhabit. We grasp them not by our senses but by our intellectual souls, which must be as eternal as they in order to grasp them.

9. Plato offers four arguments for the existence of Forms, invoking the meanings of general terms, the destruction of particulars, that we know what we mean when we speak generally, and the sameness or similarity of distinct particulars.

10. Forms are what is ultimately real. The world we perceive is like a pale reflection of the Forms, like the shadows cast on the wall by the fire or sunlight in Plato's famous metaphor of the cave. Only the philosopher truly grasps the Forms, and then has the unenviable task of trying to explain them to those who don't.

KEY TERMS

apologia
Forms
innate
nativism

particulars
psyche
Sophists
universals

REVIEW QUESTIONS

1. Who were the Sophists?

2. What was Socrates's view about the relationship between learning and moral behavior? On what charges was he brought to trial?

3. What was the Academy, and who founded it?

4. Name the four Platonic dialogues that are devoted to the life and teachings of Socrates. Briefly summarize the main theme and/or moral of each dialogue.

5. What is nativism, and how may it be invoked to defend the immortality of the soul?

6. What does it mean to describe Plato's Forms as "separated universals"?

7. Briefly summarize one of Plato's arguments for the existence of Forms.

NOTES

1. Translations of passages from *Euthyphro, Crito,* and *Phaedo* are from Hugh Tredennick, *Plato: The Last Days of Socrates* (Harmondsworth: Penguin, 1954). Reproduced by permission.

2. Much of what follows is adapted from Andrew Pessin, *Uncommon Sense: The Strangest Ideas from the Smartest Philosophers* (Lanham, MD: Rowman & Littlefield, 2012), ch. 1.

3. See Aristotle's *Metaphysics* 1078b12–34, in ed., J. L. Ackrill, *A New Aristotle Reader* (Princeton: Princeton University Press, 1987), 356.

4. The following Plato quotations are from Ed. John Cooper, *Plato: Complete Works* (Indianapolis: Hackett, 1997).

5. See G. M. A. Grube, *Plato's Thought* (Indianapolis:, Hackett, 1935/1980), pp. 5ff., for detailed discussion.

■ Reading
Apology

P L A T O

From transl., Benjamin Jowett, The Dialogues of Plato, Vol II, *3rd edition (New York: Oxford University Press, originally © 1892 by Macmillan and Co.).*

In this reading, Plato gives an account of the speeches Socrates made at his trial.

How you, O Athenians, have been affected by my accusers, I cannot tell; but I know that they almost made me forget who I was—so persuasively did they speak; and yet they have hardly uttered a word of truth. But of the many falsehoods told by them, there was one which quite amazed me; I mean when they said that you should be upon your guard and not allow yourselves to be deceived by the force of my eloquence. To say this, when they were certain to be detected as soon as I opened my lips and proved myself to be anything but a great speaker, did indeed appear to me most shameless—unless by the force of eloquence they mean the force of truth; for if such is their meaning, I admit that I am eloquent. But in how different a way from theirs! Well, as I was saying, they have scarcely spoken the truth at all; but from me you shall hear the whole truth.

. . . [F]irst, I have to reply to the older charges and to my first accusers, and then I will go on to the later ones. For of old I have had many accusers, who have accused me falsely to you during many years; and I am more afraid of them than of Anytus and his associates, who are dangerous, too, in their own way. But far more dangerous are the others, who began when you were children, and took possession of your minds with their falsehoods, telling of one Socrates, a wise man, who speculated about the heaven above, and searched into the earth beneath, and made the worse appear the better cause. The disseminators of this tale are the accusers whom I dread; for their hearers are apt to fancy that such enquirers do not believe in the existence of the gods. And they are many, and their charges against me are of ancient date, and they were made by them in the days when you were more impressible than you are now—in childhood, or it may have been in youth—and the cause when heard went by default, for there was none to answer. And hardest of all, I do not know and cannot tell the names of my accusers; unless in the chance case of a Comic poet. . . .

Well, then, I must make my defence. . . .

I will begin at the beginning, and ask what is the accusation which has given rise to the slander of me, and in fact has encouraged Meletus to prefer this charge against me. Well, what do the slanderers say? They shall be my prosecutors, and I will sum up their words in an affidavit: "Socrates is an evildoer, and a curious person, who searches into things under the earth and in heaven, and he makes the worse appear the better cause; and he teaches the aforesaid doctrines to others." Such is the nature of the accusation: it is just what you have yourselves seen in the comedy of Aristophanes [*The Clouds*], who has introduced a man whom he calls Socrates, going about and saying that he walks in air, and talking a deal of nonsense concerning matters of which I do not pretend to know either much or little—not that I mean to speak disparagingly of anyone who is a student of natural philosophy. I should be very sorry if Meletus could bring so grave a charge against me. But the simple truth is, O Athenians, that I have nothing to do with physical speculations. Very many of those here present are witnesses to the truth of this, and to them I appeal. Speak then, you who have heard me, and tell your neighbors whether any of you have ever known me hold forth in few words or in many upon such matters. . . . You hear their answer. And from what they say of this part of the charge you will be able to judge of the truth of the rest.

As little foundation is there for the report that I am a teacher, and take money; this accusation has no more truth in it than the other. Although, if a man were really able to instruct mankind, to receive money for giving instruction would, in my opinion, be an honour to him. . . . Had I the same, I should have been very proud and conceited; but the truth is that I have no knowledge of the kind.

I dare say, Athenians, that someone among you will reply, "Yes, Socrates, but what is the origin of these accusations which are brought against you; there must have been something strange which you have been doing? All these rumours and this talk about you would never have arisen if you had been like other men: tell us, then, what is the cause of them, for we should be sorry to judge hastily of you." Now, I regard this as a fair challenge, and I will endeavor to explain to you the reason why I am called wise and have such an evil fame. Please to attend then. And although some of you may think that I am joking, I declare that I will tell you the entire truth. Men of Athens, this reputation of mine has come of a certain sort of wisdom which I possess. If you ask me what kind of wisdom, I reply, wisdom such as may perhaps be attained by man, for to that extent I am inclined to believe that I am wise; whereas the persons of whom I was speaking have a superhuman wisdom, which I may fail to describe, because I have it not myself; and he who says that I have, speaks falsely, and is taking away my character. And here, O men of Athens, I must beg you not to interrupt me, even if I seem to say something extravagant. For the word which I will speak is not mine. I will refer you to a witness who is worthy of credit; that witness shall be the God of Delphi—he will tell you about my wisdom, if I have any, and of what sort it is. You must have known Chaerephon; he was early a friend of mine, and also a friend of yours . . . and he went to Delphi and boldly asked the oracle to tell him whether . . . any one was wiser than I was, and the Pythian prophetess answered that there was no man wiser. . . .

Why do I mention this? Because I am going to explain to you why I have such an evil name. When I heard the answer, I said to myself, What can the god mean? and what is the interpretation of his riddle? for I know that I have no wisdom, small or great. What then can he mean when he says that I am the wisest of men? And yet he is a god, and cannot lie; that would be against his nature. After long consideration, I thought of a method of trying the question. I reflected that if I could only find a man wiser than myself, then I might go to the god with a refutation in my hand. I should say to him, "Here is a man who is wiser than I am; but you said that I was the wisest." Accordingly I went to one who had the reputation of wisdom, and observed him—his name I need not mention; he was a politician whom I selected for examination—and the result was as follows: When I began to talk with him, I could not help thinking that he was not really wise, although he was thought wise by many, and still wiser by himself; and thereupon I tried to explain to him that he thought himself wise, but was not really wise; and the consequence was that he hated me, and his enmity was shared by several who were present and heard me. So I left him, saying to myself, as I went away: Well, although I do not suppose that either of us knows anything really beautiful and good, I am better off than he is—for he knows nothing, and thinks that he knows; I neither know nor think that I know. In this latter particular, then, I seem to have slightly the advantage of him. Then I went to another who had still higher pretensions to wisdom, and my conclusion was exactly the same. Whereupon I made another enemy of him, and of many others besides him.

Then I went to one man after another, being not unconscious of the enmity which I provoked, and I lamented and feared this: but necessity was laid upon me—the word of God, I thought, ought to be considered first. And I said to myself, Go I must to all who appear to know, and find out the meaning of the oracle. And I swear to you, Athenians . . . the result of my mission was just this: I found that the men most in repute were all but the most foolish; and that others less esteemed were really wiser and better. I will tell you the tale of my wanderings and of the "Herculean" labors, as I may call them, which I endured only to find at last the oracle irrefutable. After the politicians, I went to the poets. . . . I took them some of the most elaborate passages in their own writings, and asked what was the meaning of them—thinking that they would teach me something. Will you believe me? I am almost ashamed to confess the truth, but I must say that there is hardly a person present who would not have talked better about their poetry than they did themselves. Then I knew that not by wisdom do poets write poetry, but by a sort of genius and inspiration; they are like diviners or soothsayers who also say many fine things, but do not understand the meaning of them. The poets appeared to me to be much in the same case; and I further observed that upon the strength of their poetry they believed themselves to be the wisest of men in other things in which they were not wise. So I departed, conceiving myself to be superior to them for the same reason that I was superior to the politicians.

At last I went to the artisans. I was conscious that I knew nothing at all, as I may say, and I was sure that they knew many fine things; and here I was not mistaken, for they did know many things of which I was ignorant, and in this they certainly were wiser than I was. But I observed that even the good artisans fell into the same error as the poets; because they were good workmen they thought that they also knew all sorts of high matters, and this defect in them overshadowed their wisdom; and therefore I asked myself on behalf of the oracle, whether I would like to be as I was, neither having their knowledge nor their ignorance, or like them in both; and I made answer to myself and to the oracle that I was better off as I was.

This inquisition has led to my having many enemies of the worst and most dangerous kind, and has given occasion also to many calumnies. And I am called wise, for my hearers always imagine that I myself possess the wisdom which I find wanting in others: but the truth is, O men of Athens, that God only is wise; and by his answer he intends to show that the wisdom of men is worth little or nothing; he is not speaking of Socrates, he is only using my name by way of illustration, as if he said, He, O men, is the wisest, who, like Socrates, knows that his wisdom is in truth worth nothing. And so I go about the world obedient to the god, and search and make enquiry into the wisdom of anyone, whether citizen or stranger, who appears to be wise; and if he is not wise, then in vindication of the oracle I show him that he is not wise; and my occupation quite absorbs me, and I have no time to give either to any public matter of interest or to any concern of my own, but I am in utter poverty by reason of my devotion to the god. . . .

Someone will say: And are you not ashamed, Socrates, of a course of life which is likely to bring you to an untimely end? To him I may fairly answer: There you are mistaken: a man who is good for anything ought not to calculate the chance of living or dying; he ought only to consider whether in doing anything he is doing right or wrong— acting the part of a good man or of a bad. . . . Had Achilles any thought of death and danger? For wherever a man's place is

. . . there he ought to remain in the hour of danger; he should not think of death or of anything but of disgrace. And this, O men of Athens, is a true saying.

Strange, indeed, would be my conduct, O men of Athens, if I, who, when I was ordered by the generals whom you chose to command me at Potidaea and Amphipolis and Delium, remained where they placed me, like any other man, facing death—if now, when, as I conceive and imagine, God orders me to fulfill the philosopher's mission of searching into myself and other men, I were to desert my post through fear of death, or any other fear; that would indeed be strange, and I might justly be arraigned in court for denying the existence of the gods, if I disobeyed the oracle because I was afraid of death, fancying that I was wise when I was not wise. For the fear of death is indeed the pretence of wisdom, and not real wisdom, being a pretence of knowing the unknown; and no one knows whether death, which men in their fear apprehend to be the greatest evil, may not be the greatest good. Is not this ignorance of a disgraceful sort, the ignorance which is the conceit that a man knows what he does not know? And in this respect only I believe myself to differ from men in general, and may perhaps claim to be wiser than they are:—that whereas I know but little of the world below, I do not suppose that I know: but I do know that injustice and disobedience to a better, whether God or man, is evil and dishonorable, and I will never fear or avoid a possible good rather than a certain evil. And therefore if you let me go now, and are not convinced by Anytus, who said that since I had been prosecuted I must be put to death (or if not that I ought never to have been prosecuted at all); and that if I escape now, your sons will all be utterly ruined by listening to my words—if you say to me, Socrates, this time we will not mind Anytus, and you shall be let off, but upon one condition, that you are not to enquire and speculate in this way anymore, and that if you are caught doing so again you shall die;—if this was the condition on which you let me go, I should reply: Men of Athens, I honor and love you; but I shall obey God rather than you, and while I have life and strength I shall never cease from the practice and teaching of philosophy, exhorting anyone whom I meet and saying to him after my manner: You, my friend,—a citizen of the great and mighty and wise city of Athens,—are you not ashamed of heaping up the greatest amount of money and honor and reputation, and caring so little about wisdom and truth and the greatest improvement of the soul, which you never regard or heed at all? And if the person with whom I am arguing, says: Yes, but I do care; then I do not leave him or let him go at once; but I proceed to interrogate and examine and cross examine him, and if I think that he has no virtue in him, but only says that he has, I reproach him with undervaluing the greater, and overvaluing the less. And I shall repeat the same words to everyone whom I meet, young and old, citizen and alien, but especially to the citizens, inasmuch as they are my brethren. For know that this is the command of God; and I believe that no greater good has ever happened in the state than my service to the God. For I do nothing but go about persuading you all, old and young alike, not to take thought for your persons or your properties, but first and chiefly to care about the greatest improvement of the soul. I tell you that virtue is not given by money, but that from virtue comes money and every other good of man, public as well as private. This is my teaching, and if this is the doctrine which corrupts the youth, I am a mischievous person. But if anyone says that this is not my teaching, he is speaking an untruth. Wherefore, O men of Athens, I say to you, do as Anytus bids or not as Anytus bids, and either acquit me or not; but whichever you do, understand that I shall never alter my ways, not even if I have to die many times. . . .

And now, Athenians, I am not going to argue for my own sake, as you may think, but for yours, that you may not sin against the God by condemning me, who am his gift to you. For if you kill me you will not easily find a successor to me, who, if I may use such a ludicrous figure of speech, am a sort of gadfly, given to the state by God; and the state is a great and noble steed who is tardy in his motions owing to his very size, and requires to be stirred into life. I am that gadfly which God has attached to the state, and all day long and in all places am always fastening upon you, arousing and persuading and reproaching you. . . . When I say that I am given to you by God, the proof of my mission is this:—if I had been like other men, I should not have neglected all my own concerns or patiently seen the neglect of them during all these years, and have been doing yours, coming to you individually like a father or elder brother, exhorting you to regard virtue; such conduct, I say, would be unlike human nature. If I had gained anything, or if my exhortations had been paid, there would have been some sense in my doing so; but now, as you will perceive, not even the impudence of my accusers dares to say that I have ever exacted or sought pay of anyone; of that they have no witness. And I have a sufficient witness to the truth of what I say—my poverty.

Some one may wonder why I go about in private giving advice and busying myself with the concerns of others, but do not venture to come forward in public and advise the state. I will tell you why. You have heard me speak at sundry times and in divers places of an oracle or sign which comes to me, and is the divinity which Meletus ridicules in the indictment. This sign, which is a kind of voice, first began to come to me when I was a child; it always forbids but never commands me to do anything which I am going to do. . . .

I can give you convincing evidence of what I say, not words only, but what you value far more—actions. Let me relate to you a passage of my own life which will prove to you that I should never have yielded to injustice from any fear of death. . . . [Socrates relates a story of how, when he was a senator, he stood up for justice against death threats] . . . and then I showed, not in word only but in deed, that . . . I cared not a straw for death, and that my great and only care was lest I should do an unrighteous or unholy thing. . . .

I have been always the same in all my actions, public as well as private, and never have I yielded any base compliance to those who are slanderously termed my disciples, or to any other. Not that I have any regular disciples. But if anyone likes to come and hear me while I am pursuing my mission, whether he be young or old, he is not excluded. Nor do I converse only with those who pay; but anyone, whether he be rich or poor, may ask and answer me and listen to my words; and whether he turns out to be a bad man or a good one, neither result can be justly imputed to me; for I never taught or professed to teach him anything. And if anyone says that he has ever learned or heard anything from me in private which all the world has not heard, let me tell you that he is lying. . . .

Well, Athenians, this and the like of this is all the defence which I have to offer. . . .

[Socrates is convicted.]

There are many reasons why I am not grieved, O men of Athens, at the vote of condemnation. I expected it, and am only surprised that the votes are so nearly equal; for I had thought that the majority against me would have been far larger; but now, had thirty votes gone over to the other side, I should have been acquitted. And I may say, I think, that I have escaped Meletus. I may say more; for without the assistance of Anytus and Lycon, anyone may see that he would not have had a fifth part of the votes, as the law requires, in which case he would have incurred a fine of a thousand drachmae.

And so he proposes death as the penalty. And what shall I propose on my part, O men of Athens? Clearly that which is my due. And what is my due? What returns shall be made to the man who has never had the wit to be idle during his whole life; but has been careless of what the many care for—wealth, and family interests, and military offices, and speaking in the assembly, and magistracies, and plots, and parties. Reflecting that I was really too honest a man to be a politician and live, I did not go where I could do no good to you or to myself; but where I could do the greatest good privately to every one of you, thither I went, and sought to persuade every man among you that he must look to himself, and seek virtue and wisdom before he looks to his private interests, and look to the state before he looks to the interests of the state; and that this should be the order which he observes in all his actions. What shall be done to such a one? Doubtless some good thing, O men of Athens, if he has his reward; and the good should be of a kind suitable to him. What would be a reward suitable to a poor man who is your benefactor, and who desires leisure that he may instruct you? There can be no reward so fitting as maintenance in the Prytaneum, O men of Athens, a reward which he deserves far more than the citizen who has won the prize at Olympia in the horse or chariot race. . . .

Perhaps you think that I am braving you in what I am saying now. . . . But this is not so. I speak rather because I am convinced that I never intentionally wronged anyone, although I cannot convince you—the time has been too short; if there were a law at Athens, as there is in other cities, that a capital cause should not be decided in one day, then I believe that I should have convinced you. But I cannot in a moment refute great slanders; and, as I am convinced that I never wronged another, I will assuredly not wrong myself. I will not say of myself that I deserve any evil, or propose any penalty. Why should I? Because I am afraid of the penalty of death which Meletus proposes? When I do not know whether death is a good or an evil, why should I propose a penalty which would certainly be an evil? Shall I say imprisonment? And why should I live in prison, and be the slave of the magistrate of the year. . . ? Or shall the penalty be a fine, and imprisonment until the fine is paid? There is the same objection. I should have to lie in prison, for money I have none, and cannot pay. And if I say exile . . . I must indeed be blinded by the love of life, if I am so irrational as to expect that when you, who are my own citizens, cannot endure my discourses and words, and have found them so grievous and odious that you will have no more of them, others are likely to endure me. No, indeed, men of Athens, that is not very likely. And what a life should I lead, at my age, wandering from city to city, ever changing my place of exile, and always being driven out! For I am quite sure that wherever I go, there, as here, the young men will flock to me; and if I drive them away, their elders will drive me out at their request; and if I let them come, their fathers and friends will drive me out for their sakes. . . .

[A vote is taken, and Socrates is condemned to death. Socrates makes a closing address to those assembled.]

Not much time will be gained, O Athenians, in return for the evil name which you will get from the detractors of the city, who will say that you killed Socrates, a wise man; for they will call me wise, even although I am not wise, when they want to reproach you. If you had waited a little while, your desire would have been fulfilled in the course of nature. For I am far advanced in years, as you may perceive, and not far from death. I am speaking now not to all of you, but only to those who have condemned me to death. And I have another thing to say to them: You think that I was convicted because I had no words of the sort which would have procured my acquittal—I mean, if I had thought fit to leave nothing undone or unsaid. Not so; the deficiency which led to my conviction was not of words—certainly not. But I had not the boldness or impudence or inclination to address you as you would have liked me to do, weeping and wailing and lamenting, and saying and doing many things which you have been accustomed to hear from others, and which, as I maintain, are unworthy of me. I thought at the time that I ought not to do anything common or mean when in danger: nor do I now repent of the style of my defence; I would rather die having spoken after my manner, than speak in your manner and live. For neither in war nor yet at law ought I or any man to use every way of escaping death. Often in battle there can be no doubt that if a man will throw away his arms, and fall on his knees before his pursuers, he may escape death; and in other dangers there are other ways of escaping death, if a man is willing to say and do anything. The difficulty, my friends, is not to avoid death, but to avoid unrighteousness; for that runs faster than death. I am old and move slowly, and the slower runner has overtaken me, and my accusers are keen and quick, and the faster runner, who is unrighteousness, has overtaken them. And now I depart hence condemned by you to suffer the penalty of death,—they too go their ways condemned by the truth to suffer the penalty of villainy and wrong; and I must abide by my award—let them abide by theirs. I suppose that these things may be regarded as fated,—and I think that they are well. . . .

Wherefore, O judges, be of good cheer about death, and know of a certainty, that no evil can happen to a good man, either in life or after death. He and his are not neglected by the gods; nor has my own approaching end happened by mere chance. But I see clearly that the time had arrived when it was better for me to die and be released from trouble; wherefore the oracle gave no sign. For which reason, also, I am not angry with my condemners, or with my accusers; they have done me no harm, although they did not mean to do me any good; and for this I may gently blame them.

Still, I have a favour to ask of them. When my sons are grown up, I would ask you, O my friends, to punish them; and I would have you trouble them, as I have troubled you, if they seem to care about riches, or anything, more than about virtue; or if they pretend to be something when they are really nothing,—then reprove them, as I have reproved you, for not caring about that for which they ought to care, and thinking that they are something when they are really nothing. And if you do this, both I and my sons will have received justice at your hands.

The hour of departure has arrived, and we go our ways—I to die, and you to live. Which is better God only knows.

REVIEW AND DISCUSSION QUESTIONS

1. Does Socrates agree, in the end, that no one is wiser than he?
2. Do you think Socrates was correct in accepting his sentence the way he did?
3. How would Socrates be regarded by society today? Can you think of any modern individuals who are similar to Socrates?

PART II

PHILOSOPHY'S METHOD

ONE CAN ACQUIRE no greater skill in life than the ability to think well. Contrary to what many believe, this is not a skill that comes naturally, nor is it one we exercise often. Although it is not a natural skill, it is has been integral to philosophy from its beginning—so much so, that to philosophize and to think well have come to be regarded as almost synonymous.

Still, thinking well did not achieve the rank of a distinct discipline until the arrival of Plato's great student Aristotle, whose work transformed it into the major discipline it has become.

ARISTOTLE (384–322 B.C.E.)

Aristotle was born at Stagira, a Macedonian city some two hundred miles north of Athens. When he was born, Plato was forty-five years old, and Socrates had been dead fifteen years. Aristotle's parents died while he was young, and he was given a home and an education by a family friend. At eighteen, he was sent to Plato's Academy in Athens, where he remained for the next twenty years, first as a student and then as a colleague of Plato's. When Plato died in 347 B.C.E., Aristotle left the Academy. He went to Assos, on the coast of Asia Minor, to teach at a school established by its philosophically sympathetic ruler, Hermias. Aristotle taught there for three years. He married Hermias's daughter and they had two children, a son, Nicomachus, and a daughter, Pythias.

After spending another two years on the neighboring island of Lesbos, Aristotle was invited by Philip of Macedonia to oversee the education of his son Alexander, then thirteen.

ARISTOTLE

Aristotle spent seven years tutoring the young prince, ending with the death of Philip in 336 B.C.E. Alexander ascended to the throne of Macedonia, which by then dominated all Greece, and began his spectacular career as the conquerer of Persia, earning his name of Alexander the Great.

Aristotle returned to Athens and founded his own school, the Lyceum. His system of philosophy came to be known as the **peripatetic philosophy**—apparently from his habit of teaching while walking up and down its covered walk. Aristotle spent the next twelve years at the Lyceum, where he started a library (the first in history), made vast collections of scientific data (much of it coming to him from Alexander's expeditions), and built dorms to accommodate the growing number of students. The Lyceum quickly outstripped the Academy in fame. The two schools were very different in their orientation, each tending to reflect the temperament of its founder: the Academy was devoted to the study of the rational sciences (mathematics and astronomy) while the Lyceum focused on the empirical sciences, especially biology.

Aristotle's work at the Lyceum ended in 323 B.C.E. with Alexander's sudden death. In a wave of anti-Macedonian feeling, he was marked down as an associate of Alexander by the rebellious Athenians, and they drew up a charge against him, similar to that which had been brought against Socrates earlier. Not wanting to give the Athenians another chance of sinning against philosophy (he allegedly remarked), he returned to his country estate, where he died at the age of sixty-two.

Aristotle's ability was recognized by Plato, who called him the *nous* (the "brain" or "mind") of the school. And Aristotle always spoke highly of Plato. He said of him that he was a man "whom bad men have not even the right to praise, and who showed in his life and teachings how to be happy and good at the same time."[1]

Aristotle is known variously as "The Stagirite," after his birthplace; "The Peripatetic," from his habit of teaching; and "The Philosopher," the name given to him by St. Thomas Aquinas (1225–1274 C.E.) to indicate that there was no other.

THE SOPHISTS AGAIN

The study of logic, or thinking well, can be said to have begun when Aristotle, observing his teacher Plato debating with the still ubiquitous Sophists, found himself challenged by their ability to outwit all comers. He decided to examine what it was that enabled these "experts," as they were called, to accomplish their feats.

The result was a work on logic—one of eventually six—titled *Of Sophistical Refutations*. The title hints at its contents, for what we have here is a manual in which Aristotle sets out to expose the tactics the Sophists used to gain their verbal victories.

To call someone a sophist today is not, of course, to pay them a compliment: a "sophist" is someone who is clever and tricky, who engages in fallacious reasoning in order to outmaneuver or deceive an opponent. Plato himself left us some descriptions of them in action. A particularly memorable one is in the dialogue *Euthydemus*. Since it contains some of the logical moves that will occupy us in this and the next chapter, let us spend some moments with it.

The dialogue opens with Socrates relating his encounter with two recent arrivals in Athens, the Sophists Euthydemus and Dionysodorous. They have encountered a young boy, Cleinias, and are busy questioning him. Socrates is there, and so is Cleinias's friend, a youth called Ctessippus, who will later get clobbered when he tries to come to his friend's rescue. A large crowd enjoys the spectacle.

The questioning begins with Euthydemus asking Cleinias who learns things best, the wise or the unwise? The boy, understanding *wise* to mean "intelligent," naturally replies that it is the wise who learn best and not the unwise. By playing fast and loose with the meaning of the word, shifting from one meaning to another, the Sophists soon get Cleinias to deny what he has just affirmed, subsequently to affirm it once again, then to deny it, until he is completely befuddled—to the amusement of the crowd. Finished with Cleinias, they turn to Socrates:

DIONYSODOROUS: Reflect, Socrates: you may have to deny your words.
SOCRATES: I have reflected, and I shall never deny my words.
DIONYSODOROUS: Well, and so you say that you wish Cleinias to become wise?
SOCRATES: Undoubtedly.
DIONYSODOROUS: And he is not wise as yet?
SOCRATES: At least his modesty will not allow him to say that he is.
DIONYSODOROUS: You wish him to become wise and not to be ignorant? You wish him to be what he is not, and no longer to be what he is? . . . You wish him no longer to be what he is? Which can only mean that you wish him to perish! Pretty lovers and friends they must be who want their favorite not to be, that is, to perish!

Socrates, momentarily baffled, yields to Cleinias's friend Ctessipus, and the Sophists then pounce on him.

DIONYSODOROUS: If you will answer my questions, I will soon extract the same admissions from you, Ctessippus. You say you have a dog.
CTESSIPPUS: Yes, a villain of a one.
DIONYSODOROUS: And he has puppies?
CTESSIPPUS: Yes, and they are very like himself.
DIONYSODOROUS: And the dog is the father of them?
CTESSIPPUS: Yes, I certainly saw him and the mother of the puppies come together.
DIONYSODOROUS: And he is not yours?
CTESSIPPUS: To be sure he is.
DIONYSODOROUS: Then he is a father, and he is yours; ergo, he is your father, and the puppies are your brothers.

Plato is engaging in comedy here. In the course of the dialogue, the Sophists prove, among other things, that it is impossible to tell a lie since a lie is "that which is not" and thus can have no existence, that good men speak evil since they would not be good if they did not speak evil of evil things, and that everything visible "has the quality of vision" and hence can see. Of course not all Sophists were as easy to ridicule, nor were the fallacies committed by them always as easy to spot as those here. Nevertheless, this was the task that

Tweedledum: I know what you're thinking about; but it isn't so, nohow.
Tweedledee: Contrariwise. If it was so, it might be; and if it were so, it would be; but as it isn't, it ain't. That's logic.

—**Lewis Carroll**, *Through the Looking Glass* (1871)

Aristotle now set himself, for he recognized that errors in logic, although sometimes amusing, can cause serious problems—for individuals, for groups, and for nations.

THE SCIENCE OF LOGIC

In his various logical works, Aristotle discovered something else about language and thinking that was of enormous importance. Certainly we can be led astray easily by people like the Sophists or by their modern-day counterparts, and a study of their tactics is essential. But we must also learn to develop a healthy respect for the structures built into our language and even the content packed into our words and idioms. Rules govern the use of language, rules that determine what we may or may not say. We violate them only at our peril.

Aristotle went on to show how limited in fact we are by the way we talk. He demonstrated this limitation by examining the main units of language with which we do most of our thinking: the categorical proposition and the arguments, called *syllogisms*, that employ those propositions. By **categorical proposition**, Aristotle meant simply the simple declarative sentences that we all regularly employ: *The table is brown*, or *The sky is clear*. A **syllogism** is an argument composed of such sentences.

Few of us in fact are aware that much of our reasoning is syllogistic. This easily escapes us because our reasoning is often highly abbreviated and its structure is not always explicit. Even an epithet like "Liar!" hurled at someone is in essence an argument—and a formally valid one at that. For, unpacked, what it contains is the following reasoning:

All people who try to deceive others by uttering what they know to be false are liars.
You are such a person.

Therefore, you are a liar.

Although the categorical proposition is only one way we express our thought, it is nevertheless the main one, accounting for much of our reasoning. Aristotle discovered a surprising thing about it: although we may believe that the vast number of words in our language would allow us to compose an unlimited number of different propositions and arguments, in fact the number of different types of propositions we can construct is quite limited, and their combinations in possible argument forms can be determined exactly.

> Thinking consists of journeys through the mazes of our linguistic forms, and logic is the study of the relations that obtain in and among these forms.
>
> —Source unknown

Aristotle went on to determine just how many argument forms the various combinations of categorical propositions make possible. He found the number to be exactly 256. So much for freedom of thought! More depressing still was the further discovery that of these 256 argument forms, only some 15 are valid.

People had engaged in and reflected on reasoning long before Aristotle came around, but we can see why he is considered the founder of logic—for he was the first to make a science of it.

LOGIC AS THE STUDY OF ARGUMENT

Now is a good time for a quick review of some material in Chapter 1. Logic is the study of **argument**, that is, pieces of reasoning in which one or more statements are offered as logical support for (reasons to believe in the truth of) some other statement. (We shall use *statement* and *proposition* interchangeably.) The statement being supported is the **conclusion** of the argument; the reasons supporting the conclusion are called **premises**. We may say, "This is so (conclusion) because that is so (premise)." Or, "This is so and this is so (premises), therefore that is so (conclusion)." Premises are often preceded by such words as *because, for, since,* or *on the ground that*; conclusions by such words as *therefore, hence, consequently,* and *it follows that.* When representing arguments explicitly, we shall use a line to separate the premises from the conclusion, as we did in the example displayed above.

The first step toward understanding arguments, then, is learning to identify premises and conclusions. To do so, first look for indicator words such as those just listed. In arguments where such words are absent, try to find the conclusion by determining the main point the argument is trying to establish. That will be its conclusion; the rest will be supporting grounds or premises.

Distinguishing the conclusion from the premise(s) in the following two arguments is easy, thanks to the convenient indicator words *for* and *hence*:

> Robert will not do well in this course, for he is having a hard time concentrating on course work this semester and has hardly attended any classes.

> She has antagonized nearly everyone on the committee; hence it is unlikely that she will be granted the promotion.

In the following two examples, however, no indicator words are present:

> There are no foxes in this area. We haven't seen one all day.

> All Democrats favor public housing. Senator Smith favors it; he must be a Democrat.

To distinguish the premise from the conclusion in cases of this sort, ask yourself such questions as, What is being *argued for*? and What is the person trying to *persuade us of*? In the first example what is being argued for is not that "we haven't seen a fox all day"—for that point is presumably not in debate—but rather that, in light of this fact, there must be no foxes in this area. *That* is the conclusion of the argument. Similarly, what is being argued for in the second example is not that "all Democrats favor public housing," nor that "Senator Smith favors it"— for here these are assumed to be shared statements of fact—but rather that, given these facts, Smith must be a Democrat.

The following is a more difficult example. In 1960, at the height of the Cold War, J. Edgar Hoover (then director of the FBI) released the following statement:

> It is an incontestable fact that our country is the ultimate, priceless goal of international communism. The leaders of international communism have vowed to achieve world domination. This cannot be until the Red Flag is flown over the United States. (http://ner.stparchive.com/Archive/NER/NER07141960P08.php)

To determine the premises and conclusion in this argument, ask yourself what the main thrust of it is. Is it to persuade us of the fact that "the leaders of international communism have vowed to achieve world domination"? This hardly seems so, being offered, as it is, as a simple statement of fact. Is it that such world domination cannot be achieved until the communists' "Red Flag is flown over the United States"? Again, hardly so since this, too, is offered as a presumed fact, a clear necessary condition for achieving world domination. We come, then, to the remaining statement, the opening one: that it is "an incontestable fact that our country is the ultimate, priceless goal of international communism." Despite the use of the phrase *incontestable fact*, what we have here is *not* a statement of fact but a conclusion gathered from the facts offered. From both its tone and its content, this is what the argument aims to convince us of. Thus understood, we might rearrange the argument for greater clarity:

> Communist leaders have vowed to achieve world domination.
> They cannot achieve world domination unless they rule over the United States.
> ----------
> Therefore, (conquering) the United States is their ultimate goal.

Finding the conclusion when it has no obvious indications will not always be easy or certain. To do so we must attend carefully to the content and tone of the argument and to the direction of its reasoning.

■ EXERCISES[2]

Determine the conclusion and the premises in the following arguments.

1. Since all rational beings are responsible for their actions and since all human beings are rational, it follows that all human beings are responsible for their actions.

2. Mario does not attend church, for he is an atheist, and atheists do not attend church.

3. If people are successful, then they are keenly interested in their work and not easily distracted from it. We may therefore conclude that no one who is successful is easily distracted when working.

4. The city should reimburse him for his hospital expenses for the simple reason that the accident took place while he was engaged in city business.

5. Because only those who can quote large chunks of that material can pass a test on it, it is useless for me to try, for I know hardly any of it by heart.

6. Today I will be master of my emotions. The tides advance; the tides recede. Winter goes and summer comes. Summer wanes and the cold increases. The sun rises; the sun sets. The moon is full; the moon is black. The birds arrive; the birds depart. Flowers bloom; flowers fade. Seeds are sown; harvests are reaped. All nature is a circle of moods and I am a part of nature and so, like the tides, my moods will rise; my moods will fall. Today I will be master of my emotions. (Og Mandino, *The Greatest Salesman in the World* [1968])

7. Stephen ought to exercise more. It would be good for his condition.

8. Tiffany must be in the shower, because she hasn't replied to my text yet.

9. I no longer believe those who say that a poor politician could be a good president, "if he could only be appointed to the job." Without the qualities required of a successful candidate—without the ability to rally support, to understand the public, to express its aspirations—without the organizational talent, the personal charm, and the physical stamina required to survive the primaries, the convention, and the election—no man would make a great

president, however wise in other ways he might be. (Theodore G. Sorensen, *Decision-Making in the White House* [1963])

10. The day *may* come when the rest of the animal creation may acquire those rights which never could have been withholden from them by the hand of tyranny. The French have already discovered that the blackness of the skin is no reason why a human being should be abandoned without redress to the caprice of a tormentor. It may one day come to be recognized that the number of the legs, the villosity of the skin, or the termination of the *os sacrum*, are reasons equally insufficient for abandoning a sensitive being to the same fate. What else is it that should trace the insuperable line? Is it the faculty of reason, or perhaps the faculty of discourse? But a full-grown horse or dog is beyond comparison a more rational, as well as a more conversable animal, than an infant of a day, or a week, or even a month, old. But suppose they were otherwise, what would it avail? The question is not, Can they *reason*? nor Can they *talk*? but, Can they *suffer*? (Jeremy Bentham, *The Principles of Morals and Legislation* [1789])

DISTINGUISHING ARGUMENTS FROM NON-ARGUMENTS

As we have seen, an argument is a piece of reasoning in which one or more statements are offered as support for some other statement. If a passage makes no claim supported by such reasons, it is not an argument. Thus, questions are not arguments, nor are announcements, complaints, compliments, apologies, and so on. Or put differently, we use language to do many things, only a subset of which involve arguments.

Consider the following typical examples of ordinary communication:

Every scene of *House of Cards* was thrilling for me. It makes me want to go into politics, or film-making. Or maybe both.

I spent $125 for a kabbalah seminar and the leader showed up in a biker's jacket, jeans, and a T-shirt for legalizing pot, with Madonna's little red string dangling on his wrist like an afterthought. He said some interesting things, but overall it felt like a scam.

The sincerest satisfaction in life is doing and not in dodging duty; in meeting and solving problems, in facing facts, in being a dependable person.

The first is an expression of enthusiasm, the second is a complaint, and the third is merely an assertion without any attempt to persuade us of it. None of these, then, is an argument. They simply fulfill other communicative functions.

More difficult cases are those where reasons are indeed offered but more in way of clarification rather than justification. Although appearing like arguments, such passages are often no more than a collection of statements, one expanding on the other. Consider, for example, the following remark by nationally syndicated televangelist James Robison (b. 1943):

Women have great strengths, but they are strengths to help the man. A woman's primary purpose in life and marriage is to help her husband succeed, to help him be all God wants him to be.

Robison's main point is that a woman's role in life is to help the man, a point he then simply reaffirms and expands on. This is, essentially, a slightly elaborated but unsupported statement of an opinion, not an argument.

The same is true of this oft-quoted aphorism of Francis Bacon (1561–1626):

> He that hath wife and children hath given hostages to fortune; for they are impediments
> to great enterprise, either of virtue or mischief.

Bacon here is primarily simply explaining what he means with that poetic phrase "hostages to fortune": wife and children are impediments to a man's endeavors. He is not giving us reasons to believe it is *true* that they are impediments, so he is not giving an argument.

But cases will not always be so clear-cut, and often enough, you will encounter examples where explanation and justification simply blend into each other:

> We are sorry but we tried and tried and we find that the stains on your hoodie cannot
> be removed without possibly damaging the color or fabric. This has been called to your
> attention so that you will know it has not been overlooked.

This passage can be said both to communicate that the stains have not been removed as well as to offer a reason justifying why they have not. Although the former is probably its main object, the explanation is of such a nature that it can function as a reason—that is, constitute an argument—as well (and would, no doubt, be invoked as such were the need to arise).

It would seem best to evaluate examples like these in light of their primary intention. If, as in the case above, the intention is to explain rather than justify, then, strictly speaking, the passage is not an argument.

■ EXERCISES

Which of the following are arguments, and which are non-arguments? If they are not arguments, explain what they are; if they are arguments, say why.

11. There used to be an actor named Corey Feldman. I can't think of any movies he was in, but he had something to do with Michael Jackson, the singer. What ever happened to him?

12. We must stop the homosexuals dead in their tracks—before they get one step further toward warping the minds of our youth. The time for us to attack is now! The enemy is in our camp! (Jerry Falwell (1933–2007), founder of the Moral Majority)

13. The main issue in life is not the victory but the fight. The essential thing is not to have won but to have fought well. (Baron Pierre de Coubertin (1863–1937), founder of the modern Olympic Games)

14. Sex deepens love and love deepens sex, so physical intimacy transforms everything and playing with it is playing with fire. Men try to ignore the fact that making love creates bonds, creating dependencies where there were none before, and women who try to ignore it with them deny their basic needs. (Merle Shain, *Some Men Are More Perfect Than Others* [1984])

15. I must study politics and war that my sons may have liberty to study mathematics and philosophy. My sons ought to study mathematics and philosophy, geography, natural history, naval architecture, navigation, commerce, and agriculture, in order to give their children a right to study painting, poetry, music, architecture, statuary, tapestry, and porcelain. (John Adams [1735–1826], U.S. President. Letter, May 1780, to his wife Abigail Adams)

16. Oh, come with old Khayyam, and leave the Wise
   To talk; one thing is certain, that life flies;
   One thing is certain, and the Rest is Lies;
   The Flower that once has blown for ever dies.
   Ah, make the most of what we yet may spend,
   Before we too into the Dust descend;
   Dust into Dust, and under Dust, to lie,
   Sans Wine, sans Song, sans Singer—and sans End!

(from *The Rubaiyat of Omar Khayyam*, translated by Edward FitzGerald [1809–1883])

17. As many states have started to recognize, you shouldn't have legislation against a thing that so many people regularly do. And today many, many people smoke marijuana. So marijuana should be legalized.

18. It is important that you study this book thoroughly. . . . The state insurance departments which administer insurance examinations take seriously their responsibility to protect the public from unqualified persons. For that reason, life insurance examinations cannot be considered easy to pass. Prospective agents who take their task of studying lightly have been surprised to learn that they have failed examinations. . . . While examinations cannot be considered easy, neither should they be considered unreasonably difficult. The purpose of the examination is to test your knowledge of the type of information contained in this book. If you study thoroughly, you have a good chance of passing. (Gary H. Snouffer, *Life Insurance Agent* [1979])

19. The only creatures on earth that have bigger—and maybe better—brains than humans are the Cetacea, the whales and dolphins. Perhaps they could one day tell us something important, but it is unlikely that we will hear it. Because we are coldly, efficiently and economically killing them off. (Jacques Cousteau [1910–1997])

20. What happens to cigarette smoke in the air? It is immediately diluted by surrounding air. And measurements of cigarette smoke in the air, taken under realistic conditions, show again and again that there is minimal tobacco smoke in the air we breathe. In fact, based on one study, which measured nicotine in the air, it has been said that a nonsmoker would have to spend 100 straight hours in a smoke-filled room to consume the equivalent of a single filter-tipped cigarette. So, does cigarette smoke endanger nonsmokers? In his most recent report, the Surgeon General, no fan of smoking, said that the available evidence is not sufficient to conclude that other people's smoke causes disease in nonsmokers. In our view, the decision to smoke should be based on mature and informed individual freedom of choice.

21. Although we do not know if other influenza vaccines can cause Guillain-Barre syndrome (GBS), this risk may be present for all of them. Little is known about the exact causes of GBS, but clearly the great majority of the several thousand GBS cases each year in the United States are not due to influenza vaccine. The risk of GBS from the vaccine is very small. This risk should be balanced against the risk of influenza and its complications. The risk of death from influenza during a typical epidemic is more than 400 times the risk of dying from any possible complications of influenza vaccine injections.

ELIMINATING VERBIAGE

As some of the exercises make clear, ordinary arguments often include a great deal of repetition, verbosity, and irrelevance. To see more clearly what such arguments are about you must scrape away a good deal of this material from them. Sometimes this may simply involve ignoring a long introduction, as in the example from exercise 6:

> Today I will be master of my emotions. The tides advance; the tides recede. Winter goes and summer comes. Summer wanes and the cold increases. The sun rises; the sun sets. The moon is full; the moon is black. The birds arrive; the birds depart. Flowers bloom; flowers fade. Seeds are sown; harvests are reaped. All nature is a circle of moods and I am a part of nature and so, like the tides, my moods will rise; my moods will fall. Today I will be master of my emotions.

What this argument basically asserts is contained in its second-to-last sentence: "All nature is a circle of moods and I am part of nature and so, like the tides, my moods will rise; my moods will fall." For purposes of logical evaluation, all the preceding material is irrelevant, however poetic and moving it may be.

Conclusions, too, may needlessly repeat what has already been stated. The insurance example in exercise 18 is an example of this: its last three sentences, at least, add nothing that was not already stated previously. Often, too, an example is simply verbose throughout and needs to be abbreviated and/or rearranged significantly before its structure can be observed clearly, as in the cigarette smoke example in exercise 20.

Revising the three arguments in exercises 6, 18, and 20 along such lines, we find that they essentially state the following:

6.
All nature is a circle of moods.
I am part of nature.

Therefore, I, too, will be subject to such swings of mood.

18.
Insurance examinations are not easy to pass without proper preparation.

Therefore, prepare for them (by studying this book) if you desire to pass them.

20.
According to a recent study, cigarette smoke is immediately diluted by surrounding air.
This is also affirmed by the Surgeon General.

Therefore, second-hand smoke does not represent a serious danger to nonsmokers.

In eliminating verbiage, you will at times need to discard some of the elegance of the original. But this is a worthwhile sacrifice for the sake of logical clarity.

■ EXERCISES

Rewrite the following arguments as concisely as possible, clarifying their meaning and arranging the premises and conclusion in their logical order. (You will recognize some of these from earlier exercises.)

22. I no longer believe those who say that a poor politician could be a good president, "if he could only be appointed to the job." Without the qualities required of a successful candidate—without the ability to rally support, to understand the public, to express its aspirations—without the organizational talent, the personal charm, and the physical stamina required to survive the primaries, the convention, and the election— no man would make a great president, however wise in other ways he might be. (Theodore G. Sorensen, *Decision-Making in the White House* [1963])

23. The day *may* come when the rest of the animal creation may acquire those rights which never could have been withholden from them by the hand of tyranny. The French have already discovered that the blackness of the skin is no reason why a human being should be abandoned without redress to the caprice of a tormentor. It may one day come to be recognized that the number of the legs, the villosity of the skin, or the termination of the *os sacrum*, are reasons equally insufficient for abandoning a sensitive being to the same fate. What else is it that should trace the insuperable line? Is it the faculty of reason, or perhaps the faculty of discourse? But a full-grown horse or dog is beyond comparison a more rational, as well as a more conversable animal, than an infant of a day, or a week, or even a month, old. But suppose they were otherwise, what would it avail? The question is not, Can they *reason*? nor Can they *talk*? but, Can they *suffer*? (Jeremy Bentham, *The Principles of Morals and Legislation* [1789])

24. Although we do not know if other influenza vaccines can cause Guillain-Barre syndrome (GBS), this risk may be present for all of them. Little is known about the exact causes of GBS, but clearly the great majority of the several thousand GBS cases each year in the United States are not due to influenza vaccine. The risk of GBS from the vaccine is very small. This risk should be balanced against the risk of influenza and its complications. The risk of death from influenza during a typical epidemic is more than 400 times the risk of dying from any possible complications of influenza vaccine injections.

25.   Oh, come with old Khayyam, and leave the Wise
      To talk; one thing is certain, that life flies;
      One thing is certain, and the Rest is Lies;
      The Flower that once has blown for ever dies.
      Ah, make the most of what we yet may spend,
      Before we too into the Dust descend;
      Dust into Dust, and under Dust, to lie,
      Sans Wine, sans Song, sans Singer—and sans End!

(from *The Rubaiyat of Omar Khayyam*, translated by Edward FitzGerald [1809–1883])

26. Because the father of poetry was right in denominating poetry an imitative art, these metaphysical poets will, without great wrong, lose their right to the name of poets, for they copied neither nature nor life. (Samuel Johnson, *Life of Cowley* [1781])

27. The Abbé . . . had just said, "Do you know, ladies, my first penitent was a murderer," when a nobleman of the neighborhood entered the room and exclaimed, "You there, Abbé?

Why, ladies, I was the Abbé's first penitent, and I promise you my confession astonished him." (Story by William Thackeray [1811–1863])

28. Surely also there is something strange in representing the man of perfect blessedness as a solitary or a recluse. Nobody would deliberately choose to have all the good things in the world, if there was a condition that he was to have them all by himself. Man is a social animal, and the need for company is in his blood. Therefore the happy man must have company, for he has everything that is naturally good, and it will not be denied that it is better to associate with friends than with strangers, with men of virtue than with the ordinary run of persons. We conclude then that the happy man needs friends. (Aristotle, *Ethics*)

29. Forty years ago, it took farmers three to four months and five pounds of natural feed to produce one pound of chicken meat. Today, it takes nine weeks and two and a half pounds of "doctored feed" to achieve the same results. The breeders are experimenting with techniques to do it with two pounds of feed. Today, 90 percent of all chickens eat arsanilic acid, an arsenic substance mixed into the feed as a growth stimulant. This substance is toxic to humans but not to the chickens. To help chickens resist disease before they make it to the supermarket, they are given antibiotics. The Food and Drug Administration also permits breeders to dip the slaughtered hens into an antibiotic solution designed to increase the shelf life of the chicken. Many other drugs and additives are often added to poultry feed, among them tranquilizers, aspirin, and hormones. How many of these chemicals come to affect us no one really knows.

30. *Nothing* in the world—indeed nothing even beyond the world—can possibly be conceived which could be called good without qualification except a *good will.* Intelligence, wit, judgment, and the other talents of the mind, however they may be named, or courage, resoluteness, and perseverance as qualities of temperament, are doubtless in many respects good and desirable. But they can become extremely bad and harmful if the will, which is to make use of these . . . is not good. It is the same with the gifts of fortune. Power, riches, honor, even health, general well-being, and the contentment with one's condition which is called happiness, make for pride and even arrogance if there is not a good will to correct their influence on the mind and on its principles of action. . . . [T]he sight of a being adorned with no feature of a pure and good will, yet enjoying uninterrupted prosperity, can never give pleasure to a rational impartial observer. Thus the good will seems to constitute the indispensable condition even of worthiness to be happy. (Immanuel Kant, *Foundations of the Metaphysics of Morals* [1785])

SUPPLYING MISSING COMPONENTS

Sometimes an argument's basic structure may be obscured by excess verbiage, but sometimes it may also be obscured by too *little,* if it has missing components. Such arguments may appear stronger than they are because we are unaware of important assumptions on which they rest. These assumptions need to be dug out and made explicit. Once made explicit, it will be easier to determine the role these missing components play in the argument and to what degree the argument depends on them.

It will be easier to find these missing components if we keep in mind that many arguments consist of a statement of a general principle, the citing of a case of it, and a conclusion inferring that the general principle applies to the case in question. The following is a classic example:

> All men are mortal. (the general principle)
> Socrates is a man. (a case)
> ----------
> Therefore, Socrates is mortal. (the conclusion)

In the previous exercises, examples 26 and 28 conform very much to this pattern. In abbreviating and ordering them, what you got was probably fairly close to the following:

> 26.
> Poetry is an imitative art.
> Metaphysical poetry is not imitative.
> ----------
> Therefore, metaphysical poetry is not poetry.

> 28.
> To be happy is to have the things you need.
> One of the things you need most is friends.
> ----------
> Therefore, to be happy you need friends.

Arguments of this type may lack the statement of the general principle (called the **major premise),** explicit reference to the case in question (the **minor premise**), or even the conclusion. Here are some examples:

> 1. These are natural foods and therefore good for you.

Omitted here is the major premise. Once added, we get:

> All natural foods are good for you. (major premise)
> These foods are natural foods.
> ----------
> Therefore, these foods are good for you.

> 2. You'll make a great kindergarten teacher. People who are fond of children always do.

Omitted here is the minor premise:

> All who are fond of children make great teachers.
> You are fond of children. (minor premise)
> ----------
> Therefore, you'll make an excellent kindergarten teacher.

3. Cassius has a lean and hungry look; such men are dangerous.

Omitted here is the conclusion:

All who have lean and hungry looks are dangerous.
Cassius has such a look.

Therefore, Cassius is dangerous. (conclusion)

Sometimes such omissions are innocent, done for the sake of elegance or brevity. But other times what is omitted is highly questionable, and omitted for that very reason:

4. This must be a good book; it was chosen by Amazon as a "must-read."

Omitted here is the major premise, "All books chosen by Amazon as 'must-reads' are good." To state it explicitly, we can see, is to call attention to it and risk having it questioned.

5. All alcoholics are short lived; therefore Jim won't live long.

6. Cowardice is always contemptible, and this was clearly a case of cowardice.

Although the missing components easily spring to mind in these examples, it still helps not to state them explicitly, for to do so is, again, to call attention to them and risk a challenge.

More difficult cases, and more frequent, are the more verbose examples. Often, benefits hang in the balance—the opportunity for gain, influence, deception—and hence a greater effort is made to hide the assumptions on which the argument rests. Because such arguments are more complicated, it is easy to lose track of the missing components. The following is an advertisement for a podcast dealing with loneliness:

Almost everyone feels lonely at times, and for many it is a constant companion. From the little child who feels he has no friends to the elderly who feel resigned to a cold empty feeling. Teenagers often feel they are nobody and young adults feel friendless. This remarkable program is not only comforting news but also contains an innovative approach to dealing with this emptiness.

Restating this argument, we get this:

Everyone suffers from loneliness.
This program is a cure for loneliness.

Therefore, this program will relieve your loneliness.

It is the conclusion that we now see has been omitted, and for good reason. To state it explicitly might raise a question in your mind as to whether indeed this program, although it supposedly has helped others, will help specifically *you*.

Of course not all omissions of this sort are questionable. Often a person will omit a component because it is simply too obvious to state explicitly. Sometimes it may be done for dramatic reasons, and occasionally it occurs because the person wishes to be cautious. Exercises 24 (the Guillain-Barre syndrome [GBS] case) and 29 (the poultry case) were of this last sort. Both writers seem hesitant to state their conclusions. In the former we are told that the risk of death from influenza during an epidemic is far greater than the risk of dying from the complications of the vaccine, and it is left to us to infer that vaccination is the wiser choice. In the poultry example, we are informed that poultry are fed and treated with large doses of potentially harmful chemicals; the conclusion that it might be wiser to avoid eating such chicken is, again, merely implied and not explicitly stated.

Such hesitancy, if that is all it is, may be defensible from the point of view of scientific reserve or legal caution; in logic, however, one must always make it a point to know clearly what is being asserted and what one is being asked to assent to.

■ EXERCISES

Supply the missing components in the following arguments. If these components throw the argument into suspicion, explain how and why.

31. Obama criticizes free markets; he must be a socialist.
32. She is a Phi Beta Kappa, so she must have been a bookworm.
33. The climate change crisis, being human made, can be human solved.
34. Our ideas reach no farther than our experience; we have no experience of divine attributes and operations; I need not conclude my syllogism; you can draw the inference yourself. (David Hume, *Dialogues concerning Natural Religion* [1779])
35. We do not want a democracy in this land, because if we have a democracy a majority rules. (Televangelist Charles Staney [b. 1932])
36. Death cannot be an evil, being universal. (J. W. von Goethe [1749–1832])
37. No person is free, for everyone is a slave either to money or to fortune.
38. Nothing intelligible puzzles me, but logic puzzles me.
39. He cannot possibly have a computer since he doesn't have an e-mail address.
40. He would not take the crown; therefore 'tis certain he was not ambitious. (Shakespeare, *Julius Caesar* [c.1599])
41. Blessed are the meek, for they shall inherit the earth.

DISTINGUISHING DEDUCTIVE AND INDUCTIVE ARGUMENTS

Having separated premises from conclusions, distinguished between arguments and nonarguments, eliminated excess verbiage, and supplied missing components, we must now ask the two crucial questions of any argument. Are the premises true, and does the conclusion really follow from them?

Regarding the first question, we want to know whether the facts stated by the argument are really so. Premises, after all, are the foundation of an argument. If they are unreliable or shaky, the argument built on them will be no better.

As for the second question, however, there's another way an argument can go wrong: when the premises fail to support the conclusion, that is, fail to give reason to believe the conclusion is true. A premise can support a conclusion fully:

All men are mortal.
Socrates is a man.

Therefore, Socrates is mortal.

Partially:

Most Scandinavians are blond.
My cousin Christine is Scandinavian.

Therefore, she must be blond.

Or not at all:

Be sure to use a SodaStream soda maker.
Celebrities like Scarlett Johansson do.

We will consider sometimes tempting but overall misleading arguments of the third type in the next chapter. Here let us consider the first two. The first is an example of a **deductive argument**, or one in which the conclusion is presented as following from the premises with certainty or necessity. The second is an example of an **inductive argument**, in which the conclusion is presented as following from the premises with merely a high degree of probability.

Two examples will help illustrate this distinction:

All the beans in this bag are black.
All these beans are from this bag.

Therefore, all these beans must be black.

All these beans are from this bag.
All these beans are black.

Therefore, all the beans in the bag must be black.

Here only the first has a conclusion that follows with certainty from its premises, and is therefore deductive; the conclusion of the second argument follows only with some probability from its premises, so it is inductive.

One difference between deductive and inductive arguments is that the premises in a good deductive argument contain all the information needed to reach the conclusion. In the conclusion of an inductive argument, on the other hand, we must venture beyond the information contained in the premises. Thus, our conclusion can never be fully necessary or certain.

This classic inductive argument highlights this issue of certainty:

The sun has risen every morning since time immemorial.

Therefore, the sun will rise tomorrow morning.

We may feel sure that the sun will rise tomorrow, yet logically speaking the premises only make this conclusion probable, not necessary. That's because the conclusion asserts a fact going beyond what's contained in the premises: the premises make assertions only about the past, but assert nothing about what will happen in the future. The premises do not therefore rule out the possibility of the sun *not* rising, so the claim that it *will* rise is only probable, not necessary.

> The man who has fed the chicken every day throughout its life at last wrings its neck instead.
>
> —**Bertrand Russell** (1872–1970)

In deductive reasoning, the premises do contain all the information that we seek to draw out or unfold. We attempt not to go beyond the premises but to understand more specifically what they contain. Consider:

If there are 50,001 people in a town,
And if no person can have more than 50,000 hairs on his or her head,
And if no one is completely bald,
Then at least two people in town have the same number of hairs on their heads.

This example illustrates the precision of which deduction is capable. Whereas inductive conclusions expand the content of their premises at the sacrifice of necessity, deductive conclusions achieve necessity by sacrificing expansion of content. Most of the arguments one encounters in daily life are of the inductive type. Both types of arguments, however, are alike in having premises and a conclusion, and hence both must be evaluated in light of our two basic questions—Are the premises true? Does the conclusion follow from them?

(In chapter 9, we will explore the famous critiques of both forms of reasoning offered by David Hume [1711–1776].)

■ EXERCISES

Determine whether the following arguments are deductive or inductive. Explain.

42. There are no foxes in this area, since we haven't seen one all day.

43. Tiffany must be in the shower, because she hasn't replied to my text yet.

44. Because the father of poetry was right in denominating poetry an imitative art, these metaphysical poets will, without great wrong, lose their right to the name of poets, for they copied neither nature nor life. (Samuel Johnson, *Life of Cowley* [1781])

45. Everyone in the first year advanced chemistry class needed to have had one year of high school chemistry as a prerequisite. Since Hannah is in that class, she must have had one year of high school chemistry.

46. The house across the street has shown no signs of life for several days. Some rain-soaked newspapers lie on the front steps. The grass badly needs cutting. The people across the street must be away on a trip.

47. All life requires water. There is no water on Venus. Therefore, there is no life there.

48. Brandon will not be able to drink at the frat party, for he is nineteen and only persons over the age of twenty-one will be able to drink there.

49. "How . . . did you know all that, Mr. [Sherlock] Holmes?" he asked. "How did you know . . . that I did manual labor? It's true as gospel, for I began as a ship's carpenter."

"Your hands, my dear sir. Your right hand is quite a size larger than your left. You have worked with it and the muscles are more developed." (Arthur Conan Doyle, "The Red-Headed League" [1891])

50. Our ideas reach no farther than our experience; we have no experience of divine attributes and operations; I need not conclude my syllogism; you can draw the inference yourself. (David Hume, *Dialogues concerning Natural Religion* [1779])

51. Since many drug addicts who came through the courts admit that they started on pot, pot likely causes hard-core drug addiction.

52. You are wise; or else you love not, for to be wise and love exceed man's might; that dwells with gods above. (Shakespeare, *Troilus and Cressida* [1602])

EVALUATING ARGUMENTS: TRUTH, VALIDITY, AND SOUNDNESS

People are sometimes heard to say, "That may be logical, but it's not true," or "What's logical isn't always right." Both of these statements are legitimate, yet they do not mean that logic is unconcerned with truth. Indeed, logic defines truth rigorously and separates it from two other concepts (validity and soundness) with which it is sometimes confused in ordinary speech. Together, these three concepts provide a basis for evaluating any argument.

Let's briefly review these concepts from chapter 1. Validity, in general, is a matter of the correctness of an inference, that is, with whether the conclusion *follows* from its premises. More specifically, a **valid argument** is one where the conclusion does follow with necessity from the premises, as we saw with good deductive arguments. An **invalid argument** would be one where the conclusion doesn't follow with necessity: the premises may well be true and yet the conclusion could be false.

Truth, on the other hand, concerns whether those premises and conclusion accord *with the facts.* You can start with true premises but reach a false conclusion (because you reason badly) or you can reason correctly (or validly) while reaching a false conclusion (because one or more of your premises are false). **A sound argument** is one where the premises are true and the conclusion is validly drawn. Or put differently: a sound argument is a valid argument whose premises are also all true. (Quick test: The conclusion of a sound argument must always be true—why?)

As we've defined the terms, inductive arguments can never be valid, for they never support their conclusions with necessity or certainty. That doesn't mean they can't be *good* arguments, however. They can be, when they support their conclusions with an adequately high degree of probability. That the sun will rise tomorrow does not follow with necessity from the fact that it has always arisen in the past, but you still would be wise to infer that it will, based on its past behavior (though see the Hume discussion of inductive arguments in chapter 9).

If you want *validity*, however, you'll have to stick with deductive arguments. Let's have a brief look next at a few classic examples of valid deductive arguments.

Some Classic Examples of Valid Deductive Arguments

The first is known by the name of **modus ponens**, and takes the following general form:

If P, then Q
P

Therefore, Q

You get a particular example of a *modus ponens* argument when you substitute particular statements or propositions for the P and for the Q:

If God exists, then gay marriage is forbidden.
God exists.

Therefore, gay marriage is forbidden.

This would be a *modus ponens* argument, with P = "God exists" and Q = "Gay marriage is forbidden." Since any argument of the *modus ponens* form is a valid one, the argument just displayed is indeed valid. (There of course remains the question of whether its premises are true.)

A second classic valid deductive argument is **modus tollens**, which takes this form:

If P, then Q
Not-Q

Therefore, not-P

Again, you get a particular example of a *modus tollens* argument when you substitute particular statements for the P and Q:

If it was recently raining, then the streets would be wet.
The streets are not wet.

Therefore, it has not been recently raining.

Here basically P = "It was recently raining," and Q = "The streets are wet." (Not-Q would be the negation of Q, or "The streets are *not* wet"; similarly for Not-P.) Again, it's a valid form of argument, so the only question about accepting its conclusion would be whether indeed both premises are true.

You'll notice that *modus ponens* and *modus tollens* are similar, in that they share the first premise, "If P, then Q." A statement of this form is called a **conditional statement**: P is offered as the condition upon which Q follows. The condition is also called the **antecedent** of the statement, while the statement that follows upon it is called the **consequent**. In our last example, "It was recently raining" is the antecedent and "The streets are wet" is the consequent.

But if *modus ponens* and *modus tollens* share the conditional statement as the first premise, they differ in their next step: *modus ponens* affirms the antecedent P, that is, it holds it to be true, while *modus tollens* denies the consequent Q, that is, it negates it or holds it to be false. Doing so then leads them to their very different conclusions, where *modus ponens* ends up supporting the truth of Q while *modus tollens* ends up denying the truth of P. So they start off similarly, but end up in quite different places.

Both forms of argument share another feature. They are each easily (and in fact often) confused with a corresponding *invalid* form of argument. Consider the following form of argument:

> If P, then Q
> Q
> ----------
> Therefore, P

This form is known as **affirming the consequent**, by its second premise, which affirms the consequent of the conditional in the first premise. It looks a lot like *modus ponens*, but it is invalid. To see why, let's substitute particular statements for the P and Q:

> If it was recently raining, then the streets would be wet.
> The streets are wet.
> ----------
> Therefore, it was recently raining.

While both premises may be true, the conclusion doesn't follow. Perhaps the streets are wet for some reason other than rain, such as an opened fire hydrant.

Similarly, there's an invalid argument that resembles *modus tollens*:

> If P, then Q
> Not-P
> ----------
> Therefore, Not-Q

This form is known as **denying the antecedent**, which is what the second premise does. But again, to observe its invalidity let's substitute particular statements:

> If it was recently raining, then the streets would be wet.
> It has not been recently raining.
> ----------
> Therefore, the streets are not wet.

Again, the conclusion doesn't follow even if the premises are true. The streets might be wet for some other reason, despite the lack of rain.

Let's now mention briefly two other classic forms of valid deductive argument, widely used throughout the history of philosophy.

There's **hypothetical syllogism**, which is any argument of this form (where P, Q, and R get substituted with particular statements):

If P, then Q
If Q, then R

Therefore, if P, then R

Denying the antecedent **in action:**

The great philosopher René Descartes (of "I think, therefore I am" fame) was seated in a pub. The bartender asked if he would like something to drink. "I think not," Descartes replied, and *poof!* went out of existence.

Though this one is a little harder to get comfortable with, it may help to think of it this way. The first premise is saying "if statement P is true, then statement Q would be true"; the second is saying "if statement Q is true, then statement R would be true." Then ask yourself what happens if P is true? Well, by the first premise Q would be true; but then by the second premise, R would also be true. So if P is true, then R would be true—which is precisely the validly drawn conclusion.

Then, lastly, there's **disjunctive syllogism:**

Either P or Q (or both)
Not-P

Therefore, Q

Again, the first premise is asserting that at least one of the statements is true (and possibly both); the second premise tells you the first statement P is not true; well, if at least one is true and it isn't the first, then it follows validly that the second statement Q is true, which is the conclusion.

Evaluating Arguments: Strategy

Having said all this, then, let's not forget: to logically accept the conclusion of an argument, we must be sure of *two* things. The argument must be valid, that is, the conclusion must follow from the premises, as it does in the examples just above. But further, we must also know that the premises themselves are true, not false. Nothing we said in the previous section addressed the truth of the premises.

Or we may put it slightly differently. The fact that the conclusion follows from the premises doesn't guarantee the conclusion is true. It may be false, if a premise from which it follows is itself false, and thus infects the conclusion with its own falsity. Similarly, a conclusion *in*validly inferred from its premises is not on that account false, since it might simply happen to be true anyway. Consider:

Justin Bieber will not live forever.

Therefore, the sky is blue.

This is clearly an invalid argument, since the premise gives us no reason to believe in the truth of the conclusion, as the two statements are utterly unrelated. And yet the conclusion is perfectly true anyway.

Knowing that something can follow from something else even though what it follows from is false can be useful. For this means that if you do not believe a conclusion seemingly validly derived from a premise, it is possible that you simply reject the premises from which it is deduced. The trouble may therefore lie in the premises.

Consider, for example, the following argument:

Abortion is the destruction of a human fetus, and the destruction of a human fetus is the taking of a human life. If, therefore, the taking of a human life is murder, then so is abortion.

Suppose you do not accept the conclusion that abortion is murder. How might you respond to the argument? Well, if you think the conclusion is false then either (a) the argument must have one or more false premises, or else (b) the conclusion doesn't follow from the premises, or (c) both. So, first, identify clearly the premises and conclusion of the argument. Next, determine whether you believe all the premises are true. If not, then you have refuted the argument. If they are, then determine whether the conclusion follows validly, that is, with necessity, from those premises. If not, then again you have refuted the argument.

But what if the conclusion *does* follow from true premises? Then something very important might happen. You, as a rational person, might have to change your mind. For if the premises are true and the conclusion is validly inferred, then the argument is sound—and the conclusion of a sound argument must be true (if you think about it).

■ **EXERCISES**

Do the conclusions in the following arguments follow validly from their premises? If so, how might you still challenge their soundness?

53. Every event in the world is caused by other events. Human actions and decisions are events in the world. Therefore, every human action and decision is caused by other events.

54. Thinking is a function of man's immortal soul. God has given an immortal soul to every man and woman, but not to any other animal or to machines. Hence no animal or machine can think. (A. M. Turing, "Computing Machinery and Intelligence" [1950])

55. Our ideas reach no farther than our experience; we have no experience of divine attributes and operations; I need not conclude my syllogism; you can draw the inference yourself. (David Hume, *Dialogues concerning Natural Religion* [1779])

56. You are wise; or else you love not, for to be wise and love exceed man's might; that dwells with gods above. (Shakespeare, *Troilus and Cressida* [1602])

SUMMARY

1. Aristotle founded the science of logic. Logic is the study of thinking well, or of argument. Every argument consists of premises and a conclusion.

2. Not all arguments display their structure clearly or simply. It can take some work even to identify a passage *as* an argument, and then to identify its premises and conclusions. Often you need to eliminate excess verbiage, and expose hidden components.

3. Deductive arguments purport to support their conclusions with certainty, while inductive ones only with some degree of probability. In deductive arguments all the information relevant to the conclusion is contained within the premises, while in inductive arguments, the conclusion goes beyond what's contained in the premises.

4. When evaluating an argument, we examine whether its premises are all true, and whether its conclusion follows (with necessity) from its premises. If the conclusion does follow with necessity, the argument is valid; if the premises are also all true, the argument is also sound.

5. Some classic valid deductive argument forms are *modus ponens* and *modus tollens*. Other valid forms include hypothetical syllogism and disjunctive syllogism.

6. *Modus ponens* is easily confused with the invalid form of argument known as *affirming the consequent. Modus tollens* is easily confused with the invalid form of argument *denying the antecedent.*

7. Something may follow from something else without being true. Whether or not a conclusion is true will also depend on whether the premises it follows from are true. In short, a conclusion may be validly drawn, but false.

KEY TERMS

affirming the consequent	invalid argument
antecedent	major premise
argument	minor premise
categorical proposition	*modus ponens*
conclusion	*modus tollens*
conditional statement	*nous*
consequent	peripatetic philosophy
deductive argument	premise
denying the antecedent	sound argument
disjunctive syllogism	syllogism
hypothetical syllogism	truth
inductive argument	valid argument

REVIEW QUESTIONS

1. Whose system of philosophy was known as "the peripatetic philosophy"?

2. The study of the strategies and tactics of what school led Aristotle to develop the science of logic?

3. What are "categorical propositions" and "syllogisms"?

4. What is the difference between a deductive argument and an inductive argument?

5. Provide examples of (a) a valid argument with a false conclusion, and (b) an invalid argument with a true conclusion.

6. The conclusion of a sound argument must always be true. Why?

ANSWERS TO EXERCISES

1. P1: All rational beings are responsible for their actions. P2: All human beings are rational. C: All human beings are responsible for their actions.

2. P1: Atheists do not attend church. P2: Mario is an atheist. C: Mario does not attend church.

3. P: If people are successful, then they are keenly interested in their work and not easily distracted from it. C: No one who is successful is easily distracted when working.

4. P1: The city should reimburse hospital expenses for anyone injured while engaged in city business. P2: He was injured while engaged in city business. C: The city should reimburse his hospital expenses.

5. P1: Only those who can quote large chunks of that material can pass a test on it. P2: I know hardly any of it by heart. C: It is useless for me to try to pass a test on it.

6. P1: All nature is a cycle of moods. P2: I am part of nature. C: I, too, will be subject to swings of mood.

7. P1: More exercise is good for people with that condition. P2: Stephen has that condition. C: Stephen ought to exercise more.

8. P: Tiffany hasn't responded to my text yet. C: Tiffany is in the shower.

9. P1: To be a good president requires organizational talent, personal charm, physical stamina, and so on. P2: Only good politicians have all these qualities. C: Only a good politician can make a good president.

10. P1: Animals are similar to humans in being susceptible to suffering. P2: This is a crucial similarity. C: Basic rights enjoyed by humans should not be withheld from animals.

11. An inquiry, not an argument.

12. If the emphasis is simply on acting against the advance of gay rights, then this is more of a diatribe, not an argument; but if the emphasis is specifically on acting *now* (as opposed to delaying), then it may well be an argument, persuading its audience to act quickly.

13. Not an argument. The second statement merely elaborates on the first.

14. An argument attempting to persuade us both that "physical intimacy transforms everything" and "playing with it is playing with fire."

15. Appears to be more of an explanation than an argument, more interested in expressing a certain point of view rather than persuading us of a particular conclusion.

16. An argument: Life passes one by very quickly into an endless death; therefore, make the most of what remains.

17. This is an argument, consisting of a conclusion (that marijuana should be legalized) and two premises (the rest).

18. An argument: Insurance examinations are not easy to pass without preparation. Therefore, prepare for them (by carefully studying this book) if you desire to pass them.

19. More of an explanation than an argument, lamenting a certain state of affairs.

20. An argument attempting to persuade that secondary cigarette smoke is not harmful to nonsmokers (and, further, consequently, there should be less public restriction on smoking).

21. An argument attempting to persuade you to take the influenza vaccine.

22. P1: To be a good president requires organizational talent, personal charm, physical stamina, and so on. P2: Only good politicians have all these qualities. C: Only a good politician can make a good president.

23. P1: Animals are similar to humans in being susceptible to suffering. P2: This is a crucial similarity. C: Basic rights enjoyed by humans should not be withheld from animals.

24. P1: Vaccines protect against influenza with minimal side effects. P2: The risk of death from influenza is great without vaccine. C: People should be vaccinated against influenza.

25. P1: Life passes one by very quickly into an endless death. C: Make the most of what remains.

26. P1: Poetry is an imitative art. P2: Metaphysical poets imitate neither life nor nature. C: Metaphysical poets are not poets.

27. P1: The Abbé's first penitent was a murderer. P2: The nobleman was the Abbé's first penitent. C: The nobleman was a murderer.

28. P1: Human beings are social animals and need the company of other human beings to be happy. P2: The company of friends is better than that of strangers. C: To be happy, a person needs friends.

29. P1: Today's chickens are fed chemical additives that are toxic to humans. P2: After slaughter they are also dipped in antibiotic solutions that may be toxic to humans. C: Eating non-organically bred chickens may be hazardous to one's health.

30. P1: Intelligence, wit, judgment, courage, and so on are good but can become bad if combined with a bad will. C: Only a good will itself is good without qualification.

31. Major premise: All who criticize free markets are socialists. (A questionable premise, not allowing for the possibility of non-socialist critique of free markets.)

32. Major premise: All Phi Beta Kappas are bookworms. (We cannot assume that all PBKs are bookworms.)

33. Major premise: All human-made crises can be human solved. (Questionable, for some human-made crises—such as climate change, or nuclear holocaust—may result in the extinction of all life on earth.)

34. Conclusion: We can have no ideas of divine attributes and operations.

35. Minor premise: We don't want the majority to rule. (Reverend Staney may not want this, but the rest of us may feel differently about it.)

36. Major premise: Nothing that is universal is evil. (A very large assumption that surely needs further defense.)

37. Major premise: To be a slave to either money or fortune is not to be free. (The truth of this premise will depend on how we understand the words *slave, fortune,* and *free.*)

38. Conclusion: Logic is not intelligible. (This does follow from the premises. If we don't accept this conclusion, we must, as we will soon see, question the truth of the premise[s].)

39. Major premise: All who have computers have e-mail addresses. (It's at least possible that he has a computer despite not having an e-mail address.)

40. Major premise: All who are ambitious *would* take the crown. (The assumption seems reasonable, though some might question it.)

41. Major premise: All who inherit the earth are blessed. (Again, the assumption seems reasonable, though some might question it.)

42. Inductive. The fact that they haven't seen any foxes makes it only probable, not certain, that there aren't any in the area. (The people may not be very observant, or the foxes may be avoiding them.)

43. Inductive. The fact that she doesn't answer the text promptly doesn't necessarily mean she is in the shower. (She might have other reasons for not answering.)

44. Deductive. The conclusion is asserted to follow necessarily from the premises. (If all poetry is imitative and metaphysical poetry is not imitative, then it is not poetry. But is it the case that all poetry is imitative?)

45. Deductive. Given that the premises are true, the conclusion follows with certainty.

46. Inductive. The people may be at home but have other reasons for not taking care of these things. (Perhaps they are ill, or tending to more pressing matters.)

47. Deductive. If all life requires water and there is no water on Venus, then it follows necessarily that there is no life on that planet. (But is it true that all life requires water?)

48. Deductive. If only people over twenty-one can drink and Brandon is only nineteen, then it follows necessarily that he cannot drink.

49. Inductive. He may simply have been born with one hand larger than the other, without having done manual labor.

50. Deductive. The conclusion is asserted to follow necessarily from the premises.

51. Inductive. That conclusion does not necessarily follow from those premises, as the word *likely* suggests. (Not every pot smoker becomes a drug addict; and not every drug addict begins with pot smoking.)

52. Deductive. The premise states that it is not possible simultaneously to be wise and to love; the conclusion merely restates this (hence does not go beyond what the premise asserts).

53. The conclusion does follow with certainty from the premises. But is it the case that human actions and decisions are just like other (physical) events? The law of causality may apply to physical but perhaps not to mental events.

54. If thinking is a function of our immortal soul, and if God has given an immortal soul only to human beings, then it follows validly that only human beings can think. But perhaps thinking is not restricted to immortal souls; or perhaps God has also given this capacity to other creatures as well. (Turing, by the way, does not endorse the argument in question; he raises it to respond to it.)

55. If all our ideas come from experience and if we have no experience of God, then it follows that we can have no idea of God. But is it the case that absolutely all our ideas come from (or originate only from) experience? (See chapter 9 for more on Hume.)

56. If it is impossible to be both wise and to love (at the same time), then it follows that if I love, I am not wise, and if I am wise, I do not love. But *is* it impossible to do both or have both?

NOTES

1. Fragment 623. (Rose, *Aristotelis Fragmenta.* Berlin, 1870 ed.) Quoted in Frederick Copleston, *A History of Philosophy: Greece and Rome* (New York: Paulist Press, 1946), p. 266.

2. Answers appear at the end of the chapter.

■ Reading
"What the Tortoise Said to Achilles"

Lewis Carroll

Mind 4, No. 14 (April 1895), 278–80.

In this reading, Carroll raises a profound problem for understanding how deductive arguments can ever succeed in being valid.

Achilles had overtaken the Tortoise, and had seated himself comfortably on its back.

"So you've got to the end of our race-course?" said the Tortoise. "Even though it does consist of an infinite series of distances? I thought some wiseacre or other had proved that the thing couldn't be done?"

"It *can* be done," said Achilles. "It *has* been done! *Solvitur ambulando.* You see the distances were constantly *diminishing*; and so—"

"But if they had been constantly *increasing*?" the Tortoise interrupted, "How then?"

"Then I shouldn't be *here*," Achilles modestly replied; "and you would have got several times round the world, by this time!"

"You flatter me—*flatten*, I *mean*" said the Tortoise; "for you are a heavy weight, and *no* mistake! Well now, would you like to hear of a race-course, that most people fancy they can get to the end of in two or three steps, while it *really* consists of an infinite number of distances, each one longer than the previous one?"

"Very much indeed!" said the Grecian warrior, as he drew from his helmet (few Grecian warriors possessed *pockets* in those days) an enormous notebook and a pencil. "Proceed! And speak *slowly*, please! *Shorthand* isn't invented yet!"

"That beautiful First Proposition of Euclid!" the Tortoise murmured dreamily. "You admire Euclid?"

"Passionately! So far, at least, as one *can* admire a treatise that won't be published for some centuries to come!"

"Well, now, let's take a little bit of the argument in that First Proposition—just *two* steps, and the conclusion drawn from them. Kindly enter them in your notebook. And in order to refer to them conveniently, let's call them *A, B,* and *Z*:—

(*A*) Things that are equal to the same are equal to each other.
(*B*) The two sides of this Triangle are things that are equal to the same.
(*Z*) The two sides of this Triangle are equal to each other.

Readers of Euclid will grant, I suppose, that *Z* follows logically from *A* and *B,* so that any one who accepts *A* and *B* as true, *must* accept *Z* as true?"

"Undoubtedly! The youngest child in a High School—as soon as High Schools are invented, which will not be till some two thousand years later—will grant *that.*"

"And if some reader had *not* yet accepted *A* and *B* as true, he might still accept the *sequence* as a *valid* one, I suppose?"

"No doubt such a reader might exist. He might say 'I accept as true the Hypothetical Proposition that, *if A* and *B* be true, *Z* must be true; but, I *don't* accept *A* and *B* as true.' Such a reader would do wisely in abandoning Euclid, and taking to football."

"And might there not *also* be some reader who would say 'I accept *A* and *B* as true, but I *don't* accept the Hypothetical'?"

"Certainly there might. *He*, also, had better take to football."

"And *neither* of these readers," the Tortoise continued, "is *as yet* under any logical necessity to accept *Z* as true?"

"Quite so," Achilles assented.

"Well, now, I want you to consider *me* as a reader of the *second* kind, and to force me, logically, to accept *Z* as true."

"A tortoise playing football would be—" Achilles was beginning . . .

"—an anomaly, of course," the Tortoise hastily interrupted. "Don't wander from the point. Let's have *Z* first, and football afterwards!"

"I'm to force you to accept *Z*, am I?" Achilles said musingly. "And your present position is that you accept *A* and *B*, but you don't accept the Hypothetical—"

"Let's call it *C*," said the Tortoise.

"—but you *don't* accept

(*C*) If *A* and *B* are true, *Z* must be true."

"That is my present position," said the Tortoise.

"Then I must ask you to accept *C*."

"I'll do so," said the Tortoise, "as soon as you've entered it in that notebook of yours. What else have you got in it?"

"Only a few memoranda," said Achilles, nervously fluttering the leaves: "a few memoranda of—of the battles in which I have distinguished myself!"

"Plenty of blank leaves, I see!" the Tortoise cheerily remarked. "We shall need them *all!*" (Achilles shuddered.) "Now write as I dictate:—

(*A*) Things that are equal to the same are equal to each other.
(*B*) The two sides of this Triangle are things that are equal to the same.
(*C*) If *A* and *B* are true, *Z* must be true.
(*Z*) The two sides of this Triangle are equal to each other."

"You should call it *D*, not *Z*," said Achilles. "It comes *next* to the other three. If you accept *A* and *B* and *C*, you *must* accept *Z*."

"And why *must* I?"

"Because it follows *logically* from them. If *A* and *B* and *C* are true, *Z must* be true. You don't dispute *that*, I imagine?"

"If *A* and *B* and *C* are true, *Z must* be true," the Tortoise thoughtfully repeated. "That's *another* Hypothetical, isn't it? And, if I failed to see its truth, I might accept *A* and *B* and *C*, and *still* not accept *Z*, mightn't I?"

"You might," the candid hero admitted; "though such obtuseness would certainly be phenomenal. Still, the event is *possible*. So I must ask you to grant *one* more Hypothetical."

"Very good. I'm quite willing to grant it, as soon as you've written it down. We will call it

(*D*) If *A* and *B* and *C* are true, *Z* must be true.

Have you entered that in your notebook?"

"I *have*!" Achilles joyfully exclaimed, as he ran the pencil into its sheath. "And at last we've got to the end of this ideal race-course! Now that you accept A and B and C and D, *of course* you accept Z."

"Do I?" said the Tortoise innocently. "Let's make that quite clear. I accept A and B and C and D. Suppose I *still* refused to accept Z?"

"Then Logic would *force* you to do it!" Achilles triumphantly replied. "Logic would tell you 'You can't help yourself. Now that you've accepted A and B and C and D, you *must* accept Z!' So you've no choice, you see."

"Whatever Logic is good enough to tell me is worth *writing down*," said the Tortoise. "So enter it in your book, please. We will call it

(E) If A and B and C and D are true, Z must be true.

Until I've granted *that*, of course I needn't grant Z. So it's quite a *necessary* step, you see?"

"I see," said Achilles; and there was a touch of sadness in his tone.

Here the narrator, having pressing business at the Bank, was obliged to leave the happy pair, and did not again pass the spot until some months afterwards. When he did so, Achilles was still seated on the back of the much-enduring Tortoise, and was writing in his notebook, which appeared to be nearly full. The Tortoise was saying, "Have you got that last step written down? Unless I've lost count, that makes a thousand and one. There are several millions more to come. And *would* you mind, as a personal favour, considering what a lot of instruction this colloquy of ours will provide for the Logicians of the Nineteenth Century—*would* you mind adopting a pun that my cousin the Mock-Turtle will then make, and allowing yourself to be re-named *Taught-Us*?"

"As you please!" replied the weary warrior, in the hollow tones of despair, as he buried his face in his hands. "Provided that *you*, for *your* part, will adopt a pun the Mock-Turtle never made, and allow yourself to be re-named *A Kill-Ease*!"

REVIEW AND DISCUSSION QUESTIONS

1. What famous paradox (discussed in chapter 2) does the passage refer to at the beginning?

2. The Tortoise is raising a very difficult problem or paradox for all deductive arguments, by challenging the idea that any finite argument can be valid. Explain exactly what the problem is.

■ Reading

"Newcomb's Problem and Two Principles of Choice" (1969)

ROBERT NOZICK

From ed. Nicholas Rescher, Essays in Honor of Carl G Hempel *(Springer, 1969), 114–17. Reprinted with permission.*

In this reading, Nozick introduces a scenario that pits a powerful inductive argument against a powerful deductive argument.

Suppose a being in whose power to predict your choices you have enormous confidence. (One might tell a science-fiction story about a being from another planet, with an advanced technology and science, who you know to be friendly, etc.) You know that this being has often correctly predicted your choices in the past (and has never, so far as you know, made an incorrect prediction about your choices), and furthermore you know that this being has often correctly predicted the choices of other people, many of whom are similar to you, in the particular situation to be described below. One might tell a longer story, but all this leads you to believe that almost certainly this being's prediction about your choice in the situation to be discussed will be correct.

There are two boxes, (Bl) and (B2). (Bl) contains $1,000. (B2) contains either $1,000,000 ($M), or nothing. What the content of (B2) depends upon will be described in a moment. You have a choice between two actions:

(1) taking what is in both boxes
(2) taking only what is in the second box.

Furthermore, and you know this, the being knows that you know this, and so on:

(I) If the being predicts you will take what is in both boxes, he does not put the $M in the second box.
(II) If the being predicts you will take only what is in the second box, he does put the $M in the second box.

The situation is as follows. First the being makes its prediction. Then it puts the $M in the second box, or does not, depending upon what it has predicted. Then you make your choice. What do you do?

There are two plausible looking and highly intuitive arguments which require different decisions. The problem is to explain why one of them is not legitimately applied to this choice situation. You might reason as follows:

First Argument: If I take what is in both boxes, the being, almost certainly, will have predicted this and will not have put the $M in the second box, and so I will, almost certainly, get only $1,000. If I take only what is in the second box, the being, almost certainly, will have predicted this and will have put the $M in the second box, and so I will, almost certainly, get $M. Thus, if I take what is in both boxes, I, almost certainly, will get $1,000. If I take only what is in the second box, I, almost certainly, will get $M. Therefore I should take only what is in the second box.

Second Argument: The being has already made his prediction, and has already either put the $M in the second box, or has not. The $M is either already sitting in the second box, or it is not, and which situation obtains is already fixed and determined. If the being has already put the $M in the second box, and I take what is in both boxes, I get $M +$1,000, whereas if I take only what is in the second box, I get only $M. If the being has not put the $M in the second box, and I take what is in both boxes I get $1,000, whereas if I take only what is in the second box, I get no money. Therefore, whether the money is there or not, and which it is is already fixed and determined, I get $1,000 more by taking what is in both boxes rather than taking only what is in the second box. So I should take what is in both boxes.

Let me say a bit more to emphasize the pull of each of these arguments:

The First: You know that many persons like yourself, philosophy teachers and students, etc., have gone through this experiment. All those who took only what was in the second box, including those who knew of the second argument but did not follow it, ended up with $M. And you know that all the shrewdies, all those who followed the second argument and took what was in both boxes, ended up with only $1,000. You have no reason to believe that you are any different . . . than they are. Furthermore, since you know that I have all of the preceding information, you know that I would bet, giving high odds, and be rational in doing so, that if you were to take both boxes you would get only $1,000. And if you were to irrevocably take both boxes, and there were some delay in the results being announced, would not it be rational for you to then bet with some third party, giving high odds, that you will get only $1,000 from the previous transaction? Whereas if you were to take only what is in the second box, would not it be rational for you to make a side bet with some third party that you will get $M from the previous transaction? Knowing all this . . . do you really want to take what is in both boxes, acting against what you would rationally want to bet on?

The Second: The being has already made his prediction, placed the $M in the second box or not, and then left. This happened one week ago; this happened one year ago. Box (Bl) is transparent. You can see the $1,000 sitting there. The $M is already either in the box (B2) or not (though you cannot see which). Are you going to take only what is in (B2)? To emphasize further, from your side, you cannot see through (B2), but from the other side it is transparent. I have been sitting on the other side of (B2), looking in and seeing what is there. Either I have already been looking at the $M for a week or I have already been looking at an empty box for a week. If the money is already there, it will stay there whatever you choose. It is not going to disappear. If it is not already there, if I am looking at an empty box, it is not going to suddenly appear if you choose only what is in the second box. Are you going to take only what is in the second box, passing up the additional $1000 which you can plainly see? Furthermore, I have been sitting there looking at the boxes, hoping that you will perform a particular action. Internally, I am giving you advice. And, of course, you already know which advice I am silently giving to you. In either case (whether or not I see the $M in the second box) I am hoping that you will take what is in both boxes. You know that the person sitting and watching it all hopes that you will take the contents of both boxes. Are you going to take only what is in the second box, passing up the additional $1,000 which you can plainly see, and ignoring my internally given hope that you take both? . . .

I should add that I have put this problem to a large number of people, both friends and students in class. To almost everyone it is perfectly clear and obvious what should be done. The difficulty is that these people seem to divide almost evenly on the problem, with large numbers thinking that the opposing half is just being silly.

Given two such compelling opposing arguments, it will not do to rest content with one's belief that one knows what to do. Nor will it do to just repeat one of the arguments, loudly and slowly. One must also disarm the opposing argument; explain away its force while showing it due respect.

REVIEW AND DISCUSSION QUESTIONS

1. Briefly summarize the scenario in question, and the arguments for each choice. Which argument is inductive, and which argument is deductive?

2. Which choice would you make? Why do you think the argument for that choice is stronger than the argument for the other choice?

FALLACIES ARE ARGUMENTS that may appear to be sound but for various reasons are not. Aristotle, who was the first to explore these common errors of reasoning, divided them into two groups: those that have their source in language and those whose source lies outside. Although many thinkers have followed Aristotle's classification, neither the list of fallacies he compiled nor their treatment has remained fixed. And indeed it seems more accurate to say that *all* the fallacies have their source in language—though they differ in just which aspects of language are responsible in each case. In one group of fallacies, for example, the **fallacies of ambiguity**, it is the ambiguity of the words used that proves deceiving. In the **fallacies of presumption**, what deceives is the arguments' similarity to valid argument forms. Finally, in the **fallacies of relevance**, it is the emotional appeal of the language that deceives.

Often the very thing responsible for the fallacy is what makes the argument appealing to us. That is why we are so often deceived by fallacies, why, despite their being unsound, they are psychologically persuasive. And this is so not only because they evoke such attitudes as pity, fear, reverence, disapproval, and enthusiasm (which tend to blind us to the logical merits of the case being argued) but also because they are often subtle and complex.

To learn how to deal with these cases, it is sometimes helpful to use somewhat absurd examples. Using such examples does not imply that you or anyone else is ever likely to commit the fallacies in these extreme guises. These examples serve rather to magnify the structure of the fallacy so that we may see it more clearly.

Consider, for example, the following absurd argument: "Everything that runs has feet; the river runs; therefore, the river has feet." This argument may appear sound because we do say such things as "the river runs." Of course, when we do so, we do not mean that it has feet on which it runs, but merely that it flows. Although this is an absurd example, the persuasiveness of many subtle arguments depends on this same device: a key term switched in meaning at a critical point in an argument.

For a more subtle example, consider the case of the evangelist who challenges you, "If you believe in the miracles of science, then why not believe in the miracles of the Bible? As a student of science and logic, you ought to be consistent." If he truly believes in this argument, he has come to do so by failing to see that the word *miracle* as used in science means something quite different from its religious use. Used literally in the latter, a *miracle* is any occurrence that goes against the laws of nature. But used metaphorically in the "miracles of science," the term means "great discovery" or "outstanding achievement." This being so, you might reply, you are not being inconsistent in believing in the miracles of science and not in the miracles of the Bible.

We can use the same devices responsible for these logical traps for the expression of our sense of humor, too. "Good steaks are rare these days, so don't order yours well done"; "Diamonds are seldom found in this country, so be careful not to mislay your engagement ring"; "Your argument is sound—nothing but sound." In these cases we are not deceiving with the words *rare, found,* and *sound,* we are rather punning with them.

> We must all hang together, or assuredly we shall all hang separately.
>
> **—Benjamin Franklin** (1706–1790)

THE FALLACIES OF AMBIGUITY

The fallacies generally discussed under this category include amphiboly, accent, and equivocation. What tends to deceive us here is the confusing nature of the language in which the argument is expressed. Each type of confusion arises from an important aspect of the nature of sentences: *amphiboly* explores the consequences of not taking sufficient care with the way we structure our statements, *accent* explores what can go wrong when we mistake the context of a statement and so fail to understand it in the way it was intended, and *equivocation* explores the errors resulting from the fact that many words have multiple meanings.

One of the benefits of studying these three fallacies is that it helps people develop their ability to express themselves with greater clarity and precision. In dealing with them, your goal, therefore, should not simply be to identify the fallacy but rather to develop the skill of explaining clearly why this or that particular argument is less than sound.

Amphiboly

Language admits of different sorts of ambiguity and each major kind receives its own name. **Amphiboly** is the term attached to fallacies or deceptions that result from faulty or careless sentence structure. The carelessness may be intentional, as in the case of the title of the music album *Best of the Beatles,* which misled many people into thinking they were getting the best songs of the Beatles. In fact what they got was the music of Pete Best, who had been a member of the Beatles early in their career.

Shakespeare loved to exploit this particular ambiguity for dramatic effect. In *Henry VI* (II.iv) a witch prophesies that "The Duke yet lives that Henry shall depose," which leaves it unclear whether the Duke will depose Henry or Henry will depose the Duke. To make it clear, the word *that* would have to be replaced with either *who* or *whom.* Another use of this kind of ambiguity occurs in the play *Macbeth.* The witches tell Macbeth,

> Be bloody, bold, and resolute; laugh to scorn
> The power of man, for none of woman born
> Shall harm Macbeth.

The phrase "none of woman born" turns out to be a deception when Macbeth discovers, all too late, that his murderer, Macduff, had been "untimely ripped from his mother's womb" and thus torn of woman and not literally born of her.

It is because of the inherent ambiguity in our language that when we are asked to swear an oath, we promise not only to tell the truth (for we might then only tell part of it) and not only to tell the whole truth (for we might then throw in a few lies as well) but "to tell the truth, the whole truth, and nothing but the truth," which takes care of all contingencies.

■ EXERCISES¹

Explain briefly how the following examples illustrate amphiboly.

1. It would be a great help toward keeping the churchyard in good order if others would follow the examples of those who clip the grass on their own graves.

2. Bush's are the finest vegetarian baked beans you ever ate. So when you buy vegetarian baked beans, be sure Bush is on the can.

3. Classified ad on Craigslist: "Wanted Smart Young Man for Butcher. Able to Cut, Skewer, and Serve a Customer."

4. Headline: Nude Patrol OK'd for Muir Beach.

5. Report of social worker: Woman still owes $145 for a funeral she had recently.

6. Dr. William Smith read a paper on "Idiots from Birth." There were over 200 present.

Accent

Accent is the name for those fallacies that arise from ambiguity or confusion in emphasis. The fallacy can take three forms, resulting (1) from confusion about the tone of voice a statement was meant to be spoken in, (2) from confusion about where the stress was meant to be placed in a remark, and (3) when a passage is taken out of context and thus given an unintended emphasis.

In one of the transcripts of the famous Watergate tapes, John Dean warns Richard Nixon against getting involved in a cover-up, and Nixon replies, "No—it is wrong, that's for sure." But what inflection was in Nixon's voice when he said this? Was it said in a serious tone, or ironically? If the latter, this remark might be evidence of his involvement in the cover-up.

It is because tone of voice adds a dimension to language that clerks of court usually read testimony in a monotone, trying to keep out any inadvertent indications of their own feelings about the matter read.

The following are somewhat more mundane examples of the fallacy in this first form. "I cannot praise this book too highly" (meaning what? that it is impossible to praise it at all or enough?); "You never looked better" (meaning what? that you always look that way, namely, bad, or that you were never more beautiful?); "I wish you all the good fortune you deserve" (meaning what?).

Ambiguities with tone of voice apply to stress as well. Thus, to consider an artificial example, if we were to emphasize the word *friends* in the statement "We should not speak ill of our friends," we might be saying that it is all right to speak ill of our enemies; if we emphasize the word *speak*, we might be saying that it is all right to think ill of them; and so on. The same applies to a statement such as "men were created equal." If we stressed *men*, we might thereby imply that women were not created equal; if we stressed *were created*, we might suggest that although that is the way they started out, they are no longer so.

As these examples indicate, the fallacy of accent arises either when a wrong or unintended stress is placed on some word or phrase in a statement or when a statement is read in an

---

1. Answers appear at the end of the chapter.

unintended tone of voice. As such, the fallacy is unlike amphiboly, whose ambiguity is due not to emphasis or intonation but to misplaced words or faulty sentence structure.

How can we avoid this fallacy? Sometimes it will simply be unavoidable. We cannot foretell how our words will be used or abused or understood or misunderstood on some future occasion. We can, however, take some precautions. We can provide a background or context that will be difficult to distort. It need not be anything elaborate. The addition of another emphatic word will sometimes do it.

As with the fallacy of amphiboly, the fallacy of accent can also be exploited for humor. A notable example is the poor worker in Charlie Chaplin's classic film *The Great Dictator* (1940) who sarcastically growled, "This is a *fine* country to live in" and was promptly arrested by the dictator's police. He managed to get himself off, however, by pleading that all he said was "This is a fine country to live in"—meaning that it was a wonderful place.

Accent is obviously more a reader's than a writer's fallacy. The authors of a particular statement presumably know what emphasis they wish to give to it or how they want it to be understood, and were they present to translate it into spoken words, they would be able to make that meaning clear to readers.

The fallacy of accent can be found in one further form. This occurs when the content of a passage is distorted by presenting its components out of context. This is a favorite device of blurb writers, journalists, and politicians. The damage and misinformation conveyed by dishonest captions, misleading headlines, and misquotations can be enormous. When Barack Obama was running for his first term as president, his opponent John McCain quoted him as saying that our troops in Afghanistan were "just air-raiding villages and killing civilians." What Obama had *actually* said was "We've got to get the job done there and that requires us to have enough troops so that we're not just air-raiding villages and killing civilians." Out of context it sounded like Obama was claiming the troops were doing that activity; in context he was defending the large deployment so as to prevent that activity.

Similarly for advertisements and endorsements, a drama critic might write that she "liked all of the play except the lines, the acting, and the scenery," only to find herself quoted the next morning that she "liked all of the play." One critic wrote that the television show *Lost* was "the most confusing, asinine, ridiculous—yet somehow addictively awesome—television show of all time." By the time it was quoted by the network producing the show it became merely, "The most addictively awesome television show of all time."

There is no way to be sure that others will use your words responsibly, but at least you can be sure to do so with others' words. If you supply a direct quotation you should always indicate any omission of words or phrases by the use of ellipsis points. Not to do so is to tell only half the story and with it only half the truth. In addition, you should make a sincere effort to capture both the tone and flavor of the original in your paraphrases, providing as well the proper context of the remark in question.

■ **EXERCISES**

Explain briefly how the following sentences might be subject to the fallacy of accent.

7. Only Hollywood could produce a film like this.

8. Member of audience after sitting through a five-hour performance of Wagner's opera *Parsifal*: "I can't believe I heard the whole thing!"

9. What are you doing this weekend? The usual?

10. Thou shalt not bear false witness against thy neighbor.

11. Be courteous to strangers.

12. Federal regulation: Warning: Under Title 18 U.S. Code: It Is a Federal Offense to Assault a Postal Employee While on Duty.

13. School sign: Slow Children Crossing.

14. Speaker: Lincoln could not have been such a fine man, for didn't he say that "You can fool some of the people all of the time"?

Equivocation

We have seen how ambiguity of sentence structure gives rise to the fallacy of amphiboly and how ambiguity concerning emphasis gives rise to the fallacy of accent. Now we want to note how confusion arises from the ambiguity of the words themselves.

The fallacy of **equivocation** occurs when a word shifts in its meaning during the course of the argument. If the change in meaning is subtle, the conclusion of the argument will seem to follow from the premises, and the argument will seem more convincing than it deserves to be.

A rather absurd example uses the term *man* equivocally to construct a seemingly sound argument: "Only man is rational; no woman is a man; therefore, no woman is rational." This argument would be valid if the term *man* had the same meaning each time it occurred. However, for the first premise to be true, *man* must mean "human being," whereas for the second premise to be true, *man* must mean "male." Thus, if the premises are to have any plausibility, the term *man* must shift its meaning—but then the conclusion doesn't follow.

A good test to apply to arguments we suspect of equivocation is to make them stick to the original meanings of their terms and see whether they still make sense. An argument that turns on equivocation will not. If we make the term *man* mean "male" throughout the example, the first premise will then read, "Only males are rational." We need not go further because we immediately reject this premise as either false or for assuming the very point to be proven. On the other hand, if we make the term *man* mean "human being" throughout the argument, the second premise becomes "No woman is a human being." Here again, we need go no further, for we immediately reject this false claim.

The fallacy of equivocation is especially easy to commit when the key term is a figure of speech or a metaphor. By interpreting the metaphor literally, we can sometimes persuade ourselves that the argument is stronger than it really is. Consider this:

> It is the clear duty of the press to publish such news as is in the public interest. There can be no doubt about the public interest taken in the brutal murder of the Countess and concerning the details of her private life leading up to the murder. The press would have failed in their duty if they had refrained from publishing these matters.

The arguer here apparently does not realize that what is "in the public interest" is not quite the same thing as what the public is interested in. The former is a metaphorical expression meaning "what is for the public good," while the latter simply means what the public is curious about.

The warning against being misled by figures of speech should not be mistaken as a warning against their use. Language is filled with figures of speech, and it is not possible to avoid them entirely. Nor should we try to. Our speech and writing would be much poorer without them. Not only do they make for pointed expression, economy, and tact, but often a figure of speech is the only way of saying precisely what we wish to say.

Equivocation, however, is not confined to figurative expressions. On the contrary, since many words have more than one meaning, any one of them can occasion the fallacy. An absurd example would be the following: "Some birds are domesticated; my parrot is domesticated; my parrot, therefore, is some bird!" As this example shows, even such a common and simple word as *some* can lend itself to equivocation. Here *some* is used first quantitatively, to mean "a number of," and then qualitatively, to mean "a magnificent bird." Although probably no one would ever become confused over this, the example brings out the point that almost any word can either be exploited for its ambiguity or be itself ambiguous, so that it occasions mistakes in thinking.

Still, the widespread ambiguity of language is not really a defect we should wish to remedy. It is one of the major vehicles for the expression of wit and would be missed were it possible to eliminate it from language.

■ EXERCISES

Explain how the following examples illustrate equivocation.

15. There are laws of nature. Laws need lawgivers. Therefore, there is a cosmic lawgiver.

16. I have the right to publish my opinions concerning the present administration. What is right for me to do I ought to do. Hence I ought to publish them.

17. Jane: That old copper kettle isn't worth anything. You can't even boil water in it. Mary: It is worth something. It's an antique.

18. Birth control is race suicide, for when no children are born, as happens when you practice birth control, the human race must die out.

19. Anyone who is old enough to go into the army and fight for his country is a mature person, and anyone old enough to vote is a mature person, too. Hence, anyone old enough to fight is old enough to vote.

20. I do not believe in the possibility of eliminating the desire to fight from humankind because an organism without fight is dead or moribund. Life consists of tensions. There must be a balance of opposite polarities to make a personality, a nation, a world, or a cosmic system.

21. In our democracy all people are equal. The Declaration of Independence states this clearly and unequivocally. But we tend to forget this great truth. Our society accepts the principle of competition. And competition implies that some people are better than others. But this implication is false. The private is just as good as the general; the file clerk is just as good as the executive; the scholar is no better than the dunce; the philosopher is no better than the fool. We are all born equal.

THE FALLACIES OF PRESUMPTION

Whereas confusing language is what deceives in the fallacies of ambiguity, it is the misleading resemblance to valid argument forms that deceives in the fallacies of presumption. We saw a pair of these in chapter 4, the fallacies of affirming the consequent and denying the antecedent, which looked confusingly like the valid argument forms *modus ponens* and *modus tollens* respectively. As a further example now, the argument "Exercise is good; therefore Nora should do more of it, for it will be good for her" looks deceptively like the valid argument "All men are mortal; Socrates is a man; therefore, Socrates is mortal." However, the statement "Exercise is good" is an unqualified generalization that may not apply to Nora, who may suffer from a heart condition (say) and has been told by her doctor not to exercise.

What is most characteristic of the fallacies of presumption is that facts relevant to the argument have not been represented correctly in the premises. This inappropriate treatment of the facts may take the form of overlooking, evading, or distorting them. Overlooking the facts gives rise to the fallacies of sweeping generalization, hasty generalization, and bifurcation. Evading the facts takes the form of begging the question. Distorting the facts occurs with the fallacies of false analogy and false cause.

Overlooking the Facts

In the fallacy of **sweeping generalization**, the error lies in assuming that what is true under certain conditions must be true under all conditions. Consider this example:

> Everyone has a right to his or her own property. Therefore, even though Smith has been declared insane, you had no right to take away his weapon.

The first premise in this argument is a general principle that is widely accepted. It does not apply, however, in the specific case in which a person has lost his reason—especially when the piece of property is a weapon.

The source of this fallacy's persuasive power is that it resembles valid arguments in which individual cases do fall under a general rule. Nevertheless, a generalization applies only to individual cases that properly fall under it. It does not necessarily apply to *all* individual cases.

To argue, therefore, that "since horseback riding and mountain climbing are healthful exercises, Zach ought to do more of them because it will be good for his heart trouble" would be to commit this fallacy, for what is good for a person's health normally is not good where special conditions prevail. And the same is true of the following argument: "It is my duty to do unto others as I would have them do unto me. If I were puzzled by a question in an examination, I would like my neighbor to help me out. So it is my duty to help this person beside me who is stuck." Here our reply should be that to do one's duty in such circumstances would be *not* to help the person. This is an examination, and the point of it is to find out what each one knows by himself or herself.

Arguments of the kind we are examining here have two parts to them: a rule and a case. If the argument in question is invalid, it is because the case to which the rule is being applied is exceptional and therefore does not fall under the given rule. To expose them, therefore, you must isolate the rule and show that, understood properly, it cannot be applied to the case in question.

■ **EXERCISES**

Explain how each of the following demonstrates the fallacy of sweeping generalization.

22. I don't care if he did weigh three times as much as you. A good scout always tries to help. You should have jumped into the water and tried to save him.

23. Narcotics are habit forming. Therefore, if you allow your physician to ease your pain with an opiate you will become a hopeless drug addict.

24. No one who lives on terms of intimate friendship and confidence with another is justified in killing him. Brutus, therefore, did wrong in assassinating Caesar.

25. The president should get rid of his advisers and run the government by himself. After all, too many cooks spoil the broth.

26. The American secretary of state in 1939, refusing to grant asylum to Jewish refugees on the ship the *St. Louis* (whose forced return to Germany meant certain death): "I took an oath to protect the flag and obey the laws of my country and you are asking me to break those laws."

The fallacy of **hasty generalization** is the reverse of the fallacy we have just examined. This fallacy is committed whenever some isolated or exceptional case or event is used as the basis for a general conclusion.

For example, a woman argues, "I had a bad time with my ex-husband. From that experience I learned that men were no good." And someone else complains, "I've only known one surgeon, and he was incredibly arrogant. I wouldn't want to associate with any of them." The arguments in both cases are invalid because they assume that what is true under certain conditions is true under all conditions. At most, the evidence warrants only a specific, not a general, conclusion. And this is typical of the fallacy: unlike sweeping generalization, which results when a rule or a generalization is misapplied, the fallacy of hasty generalization results when a particular case is misused.

Of course, in generalizing we should remember that it is not possible (or necessary) to consider all the cases involved. Nevertheless, unless a sufficiently large number of cases are examined, the conclusion cannot be relied upon. A small sample may not be at all representative, but rather quite exceptional. The following would be an absurd example: "They just don't care about traffic law enforcement in this town, for they let ambulances go at any speed they like and let them run red lights, too." This is absurd, of course, because there are good reasons for permitting ambulances to do these things. No such conclusion can therefore be built on the basis of such unrepresentative examples of supposed law violation.

The fallacy of hasty generalization is also committed when we select and consider only the evidence that favors our position and ignore all the evidence that would throw doubt on it. Consider the following: "State-owned industries encourage inefficiency. All state-owned industries should therefore be abolished." Even if it were true that state-owned industries encourage inefficiency, this is hardly a sufficient basis for the drastic action recommended. To try to get rid of these abuses by abolishing the industries in which they tend to flourish would be like the proverbial throwing out the baby with the bathwater.

■ **EXERCISES**

Explain how each of the following demonstrates the fallacy of hasty generalization.

27. The customer service people at Best Buy are incompetent. They screwed up two of my orders during my holiday shopping.

28. Doctors are all alike. They really don't know any more than you or I do. This is the third case of misdiagnosis I have heard of in the last month.

29. She is fond of children and so will undoubtedly make a fine kindergarten teacher.

30. He speaks so beautifully. He must have studied acting.

31. High tariffs enable our industries to grow strong; they ensure high wages to the workers, and they increase federal revenues. High tariffs, therefore, are a benefit to the nation.

The fallacy of **bifurcation** refers to a fallacy that presumes that a certain distinction or classification is exhaustive when other alternatives are possible. The fallacy is sometimes referred to as the "either/or fallacy" or the "black or white fallacy." (This fallacy might also get some of its force from its resemblance to the valid argument form *disjunctive syllogism*, which we looked at in chapter 4.)

In some cases of either/or, there *is* no middle course between the two extremes noted. The two poles of the proposition exhaust all the possibilities, and therefore if one of them is true, the other must be false and vice versa: "Either the man is dead or he is alive"; "Either it is your birthday today or it is not."

However, polar terms that go into the formation of many propositions do *not* exhaust all the possibilities. The result is the fallacy of bifurcation. The famous debates over the atomic bomb gave rise to many examples of the fallacy. Some argued that either we must have war against the (then) Soviet Union before it had the atom bomb or the Soviet Union would end up conquering us. Their opponents countered that these didn't exhaust the options, for peaceful co-existence was possible. In the contemporary vein, some enthusiastically patriotic people endorse the slogan "America: Love It or Leave It." Opponents may counter that there is a middle ground, as there is room to criticize one's country even while choosing to remain in it.

Because our vocabulary is replete with polar terms, the tendency to bifurcate is common. We are thus prone to people the world with the *rich* and the *poor*, the *good* and the *bad*, the *normal* and the *abnormal*, those *with us* or *against us*, forgetting that between these extremes are many gradations—any one of which could be further alternatives to the either/or proposed. From a logical point of view, what is objectionable about overlooking the middle ground is that there is no necessary connection between the two polar extremes in question. The fact that we do not want our soup cold does not mean, nor does it logically follow, that we want it hot; it is not necessarily the case that if something is not good it must be bad. It could be neither good nor bad but a bit of both.

It is, however, in the context of political debate that the fallacy is most often committed. It is typical for opponents to characterize each other as adopting extreme positions. ("Republicans are for the rich and against the poor, Democrats are for the poor and against the rich.") But of course (one hopes) most politicians are ultimately for *everybody*, even if they disagree on the policies to adopt for promoting the general good.

■ EXERCISES

Explain how the following illustrate the fallacy of bifurcation.

32. There are only two kinds of people in the world: winners and losers.

33. Either he knew everything that was going on, in which case he's a liar, or he's a fool.

34. God doesn't tolerate indecision in the cosmic sense. You must be either committed to Christ or fall in with the Devil.

35. It seems to me that one is either for the War on Terror or against it. Either we continue to be on the offensive across the globe, or we sit back and wait to be attacked.

36. We can continue to use fossil fuels or we can save our environment.

Evading the Facts

In the second category of the fallacies of presumption, evading the facts, the error lies not in overlooking facts but in seeming to deal with all relevant facts without actually doing so. Such arguments deceive by inviting us to assume that the facts are as they have been stated in the argument when they are quite otherwise.

In its simple form, the fallacy of **begging the question** is committed when instead of providing proof for our assertion we simply repeat it or assume it. If the statement or argument is brief, not many will be fooled by it. Thus, if we should argue, "The belief in God is universal because everybody believes in God," it would be apparent that since *universal* means *everybody*, all we have done is reaffirm that the belief in God is universal without having confirmed or proved it. The same would be true if we argued, "Honesty is praiseworthy because it deserves the approval of all." Again, since *praiseworthy* means *deserving of approval*, we have merely repeated in our premise (which should contain our evidence) the very conclusion ("Honesty is praiseworthy") to be established. The argument therefore lacks evidence and is no real argument. The same would be true if, finally, we argued, "Miracles are impossible, for they cannot happen." Here, too, all we have done is reassert the same point we began with.

Of course, to assert, or even reassert, something is not in itself objectionable. What makes arguments of this sort objectionable is that they suggest they *have* done more than this: they imply that by reasserting the point they have somehow established or confirmed it. This strategy can be psychologically effective, to be sure, as repetition does make something more believable. But again, merely repeating a point is not in fact to support it, and that's what makes this a fallacy.

> If you repeat a lie often enough, people will believe it, and you will even come to believe it yourself.
>
> —attributed to **Joseph Goebbels** (1897–1945), Nazi Minister of Propaganda

As obvious as this error may seem, it is surprisingly common. Nor does it spare the mighty. It was one of President Calvin Coolidge's misfortunes to provide logicians with a classic example. He once remarked, "When large numbers of people are out of work, unemployment results." True, but only because large numbers of people being out of work just *is* unemployment.

Sometimes the same sort of maneuver might be used to another rhetorical end, of course: not as a logical fallacy but as a form of evasion, or even wit. Thus, in reply to a reporter's question as to why presidential candidate Hubert Humphrey lost in the 1968 elections, Mayor Richard Daley of Chicago replied, "He lost it because he didn't get enough votes." True enough, but again, losing just *is* not getting enough votes. But here the reply is amusing and meant to be so. That is why it is not a fallacy, for it is rather feigning the error than committing it.

Often quite flagrant examples of this fallacy will escape detection if the statements involved are drawn out. Our memories, not always very good, fail to make the repetition immediately apparent to us. Consider the following example:

Free trade will be good for this country. The reason for this is patently clear. Is it not obvious that unrestricted commercial relations would bestow upon all sections of this community the advantages and benefits which result when there is an unimpeded flow of goods between nations?

Since "unrestricted commercial relations" is simply a more verbose way of saying "free trade," and "would bestow upon all sections of this community the advantages and benefits" is a more verbose way of saying "good for this country," the argument merely says, in effect, that "free trade will be good for this country, because free trade will be good for this country." Unfortunately, many arguments consist of such restatements. Language can hide this from us because of the numerous synonyms it contains.

Let's note one further form in which this fallacy appears. A person might try to establish a particular proposition by subsuming it under a generalization. Should the generalization itself be questionable, then the argument is fallacious. Consider the following argument: "Democracy is the best form of government because it alone takes care of the interests of the common people." Here the conclusion ("Democracy is the best form of government") is made to rest upon a principle ("it alone takes care . . .") that is much wider and more questionable than the conclusion itself. Obviously, if the conclusion needs proving, how much more so does the premise!

■ EXERCISES

Explain how each of the following illustrates the fallacy of begging the question.

37. School isn't worthwhile because education doesn't pay off.

38. Death for traitors is properly justified because it is right to put to death those who betray our country.

39. To allow everyone unbounded freedom of speech must always be, on the whole, advantageous to the state. You ask why? Well, it is highly conducive to the interest of the community that each individual should enjoy an unlimited liberty of expressing his or her sentiments.

40. A: He talks with angels. B: How do you know? A: He said he did. B: But suppose that he lied! A: No way! How could anyone lie who is capable of talking with angels?

41. Chris cannot have lied when he said he was my cousin, for no cousin of mine would ever tell a lie.

42. Moral beliefs are unjustified because they are not verifiable in sense experience.

Distorting the Facts

The third type of fallacies of presumption includes those that, rather than overlook or evade relevant facts, actually distort them. In the fallacy of **false (or imperfect) analogy**, certain cases are made to appear more similar than they really are. The fallacy of **false cause** makes it appear that two events are causally connected in a way they are not.

Perhaps no other technique of reasoning has been more helpful or harmful than reasoning by analogy. Analogy is a method of reasoning in which facts that are obscure or difficult to understand are explained by comparing them to facts that are already known or better understood and to which they bear some likeness. In an argument, analogy suggests that because two things or situations are similar in certain respects, they must therefore be similar in other respects. Now, drawing attention to such similarities can be useful, as long as we are careful that the two things being compared resemble each other in important respects and differ only in trifling ones. If, on the contrary, they resemble each other in unimportant ways and differ in important ones, then there is no meaningful analogy between them. Merely to seize upon some slight similarity between two things and then to conclude on that basis that what is true of one is also true of the other leads to the fallacy of false analogy.

Consider the following extreme but not necessarily absurd example:

> It is right to force people to accept the gospel for their own good, just as force must be used to prevent a crazy person from throwing himself over the edge of a steep cliff.

This is not much of an argument even for those for whom the truth of the gospel is not a matter of doubt. In the one case it is a matter of saving a crazy person from killing himself, and in the other, the person involved presumably is not crazy. In other words, even if we were to grant that just as we are obligated to do all we can to save people for this life, so we are obligated to do all we can to save them for the afterlife, it still would *not* follow that just as force is allowed in the "this life" cliff case, so force should be permitted in the "gospel" afterlife case. In the one we are dealing with a person who has lost his reason, and in the other we are dealing with rational people who should be allowed, therefore, to make up their own minds about such things.

As in all cases of false or imperfect analogy, the one we have just examined is faulty because the two things that are compared resemble each other only in trifling ways and differ in significant ones. To expose imperfect analogy, all you must do is simply point this out. In the case of some analogies this is not difficult:

> Why should we worry over a few thousand people who were cheated or ruined when our great industrial enterprises, railroads, and pipelines were being built? It may be that they suffered an injustice, but, after all, you can't make an omelet without breaking a few eggs.

Here one might point out that even if it were true that it is just as impossible to build great industrial enterprises without causing pain as it is to make an omelet without breaking eggs, the two cases are not comparable—for to break eggs is not to cause them any pain, while to build great empires by destroying people's lives is.

Of course, not every analogy is an argument *by* analogy. Often analogies are constructed merely for illustrative purposes or to lend color to a position supported in other ways. Such analogies may still mislead, but no more weight should be placed on them than their authors intend them to carry. The following lyric from the famous band the Grateful Dead is a case in point: "Sometimes your cards ain't worth a dime if you don't lay 'em down." This isn't merely a piece of poker advice, but some (not very concrete) life wisdom, based on an analogy between poker and certain real life situations. But no argument of any sort is being offered here.

In fact, strictly speaking, it is not really possible to make a *perfectly* compelling argument by analogy at all. Two things may be similar in many different ways, but the similarities noted cannot alone prove that the two things will resemble each other in some further property. Analogy may help us see that it is likely that they will, but it cannot definitively *establish* that they will. Arguments by analogy, therefore, are inductive arguments, unable to establish their conclusions with necessity.

A last example will illustrate this point. Though there are perhaps important similarities between the structure of a living body and the structure of a political body, it was perhaps a misleading analogy (due to a misleading metaphor) that led King James I to argue,

If you cut off the head of a body, the other organs cannot function, and the body dies. Similarly, if you cut off the head of the State, the State may flop around awhile, but it is due to perish in time or become easy prey to its neighbors.

Even good analogies only go so far. King James apparently overlooked the fact that while a body certainly cannot grow a new head, a state easily can—by appointing another ruler.

■ **EXERCISES**

Explain how each of the following illustrates the fallacy of false analogy.

43. President Truman: "We should never have stopped [testing of nuclear weapons]. Where would we be today if Thomas Edison had been forced to stop his experiments with the electric bulb?"

44. Why should we punish human beings for their actions? Whatever they do is an expression of their nature, and they cannot help it. Are we angry with the stone for falling and the flame for rising?

45. Philosopher Sidney Hook (1902–1989): "A philosopher in his own life need be no more wise than a physician needs to be healthy."

46. Advertisement for skin lotion: "You've seen land crack when it loses its essential moisture; the same thing can happen to your skin when it loses its moisture."

47. If we find it necessary to tip waiters and hotel maids for a job well done, why should we not similarly reward doctors and professors?

Although the fallacy of false cause can assume different forms, all are essentially a matter of mistakenly believing that because something occurred just prior to something else, it was therefore its cause. Much more knowledge is required to be able to identify the cause than the mere fact that it occurred even just a split second before the given event. In short, sequence alone is no proof of causation.

Although once quite widespread, false cause has slipped in frequency over the years because of the impact of education on the general public. People are still inclined to commit it, but not in the crude forms in which they once did. We no longer argue, as the nineteenth-century reformer did, that because every sober and industrious farmer owned at least one cow and those who had no cows were usually lazy and drunken, a cow should be given to any farmer who had none in order to make him sober and industrious.

Today we encounter more subtle versions of the fallacy:

In 1995 the number of television programs depicting crimes of violence increased 12 percent as compared with the figures of 1994. Subsequently, the Department of Justice index of juvenile delinquency showed a corresponding increase. Hence, the evidence shows that a stricter control of television crime programs would result in a lowering of the juvenile crime rate.

What we might say in response to this argument is that the fact that a rise in the crime rate followed a rise in the number of crime television programs is not sufficient to establish a causal connection. The rise in crime might have been due to any number of different factors, such as a rise in population or changes in economic conditions.

It is also important to note that two events may be causally related though neither is the cause of the other, for example if both are effects of a third event. Consider the ibis. The ancient Egyptians worshipped this bird because at a certain time each year, shortly after ibises migrated to the banks of the Nile, the river would overflow its banks and irrigate the land. The birds were credited with magical powers, when in fact both their migration and the overflow of the river were effects of a common cause, the change in seasons.

If immediate temporal succession is an insufficient basis for establishing causal connection, more remote temporal succession gives even less warrant for causal connection. Thus the fact, to take some broad examples, that humans follow the apes in the succession of primates is no proof that we are descended from apes; nor is the fact that because the Roman Empire declined and fell after the appearance of Christianity proof that Christianity was the cause of its decline and fall.

Let us consider a more contemporary example. Many studies suggest that babies who are breast-fed (as opposed to bottle-fed) typically grow up to have various health and cognitive advantages over those who aren't breast-fed. That might suggest the conclusion that breast-feeding *causes* children to be healthier and smarter, in a word. But more cautious critics point out that families who breast-feed their children already are typically healthier and wealthier than those who do not or cannot. It may therefore be *those* facts—that the children are being raised in healthy, wealthy homes—that causes the outcomes, not the breast-feeding itself. Mere correlation does not entail causation.

Indeed, one can find no lack of interesting correlations where it's implausible to imagine causation. Statistics show, for example, that between the years 1999 and 2009, U.S. spending on science, space, and technology correlates closely with the number of suicides by hanging, strangulation, and suffocation; that the divorce rate in Maine correlates with the per capita consumption of margarine in the United States; and that the revenue generated by arcades correlates with the number of computer science doctorates awarded. (For many other examples, see www.tylervigen.com/.)

■ **EXERCISES**

Explain how each of the following illustrates the fallacy of false cause.

48. No sooner did the government start to fluoridate the water than my friends began dying of heart disease. It just doesn't pay to tamper with nature.

49. Your boss has a bigger vocabulary than you have. That's why she's your boss.

50. From early Greek physics: Night is the cause of the extinction of the sun, for as evening comes on, the shadows arise from the valleys and blot out the sunlight.

51. If strong law enforcement really prevented crime, then those areas where police patrols are most frequent would be the safest and the best protected. Actually, the reverse is true, for in such areas even one's life is in danger, and crimes of all kinds are more common than in other areas where police patrols are infrequent.

52. In the oil-embargoed 1970s the president of the Women's Christian Temperance Union said that people were turning to drink to escape the worries of the troubled economy. "Liquor

dealers admit that since the energy crisis began, the consumption of alcoholic beverages has greatly increased," said Mrs. Fred Tooze, head of the national anti-alcohol group. Mrs. Tooze said the need to conserve gasoline would cause people to stay home and drink more, creating broken homes and harming the mental capacity of the nation's workforce.

FALLACIES OF RELEVANCE

Fallacies of relevance are arguments in which the premises, despite appearances, do not actually bear upon the conclusions drawn in the arguments. These fallacies might well be called fallacies of *ir*relevance, for all of them introduce some piece of irrelevance that tends to confuse. What unites this last set of fallacies is that in all of them the irrelevance is an attempt to obscure the real issue by stirring up our emotions. Fallacies of relevance derive their persuasive power from the fact that, when feelings run high, almost anything will pass as an argument.

The five fallacies selected for examination here include the genetic fallacy, abusive *ad hominem*, circumstantial *ad hominem*, *tu quoque*, and poisoning the well. This list is not exhaustive and probably represents only a small fraction of types of irrelevance.

Genetic Fallacy

Genetic fallacy is a type of argument in which an attempt is made to prove a conclusion false by condemning its source, or genesis. Such arguments are fallacious because how an idea originated is irrelevant to its value. Thus, it would be fallacious to argue that since chemical elements are involved in all life processes, life is therefore nothing more than a chemical process, or that since early religious beliefs were based in superstition, religion is nothing but superstition. Genetic accounts of an issue may be true, and they may be illuminating as to why the issue has assumed its present form, but they are irrelevant to its merits.

Here are some examples:

This scholarship aid proposal is calculated to exploit poor students, for it was written by a committee composed only of members of the faculty and administration. No scholarship students were on that committee.

We must take Schopenhauer's famous essay denouncing women with a grain of salt. Any psychiatrist would at once explain this essay by reference to the strained relationship between Schopenhauer and his mother.

Just because the committee had no scholarship students on it does not itself mean that the proposal doesn't reflect the interests of that group (though it might encourage us to examine it carefully). Similarly, the twentieth-century popularity of psychoanalysis helped promote the appeal to underlying motivations that is found in this second argument. Although it may be true that a source's motives may weaken his or her credibility, motives are irrelevant to the credibility of the argument itself. Arguments are sound not because of who proposes them (or why) but by virtue of their internal merit. If the premises of an argument prove its conclusion, they do so no matter who happens to formulate the argument or why. If they do not, the greatest logician cannot make them sound.

Abusive Ad Hominem

A variant of the genetic fallacy is the **abusive *ad hominem*** ("against the person"), which draws attention to the source of an idea by attacking the advocate of that idea:

> This theory about a new cure for cancer has been introduced by a woman known for her spiritual healing sympathies. Don't pay attention to it.

> The senator is now saying that big corporations shouldn't pay more taxes. That's what you'd expect from a politician who's lived in Washington for a few years and has forgotten all about the people back home.

> In reply to his argument, I need only say that two years ago he vigorously defended the very position he now opposes so adamantly.

Turning attention away from the claims made within the arguments to the people *making* the claims is characteristic not only of everyday discussions but of many of our political debates as well. Rather than discuss political issues soberly, rivals find it easier to discuss personalities and smear each other. This tactic can be effective because a suspicion once raised is difficult to put to rest. It is not surprising, therefore, that abusive *ad hominem* is common in debates among people seeking office.

When feelings run high, such abusive tactics can persuade. Making an opponent appear suspicious, ridiculous, or inconsistent suggests that his or her argument must be unsound because he or she cannot be trusted. But again, this is a fallacy—the merit of the argument depends only on its premises and conclusions, not on the person making it.

Circumstantial Ad Hominem

Occasionally, instead of engaging in direct abuse, an opponent will try to undercut a position by suggesting that the views being advanced merely serve the advocate's own interests. Logicians call this the **circumstantial *ad hominem*** fallacy.

Someone might point out, for example, that a manufacturer's argument in favor of tariff protection should be rejected on the ground that, as a manufacturer, the individual *would* favor a protective tariff. Rather than offering actual reasons to reject the opponent's argument, such moves offer only self-interested reasons for expecting one's opponent to endorse the conclusion.

Although charging an opponent with having vested interests can be seen as a form of reproach, the nonabusive form of this fallacy differs from the abusive form in that abuse is only incidental, not central, to circumstantial *ad hominem*. Take this argument:

> It is true that several college professors have testified that these hallucinogenic drugs are harmless and nonaddictive, but these same professors have admitted to taking drugs themselves. We should certainly disregard their views.

Here again, an irrelevancy has been introduced in order to divert attention from the real issue.

Tu Quoque

We have now examined three fallacious ways to undermine a person's credibility: deflation (genetic fallacy), straight-out insult (abusive *ad hominem*), and insinuation (circumstantial *ad hominem*). The remaining two fallacies of relevance are a bit more complex.

The first of these goes by the Latin name ***tu quoque*** (pronounced "tu kwokway"), meaning "you, also." In idiomatic English, it means "look who's talking." The thrust of the *tu quoque* fallacy is that an opponent's argument is worthless because the opponent has failed to follow his or her own advice: "Look who's telling me to stop smoking! You smoke more than I do." Although the fact that the suggestion comes from a fellow smoker may weaken its moral force, it does not undermine the argument. The contention that smoking is unhealthful may still be true whether or not the person saying so is a smoker.

We have a natural tendency to want others to practice what they preach. But practice is irrelevant to the merits of an argument. The following retort seems reasonable enough at first glance, but it has no place in logical discourse: "If you think income equality is such a great idea, why don't you give up your job?" But of course there may be many reasons that someone who advocates for general income equality might legitimately not give up his or her job while doing so.

It is only a step from an argument charging, "You do it, too!" to one that charges, "You would do the same thing if you got a chance." Notice this shift between the next two arguments:

Far too much fuss has been made over the CIA's espionage abroad. Other countries are just as deeply engaged in spying as we are.

It may be true that Iran hasn't yet carried out any espionage activities in the United States, but it would if it had the chance. Let's beat Iran to it, I say.

The fallacy is fundamentally the same in each case. Whether someone else is already acting in a manner counter to the conclusion at issue or whether someone else would act in such a manner if the opportunity arose has no bearing on whether the conclusion in question is right or wrong. As in all fallacies based on personal attack, any considerations of those who hold a position or who originated a position or who are opposed to a position must be viewed as irrelevant.

Poisoning the Well

The final fallacy of this sort is known as **poisoning the well**. The expression refers to an ancient wartime practice of pouring poison into sources of fresh water before an invading army, to diminish the attacking army's strength. In the fallacy, similarly, an attempt is made to place the opponent in a weakened position from which he or she is unable to reply. This form of the fallacy was identified by John Henry Cardinal Newman (1801–1890), who protested when his opponent insisted that he (Newman) did not place the highest value on truth—for once the opponent did that, then anything Newman said in his own defense could simply be dismissed as untrue!

Consider how these accusations poison the well:

Don't listen to him; he's a liar!

"The lady doth protest too much, methinks." (Shakespeare, *Hamlet* [1603])

This man denies being a member of the opposition. But we know that members of the opposition have been brainwashed to deny under any circumstances that they belong to the opposition.

Anyone attempting to rebut these arguments would be hard pressed to do so, for anything he or she said would only seem to strengthen the accusation against the person saying it. If you're a liar, then anything you say in your defense might be dismissed as a lie; the more you protest, the more you are guilty of the accusation. But of course all these charges don't prove their points at all. In a very unfair way they merely make it difficult for you to prove your point. In some respects they defend their points only by discrediting in advance the possibility of criticizing them, and thus by precluding genuine reasoned discussion.

> Those who disagree with me when I say that mankind is corrupt prove that they are already corrupted.
>
> —**Friedrich Nietzsche** (1844–1900)

It should be pointed out that there are occasions on which it *is* appropriate to question a person's character. In a court of law, for example, it would not be irrelevant to point out that a witness is a chronic liar. But even so, while this information would reduce the credibility of the person's testimony, it would not in itself prove that testimony false. Even chronic liars can tell the truth, and we would be guilty of a breach of logic were we to argue that what a person says is a lie simply because he or she has often lied in the past.

■ EXERCISES

Identify which relevance fallacy each of the following illustrates and explain how it commits that fallacy.

53. Present economic policies are rapidly placing this country in a bad condition. This is mainly due to some of the ex–White House advisers connected with the former administration, plus some of the intellectuals still in power. These people are evidently very egotistical and smug, entirely out of contact with the American people and Congress.

54. Humans are made of nothing but atoms, and since atoms have no free will, humans don't either.

55. A: Of course you would favor reduced real estate taxes because you would benefit personally by such a reduction. B: Of course you are against such a reduction because you own no real estate.

56. A top foreign authority on U.S. affairs showed irritation at Americans over the human rights issue. "What right do they have to preach freedom and democracy, when their society is ravaged by income inequality and their prisons are disproportionately filled with minorities?"

57. A: I don't think I really matter to you. B: Now why are you saying that? I'm doing the best I can. A: Well, I just feel taken for granted. B: I think you are insatiable. There is never enough. A: See, this is proof of what I just said. I don't really matter to you. If I did you wouldn't talk this way to me.

SUMMARY

1. The common fallacies are traditionally divided into three groups: fallacies of ambiguity, presumption, and relevance.

2. Fallacies of ambiguity stem from the use of language having more than one meaning. These include amphiboly, accent, and equivocation.

3. Fallacies of presumption are arguments in which unfounded or unproven assumptions are smuggled in under the guise of valid argument forms. These include sweeping generalization, hasty generalization, bifurcation, begging the question, false (or imperfect) analogy, and false cause.

4. Fallacies of relevance are arguments in which the premises are not in fact fully relevant to the alleged conclusion. These include genetic fallacy, abusive *ad hominem*, circumstantial *ad hominem*, *tu quoque*, and poisoning the well.

KEY TERMS

abusive *ad hominem*	fallacies of presumption
accent	fallacies of relevance
amphiboly	false cause
begging the question	false (imperfect) analogy
bifurcation	genetic fallacy
circumstantial *ad hominem*	hasty generalization
equivocation	poisoning the well
fallacy	sweeping generalization
fallacies of ambiguity	*tu quoque*

REVIEW QUESTIONS

1. What are the three major categories of fallacies, and what distinguishes each of them?
2. Identify the three fallacies of ambiguity.
3. What fallacies are included under the category of presumption?
4. Which of the fallacies of presumption discussed in the text evade the facts? Which overlook the facts? Which distort the facts?
5. What is reasoning by analogy?
6. What are the five fallacies of relevance examined in the text?

ANSWERS TO EXERCISES

1. Whose example are we to follow here: the dead who clip the grass on "their" own graves, or those who keep the graves of "their" loved ones trimmed so neatly?

2. Should Bush himself be on the can, or Bush's *picture*?

3. Is the butcher to cut and skewer the customer?

4. Are the patrollers looking for nude people on the beach, or themselves nude?

5. If it is the woman's own funeral they mean here, they will find it hard to collect.

6. This sounds like the 200 present were also the subject of the paper.

7. Said in a serious tone, it means only Hollywood could produce such a great film; said sarcastically, it means that only Hollywood could produce such a terrible film.

8. Said in an excited tone, the remark is an expression of great satisfaction; said in a dreary tone, it is an expression of disbelief and disgust.

9. Said in an expectant tone of voice, it means one thing; said in a tone of boredom it means quite another sort of thing.

10. If the stress is on *thou*, it implies that although *you* may not bear false witness, someone else may; if the stress is on *thy*, it implies that it may be all right to bear false witness against

someone else's neighbor; if the stress is on *false*, then the intended meaning is conveyed, that you must not speak falsehoods against others but you may, of course, speak the truth.

11. Stress the word *strangers*, and it implies that one should be courteous only to strangers (but not to family or friends); unstressed, it implies that one should be courteous to everyone, including strangers.

12. Is it a federal offense to assault a postal employee only while he or she is on duty? Or while *you* are on duty? Or that it is a federal offense only in the case of assaulting a *postal employee* (but other employees are fine to assault)?

13. Stress *slow*, and the statement directs drivers to slow down; with no stress, the statement may be describing the type of children in the area.

14. Lincoln is being quoted out of context. What he reputedly said was "You can fool all the people some of the time, and some of the people all of the time, but you cannot fool all the people all of the time." In context, Lincoln is not endorsing fooling people but condemning it.

15. Since by "laws of nature" we mean "regularities of behavior" and not literal legislation, it does not follow that their existence requires a cosmic lawgiver.

16. *Right* can mean privilege as well as duty. Here in its first occurrence it is used in the former sense; in the second occurrence, it is used in the latter sense. So just because you have a right to do something, it doesn't mean you ought to.

17. Jane and Mary are speaking equivocally here: Mary uses the word *worth* in its monetary sense, Jane in its practical sense.

18. Here, the *birth control* that would be "race suicide" (large-scale enforced prohibitions on reproduction) is not the same as the *birth control* that individuals may choose to use.

19. The argument turns on the equivocal use of the word *mature*: just because a person may be physically mature to perform a certain task at a certain age does not mean that he or she is emotionally or intellectually mature at that age as well.

20. Since by the phrase "desire to fight" we mean violence and war and not merely drive or spirit ("without fight"), it may be possible to eliminate the one (violence) without necessarily doing away with the other—the will to live.

21. Since by the phrase "all people are equal" we mean that all are equal before the law and not that all are born with the same abilities ("born equal"), we are not being inconsistent in believing in the one (that the law should treat everyone alike) and not in the other (that society should reward everyone the same). (See chapter 11 for more discussion of these ideas.)

22. Certainly we ought to try to come to one another's assistance, but in this particular case, unless the accused Boy Scout is a powerful swimmer, the attempt to save a bigger boy might have resulted in tragedy for both.

23. Narcotics are habit forming, but the circumstances here are special: the drug will be administered by one with the proper knowledge, under guarded conditions. It is therefore not likely to lead to the same results as self-administered doses.

24. Normally a person who lives with another on terms of friendship should not wish to harm him. Here, however, the person involved was a threat to Rome and the lives of its citizens.

25. Running a government is not like making a broth. No one person can master all that is involved but must depend on the advice and skill of many different people. What applies to a broth hardly therefore applies to the duties and responsibilities of a president.

26. The secretary of state's reasoning was specious, as he was undoubtedly aware, since the circumstances were special and mitigating. The *St. Louis's* sad mission ended in the ship's

return to Europe and subsequently in the demise of most of its passengers in Auschwitz, Treblinka, and other death camps.

27. Two screwed up orders are hardly sufficient to condemn the entire customer service department. An added factor was the time when this occurred—the holiday rush season.

28. When one considers how many doctors there are and how many diagnoses are made in the course of a month, three such faulty diagnoses hardly justify the general conclusion that all doctors are alike or that they do not know any more than we do.

29. Although being fond of children is important, it alone could not guarantee the person would make a fine kindergarten teacher. Other traits are also necessary: intelligence, dedication, patience, and so on. Put differently, just because some people fond of children make good kindergarten teachers doesn't mean they all would.

30. Just because some who speak beautifully have studied acting doesn't mean all who do have studied acting.

31. What is stated may be true, but it is only part of the story. What is neglected is some recognition of the need and value of international trade, and thus the possible *harms* of high tariffs. Other nations are able to do some things better and more economically than the United States can (for example), and it may make sense to let them produce these things and sell them here in exchange for things we have that they need or that we can produce more economically than they. So high tariffs might be useful in some cases or industries, but perhaps not in general.

32. No one is always either a "winner" or a "loser." Sometimes we succeed, sometimes we do not, and often we neither completely win nor completely lose.

33. Another possibility is that his lack of awareness of what was going on does not make him a fool, for the evidence may have been cleverly hidden from him or simply not easy to get.

34. This argument assumes that "sinner" and "saint" are the only alternatives, whereas most people do fall somewhere in between.

35. A typical example of oversimplification and of thinking in black and white terms. There are more moderate ways of defending against terrorism that perhaps don't involve "going on the offensive across the globe."

36. Are these the only possibilities? Perhaps we should decrease our consumption of fossil fuels, but "saving the environment" may not require eliminating their use altogether.

37. The second part of the statement (the premise) essentially just repeats the first part (the conclusion), with the result being that nothing is confirmed.

38. Since "those who betray our country" is another way of saying "traitor" and "right" is the same as "properly justified," the premises of the "argument" simply repeat what has been asserted in the conclusion without supporting the conclusion.

39. "Each individual should enjoy an unlimited liberty of expressing his or her sentiments" is simply another way of expressing "everyone" should be allowed "unbounded freedom of speech," and the phrase "highly conducive to the interests of the community" is another way of saying "advantageous to the state"; thus, nothing new is presented in support of the original claim.

40. If we grant that he talks with angels then we may believe that he does not lie; but granting that he talks with angels first presumes that he is not lying, which is the very point allegedly being proved!

41. How do we know that no cousin of his would lie? Or that that person, claiming to be his cousin, *is* his cousin? Both these questions are begged.

42. This statement assumes that only things verifiable in sense experience are justifiable. What evidence is there for this large assumption? Here it is only assumed, not established.

43. These are two vastly different cases. Experimenting with electric bulbs posed no great danger to anyone, whereas the testing of nuclear weapons threatens the lives of millions.

44. One cannot compare a human being to a stone or a fire. Stones and fires perform as they do *only* as the result of the force of natural law on them. Human beings, having intelligence, have a measure of choice and therefore can be held at least partly responsible for their actions.

45. A doctor may not be entirely healthy, yet he may still be able to help his patients by imparting his knowledge to them; a philosopher who is totally lacking in wisdom may have little to impart to his students.

46. Skin and land are also very different in nature. The body produces its own oils and moisturizers, while the land is dependent solely on external sources for moisture. Our skin has internal sources that naturally prevent it from drying up completely and cracking, as opposed to what the advertisement would like us to believe.

47. Waiters and hotel maids typically receive lower wages, partly on the assumption that they will receive tips to supplement their income; doctors and professors typically receive better wages, thus obviating the need for tips.

48. The simultaneous occurrence of fluoridation and heart disease in the speaker's friends does not mean that one is the cause of the other. His friends may have died from heart disease because they did not take proper care of themselves.

49. There are many other reasons that may have generated your boss's success besides her vocabulary: her intelligence, experience, initiative, and so on.

50. Cause and effect are reversed here: the sun setting causes the shadows, which then seem to blot out the sunlight, and not the other way around (night with its shadows causing the setting of the sun).

51. Although it is true that in areas where police patrols are frequent, crimes are more common, it is not because law enforcement fails to prevent crime. More likely, it is because a high-crime area is more frequently patrolled—otherwise the crime rate would be even higher. If the police stay long enough, the crime rate will go down.

52. As in exercise 48, even a simultaneous increase in alcoholism along with the energy crisis does not mean a causal relationship exists between them.

53. Abusive *ad hominem*. Instead of examining the economic policies themselves, the arguer attacks the "advisers" and "intellectuals" who devised the policies.

54. Genetic fallacy. Because we are composed or made up of atoms (which lack free will), it does not follow that we have all the same properties as atoms (i.e., that we lack free will).

55. Circumstantial *ad hominem*. In this interchange, each believes that the other will take a certain position on the tax issue only because of his or her circumstances, when this may not be the case at all.

56. *Tu quoque.* Perhaps the United States lacks a perfect record in domestic human rights, but this does not invalidate its efforts to promote human rights elsewhere or in general.

57. Poisoning the well. Matters are arranged in such a way that anything the other person says is taken as proof of the original contention—here that he or she doesn't matter very much.

■ Reading
"A Mad Tea-Party"

Lewis Carroll

From Alice's Adventures in Wonderland *(1865).*

An entertaining sample of strange thinking and reasoning.

There was a table set out under a tree in front of the house, and the March Hare and the Hatter were having tea at it: a Dormouse was sitting between them, fast asleep, and the other two were using it as a cushion, resting their elbows on it, and talking over its head. "Very uncomfortable for the Dormouse," thought Alice; "only as it's asleep, I suppose it doesn't mind."

The table was a large one, but the three were all crowded together at one corner of it. "No room! No room!" they cried out when they saw Alice coming.

"There's *plenty* of room!" said Alice indignantly, and she sat down in a large arm-chair at one end of the table.

"Have some wine," the March Hare said in an encouraging tone.

Alice looked all round the table, but there was nothing on it but tea. "I don't see any wine," she remarked.

"There isn't any," said the March Hare.

"Then it wasn't very civil of you to offer it," said Alice, angrily.

"It wasn't very civil of you to sit down without being invited," said the March Hare.

"I didn't know it was *your* table," said Alice: "it's laid for a great many more than three."

"Your hair wants cutting," said the Hatter. He had been looking at Alice for some time with great curiosity, and this was his first speech.

"You should learn not to make personal remarks," Alice said with some severity: "it's very rude."

The Hatter opened his eyes very wide on hearing this; but all he *said* was, "Why is a raven like a writing-desk?"

"Come, we shall have some fun now!" thought Alice. "I'm glad they've begun asking riddles—I believe I can guess that," she added, aloud.

"Do you mean that you think you can find out the answer to it?" said the March Hare.

"Exactly so," said Alice.

"Then you should say what you mean," the March Hare went on.

"I do," Alice hastily replied; "at least—at least I mean what I say—that's the same thing, you know."

"Not the same thing a bit!" said the Hatter. "Why, you might just as well say that 'I see what I eat' is the same thing as 'I eat what I see'!"

"You might just as well say," added the March Hare, "that 'I like what I get' is the same thing as 'I get what I like'!"

"You might just as well say," added the Dormouse, which seemed to be talking in its sleep, "that 'I breathe when I sleep' is the same thing as 'I sleep when I breathe'!"

"It *is* the same thing with you," said the Hatter, and here the conversation dropped, and the party sat silent for a minute, while Alice thought over all she could remember about ravens and writing-desks, which wasn't much.

The Hatter was the first to break the silence. "What day of the month is it?" he said, turning to Alice: he had taken his watch out of his pocket, and was looking at it uneasily, shaking it every now and then, and holding it to his ear.

Alice considered a little, and then said, "The fourth."

"Two days wrong!" sighed the Hatter. "I told you butter wouldn't suit the works!" he added, looking angrily at the March Hare.

"It was the *best* butter," the March Hare meekly replied.

"Yes, but some crumbs must have got in as well," the Hatter grumbled: "you shouldn't have put it in with the bread-knife."

The March Hare took the watch and looked at it gloomily: then he dipped it into his cup of tea, and looked at it again: but he could think of nothing better to say than his first remark, "It was the *best* butter, you know."

Alice had been looking over his shoulder with some curiosity. "What a funny watch!" she remarked. "It tells the day of the month, and doesn't tell what o'clock it is!"

"Why should it?" muttered the Hatter. "Does *your* watch tell you what year it is?"

"Of course not," Alice replied very readily: "but that's because it stays the same year for such a long time together."

"Which is just the case with *mine*," said the Hatter.

Alice felt dreadfully puzzled. The Hatter's remark seemed to her to have no sort of meaning in it, and yet it was certainly English. "I don't quite understand you," she said, as politely as she could.

"The Dormouse is asleep again," said the Hatter, and he poured a little hot tea upon its nose.

The Dormouse shook its head impatiently, and said, without opening its eyes, "Of course, of course: just what I was going to remark myself."

"Have you guessed the riddle yet?" the Hatter said, turning to Alice again.

"No, I give it up," Alice replied. "What's the answer?"

"I haven't the slightest idea," said the Hatter.

"Nor I," said the March Hare.

Alice sighed wearily. "I think you might do something better with the time," she said, "than wasting it in asking riddles that have no answers."

"If you knew Time as well as I do," said the Hatter, "you wouldn't talk about wasting *it*. It's *him*."

"I don't know what you mean," said Alice.

"Of course you don't!" the Hatter said, tossing his head contemptuously. "I dare say you never even spoke to Time!"

"Perhaps not," Alice cautiously replied; "but I know I have to beat time when I learn music."

"Ah! That accounts for it," said the Hatter. "He won't stand beating. Now, if you only kept on good terms with him, he'd do almost anything you liked with the clock. For instance, suppose it were nine o'clock in the morning, just time to begin lessons: you'd only have to whisper a hint to Time, and round goes the clock in a twinkling! Half-past one, time for dinner!"

("I only wish it was," the March Hare said to itself in a whisper.)

"That would be grand, certainly," said Alice thoughtfully; "but then—I shouldn't be hungry for it, you know."

"Not at first, perhaps," said the Hatter: "but you could keep it to half-past one as long as you liked."

"Is that the way *you* manage?" Alice asked.

The Hatter shook his head mournfully. "Not I!" he replied. "We quarrelled last March—just before *he* went mad, you know—" (pointing with his teaspoon at the March Hare), "—it was at the great concert given by the Queen of Hearts, and I had to sing. . . . Well, I'd hardly finished the first verse," said the Hatter, "when the Queen bawled out 'He's murdering the time! Off with his head!'"

"How dreadfully savage!" exclaimed Alice.

"And ever since that," the Hatter went on in a mournful tone, "he won't do a thing I ask! It's always six o'clock now."

A bright idea came into Alice's head. "Is that the reason so many tea-things are put out here?" she asked.

"Yes, that's it," said the Hatter with a sigh: "it's always tea-time, and we've no time to wash the things between whiles."

"Then you keep moving round, I suppose?" said Alice.

"Exactly so," said the Hatter: "as the things get used up."

"But what happens when you come to the beginning again?" Alice ventured to ask.

"Suppose we change the subject," the March Hare interrupted, yawning. "I'm getting tired of this. I vote the young lady tells us a story."

"I'm afraid I don't know one," said Alice, rather alarmed at the proposal.

"Then the Dormouse shall!" they both cried, "Wake up, Dormouse!" And they pinched it on both sides at once.

The Dormouse slowly opened its eyes. "I wasn't asleep," it said in a hoarse, feeble voice, "I heard every word you fellows were saying."

"Tell us a story!" said the March Hare.

"Yes, please do!" pleaded Alice.

"And be quick about it," added the Hatter, "or you'll be asleep again before it's done."

"Once upon a time there were three little sisters," the Dormouse began in a great hurry; "and their names were Elsie, Lacie, and Tillie; and they lived at the bottom of a well—"

"What did they live on?" said Alice, who always took a great interest in questions of eating and drinking.

"They lived on treacle," said the Dormouse, after thinking a minute or two.

"They couldn't have done that, you know," Alice gently remarked. "They'd have been ill."

"So they were," said the Dormouse; "*very* ill."

Alice tried a little to fancy to herself what such an extraordinary way of living would be like, but it puzzled her too much: so she went on:

"But why did they live at the bottom of a well?"

"Take some more tea," the March Hare said to Alice, very earnestly.

"I've had nothing yet," Alice replied in an offended tone: "so I can't take more."

"You mean you can't take *less*," said the Hatter: "it's very easy to take *more* than nothing."

"Nobody asked *your* opinion," said Alice.

"Who's making personal remarks now?" the Hatter asked triumphantly.

Alice did not quite know what to say to this: so she helped herself to some tea and bread-and-butter, and then turned to the Dormouse, and repeated her question. "Why did they live at the bottom of a well?"

The Dormouse again took a minute or two to think about it, and then said, "It was a treacle-well."

"There's no such thing!" Alice was beginning very angrily, but the Hatter and the March Hare went, "Sh! Sh!" and the Dormouse sulkily remarked, "If you can't be civil, you'd better finish the story for yourself."

"No, please go on!" Alice said very humbly, "I won't interrupt you again. I dare say there may be *one*."

"One, indeed!" said the Dormouse indignantly. However, he consented to go on. "And so these three little sisters—they were learning to draw, you know—"

"What did they draw?" said Alice, quite forgetting her promise.

"Treacle," said the Dormouse, without considering at all, this time.

"I want a clean cup," interrupted the Hatter: "let's all move one place on."

He moved on as he spoke, and the Dormouse followed him: the March Hare moved into the Dormouse's place, and Alice rather unwillingly took the place of the March Hare. The Hatter was the only one who got any advantage from the change; and Alice was a good deal worse off than before, as the March Hare had just upset the milk-jug into his plate.

Alice did not wish to offend the Dormouse again, so she began very cautiously: "But I don't understand. Where did they draw the treacle from?"

"You can draw water out of a water-well," said the Hatter; "so I should think you could draw treacle out of a treacle-well—eh, stupid?"

"But they were *in* the well," Alice said to the Dormouse, not choosing to notice this last remark.

"Of course they were," said the Dormouse: "well in."

This answer so confused poor Alice, that she let the Dormouse go on for some time without interrupting it.

"They were learning to draw," the Dormouse went on, yawning and rubbing its eyes, for it was getting very sleepy; "and they drew all manner of things—everything that begins with an M—"

"Why with an M?" said Alice.

"Why not?" said the March Hare.

Alice was silent.

The Dormouse had closed its eyes by this time, and was going off into a doze; but, on being pinched by the Hatter, it woke up again with a little shriek, and went on: "—that begins with an M, such as mouse-traps, and the moon, and memory, and muchness—you know you say things are 'much of a muchness'—did you ever see such a thing as a drawing of a muchness?"

"Really, now you ask me," said Alice, very much confused, "I don't think—"

"Then you shouldn't talk," said the Hatter.

This piece of rudeness was more than Alice could bear: she got up in great disgust, and walked off: the Dormouse fell asleep instantly, and neither of the others took the least notice of her going, though she looked back once or twice, half hoping that they would call after her: the last time she saw them, they were trying to put the Dormouse into the tea-pot.

"At any rate I'll never go *there* again!" said Alice, as she picked her way through the wood. "It's the stupidest tea-party I ever was at in all my life!"

Just as she said this, she noticed that one of the trees had a door leading right into it. "That's very curious!" she thought. "But everything's curious to-day. I think I may as well go in at once." And in she went.

Once more she found herself in the long hall, and close to the little glass table. "Now, I'll manage better this time," she said to herself, and began by taking the little golden key, and unlocking the door that led into the garden. Then she set to work nibbling at the mushroom (she had kept a piece of it in her pocket) till she was about a foot high: then she walked down the little passage: and *then*—she found herself at last in the beautiful garden among the bright flower-beds and the cool fountains.

REVIEW AND DISCUSSION QUESTION

1. Identify examples of fallacious reasoning in the text, either of the kinds discussed in chapter 5 or of other kinds.

PART III

PHILOSOPHY'S MAIN QUESTIONS

What Are We Like, and What Should We Do?

CHAPTER SIX

A S WE SAW in chapter 1, the domain of inquiry we call **ethics** addresses these sorts of questions: What is a good life? How should we order our lives? What goals should we seek? Which actions are right or good, and which are wrong or bad? These questions are distinguishable from the questions of metaphysics and epistemology in that they are **normative** in nature. They concern the *norms* of human life, in the sense of how things *should* or *ought* to be (whether they are that way or not). They concern standards or ideals of character and behavior, independently of whether we manage to achieve those ideals. A psychologist might argue that human beings are fundamentally selfish, or a metaphysician may argue that the mind is distinct from the body, but it is the ethicist who explores whether we *should* (or should *not*) be selfish, and whether a life of the mind is better than one focused on the body.

The study of ethics over the centuries has tended to take three different (if interrelated) directions. It has occupied itself with the practical problem of what sorts of actions (or life) we should pursue (**practical** or **applied ethics**), it has considered the underlying theoretical reasons for the proper lines of conduct (**ethical theory**), and, last, it has inquired into the very meanings of ethical concepts themselves, such as *good*, or *right* (**metaethics**). While these pursuits are so closely related that it isn't really possible to do any one without the others, different historical periods have nevertheless differed in their emphases: many of today's thinkers are concerned with metaethics, thinkers of recent centuries tended to stress ethical theory, and ancient thinkers tended to focus on the practical matter of what life is best to live.

To illustrate the latter, let's return to Aristotle and his work, *Nicomachean Ethics*.

ARISTOTLE'S ETHICS

Aristotle believed that all living things are endowed with certain capacities or potentialities and that their well-being lies in realizing these potentialities. The acorn has the potentiality of becoming an oak tree, and its well-being lies in attaining that final state, which it is drawn to achieve by its nature. What is true of all of nature is true of humans, who have the added capacity of being conscious of the goals they try to realize.

Ethics, as the study of proper human conduct, must therefore begin with an investigation of the goals at which people naturally aim. There is fundamentally, however, only one such goal: happiness. But since nobody can be happy without being good (Aristotle thinks), the study of happiness requires a study of goodness. *Nicomachean Ethics* is therefore devoted to both.

Goodness and Happiness

Aristotle begins by distinguishing between two types of goals, or *ends*: (1) those that are good in themselves and are desired for themselves alone, and (2) those that are good as means toward other ends (that may or may not be good in themselves). Some ends are *intrinsically good*, we might say, while others are only *instrumentally good*. Money, for example, is for most an instrumental good, desired not for itself but for the things it enables us to obtain; a miser, on the other hand, might make it an intrinsic good by desiring it for itself alone.

Yet even here we must be clear, for the miser is typically someone who derives great pleasure from hoarding money. If he hoards the money in order to get this pleasure, the money is still only an instrumental good—good only in its capacity to get something else, pleasure. If, on the other hand, he wants the money independently of anything it might gain him (material goods, security, or pleasure), he is considering it an intrinsic good, to be pursued purely for itself.

Not all goods are desired only as means, obviously, for this would involve an infinite and meaningless progression: one thing desired only because of some other thing, desired only because of still some other thing, and so on. There must be some things that are desired for their own sake. And among these, there must be one that is valued more than the others.

> Tell me, Socrates, what does he desire who loves good things? That he may have them, said I. And what will he have when he has the good things? This is easier to answer, said I; he will be happy. Yes, he said, it is through getting good things that the happy become happy. And now we have no need to go on and ask why man wishes to be happy, for we have come to the final point in our inquiry.
>
> —**Plato** (429–347 B.C.E.), *Symposium*

This, Aristotle observes, is happiness:

> Though apparently there are many ends, we choose some of them, e.g. wealth . . . because of something else; hence it is clear that not all ends are complete. But the best good is apparently something complete. Hence, if only one end is complete, this will be what we are looking for; and if more than one are complete, the most complete of these will be what we are looking for. . . .
>
> An end pursued in itself, we say, is more complete than an end pursued because of something else; and an end that is never choiceworthy because of something else is more complete than ends that are choiceworthy both in themselves and because of this end; and hence an end that is always [choiceworthy, and also] choiceworthy in itself, never because of something else, is unconditionally complete. . . .
>
> Now happiness more than anything else seems unconditionally complete, since we always [choose it, and also] choose it because of itself, never because of something else.
>
> Honour, pleasure, understanding and every virtue we certainly choose because of themselves, since we would choose each of them even if it had no further result, but we also choose them for the sake of happiness, supposing that through them we shall be happy. Happiness, by contrast, no one ever chooses for their sake, or for the sake of anything else at all. (Book I, vii)[1]

Although everyone (Aristotle notes) seems to be in agreement about this, not everyone has quite the same conception of happiness, and so further analysis is necessary. But before proceeding, he cautions us not to expect that the investigation will have the precision found in a science like mathematics. We must look for precision only to the degree that the subject itself admits, and while we should demand absolutely certain proofs from a mathematician, we cannot expect the same in ethics or human affairs generally.

Now happiness, for Aristotle, is not some momentary feeling or sensation. It is something more substantial and lasting. When we remark of someone that he has had a happy life, what we mean is that he has overall lived well, that he has realized his aims and ambitions as a human being. The question now is, What is it to live well, as a human being?

To answer this question, Aristotle returns to his basic premise about the nature of living things. A living thing lives well, has a successful life, if it has attained its nature, if it has realized its potentialities. Since the potentialities of different things are different (the potentiality of an acorn differs from that of a cow), living well will be different for different things. Each thing must aim to achieve the potentialities distinct to it.

A human could not be said to live well if he or she only realized those of his or her potentialities shared with all other living things; if, say, he or she lived a life of only eating and drinking and reproducing. For a human to be happy, the potentialities distinctive of us must be attained. In the case of humankind this is obviously *reason*, our ability to think and draw conclusions. The truly good life for a human being must therefore involve the exercise, development, and perfection of reason.

PLATO AND ARISTOTLE

Some object here that reason is not the only thing distinctive of humankind. For one thing we have, in addition, a moral sense, and for another we are capable of laughter. Further, it seems increasingly apparent that reason is not actually distinctive to us but is shared by some other primates. Still, even if so, reason may be distinctive to humans at least in the degree to which it is present; and even if it is not our only distinguishing characteristic, it is surely a key one.

But now while our happiness (for Aristotle) lies in the development, perfection, and exercise of our higher capacities, our other needs must also be satisfied. In fact, they have to be satisfied first. For even if we do not live to eat, so to speak, we have to eat to live. Nor is it only a matter of merely eating. A truly happy life requires the sunshine of prosperity:

Nonetheless, happiness evidently also needs external goods to be added [to the activity], as we said, since we cannot, or cannot easily, do fine actions if we lack the resources.

For, first of all, in many actions we use friends, wealth and political power just as we use instruments. Further, deprivation of certain [externals]—e.g. good birth, good children, beauty—mars our blessedness; for we do not altogether have the character of happiness if we look utterly repulsive or are ill-born, solitary or childless, and have it even less, presumably, if our children or friends are totally bad, or were good but have died.

And so, as we have said, happiness would seem to need this sort of prosperity added also. (Book I, viii)

Aristotle ends this passage by reminding us not to make the mistake of equating happiness with the possession of such external goods. Although they are necessary for attaining happiness, they are not sufficient. All of us know many who have had material goods in abundance and yet have missed happiness.

(Still, note how Aristotle's treating these external goods as necessary for a good life differs from our typical perspective today. We tend to think that living a good life means being a good person, and being a good person has little to do with whether you are good-looking, of "low birth," or single. Perhaps he is right that being "happy" requires these things, or at least is aided by them. But then is "being happy" to be equated with "living a good life"?)

Now the perfection of our reason, Aristotle goes on to explain, enables us to develop two main kinds of desirable qualities (or *virtues*), whose exercise brings us happiness. The first set, called the **intellectual virtues**, includes our ability to discover and recognize truths, including the rules of life we ought to follow; the second set, the **moral virtues,** deals with our ability to control our appetites and passions so that they will obey the rules our intellects recognize as good.

Moral Virtues

Aristotle first takes up the moral virtues.

We must learn to control our feelings, emotions, and impulses, he suggests, in order ultimately to make the most effective use of our reason. But controlling these is not something we are born able to do, rather, we learn to do it gradually. We are not born brave, for example, able to control our fear. We must learn to become brave, and we learn this by doing brave things. Furthermore, these passions of ours are in themselves neither good nor bad, but become so depending on the degree of their expression. Dampening our sense of fear so far that we become rash and foolhardy is just as bad as allowing this fear to overwhelm us so that we become timid and cowardly. Both extremes are equally bad. The person of good moral character is one who has learned to act bravely not by eliminating fear but by controlling it.

This is also true for the other moral qualities. They are, generally, means or points of balance between two extremes, each extreme being a *vice* either of excess or of defect. Modesty is thus the mean between pride (too much vanity) and humility (too little); ambition is the mean between greed (too much) and sloth (too little); and so forth.

First, then, we should observe that these sorts of states naturally tend to be ruined by excess and deficiency. We see this happen with strength and health. . . . For both excessive and deficient exercises ruin strength; and likewise, too much or too little eating or drinking ruins health, while the proportionate amount produces, increases and preserves it.

The same is true, then, of temperance, bravery and the other virtues. For if, e.g., someone avoids and is afraid of everything, standing firm against nothing, he becomes cowardly, but if he is afraid of nothing at all and goes to face everything, he becomes rash. Similarly, if he gratifies himself with every pleasure and refrains from none, he becomes intemperate, but if he avoids them all, as boors do, he becomes some sort of insensible person. Temperance and bravery, then, are ruined by excess and deficiency but preserved by the mean. (Book II, ii)

We have said enough, then, to show that virtue of character is a mean and what sort of mean it is; that it is a mean between two vices, one of excess and one of deficiency; and that it is a mean because it aims at the intermediate condition in feelings and actions.

Hence it is hard work to be excellent, since in each case it is hard work to find what is intermediate; e.g. not everyone, but only one who knows, finds the midpoint in a circle. So also getting angry, or giving and spending money, is easy and anyone can do it; but doing it to the right person, in the right amount, at the right time, for the right end, and in the right way is no longer easy, nor can everyone do it. Hence [doing these things] well is rare, praiseworthy and fine. (Book II, ix)

Although much of *Nicomachean Ethics* is devoted to the analysis of this doctrine of the **golden mean** (as it has come to be called), Aristotle's most memorable illustration of it is in his *Rhetoric*, in the description of the three main stages of life as represented in the Youthful Man, the Elderly Man, and the Man in His Prime. In terms of the major virtues, the Youthful Man represents the excess, the Elderly Man the defect, and the Man in His Prime the mean.

We shall omit quoting here his sketch of the Youthful Man, since it merely contains the opposite of his description of the Elderly Man. Aristotle, however, finds the Youthful Man's innocence, ignorance, and inexperience engaging. The Youthful Man, he says, is also passionate, brave, noble, and disinterested, but only because he does not yet know life as it is. And this is precisely what the elderly do know, and that knowledge has a desolating effect:

They have lived many years; they have often been taken in, and often made mistakes; and life on the whole is a bad business. The result is that they are sure about nothing and underdo everything. They "think" but they never "know"; and because of their hesitancy they always add a "possibly" or a "perhaps," putting everything this way and nothing positively.

They are cynical . . . Further, their experience makes them distrustful and therefore suspicious of evil. Consequently they neither love warmly nor hate bitterly, but following the hint of Bias, they love as though they will some day hate and hate as though they will some day love.

They are small-minded, because they have been humbled by life: their desires are set upon nothing more exalted or unusual than what will help them to keep alive. They are not generous, because money is one of the things they must have, and at the same time their experience has taught them how hard it is to get and how easy to lose. They are cowardly, and are always anticipating danger; unlike that of the young, who are warmblooded, their temperament is chilly. . . .

[T]hey guide their lives too much by consideration of what is useful and too little by what is noble—for the useful is what is good for oneself, and the noble what is good absolutely.

They are not shy, but shameless rather; caring less for what is noble than for what is useful, they feel contempt for what people may think of them. (*Rhetoric*, Book II, Chapter 13)[2]

It would be interesting to discuss whether any of his analysis of the elderly rings true today. Meanwhile, his sketch of the Man in His Prime is briefer:

> As for Men in their Prime . . . they have a character between that of the young and that of the old, free from the extremes of either. They have neither that excess of confidence which amounts to rashness, nor too much timidity, but the right amount of each. They neither trust everybody nor distrust everybody, but judge people correctly. Their lives will be guided not by the sole consideration either of what is noble or what is useful, but by both; neither by parsimony nor by prodigality, but by what is fit and proper. So, too, in regard to anger and desire; they will be brave as well as temperate, and temperate as well as brave; these virtues are divided between the young and the old; the young are brave but intemperate, the old temperate but cowardly. To put it generally, all the valuable qualities that youth and age divide between them are united in the prime of life, while all their excesses or defects are replaced by moderation and fitness. The body is in its prime from thirty to five-and-thirty; the mind about forty-nine. (*Rhetoric*, Book II, Chapter 14)

It is important to realize that the mean is not a rigid mathematical middle but a relative thing, differing for people of different temperaments and under different conditions. Finding one's mean, therefore, requires experience and maturity: after a certain amount of practice in, say, generosity or courage, one comes to find the mean in any given case almost instinctively. It may well be, too, that different individuals reach their "primes" at different points in life, despite Aristotle's closing remark.

Aristotle also point outs that there are some moral virtues to which the doctrine of the mean does not apply, for their very nature already implies either their badness or goodness. Goodness and honesty are simply good, period, and not a matter of having the right amount of something; theft, envy, and spite are simply bad.

Intellectual Virtues

If the mean is a relative thing that differs for different people (and even for the same person in different situations), how does one go about determining it? Aristotle replies that it requires knowledge and wisdom, and thus to attain happiness we need to attend not only to the moral virtues but also to the intellectual virtues, such as prudence, foresight, and wisdom.

However, what Aristotle now says about the attainment of these intellectual virtues is discouraging, for it soon becomes apparent that if he is right, only a few of us can hope to achieve true happiness. For the perfection of the intellectual virtues, although indispensable in keeping the passions in check, is described as having a value and purpose all its own. The goodness of intellect that makes possible the goodness of character, which brings happiness, is itself intrinsically finer and higher than anything else available to us.

> The life which is unexamined is not worth living.
>
> —**Socrates** (470–399 B.C.E.)

What follows is not an account of the use of intelligence in the formation of character but an eloquent description and defense of the contemplative life. Summarizing its values, and doing so in a manner suggestive of Plato's description of the philosopher emerging from "the cave" (recall chapter 3), Aristotle declares that the contemplative life is superior to the merely practical life because "the intellect is the highest thing in us, and the objects that it apprehends are the highest things that can be known"; it is more lasting than other activities and purer and more pleasurable than them, and, as the highest human activity, it is most like that of the gods and tends to bring us closer to them:

> The person whose activity expresses understanding and who takes care of understanding would seem to be in the best condition, and most loved by the gods. For if the gods pay some attention to human beings, as they seem to, it would be reasonable for them to take pleasure in what is best and most akin to them, namely understanding; and reasonable for them to benefit in return those who most of all like and honour understanding, on the assumption that these people attend to what is beloved by the gods, and act correctly and finely.
>
> Clearly, all this is true of the wise person more than anyone else; hence he is most loved by the gods. And it is likely that this same person will be happiest; hence the wise person will be happier than anyone else on this argument too. (Book X, viii)

The highest activity a human is capable of turns out, quite interestingly, to be divine rather than human. Nevertheless, this opinion may strike some as overly intellectual and elitist. After all, there are many people who would be simply incapable of the kind of happiness, let alone "blessedness," here described, including people of ordinary intellects and, working downward, the mentally disabled. Does this mean their lives are of no value, or will be of no value, to themselves or others? Are ordinary people incapable of living "the good life," or "good lives" at all?

The ethical position taken by Aristotle indeed excludes many. For if Aristotle is correct, the best human life is possible only to a very few people, those who have the requisite intellect as well as the other necessary qualities of health, wealth, family, and so on. One might ask, Why should we believe that there is only one true road to happiness and that it is produced only by this single activity? Why should not a life devoted to service and good works, to the appreciation and production of beautiful things, lead to an equally happy and fulfilling life? Certainly most of us would believe that composers, sculptors, painters, and so on, have it in their power to achieve the same heights of human perfection as scientists and philosophers. And why draw the line at artists? The social activist, the reformer, the teacher, even the craftsperson—why should we think that true happiness is eternally closed to them?

Aristotle's selection of the intellectual life as the supremely happy one displays, perhaps, an element of bias, as that happens to be *his* life. This does not mean that the view must be mistaken (as we saw in our discussion of fallacies). But it does raise the point that there is often a close relation between a philosopher's thought and the cultural setting in which it arises. For Aristotle's analysis of virtue as a mean between extremes seems aimed to provide a philosophical justification of the moral convictions of his own age and culture, as conveyed, for example, in the famous Delphic exhortation, "Nothing in excess."

Although living at a different time and place, we still find this rule commendable. But what a modern reader may find less commendable about Aristotle's ethical doctrine is not its cultural ethnocentrism but its self-centeredness. Apparently, the happiness the virtuous person is to seek is not anyone else's but his or her own. We ought, implies Aristotle, to look after only ourselves, to procure a good life for ourself. Aristotle does indeed instruct us in such altruistic virtues as honesty, generosity, friendship, and so on, but their justification is not that they will increase the general happiness but that these things are desirable for the individual to have.

Then again (and in Aristotle's defense), if it is true that in order to obtain happiness one must cultivate and realize certain potentialities, then such happiness can be obtained only by attending to oneself. A society that recognized this might design itself in order to maximize the possibility of individuals' obtaining their happiness. And if such happiness were realized by many, the society could not help but benefit.

Still, we might nevertheless ask, What happens when one person's good and the good of others come into conflict? What ought one to do then? It is one of the limitations of Aristotle's ethics that he hardly addressed this problem, much less answered it.

KANT'S ETHICS

We now skip ahead two millennia.

"Ethics," says Immanuel Kant (1724–1804), turning from Aristotle's emphasis on practical ethics toward ethical theory, "is not the doctrine of how to make ourselves happy, but of how we are to be worthy of happiness." To make happiness the supreme principle of morality, Kant thinks, is to miss what is central to it: the obligation we are all under to do what is right. For there is nothing morally admirable about a person seeking his own happiness, but there is something worthy of admiration about a person who, in the face of dangers, does his duty and does it for no other reason than that it is his duty. The difference between the moral and immoral person, furthermore, is not that one is wise and the other foolish, that one knows what will lead to happiness and the other doesn't. It's that one is good and the other is bad. One does what is right, whether it will bring him happiness or not, and the other is concerned only with his welfare.

IMMANUEL KANT

A Good Will

But what makes a person good? Possession, Kant answers, of the only thing that is good without qualification, and this is a "good will." Determining what this "good will" is constitutes the task of Kant's book *Foundations of the Metaphysics of Morals* (1785). It opens with these remarks:

> Nothing can possibly be conceived in the world . . . which can be called good, without qualification, except a Good Will. Intelligence, wit, judgment, and the other talents of the mind, however they may be named, or courage, resolution, perseverance, as qualities of temperament, are undoubtedly good and desirable . . . but these gifts of nature

may also become extremely bad and mischievous if the will which is to make use of them . . . is not good. It is the same with the gifts of fortune. Power, riches, honor, even health, and the general well-being and contentment with one's condition which is called happiness, inspire pride . . . if there is not a good will to correct the influence of these on the mind. . . . The sight of a being who is not adorned with a single feature of a pure and good will, enjoying unbroken prosperity, can never give pleasure to an impartial rational spectator. Thus a good will appears to constitute the indispensable condition even of being worthy of happiness.

Kant does not deny, as we see here, that there are many things in the world that may be regarded as good, but he maintains that none of them is absolutely good. These things are morally good only if the will that directs them is good, and unless so directed they may in fact turn out to be bad (as in the case of great intelligence in a criminal).

A **good will**, then, does not derive its goodness from being directed to the attainment of intelligence, courage, or wealth, for these are good only when directed by a will that is already good. The goodness of the will is derived rather from the use of such faculties as intelligence, courage, and wealth in the service of duty.

What does this mean? A will to act from duty, Kant explains, follows the dictates not of desire or inclination but of pure reason. It is the will of one who does the right thing not because that is what he or she wants to do, or because of the good consequences that will follow from it, but because it is what pure reason demands of him or her. And only actions springing from such a motive are deserving of moral praise and respect.

Consider some examples. Suppose you were accosted by a homeless person and you gave him money, but only because you wished to be rid of him. Kant would say of such an action that, although not morally bad, it does not deserve moral praise. You may have acted in accordance with duty (you did what was right) but not from a sense of duty (*because* it was right).

Or suppose you are playing chess and a child walks up to the table and randomly moves one of your pieces. Suppose that the move happens not only to be a permissible one but also an excellent one. Now, we can say of the child that he has made a move, a good move, that was in accordance with the rules. However, to make a move *from* the rules (or duty) would require not only knowledge of the game, its permitted moves, and its goals, but also the will to follow its rules.

Returning now to the first example, suppose you were a completely warmhearted person who delighted in spreading joy, and you gave this homeless person money simply because you wanted to. Kant would say of this action that, while not bad, it was not morally praiseworthy, either, since you did it for the gratification of your own desire. Such actions may deserve encouragement but not moral esteem.

But now suppose that you gave this person money not because you wanted to get rid of him or because you felt kindly toward him but because you felt duty bound to do so. You felt obligated to do it independently of your own interests and desires. Then and only then, says Kant, would your action have moral worth, for actions arising from that motive spring from a good will.

The Categorical Imperative

To make the meaning of such a will still clearer, Kant goes on to distinguish between two types of obligations or *imperatives*, as he calls them, that may direct our will. The first of these are **hypothetical imperatives** that command us to do certain things *if* we want to achieve certain ends. If it is our goal to become a concert musician, for example, we must practice at least so many hours each day. If that isn't our goal, the obligation to practice simply doesn't apply. Similarly, someone may tell you that you must go see the new play if you want to see good theater. But again, if you don't particularly desire to see good theater, then the imperative to see the new play evaporates.

Hypothetical imperatives, in short, are obligations we have that are conditional on certain wishes or desires or interests we may have, and should we cease to have those, they cease to bind us. The "oughts" that figure in them are therefore not *moral* oughts. If we don't care to become concert artists, we are not doing anything morally wrong in not practicing.

But when *ought* is used in a moral sense, the imperative is not hypothetical but unconditional, or a **categorical imperative**. For example, when we say to someone, "You ought to pay your debts," we mean that he ought to do so whether or not he wants to, or whether or not he will gain something by doing it. Such a categorical imperative is unconditional and is not preceded or followed by an *if*. Were we to add an *if* to it (as in, "If you want people to trust you"), it becomes a hypothetical imperative and ceases to be moral. People who pay their debts for that conditional reason, Kant would say, are not acting from a pure motive and therefore are not acting morally. That is not to say that they are acting immorally. It is merely that an act motivated in this way is not worthy of moral esteem.

But why, you might ask, should we be moral? Why should we unconditionally be honest, pay our debts, and so on? Why exactly should we do what these categorical imperatives command?

Kant's answer is ultimately not unlike that given by Aristotle, although its elaboration is very different. It is that it would be unworthy of us as human beings to do otherwise. For to be human, Kant explains, is to be rational, and to act as a human being is to act rationally. It is to possess a will that is motivated not by impulses or feelings but by reason. Since the essence of reason (unlike impulses and feelings) is consistency, and since the test of consistency is universal validity, in order to be rational an action must be motivated by a universally valid and binding principle of conduct. Indeed, just as reason in the realm of science and mathematics produces principles that are universally and necessarily true, so too the principles issued by reason in the realm of human conduct must be universally valid and binding. And to say they are universally binding, that they are binding, *period*, is to say that they are unconditional.

So to be rational in conduct is to act on principles that can be willed to be universal, that apply to every situation and person equally. The rational person will not act on one principle in one situation and on another in a precisely similar situation. Nor would the rational person try to make an exception in his or her own case, for that, too, would be inconsistent. For the rational (and therefore moral) person will realize that whatever is morally right for him or her is right for all, and that whatever is morally wrong for him or her is also morally wrong for all.

That, for Kant, is the essence of what it is to be moral.

Kant's fundamental principle of morality thus becomes this, that you should act as you would have all others act when in the same circumstances. Or, as he expressed it, "Act on that **maxim** (rule) and that maxim only, which you can at the same time will to be a universal law."

This, then, is Kant's supreme principle of morality, his **principle of universality**, as it has come to be called. It is also what he means when he says that to have a good will is to act out of respect for law, not out of respect for some particular law but for law as such: respect for universality, which is the form of law, that has no exceptions and is the same for all. Those who act in this manner do what reason demands of them, and so can be said to act from a sense of duty, from a motive that is pure.

Kant offers the following example:

> A man finds himself forced by need to borrow money. He well knows that he will not be able to repay it, but he also sees that nothing will be loaned him if he does not firmly promise to repay it at a certain time. He desires to make such a promise, but he has enough conscience to ask himself whether it is not improper and opposed to duty to relieve his distress in such a way. Now, assuming he does decide to do so, the maxim of his action would be as follows: When I believe myself to be in need of money, I will borrow money and promise to repay it, although I know I shall never do so. Now this principle of self-love or of his own benefit may very well be compatible with his whole future welfare, but the question is whether it is right. He changes the pretension of self-love into a universal law and then puts the question: How would it be if my maxim became a universal law? He immediately sees that it could never hold as a universal law of nature and be consistent with itself; rather it must necessarily contradict itself. For the universality of a law which says that anyone who believes himself to be in need could promise what he pleased with the intention of not fulfilling it would make the promise itself and the end to be accomplished by it impossible; no one would believe what was promised to him but would only laugh at any such assertion as vain pretense. (p. 40)

Or to put it simply, Kant's principle of universality requires us to ask of some possible action the classic question: "What if everybody behaved that way?"

His formulation, however, makes us see more clearly that what is wrong with everybody behaving that way is not that it would be unpleasant if they did, or even that if it would be wrong for them it would be wrong for you, but rather that it would make lying, breaking promises, and so on self-defeating. For if everybody lied, nobody would believe anybody, and then lying, which requires belief to be effective, would become impossible. Willing such a thing

---

[Kant] is not arguing against lying on the grounds that if I lie, others will soon lose confidence in me and eventually won't believe my promises. Nor is he arguing against lying on the grounds that my lie will contribute to a general practice of lying, which in turn will lead to a breakdown of trust and the destruction of the practice of promising. These considerations are basically utilitarian. Kant's point is more subtle. He is saying that there is something covertly self-contradictory about the state of affairs in which, as a law of nature, everyone makes a false promise when in need of a loan. Perhaps Kant's point is this: Such a state of affairs is self-contradictory because, on the one hand, in such a state of affairs everyone in need would borrow money on a false promise, and yet, on the other hand, in that state of affairs no one could borrow money on a false promise—for if promises were always violated, who would be silly enough to loan any money? . . . [I]n that (allegedly impossible) state of affairs there would be promises, since those in need would make them, and there would also not be promises, since no one would believe that anyone was really committing himself to future payment by the use of the words "I promise." So, as Kant says, the generalized form of the maxim "annuls itself." It cannot be a law of nature.

—**Fred Feldman**, *Introductory Ethics* (1978)

as a rule would ultimately contradict itself, for the behavior can only function as the exception, not as the rule itself.

But this is precisely what the immoral person does, in fact, want. He wants to make an exception in his own favor in respect to a rule that others must observe if he is to succeed in gaining his ends. It is not that he doesn't know the principle behind his action or the nature of the principle it would contradict. He knows all this but wishes to be treated differently. On the other hand, the moral person does not try to make any exceptions for himself. He treats himself and others on the same basis. And for Kant that is ultimately the test of what is right and wrong, moral and immoral.

As inspiring an account of ethics as this may be, it is not without its difficulties. Let us consider here only those surrounding the ambiguity of the term *universal*. Suppose one were to agree to act on Kant's principle of universality. One agreed to do only those things that can be universalized and not to do anything that cannot. But by taking *very specific* circumstances into account, we could easily cheat. We could will that if anyone ever found himself in *exactly* the circumstances we now find ourselves in, he may lie. ("Anyone who is dressed like me, with my name, in these circumstances, may lie . . .") In such a case the principle would not appear to forbid lying, yet by extending to anyone in this kind of situation the same privilege, it would continue to be "universal."

Kant's intention, pretty clearly, was to forbid such a thing as lying entirely, in all circumstances. But that would be possible only if his principle were taken in its most general sense (do not lie now, unless you are willing that anyone should lie at any time in any situation). But taken in such an unqualified sense, the principle suffers from the opposite difficulty—it is now too rigorous for most people. For suppose telling a lie will save an innocent life. Most of us would probably justify such a lie, while Kant in fact disagrees, in a famous essay on the subject (see the adjacent quote). So for most people, then, Kant's principle seems either too restrictive or too permissive, and in cases of conflict between maxims (between telling the truth or saving a life) it appears unhelpful.

The Role of Reason

But let us now note the way Kant's theory deals with another type of objection. Suppose someone inquired of Kant's theory, "But why should we treat each other equally? Why indeed

---

For instance, if you have by a lie hindered a man who is even now planning a murder, you are legally responsible for all the consequences. But if you have strictly adhered to the truth, public justice can find no fault with you, be the unforeseen consequence what it may. It is possible that whilst you have honestly answered Yes to the murderer's question, whether his intended victim is in the house, the latter may have gone out unobserved, and so not have come in the way of the murderer, and the deed therefore have not been done; whereas, if you lied and said he was not in the house, and he had really gone out (though unknown to you) so that the murderer met him as he went, and executed his purpose on him, then you might with justice be accused as the cause of his death. For, if you had spoken the truth as well as you knew it, perhaps the murderer while seeking for his enemy in the house might have been caught by neighbors coming up and the deed been prevented.

—**Kant**, *On a Supposed Right to Tell Lies from Benevolent Motives* (1797)

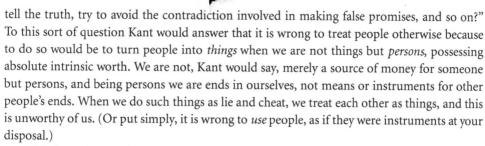

tell the truth, try to avoid the contradiction involved in making false promises, and so on?" To this sort of question Kant would answer that it is wrong to treat people otherwise because to do so would be to turn people into *things* when we are not things but *persons*, possessing absolute intrinsic worth. We are not, Kant would say, merely a source of money for someone but persons, and being persons we are ends in ourselves, not means or instruments for other people's ends. When we do such things as lie and cheat, we treat each other as things, and this is unworthy of us. (Or put simply, it is wrong to *use* people, as if they were instruments at your disposal.)

This formulation of the principle of universality instructs us, therefore, "Act so that you treat all persons always as an end and never as a means only." The principle doesn't say *never* treat anyone "as a means," but never "as a means *only*." There are times when we serve each other's needs. This is unavoidable. But we can avoid treating each other as *mere* means.

It is of course our possession of reason that endows humans with absolute worth and thus places them in this unique position in the hierarchy of creation. To illustrate this, Kant compares humans first with non-human animals, then with God.

As we saw, a good will derives its goodness from working in the service of duty. Reason, however, as we well know, does not always determine the direction of our will but does so only within limits. Not having full control over our will, we come to experience the dictates of reason as *obligation*—a feeling only we can experience, that expresses itself in the form of a command or an imperative. When we follow the dictates of reason against the urges of desire and inclination, when we do what reason demands, our will can be said to be morally good.

Animals, not being subject to this conflict between duty and inclination, are incapable of that experience of obligation. An animal may find itself torn between one want and another, but never between want and duty. An animal, being wholly determined by its natural inclinations, can therefore be said to be innocent and not, like us, either morally good or evil.

At the other extreme, God, being perfect, has a will that is perfectly rational. His will and His reason coincide, and there is never any tension between them. While an animal is below the level of duty, God is above it. God not only knows the moral law, but can have no desires that could possibly conflict with that law. God thus acts in conformity with the moral law, but does so as a matter of course. God's will is therefore holy. Humans, on the other hand, who never perform their duty as a matter of course but are always subject to desire, may be morally good but never holy. We, therefore, unlike animals or God, are creatures who belong to two worlds at once—the world of sense (desire) and the world of reason (duty)—and thus are neither innocent nor holy but, depending on whether we do what reason commands, either good or evil.

> Even if a civil society were to be dissolved by the consent of all its members . . . the last murderer remaining in prison would first have to be executed, so that each has done to him what his deeds deserve and blood guilt does not cling to the people for not having insisted upon this punishment; for otherwise the people can be regarded as collaborators in his public violation of justice.
>
> —**Kant**, *The Metaphysics of Morals* (1797)

We are thus inevitably led to the most fundamental question of all, "Are people actually free to do what reason demands?" Kant takes this question up more fully in his *Critique of Practical Reason* (1788). The conclusions he arrives at are as follows:

(1) We must be free since the obligation to be moral (to do what reason demands) would make no sense were we not free to carry out such demands;

(2) Our souls must be immortal, for we are enjoined by reason to seek perfection, but this life alone is too brief to achieve it; hence, we must survive this life to continue our striving toward that goal; and

(3) God must exist. For our moral obligation is to bring about the highest good, and a world reflecting the highest good would be one where good people are happy. But we can only be morally obliged to do something if it is possible for it to come into being; and such a world would be possible only if there exists a Being capable of ensuring that happiness is apportioned to goodness. If we have genuine moral obligations, in short, then God must exist. (For more detail on this "moral argument for the existence of God," see chapter 7.)

Kant is careful to point out that these are only postulates; he does not consider these conclusive proofs that we are free, our soul is immortal, and that God exists. But if we cannot know that they are true, we also cannot know that they are not. Hence, believing them is not unreasonable.

Now these postulates obviously represent some of the major tenets of Western, Judeo-Christian teaching about our earthly duties and future rewards. Kant's ethics, like Aristotle's, reflect his age and culture. But still, a philosophy is not merely a summary and reflection of the thought and experience of a particular period and people. Often it is groundbreaking, anticipating developments yet to take place or whose full impact has yet to be felt, and this is certainly the case with Kant's philosophy. If it is not difficult, therefore, to recognize in his postulates and in his principle of universality the influence of his religious heritage, it is also not difficult for us to see his principle that we treat all persons as ends and never merely as means as a driving force in the growing egalitarian ideal represented by the great social and political events of his age: the Industrial Revolution, and the American and French revolutions.

THE UTILITARIAN THEORY

The full impact of the social and political changes of the late 1700s was not yet fully clear at the time of Kant's writing. When they became clearer in the next century, ethical theories arose that were perhaps better suited to them than was Kant's. A society of plenty with a growing awareness of its rights had arisen, and *utilitarianism* became its philosophical voice.

Recall that an "ethical theory" is an account of the underlying theoretical reasons for the proper lines of conduct. Now one simple way to illustrate what this means is this. Make a short list of some actions you consider to be uncontroversially morally good ones, and another list of uncontroversially morally bad ones. (Your first list might include "being kind," "telling the truth," "helping those in need"; your second, "stealing," "lying," "murdering," etc.) Then ask yourself just what it is that the members of each list have in common, by *virtue* of which they are "good" and "bad" respectively. Presumably these lists aren't purely random or arbitrary. There's some *reason* that being kind and helping others belong on the good list while lying and murdering belong on the bad list. Well, ethical theory is the attempt to determine what that reason is; and utilitarianism is a particularly clear and concrete example of an ethical theory. (You might recall from chapter 3 that Plato's *Euthyphro* dealt with similar issues.)

Jeremy Bentham (1748–1832)

Jeremy Bentham was the founder of utilitarianism. The son of a well-to-do London lawyer, Bentham was sent to Oxford for a legal career, but his sensitivity to the plight of the working people of his time made him abandon a legal career in favor of one of legal reform. And there was much to reform. Conditions in England (soon to be described by Charles Dickens [1812–1870]), with its workhouses, debtors' prisons, and slums, were shocking, and Bentham determined to correct them, by working out a scientific system of law. He produced a series of writings, the most famous of which was *An Introduction to the Principles of Morals and Legislation* (1789). There soon formed around him a group of like-minded intellectuals who, fired by his humanitarian ideals, pressed for social and political reforms. Bentham died just as Parliament was about to pass its first reform bill—a landmark piece of legislation and a notable personal triumph for the man who had paved the way for its realization.

Principles opens with this statement: "Nature has placed mankind under the governance of two sovereign masters, pain and pleasure. It is for them alone to point out what we ought to do, as well as to determine what we shall do."

This brief statement asserts two separate doctrines. One is descriptive, claiming that what in fact motivates our actions is our desire for pleasure (and ultimately happiness); this doctrine may be called **psychological hedonism**. The other is normative, claiming ultimately that pleasure and happiness *should* be the ultimate aim of our actions; this may be called **ethical hedonism**. You might wonder whether the psychological doctrine renders the ethical one pointless, for if pain and pleasure (or happiness) in fact fully determine our decisions, there would seem to be no point in saying what we *ought* to do, the matter having already been decided. The advice would seem either unnecessary or futile.

But Bentham embraces these two doctrines purposely, their tension being for him only apparent. We are indeed guided by our desire for pleasure and happiness, but we are also burdened with mistaken notions of what

JEREMY BENTHAM

happiness truly is. Thus his investigation is neither unnecessary nor doomed to failure. The pleasure or happiness he has in mind, as he soon tells us, is not each person's own happiness or pleasure but rather, in the words of his famous slogan, "the greatest happiness of the greatest number." In considering a course of action, what we have to be concerned with is the amount of pleasure the action is likely to bring to all those whose interests are at stake.

This is Bentham's **principle of utility**, also known as **utilitarianism**. It maintains that there is only one way to determine whether something is right or wrong, good or bad, and this is by considering its usefulness or "utility" in bringing about pleasant results. An action is good or right if it brings about more overall pleasure or happiness than any other possible action; it is wrong if some other action could have produced more pleasure or happiness. This then becomes the simple central principle of his ethical theory: it determines and explains (to invoke our earlier example) which actions go on the "good" list and which ones on the "bad" list.

Since, according to Bentham, what is right and good is that which produces the most happiness, and happiness is simply a condition in which pain is outweighed by pleasure, it is important to arrive at as clear an understanding of the nature of pleasure as possible. Bentham proposes a kind of **hedonic calculus**, as he calls it, to evaluate pleasures, based on the seven ways (he thinks) in which pleasures vary, as reflected in the following questions:

(1) How intense are the pleasures?
(2) How long can we expect them to last?
(3) How certain are we they will occur?
(4) How immediate or remote are they?
(5) What is their chance of being followed by sensations of the same kind?
(6) What is their chance of being followed by sensations of the opposite kind?
(7) How many other people will share in them?

One striking feature of Bentham's list is that he deliberately omits an important aspect of pleasure: its *quality*. No kind of pleasure is any more or less valuable than any other. The only thing that matters is the quantity of pleasure, not its quality. Thus a child's game of "pin the tail on the donkey" may be as ethically valuable as Shakespeare's poetry, the quantity of pleasure being about equal (say). This omission of "quality" led his critics to call his theory a "pig philosophy," as if a pig's pleasure is morally comparable to our own. But Bentham was undaunted. The source of pleasure, he felt, is irrelevant. What matters is the amount of it after any unpleasantness or pain has been subtracted.

So Bentham proposes that we measure and calculate our pleasures and pains in the same spirit that scientists measure and calculate the motion of bodies in space. But has, or would, anyone ever actually engage in this kind of calculation? Bentham writes,

> There are some who may look upon the nicety employed in the adjustment of such rules as so much labor lost: for gross ignorance, they will say, never troubles itself about laws, and passion does not calculate. But the evil of ignorance admits of cure: and when matters of such importance as pain and pleasure are at stake, and these in the highest degree, who is there that does not calculate? Men calculate, some with less exactness, indeed, and some with more: but all men calculate. (*Principles*, Introduction)

Although all people thus calculate, they do not unfortunately all do so in the right way, for they calculate their own pleasure or happiness, not, as they should, the greatest happiness of the greatest number. It would be a simple matter to get them to calculate properly, says Bentham, if they were not by nature egoistic and selfish, but they are and we cannot change them.

What, then, is to be done? How are we to reconcile this ideal of aiming to maximize overall happiness with the reality of our self-serving egoism?

Seeing this as the main problem not only of ethics but of government as well, Bentham designs a proposal for both. It is true, he says, that we cannot change people. Nevertheless, we can get them to behave in a manner that will be for the good of all by making this course of action pay them personally. We can see to it that to deviate from the path of social good costs a person so much that he or she won't do so. By seeking his or her own good, such a person will then act in a way as to realize the maximum good for society.

Bentham did not need to look far for such a system of "sanctions," as he calls them. There were, first of all, the sanctions already found in physical nature, operating to bring happiness to people who act in one way (eat moderately) and pain when they act in another (overeat). Then there were the political and legal sanctions exacted by the law, the social sanctions of public opinion, and, finally, the sanctions of religion with its fear of divine punishment and promise of heavenly reward.

But the trouble is, Bentham argues, that in any existing society the sanctions applying to conduct are irrational. They have developed haphazardly and are now themselves the cause of much misery. They need to be made more reasonable by being brought into an orderly system on the basis of some first principle. Take, for example, he says, the penal laws. Describing the shocking prison conditions at the time, Bentham points out the unnecessary severity of the punishments. They inflict more pain than necessary in order to redirect conduct into socially desirable lines. Since pain is always evil, this is wrong. We need to inflict just that amount necessary to prevent a greater evil. To use more is unjustified and irrational.

The same is true of the other areas of our life, he urges, arguing both for a different sort of government and less of it. As to the former, he defends democracy over monarchy, for only where there is an identity between the rulers and the ruled will their interests be the same and the greatest happiness of the greatest number be assured. As for less government, he argues that much of what the government tries to control is really a matter of private morals and not its business at all.

Although our stress here is on Bentham's work as a theory of ethics, his own overall aim in analyzing pleasure and developing the hedonic calculus is quite ambitious: to apply them to legal, social, and political reform, and in so doing bring about a more humane and just society. This same reformist tendency was characteristic of all the utilitarians who gathered around him. Feeling compassion for the misery of the overworked poor, angered by the complacency of factory owners, and offended by the injustice of the prevailing economic system, they aimed to change the organization of society that gave rise to these conditions. Like Bentham, they were convinced that reform could be achieved only if based on sound principles concerning the nature of human motivation, law, society, and government. They therefore studied not only ethics but such disciplines as psychology, education, and politics, making contributions to each. In all these investigations, their basic principle remained the same, that of utility: only those actions and laws are morally correct that promote the greatest happiness of the greatest number.

John Stuart Mill (1806–1873)

While Bentham's principle of utility may sound appealing at first, it turns out that it needed careful refining before it could gain more widespread acceptance. And none was more influential at that task than John Stuart Mill.

Mill was the son, in fact, of Bentham's immediate disciple, James Mill (1773–1836), a reputed scholar in his own right. The senior Mill made contributions in psychology and education, arguing that the civil liberties and democratic ideals he shared with Bentham could be realized by properly conducted education.

The birth of his son John in 1806 gave him an opportunity to test his theories. He subjected the boy to studies that still seem remarkable to us, and with remarkable results.

Home-schooling him, James had John learn Greek at the age of three, arithmetic and English grammar soon after, and Latin when the boy reached the ripe old age of four. By age seven, John had composed a work on the history of Rome, replete with footnotes. At the age of twelve, he set to work on logic, economics, and philosophy. Nor, of course, was he spared the systematic study of utilitarian principles: at the age of eighteen he landed in jail for handing out birth control pamphlets in a working-class slum. So intense was his personal tutoring that Mill was later to say that it put him a quarter of a century ahead of his contemporaries. However it also took its toll, for at the age of twenty he suffered a mental breakdown that he attributed to the overdevelopment of intellect without a parallel development of the emotions. He tried to correct this imbalance by immersing himself in the writings of Coleridge, Carlyle, and Wordsworth, the English romantic poets and essayists.

He also had a long romance with the married Mrs. Harriet Taylor, which began when he was twenty-five and whom he married many years later when her husband died. Aside from Bentham, she was the most dominant influence in his life and, essentially, the coauthor of some of his works.

Of Mill's works, his best known is *On Liberty* (1859), whose elaborately reasoned defense of the right of individuals to think and act for themselves has never been surpassed. The case for liberty, Mill argues here, is its utility, its power to create, maintain, and augment the greatest happiness of the greatest number. In memorable words in its introduction, he says,

JOHN STUART MILL

The object of this Essay is to assert one very simple principle as entitled to govern absolutely the dealings of society with the individual in the way of compulsion and control, whether the means used be physical force in the form of legal penalties, or the moral coercion of public opinion. That principle is, that the sole end for which mankind are warranted, individually or collectively, in interfering with the liberty of action of any of their number, is self-protection. That the only purpose for which power can be rightly exercised over any member of a civilized community, against his will, is to prevent harm to others. His own good, either physical or moral, is not a sufficient warrant. He cannot rightfully be compelled to do or forbear because it will be better for him to do so, because it will make him happier, because, in the opinions of others, to do so would be wise or even right. These are good reasons for remonstrating with him or reasoning with him, or persuading him, or entreating him, but not for compelling him, or visiting him with any evil in case he do otherwise. To justify that, the conduct from which it is desired to deter him must be calculated to produce evil to someone else. The only part of the conduct of anyone, for which he is amenable to society, is that which concerns others. In the part which merely concerns himself, his independence is, of right, absolute. Over himself, over his own body and mind, the individual is sovereign.

Mill defended this ideal of liberty again two years later, in *Considerations on Representative Government* (1861). Finally, in another work, almost a century ahead of its time—*The Subjection of Women* (1869)—he extended the argument to the position of women in the modern world. This work protests their political, economic, social, and professional subjection, and argues for their emancipation. Overall, he argues, the subjection of women works against the greatest happiness of the greatest number, and their emancipation works for it.

Bentham's principle of utility clearly made a profound impression on Mill. As he tells us in his posthumously published *Autobiography*,

> This principle gave unity to my conceptions of things. I now had opinions, a creed, a doctrine, a philosophy, in one among the best senses of the word a religion; the inculcation and diffusion of which could be made the principal outward purpose of a life. And I had a grand conception laid before me of changes to be effected in the condition of mankind through that doctrine. The vista of improvement which Bentham opened was sufficiently large and brilliant

to light up my life as well as to give a definite shape to my aspirations.

Mill's Dedication of On Liberty to His Wife Harriet

To the beloved and deplored memory of her who was the inspirer, and in part the author, of all that is best in my writings— the friend and wife whose exalted sense of truth and right was my strongest incitement, and whose approbation was my chief reward—I dedicate this volume. Like all that I have written for many years, it belongs as much to her as to me; but the work as it stands has had, in a very insufficient degree, the inestimable advantage of her revision; some of the most important portions having been reserved for a more careful reexamination, which they are now never destined to receive. Were I but capable of interpreting to the world one half the great thoughts and noble feelings which are buried in her grave, I should be the medium of a greater benefit to it, than is ever likely to arise from anything that I can write, unprompted and unassisted by her all but unrivaled wisdom.

But Bentham's version of the principle had stirred up many critics, and in his own work, *Utilitarianism* (1861), Mill set out to refine it in a way that would answer these critics. Mill introduced two major modifications, one concerning Bentham's psychological hedonism, the other concerning his ethical hedonism.

Concerning the first, Mill argued that we are not necessarily so made as to seek only our own happiness. Whereas Bentham tended to reduce our occasional altruistic feelings to self-interest, Mill believed they were founded in a primitive gregarious instinct we all have. We are naturally altruistic, he says, and often find our individual happiness by promoting the happiness of the group. Nevertheless, the more room the world has in it for the self-development of different individual characters, the better chance everyone has to be happy. The greatest happiness of the greatest number can thus be attained only under conditions of the greatest possible individual freedom; hence Mill's advocacy of personal freedom, his defense of civil liberties, and his abhorrence of government paternalism.

Concerning Bentham's ethical hedonism, Mill rejected Bentham's purely quantitative approach to the hedonic calculus. Pleasures *do* differ in quality, Mill insisted, and this difference affects their value. Human beings have capacities for pleasures of many kinds. We have animal appetites, but we also have higher faculties. The pleasures derived from the exercise of our higher faculties are intrinsically better than purely sensuous pleasures. (The early Greek philosopher Epicurus [341–270 B.C.E.] had also distinguished between the "higher pleasures," the rational and the aesthetic, and the "lower pleasures," eating, drinking, and generally sensual pleasures. Recall, too, Aristotle's view of the good life, above.) Persons who have experienced both kinds of pleasure know this to be so:

> It is quite compatible with the principle of utility to recognize the fact, that some kinds of pleasure are more desirable and more valuable than others. It would be absurd that while, in estimating all other things, quality is considered as well as quantity, the estimation of pleasures should be supposed to depend on quantity alone.
>
> —**John Stuart Mill**, *Utilitarianism* (1861)

> Few human creatures would consent to be changed into any of the lower animals, for a promise of the fullest allowance of a beast's pleasures; no intelligent human being would consent to be a fool, no instructed person would be an ignoramus, no person of feeling and conscience would be selfish and base, even though they should be persuaded that the fool, the dunce, or the rascal is better satisfied with his lot than they are with theirs.

And so Mill comes to the conclusion that he expressed in the following famous words:

> It is better to be a human being dissatisfied than a pig satisfied; better to be Socrates dissatisfied than a fool satisfied. And if the fool, or the pig, are of a different opinion, it is because they only know their own side of the question. The other party to the comparison knows both sides.

This issue is, of course, of great practical consequence. In distributing tax money, for just one example, how we decide such questions will determine whether to subsidize opera houses and art galleries that cater to refined tastes and that few people enjoy, or to use such monies to build sports arenas or house the poor.

But aside from the practical consequences, Mill's modification seems to constitute an abandonment of pure hedonism. If pleasures are now to be graded not for their quantity but for their quality, then pleasure itself is no longer the sole criterion determining our choices, and what is "good." Pleasures themselves must be judged in the light of some *further* qualities they may or may not have.

We see this implication again when Mill argues that aiming for happiness is the most "desirable" mode of conduct for human beings. How can we prove, he asks, that happiness is indeed the true and desirable end of human life and conduct? To this Mill replies, in an oft-quoted passage,

> The only proof capable of being given that an object is visible, is that people actually see it. The only proof that a sound is audible, is that people hear it: and so of the other sources of our experience. In like manner, I apprehend, the sole evidence it is possible to produce that anything is desirable, is that people do actually desire it.

Some critics charge, however, that *desirable* cannot be compared with *visible* and *audible* in this way, since "desirability" is not related to "desired" in the same way that "visible" is to "seen." Whereas *visible* means simply that something is capable of being seen, *desirable* has a moral implication, that something is *worthy* of being desired, that it *ought* to be desired. Thus while a thing's being seen does prove that it is visible, it does not follow that a thing's being desired proves it is desirable, that is, worthy of being desired. Many people may desire heroin, but heroin is hardly *desirable* in the moral sense.

To establish that some pleasure is desirable (or more desirable than some other) involves more than establishing the bare fact that many desire it; there must be some further feature of the pleasure that makes it desirable, which other pleasures may lack. But then pleasure as such is no longer the standard of value, and something else takes its place. This, again, is the surprising consequence of Mill's modification of Bentham's hedonism.

SOME CRITICISMS OF UTILITARIANISM

Utilitarianism is an appealing theory on many levels. On a first pass through, it is simple and clear, it fits many of our ethical intuitions, and it does seem plausible that (as Aristotle suggested) happiness is our fundamental, intrinsic value, something we value for its own sake and for the sake of which we value other things. Indeed even those inclined to look to religion for morality may be comfortable with utilitarianism, for even if God is the ultimate source of morality it is not unreasonable to imagine that, being benevolent, He might well structure morality so as to maximize human happiness.

Nevertheless, utilitarianism confronts its share of problems.

First, there are questions about the hedonism at its core. Bentham adopted psychological hedonism, the view that we are simply endowed by nature so that we pursue pleasure and avoid pain. To many, however, this appears as an astounding generalization about human motivation. It is one thing to say that a person gets pleasure from his action, but quite another to say that the expectation of that pleasure is the reason for acting. We may go to great lengths to help a friend when he is ill, for example. When he gets well, we do derive great pleasure, but that doesn't mean that our reason for acting *was* that pleasure. (Perhaps we acted for our *friend's* pleasure; or recall Kant's point above about being motivated by duty.)

To disprove psychological hedonism conclusively, we need to find cases of truly altruistic acts, acts impossible to ascribe to any self-interested motives. Are there such acts? Consider the case of the soldier who dives on a hand grenade to save his fellow soldiers. Many such cases are well recorded. The psychological hedonist cannot say that the soldier did it for the sake of any future pleasure or to avoid future pain, since the soldier knows he won't have any of either. Such acts as these are clearly altruistic, and therefore count against psychological hedonism. (On the issue of our motives, then, Mill seems closer to the truth than Bentham.)

As for ethical hedonism, we might further characterize this doctrine as requiring these two theses: (1) that happiness is intrinsically good and (2) that it is the only thing that is intrinsically good. But if the first is correct, what shall we say of the sadist who derives his happiness from torturing others? We would normally regard such happiness as bad, derived as it is from pain. So happiness is *not* always good, and therefore not intrinsically good. And if the second thesis is correct, what shall we say about such things as the development of our intellectual or artistic capacities? Are these not good in themselves, apart from any happiness that may (or may not) be associated with them? Many would claim that they indeed are. And of those ethical hedonists who, like Bentham, equate pleasure with happiness, might we not ask whether happiness does not ordinarily include more than just pleasure?

Let's now turn to some specific implications of utilitarianism.

First, consider the problem of the **tyranny of the majority**, to use the phrase of the second U.S. president, John Adams (1735–1826). Adams's worry was that once a democracy grants to the majority the power to dictate the rules, then the majority would be empowered to do whatever they wanted to the minority. So suppose (for a thought experiment) that everyone really despises old Uncle Fred, and maybe even legitimately so (he *is* really annoying, and consumes a lot of family resources). So everyone votes to kill him. Is it morally acceptable to put (innocent) old Uncle Fred out of his misery like this? If the utilitarian merely performs Bentham's hedonic calculus, the answer would seem to be yes: killing him makes a lot of people happy, far outweighing the unhappiness briefly suffered by Fred. Yet to most people the correct answer seems to be no. Uncle Fred has the right to life, or at least not to be murdered in this way. So utilitarianism seems to conflict with a basic right that people have. (Indeed the very idea of any *rights* at all may be problematic for utilitarianism, for a **right** is something that cannot be violated no matter *how* much happiness violating it would produce.)

Or consider a similar case. Suppose you have to make a terrible choice. A train is barreling down a track. You are standing at a fork ahead in the track. If you do nothing, the train will run over ten children playing on the track. But if you flick the switch at the fork, diverting the train to the other track, the train will run over a single child playing there. What is the morally right thing to do? The utilitarian, aiming to maximize happiness (in this case to minimize unhappiness), would seem to conclude you must flip the switch: it is right to kill one in order to save ten. (Most people share this intuition.) But now suppose there are ten children dying because of different organs failing. One desperately needs a heart transplant, another a kidney, another a lung, and so on. You are able, with the flick of a switch, to arrange the capture of one child, to kill him, and to transplant his organs to save the lives of the ten. Should you? There are many details you could vary here, but the utilitarian seems to have to give the same answer as in the train case: it is right to kill one in order to save ten. But now most people do *not* share this intuition. If they are right, then there must be more to morality than simply maximizing happiness. (There is much to discuss here; for more on these issues, see chapter 11.)

To illustrate a second problematic implication of utilitarianism, suppose there is a burning motel and your parents are in one room and a family of four is in another room. You have time to rescue the occupants of only one room. Who should you rescue? The hedonic calculus suggests that you should rescue the four: four people are twice as many as two, and all else being equal, rescuing them would produce more overall happiness than rescuing your parents. But most people feel not only that they *would* rescue their parents but that they *should* rescue their parents; that even if doing so produces less happiness, one's parents count more than complete strangers. There are various reasons why (many think) utilitarianism goes wrong here, but the simple point is that it does, for it gives the wrong moral verdict. So there must be more to morality than just adding up happiness.

Third, to anticipate our discussion in chapter 11, suppose you were passing a shallow pond and observed a small child starting to drown. You are wearing your expensive new shoes, which would be ruined were you to wade in to rescue the child. Should you save the child? (Easy one: of course!) Why? Because the overall happiness produced by the life saved far outweighs the unhappiness of losing those shoes. So far, utilitarianism agrees with our intuitions. But now consider that trip to the movies you took this weekend. (Or your buying your shoes in the first place!) The $15 or $20 you spend at the movies (with popcorn) could in fact save the life of a starving child in a developing country, and the money your shoes cost could save many lives. So utilitarianism suggests that you are behaving morally wrongly in going to the movies, or buying nice shoes—or, if you think about it, in doing almost anything you do. Basically anything short of extreme saintliness comes out to be a moral wrong! But to many, utilitarianism gets it wrong here. While it may be a moral good to sacrifice much for ourselves for the sake of saving lives, we are not morally *obliged* to do so, even if greater overall happiness is generated thereby.

Finally, and most fundamentally, we return to the question whether happiness really is our basic value. Robert Nozick (1938–2002) imagined a machine that could give you any experience you desired: the sensations of skiing downhill, the taste of a chocolate cake, the experience of coming onstage to accept a Nobel Prize, and so on. (While in the machine you wouldn't know you were in the machine, as it would all seem perfectly real to you.) He then asked whether you would choose to enter the machine for an extended period of time, say, two years, or more, or even the rest of your life, choosing any or all of the experiences you would want to have. Would you? While almost everyone would go inside for a brief time, most people would not choose to spend their lives in the machine, and for lots of different reasons.

But that suggests the following argument. If happiness were our fundamental value, we would all choose to live in the machine the rest of our lives. Why? Because the machine could give us any experience we wanted, including that of being blissfully happy. But if we choose not to go into the machine for the rest of our lives, then that must be because even being blissfully happy for life is not what matters to us most. What matters most may vary from person to person, but the point is the same: happiness is *not* what we ultimately value most. And since utilitarianism is based on the idea that it is, utilitarianism has a problem at its core.

These are serious challenges to utilitarianism, to be sure. But they don't quite refute utilitarianism so much as call for it to respond, and perhaps to refine itself in order to deal with them. Indeed utilitarians have much they can say (and do say) in response to each of these challenges. What is clear, though, is that utilitarianism as we have so far stated it—aim for the greatest happiness for the greatest number—is too simple to work. But that doesn't mean that some more sophisticated version of the theory won't work. So consider these challenges not as refutations but simply the next steps in a long conversation about ethics.

SUMMARY

1. Ethics concerns the norms of human conduct. Its study has tended to take three distinct (though related) directions: practical ethics, ethical theory, and metaethics. Ancient thinkers tend to stress the first, more modern thinkers the second, and contemporary thinkers the third.

2. Aristotle believed that the best thing to strive for in life, the good life, was happiness. But happiness cannot be achieved without realizing our highest capacities, which for us is reason. The good life, the happy life, is therefore one devoted to the exercise, development, and perfection of reason. Attaining this involves possessing certain external goods (like health, wealth, good fortune) and mastering both moral and intellectual virtues. Moral virtues are generally determined by the doctrine of the golden mean.

3. Immanuel Kant argued that ethics is not about how to achieve happiness but rather how we might become worthy of it. To become so worthy, he argued, is to have a good will; to have a good will, we must learn to act not out of our interests or desires but out of duty. Duty is thus reflected not in hypothetical imperatives but in unconditional, categorical imperatives.

These in turn are generated by reason, and thus must be consistent and universally valid or binding. The test for a given maxim or rule is the principle of universality: you should act only on those maxims which you can will to be a universal law. The moral person sees herself as worthy of no more or less than anyone else, thus does not seek to make exceptions for herself. In another formulation, Kant stated his basic principle as demanding that we act so as to treat other people always as ends, and not merely as means for our own ends.

4. According to utilitarianism, as developed in the nineteenth century, the right action is that which produces the overall greatest happiness of the greatest number, with happiness often being equated with pleasure. Jeremy Bentham sought to use this principle as the basis for social, political, and legal reform, along the way working out a detailed hedonic calculus. The idea was to structure society so as to motivate people, motivated by their self-interest, to work toward maximizing general happiness.

5. John Stuart Mill modified Bentham's utilitarianism. He argued that people are not always motivated by self-interest, and that it was necessary to distinguish the quality of pleasures from their quantity. Mill employed utilitarian considerations to argue for individual liberty, including the emancipation of women.

6. Despite its intuitive appeal, utilitarianism confronts several challenges. These include the tyranny of the majority (old Uncle Fred), the thought that not everyone should count equally in the calculations (the burning motel), that utilitarianism implies that most ordinary behavior is morally wrong (the shallow pond), and that happiness just isn't what matters most to us (the experience machine).

KEY TERMS

categorical imperative	metaethics
ethical hedonism	moral virtues
ethical theory	normative
ethics	practical (or applied) ethics
golden mean	principle of universality
good will	principle of utility
hedonic calculus	psychological hedonism
hypothetical imperative	right (n.)
intellectual virtues	tyranny of the majority
maxim	utilitarianism

REVIEW QUESTIONS

1. What are the three directions ethical investigation has taken in philosophy's history? What questions characterize each type of investigation? What historical period is associated with each type?

2. What is Aristotle's conception of the good or happy life?

3. What is Aristotle's doctrine of the golden mean?

4. What is the difference between a hypothetical imperative and a categorical imperative? Which kind does Kant believe best captures our moral obligations, and why?

5. What is the difference between psychological hedonism and ethical hedonism? How did Mill respond to Bentham with respect to these doctrines?

6. Briefly summarize three of the challenges confronting utilitarianism.

NOTES

1. Excerpts from *Nicomachean Ethics*, trans., Terence Irwin (Indianapolis, IN: Hackett Publishing Company, 1985).

2. From Aristotle's *Rhetoric*, trans. W. Rhys Roberts, in Richard McKeon, ed., *The Basic Works of Aristotle* (New York: Random House, 1941).

■ Reading

Nicomachean Ethics

ARISTOTLE

From Aristotle, Nicomachean Ethics, *transl., Terence Irwin (Indianapolis: Hackett Publishing Co., 1985), pp. 1–2, 13–17, 30–35, 44–47, 284–87. Reprinted with permission.*

This excerpt contains some of the key points in Aristotle's ethics, including his account of the good life and of the moral and intellectual virtues.

Every craft and every investigation, and likewise every action and decision, seems to aim at some good; hence the good has been well described as that at which everything aims. . . .

Suppose, then, that (a) there is some end of the things we pursue in our actions which we wish for because of itself and because of which we wish for the other things; and (b) we do not choose everything because of something else, since (c) if we do, it will go on without limit, making desire empty and futile; then clearly (d) this end will be the good, i.e., the best good. . . .

The demand for exactness must be limited by the nature of ethics

Our discussion will be adequate if its degree of clarity fits the subject-matter; for we should not seek the same degree of exactness in all sorts of arguments alike, any more than in the products of different crafts. . . .

The proper aim of ethical theory

Since these, then, are the sorts of things we argue from and about, it will be satisfactory if we can indicate the truth roughly and in outline; since [that is to say] we argue from and about what holds good usually [but not universally], it will be satisfactory if we can draw conclusions of the same sort. . . .

1.51 Characteristics of the good

(1) The good is the end of action

But let us return once again to the good we are looking for, and consider just what it could be, since it is apparently one thing in one action or craft, and another thing in another; for it is one thing in medicine, another in generalship, and so on for the rest.

What, then, is the good in each of these cases? Surely it is that for the sake of which the other things are done; and in medicine this is health, in generalship victory, in housebuilding a house, in another case something else, but in every action and decision it is the end, since it is for the sake of the end that everyone does the other things.

And so, if there is some end of everything that is pursued in action, this will be the good pursued in action; and if there are more ends than one, these will be the goods pursued in action.

Our argument has progressed, then, to the same conclusion [as before, that the highest end is the good]; but we must try to clarify this still more.

(2) The good is complete

Though apparently there are many ends, we choose some of them, e.g. wealth, flutes and, in general, instruments, because of something else; hence it is clear that not all ends are complete. But the best good is apparently something complete. Hence, if only one end is complete, this will be what we are looking for; and if more than one are complete, the most complete of these will be what we are looking for.

CRITERIA FOR COMPLETENESS

An end pursued in itself, we say, is more complete than an end pursued because of something else; and an end that is never choiceworthy because of something else is more complete than ends that are choiceworthy both in themselves and because of this end; and hence an end that is always [choiceworthy, and also] choiceworthy in itself, never because of something else, is unconditionally complete.

(3) Happiness meets the criteria for completeness, but other goods do not

Now happiness more than anything else seems unconditionally complete, since we always [choose it, and also] choose it because of itself, never because of something else. Honor, pleasure, understanding and every virtue we certainly choose because of themselves, since we would choose each of them even if it had no further result, but we also choose them for the sake of happiness, supposing that through them we shall be happy. Happiness, by contrast, no one ever chooses for their sake, or for the sake of anything else at all.

(4) The good is self-sufficient; so is happiness

The same conclusion [that happiness is complete] also appears to follow from self-sufficiency, since the complete good seems to be self-sufficient. . . .

Anyhow, we regard something as self-sufficient when all by itself it makes a life choiceworthy and lacking nothing; and that is what we think happiness does.

(5) The good is most choiceworthy; so is happiness

Moreover, [the complete good is most choiceworthy, and] we think happiness is most choiceworthy of all goods, since it is not counted as one good among many. If it were counted as one among many, then, clearly, we think that the addition of the smallest of goods would make it more choiceworthy; for [the smallest good] that is added becomes an extra quantity of goods [so creating a good larger than the original good], and the larger of two goods is always more choiceworthy. [But we do not think any addition can make happiness more choiceworthy; hence it is most choiceworthy.]

Happiness, then, is apparently something complete and self-sufficient, since it is the end of the things pursued in action.

1.52 A clearer account of the good: the human soul's activity expressing virtue

But presumably the remark that the best good is happiness is apparently something [generally] agreed, and what we miss is a clearer statement of what the best good is.

(1) If something has a function, its good depends on its function

Well, perhaps we shall find the best good if we first find the function of a human being. For just as the good, i.e. [, doing] well, for a flautist, a sculptor, and every craftsman, and, in general, for whatever has a function and [characteristic] action, seems to depend on its function, the same seems to be true for a human being, if a human being has some function.

(2) What sorts of things have functions?

Then do the carpenter and the leatherworker have their functions and actions, while a human being has none, and is by nature idle, without any function? Or, just as eye, hand, foot and, in general, every [bodily] part apparently has its functions, may we likewise ascribe to a human being some function besides all of theirs?

(3) The human function

What, then, could this be? For living is apparently shared with plants, but what we are looking for is the special function of a human being; hence we should set aside the life of nutrition and growth. The life next in order is some sort of life of sense-perception; but this too is apparently shared, with horse, ox and every animal. The remaining possibility, then, is some sort of life of action of the [part of the soul] that has reason.

Clarification of "has reason" and "life"

Now this [part has two parts, which have reason in different ways], one as obeying the reason [in the other part], the other as itself having reason and thinking. [We intend both.] Moreover, life is also spoken of in two ways [as capacity and as activity], and we must take [a human being's special function to be] life as activity, since this seems to be called life to a fuller extent.

(4) The human good is activity expressing virtue

(a) We have found, then, that the human function is the soul's activity that expresses reason [as itself having reason] or requires reason [as obeying reason]. (b) Now the function of F, e.g. of a harpist, is the same in kind, so we say, as the function of an excellent F, e.g. an excellent harpist. (c) The same is true unconditionally in every case, when we add to the function the superior achievement that expresses the virtue; for a harpist's function, e.g. is to play the harp, and a good harpist's is to do it well. (d) Now we take the human function to be a certain kind of life, and take this life to be the soul's activity and actions that express reason. (e) [Hence by (c) and (d)] the excellent man's function is to do this finely and well. (f) Each function is completed well when its completion expresses the proper virtue.

(g) Therefore [by (d), (e) and (f)] the human good turns out to be the soul's activity that expresses virtue.

(5) The good must also be complete

And if there are more virtues than one, the good will express the best and most complete virtue. Moreover, it will be in a complete life. For one swallow does not make a spring, nor does one day; nor, similarly, does one day or a short time make us blessed and happy. . . .

1.92 A discussion of virtue requires a discussion of the soul

It is clear that the virtue we must examine is human virtue, since we are also seeking the human good and human happiness. And by human virtue we mean virtue of the soul, not of the body, since we also say that happiness is an activity of the soul. . . .

[We] have discussed the soul sufficiently [for our purposes] in [our] popular works as well [as our less popular], and we should use this discussion.

1.93 The rational and nonrational parts of the soul

We have said, e.g., that one [part] of the soul is nonrational, while one has reason. Are these distinguished as parts of a body as everything divisible into parts are? Or are they two only in account, and inseparable by nature, as the convex and the concave are in a surface? It does not matter for present purposes. . . .

1.94 The division of the virtues corresponds to the parts of the soul

The distinction between virtues also reflects this difference. For some virtues are called virtues of thought, others virtues of character; wisdom, comprehension and intelligence are called virtues of thought, generosity and temperance virtues of character.

For when we speak of someone's character we do not say that he is wise or has good comprehension, but that he is gentle or temperate. [Hence these are the virtues of character.] And yet, we also praise the wise person for his state, and the states that are praiseworthy are the ones we call virtues. [Hence wisdom is also a virtue.]

2. Virtues of Character in General

2.1 How a Virtue of Character Is Acquired

Virtue, then, is of two sorts, virtue of thought and virtue of character. Virtue of thought arises and grows mostly from teaching, and hence needs experience and time. Virtue of character [i.e., of ethos] results from habit [ethos]; hence its name "ethical," slightly varied from "ethos."

Virtue comes about, not by a process of nature, but by habituation

Hence it is also clear that none of the virtues of character arises in us naturally.

(1) What is natural cannot be changed by habituation

For if something is by nature [in one condition], habituation cannot bring it into another condition. A stone, e.g., by nature moves downwards, and habituation could not make it move upwards, not even if you threw it up ten thousand times to habituate it; nor could habituation make fire move downwards, or bring anything that is by nature in one condition into another condition.

Thus the virtues arise in us neither by nature nor against nature, but we are by nature able to acquire them, and reach our complete perfection through habit.

(2) Natural capacities are not acquired by habituation. . . .

Virtues, by contrast, we acquire, just as we acquire crafts, by having previously activated them. For we learn a craft by producing the same product that we must produce when we have learned it, becoming builders, e.g., by building and harpists by playing the harp; so also, then, we become just by doing just actions, temperate by doing temperate actions, brave by doing brave actions. . . .

(4) Virtue and vice are formed by good and bad actions

Further, just as in the case of a craft, the sources and means that develop each virtue also ruin it. For playing the harp makes both good and bad harpists, and it is analogous in the case of builders and all the rest; for building well makes good builders, building badly, bad ones. If it were not so, no teacher would be needed, but everyone would be born a good or a bad craftsman.

It is the same, then, with the virtues. For actions in dealing with [other] human beings make some people just, some unjust; actions in terrifying situations and the acquired habit of fear or confidence make some brave and others cowardly. The same is true of situations involving appetites and anger; for one or another sort of conduct in these situations makes some people temperate and gentle, others intemperate and irascible.

Conclusion: The importance of habituation

To sum up, then, in a single account: A state [of character] arises from [the repetition of] similar activities. Hence we must display the right activities, since differences in these imply corresponding differences in the states. It is not unimportant, then, to acquire one sort of habit or another, right from our youth; rather, it is very important, indeed all-important.

2.23 Definition of virtue

Virtue, then, is (a) a state that decides, (b) [consisting] in a mean, (c) the mean relative to us, (d) which is defined by reference to reason, (e) i.e., to the reason by reference to which the intelligent person would define it. It is a mean between two vices, one of excess and one of deficiency.

It is a mean for this reason also: Some vices miss what is right because they are deficient, others because they are excessive, in feelings or in actions, while virtue finds and chooses what is intermediate.

Hence, as far as its substance and the account stating its essence are concerned, virtue is a mean; but as far as the best [condition] and the good [result] are concerned, it is an extremity.

The definition must not be misapplied to cases in which there is no mean

But not every action or feeling admits of the mean. For the names of some automatically include baseness, e.g., spite, shamelessness, envy [among feelings], and adultery, theft, murder, among actions. All of these and similar things are called by these names because they themselves, not their excesses or deficiencies, are base.

Hence in doing these things we can never be correct, but must invariably be in error. We cannot do them well or not well—e.g., by committing adultery with the right woman at the right time in the right way; on the contrary, it is true unconditionally that to do any of them is to be in error.

[To think these admit of a mean], therefore, is like thinking that unjust or cowardly or intemperate action also admits of a mean, an excess and a deficiency. For then there would be a mean of excess, a mean of deficiency, an excess of excess and a deficiency of deficiency. Rather, just as there is no excess or deficiency of temperance or of bravery, since the intermediate is a sort of extreme [in achieving the good], so also there is no mean of these [vicious actions] either, but whatever way anyone does them, he is in error. For in general there is no mean of excess or of deficiency, and no excess or deficiency of a mean. . . .

2.31 Classification of virtues of character

Virtues concerned with feelings

(1) First, in feelings of fear and confidence the mean is bravery. The excessively fearless person is nameless (and in fact many cases are nameless), while the one who is excessively confident is rash; the one who is excessively afraid and deficient in confidence is cowardly.

(2) In pleasures and pains, though not in all types, and in pains less than in pleasures, the mean is temperance and the excess intemperance. People deficient in pleasure are not often found, which is why they also lack even a name; let us call them insensible.

Virtues concerned with external goods

(3) In giving and taking money the mean is generosity, the excess wastefulness and the deficiency ungenerosity. Here the vicious people have contrary excesses and defects; for the wasteful person spends to excess and is deficient in taking, whereas the ungenerous person takes to excess and is deficient in spending. At the moment we are speaking in outline and summary, and that suffices; later we shall define these things more exactly. . . .

Virtues concerned with social life

(7) Anger also admits of an excess, deficiency and mean. These are all practically nameless; but since we call the intermediate person mild, let us call the mean mildness. Among the extreme people let the excessive person be irascible, and the vice be irascibility, and let the deficient person be a sort of inirascible person, and the deficiency be inirascibility. . . .

13.3 Theoretical Study Is the Supreme Element of Happiness

If happiness, then, is activity expressing virtue, it is reasonable for it to express the supreme virtue, which will be the virtue of the best thing.

The best is understanding, or whatever else seems to be the natural ruler and leader, and to understand what is fine and divine, by being itself either divine or the most divine element in us.

Hence complete happiness will be its activity expressing its proper virtue; and we have said that this activity is the activity of study. This seems to agree with what has been said before, and also with the truth.

13.31 The activity of theoretical study is best

For this activity is supreme, since understanding is the supreme element in us, and the objects of understanding are the supreme objects of knowledge.

13.32 It is most continuous

Besides, it is the most continuous activity, since we are more capable of continuous study than of any continuous action.

13.33 It is pleasantest

We think pleasure must be mixed into happiness; and it is agreed that the activity expressing wisdom is the pleasantest of the activities expressing virtue. At any rate, philosophy seems to have remarkably pure and firm pleasures; and it is reasonable for those who have knowledge to spend their lives more pleasantly than those who seek it.

13.34 It is most self-sufficient

Moreover, the self-sufficiency we spoke of will be found in study above all. For admittedly the wise person, the just person and the other virtuous people all need the good things necessary for life. Still, when these are adequately supplied, the just person needs other people as partners and recipients of his just actions; and the same is true of the temperate person and the brave person and each of the others.

But the wise person is able, and more able the wiser he is, to study even by himself; and though he presumably does it better with colleagues, even so he is more self-sufficient than any other [virtuous person].

13.35 It aims at no end beyond itself

Besides, study seems to be liked because of itself alone, since it has no result beyond having studied. But from the virtues concerned with action we try to a greater or lesser extent to gain something beyond the action itself.

13.36 It involves leisure

Happiness seems to be found in leisure, since we accept trouble so that we can be at leisure, and fight wars so that we can be at peace. Now the virtues concerned with action have their activities in politics or war, and actions here seem to require trouble. . . .

But the activity of understanding, it seems, is superior in excellence because it is the activity of study; aims at no end beyond itself; has its own proper pleasure, which increases the activity; and is self-sufficient, leisured and unwearied, as far [as these are possible] for a human being. And whatever else is ascribed to the blessedly happy person is evidently found in connection with this activity.

Hence a human being's complete happiness will be this activity, if it receives a complete span of life, since nothing incomplete is proper to happiness.

13.37 It is a god-like life

Such a life would be superior to the human level. For someone will live it not in so far as he is a human being, but in so far as he has some divine element in him. And the activity of this divine element is as much superior to the activity expressing the rest of virtue as this element is superior to the compound. Hence if understanding is something divine in comparison with a human being, so also will the life that expresses understanding be divine in comparison with human life.

We ought not to follow the proverb-writers, and "think human, since you are human," or "think mortal, since you are mortal." Rather, as far as we can, we ought to be pro-immortal, and go to all lengths to live a life that expresses our supreme element; for however much this element may lack in bulk, by much more it surpasses everything in power and value. . . .

13.38 It realizes the supreme element in human nature

Moreover, each person seems to be his understanding, if he is his controlling and better element; it would be absurd, then, if he were to choose not his own life, but something else's. And what we have said previously will also apply now. For what is proper to each thing's nature is supremely best and pleasantest for it; and hence for a human being the life expressing understanding will be supremely best and pleasantest, if understanding above all is the human being. This life, then, will also be happiest.

REVIEW AND DISCUSSION QUESTIONS

1. Why does Aristotle think of happiness as our final or ultimate goal?

2. In what ways does Aristotle's account of the good life differ from that held by many people today, in our twenty-first-century world?

3. Is the life of the mind, devoted to intellectual study, the best kind of human life? Are there others that are equally good, and if so, why?

■ Reading
"Santa and Scrooge"

ANDREW PESSIN

From The 60-Second Philosopher *(Oxford, UK: Oneworld Publications, 2009), Chapter 45. Reprinted with permission.*

A little thought experiment that might be useful to reflect on the differences between the ethics of Aristotle and Kant.

Some people, looking for an inspiring role model, turn to religion and ask themselves, "What would Jesus do?" But it seems to me that Jesus himself probably wouldn't ask that. So what about the next best person: Santa?

Well, generosity is a good thing; I'm not questioning that. But we never learn just why Santa gives, and we cannot morally evaluate him without knowing his motivations. According to some, the actual historical source of the Santa legend originally gave only to the poor. That's admirable, but there's a long way between that and rewarding every little brat on the planet, including the rich ones. And with respect to today's Santa—who rewards those who behave and punishes those who don't—well if children behave well only to get the latest video game then we're hardly teaching them genuine morality. And if Santa is the key enabler there, so much the worse for Santa.

OK, let's give him the benefit of the doubt. Suppose we simply grant that Santa gives out of his pure and natural generosity. Would that make him an ideal role model?

Maybe. But there's another possibility. Consider Dickens' famous character Scrooge. Scrooge is not exactly a generous person. He is, well, a real scrooge. But let's alter the details of the story a bit. By the end of his experience he remains the same basic character he is: grouchy, unpleasant, and decidedly ungenerous. But now the philosopher within him has reached the conclusion that being generous is a good and admirable virtue. Unlike Santa he doesn't *feel* like being generous, and he has to overcome something within him in order to be generous. But he does so because he is now guided by what is right rather than by how he feels.

So now who is more admirable: the generous person who gives easily, naturally, or the person who has to overcome even his own natural antipathy in order to act generously?

I wonder what Santa and Scrooge would say.

REVIEW AND DISCUSSION QUESTIONS

1. How might Aristotle and Kant answer the question of which character is more admirable, and why?

2. What is your view, and why?

■ Reading

"Of What Sort of Proof the Principle of Utility Is Susceptible"

JOHN STUART MILL

From Utilitarianism *(1861), in* Utilitarianism *(London: Parker, Son, and Bourn West Strand, 1863), pp. 51–57.*

In this excerpt Mill argues that happiness is and should be the single ultimate aim of our actions.

It has already been remarked, that questions of ultimate ends do not admit of proof, in the ordinary acceptation of the term. To be incapable of proof by reasoning is common to all first principles; to the first premises of our knowledge, as well as to those of our conduct. But the former, being matters of fact, may be the subject of a direct appeal to the faculties which judge of fact—namely, our senses, and our internal consciousness. Can an appeal be made to the same faculties on questions of practical ends? Or by what other faculty is cognizance taken of them?

Questions about ends are, in other words, questions about what things are desirable. The utilitarian doctrine is, that happiness is desirable, and the only thing desirable, as an end; all other things being only desirable as means to that end. What ought to be required of this doctrine—what conditions is it requisite that the doctrine should fulfill—to make good its claim to be believed?

The only proof capable of being given that an object is visible, is that people actually see it. The only proof that a sound is audible, is that people hear it: and so of the other sources of our experience. In like manner, I apprehend, the sole evidence it is possible to produce that anything is desirable, is that people do actually desire it. If the end which the utilitarian doctrine proposes to itself were not, in theory and in practice, acknowledged to be an end, nothing could ever convince any person that it was so. No reason can be given why the general happiness is desirable, except that each person, so far as he believes it to be attainable, desires his own happiness. This, however, being a fact, we have not only all the proof which the case admits of, but all which it is possible to require, that happiness is a good: that each person's happiness is a good to that person, and the general happiness, therefore, a good to the aggregate of all persons. Happiness has made out its title as *one* of the ends of conduct, and consequently one of the criteria of morality.

But it has not, by this alone, proved itself to be the sole criterion. To do that, it would seem, by the same rule, necessary to show, not only that people desire happiness, but that they never desire anything else. Now it is palpable that they do desire things which, in common language, are decidedly distinguished from happiness. They desire, for example, virtue, and the absence of vice, no less really than pleasure and the absence of pain. The desire of virtue is not as universal, but it is as authentic a fact, as the desire of happiness. And hence the opponents of the utilitarian standard deem that they have a right to infer that there are other ends of human action besides happiness, and that happiness is not the standard of approbation and disapprobation.

But does the utilitarian doctrine deny that people desire virtue, or maintain that virtue is not a thing to be desired? The very reverse. It maintains not only that virtue is to be desired, but that it is to be desired disinterestedly, for itself. Whatever may be the opinion of utilitarian moralists as to the original conditions by which virtue is made virtue; however they may believe (as they do) that actions and dispositions are only virtuous because they promote another end than virtue; yet this being granted, and it having been decided, from considerations of this description, what *is* virtuous, they not only place virtue at the very head of the things which are good as means to the ultimate end, but they also recognise as a psychological fact the possibility of its being, to the individual, a good in itself, without looking to any end beyond it; and hold, that the mind is not in a right state, not in a state conformable to Utility, not in the state most conducive to the general happiness, unless it does love virtue in this manner—as a thing desirable in itself, even although, in the individual instance, it should not produce those other desirable consequences which it tends to produce, and on account of which it is held to be virtue. This opinion is not, in the smallest degree, a departure from the Happiness principle. The ingredients of happiness are very various, and each of them is desirable in itself, and not merely when considered as swelling an aggregate. The principle of utility does not mean that any given pleasure, as music, for instance, or any given exemption from pain, as for example health, is to be looked upon as means to a collective something termed happiness, and to be desired on that account. They are desired and desirable in and for themselves; besides being means, they are a part of the end. Virtue, according to the utilitarian doctrine, is not naturally and originally part of the end, but it is capable of becoming so; and in those who love it disinterestedly it has become so, and is desired and cherished, not as a means to happiness, but as a part of their happiness.

To illustrate this farther, we may remember that virtue is not the only thing, originally a means, and which if it were not a means to anything else, would be and remain indifferent, but which by association with what it is a means to, comes to be desired for itself, and that too with the utmost intensity. What, for example, shall we say of the love of money? There is nothing originally more desirable about money than about any heap of glittering pebbles. Its worth is solely that of the things which it will buy; the desires for other things than itself, which it is a means of gratifying. Yet the love of money is not only one of the strongest moving forces of human life, but money is, in many cases, desired in and for itself; the desire to possess it is often stronger than the desire to use it, and goes on increasing when all the desires which point to ends beyond it, to be compassed by it, are falling off. It may, then, be said truly, that money is desired not for the sake of an end, but as part of the end. From being a means to happiness, it has come to be itself a principal ingredient of the individual's conception of happiness. The same may be said of the majority of the great objects of human life—power, for example, or fame; except that to each of these there is a certain amount of immediate pleasure annexed, which has at least the semblance of being naturally inherent in them; a thing which cannot be said of money. Still, however, the strongest natural attraction, both of power and of fame, is the immense aid they give to the attainment of our other wishes; and it is the strong association thus generated between them and all our objects of desire, which gives to the direct desire of them the intensity it often assumes, so as in some characters to surpass in strength all other desires. In these cases the means have become a part of the end, and a more important part of it than any of the things which they are means to. What was once desired as an instrument for the attainment of happiness, has come to be desired for its own sake. In being desired for its own sake it is, however, desired as *part* of happiness. The person is made, or thinks he would be made, happy by its mere possession; and is made unhappy by failure to obtain it. The desire of it is not a different thing from the desire of happiness, any more than the love of music, or the desire of health. They are included in happiness. They are some of the elements of which the desire of happiness is made up. Happiness is not an abstract idea, but a concrete whole; and these are some of its parts. And the utilitarian standard sanctions and approves their being so. Life would be a poor thing, very ill provided with sources of happiness, if there were not this provision of nature, by which things originally indifferent, but conducive to, or otherwise associated with, the satisfaction of our primitive desires, become in themselves sources of pleasure more valuable than the primitive pleasures, both in permanency, in the space of human existence that they are capable of covering, and even in intensity.

Virtue, according to the utilitarian conception, is a good of this description. There was no original desire of it, or motive to it, save its conduciveness to pleasure, and especially to protection from pain. But through the association thus formed, it may be felt a good in itself, and desired as such with as great intensity as any other good; and with this difference between it and the love of money, of power, or of fame, that all of these may, and often do, render the individual noxious to the other members of the society to which he belongs, where there is nothing which makes him so much a blessing to them as the cultivation of the disinterested love of virtue. And consequently, the utilitarian standard, while it tolerates and approves those other acquired desires, up to the point beyond which they would be more injurious to the general happiness than promotive of it, enjoins and requires the cultivation of the love of virtue up to the greatest strength possible, as being above all things important to the general happiness.

It results from the preceding considerations, that there is in reality nothing desired except happiness. Whatever is desired otherwise than as a means to some end beyond itself, and ultimately to happiness, is desired as itself a part of happiness, and is not desired for itself until it has become so. . . .

We have now, then, an answer to the question, of what sort of proof the principle of utility is susceptible. If the opinion which I have now stated is psychologically true—if human nature is so constituted as to desire nothing which is not either a part of happiness or a means of happiness, we can have no other proof, and we require no other, that these are the only things desirable. If so, happiness is the sole end of human action, and the promotion of it the test by which to judge of all human conduct; from whence it necessarily follows that it must be the criterion of morality, since a part is included in the whole.

REVIEW AND DISCUSSION QUESTIONS

1. What is Mill's primary claim in the text, and how does he defend it?

2. In your view, is happiness the sole end of human action? Or are there other things we either do, or should, aim at, that may be entirely independent of happiness?

■ Reading
"The Experience Machine"

ROBERT NOZICK

From Anarchy, State, and Utopia *by Robert Nozick, copyright © 1974, pp. 42–44. Reprinted by permission of Basic Books, a member of The Perseus Books Group.*

In this excerpt Nozick explores what matters to us most, ultimately.

There are also substantial puzzles when we ask what matters other than how *people's* experiences feel "from the inside." Suppose there were an experience machine that would give you any experience you desired. Superduper neuropsychologists could stimulate your brain so that you would think and feel you were writing a great novel, or making a friend, or reading an interesting book. All the time you would be floating in a tank, with electrodes attached to your brain. Should you plug into this machine for life, preprogramming your life's experiences? If you are worried about missing out on desirable experiences, we can suppose that business enterprises have researched thoroughly the lives of many others. You can pick and choose from their large library . . . of such experiences, selecting your life's experiences for, say, the next two years. After two years have passed, you will have ten minutes or ten hours out of the tank, to select the experiences of your *next* two years. Of course, while in the tank you won't know that you're there; you'll think it's all actually happening . . . Would you plug in? *What else can matter to us, other than how our lives feel from the inside? . . .*

What does matter to us in addition to our experiences? First, we want to *do* certain things, and not just have the experience of doing them. . . . (But *why* do we want to do the activities rather than merely to experience them?) A second reason for not plugging in is that we want to *be* a certain way, to be a certain sort of person. Someone floating in a tank is an indeterminate blob. There is no answer to the question of what a person is like who has long been in the tank. Is he courageous, kind, intelligent, witty, loving? It's not merely that it's difficult to tell; there's no way he is. Plugging into the machine is a kind of suicide. . . . Why should we be concerned only with how our time is filled, but not with what we are?

Thirdly, plugging into an experience machine limits us to a man-made reality, to a world no deeper or more important than that which people can construct. There is no *actual* contact with any deeper reality, though the experience of it can be simulated. Many persons desire to leave themselves open to such contact and to a plumbing of deeper significance. This clarifies the intensity of the conflict over psychoactive drugs, which some view as mere local experience machines, and others view as avenues to a deeper reality. . . .

We learn that something matters to us in addition to experience by imagining an experience machine and then realizing that we would not use it. We can continue to imagine a sequence of machines each designed to fill lacks suggested for the earlier machines. For example, since the experience machine doesn't meet our desire to *be* a certain way, imagine a transformation machine which transforms us into whatever sort of person we'd like to be. . . . Surely one would not use the transformation machine to become as one would wish, and thereupon plug into the experience machine! So something matters in addition to one's experiences *and* what one is like. . . . Is it that we want to make a difference in the world? Consider then the result machine, which produces in the world any result you would produce. . . . We shall not pursue here the fascinating details of these or other machines. What is most disturbing about them is their living of our lives for us. . . . Perhaps what we desire is to live (an active verb) our-selves, in contact with reality. (And this, machines cannot do *for* us.) Without elaborating on the implications of this[,] . . . we need merely note the intricacy of the question of what matters *for people* other than their experiences.

REVIEW AND DISCUSSION QUESTIONS

1. Although Nozick is not explicitly addressing utilitarianism here, in what way(s) might this excerpt constitute a fundamental challenge for utilitarianism?

2. Would *you* go into the machine, for any extended period of time? Why not?

■ Religion

The Nature and Existence of God

L
OTS OF PEOPLE have believed, and do believe, in the existence of God, and lots of people haven't, and don't. But in fact most people of both camps don't have a very clear idea of exactly what it is they believe or disbelieve. That's because having a clear idea of what "God" is supposed to be requires doing some philosophical thinking, and thinking is hard; plus most people have neither the freedom nor leisure to do it, even if they have the aptitude. Still, *some* philosophers have managed to do it, and when you study their work you'll soon realize that **theism**—the doctrine that God exists—is more complicated than you think. But then again, so is **atheism**, the negation of that doctrine.

In this chapter, we'll survey some **philosophical theology**, or philosophical attempts to clarify the nature, and investigate the existence, of God. To say these are *philosophical* attempts is to say they are governed not merely by revelation and tradition but also by rational reflection.

A BRIEF HISTORY OF PHILOSOPHICAL THEOLOGY, 427 B.C.E.–1600 C.E. [1]

Although the ancient Greeks were **polytheists** believing in many gods—not **monotheists** believing in the one God of Judaism, Christianity, and Islam—the writings of Plato and Aristotle clearly suggest something like that single supreme being. Plato speaks of a "divine craftsman" who designed the cosmos, for example, and Aristotle of an "unmoved mover" responsible for all motion and change. More importantly, these two attributes—of designing the cosmos and causing motion, as well as others—would eventually become incorporated into the monotheist conception of God, forming something like its essence.

Much of that incorporating occurred during the medieval period of philosophy. Contrary to its unfair "Dark Ages" nickname, the medieval period in fact was home to great intellectual activity, particularly in philosophical theology. Far from relying on "blind faith," truly impressive philosophical work was done, for one thing, in making sense of various religion-specific doctrines. For example, Jewish thinkers analyzed the *mitzvot* (God's commandments to maintain a kosher diet, observe the Sabbath, etc.), Muslim thinkers debated whether the Qur'an (their scripture) was created or eternal, and Christian thinkers attempted to clarify the doctrines of the Trinity (that God is simultaneously three and one) and the Eucharist (that bread is converted into Christ's body despite not changing perceivably). More generally, thinkers from all three traditions worked hard, often in response to each other, to construct the great monotheistic doctrine that was common to them. This they did both by developing rational proofs of God's existence and by articulating detailed conceptions of God's key attributes: power, knowledge, goodness, and so on. In doing this they also were required to develop sophisticated theories about time, space, the soul, freedom, morality, and more.

Much of this work was inspired by the ancient Greeks. Plato's philosophy had a great influence on Augustine (354–430 C.E.) for example, who is sometimes called the first medieval philosopher. And while most of Aristotle's works were lost during the first millennium C.E., they were rediscovered early in the second, and created nothing short of an intellectual tsunami. For despite the affinity between his "unmoved mover" and the Western God, there were also many points of conflict. Aristotle seemed to hold (for example) that the cosmos was not created but eternal and that the soul is not separable from the body, while the Church taught that God created the cosmos *ex nihilo* (from nothing) and that the soul could survive the death of the body.

Initially the Christian authorities attempted to suppress Aristotle's works, but soon realized that this only kindled people's interest in them. Thus they soon adopted a new strategy: rather than condemn Aristotle, they aimed to reconcile what he wrote with Christianity. And perhaps no one did more toward that aim than St. Thomas Aquinas (1225–1274), whose massive work *Summa Theologica* summarized all aspects of Christian theology. Aquinas did such a fine job reconciling Aristotle and Christianity, in fact, that by the fourteenth century or so, Aristotle's works were moved from the list of banned books onto the list of required reading.

Nor was the medieval Church alone in having to confront the works of Aristotle. Similar crises arose for Judaism and Islam, and were ultimately met by their own thinkers in similar ways. The Muslim thinkers Avicenna (980–1037) and Averroes (1126–1198), and the Jewish thinker Maimonides (1135–1204), did

AQUINAS, WITH ARISTOTLE (LEFT) AND PLATO (RIGHT)

for their respective religions what Aquinas did for his, and indeed served as inspiration for the latter.

The synthesis of Aristotle and Christianity was the dominant theme of the medieval period in Europe, lasting through the next four centuries after Aquinas. According to some, this was the golden age of philosophical theology. But even so, the discipline continued to flourish once the early modern period began in the seventeenth century, even as it confronted challenges raised by the rise of modern science and by philosophers growing slowly comfortable with the idea of atheism; and it continues to flourish today, even as atheism becomes perhaps the reigning intellectual norm.

So let's have a look at what happens when philosophy meets theology.

We said that philosophical theology attempts to clarify the nature and investigate the existence of God. By "clarify the nature of God" we mean identify and explain the properties or attributes God is thought to have, such as power, knowledge, and goodness. By "investigate the existence of God" we refer to attempts to prove God's existence by rational means. We'll begin with the latter, and return to the former later.

Proofs of God's existence fall into several categories. **Ontological arguments** claim that the very concept or definition of God entails God's existence. **Cosmological arguments** claim that various features of the cosmos (such as motion, causation, the contingency of events, etc.) demonstrate God's existence. **Teleological arguments** (also known as **design arguments**) claim that the order or beauty or apparent "design" in the cosmos require the existence of an orderer or designer, that is, God. **Moral arguments** claim that the existence of objective morality is possible only if God exists. And finally **prudential arguments** claim not directly that God exists, but that it is rational (in the sense of wise, or prudent) to believe in God's existence.

ANSELM OF CANTERBURY

ST. ANSELM'S ONTOLOGICAL ARGUMENT

Anselm of Canterbury (1033–1109) was a monk and philosopher who served as Archbishop of Canterbury, England, from 1093 until his death. He accomplished many things, but none more notorious than his *ontological argument* for God's existence, appearing in his work *Proslogion*, written by 1078. What makes this argument so astounding—if it works—is that it seems to do something impossible: prove something exists merely by thinking about it. Normally if you want to prove something exists you have to go find it. If you wonder whether life exists on other planets, or the quarks of physics exist, you need to make observations, do experiments, look for evidence. But the ontological argument for God's existence proceeds by pure thought alone.

Anselm begins with the idea of God, that is, a description of what God *is*: a being than which none greater can be conceived or thought. (For short we'll refer to God as "the Greatest Conceivable Being.") Note that even the atheist can agree with this description, for when the atheist *denies* the existence of God, it is the existence of the Greatest Conceivable Being he or she is denying. Note, too, that this description isn't meant to be complete, as it says nothing about any other attributes God might have (such as power, knowledge, etc.). It is a minimal description meant to capture the essence of God. Whatever *else* God might be, He must be the Greatest Conceivable Being.

Next Anselm observes that whatever you have an idea of exists at least in your mind, even if you don't think it exists in reality, outside your mind. The painter has his painting "in his mind," typically, even before he paints it; after he paints it, the painting exists both in his mind (as an "idea") and outside his mind, in reality. Since we have the idea of God, then, the Greatest Conceivable Being exists *at least* in the mind.

But now, Anselm argues, you cannot legitimately think that the Greatest Conceivable Being exists *only* in the mind.

Why not? Suppose you think that it exists only in your mind. You could then easily conceive of its being greater than it is, namely by conceiving it to exist in reality as well. (For surely a being is greater when it really exists than when it merely exists in someone's mind!) To suppose that the Greatest Conceivable Being exists only in the mind, in other words, is to suppose that the *Greatest Conceivable Being* (in your mind) is not the Greatest Conceivable Being (because you could conceive of its being greater). But that is to contradict yourself, for it is to hold that the thing in your mind is simultaneously the Greatest Conceivable Being and not the Greatest Conceivable Being. And if there is one rule that no philosophers (not even atheists) should reject, it is the **Law of Non-Contradiction**: you may never legitimately contradict yourself. Any claim that leads you to contradict yourself, therefore, must be false.

And what claim led you into that contradiction? The one at the start of the previous paragraph: "suppose you think that the Greatest Conceivable Being exists *only* in your mind." It is that supposition that leads to the conclusion that the thing in your mind both is, and is not, the Greatest Conceivable Being. Since we must reject any claim that leads us to a contradiction, we must reject that claim.

So it is *false* that the Greatest Conceivable Being exists *only* in your mind. But then there is only one other place for it to exist in addition to existing in your mind, namely in reality. So the Greatest Conceivable Being exists in reality. And since God *is* the Greatest Conceivable Being, by our definition, we've got our proof: God exists.

Some Reflection on the Ontological Argument

Now the ink on Anselm's parchment was not even dry before the responses started coming in. A fellow monk named Gaunilo felt the argument must fail, for you could do the same sort of reasoning to prove anything at all existed (he claimed), even when you knew it didn't. (He used reasoning similar to Anselm's to prove that the "Greatest Conceivable Island" exists, when it clearly doesn't, but you could substitute the Greatest Conceivable *anything*.) What Gaunilo did not do, however, is explain just how or *why* the argument fails, and indeed Anselm responded by arguing that the style of reasoning only worked when applied to God alone.

Two centuries later Aquinas also objected that the argument cannot prove that God "actually exists, unless it be admitted that there actually exists something than which nothing greater can be [conceived]; and this precisely is not admitted by those who hold that God does not exist."[2] Aquinas charges that the ontological argument begs the question, in other words, by assuming the very point it needs to prove. (See chapter 5 for *begging the question*.) The problem is that, to many, Aquinas's remark doesn't refute Anselm so much as simply dismiss him. Like Gaunilo, Aquinas insists that the argument must fail without explaining just where it goes wrong.

It wasn't until seven centuries after Anselm that Immanuel Kant (1724–1804), whose work we'll examine in chapter 9, finally figured out where Anselm's argument goes wrong. Or at least that's what many initially thought. Two centuries after Kant, Norman Malcolm (1911–1990) and Alvin Plantinga (b. 1932) resurrected the ontological argument over Kant's objections, as we'll see in chapter 10. While that debate is beyond our scope here, the main point is that Anselm's simple argument has been inspiring heated debate for almost a millennium now, with no sign of slowing down.

St. Thomas Aquinas's Cosmological Arguments

Aquinas (1225–1274) was born not far from Rome. At age nineteen he joined the Dominican Order of the Catholic Church, and eventually ended up at the University of Paris, where he assumed a prestigious chair of theology. While some of his voluminous writings were initially controversial due to his sympathies for Aristotle, they soon became essential Catholic readings, and he went on to be canonized in 1323.

That Aquinas was no more convinced by Anselm's argument than was Gaunilo brings out an important philosophical point. If you are a theist, it doesn't follow that you must accept every argument for theism. The philosopher proceeds by making and evaluating arguments. You may well accept a certain proposition, but that doesn't mean that every argument supporting that proposition is a good argument. You won't find a more committed theist than Aquinas, of course, but since he is also a philosopher, he will evaluate the arguments as he sees them. Indeed you can still be a theist yet believe that *every* argument for theism fails, as we'll see below. In that case you will simply hold that theism is not or cannot be grounded in rational argument.

As it turns out, however, Aquinas does think that some arguments for theism succeed, just not Anselm's. What's necessary (he holds) is a very different kind of argument than Anselm's. You can't prove God exists merely by thinking about the idea or definition of God, but you can perhaps prove God exists in roughly the manner we prove other things exist: on the basis of evidence. The basic idea of *cosmological arguments* for the existence of God is simple. Certain features of the cosmos, of the world we inhabit, can only be adequately explained if God exists. Those features of the world are therefore evidence of God's existence. As Aquinas puts it, "[F]rom every effect the existence of the cause can be clearly demonstrated, and so we can demonstrate the existence of God from His effects."[3]

Which features of the world does Aquinas have in mind? Aquinas famously argues that the existence of God can be proved "five ways," namely by five features: motion, causation, possibility/necessity, the "gradation" in things, and the governance or "design" of the world. Without these features, he thinks, we would have no way of knowing of God's existence, since it is not something we can know of directly: we have no direct insight, or intuition, or vision of God, and can in no direct way grasp God's essence or nature. (That's partly why he thinks that Anselm's ontological argument cannot succeed.) Rather, we can infer God's existence only from those features of the world that God created that point to Him.

While each of the five arguments has its own points of interest, we'll sketch just the first as a paradigm example of a cosmological argument.

Aquinas's "First Way" concerns change in general, and motion in particular. Wherever we look in our world, we observe things in motion. How did it come to be so? We can account for any individual body's movement by observing what adjacent body set it in motion, say, by collision. But how about *that* body—what set *it* in motion? Some third body, presumably, again by collision. But then what set that third body in motion? Either we end up with an **infinite regress**—here, a never-ending sequence where each body is moved by a preceding body, forever—or there must be a **First Mover**, a being that can initiate motion on its own without itself being moved by a preceding being. Aquinas argues that there cannot be an infinite regress, so there must be a First Mover: "And this is what we all understand God to be."

There are two key questions here. First, why must the First Mover be *God*, as opposed to some other being such as (say) a body, or another mind, or even just a law of nature? Second, why must there be a First Mover at all? That is, why does Aquinas reject the possibility of the infinite regress of movers?

As for the first, recall (from chapter 2) that a similar issue confronted the early atomists. What made the tiny little atoms composing the world move about the way they do? Was someone moving them about, pushing them? No, the atomists said: atoms move because motion is simply natural to them.

So why isn't this answer sufficient for Aquinas? Because answering the question "Why does a thing move?" by saying "it's natural" amounts to merely saying "it just *does* move"— which is no real answer at all. Nor does this point apply only to the atomists. As long as you identify the First Mover with anything other than God, the only answer to the question why *it* moves will be, "it's natural." But what Aquinas seeks, as a philosopher, is *understanding*, to discover the extent to which phenomena are intelligible, make sense, can be explained. As soon as you say "it just does" you have given up the quest for understanding and simply stated a brute raw fact. You may have to do that eventually—who says that the infinite being who is God must create a world that is intelligible to us?—but you shouldn't do it prematurely.

The same quest for understanding is also what answers our second question, about why Aquinas rejects the infinite regress.

To illustrate, imagine a moving sequence of railroad cars tightly linked to each other, ending in a caboose, *c*. We ask ourselves, what explains the motion of the caboose? Well, it has no internal cause of motion, that is, it has no engine, so it cannot move itself. If it is moving, then it is only because it is being pulled by the car before it to which it is linked, *c-1*. But now we ask the same question: what explains the motion of *c-1*? (For if that motion is unexplained, then so is the motion of the caboose, which depends on that motion.) If *c-1* too lacks an engine, then it cannot move except insofar as it is pulled by the car before it, *c-2*. Now suppose for a moment this sequence went on to infinity, so each car moves only insofar as it is pulled by the car before it, to infinity. On this scenario, have we explained the motions of *c*, and *c-1*, and *c-2*, and so forth?

You might be tempted to say yes. After all, the motion of each car is sort of explained by the fact that it is linked to the moving car before it. But Aquinas suggests no. *For as long as each car in the infinite sequence lacks an engine*, he thinks, we simply cannot explain why the train *as a whole* is moving. An infinite sequence of cars could just as well be at rest as at motion. If it consists only of engineless cabooses, then it would be incapable of moving itself, despite its infinite length.

The conclusion is inescapable. If motion is to be explainable, there cannot be an infinite sequence of things each of which lacks an internal cause of motion, an "engine," or some feature which can generate motion. Somewhere—either at the head of the train, or perhaps even outside it altogether—there must exist a locomotive, a "First Mover," something which can move other things but which, as Aquinas puts it, "is moved by nothing else."

That's why Aquinas rejects the infinite regress. It would leave motion unexplained. But this also returns us to the first question, about why the First Mover must be God. For (as we noted) it must be something *different* in kind from the ordinary bodies we find around us. None of those bodies are self-explanatory. Any ordinary finite body in the world around us could just as easily not exist as exist, could just as easily not move as move. Ordinary bodies are therefore like that caboose, insofar as nothing about their intrinsic nature explains why they exist or move. So whatever it is that serves as the First Mover, it must something far greater than an ordinary body. That might not get us all the way to the monotheistic "God," but it's enough to suggest the First Mover must be different in nature from everything in the created universe.

If the motion in the world is to be intelligible, then, there must be a First Mover.

Some Reflection on Aquinas's Cosmological Argument

But why should we believe that *anything* in the world must be intelligible? (And if unintelligibility is okay, then the motion in the world proves nothing. It could just simply be the way things are, requiring no further explanation.)

This naturally becomes a very deep debate over the subsequent centuries. Philosophical theologians tend to support the idea that the world should be intelligible to us (see chapter 10 for this theme), but can you *argue* for the intelligibility? A rational God, you might suggest, does nothing arbitrarily, but always acts for reasons. A God who is good always seeks the best, and a God who is intelligent will know how to achieve the best; and so we might expect that the world He creates will reflect His aims, His methods, His reasons—and to say that, is to say we might expect the world to be intelligible, at least to some degree.

But then again, the preceding suggests that we might believe the world should be intelligible on the assumption that a rational God exists who has created it. But then the argument that the world is intelligible already *assumes* the existence of God, and cannot therefore be used in a proof for God's existence without committing the fallacy, again, of begging the question. In short, Aquinas's argument proves God exists only if you assume that motion is intelligible, but you would probably believe that only if you already believe in the existence of God. Thus you must assume the existence of God in order to prove the existence of God!

Even worse, the defense of the world's intelligibility assumed that God is rational. But who says God must be rational, particularly in ways we could understand? As we'll see below, such a claim may ultimately lead to the atheist's most aggressive charge, namely the "problem of evil." If you assume that God must be rational, good, intelligent, and so on, then any evidence that the world does *not* reflect those virtues becomes evidence that God does not exist. One glance at the evil and suffering that permeates the long history of the world might well provide that evidence. If God must be rational, then our inability to understand why evil exists becomes an argument that God does not exist.

You shouldn't conclude from these concerns, however, that Aquinas's argument must immediately be rejected. Rather, as we saw with utilitarianism in the previous chapter, these concerns are challenges to be met, issues to be responded to, in the next steps in the conversation. And indeed that is how philosophical theists go on to respond: by exploring more deeply the nature of intelligibility and our reasons for believing the world to be intelligible, by exploring the degree to which God (and His actions) may (or need not) be intelligible after all, and so on.

William Paley's Biological Teleological Argument

We now move up five centuries to the next classic argument for theism. Of course plenty happened in the long interval between Aquinas and William Paley (1743–1805), including much discussion of Anselm's ontological argument, a new cosmological argument from René Descartes (1596–1650), and sophisticated analyses of God's attributes from great medieval philosophers such as John Duns Scotus (1270–1308), William of Ockham (c.1287–1347), and Francisco Suárez (1548–1617). But given our limited space, plus the fact that Paley's work is echoed in contemporary discussions of "intelligent design," he shall be our next stop.

Paley was an English clergyman and philosopher, educated at Cambridge University, who eventually became Archdeacon at Carlisle. He wrote several influential books, including *The Principles of Moral and Political Philosophy*, published in 1785. But for us his more important work is *Natural Theology; or, Evidences of the Existence and Attributes of the Deity*, published in 1802. **Natural theology**, as the subtitle suggests, is the study of nature as a guide to the existence and attributes of God, and the overall theme of his book was to show that God's design of creation could be seen in the general happiness or well-being that was evident in both the physical and social order. An important component of this project is captured in the argument for which he is most famous, his biological teleological argument with the "divine watchmaker" analogy at its heart.

WILLIAM PALEY

The strange word *teleological* is derived from the Greek word *telos*, which can be translated as order, purpose, goal, function, or design. The basic idea of a teleological argument is that the natural world displays certain kinds of order and regularity that couldn't be explained unless there were an intelligent being responsible for ordering it. Imagine you were to walk into a closet and find all the clothes neatly folded, hung, categorized, the shirts together, the skirts together, and so on. You would never think it got to be that way by random chance, but would instead conclude that some person had organized it. So, too, once you appreciate the order and regularity of the world as a whole you should conclude that there exists some intelligent being responsible for ordering it—who, since it's the whole world we're talking about, would be God. Since Paley focuses on the order displayed by living things, we'll call his a *biological* teleological argument. (In chapter 10, we'll explore a twenty-first-century teleological argument based in physics.)

Here's the basic idea.[4]

Suppose that you came upon a stone in some desolate place. Were you asked how it might have come to be there, you might answer that for all you knew it had simply always been there. But now suppose, instead, that you came upon a watch. You wouldn't in the slightest be tempted by the same answer, Paley thinks. Why not? Because the watch—being an extremely complex object, with many subtle parts all intricately coordinated toward serving a clear purpose—is obviously the product of some intelligent designer. It couldn't have "always been there." It must have had a maker or designer at some time and place.

But what if you had never seen such a thing made, or didn't fully understand how it worked, or if it had parts whose function you could not quite discover? The conclusion would not change, for there is adequate evidence of its being deliberately designed in those parts you do recognize. If anything, your admiration for its designer might only increase, for that designer would appear to have skills and intelligence that surpassed your own. And what if you now discovered that the watch had another remarkable property: the ability to produce another watch similar to itself? This discovery, too, would only increase your admiration for the designer, for the same reason. True, when asked "how did *this* watch come to be?" you might now answer that it came to be (at least most immediately) from whatever preceding watch may have produced it. But even so, and even if the preceding watch was in turn produced by an even earlier watch, you would know that that process could not go on forever. For each watch reflects evidence of intentional design, as does the sequence as a whole; so at some point the sequence must have been initiated by a maker or designer.

But all this also applies to the actual natural world.

For just one example, consider the human eye. It's an extremely complex organ, with many subtle parts all intricately coordinated toward serving its clear purpose, to provide sight. It is therefore impossible to study the eye—or the heart, or the lungs, or any organ of any organism—and not be moved toward the conclusion that it had an intelligent designer. Nor (as we saw) will it weaken that conclusion if we don't fully understand how the eye works or if there are parts whose functions we cannot discover; those should only *increase* our admiration for the designer. Indeed the more one studies biology the more complex and finely-tuned living things turn out to be and the more forcefully we are driven to the conclusion that they have been designed. And of course living things have the ability to reproduce, like the imaginary watch. That means that plants and animals are not merely exquisitely structured to survive and function but *also* have this additional remarkable capacity. Even more impressive evidence of their even more impressive designer!

Putting it all together, then, Paley's argument is based on an analogy. Given that a watch is an intricately ordered thing and that its order is imparted to it by the watchmaker, so too the intricately ordered eyeball, and ultimately organism, suggest the delicate hand of the cosmic designer. If the discovery of that watch would lead you to conclude it had a designer, then, our observations of the biological world should lead us to conclude that *it* too has a designer, namely, obviously, God.

Some Reflection on Paley's Biological Teleological Argument

There is much to intrigue in Paley's argument, to be sure. One point of particular contemporary interest in it is that while people today often think that science is in conflict with religion, Paley's view is that the more you study the science the more you will be moved to theism. So, too, he also seems to demand the intelligibility of the natural world as we saw in Aquinas. Were there to be an infinite regress of watches producing watches (or animals producing animals), something would remain unexplained, namely why that whole sequence exists at all, rather than not.

But while that demand tugs on the intellect, to many it spells the downfall of this particular argument. To see why we'll turn to Paley's contemporary, David Hume (1711–1776). Hume's epistemology and metaphysics we'll explore in chapter 9; for now we'll merely look at his critique of Paley in his *Dialogues concerning Natural Religion*, only published in 1779 after his death, due to its antagonistic attitude toward religion. The gist of Hume's critique is that Paley relies on an unreliable analogy (recall *false analogy* from chapter 5), but there are many other insights along the way.[5]

So, Hume observes, Paley's argument depends first of all on an analogy between the world as a whole and the human artifacts we know to be caused by designers. But in general we can only reason from effects back to their causes in this way when we have observational experience of the effects following from their causes. With artifacts we have often witnessed their production by human beings. But when the effect is (as in the case of the world) singular, individual, and without specific resemblance to any artifact, and where there is no possibility of observing the production process, we simply cannot reason backward to its cause.

This becomes clearer when we examine how little the world can really teach us, at least if we restrict ourselves to concluding nothing more about its cause than is strictly warranted by the effect itself. We ought to renounce (for example) the *infinity* of this alleged designer; for since the world is, as far as we can tell, finite in proportion and nature, we may not infer anything greater of its cause. Nor can we infer the designer's *perfection* or his freedom from mistakes. For even religious philosophers (in their defensive mode) admit that the world is riddled with *im*perfections. If they insist that the world's "order" demonstrates it has a designer then they must also admit that *its* imperfections demonstrate *his*.

Yet even supposing the world were perfect we still couldn't infer its designer's perfection, since for all we know he brought the world about very inefficiently, by trial and error, by creating a long series of universes all botched and bungled until he finally got it right. And how could we infer that there was just *one* designer? Complex structures designed and made by humans typically are brought about by whole teams of individuals. If religious philosophers insist on the analogy between the world and our artifacts then they ought to reason their way to polytheism, to the belief in *multiple* deities.

In fact we can't legitimately infer there is any designer at all. For all we know, the material world has for eons been undergoing randomly changing arrangements of its innumerable particles all on its own. Some of these arrangements appear "ordered" and others do not; and obviously that arrangement which includes ourselves must appear "ordered," since we could only exist on the supposition of order. But that hardly means this order was intentionally designed. It might just be the random product of a long but random series of variations. No designer necessary.

In short, Hume concludes, if you are to reach your theistic conclusions based on your observations of nature, then using the world as your premise means that in the end it will also be your conclusion. No amount of reasoning can legitimately take us to belief in anything beyond the world itself.

It's in Hume's latter points that the issue of intelligibility is raised. For what Hume is suggesting is something quite profound, namely that structures which *appear* to display order may in fact have arisen by random processes. So noted, Hume could grant the impressive apparent order of the eyeball—as Paley put it, the existence of many distinct parts, all fine-tuned toward achieving some end, such as "seeing"—while denying that the conclusion follows, the existence of an orderer.

In making this point, of course, Hume is anticipating philosophically the revolutionary empirical discovery made three-quarters of a century later. In 1859 Charles Darwin published *On the Origin of Species*, establishing his theory of evolution by natural selection. While the details get complex (particularly in the sophisticated science of today), the basic idea in Darwin is the same as Hume's. The appearance of biological order does not require an orderer, but might arise merely by random processes governed by natural selection. Or not merely "might" arise: Darwin argues (as do many twenty-first-century scientists) that a close study of biology gives strong evidence that this is in fact *how* the apparent order in biology arose.

With the great success of Darwin's theory, Paley's argument was largely thought to be refuted. But interestingly, philosophical history has a tendency to repeat itself. Kant's powerful refutation knocked down the ontological argument for a century or two, but then it got back up. So, too, with Paley's argument. In the twenty-first century, teleological arguments have enjoyed a serious renaissance. Some of this falls under the familiar label of **intelligent design**, a general umbrella term for movements that see the world as requiring an intelligent cause, and not merely as the product of undirected evolution. Much work has been done to reconcile Darwin's theory with God's design of the biological world. Other work suggests that Darwin's theory cannot explain certain aspects of biology, those involving "irreducible complexity." Interestingly, too, there's recent work arguing that the world as conceived by Darwin would be unintelligible in a way that the world as conceived by Paley is not, and therefore it's less rational to believe in it. And finally, as we noted, the teleological argument has been drafted in a form invoking the order displayed not in biology but in physics. The crucial difference is that, in doing so, the Darwinian objection cannot even get off the ground.

But we'll have a look at all this in chapter 10.

Immanuel Kant's Moral Argument

We'll examine the work of Kant (1724–1804) in more detail in chapter 9, so here we'll just look at his moral argument for theism, an argument based on considerations familiar from our discussion of his ethics in chapter 6. Or perhaps more precisely, it's not an argument that morality "proves" the existence of God so much as that morality obliges us to believe in it.[6]

Now moral agents, it seems clear, ought to promote the realization of the highest good. For surely we would not be acting rightly if we sought to bring about less than the highest good. But **ought implies can**, as philosophers like to say: one cannot say that someone "ought" to do a particular action unless that action is actually possible for him or her. For example, we would not say of you that you were morally obliged to end world hunger, for that isn't remotely possible for you. At most we might say you were obliged to make small steps in that direction, such as giving to charities.

But if we ought to promote the realization of the highest good and if ought implies can, it follows that it must be possible for us to promote the realization of the highest good.

But now the highest good has two components. The first is moral virtue, and this is entirely in our power. But the second is this, that the world would not in fact manifest the highest good unless its moral agents were also *happy*, and happy in strict proportion to their virtue. To be sure, it is not to become happy that we act morally. As we saw for Kant, morality is a matter of doing what is right for its own sake, not in order to promote our happiness. But imagine a world where the virtuous people suffered grossly and the evil people prospered! Clearly something would be wrong about such a world. Just as clearly, therefore, the highest good for the world would be one where one's happiness is proportional to one's virtue.

But we ourselves do not directly control most of what goes on in the world. We do not have power over the laws of nature, for example. There is therefore nothing in our power to ensure that happiness be distributed in proportion to virtue. And if we just look around it may seem very questionable that happiness in fact is so distributed. But for that even to be *possible*, to be something it is reasonable to hope for in the long run, it's clear we need to believe in a being who could bring it about: a being who obviously must be supremely good and powerful and in charge of the causal structure of the world.

For the highest good even to be possible, in short, God must exist. And it is possible: we are obliged to promote it as we saw, and could not be so obliged unless it were possible.

It follows that God exists.

Or at least we must believe it to be so. For we are obliged to aim for the highest good and we would be incapable of aiming for that unless we believed that it were possible. Putting it this way may not quite prove that God in fact exists. But it would make belief in God morally necessary for us: something we must believe as strongly as we believe in morality in the first place.

Some Reflection on Kant's Moral Argument

"If there is no God, then everything is permitted." This idea, famously expressed by a character in the novel *The Brothers Karamazov* by Fyodor Dostoevsky (1821–1881) and later echoed by existentialist Jean-Paul Sartre (1905–1980), in fact traces back a long way, at least to Plato's *Euthyphro* (as we saw), for it amounts to the idea that morality depends in some way on God. How to work out that "way" is no small task, as we also saw, and Kant's argument doesn't try. Instead it merely shows that our conceptions of morality and of God are closely connected, so that a rational person who believes in the existence of genuine morality—that there is a real, objective difference between good and bad—must also believe in the existence of God.

There's another way to express this idea, due to contemporary philosopher George Mavrodes (b. 1926). Suppose, for the moment, that the world was as some ancient atomists and some contemporary atheists believe it is: just a collection of physical particles zipping around. There is no God, there aren't even minds, there is just physical matter in its permutations and motions. In such a world it is hard to imagine there could exist any normative truths, truths about how things "ought" to be. There are just descriptive truths, about how things are: this particle moving this way, that particle moving that way. But if there are no normative truths, there are no moral truths. A purely material world would lack morality.

Suppose you now added minds to the mix. So there are physical particles, and some of them make up brains, and some of those brains have minds associated with them (either produced by the particles, or as a separate substance of some sort). Would this world display normative truths? True, we with minds might have feelings of moral obligations, and we may even argue that our self-interest dictates our morality (so we "ought" to act in ways that will make us happier, to echo Aristotle and the utilitarians). But feelings of obligation are not real obligations. Often enough we may be really morally obliged to act a certain way without feeling that we are. And self-interest cannot be equated with morality, for as Kant earlier argued, often we are morally obliged to act in ways that go against our self-interest. A world with only matter and our minds, in other words, cannot account for genuine morality.

If there is genuine morality, then, there must be more to the world than matter and our minds. Though details still need working out, it is only when you accept the existence of a God that you can begin to make sense of the idea that minds and persons have genuine value, and correspondingly are subject to genuine moral obligations.

But now again, as we saw with Aquinas and Paley, there is a pretty big "if" in play here: *if* there is genuine morality. . . . For most of the history of philosophy as we've seen it so far, the real existence of morality was not in question. From Aristotle through medieval Christian ethics to Kant, there was no doubt that there is a genuine, objective difference between good and bad, right and wrong. In fact it is roughly with Hume (whose work on ethics we did not look at) that the objectivity of ethics starts coming into question; and indeed the nineteenth-century utilitarians are perhaps well along the path of giving up that objectivity insofar as they ground ethics in terms of human happiness, a very subjective phenomenon. As we will see in chapter 10, in the twenty-first century the objectivity of ethics becomes front and center as philosophers turn their attention to *metaethics*.

Blaise Pascal's Prudential Argument

We now jump back a century to Blaise Pascal (1623–1662). This chronological disorder is hopefully compensated for by the improved logical order, for Pascal's argument is really quite different from the ones we have been looking at and belongs at the end. For Pascal's argument starts from the premise that, strictly speaking, proving God's existence is *not* possible.

That a theist might believe that God's existence is not provable is neither particularly shocking nor unprecedented. The early Christian thinker Boethius (480–524 C.E.) held, for example, that God's existence was the proper realm of faith and not of reason. Many theists rejected (with Aquinas) Anselm's ontological argument, feeling that God's existence can't be proved just by thinking about God. But even Aquinas's empirical arguments may not ultimately fare much better. Whatever exactly God is, He is not thought to be like any of the other things in our cosmos. He is neither finite nor physical, so we shouldn't expect to discover Him explicitly lurking somewhere, as we might discover a quark or an alien life form. Nor must we insist that God leave definitive traces of His existence within the cosmos. Given His infinite non-physical being, we may not even have a clear idea of what definitive traces should look like; and anyway God may have good reasons for not making His existence *too* obvious. Or maybe God doesn't even *need* reasons to do things. As an infinite being beyond our intellectual grasp, it may be inappropriate to insist that He behaves in ways that we can understand.

Or maybe our minds just aren't structured, cognitively, to prove that God exists, as Kant argues in some of his work. (That's why his moral argument connected our belief in God to belief in morality, rather than framed itself as a proof of God's existence.)

Or maybe we just aren't smart enough to prove God exists. After all, it took a long time before humanity produced an Einstein smart enough to figure out the two theories of relativity; maybe we just haven't produced anyone smart enough yet to offer a compelling proof of theism.

Enter Blaise Pascal. Born in Clermont, France, to a devout Catholic family, by age fifteen he had already composed works on geometry and physics that were admired by the learned world of his time. Then on November 23, 1654, at the age of thirty-one, he had a mystical experience that transformed him completely. He began to lead a life of austerity, almsgiving, and prayer. He spent his days reflecting on the Christian faith, and on the purpose of life. He jotted down his thoughts in short fragments that he hoped some day to publish in completed form. Death came, at age thirty-nine, before the book could be completed. What was left were hundreds of loosely grouped thoughts, aphorisms, and jottings on what it means

BLAISE PASCAL

to be a Christian, how to find God, and the secret of human happiness. These fragments were subsequently published in 1669 under the French title *Pensées* (Thoughts).

Pascal, too, felt that all attempts at rational proof of God's existence were doomed to fail. That's because they rely on reason, which is not ultimate. A much superior resource is faith, and our appeal should be directed to it. As he puts it, "Proofs only convince the mind"; they make "little impression" on the heart. Such proofs may establish the existence of "a God considered as great, powerful, and eternal," a cold philosophers' God, as it were, but they cannot establish the existence of "the God of Abraham, the God of Isaac, the God of Jacob," the personal God with whom one has a relationship. Pascal doesn't deny that the world reveals some evidence of God's presence. The evidence, however, is ambiguous, as there are traces of design and order but also of disorder, evil, and chaos. Whether the one (the order) or the other (the chaos) impresses itself on us depends on prior faith on our part. In short, the evidence is real enough, but it is sufficient to convince only those who approach it with a deep longing for God. For God can be grasped only by the heart. He is not present to those who don't already love Him.

There is deep psychological insight here. Objective proofs of God's existence (and against it), Pascal observes, are not compelling. What matters is the frame of the mind of the person reflecting on the arguments, not just the arguments themselves. So for a proper approach to God, one must consider the psychological angle.

Our wretchedness and misery, in fact, is largely our own fault: it comes from having turned away from God and sought our satisfaction in other things. But this is something we have done freely, and are free to undo. In fact, the ambiguity of all the physical evidence of God's existence makes sense. Were it otherwise, the evidence of His existence would overwhelm us and compel us to acknowledge Him. He withholds such evidence, for we must come to Him freely on our own accord.

It is in this context that Pascal offers his prudential argument. It is not an argument that God exists, for no such argument can succeed, but rather that it is rational to believe in God's existence, in the sense of wise, or prudent. The idea is that once people realize it is prudent to believe in God, they will begin taking the necessary psychological steps for doing so, by living a "godly life," a morally better life, joining a church, studying scripture. Belief in God cannot come directly from proof, but it can eventually come from living a life conducive to believing.

So what is his prudential argument? Pascal sketches it as a wager, now known as **Pascal's wager**. Though you cannot *know* whether God exists, you still must make a choice about how to live, either a godly life or a godless one. As a rational person seeking your best interest, which way should you bet, so to speak?

Suppose you choose the godly life. Now, either God exists or He does not. If God does exist, then you hit the jackpot: infinite reward in heaven. But if He does not, what have you suffered? You've lost some time perhaps, and guided your life by a false belief (that God exists). That is a loss, but a small one, and immediately balanced by the fact that you've still ended up living a pretty good life, of faith, kindness, and community. And surely a rational person would risk a small loss, itself balanced by good benefits, in order to obtain an infinite reward?

Now suppose you choose the godless life. You avoid church, you are mean and selfish and do bad things. If God does not exist, then you may perhaps gain a few things, maybe some money, free time on Sundays, and the like, though of course these also come at the risk of social ostracism, jail, and so on. But if God does exist, then you *lose* big: infinite damnation.

Pascal's Wager

	God exists	**God does not exist**
Choose godly life	Infinite payoff	Minor loss, if that
Choose godless life	Infinite penalty	Minor gain, if that

by Andrew Pessin

And surely no rational person would risk an infinite loss for the sake of a small possible gain, particularly when that gain itself comes with its own risks?

Put these together and the choice is clear. The rational person seeking his or her best interest should choose the godly life. For that choice risks a very small loss (if it even is a loss) for the sake of an infinite gain, while the opposite choice risks an infinite loss for the sake of a very small gain (if it even is a gain).

Pascal understands that you cannot force belief. Nor can you simply choose what to believe. Belief in God is ultimately a matter of feeling, of the heart, and as one of his most famous aphorisms puts it, "The heart has its reasons which reason itself does not know" (*Pensées* #680). What you can do is simply realize it is more rational for you to choose the godly life, and then let belief in God follow.

Some Reflection on Pascal's Prudential Argument

One take-home point from Pascal is this, that a philosophical theist need not support *any* particular proofs of God's existence, for perhaps they all fail. But there may yet be other reasons to believe God exists, prudential reasons, distinct from any proofs *for* His existence.

The deeper point is his insight about the psychology of belief. From Socrates onward most philosophers have held that beliefs—at least about philosophical matters—were in the domain of reason. To say that, is to say that reason, or reasoning, can produce belief, and thus the goal of philosophizing, of reasoning carefully, was to produce true beliefs. To be sure, the religious philosophers dominating the medieval period understood that some or many religious beliefs might be holdable only on faith, not on reason; but even there the point was usually that these beliefs were in some sense *beyond* reason, not that reason was incapable of producing belief. What Pascal is suggesting is that reason may be less powerful than we thought, that in some matters it may not be capable of producing belief after all.

[I]n some ninety-nine percent of cases the religion which an individual professes . . . depends upon the accidents of birth. Someone born to Buddhist parents in Thailand is very likely to be a Buddhist, someone born to Muslim parents in Saudi Arabia to be a Muslim, someone born to Christian parents in Mexico to be a Christian, and so on.

—**John Hick** (1922–2012), *An Interpretation of Religion*

The still deeper point from Pascal is that the very objectivity of knowledge may be called into question. Two people can look at the same argument and one finds it compelling while the other finds it sterile. Or they can look at the same events in the world and one sees them as evidence for God's existence while the other does not. What explains these different responses? Their differing personalities, dispositions, upbringings, and so forth. If you already *feel* that God exists, then arguments for God's existence may well seem more persuasive to you; if you don't, then not. If you were brought up in a religious environment then you are more likely to see God's handiwork everywhere; if not, then not. But then it seems that what people believe is more a matter of who they are and where they come from, and less a matter of reasoning and evidence.

And while Pascal's focus is on religious belief, there's a real question about how far his insight extends. Today many philosophers now believe that objective knowledge is not even possible in fields such as science, that our standards for reasoning and evidence are culture-sensitive, affected by psychological and sociological factors. What we are convinced by is, again, less a matter of objective evidence and more a matter of who we are. So while Pascal may have limited his wager to convincing people it is wiser to choose a godly life, the insights motivating his approach have potentially wide-ranging implications.

GOD'S NATURE

We now turn to the second component of philosophical theology, the attempt to clarify God's nature, to identify and explain the properties or attributes God is thought to have. This task is essential for any philosophical theist *or* atheist. You can't meaningfully affirm or reject the existence of God without saying something about what you take God to *be*.

So what attributes does God have? Most people quickly name at least three: power, knowledge, and goodness. But the God of Western monotheism doesn't merely have *some* power, knowledge, and goodness; rather, something like *infinite* power, *infinite* knowledge, and *infinite* or *perfect goodness*. While we shall focus on these because they are the most widely known, philosophers actually assign many other attributes to God as well. God is thought to be (among others) **omnipresent** (everywhere), **eternal** (timeless), **immutable** (incapable of changing), **impassible** (incapable of feeling pain or emotion), **incorporeal** (non-physical), **impeccable** (incapable of sin), **simple** (not composed of parts), and so on.

God's Power

The fancy word here is **omnipotent**, which might be most immediately defined as "all-powerful." The Western God is surely thought to be omnipotent. The only question is what exactly that means. "All-powerful," as well as "infinitely powerful," turn out to be less illuminating than you might think.

To see why, we can do no better than return to Aquinas. God is "all-powerful," Aquinas observes, but there seem to be some things He actually cannot do. Since He is also perfectly good, that suggests that He cannot sin. Nor can He change the past, since it no longer exists and thus is not available for Him to exert causal power over. And finally there is the puzzle best exemplified by this famous paradoxical question. Could God create a stone so heavy He could not lift it? There seem to be only two possible answers, either yes or no. If no, then there is something God cannot do: create that stone. But if yes, then there could be something God cannot do: lift that stone. So either way, there could be things God cannot do. But then does this not show that God is not in fact "all-powerful"?

To answer, Aquinas notes, we must clarify what it means to be omnipotent. It is this, that an omnipotent being can do all things that are possible to do. But which things are these? Things that are **logically possible**, namely things that do not involve any logical contradictions.

To illustrate, consider the idea of a "married bachelor." This phrase in fact involves a contradiction: since a "bachelor" is an unmarried man, a "married bachelor" would be a man who is both married and unmarried, which of course makes no sense. In fact, *no* contradictory expressions make any sense. Someone who asked you to produce a married bachelor, or a round square, or who told you to simultaneously speak and not speak, would be speaking nonsense.

But if contradictory expressions are nonsense, they are meaningless. If someone demands that you produce a married bachelor, they are literally demanding nothing. They may as well be grunting meaninglessly at you. It therefore makes no sense to imagine a being having the ability to *produce* contradictory things, for that is not even a meaningful ability to have. So for a being to be "all-powerful," to be able to do all possible things, it need not be able to do contradictory things.

And that is the solution.

No, Aquinas observes, God cannot sin. But to be able to sin is to be limited in one's power to do as one morally should do—and it would be a contradiction for a being unlimited in power to be limited in power in this way. So the omnipotent God, whose omnipotence does not require His ability to do contradictory things, need not be able to sin. Similar considerations apply to changing the past. To be able to change the past is to be able to make some past event both have occurred and not have occurred, which is a contradiction. So God cannot do it, but omnipotence does not require being able to do it.

And finally, similarly, for the stone. A stone so heavy that a being who could lift all stones could not lift it would be both unliftable by Him (because so heavy) and liftable by Him (because He can lift all possible stones). But that is a contradiction, so God could not create that stone any more than He could create a married bachelor. But that is no limit on His power, because married bachelors, and such stones, are literally meaningless. He cannot produce them, but not because His power—to do all logically possible things—is limited, but because these are not, in themselves, logically possible things to do.

So there's some clarification. To say God is omnipotent is to say, according to Aquinas, that He can bring about everything that is logically possible.

Not surprisingly, some philosophical theists (from Aquinas's time to this very day) are dissatisfied with Aquinas's answer. Some argue that restricting God's power to the logically possible *does* amount to limiting it, that an omnipotent God should be able to produce contradictory things. Those debates quickly get into some deep metaphysical issues, beyond the scope of our present discussion.

God's Knowledge

Here the fancy word is **omniscient**, which might be defined as "all-knowing" or "possessing infinite knowledge." But again, just what these mean is not fully clear. There is much to explore here, but we'll examine just one aspect of the issue, the famous problem of reconciling God's foreknowledge with our free will.

What is the problem? If God is all-knowing, then His knowledge must include infallible **foreknowledge**, that is, perfect knowledge of the future. But if God infallibly knows the future, then He knows in advance everything that will happen, including our own actions. He knows with perfect certainty (for example) that next Friday morning at 9:37 a.m. you will step into your closet and choose your blue shirt. But if He knows this with perfect certainty, this action is inevitable, or unavoidable. You are not able *not* to do this. And if you are not able not to do it, if you cannot help but do it, then you do not do it freely. Since this reasoning generalizes to all your actions, then you never act freely.

God's foreknowledge thus rules out our acting freely.

Or you could put the problem in reverse. Suppose we *do* act freely. Suppose next Friday at 9:36 a.m. it is completely open, completely undetermined, what you will do next, whether you will choose the blue shirt, or yellow shirt, or no shirt at all. If so, the argument goes, then not even God can know what will happen. If it is completely undetermined what will happen, then there is nothing for Him *to* know. There is no future there to be known. So our being able to act freely, then, rules out God's having foreknowledge.

So which is it—is God omniscient (and thus possessed of foreknowledge), or are we able to act freely?

It won't surprise you to learn that there is a long history of discussion of this issue. It traces as far back as Aristotle (4th century B.C.E.), it became a major topic of discussion from St. Augustine (4th century C.E.) onward, the medieval period was filled with arguments on the subject, and the debate continues to this day, having produced more different positions on the issue than you would imagine possible. Must a philosophical theist hold that God is omniscient? Must omniscience include foreknowledge? Does foreknowledge require that the future be predetermined in this way? Does the future being predetermined truly rule out our free action? Must a philosophical theist hold that human beings are capable of free action? Just what exactly does it mean to say we act freely? And so on. Here, for the sake of illustration, we'll simply sketch Augustine's response to the problem, but know that it is just one of many possible moves available to the philosophical theist.

ST. AUGUSTINE

Augustine was responding to the problem as it had been posed by the pre-Christian Roman orator Cicero (106–43 B.C.E.). Cicero observed that if God knows the future, then everything that occurs must necessarily occur; and events occur necessarily only if they are *caused* to occur by preceding events, which *make* them occur. So if God knows all future events, then all future events have preceding causes, which in turn have preceding causes; and so (reversing direction) there will be a causal chain leading from original creation all the way through every event to the end of time. But if, then, everything we do we are caused to do by earlier events, leading all the way back to creation, then we never have any choice about what we do. Our actions are ultimately caused by a long series of events that is entirely out of our control. In short, if God has foreknowledge, then there exists a causal chain; and if there is a causal chain, then we do not act freely. By the valid argument form of *hypothetical syllogism* (see chapter 4): if God has foreknowledge, then we do not act freely. Cicero then argues that our freedom is more important than God's foreknowledge, so he keeps the former and rejects the latter.

But giving up God's foreknowledge is not an option for Augustine. His Christian faith demands it. But neither is giving up our freedom, for that is equally important from a

Christian perspective. So he must find some way to reconcile God's foreknowledge with our freedom.

Interestingly, he begins by granting the first part of Cicero's argument. If God has foreknowledge, then there is indeed a long causal chain stretching back to creation that determines everything that will happen. But what Augustine denies is that even this predetermination of our actions takes away our freedom.

To understand why, he explains, we must understand what free action *is*. Cicero's worry is that if our actions are caused by earlier events then they are not truly in our control, but what does it mean for something to be "in our control"? Something is in our control if it will occur if we want or will it to, and won't occur if we don't. The only time something is *not* in our control is if it would occur whether we want or will it to occur or not. So, dying is not in your control: you will die, whether you want to or not. That you plummet to the ground after falling from a cliff is not in your control, because gravity ensures you will fall whether you want to or not.

But most of our actions are not like this. Most of what you do, you do because you want to, and wouldn't do if you didn't want to. Suppose you choose that blue shirt next Friday morning. Why did you choose that blue shirt? Because at the moment of choosing that's the shirt you wanted to wear. Had you wanted to wear a different shirt, or no shirt at all, you would not have chosen the blue shirt. So your choosing that shirt was in your control after all. You chose it because you wanted to. And if it was in your control, then you chose it freely.

What about the fact that the choice was "determined"? That there was a causal chain of events that produced the choice? It doesn't matter, Augustine responds. What matters for freedom is whether your actions flow from your will, from your own wants and desires. If they do, then they are free, otherwise not. It simply does not matter where your wants and desires themselves come from, or if they are determined or caused.

The position sketched here is known as **compatibilism**, and holds that our acting freely is compatible with our actions being causally predetermined. Whether or not this account of free action is satisfactory continues to be discussed to this day. But here we merely note how, if it is satisfactory, it solves the problem. God can be omniscient, and know the future; yet even if knowing the future means there is a causal chain predetermining all our actions, we can still act freely anyway.

God's Goodness, and the Problem of Evil

We now come to what many see as *the* problem for theism. Indeed it may also serve as the primary argument specifically for atheism. Usually atheists don't argue *for* atheism so much as *against* theism, critiquing what theists say. But here they go on the offensive, and try actively to *disprove* God's existence. It's also where they are most successful. Many people have given up their belief in God due to the problem of evil.

The issues can get complex, but they can also be presented simply. Just what, exactly, can a theist say about the occurrence of evil things like pain, suffering, injustice, and death? In particular when these occur on large scales, or to innocent people (such as children), or for no apparent reason? Although there are many ways to frame the problem, one is as a challenge to God's goodness. How exactly can God be good, or *infinitely* good, if He produces or permits such terrible things? And since God's goodness is supposed to be one of His essential or defining attributes, then if the existence of these terrible things refutes His goodness, doesn't that amount to disproving His existence altogether?

While the problem, so stated, is intuitive, it's useful to spell it out in more detail, since that will help clarify the different ways that theists might respond to it. Overall, the problem might be presented as an argument the atheist might make:

If God exists with His attributes, then there should exist no evil.
There does exist evil.

Therefore, God does not exist.

The existence of evil, then, seems to refute the existence of God. Since this argument is of the form *modus tollens* (see chapter 4), it is a valid argument. The question is only whether it is sound, whether the premises are true. For most philosophers, the controversial premise is the first one. Why should the existence of God entail that there exists no evil?

To see why, we need a supporting argument:

God is omnipotent
Therefore, God can do all possible things
God is omniscient
Therefore, God knows everything occurring or about to occur
God is perfectly good
Therefore, God is benevolent, and wants there to be no evil

Therefore, there exists (or should exist) no evil

So we start from some of the key attributes of God, and argue that, if God exists and has these attributes, then there should be no evil. Going in reverse: if God is perfectly good then He is benevolent (literally "wishes well"), so He wants there to be no evil. But if He is omniscient He knows about every possible evil that may be about to occur, and if He is omnipotent He is capable of preventing it. Put all three together, and He should be able to create a world that has no evil in it. So if He exists with those attributes, there should be no evil. But if there is evil, it must be because He lacks one or more of those attributes. But a God lacking one of these would not be *the* Western monotheist God. That would amount to God not existing.

That is **the problem of evil**. It is a very old problem. It dates back at least to the earliest Biblical times, and probably all the way back to roughly one second after the first human being had the idea of the monotheist God in the first place.

So how might the philosophical theist respond?

Well, first of all, she might not be able to. Just as we saw earlier that rationally proving God's existence may not be within our capacity, it's not unreasonable to believe that ultimately God's reasons and actions are also beyond our capacity to grasp. We may simply not be able to understand why God inflicts or permits the evils He does. So the existence of evils does not absolutely disprove God's existence, although if you take this route, you are admitting the limits of your rationality here. Your belief in God would be less a philosophical position and more a matter of faith.

But you shouldn't give up right away, because many strategies have been developed over the centuries that theists have been thinking about this problem. To develop a response to the problem of evil is to construct a **theodicy**. The word *theodicy* was coined by the seventeenth century philosopher G. W. Leibniz, from two Greek words—*theos* and *dike*—meaning "God" and "justice." Leibniz imagined bringing God to justice for all the evils in the world, putting Him on trial and demanding He justify His actions. Thus, a theodicy is an attempt to defend the goodness of God given all the evils, and there are ultimately many versions to consider.

Nor must you restrict yourself to just one, for different theodicies may apply to different scenarios. It is common, for example, for philosophers to distinguish between different *kinds* of evils. **Natural evils** are the terrible things that nature inflicts, without the direct involvement of human beings: earthquakes, floods, epidemics. **Moral evils** are the terrible things that human beings inflict upon each other: stealing, assaulting, murdering. It may well turn out that the theodicy you find plausible for one kind of evil does not work for the other, or vice versa.

On the surface we can see why. Natural evils seem directly attributable to God, for it is presumably He who directly causes the earthquakes and floods, He who creates the tsunamis and mudslides that kill thousands, including children. So here we might ask how it is possible for the perfectly good God to directly do evil, terrible things to people. Moral evils, on the other hand, are directly attributable to human beings. Here the question is not how it's possible for God to do these, but how or why God *permits* these to be done. Both His doing and His permitting evil are problems for the theist, but they may be different problems, requiring different solutions.

So, then, what are some theodicies?

One kind disputes the second premise of the original argument, that evil even exists. (If there is no evil, then there is no problem of evil!) While that is a pretty hard claim to accept, it's not without precedent. We saw in chapter 3, for example, Plato's view that the world of the Forms, perceived via the intellect, was genuine reality, while the world as it appears to us via our senses is a kind of shadowy illusion. Well, many of the evils we suffer are pains we receive through our senses. If those pains are in any way not real, then we have no problem.

A bit more plausible might be this view, expressed in different forms by Augustine (as we'll see below) and the medieval Jewish thinker Maimonides (1135–1204).

At least a lot of what we think is "evil," they suggest, really isn't, but we only think it is

MAIMONIDES

by wrongly taking a self-centered view of the world. If something happens against our personal desires or interests we condemn it as evil, as if our desires or interests were all that mattered. You might be reasonably smart, good-looking, and rich, but you could always be more so, and others in fact *are*. No fair, you feel, that you've got the shorter end of the stick! But of course, your being less smart or good-looking than someone else is not a *genuine* evil. *You* might not like it, but the world overall just might be better off with things as they are; or at least,

Maimonides suggests, the world is not made *worse* just because some beings enjoy less goodness than others, but rather more beautiful by the great variety of beings it contains.

Still, this form of theodicy has never enjoyed broad support. There may be an important psychological insight in Maimonides's point, but at best it works only in a small number of cases. An innocent person getting murdered, and a baby born with a painful terminal disease, are suffering genuine evils that cannot be analyzed away as resulting from their self-centeredness. And the Platonic approach seems even less satisfying. Even if we are only suffering from a kind of illusion of evil, isn't that illusion *itself* rather evil? Even a horrible nightmare is no less frightening, and thereby painful, simply because it isn't actually true.

A far more widely accepted strategy is the **greater goods theodicy**. The idea is simple, that the reason God either produces or permits evils is that, in doing so, He is able to bring about some even greater good. A surgeon (for example) would rightly inflict the pain of amputation on a patient in order to save his life. This strategy works as a response to the supporting argument above by clarifying its third main premise, that God is perfectly good. God *is* perfectly good, it insists, and therefore benevolent. But it is false (it now asserts) to claim that a benevolent being "wants there to be no evil." Rather, a benevolent being wants there to be no *unnecessary* evil, or wants there to be no evil *all else being equal*; or, perhaps, a benevolent being wants to obtain the best overall outcome. If a certain evil is required in order to bring about some greater good, then the benevolent being, seeking the greater good, would permit the evil.

And while there are many forms this kind of theodicy could take, depending on which greater goods you believe God obtains by means of various evils, two points apply to all.

First, the evil in question must be *necessary* in order to bring about the greater good. The greater good must be obtainable in no other way than by that evil. For if God could obtain the greater good without allowing the evil, His benevolence would require him to. (If the surgeon could save the life without amputating the limb, he would not be acting benevolently by amputating the limb anyway.)

Second, the good in question must genuinely outweigh the evil that is required for it. God would not be justified in permitting some terrible events just to bring about some small good, any more than the surgeon would be justified in amputating the limb just so you could get out of going to a boring class the next morning.

With those remarks in mind, let's look at three versions of the greater goods theodicy.

Freedom

Many philosophical theists are attracted to this version, which traces back at least as far as Augustine. (Keep Augustine's compatibilist doctrine of human freedom in mind below.) As usual, the basic idea is simple even if the implications may not be. Human beings' having free will, our being able to act freely, is a great good; and it is in order to allow the great good of our free will that God permits all the evils that we do. Free will, in short, is the greater good for the sake of which it is necessary to permit our evils. This strategy is limited to moral evils, as it says nothing about natural evils; but if it should work at least for moral evils, that would be a great start.

For Augustine the strategy has certain advantages. If we leave aside the problem of natural evils for now, it allows Augustine to solve another problem. Augustine holds both that God, in being *perfectly* good, in having *zero* evil within Him, can create only good things, *and* that God in fact creates *everything*. But if God creates only good things and God creates everything, shouldn't there only exist good things? Not necessarily. For one of the good things God creates is the human free will. That will, in being free, can and does sometimes perform evil actions. But these evil actions are not further things in the world. Rather, they are misuses of the good thing which is free will.

But wait, you might object, isn't the evil we perform genuine evil? Doesn't that mean that we are producing something real, in which case God does not create *everything* after all?

Augustine does some heavy metaphysical lifting in his response, which in effect joins the freedom defense with the earlier "deny the reality of evil" defense. Evil, Augustine holds, is not a thing that positively exists in its own right. Rather, it is an absence, a nothingness, a *privation* as the philosophers say. It is like the hole in your donut, which is not another part of the donut, or another kind of donut, but simply where *there is no donut*. So, too, evil is not something that God (or anyone) actively creates. It is where God leaves off creating.

To continue the analogy, suppose God created the human will as a sort of donut. Every part of the will that has actual existence is good because God creates nothing that is not good. The will itself is a good thing. But God could leave gaps in the will, so to speak, allowing the will to determine its own behavior, in ways that either comport with God's wishes or not. The human will doesn't produce anything, it merely behaves certain ways. Should it misbehave, behave in bad ways, it is performing evilly but not creating evil. In this way the free human will is the source of (and has responsibility for) various kinds of evils without challenging the fact that God creates only the good.

It should be noted here that Augustine also believes that the human will cannot act in any truly good ways apart from the grace of God. This is an implication of the Augustinian doctrine of *original sin*. Given that humanity is in a fallen state from the time of Adam and Eve, the human will cannot but act badly because it is corrupt from the outset, an inheritance from the human condition. On its own, without God's positive input in the form of grace, it will always choose to pursue evil pleasures rather than act in accordance with God's wishes. Since God (in these instances) is not participating in the evil actions, the responsibility for them lies completely with the agent. But when an agent does behave rightly, does act in good ways, it is only because he is acting under and because of the grace of God. So evil behavior, misbehaving, is what you get when God is not directly involved, while good behavior is what you get when He is.

So at least with respect to moral evils, they are due entirely to human beings, and to our enjoying (but misusing) our freedom of will. God could of course eliminate those evil actions by eliminating our free will. But that would be to throw the baby out with the bathwater, as per the greater goods strategy, since the goodness of human freedom significantly outweighs the evils we perform with that freedom—or so Augustine thinks.

Various versions of the freedom theodicy became the dominant approach to the problem of evil from the medieval Catholic Church through the contemporary Catholic and Protestant versions of the faith. But it has not been without its detractors. One of those was the philosopher and theologian Friedrich Schleiermacher (1768–1834). On Schleiermacher's view, the freedom theodicy does not take seriously the argument presenting the problem. For him, that God is omnipotent and perfectly good does entail that He would create flawlessly. Thus, He would not create entities that possess "holes," which misbehave and bring about all those evils. For him, then, there are only two options to explain the existence of evil: either creation went wrong on its own, or the real responsibility for evil belongs to God. But the former implies that the world is somehow out of God's control, and thus challenges God's omnipotence, while the latter challenges God's goodness. If God with His foreknowledge created beings with "holes" who could produce evil, then He is personally responsible for the evil He foreknew they would do. We should hardly call Him *good* or *benevolent* when He is fully responsible for the evil outcomes. So, Schleiermacher concludes with our argument above, given the existence of evil (whatever the metaphysics of evil may be), then God cannot simultaneously be omnipotent, omniscient, and perfectly good.

There is plenty more to think about here, as well. Is freedom so valuable that it outweighs the evil people commit with it? In particular is the sort of compatibilist freedom that Augustine endorses really so valuable? And is it truly necessary for God to permit these evils in order to allow our free will?

But let's move on to our next greater goods theodicy.

Soul-Making

This strategy is due to the early Christian theologian Irenaeus (130–202 C.E.), called a **soul-making theodicy**.

A famous saying from the philosopher Friedrich Nietzsche (1844–1900)—borrowed in recent songs from Kelly Clarkson and Kanye West—is this: "What does not kill me makes me stronger."[7] It reflects a central aspect of the Irenaean theodicy, namely that God is constantly reworking and improving the human beings He created. Though we were initially created "in the image of God," as the book of *Genesis* says, that initial state was not the final stage of our development. The human soul is still unrefined. It must be cultivated until we come more closely and fully to resemble God, and manifest Godliness. Suffering and "evil" are not somehow blemishes on creation but rather essential tools God uses to perfect human souls.

In order to develop a properly moral character, Irenaeus holds, a person must be able to freely develop, to freely move toward God. If this is so, then freedom is a necessary feature of creation, as in our previous theodicy. But now in order to have the opportunity to behave morally, a person must also have the opportunity to behave in the opposite fashion. Thus, not only is freedom necessary, but so too is what we perceive as evil.

But then we require a different view of the nature of creation itself. When God creates and calls that creation *good*, in *Genesis*, God cannot mean that it is good in the sense of absence of evil, suffering, or pain. Instead, it is created for a *good purpose*. That purpose, the creation of mature and moral souls, is such that it requires a diverse and potentially painful world. However, the purpose is good, and that good purpose puts into context any of the suffering necessary for the refining of the soul.

In short, the greater good is the production of a mature, moral soul, and evils and suffering are necessary means for that production. We could not become true moral agents, and develop serious moral character, unless we endure obstacles, suffering, and challenges, that is, "evil." The good of our becoming true moral agents outweighs the evil necessary for it.

Now the soul-making strategy has some advantages over the freedom approach. For one, it applies to natural evils as well as moral evils, for both evils may serve to build souls. It also fits with the intuition, just expressed, that developing moral character requires experiencing suffering and setbacks. But whether it succeeds as a philosophical theodicy is another question.

Recall the two points we made about greater goods theodicies in general. The evils must be necessary in order to bring about the greater good, and the good must genuinely outweigh the evil. Is it absolutely necessary to suffer in order to obtain a good character? It doesn't seem so. At least some people seem to be born of sturdy moral stock, and if it's possible to have character without suffering, then suffering seems superfluous. Moreover, is having a good moral character so good that it outweighs the evils, the many terrible evils? Perhaps in some cases, where the process is successful, but often it isn't. Many people suffer from afflictions and, rather than become stronger or better, are crushed or destroyed by them. Consider the thousands, including children, who perish from earthquakes, floods, and starvation. What then? And given the requirement of freedom shared with the earlier theodicy, might not individuals be given some choice in the matter: would you like an easy, pain-free life without moral character, or would you like to suffer great harms in order to have the opportunity to acquire character? Some, or many, may prefer the former.

Again, theodicies are not mutually exclusive. You can choose a combination of them. Perhaps the freedom strategy works in some cases, perhaps the soul-making strategy works in some others. That would be a start. The problem is that neither seems able to cover enough cases. Both seem restricted to a nearly impossible task: take every single, individual instance of evil and try to determine what greater good comes from that particular evil. To avoid this task, the next strategy has a much wider vision.

The Best Possible World

Although this strategy was first really developed by Nicolas Malebranche (1638–1715), it is most widely associated with G. W. Leibniz. Indeed the famously sharp-tongued writer Voltaire (1694–1778), in his satirical novel *Candide*, notoriously lampooned Leibniz for holding the view. (To be fair to Leibniz, however, Voltaire does not do the view justice.)

An important point before we start, that applies to theodicies in general, is this. Theodicies are always defensive in nature. They are not trying to prove that God exists. Rather, they are merely undermining the atheist's proof that He does not. This makes their job a little easier. You don't have to show precisely how any given evil is outweighed by a specific greater good, for example, you merely have to show that the given evil does not absolutely disprove the possibility of some greater good. The two previous theodicies were limited because they weren't plausible: by focusing on specific particular evils it often doesn't seem likely that a specific greater good comes from them. By widening his scope, Leibniz avoids this problem.

For what should be evaluated, he holds, is not some individual event or action. Instead it is the world *as a whole*. And by "world" we mean "history of the world," from beginning to end, from its creation to however it ends (if it does). Leibniz observes that what we should expect the omnipotent, omniscient, and perfectly good God to create

> The optimist says this is the best of all possible worlds. The pessimist agrees.
>
> —Joke

is, of course, the best overall possible world, the best overall world that could be created, the best overall sequence of events from beginning to end. Of course we cannot prove directly that the world we live in is the best possible world. At minimum we don't know enough about it. We don't know what happened in most of history, we don't know most of what's happening on the globe at this moment, and we surely have no idea what will happen in the future.

But for a theodicy, playing defense, we don't have to. All we need to show is that no one can prove that this *isn't* the best possible world.

All the evils we observe may provide reasonable ground for skepticism. In fact it may seem easy to convince ourselves that this is not the best possible world. Just take some small evil, and imagine the world has gone the way it has except that this evil didn't occur. This morning you stubbed your toe. Wouldn't a world exactly like our actual world up to that moment, but where you didn't stub your toe, be a slightly better world, free of one tiny little unnecessary pain? Or, upping the scale, couldn't one or more of the wars that devastated the twentieth century have been avoided, sparing all the unnecessary suffering, and thus producing an overall better world? As long as some better overall world is possible, the skeptic maintains, then this actual world is not the best possible.

But don't be misled by those simple thought experiments, Leibniz warns. For once you factor in two key points, those thought experiments become less persuasive. First, there is our now familiar point about greater goods. Sometimes evils are necessary means in order to obtain greater goods. Then there is his second point. In his metaphysics (as we'll see in chapter 8), the world displays a fixed causal order, much as in Cicero and Augustine. Every event that occurs is caused to occur by an earlier event, in turn caused by an earlier event; thus every event is causally predetermined, and, most importantly, the sequence of events in the world stands or falls *as a whole.*

What this means, then, is that you cannot imagine the world being exactly the same as it was up to a certain moment and then being different otherwise. Given the causal order and causal laws, if a certain event occurs then the next predetermined event must necessarily occur. You cannot have the first event without the second event. But then the skeptic's thought experiments must fail. You cannot imagine the world being exactly the same up to the point where you stubbed your toe, but then you don't stub your toe. But then your sense that you could easily imagine a better possible world than our world is misleading, for the world you just imagined *is not a possible world.* If there is to be a better possible world, it would have to be an entirely different world, all the way from beginning to end.

And not only is it much harder to imagine such a world, Leibniz suggests, but we couldn't even have any confidence that such a world would be better, overall, than ours. Why not? Because of the first point, that sometimes evils are necessary for greater goods. For all we know, the evils we witness in our actual world are necessary for some greater goods. Those greater goods don't have to be immediate, and they don't have to apply to the individuals suffering the evils. For all we know, the great evil suffered by the children who perished in the Holocaust will lay the ground for some series of wonderful events five hundred or a thousand years for now. Or perhaps it will somehow lay the ground for the eventual redemption of all creation. Here is where Leibniz avoids the problems of the earlier theodicies: you don't have to reward the specific evil suffered by an individual with a specific greater good for that individual. The reward may be much further down the line, and apply to the world as a whole.

For all we know . . . Of course we cannot directly prove (as we said) that this is the best overall possible world, that some overall greater good *will* occur for which the current evils are necessary. But again, we don't have to, for neither can the atheist prove that this *isn't* the best possible world. For the sheer existence of evils cannot prove this isn't the best possible world as long as it is *possible* that these evils may produce some overall greater good somewhere down the line. And as long as it cannot be proven that this isn't the best possible world, then the existence of evils cannot disprove the existence of God.

Leibniz's **best possible world theodicy** is rightly influential, and no doubt succeeds in some sense. He is surely correct that we cannot *prove* this is not the best possible world. And indeed it may provide consolation for some: if you have independent reasons to believe that God exists—perhaps one of the earlier arguments for God's existence persuades you—then you can be confident that God has, indeed, created the best possible world, despite all appearances to the contrary. But then again, this may be cold consolation for others. The degree to which God has concern for the world overall may be the degree to which God is not concerned for the individual. Perhaps the world as a whole gets redeemed down the line for the evils of the Holocaust, but that doesn't exactly benefit the people who perished.

SUMMARY

1. Philosophical theology consists of philosophical attempts to clarify the nature and interpret the existence of God.

2. Medieval philosophers did sophisticated work in philosophical theology, especially in synthesizing Aristotle's ideas with Western monotheism.

3. Proofs of God's existence fall into several categories: ontological arguments, cosmological arguments, teleological (or design) arguments, moral arguments, and prudential arguments.

4. Anselm's ontological argument proceeds by reflection on the very definition of God. Thomas Aquinas's five cosmological arguments relied on the evidence presented by various features of the world, such as motion. William Paley's biological teleological argument invoked the analogy between intelligently designed artifacts (such as watches) and the world as a whole. David Hume anticipated Darwin's critique of Paley, that the apparent order or design could arise via random processes. Immanuel Kant connected morality to God, arguing that our belief in the existence of objective morality requires us to believe in the existence of God. Finally Blaise Pascal claimed that reason was incapable of proving God's existence, but that in light of that uncertainty, it was more rational (or prudent) to live a godly life than not.

5. With respect to God's nature, Western monotheism construes God as omnipotent, but what that means exactly needs some work. According to Aquinas, omnipotence is the ability to do everything that is logically possible.

6. Western monotheism construes God as omniscient, but again, what that means needs some work. In particular, omniscience seems to include foreknowledge, but foreknowledge seems to preclude human freedom. Augustine reconciled the two by adopting a compatibilist account of freedom, but many other options are available here.

7. The problem of evil is a major problem for theists, and perhaps the main argument for atheism. The existence of natural and moral evils challenges God's goodness, or at least seems to suggest that God lacks one of his defining attributes, which amounts to denying God's existence. Various theodicies have been developed. You might deny the reality of genuine evil, showing how much of what we judge to be evil is really just something we don't like or want. More widely supported are greater goods theodicies, which justify God's doing or permitting evils by seeing them as necessary means to obtain greater goods. Candidate greater goods include human freedom, the development of moral character, and the bringing about of the best possible world.

KEY TERMS

atheism

best possible world theodicy

compatibilism

cosmological arguments

eternal

ex nihilo

First Mover

foreknowledge

greater goods theodicy

immutable

impassible

impeccable

incorporeal

infinite regress

intelligent design

Law of Non-Contradiction

logically possible

monotheism

moral arguments for theism

moral evils

natural evils

natural theology

omnipotent

omnipresent

omniscient

ontological arguments

ought implies can

Pascal's wager

philosophical theology

polytheism

the problem of evil

prudential arguments

simple

soul-making theodicy

teleological (or design) arguments

theism

theodicy

REVIEW QUESTIONS

1. Name, and briefly describe, any three kinds of arguments for theism.

2. In what way(s) did Hume's critique of Paley's argument anticipate Darwin?

3. In what sense is Pascal's argument not directly an argument that God exists?

4. According to Aquinas, why can't God create a married bachelor? Why doesn't this inability take away God's omnipotence?

5. In what way does Cicero think that God's foreknowledge would take away our free will? How does Augustine respond?

6. Name, and briefly describe, any two kinds or versions of theodicy.

NOTES

1. This section is loosely based on material in Andrew Pessin, *The God Question: What Famous Thinkers from Plato to Dawkins Have Said about the Divine* (New York: Oneworld, 2009).

2. *Summa Theologica*, I.Q2 (www.newadvent.org/summa/1002.htm).

3. *Summa Theologica*, I.Q2 (www.newadvent.org/summa/1002.htm).

4. The following summary is excerpted from Andrew Pessin, *The God Question: What Famous Thinkers from Plato to Dawkins Have Said about the Divine* (New York: Oneworld, 2009), ch. 50.

5. The following summary is excerpted from Andrew Pessin, *The God Question: What Famous Thinkers from Plato to Dawkins Have Said about the Divine* (New York: Oneworld, 2009), ch. 51.

6. The following summary is excerpted from Andrew Pessin, *The God Question: What Famous Thinkers from Plato to Dawkins Have Said about the Divine* (New York: Oneworld, 2009), ch. 54.

7. Nietzsche, "Maxims and Arrows," in *Twilight of the Idols*, transl. R. J. Hollingdale (Harmondsworth: Penguin, 1968), 8.

■ Reading
"That God Truly Exists"

ANSELM

From Proslogion, *Chapter 2. Transl., ed., Thomas Williams,* Anselm: Monologion and Proslogion *(Indianapolis: Hackett, 1995).*

This excerpt contains the text of Anselm's classic ontological argument.

Therefore, Lord, you who grant understanding to faith, grant that, insofar as you know it is useful for me, I may understand that you exist as we believe you exist, and that you are what we believe you to be. Now we believe that you are something than which nothing greater can be thought. So can it be that no such nature exists, since "The fool has said in his heart, 'There is no God'" (Psalm 14:1; 53:1)? But when this same fool he hears me say "something than which nothing greater can be thought," he surely understands what he hears; and what he understands exists in his understanding, even if he does not understand that it exists [in reality]. For it is one thing for an object to exist in the understanding and quite another to understand that the object exists [in reality]. When a painter, for example, thinks out in advance what he is going to paint, he has it in his understanding, but he does not yet understand that it exists, since he has not yet painted it. But once he has painted it, he both has it in his understanding and understands that it exists because he has now painted it. So even the fool must admit that something than which nothing greater can be thought exists at least in his understanding, since he understands this when he hears it, and whatever is understood exists in the understanding. And surely that than which a greater cannot be thought cannot exist only in the understanding. For if it exists only in the understanding, it can be thought to exist in reality as well, which is greater. So if that than which a greater cannot be thought exists only in the understanding, then that than which a greater *cannot* be thought is that than which a greater *can* be thought. But that is clearly impossible. Therefore, there is no doubt that something than which a greater cannot be thought exists both in the understanding and in reality.

REVIEW AND DISCUSSION QUESTIONS

1. In what way does Anselm's argument rely on the Law of Non-Contradiction?
2. Gaunilo claimed that the same style of argument could show that any arbitrary thing exists (which means something must be wrong with the argument). Use the same style of argument to prove that "an island than which none greater can be thought" exists.

■ Reading

Natural Theology

WILLIAM PALEY

From Natural Theology; or, Evidences of the Existence and Attributes of the Deity;
Chapters 1, 2, and 5 (1802).

> In this excerpt Paley sketches his now classic biological teleological argument for
> theism.

CHAPTER ONE

In crossing a heath, suppose I pitched my foot against a *stone* and were asked how the stone came to be there, I might possibly answer that for anything I knew to the contrary it had lain there forever; nor would it, perhaps, be very easy to show the absurdity of this answer. But suppose I had found a *watch* upon the ground, and it should be inquired how the watch happened to be in that place, I should hardly think of the answer which I had before given, that for anything I knew the watch might have always been there. Yet why should not this answer serve for the watch as well as for the stone? Why is it not as admissible in the second case as in the first? For this reason, and for no other, namely, that when we come to inspect the watch, we perceive—what we could not discover in the stone—that its several parts are framed and put together for a purpose, e.g., that they are so formed and adjusted as to produce motion, and that motion so regulated as to point out the hour of the day; that if the different parts had been differently shaped from what they are, of a different size from what they are, or placed after any other manner or in any other order than that in which they are placed, either no motion at all would have been carried on in the machine, or none which would have answered the use that is now served by it. To reckon up a few of the plainest of these parts and of their offices, all tending to one result; we see a cylindrical box containing a coiled elastic spring, which, by its endeavor to relax itself, turns round the box. We next observe a flexible chain—artificially wrought for the sake of flexure—communicating the action of the spring from the box to the fusee. We then find a series of wheels, the teeth of which catch in and apply to each other, conducting the motion from the fusee to the balance and from the balance to the pointer, and at the same time, by the size and shape of those wheels, so regulating that motion as to terminate in causing an index, by an equable and measured progression, to pass over a given space in a given time. We take notice that the wheels are made of brass, in order to keep them from rust; the springs of steel, no other metal being so elastic; that over the face of the watch there is placed a glass, a material employed in no other part of the work, but in the room of which, if there had been any other than a transparent substance, the hour could not be seen without opening the case. This mechanism being observed—it requires indeed an examination of the instrument, and perhaps some previous knowledge of the subject, to perceive and understand it; but being once, as we have said, observed and understood—the inference we think is inevitable, that the watch must have had a maker—that there must have existed, at some time and at some place or other, an artificer or artificers who formed it for the purpose which we find it actually to answer, who comprehended its construction and designed its use.

I. Nor would it, I apprehend, weaken the conclusion, that we had never seen a watch made—that we had never known an artist capable of making one—that we were altogether incapable of executing such a piece of workmanship ourselves, or of understanding in what manner it was performed; all this being no more than what is true of some exquisite remains of ancient art, of some lost arts, and, to the generality of mankind, of the more curious productions of modern manufacture. Does one man in a million know how oval frames are turned? Ignorance of this kind exalts our opinion of the unseen and unknown artist's skiff, if he be unseen and unknown, but raises no doubt in our minds of the existence and agency of such an artist, at some former time and in some place or other. Nor can I perceive that it varies at all the inference, whether the question arise concerning a human agent or concerning an agent of a different species, or an agent possessing in some respects a different nature.

II. Neither, secondly, would it invalidate our conclusion, that the watch sometimes went wrong or that it seldom went exactly right. The purpose of the machinery, the design, and the designer might be evident, and in the case supposed, would be evident, in whatever way we accounted for the irregularity of the movement, or whether we could account for it or not. It is not necessary that a machine be perfect in order to show with what design it was made: still less necessary, where the only question is whether it were made with any design at all.

III. Nor, thirdly, would it bring any uncertainty into the argument, if there were a few parts of the watch, concerning which we could not discover or had not yet discovered in what manner they conduced to the general effect; or even some parts, concerning which we could not ascertain whether they conduced to that effect in any manner whatever. For, as to the first branch of the case, if by the loss, or disorder, or decay of the parts in question, the movement of the watch were found in fact to be stopped, or disturbed, or retarded, no doubt would remain in our minds as to the utility or intention of these parts, although we should be unable to investigate the manner according to which, or the connection by which, the ultimate effect depended upon their action or assistance; and the more complex is the machine, the more likely is this obscurity to arise. Then, as to the second thing supposed, namely, that there were parts which might be spared without prejudice to the movement of the watch, and that we had proved this by experiment, these superfluous parts, even if we were completely assured that they were such, would not vacate the reasoning which we had instituted concerning other parts. The indication of contrivance remained, with respect to them, nearly as it was before.

IV. Nor, fourthly, would any man in his senses think the existence of the watch with its various machinery accounted for, by being told that it was one out of possible combinations of material forms; that whatever he had found in the place where he found the watch, must have contained some internal configuration or other; and that this configuration might be the structure now exhibited, namely, of the works of a watch, as well as a different structure. . . .

VII. And not less surprised to be informed that the watch in his hand was nothing more than the result of the laws of *metallic* nature. It is a perversion of language to assign any law as the efficient, operative cause of any thing. A law presupposes an agent, for it is only the mode according to which an agent proceeds: it implies a power, for it is the order according to which that power acts. Without this agent, without this power, which are both distinct from itself, the *law* does nothing, is nothing. The expression, "the law of metallic nature," may sound strange and harsh to a philosophic ear; but it seems quite as justifiable as some others which are more familiar to him, such as "the law of vegetable nature," "the law of animal nature," or, indeed, as "the law of nature" in general, when assigned as the cause of phenomena, in exclusion of agency and power, or when it is substituted into the place of these.

VIII. Neither, lastly, would our observer be driven out of his conclusion or from his confidence in its truth by being told that he knew nothing at all about the matter. He knows enough for his argument; he knows the utility of the end; he knows the subserviency and adaptation of the means to the end. These points being known, his ignorance of other points, his doubts concerning other points affect not the certainty of his reasoning. The consciousness of knowing little need not beget a distrust of that which he does know.

CHAPTER TWO

Suppose, in the next place, that the person who found the watch should after some time discover that, in addition to all the properties which he had hitherto observed in it, it possessed the unexpected property of producing in the course of its movement another watch like itself—the thing is conceivable; that it contained within it a mechanism, a system of parts—a mold, for instance, or a complex adjustment of lathes, baffles, and other tools—evidently and separately calculated for this purpose; let us inquire what effect ought such a discovery to have upon his former conclusion.

I. The first effect would be to increase his admiration of the contrivance, and his conviction of the consummate skill of the contriver. Whether he regarded the object of the contrivance, the distinct apparatus, the intricate, yet in many parts intelligible mechanism by which it was carried on, he would perceive in this new observation nothing but an additional reason for doing what he had already done—for referring the construction of the watch to design and to supreme art. If that construction *without* this property, or, which is the same thing, before this property had been noticed, proved intention and art to have been employed about it, still more strong would the proof appear when he came to the knowledge of this further property, the crown and perfection of all the rest.

II. He would reflect, that though the watch before him were *in some sense* the maker of the watch which was fabricated in the course of its movements, yet it was in a very different sense from that in which a carpenter, for instance, is the maker of a chair—the author of its contrivance, the cause of the relation of its parts to their use. With respect to these, the first watch was no cause at all to the second; in no such sense as this was it the author of the constitution and order, either of the arts which the new watch contained, or of the parts by the aid and instrumentality of which it was produced. We might possibly say, but with great latitude of expression, that a stream of water ground corn; but no latitude of expression would allow us to say, no stretch of conjecture could lead us to think that the stream of water built the mill, though it were too ancient for us to know who the builder was. What the stream of water does in the affair is neither more nor less than this: by the application of an unintelligent impulse to a mechanism previously arranged, arranged independently of it and arranged by intelligence, an effect is produced, namely, the corn is ground. But the effect results from the arrangement. The force of the stream cannot be said to be the cause or author of the effect, still less of the arrangement. Understanding and plan in the formation of the mill were not the less necessary for any share which the water has in grinding the corn; yet is this share the same as that which the watch would have contributed to the production of the new watch, upon the supposition assumed in the last section. Therefore,

III. Though it be now no longer probable that the individual watch which our observer had found was made immediately by the hand of an artificer, yet does not this alteration in anyway affect the inference that an artificer had been originally employed and concerned in the production. The argument from design remains as it was. Marks of design and contrivance are no more accounted for now than they were before. In the same thing, we may ask for the cause of different properties. We may ask for the cause of the color of a body, of its hardness, of its heat; and these causes may be all different. We are now asking for the cause of that subserviency to a use, that relation to an end, which we have remarked in the watch before us. No answer is given to this question by telling us that a preceding watch produced it. There cannot be design without a designer; contrivance without a contriver; order without choice; arrangement without anything capable of arranging; subserviency and relation to a purpose without that which could intend a purpose; means suitable to an end, and executing their office in accomplishing that end, without the end ever having been contemplated or the means accommodated to it. Arrangement, disposition of parts, subserviency of means to an end, relation of instruments to a use imply the presence of intelligence and mind. No one, therefore, can rationally believe that the insensible, inanimate watch, from which the watch before us issued, was the proper cause of the mechanism we so much admire in it—could be truly said to have constructed the instrument, disposed its parts, assigned their office, determined their order, action, and mutual dependency, combined their several motions into one result, and that also a result connected with the utilities of other beings. All these properties, therefore, are as much unaccounted for as they were before.

IV. Nor is anything gained by running the difficulty farther back, that is, by supposing the watch before us to have been produced from another watch, that from a former, and so on indefinitely. Our going back ever so far brings us no nearer to the least degree of satisfaction upon the subject. Contrivance is still unaccounted for. We still want a contriver. A designing mind is neither supplied by this supposition nor dispensed with. If the difficulty were diminished the farther we went back, by going back indefinitely we might exhaust it. And this is the only case to which this sort of reasoning applies. Where there is a tendency, or, as we increase the number of terms, a continual approach toward a limit, *there*, by supposing the number of terms to be what is called infinite, we may conceive the limit to be attained; but where there is no such tendency or approach, nothing is effected by lengthening the series. There is no difference as to the point in question, whatever there may be as to many points, between one series and another—between a series which is finite and a series which is infinite. A chain composed of an infinite number of links, can no more support itself, than a chain composed of a finite number of links. And of this we are assured, though we never *can* have tried the experiment; because, by increasing the number of links, from ten, for instance, to a hundred, from a hundred to a thousand, etc., we make not the smallest approach, we observe not the smallest tendency toward self support. There is no difference in this respect—yet there may be a great difference in several respects—between a chain of a greater or less length, between one chain and another, between one that is finite and one that is infinite. This very much resembles the case before us. The machine which we are inspecting demonstrates, by its construction, contrivance and design. Contrivance must have had a contriver, design a designer, whether the machine immediately proceeded from another machine or not. That circumstance alters not the case. That other machine may, in like manner, have proceeded from a former machine: nor does that alter the case; contrivance must have had a contriver. That former one from one preceding it: no alteration still; a contriver is still necessary. No tendency is perceived, no approach toward a diminution of this necessity. It is the same with any and every succession of these machines—a succession of ten, of a hundred, of a thousand; with one series, as with another—a series which is finite, as with a series which is infinite. In whatever other respects they may differ, in this they do not. In all equally, contrivance and design are unaccounted for.

The question is not simply, How came the first watch into existence?—which question, it may be pretended, is done away by supposing the series of watches thus produced from one another to have been infinite, and consequently to have had no such *first* for which it was necessary to provide a cause. This, perhaps, would have been nearly the state of the question, if nothing had been before us but an unorganized, unmechanized substance, without mark or indication of contrivance. It might be difficult to show that such substance could not have existed from eternity, either in succession—if it were possible, which I think it is not, for unorganized bodies to spring from one another—or by individual perpetuity. But that is not the question now. To suppose it to be so is to suppose that it made no difference whether he had found a watch or a stone. As it is, the metaphysics of that question have no place; for, in the watch which we are examining are seen contrivance, design, an end, a purpose, means for the end, adaptation to the purpose. And the question which irresistibly presses upon our thoughts is, whence this contrivance and design? The thing required is the intending mind, the adapting hand, the intelligence by which that hand was directed. This question, this demand is not shaken off by increasing a number or succession of substances destitute of these properties; nor the more, by increasing that number to infinity. If it be said that, upon the supposition of one watch being produced from another in the course of that other's movements and by means of the mechanism within it, we have a cause for the watch in my hand, namely, the watch from which it proceeded; I deny that for the design, the contrivance, the suitableness of means to an end, the adaptation of instruments to a use, all of which we discover in the watch, we have any cause whatever. It is in vain, therefore, to assign a series of such causes or to allege that a series may be carried back to infinity; for I do not admit that we have yet any cause at all for the phenomena, still less any series of causes either finite or infinite. Here is contrivance but no contriver; proofs of design, but no designer. . . .

The conclusion which the *first* examination of the watch, of its works, construction, and movement, suggested, was that it must have had, for cause and author of that construction, an artificer who understood its mechanism and designed its use. This conclusion is invincible. A *second* examination presents us with a new discovery. The watch is found, in the course of its movement, to produce another watch similar to itself; and not only so, but we perceive in it a system of organization separately calculated for that purpose. What effect would this discovery have or ought it to have upon our former inference? What, as has already been said, but to increase beyond measure our admiration of the skill which had been employed in the formation of such a machine? Or shall it, instead of this, all at once turn us round to an opposite conclusion, namely, that no art or skill whatever has been concerned in the business, although all other evidences of art and skill remain as they were, and this last and supreme piece of art be now added to the rest? Can this be maintained without absurdity? Yet this is atheism.

CHAPTER FIVE

Every observation which was made in our first chapter concerning the watch may be repeated with strict propriety concerning the eye, concerning animals, concerning plants, concerning, indeed, all the organized parts of the works of nature. As,

I. When we are inquiring simply after the *existence* of an intelligent Creator, imperfection, inaccuracy, liability to disorder, occasional irregularities may subsist in a considerable degree without inducing any doubt into the question; just as a watch may frequently go wrong, seldom perhaps exactly right, may be faulty in some parts, defective in some, without the smallest ground of suspicion from thence arising that it was not a watch, not made, or not made for the purpose ascribed to it. When faults are pointed out, and when a question is started concerning the skill of the artist or dexterity with which the work is executed, then, indeed, in order to defend these qualities from accusation, we must be able either to expose some intractableness and imperfection in the materials or point out some invincible difficulty in the execution, into which imperfection and difficulty the matter of complaint may be resolved; or, if we cannot do this, we must adduce such specimens of consummate art and contrivance proceeding from the same hand as may convince the inquirer of the existence, in the case before him, of impediments like those which we have mentioned, although, what from the nature of the case is very likely to happen, they be unknown and unperceived by him. This we must do in order to vindicate the artist's skill, or at least the perfection of it; as we must also judge of his intention and of the provisions employed in fulfilling that intention, not from an instance in which they fail but from the great plurality of instances in which they succeed. But, after all, these are different questions from the question of the artist's existence; or, which is the same, whether the thing before us be a work of art or not; and the questions ought always to be kept separate in the mind. So likewise it is in the works of nature. Irregularities and imperfections are of little or no weight in the consideration when that consideration relates simply to the existence of a Creator. When the argument respects His attributes, they are of weight; but are then to be taken in conjunction—the attention is not to rest upon them, but they are to be taken in conjunction with the unexceptionable evidence which we possess of skill, power, and benevolence displayed in other instances; which evidences may, in strength, number, and variety, be such and may so overpower apparent blemishes as to induce us, upon the most reasonable ground, to believe that these last ought to be referred to some cause, though we be ignorant of it, other than defect of knowledge or of benevolence in the author.

REVIEW AND DISCUSSION QUESTIONS

1. Although it's not included here, Paley makes an explicit analogy between a watch and biological organs such as eyeballs. Given what he says about the key properties of the watch, what would be the relevant analogous properties of an eyeball?

2. In what way(s) does Paley's argument already attempt to respond to anticipated objections that might be raised by Hume and Darwin?

3. In what way(s) does Paley's argument resemble Aquinas's cosmological argument about motion?

■ Reading
City of God
AUGUSTINE

From City of God, *Chapters 9 and 10 (5ᵗʰ century C.E.); transl., Marcus Dods, ed., Philip Schaff, Nicene and Post-Nicene Fathers, First Series, Vol. 2 (Buffalo, NY: Christian Literature Publishing Co., 1887). Revised and edited for New Advent by Kevin Knight, www.newadvent.org/ fathers/120105.htm. Reprinted with permission.*

In this excerpt, Augustine explains (against Cicero) why God's foreknowledge is not inconsistent with our having free will.

CHAPTER 9. CONCERNING THE FOREKNOWLEDGE OF GOD AND THE FREE WILL OF MAN, IN OPPOSITION TO THE DEFINITION OF CICERO.

The manner in which Cicero addresses himself to the task of refuting the Stoics, shows that he did not think he could effect anything against them in argument unless he had first demolished divination. And this he attempts to accomplish by denying that there is any knowledge of future things, and maintains with all his might that there is no such knowledge either in God or man, and that there is no prediction of events. Thus he both denies the foreknowledge of God, and attempts by vain arguments, and by opposing to himself certain oracles very easy to be refuted, to overthrow all prophecy, even such as is clearer than the light (though even these oracles are not refuted by him).

But, in refuting these conjectures of the mathematicians, his argument is triumphant, because truly these are such as destroy and refute themselves. Nevertheless, they are far more tolerable who assert the fatal influence of the stars than they who deny the foreknowledge of future events. For, to confess that God exists, and at the same time to deny that He has foreknowledge of future things, is the most manifest folly. This Cicero himself saw, and therefore attempted to assert the doctrine embodied in the words of Scripture, The fool has said in his heart, There is no God . . . [I]n his book on divination, he in his own person most openly opposes the doctrine of the prescience of future things. But all this he seems to do in order that he may not grant the doctrine of fate, and by so doing destroy free will. For he thinks that, the knowledge of future things being once conceded, fate follows as so necessary a consequence that it cannot be denied.

But, let these perplexing debatings and disputations of the philosophers go on as they may, we, in order that we may confess the most high and true God Himself, do confess His will, supreme power, and prescience. Neither let us be afraid lest, after all, we do not do by will that which we do by will, because He, whose foreknowledge is infallible, foreknew that we would do it. It was this which Cicero was afraid of, and therefore opposed foreknowledge. The Stoics also maintained that all things do not come to pass by necessity, although they contended that all things happen according to destiny. What is it, then, that Cicero feared in the prescience of future things? Doubtless it was this—that if all future things have been foreknown, they will happen in the order in which they have been foreknown; and if they come to pass in this order, there is a certain order of things foreknown by God; and if a certain order of things, then a certain order of causes, for nothing can happen which is not preceded by some efficient cause. But if there is a certain order of causes according to which everything happens which does happen, then by fate, says he, all things happen which do happen. But if this be so, then is there nothing in our own power, and there is no such thing as freedom of will; and if we grant that, says he, the whole economy of human life is subverted. In vain are laws enacted. In vain are reproaches, praises, chidings, exhortations had recourse to; and there is no justice whatever in the appointment of rewards for the good, and punishments for the wicked. And that consequences so disgraceful, and absurd, and pernicious to humanity may not follow, Cicero chooses to reject the foreknowledge of future things, and shuts up the religious mind to this alternative, to make choice between two things, either that something is in our own power, or that there is foreknowledge—both of which cannot be true; but if the one is affirmed, the other is thereby denied. He therefore, like a truly great and wise man, and one who consulted very much and very skillfully for the good of humanity, of those two chose the freedom of the will, to confirm which he denied the foreknowledge of future things; and thus, wishing to make men free he makes them sacrilegious. But the religious mind chooses both, confesses both, and maintains both by the faith of piety. But how so? Says Cicero; for the knowledge of future things being granted, there follows a chain of consequences which ends in this, that there can be nothing depending on our own free wills. And further, if there is anything depending on our wills, we must go backwards by the same steps of reasoning till we arrive at the conclusion that there is no foreknowledge of future things. For we go backwards through all the steps in the following order:—If there is free will, all things do not happen according to fate; if all things do not happen according to fate, there is not a certain order of causes; and if there is not a certain order of causes, neither is there a certain order of things foreknown by God—for things cannot come to pass except they are preceded by efficient causes,—but, if there is no fixed and certain order of causes foreknown by God, all things cannot be said to happen according as He foreknew that they would happen. And further, if it is not true that all things happen just as they have been foreknown by Him, there is not, says he, in God any foreknowledge of future events.

Now, against the sacrilegious and impious darings of reason, we assert both that God knows all things before they come to pass, and that we do by our free will whatsoever we know and feel to be done by us only because we will it. But that all things come to pass by fate, we do not say; nay we affirm that nothing comes to pass by fate; for we demonstrate that the name of fate, as it is wont to be used by those who speak of fate, meaning thereby the position of the stars at the time of each one's conception or birth, is an unmeaning word, for astrology itself is a delusion. But an order of causes in which the highest efficiency is attributed to the will of God, we neither deny nor do we designate it by the name of fate, unless, perhaps, we may understand fate to mean that which is spoken, deriving it from *fari*, to speak; for we cannot deny that it is written in the sacred Scriptures, God has spoken once; these two things have I heard, that power belongs unto God. Also unto You, O God, belongs mercy: for You will render unto every man according to his works. Now the expression, Once has He spoken, is to be understood as meaning immovably, that is, unchangeably has He spoken, inasmuch as He knows unchangeably all things which shall be, and all things which He will do. We might, then, use the word fate in the sense it bears when derived from *fari*, to speak, had it not already come to be understood in another sense, into which I am unwilling that the hearts of men should unconsciously slide. But it does not follow that, though there is for God a certain order of all causes, there must therefore be nothing depending on the free exercise of our own wills, for our wills themselves are included in that order of causes which is certain to God, and is embraced by His foreknowledge, for human wills are also causes of human actions; and He who foreknew all the causes of things would certainly among those causes not have been ignorant of our wills. For even that very concession which Cicero himself makes is enough to refute him in this argument. For what does it help him to say that nothing takes place without a cause, but that every cause is not fatal, there being a fortuitous cause, a natural cause, and a voluntary cause? It is sufficient that he confesses that whatever happens must be preceded by a cause. . . . [Voluntary causes] are referable either to God, or to angels, or to men . . . [and] are to be called wills. . . . [B]y the wills of men I mean the wills either of the good or of the wicked. And from this we conclude that there are no efficient causes of all things which come to pass unless voluntary causes, that is, such as belong to that nature which is the spirit of life. . . . In [God's] supreme will resides the power which acts on the wills of all created spirits, helping the good, judging the evil, controlling all, granting power to some, not granting it to others. For, as He is the creator of all natures, so also is He the bestower of all powers, not of all wills; for wicked wills are not from Him, being contrary to nature, which is from Him. . . . How, then, does an order of causes which is certain to the foreknowledge of God necessitate that there should be nothing which is dependent on our wills, when our wills themselves have a very important place in the order of causes? Cicero, then, contends with those who call this order of causes fatal, or rather designate this order itself by the name of fate; to which we have an abhorrence, especially on account of the word, which men have become accustomed to understand as meaning what is not true. But, whereas he denies that the order of all causes is most certain, and perfectly clear to the prescience of God, we detest his opinion more than the Stoics do. For he either denies that God exists . . . or if he confesses that He exists, but denies that He is prescient of future things, what is that but just the fool saying in his heart there is no God? For one who is not prescient of all future things is not God. Wherefore our wills also have just so much power as God willed and foreknew that they should have; and therefore whatever power they have, they have it within most certain limits; and whatever they are to do, they are most assuredly to do, for He whose foreknowledge is infallible foreknew that they would have the power to do it, and would do it. Wherefore, if I should choose to apply the name of fate to anything at all, I should rather say that fate belongs to the weaker of two parties, will to the stronger, who has the other in his power, than that the freedom of our will is excluded by that order of causes, which, by an unusual application of the word peculiar to themselves, the Stoics call Fate.

CHAPTER 10. WHETHER OUR WILLS ARE RULED BY NECESSITY.

Wherefore, neither is that necessity to be feared, for dread of which the Stoics labored to make such distinctions among the causes of things as should enable them to rescue certain things from the dominion of necessity, and to subject others to it. Among those things which they wished not to be subject to necessity they placed our wills, knowing that they would not be free if subjected to necessity. For if that is to be called our necessity which is not in our power, but even though we be unwilling effects what it can effect—as, for instance, the necessity of death—it is manifest that our wills by which we live up-rightly or wickedly are not under such a necessity; for we do many things which, if we were not willing, we should certainly not do. This is primarily true of the act of willing itself—for if we will, it is; if we will not, it is not—for we should not will if we were unwilling. But if we define necessity to be that according to which we say that it is necessary that anything be of such or such a nature, or be done in such and such a manner, I know not why we should have any dread of that necessity taking away the freedom of our will. For we do not put the life of God or the foreknowledge of God under necessity if we should say that it is necessary that God should live forever, and foreknow all things; as neither is His power diminished when we say that He cannot die or fall into error—for this is in such a way impossible to Him, that if it were possible for Him, He would be of less power. But assuredly He is rightly called omnipotent, though He can neither die nor fall into error. For He is called omnipotent on account of His doing what He wills, not on account of His suffering what He wills not; for if that should befall Him, He would by no means be omnipotent. Wherefore, He cannot do some things for the very reason that He is omnipotent. So also, when we say that it is necessary that, when we will, we will by free choice, in so saying we both affirm what is true beyond doubt, and do not still subject our wills thereby to a necessity which destroys liberty. Our wills, therefore, exist as wills, and do themselves whatever we do by willing, and which would not be done if we were unwilling. But when any one suffers anything, being unwilling by the will of another, even in that case will retains its essential validity, —we do not mean the will of the party who inflicts the suffering, for we resolve it into the power of God. For if a will should simply exist, but not be able to do what it wills, it would be overborne by a more powerful will. Nor would this be the case unless there had existed will, and that not the will of the other party, but the will of him who willed, but was not able to accomplish what he willed. Therefore, whatsoever a man suffers contrary to his own will, he ought not to attribute to the will of men, or of angels, or of any created spirit, but rather to His will who gives power to wills. It is not the case, therefore, that because God foreknew what would be in the power of our wills, there is for that reason nothing in the power of our wills. For he who foreknew this did not foreknow nothing. Moreover, if He who foreknew what would be in the power of our wills did not foreknow nothing, but something, assuredly, even though He did foreknow, there is something in the power of our wills. Therefore we are by no means compelled, either, retaining the prescience of God, to take away the freedom of the will, or, retaining the freedom of the will, to deny that He is prescient of future things, which is impious. But we embrace both. We faithfully and sincerely confess both. The former, that we may believe well; the latter, that we may live well. For he lives ill who does not believe well concerning God. Wherefore, be it far from us, in order to maintain our freedom, to deny the prescience of Him by whose help we are or shall be free. Consequently, it is not in vain that laws are enacted, and that reproaches, exhortations, praises, and vituperations are had recourse to; for these also He foreknew, and they are of great avail, even as great as He foreknew that they would be of. Prayers, also, are of avail to procure those things which He foreknew that He would grant to those who offered them; and with justice have rewards been appointed for good deeds, and punishments for sins. For a man does not therefore sin because God foreknew that he would sin. Nay, it cannot be doubted but that it is the man himself who sins when he does sin, because He, whose foreknowledge is infallible, foreknew not that fate, or fortune, or something else would sin, but that the man himself would sin, who, if he wills not, sins not. But if he shall not will to sin, even this did God foreknow.

REVIEW AND DISCUSSION QUESTIONS

1. What is Cicero's position on the question of whether God's foreknowledge is consistent with our having free will? What is Cicero's argument?

2. What is Augustine's compatibilist conception of human freedom, and how is it in play in his response to Cicero?

3. Augustine distinguishes between two senses of necessity. In what sense does he believe our wills are *not* ruled by necessity?

■ Reading
"Abridgement of the Argument Reduced to Syllogistic Form"
G. W. LEIBNIZ

"Abridgement of the Argument Reduced to Syllogistic Form" (1710). From Theodicy. *Transl., G. M. Duncan,* Gottfried Wilhelm Leibniz: Philosophical Works *(New Haven, 1890).*

In this excerpt Leibniz sketches the general idea of a greater goods theodicy, in particular the version invoking the best possible world.

First Objection. Whoever does not choose the best is lacking in power, or in knowledge, or in goodness. God did not choose the best in creating this world. Therefore, God has been lacking in power, or in knowledge, or in goodness.

Answer. I deny the minor, that is, the second premise of this syllogism [that God did not choose the best in creating this world].

Prosyllogism [the objector's defense of his objection]: Whoever makes things in which there is evil, which could have been made without any evil, or the making of which could have been omitted, does not choose the best. God has made a world in which there is evil, a world, I say, which could have been made without any evil, or the making of which could have been omitted altogether. Therefore, God has not chosen the best.

Answer. I grant the minor [premise] of this prosyllogism [that God made a world in which there is evil]. For it must be confessed that there is evil in this world which God has made, and that it was possible to make a world without evil, or even not to create a world at all, for its creation has depended on the free will of God; but I deny the major, that is, the first of the two premises of the prosyllogism, and I might content myself with simply demanding its proof; but in order to make the matter clearer, I have wished to justify this denial by showing that the best plan is not always that which seeks to avoid evil, since it may happen that *the evil is accompanied by a greater good.* For example, a general of an army will prefer a great victory with a slight wound to a condition without wound and without victory. We have proved this more fully in the large work by making it clear, by instances taken from mathematics and elsewhere, that an imperfection in the part may be required for a greater perfection in the whole. In this I have followed the opinion of St. Augustine, who has said a hundred times, that God has permitted evil in order to bring about good, that is, a greater good; and that of Thomas Aquinas . . . that the permitting of evil tends to the good of the universe. I have shown that the ancients called Adam's fall . . . a happy sin, because it had been retrieved with immense advantage by the incarnation of the Son of God, who has given to the universe something nobler than anything that ever would have been among creatures except for it. For the sake of a clearer understanding, I have added, following many good authors, that it was in accordance with order and the general good that God allowed to certain creatures the opportunity of exercising their liberty, even when he foresaw that they would turn to evil, but which he could so well rectify; because it was not fitting that, in order to hinder sin, God should always act in an extraordinary manner. To overthrow this objection, therefore, it is sufficient to show that a world with evil might be better than a world without evil; but I have gone even farther, in the work, and have even proved that this universe must be in reality better than every other possible universe.

REVIEW AND DISCUSSION QUESTION

1. In what way does this selection illustrate the idea raised in the main text that theodicies are "defensive" in nature?

I N CHAPTER 1 we distinguished the three main areas of philosophy. Ethics, we said, addresses normative questions about what sort of people we should be and how we should behave. Epistemology addresses questions of knowledge, about its nature and limits. And metaphysics, we said, addresses the ultimate nature of the world, asking about what sorts of things exist.

These areas, it turns out, may not be as separate from each other as these brief descriptions may imply.

In fact we already saw some connection between ethics and metaphysics, in the moral argument for God's existence in chapter 7. There it was claimed that *ought implies can*: if we *ought* to do some action (ethics), it follows that we *can* do it (metaphysics). In chapter 10 we shall explore a similarly close connection between ethics and epistemology. The basic problem will be how, exactly, we can come to *know* what is right or wrong. Our senses provide only descriptive information about what is occurring in our vicinity. But ethics is about the normative, about what *should* occur, how we *should* behave, and our senses are not equipped to tell us *that*. So where do our moral beliefs come from in the first place? Ethics requires some epistemology.

Finally there is the connection between metaphysics and epistemology. Again, we saw some of this in our discussion of philosophical theology in the previous chapter. Can God's existence (metaphysics) be proven, that is, known (epistemology)? Anselm's ontological argument claimed it could be known purely by reasoning about the idea of God; Aquinas's arguments claimed it could be known only by reasoning about features we perceive the cosmos to have; Pascal believed God's existence couldn't be proven at all. So their metaphysical conclusions were intimately entangled with their epistemological positions.

The close connection between metaphysics and epistemology in general is nowhere more evident than in the work of the great, systematic philosophers of the seventeenth and eighteenth centuries, the early modern philosophers. To this we now turn, in this chapter and the next.

BRIEF OVERVIEW OF EARLY MODERN PHILOSOPHY

A brief sketch of these two philosophical centuries may provide a useful framework for our next two chapters.

Early modern philosophy begins at the start of the seventeenth century with René Descartes (1596–1650). Often (and aptly) called "the father of modern philosophy," Descartes radically changed the nature and scope of philosophy. The five centuries before him, the medieval period, were dominated by the Christian Aristotelianism produced by Aquinas and his followers, who (you'll recall from chapter 7) had synthesized Aristotle's way of thinking about the world with Christian doctrine. In rather one fell swoop Descartes discarded the Aristotelianism, largely ignored the Christian element, and developed brand new theories of the nature of mind and of physical matter. These two metaphysical theories, generated by Descartes's new approach to epistemology, set the philosophical agenda for the next two centuries.

It is common to divide the early modern philosophers into two schools, characterized by their different emphases in epistemology: **rationalism** and **empiricism.** The word *rationalism* comes from the Latin *ratio*, for reason, while *empiricism* comes from the Greek *empeiria*, for experience, meaning primarily sensory experience. On a first pass through, roughly, empiricists hold sensory experience to be epistemologically fundamental: our ideas, beliefs, knowledge must derive from sensory experience and observation. Rationalists, to the contrary, hold reason to be fundamental: while the senses may provide useful raw material, it is only by reasoning that we can turn that material into genuine knowledge. Moreover, pure reasoning may itself be a source of knowledge, independent of sensory experience. Of the major early modern philosophers, the rationalists are Descartes, Nicolas Malebranche, Baruch Spinoza, and G. W. Leibniz, while the empiricists are John Locke, George Berkeley, and David Hume.

Concluding the early modern period is the great German thinker Immanuel Kant (1724–1804), who, instead of falling into one of the schools, is said to have *synthesized* them instead. Finding each school to have certain strengths yet subject to certain limits, Kant found a way to combine them while preserving the former and eliminating the latter. If rationalists stress reason and empiricists stress experience in epistemology, Kant carefully outlines precisely how each is necessary and each requires the other. But while this may sound simple in the abstract, it in fact involved its own serious revolution in philosophy, in turn setting the philosophical agenda for at least the next century after it.

With this in mind, let's turn, in this chapter, to rationalism, and begin with the first early modern rationalist, the father of modern philosophy.

RENÉ DESCARTES (1596–1650)

Descartes was born in 1596 in La Haye, a small town in France now called La Haye-Descartes, or simply Descartes. As a child he attended the Jesuit college of La Flèche, where he was drawn to mathematics, a field to which he was later to make important contributions. After completing his education he enlisted as a soldier in the just-beginning Thirty Years' War, eventually serving in both Protestant and Catholic armies. In November of 1619, wintering with his regiment in Germany, he had the profound contemplative experience that would result, years later, in the world's most famous philosophical slogan, "I think therefore I am." After some years in Paris establishing his reputation as a great mathematician, he moved to Holland in 1628, where he would spend two decades cementing an additional reputation as a **natural philosopher**, meaning *philosopher of nature* (today, *scientist*). Along the way, he became embroiled in many intellectual controversies, partly due to the fact that his philosophy was seen as antagonistic to many centuries' worth of Christian thought. In 1649 he was invited by Queen Christina of Sweden—though just twenty-two years old, she was the most powerful monarch in Europe, thanks to Sweden's victories in the just concluded Thirty Years' War—to become her personal tutor. What Her Highness didn't mention was that she wanted her lessons at five in the morning, in her unheated library. Soon after arriving in Stockholm, Descartes developed pneumonia and died, at fifty-four years of age.

Descartes wrote major works in many areas, including mathematics, various sciences (physics, optics, meteorology, physiology, etc.), and of course philosophy. But all of it, he thought, from the mathematics to his new metaphysical theories of mind and matter, was grounded in his epistemology. Our sketch below will be based primarily, then, on his two great works in epistemology, *Discourse on Method* (1637) and *Meditations on First Philosophy* (1641).

RENÉ DESCARTES

The latter begins with these famous words:

> Several years have now passed since I first realized how numerous were the false opinions that in my youth I had taken to be true, and thus how doubtful were all those that I had subsequently built upon them. And thus I realized that once in my life I had to raze everything to the ground and begin again from the original foundations, if I wanted to establish anything firm and lasting in the sciences. (*Meditation One*)[1]

In his quest for true knowledge, for knowledge that would be "firm and lasting," Descartes realized that he must start from scratch. We accumulate too many false beliefs and silly ideas from childhood, before we are able to evaluate them, and humankind as a whole has accumulated too many such things; and anyway, he observed, philosophers and theologians, the main epistemological authorities of the era, lacked any proper standards or methods, resulting in epistemological chaos and endless disputes about every little thing. It was necessary to discover firm methods and foundations, and the only way to do that was simply to start over.

As for firm epistemological methods, we have his *Discourse*, whose full title is *Discourse on the Method of Rightly Conducting the Reason, and Seeking Truth in the Sciences*. Descartes saw mathematics as a paradigm for knowledge, and thought that its success might transfer to other fields if they could only emulate its methods. What was therefore required was to abstract those rules responsible for its success and then apply them to philosophy and science.

Mathematics (Descartes saw) begins with simple and clear ideas whose truth the mind can apprehend directly and know with absolute certainty. It then advances step-by-step toward more complex truths, making sure that each step of the way is indisputable. The mind obtains those first truths by **intuition**, a cognitive faculty capable of producing intellectual understanding (or "visions") of such clarity that one has no doubt regarding the truth of what is apprehended. Subsequent truths are generated by deduction, or careful, clear, and certain inferences, the validity of each step of which is also apparent by intuition.

After making these observations, Descartes recorded the four main principles of his epistemological method:

> The first was never to accept anything for true for which I did not clearly know to be such . . . to comprise nothing more in my judgment than was presented to my mind so clearly and distinctly as to exclude all ground of doubt. The second, to divide each of the difficulties under examination into as many parts as possible, and as might be necessary for its adequate solution. The third, to conduct my thoughts in such order that by commencing with objects the simplest and easiest to know, I might ascend by little and little, and, as it were, step by step, to the knowledge of the more complex. . . . And the last, in every case to make enumerations so complete, and reviews so general, that I might be assured that nothing was omitted. (*Discourse on Method*, Part II)

But now if this was to be his epistemological method, what about his "foundations"? Could he find, in philosophy and science, simple, clear, and obvious truths on whose foundations, with his method, he might construct this new system of knowledge?

Enter his encounter with *radical skepticism*. A **skeptic** is one who challenges the possibility of obtaining certain kinds of knowledge; a **radical skeptic** is one who challenges the possibility of obtaining *any* knowledge. Descartes's *Meditation One* is one of the great expressions of radical skepticism in the history of philosophy. What he seeks are "firm foundations," propositions of whose truth he can be absolutely, completely certain. Which propositions might these be? *Indubitable* ones, that is, those which are literally impossible to doubt. And the way to find these, he suggests, is to try to call *everything* he believes into doubt. As long as there is the smallest possibility a given proposition might be false, however improbable that might be, he will reject it. If any propositions resist his attempt to call them into doubt, if any are indubitable—then he shall have found his foundations. Radical skepticism is the mechanism in the search for certainty.

Once he began to apply this method of doubt, he quickly saw how uncertain so much of what he had previously believed really was. Without much difficulty he could doubt authorities, doubt common sense, doubt the testimony of his senses and memory, and thus doubt all the sciences based on these sources of knowledge. Even something so initially compelling as his immediate sensory experience was questionable. While hardly anything could be clearer than "that I am sitting here next to the fire, wearing my winter dressing gown, that I am holding this sheet of paper in my hands," he writes,

> This would all be well and good, were I not a man who is accustomed to sleeping at night, and to experiencing in my dreams the very same things . . . How often does my evening slumber persuade me of such ordinary things as these: that I am here, clothed in my dressing gown, seated next to the fireplace—when in fact I am lying undressed in bed! . . . (*Meditation One*)

As there are "no definitive signs by which to distinguish being awake from being asleep," he realizes, then there is at any moment always the possibility that he is dreaming; and therefore always the possibility that his senses are completely deceiving him, about *everything*. Perhaps he does not even have a physical body, for he only knows of its existence by means of his senses. Perhaps there is no physical world at all, for he only knows of that world, too, by means of his senses. Perhaps even he . . .

That's when it hit him.

There *was* one thing he could not doubt: his own existence. True, the existence of his physical body was in doubt, but he could not doubt his own existence as a thinking thing, a mind. For him even to doubt his existence, he had to doubt; and since doubt is just a manner of thinking, in order to doubt it was necessary that he think. The very activity of doubting presupposes thinking, in short, and the activity of thinking presupposes the existence of a thinking thing. *I think, therefore I am* became the famous slogan summarizing this passage of the *Meditations*. In Latin this phrase is expressed as **cogito ergo sum**, and so Descartes's discussion here is sometimes referred to simply as the *cogito*.

The *cogito* became Descartes's starting point, his "first principle." It was his foundational certainty on the basis of which he could now go on to construct a body of knowledge.

Inquiring next what it was about his own existence that made it so indubitable to him, Descartes found it was the "clarity and distinctness" with which it forced itself upon him. He therefore decided to adopt this **clear and distinct criterion** as his criterion of truth: if it would be contradictory to deny the truth of a certain proposition, then the proposition was certainly true. Any proposition possessed of this same mode of self-evidence must be true.

What other propositions fit this criterion? In *Meditation Three* Descartes offers a new cosmological argument for God's existence, quite different from those we discussed in chapter 7. Simplified, it works like this. He finds in himself, in his mind, the idea of God, that is, of a "substance that is infinite, independent, supremely intelligent, and supremely powerful" (*Meditation Three*). The key attribute here is that God is an *infinite* substance. Where, Descartes asks, could this idea of the infinite have come from? He finds it literally contradictory that something could come into being from nothing, and therefore accepts as a basic causal principle that *nothing occurs without a sufficient cause*, namely a cause that fully explains, that makes intelligible, how the effect arose. (See chapter 7 for how cosmological arguments invoke the intelligibility of the world.) Could he himself have generated his idea of an infinite being? Surely not, for he is finite, limited in life, and in ability. If the idea of the infinite is in his mind, then only a "sufficient cause" could have put it there; it could only have been caused to be there by something that was itself infinite. Therefore the infinite substance, "God," must exist, in order to have caused his idea of it. (Descartes additionally offers his own ontological argument for God's existence.)

Note, here, how the epistemology drives the metaphysics. Descartes seeks certainty (epistemology), thus concludes, first, only that he exists as a thinking thing (metaphysics). Then he develops his clear and distinct criterion (epistemology), which in turn establishes a causal principle and God's existence (both metaphysics). In precisely the same vein he turns to the next question. What might now be said about the existence and nature of the external physical world, the one that had been called into question by the radical skepticism in *Meditation One*? After all, it was his quest for knowledge of that world, science, that inspired his endeavor in the first place.

Well, the clear and distinct criterion quickly teaches him that God could never deliberately, inescapably deceive. Such deception arises from malice, and it would be a contradiction for a perfectly good God to act out of malice. Since God created us with our senses, and via our senses we experience perceptions of a physical world, it must be that the world exists in order

From *Action Philosophers!* by Fred Van Lente and Ryan Dunlavey (Evil Twin Comics, 2009).

Used by permission.

to cause those perceptions—for if they were caused by anything other than physical bodies we would be inescapably deceived.

So far, so good, but the epistemology isn't finished yet. Most of what our sensory experiences contain is *not* clear and distinct. We have no real grasp of such properties as colors, flavors, and sounds, and the senses do regularly mislead us with illusions and misperceptions (as laid out in *Meditation One*). Thus the rationalist Descartes insists that we cannot accept the evidence of the senses as truth until it has been carefully processed by reason, the same reason which is the source of the clear and distinct criterion. God would only be deceiving us *inescapably* if our reason, properly used, were duped. But if we uncritically accept the evidence of the senses and are deceived, it is our own fault, for failing to accept only that which we grasp clearly and distinctly by reason.

So the senses can reliably teach us that physical bodies exist, but they cannot reliably teach us much about their specific nature or properties. Thus Descartes writes, immediately after his proof that the physical world exists,

> Nevertheless, perhaps not all [physical] bodies exist exactly as I grasp them by sense, since this sensory grasp is in many cases very obscure and confused. But at least they do contain everything I clearly and distinctly understand. (*Meditation Six*)

Which aspects of physical bodies *are* clearly and distinctly understood? Their mathematical properties, Descartes concludes, for only mathematical concepts, of sizes, shapes, and quantities, are appropriate subjects for clear and distinct reasoning.

That, in a nutshell, is Descartes's new theory of matter, the one that overthrows the centuries-old Aristotelian one. Physical bodies truly only possess those properties suitable for mathematics, such as sizes, shapes, and motions. With this epistemologically driven claim, physical science was set to become the mathematical endeavor it remains today.

And what's left behind? All the other properties physical bodies appear to have, that we *perceive* them to have, but which aren't mathematical and therefore aren't real: colors, flavors, sounds, smells. The apple may *look* red to you, but it really isn't. As the ancient atomists had speculated two millennia earlier (see chapter 2), it's just a bunch of colorless physical particles moving around that are causing your red perception.

So where then is the redness that you perceive? If it's not in the matter, there's only one place to put it: in the mind. And that, in a smaller nutshell, is Descartes's new theory of mind, to which we'll return shortly.

Descartes's Dualism

It isn't merely that Descartes offered new theories of matter and of mind. It's that he also saw them as fundamentally different kinds of things or *substances*. The doctrine that the world contains these two different things is known as **dualism**. This distinction of mind from matter, of *your* mind from *your* body, would come to be seen as one of Descartes's main contributions to philosophy. No previous philosopher had made the division as clearly and sharply as he had, and ever since, mind and consciousness have been part of the main subject matter of philosophical investigation.

Let's have a look at some of his arguments for dualism, then sketch his theories of the distinct natures of mind and matter.

(1) The first is a **theological argument for dualism**. The background for it is the Christian Aristotelianism that dominated the centuries before Descartes. Although the details are beyond our scope, on that view the mind or soul stood to the body roughly as the form or shape stands to a lump of clay molded into a statue. The shape of the statue is not quite identical to the lump of clay, since you can separate them from each other by remolding the clay—in which case you still have the same clay, but the shape is gone. But that isn't *really* to separate them. It's not like you can hold the shape in one hand, and the clay in the other! The shape, while not exactly the same thing as the clay, doesn't have any real existence on its own.

And that is the problem. For Christians also believed in **personal immortality**, the idea that the mind or soul can survive the death of the body. But if the mind is like the shape of the clay, it was entirely unintelligible how it could exist on its own. Personal immortality had to be understood as a miracle, something intrinsically impossible that only God could bring about. That wasn't a terrible result, since Christians don't entirely object to miracles. But philosophical theologians, as philosophers, prefer the world to be as intelligible as possible (as we saw in chapter 7), and thus to minimize the miracles, if possible.

On Descartes's view, the mind was a completely different sort of thing from matter. In fact it was a *thing*, a "substance." As the *Meditations* suggests, the mind was capable of existing even when the body didn't, a clear sign that it was really distinct from the body in a way the shape is not from the clay. And so one advantage to endorsing his dualism over the Aristotelian view was that personal immortality no longer was unintelligible, but now seemed entirely possible.

(2) **Metaphysical arguments for dualism**. Descartes offers several, though we'll look at just one. What they share is that each isolates an important property that minds have but matter lacks, or vice versa, and concludes that insofar as they differ in that property they must be different things.

The defining property of mind, Descartes suggested, was *thought*. Sometimes he used that word narrowly, to refer only to intellectual thought, the kind of thinking you do when doing mathematics. Other times he used it more broadly, to refer to all sorts of activities we think of as "mental" in nature: thinking, perceiving, feeling, remembering, imagining, and so on. What they all share for him is that they are all conscious, as the mind is always aware of itself as it does these things. So we might say that for Descartes, the defining property of mind was consciousness.

The defining property of matter, to the contrary, was **extension**. For something to be *extended* is for it to take up space, to have a certain size, and shape, and volume, as well as a particular location. Thus anything that had these properties was by definition physical or material, and everything physical had those properties.

But now note that these are very different properties. Consciousness has nothing in common with extension. "Being aware" and "having size *s*" simply have no intrinsic connection. With no connection between them, one could always conceive of something having one of the properties and lacking the other. It's surely easy to conceive of physical bodies lacking consciousness, since many already do, such as stones. But even when we think about minds, about consciousness, nothing in our thought suggests or requires that a physical body be present. To the contrary, it's also easy to conceive of disembodied minds (as Descartes does in *Meditation One*), minds disconnected from bodies, minds existing in heaven after the death of the body. So again, the epistemology drives the metaphysics. For Descartes, the fact that we can conceive of mind and matter separately (epistemology), without encountering any contradictions, shows that mind and matter are fundamentally different kinds of things (metaphysics).

(3) **Empirical argument for dualism**. Descartes believed that almost everything about the human body and human behavior could be explained in purely physical terms. Our bodies are merely complicated machines, and as science progressed we could explain such phenomena as these without ever invoking conscious minds: waking, sleep, dreams, sensations, hunger, thirst, memory, imagination, the motions of our limbs, and so on. He himself studied anatomy and physiology, and devised theories for many of these.

Yet there were two phenomena, he thought, that could *not* be explained without invoking a conscious, intellectual mind: language and reasoning. While some animals might exhibit behaviors similar to these, none remotely resembles human competence in these areas, and so these are clear signs that there is more to the human being than his or her body. Much more could be said here, of course, but lest you think Descartes's view is scientifically dated, note that his observations have actually proved prescient. For while twenty-first-century researchers have made great strides in getting computers and robots to imitate human behavior in many ways, it is precisely in the mastery of language and reason that they have struggled. The jury may still be out, but Descartes may well have been right that these cognitive capacities resist physical explanation. If so, again, then mind is something other than body.

So mind and matter are distinct. Let's now say a bit more about his understanding of each.

Descartes's Theory of Mind

The defining property of mind for Descartes, we saw, was *thought*, or consciousness. But things get really interesting when you ask just what it is, exactly, that minds are conscious *of*, according to him. The answer comes in the form of what is often called the **representational theory of mind (RTM)**.

According to RTM, the immediate object of sensation or intellect, that is, what the mind is aware of when it is perceiving or thinking, is an *idea*. This may sound all right until you think about what the mind is *not* aware of during perceiving or thinking, namely physical objects. So suppose you look out your window at the tree in the courtyard. Normally, pre-philosophically, you would say, "I see the tree in the courtyard." When you close your eyes and think about what you saw, you would say, "I am thinking about the tree in the courtyard." We normally take ourselves to perceive and think about physical objects. It is *this* that RTM rejects.

Instead what you are aware of is an **idea** of the tree. An idea is some kind of mental object, existing only in the mind. It serves as a *representation* of the tree, it stands in for the tree, refers to the tree, somehow, but it is not the tree. After all, the tree is a physical object, with a certain size and shape, located in the courtyard; your idea of the tree is a mental object, in your mind, and certainly not possessing the same size, shape, or location of the tree. In fact, as a mental object, it's not located in physical space at all. So according to RTM we are never directly aware, via sensation or thinking, of physical objects at all—only ideas.

This is probably a surprising claim to you, and you would probably be even more surprised to learn that Descartes's RTM became the dominant theory of mind for the next two centuries. (In some ways it is still flourishing in the twenty-first century, as we'll see in chapter 10.) Your next question, then, is probably this: Why on earth should anyone believe this theory?

In fact Descartes (and others) offer many arguments for RTM, but we'll only look at two. The first is the **dream argument for RTM**, suggested by Descartes's expression of radical skepticism in Meditation One. For there, you'll recall, he was concerned that there were "no definitive signs by which to distinguish being awake from being asleep." So ask yourself, for a moment, just "what" it is that you are aware of when dreaming. You are having what feels like

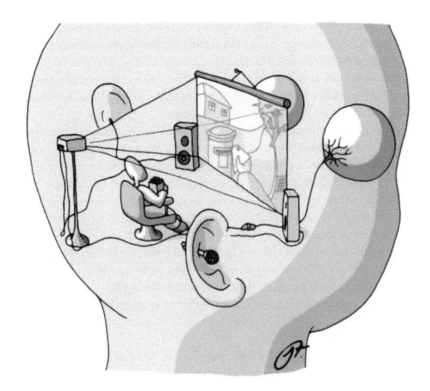

Jolyon Troscianko.
Used by permission.

a perceptual experience, it seems to you that you are looking at the tree in the courtyard, but is it really that physical tree you see? Clearly not. Your eyes are closed, you are dreaming, you may be nowhere near that tree (perhaps you are on vacation far away). And of course we often dream of things that don't even exist at all. So it seems that in dreams what we are aware of are indeed ideas, not physical objects. But if there are "no definitive signs" by which to distinguish dreams from waking states, if actually perceiving a body is indistinguishable from dreaming of the body, and if in dreams we are aware of ideas not bodies, then we should conclude that while awake, too, in actual perception we are also aware of ideas, not bodies.

A second argument we'll call a **relativity of perception argument**. There are many variations of these, and we shall discuss them in more depth in chapter 9, but for now consider just this. The color a body appears to have (for just one example) can change dramatically depending on context. The shirt looks one color under the fluorescent lights of the store, another in the daylight outside, another under the incandescent light in your closet, and so on. In fact it is well established that colors are perceived differently by different people even in the same contexts, and surely are perceived differently by different animals. But now the body itself, the shirt itself, is not changing here. It is the same shirt, even if its perceived color varies across contexts, persons, or animals. Well, if the perceived color is changing, but the physical body itself is not changing, then the perceived color must not belong to the physical body. But then it must not be the physical body you are perceiving. What you perceive when you perceive colors, then, are not bodies but *ideas*. (This would apply to other properties, too, such as flavors, sounds, and smells. And note how well this fits with Descartes's earlier argument that physical bodies have only mathematical properties [size, shape, motion], and don't truly possess color, flavor, etc.)

After establishing that the contents of the mind are ideas, then, Descartes also says more about the nature of the mind. In addition to its defining property of thought or consciousness, he identifies at least four other important properties.

(1) The mind is indubitable: an individual cannot doubt the existence of his or her own mind. This point derives from the *cogito* in *Meditation Two*.

(2) The mind is **incorrigible**: it can never make a mistake concerning what is going on inside it, although naturally it is fallible with respect to what is going on outside. If you are dreaming, for example, you cannot be mistaken that you *seem* to see a tree, that you are perceiving a tree (or tree-idea) inside your mind. But you may well be mistaken if you then believe that there really exists a physical tree outside you *that* you are seeing.

(3) The mind is **transparent**: it is fully aware of everything actively occurring in it. For Descartes, mind is consciousness. It simply doesn't make sense to him to imagine that mental objects such as ideas could exist unconsciously, or that mental activity such as thinking, perceiving, feeling, imagining, and so on, could occur unconsciously. While mental transparency is no longer widely held in the twenty-first century—thanks to Sigmund Freud (1856–1939), the founder of psychoanalysis and the "discoverer" of the unconscious mind—it was widely embraced in the centuries after Descartes, until Freud.

(4) Finally, the mind is a **simple unity**: it is indivisible, cannot be divided into distinct parts or components. Of course, the mind does have different abilities, as you can think, perceive, feel, and so forth. But you shouldn't think of these as different parts of the mind, since, Descartes points out, it is the same single *you* who does these things. It is *you* who thinks, *you* who perceives, and so on. The unity of the mind also follows from the fact that it is not physical. Physical matter (as we saw) is defined by its extension, by taking up space, and everything that takes up space can always be divided into smaller parts. If the mind is not physical then it does not take up space; if it doesn't take up space, it cannot be divided.

In short, Descartes's new theory of mind consists of RTM, the claim that the mind has these four properties, and that its defining property is thought or consciousness.

Descartes's Theory of Matter

Descartes was not the first, or only, to develop his theory of matter. The theory began at least the century before with Galileo (1564–1642), and many others contributed along with and after Descartes, including Robert Boyle (1627–1691). But Descartes did much to develop and promote the theory, so we shall treat it as his.

The theory is known as **the mechanical philosophy**. The basic idea was given earlier, that the defining property of matter is extension (taking up space), and that, therefore, the only real properties that matter has are properties that extended (spatial) things can have, such as size, shape, and motion. Its name derives from the idea that the physical world, consisting of bits of extended matter moving according to laws, colliding, joining, breaking apart, and so on, amounts to a large complicated machine.

But this basic idea generates some important questions and implications. To see some of these, we shall summarize the mechanical philosophy as a list of five separate (though related) claims. Much more could be said about each, but we shall have to be brief.

(1) The first is that all matter in the universe is the same. Sure, it *looks* as if there are many different kinds of matter. Just look at your own body: your nails, skin, hair, eyeballs, blood, bones, heart tissue, lung tissue, and so on. These seem to be very different, but ultimately they aren't, as we'll see in a moment.

(2) The defining property of matter is extension. That means (as we saw) that pieces of matter will have properties such as size, shape, and motion, but will not have properties like colors, flavors, sounds, and smells (now understood to consist only of ideas in the minds of perceivers). But it also now means that matter has two other properties. Just like space, matter is infinitely divisible. Any piece of matter can always be divided into smaller pieces, which in turn can be divided, and so on. Further, matter is intrinsically passive. If a piece of matter is just a blob taking up space, it has no internal source of motion, no engine, no power or force in it. Thus matter cannot move on its own without being moved ultimately by something which does have power or force (such as a mind).

(3) The universe is a **plenum**. A plenum, from the Latin for "fullness," is something entirely full, with no voids, vacuums, or empty spots. Again, it may look to us as if there are plenty of empty spaces, such as between you and your friend, between the earth and the moon, and so on. But the mechanical philosophy holds that all space is full of matter even if we cannot always perceive it.

(4) The differences we perceive in different regions of space—that there appear to be distinct individual bodies and that these appear to include different kinds of matter—are due to variations in motion in the plenum. This point addresses the misleading appearances in (1) and (3). That you appear to be a distinct individual from your friend is not because there is empty space between you, but because all the matter in you moves together and all the matter in her moves together. Similarly, matter moving one way may cause a red perception in us, moving another way may cause a yellow perception; matter moving slowly may look like a solid, moving quickly like a liquid. The matter is the same, but the differences in motion account for the different appearances of (for example) your nails, skin, blood, heart tissue, and so forth.

(5) God is responsible for the motion of matter in nature. Since matter is passive, it cannot move itself, so when God created the physical universe He initially put the matter into motion. He further maintains that motion by means of the laws of nature, which describe the regular ways He keeps matter moving. (We human beings, via our minds, may be partly responsible for the way matter moves within our body, but see the causation discussion below.)

Again, the crucial consequence of the mechanical philosophy is that it turned the study of nature, or science, into a mathematical discipline. Prior to the mechanical philosophy, what we call *science* was not in fact much distinguishable from philosophy (and indeed was referred to as *natural philosophy*, or philosophy of nature). It was studied largely by philosophical reflection, by thinking, as best reflected in the fact that Aristotle's own book on physics was still the main textbook in the universities two thousand years after its composition. But once the physical world was conceived via the mechanical philosophy it became something quantifiable, measurable, and thereby something you could develop sophisticated theories about, and then you could make observations and experiments to test those theories. So the mechanical philosophy not only made science mathematical, it actually enabled science to be born from philosophy. While Descartes's specific theory of physics is long outdated, its fundamental legacy, the mathematization of science, lives on to this day.

With that in mind we turn to our next great rationalist thinker.

BARUCH SPINOZA (1632–1677)

Spinoza was born in Holland, into a Portuguese Jewish family, refugees from the Spanish Inquisition. Sent to Hebrew school to study for the rabbinate, he was soon torn by doubts, unable to accept the teachings of the scriptures. Not hesitant to express his doubts, he was, by the age of twenty-four, excommunicated from the Jewish community. Spinoza spent the rest of his life in a lonely, quiet existence, earning his living by grinding lenses. He died at forty-four of tuberculosis, exacerbated by the glass dust he inhaled practicing his vocation.

Only two of Spinoza's books appeared during his lifetime: *The Principles of Descartes' Philosophy* (1663), a critique of Descartes, and the other, published anonymously, *Treatise on Theology and Politics* (1670). This second work was revolutionary, initiating the study of the Bible as a literary and historical human document, rather than supernatural one. It was also ahead of its time in advocating the separation of church and state, stressing the value of individual liberty and religious tolerance, and arguing for democracy against the claims of monarchy and aristocracy.

BARUCH SPINOZA

Spinoza's crowning achievement was the posthumously published book *Ethics*, on which he began working in 1662. This majestic work deals not only with ethics, as its title suggests, but also with physics, metaphysics, psychology, and more. He named it *Ethics* because he believed that the overall purpose of philosophical investigation is not mere speculation but moral action.

> Thank God there are no free schools or printing . . . for learning has brought disobedience and heresy into the world, and printing has divulged them. . . . God keep us from both.
>
> —**Sir William Berkeley**, governor of Virginia (mid-1600s)

Spinoza's Pantheism and Monism

The most famous (or infamous) theme of Spinoza's work was his **pantheism**, the doctrine that everything in some sense is or is part of God. During his lifetime and for at least two centuries after his death, this theme aroused intense and almost universal indignation, and led him to be despised as in fact an atheist. For Spinoza to identify the world with God amounted, after all, to his identifying God *with the world*, as expressed in his phrase, "God is nature." But the distinction between God and His creation is fundamental for Christian thinkers, so to equate God with nature was to eliminate God in *favor* of nature. And so for a long time there could be hardly any greater insult than when a philosopher was labeled a *Spinozist*.

What's interesting is that Spinoza arrived at his pantheism by following Descartes's rationalist methods, with the epistemology driving the metaphysics. Using mathematics as a paradigm—as its subtitle suggests, *Demonstrated in Geometrical Order*—Spinoza's *Ethics* started

with definitions and axioms, with simple, clear and distinct first principles, then went on methodically to prove (deduce) theorems about the nature of reality. Yet despite applying the
same epistemological methods Spinoza ends up about as metaphysically far away from Descartes as almost seems possible.

Most deeply, Descartes's dualism became transformed into a **monism**, the doctrine that the
world consists of only one kind of substance or thing. Matter and mind, Descartes's two kinds
of substance, became aspects of only one substance, which Spinoza called either *nature* or *God*.
Spinoza arrived at this conclusion, he claimed, by working out the implications of Descartes's
basic ideas more carefully than Descartes himself had done. Descartes started with the idea of
his own existence and went on to deduce the existence of God and then the physical world. But
since God is prior to everything else—at least in being the alleged creator of everything—Spinoza
began with the idea of God and then aimed to deduce whatever is true about us and the world.

And what is that idea of God? God is some kind of thing, or substance. A **substance** is
something capable of existing independently from other things. So "color" is not a substance,
because a color cannot exist except as the color of some thing; the yellow must be the yellow
of a lemon, or of a shirt. A substance, to the contrary, may generally exist with or without its
color, so the lemon itself still exists even as it turns brown.

But now not even the shirt, or the lemon, are substances either, strictly speaking. Why
not? According to Descartes's own mechanical philosophy, the physical universe is actually
a plenum. What appears to be empty space is actually filled with physical matter, even if we
can't see it. But if the whole universe is filled with matter it is quite arbitrary to carve off some
region of it, such as that lemon or that shirt, and treat it as if it were an individual thing existing
separately and independently from other things. So there aren't really any individual physical
substances. At most there is only one physical substance, namely the entire physical universe
as a whole. Things like individual lemons or shirts are just features or aspects *of* that substance.

That one physical substance, too, must be infinite. For the very idea of space, of this plenum of matter, coming to end makes no sense. If there were some end we would ask what
comes beyond it, and in doing that we are extending space beyond the alleged limit of space—
in which case we are not limiting it. Space (or the plenum) must go on forever, with no limits,
and is therefore infinite.

But now, if a substance is something that can exist independently of other things, then
there could be only one substance, strictly speaking: God, the infinite substance, who depends
on nothing for His existence and on whom all things depend for theirs. Nor could there exist
two infinite substances, since whatever is infinite extends to everywhere, and two allegedly
distinct things both extending everywhere and thus overlapping in every respect would really
just be identical. If there cannot be two distinct infinite substances, then the infinite physical
universe we just sketched must either rule out the existence of God (as an infinite substance)
or else be identified with God.

Or there's one more possibility. Since everyone holds that the physical universe does depend on God for its existence, it may not be a "substance" after all. Instead it is a feature or
aspect, or more technically a *mode* or *attribute*, *of* a substance. But what substance? Well, since
the physical world is infinite in extent and God is the one infinite substance, the answer is
clear: the physical world is a mode or attribute of God. Similar reasoning also confirms the
conclusion that Descartes's minds are also not individual substances. Rather, they too are but
modes or attributes of the one genuine substance, God.

There is both the monism and the pantheism. God becomes the one substance in the world (monism), and all things, mental or physical, thought or extension, are merely aspects of God (pantheism). In using the term *attributes* for these aspects, Spinoza explains, he means they are ways in which our intellect grasps or understands the one true infinite substance. We grasp God in terms of only these two attributes, though there are actually an infinite number of ways in which this one infinite substance can manifest itself.

Thought and extension being attributes of God, it would not quite be correct to say that God is the creator of the world. Rather, God *is* the world. Similarly, since both thought and extension are manifestations of this same basic substance, it would be incorrect to say that mind and body are separate entities. They are really one, and what occurs in one finds its correlative occurrence in the other. Consciousness is thus not separate from body. It is simply "the idea of the body."

> I am fascinated by Spinoza's pantheism, but I admire even more his contribution to modern thought because he is the first philosopher to deal with the soul and body as one, and not two separate things.
>
> —**Albert Einstein** (1879–1955)

So Descartes's own epistemological methods and resources—start with simple, clear ideas, with definitions of things like substances and God, proceed by careful deductions—result in a very different metaphysics. But Spinoza now pushes the metaphysics further, linking it with important moral consequences.

Spinoza's Necessitarianism, Determinism, and Ethics

The next metaphysical doctrine is **necessitarianism**, the doctrine that God both exists and has His nature necessarily. To say God exists necessarily is to say that there is no logical possibility of God *not* existing. If we ignore Spinoza's pantheism a moment, this would make God a very different sort of thing from all other ordinary things. You exist, but not necessarily, for there is no contradiction in your not existing, as proved by the fact that once you did not exist and presumably will one day stop existing as well. God, to the contrary, cannot *not* exist. Similarly, to say God has His nature necessarily is to say that it is not possible for God to be any different from what He is.

Necessitarianism then leads to the next metaphysical doctrine, that of **determinism**, the doctrine that everything that occurs in the world is necessarily caused to occur by earlier events, and thus pre-determined. How does determinism follow from necessitarianism? Well, if everything about God's nature is necessary, and everything in the world is just in or is some aspect of God, then everything in the world must occur necessarily in the precise order in which it does. Just as (for example) God cannot *not* bring about the best possible world (recall the best possible world theodicy from chapter 7), so too events in the world must be seen as simply unfolding in the only possible way they can. Each event is necessarily brought about by earlier events, and in turn necessarily brings about subsequent events.

These now lead to the moral implications.

Being part of God, we are not free to go our separate ways but are compelled to live lives whose destinies are fixed from eternity. This being so, we can begin to understand that nothing is in itself good or evil in some intrinsic or objective way, but rather that we only judge them to be so in relation to human interests. The illness you may suffer is not in itself a bad or evil thing, it is only something you wish you didn't have. In a way reminiscent of the theodicies we discussed, again, when you get your metaphysics right, Spinoza suggests, you will realize that to God—or from the perspective of eternity—all is fair.

The consequence is that such human emotions as hope and fear, humility and repentance, envy and hatred, are ultimately useless and futile, for the future is unalterably fixed. We can, however, free ourselves from our bondage to these emotions by knowledge, by striving through reason to achieve that identification with the order of the universe that will enable us to see how things must be the way they are. Spinoza calls this acceptance and love of our fate *the intellectual love of God*. Its reward, he says, is *blessedness*.

With the metaphysics in mind, too, we can understand Spinoza's critique of traditional religious belief. For that belief is based in the idea that events in the world have a purpose, or a goal, in the same way that teleological arguments worked (as we saw in chapter 7). But why are people so prone to believe this about nature? What prevents them from seeing that in fact nature has no particular goal in view, and that everything in it proceeds from necessity?

Partly, he answers, it is due to ignorance of natural causes and partly to the human propensity to seek and believe only that which is useful to us. We believe ourselves to be free insofar as we are aware of our ability to act on our own volitions or desires, but are ignorant of the natural causes which generate our wishes and desires. (Recall Augustine's compatibilist freedom in chapter 7.) We typically act for a goal or a purpose, to obtain that which is useful to us, and thus tend to believe that nature itself operates similarly. We seek the purposes of events, including other people's actions:

> If [people] cannot learn such [purposes] from external sources, they . . . turn to . . . themselves, and reflecting what end would have induced them personally to bring about the given event . . . necessarily judge other natures by their own. Further, as they find . . . many means which assist them . . . in their search for what is useful, for instance, eyes for seeing, teeth for chewing, . . . the sun for giving light, the sea for breeding fish, etc., they come to look on the whole of nature as a means for obtaining such conveniences. Now . . . that they found these conveniences and did not make them, they think they have cause for believing, that some other being has made them for their use. As they look upon things as means . . . they are bound to believe in some ruler or rulers of the universe endowed with human freedom, who have arranged and adapted everything for human use. They are bound to estimate the nature of such rulers . . . in accordance with their own nature, and therefore they assert that the gods ordained everything for the use of man, in order to bind man to themselves and obtain from him the highest honor. Hence also it follows, that everyone thought out for himself . . . a different way of worshipping God, so that God might love him more than his fellows, and direct the whole course of nature for the satisfaction of his . . . insatiable avarice.[2]

The incorrect understanding of the world, Spinoza concludes, leads people into superstition and then into religion. They confront hindrances, such as storms, earthquakes, diseases, and declare that such things happen because the gods are angry at some wrong done them by human beings, or at our laxity in worship. No matter that every day provides evidence that good and evil fortunes fall to the pious and impious alike; they retain their ignorance and their prejudice, that the world is governed by purpose. Spinoza's philosophy, to the contrary, teaches that such purposes are merely human figments, that we bind ourselves to illusions that we ourselves create. But once we gain the metaphysical truth, we can change our attitude toward the world, and behavior in it, accordingly.

The last of the great early modern rationalists was Gottfried Wilhelm von Leibniz, born in Leipzig, Germany, in 1646. A brilliant prodigy, at age twenty Leibniz was rejected for a law degree at the University of Leipzig because the professors were jealous of his talents. Incensed, he obtained a degree from the University of Nuremberg, then set himself to master whatever knowledge still remained—leading Frederick the Great, one of his patrons, later to describe him as a "whole academy in himself." At twenty-one, he entered diplomatic service, serving as a librarian, adviser, statesman, and international lawyer, but his greatest contributions were in mathematics, science, and philosophy. He in-vented a computing machine, for example, that anticipated modern computers, he developed a formal language modeled on mathematics that anticipated modern formal logic, and most fa-mously, in 1675–1676, he discovered both the differential and infinitesimal calculus. Though he had worked independently of similar work by Isaac Newton (1643–1727), a long and bitter dispute arose as to who stole from whom. It was at this time that Leibniz took up the librar-ianship at Hanover, a position he held until his death. When George of Hanover became King of England in 1714, Leibniz, unwelcome in En-gland because of the calculus controversy, was left behind, embittered and neglected, dying two years later at the age of seventy.

G. W. LEIBNIZ

Although Leibniz was a prolific writer, his best-known book is *Monadology* (1714), meant to serve as a short account of his metaphysics and epistemology. His work grew partly in crit-ical response to his predecessors, especially to Descartes and to another important rationalist, Nicolas Malebranche (1638–1715). But as with his predecessors, it was also partly generated by purely rational, logical considerations, with the epistemology driving the metaphysics.

Leibniz's Monads and Pre-Established Harmony

According to Leibniz, the basic substances of the universe are entities he calls **monads**, derived from the Greek for "unit." He conceives these as non-physical, endlessly diverse, cen-ters of energy, each with the capacity of reflecting (some more clearly and fully than others) the universe as a whole.

The simplest way to think of monads is as minds, but unlike Descartes's "minds" (which were associated only with human consciousness) they range far more widely in nature, from primitive to sophisticated. So what is true of our minds in general is true (to varying degrees) of all substances in the universe. They are all possessed of powers of perception, or something analogous thereto. Thus every monad perceives and represents the whole of the universe in itself, and is, as Leibniz expressed it, a "living mirror of the universe."

But each monad mirrors or represents the universe only with its own degree of clarity. It represents it, that is to say, only in its own way and from its own unique point of view. In the lowest monads, those of plants, perception is of a limited and primitive sort, with everything obscure and confused. Perception among animals is of a higher kind, one that we may call "consciousness." In our own case, "consciousness" becomes even more refined and clear, and turns into "self-consciousness." So, in short, all that exists in the universe are minds, though minds come in different categories, varying in degrees of perception.

So described, Leibniz's doctrine would be a form of **idealism**, the doctrine that all that exists is mental in nature. Having said that, we must note that there is scholarly controversy over how to interpret Leibniz here. Over the course of many years and writings Leibniz often did sound like an idealist, but he also wrote many things suggestive of the dualism we ascribed to Descartes (though recognizing the wide variety of minds). While the idealist interpretation may well be correct—on which even plants, even the inanimate "matter" composing plants, are kinds of minds—for what follows it will be easier for us to treat Leibniz as a dualist.

With that qualification, we turn next to Leibniz's most famous single doctrine. If the substances of the universe, the monads, are "mirrors of the universe," they are also (as he puts it) "windowless": nothing comes in, nothing goes out. By this Leibniz means that each substance runs on its own internal program, going through its sequence of states by inner necessity, neither determined nor influenced by anything outside it. Depending on nothing outside them, monads contain within themselves implicitly or potentially, from their creation, everything they will ever come to be. There cannot, therefore, be any causal interaction between monads.

Leibniz offers dramatic statements of this doctrine:

God originally created the [mind] . . . in such a way that everything must arise for it from its own depths, through a perfect *spontaneity* relative to itself, and yet with a perfect *conformity* relative to external things . . . [T]he perceptions or expressions of external things occur in the [mind] at a given time, in virtue of its own [internal] laws, as if in a world apart. ("New System of Nature," in transls., eds. Roger Ariew and Daniel Garber, *G. W. Leibniz: Philosophical Essays* [Indianapolis, IN: Hackett Publishing Company], 143)

Anything which occurs in . . . a substance . . . [arises] out of its own depths; for no created substance can have an influence upon any other, so that everything comes to a substance from itself (though ultimately from God). (*New Essays on Human Understanding* II.xxi, eds. Peter Remnant and Jonathan Bennett [Cambridge: Cambridge University Press], 210)

According to this system, bodies act as if there were no [minds] . . . and [minds] act as if there were no bodies; and both act as if each influenced the other. (*The Monadology*, #81, in transls., eds. Roger Ariew and Daniel Garber, *G. W. Leibniz: Philosophical Essays* [Indianapolis, IN: Hackett Publishing Company], 223)

But if the different substances of the universe are not in causal relationships to each other, what keeps things together? If the physical activity of your speaking doesn't cause the mental activity of your friend's perceiving your voice, if your (mental) desire to get something to eat doesn't cause your physical body's motion toward the refrigerator, then why or how does the world function at all?

Leibniz's reply was that the unity, or harmony, that we find was "pre-established" by God when He first created the universe. Monads are like clocks wound up together to keep the same time. Although their readings will always be perfectly correlated (having been made by a perfect maker), they don't causally influence each other. When it reads 1:12 on this clock it will read 1:12 on that clock simply because their internal programs are perfectly synchronized. Or, as Leibniz explained it, they are like "several different bands of musicians or choirs separately playing their parts, and placed in such a way that they do not see and do not even hear each other, though they nevertheless can agree perfectly, each following his own notes, so that someone hearing all of them would find a marvelous harmony there, one more surprising than if there were a connection among them."[3]

Thus, your speaking does *not* cause your friend's perceiving your voice. Rather, your internal program causes you to speak at just the moment her internal program causes her perception of your voice. Similarly, your desire to eat does not cause your body to move. Rather, your mind's program causes you to feel your desire at the moment your body's program causes it to move. There *is* genuine causation within each substance, as each substance causes its own sequence of internal states. But there is no genuine causation *between* substances. Rather, each substance runs through its sequence of internal states in perfectly synchronized harmony with all other substances.

This Leibniz refers to as the doctrine of **pre-established harmony**. It is surely an original doctrine, to the point of seeming almost absurd to many upon first hearing of it. Indeed it initially struck Leibniz that way as well:

> [S]ince I was forced to agree [by my reasoning] that it is not possible for the [mind] or any other true substance to receive [causal influence] from without . . . I was led . . . to a view that surprised me. ("New System," 143)

But of course a rational person must go where his reason leads him, even to strange places. And in this case Leibniz discovered that the more he thought about the doctrine, the better it sounded. The previous passage continues:

> I was led . . . to a view that surprised me, but which seems inevitable, and which, in fact, has very great advantages and rather considerable beauty. ("New System," 143)

So why does pre-established harmony strike Leibniz as "inevitable," something to which he is "forced to agree"? And what are some of its "great advantages"?

The Truth Argument for Pre-Established Harmony

As for the first question, there are many arguments that lead Leibniz to the position. These include its "advantages," some of which we'll look at in the causation section below. Here we'll look at just one general argument, based in a fundamental concept in logic. According to his **truth argument for pre-established harmony**, the doctrine follows directly from the nature of truth itself.[4]

What, you may ask, is "truth"?

Well, as we noted in chapter 4, truth is a matter of whether statements or sentences "accord with the facts." Proceeding a bit more methodically now, we might say that truth is something that at least some statements or sentences enjoy, while others do not. The question is what accounts for the difference between those that do and those that don't. The answer begins by observing that the relevant sentences standardly come in the form of a *subject* combined with a *predicate*: the subject is the thing the sentence is about, and the predicate is what is being said about the subject. In the sentence "Snow is white," "Snow" is the subject and "is white" is the predicate.

But now, Leibniz writes, "[A]ll true predication has some basis in the nature of things . . . Thus the subject term must always contain the predicate term."[5]

A true sentence has a "basis in the nature of things," that is, in reality itself. Thus, to say that, in such a sentence, the predicate term is "contained in" the subject term is to say that what you say about the subject really is *in* the subject. For "snow is white" to be true, then, whiteness, the thing referred to by the predicate "is white," must really be a feature of the snow itself. This is what we meant earlier in saying that truth is a matter of statements "according with the facts."

Plausible enough, surely. But now let's consider some other true sentences.

Imagine that we are contemporaries of Alexander the Great, who lived a mere thirty-three years from 356–323 B.C.E.; let us imagine that we are with him during his teenage years, say, in 340 B.C.E. It turns out that, here in 340 B.C.E., there are many true sentences that could be uttered about this adolescent: "He was born in Macedon," "He was tutored by the famous philosopher Aristotle," "He is currently sixteen years old," "He will become king in four years," "He will shortly conquer most of the known world," and so on. Notice that some of these sentences are in the past tense, some in the present, and some in the future. Of course in 340 B.C.E. we wouldn't be in a position to *know* those truths that are about his future. But those were true sentences at that time anyway, as our actual twenty-first-century perspective teaches us.

> In Leibniz, a vast edifice of deduction is pyramided upon a pin-point of logical principle. In Leibniz, if the principle is completely true and the deductions are entirely valid, all is well; but the structure in unstable, and the slightest flaw anywhere brings it down in ruins.
>
> —**Bertrand Russell** (1872–1970), *A History of Western Philosophy*

But now truth, Leibniz tells us, "has some basis in the nature of things."

If those sentences are true, then their respective predicates must be "contained" in their shared subject.

But that means that, in 340 B.C.E., it is already "contained" in Alexander himself that he *will* become king and conquer the world. Indeed everything that will *ever* happen to him after 340 B.C.E. is already "contained" in him in some way, just as whiteness is contained in snow that is currently white.

But then *that* is to say that nothing could ever come into him from outside, or causally affect him, later on, for if some effect (or property) were only to come in from outside later then it wouldn't already be contained in him *now*. But then it follows that everything about his future, if it is already contained in him now, must be generated *from* within him, just as pre-established harmony says.

To make this even clearer, let's shift our perspective: to you.

Right now you are having certain visual perceptions, such as that of reading this page. A little later you will be having different visual perceptions, such as that of putting down this book. Weeks or months or years from now, you'll have who-knows-what sorts of perceptions; we're not in a position to know our futures. Nevertheless, whatever specific perceptions will happen to you in the future, at those different times, it is true right now that you *will* have those perceptions exactly when you have them, even if you don't know it.

But a true sentence is one where the predicate is contained in the subject.

If so, it follows that all those future perceptions of yours must already be contained in you in some sense or another. What makes the sentence "snow is white" true right now is that whiteness is contained in snow; what makes "you will have perception p at later time t" true right now is that *the fact that you will have that perception at that time is itself already contained in you.*

But if the fact that you will have all those future perceptions is already built into you now, then we cannot say that those perceptions will, later, only be caused in you by something outside you. And to say that is just to say that nothing at all has causal influence over you and your perceptions. And of course similar considerations apply to every single individual thing and to everything that will happen *to* every single thing.

And that is precisely what pre-established harmony asserts. The very idea of truth, then, supports pre-established harmony.

RATIONALISM, INTELLIGIBILITY, AND CAUSATION

What the three philosophers we have just looked at shared was a supreme confidence in the faculty of reason. The human mind, they believed, is so structured that by following the proper method, it is capable of arriving at certain knowledge of reality. Unfortunately, although each claimed to use that same faculty in the same way, and each thought that what he could deduce "clearly and distinctly" with his mind reflected what existed in the world outside, they arrived at very different theories of the world. These disparate accounts ultimately led their competitors, the early modern empiricists, to question the basic, underlying premises shared by these three major rationalists.

What are these premises?

The first is a key epistemological one: that pure reason, reason used alone, is a reliable source of knowledge. We see this most explicitly in Spinoza and Leibniz, who essentially sat in their proverbial armchairs and reached their dramatic and counterintuitive accounts of the world just by reasoning about the nature of "substances" and "truth" and similar concepts. But while Descartes (as an early scientist) is more open to the role that sensory experience and empirical observation must play in the production of knowledge, even he treats reason as the final arbiter. The senses provide data about the world, but it is only when that data is processed by careful reasoning that knowledge is achieved.

The second premise is metaphysical, and more subtle, perhaps because it is even more fundamental than the first: that the world itself is intelligible, an idea we saw in chapter 7. To say the world is intelligible is to say that it is capable of being understood; and clearly, if reason is to be capable of understanding (or "knowing") the world, then the world itself must be knowable. (Note here, again, how closely intertwined metaphysics and epistemology must be. If reason is to be a reliable source of knowledge [epistemology] then the world must have a certain structure that makes it knowable [metaphysics].)

Now what it means for the world to be "understood" is a complicated question, but we can make an initial entry into it. At least one sense in which we understand how or why things occur in the world involves *causation*. Suppose a given event occurs: a volcano erupts, a leaf falls, you hear Josh calling you, your arm moves toward the refrigerator door. We feel we partly understand how or why these events occur when we grasp their causes. Sometimes we look to the sciences to reveal causes. Geologists will talk about heat and magma, botanists will talk about the chemical processes inside leaves, neuroscientists work out how sound makes neurons fire and produce perceptions. Sometimes we just look inside, reflecting on our own experience. Your arm moved toward the refrigerator because you were hungry and wanted a snack, and those mental states caused the bodily motion.

Understanding the world, then, at least partly involves grasping what causes what, or the causal relations between events. It was not for nothing that David Hume (1711–1776) called causation the "cement of the universe," since it's what holds everything together—and to grasp how everything holds together is to understand it. No wonder, then, that early modern rationalists devoted a great deal of their time to thinking about causation.

Rationalist Debates on the Nature of Causation

There are two closely related questions in play here.

First, just what is the nature of the causal relation? When we say that a given event *causes* another event, just what exactly do we mean? (We'll return to this question below.)

Second, between just which sorts of events does this relation actually obtain? Given that most philosophers of the period followed Descartes in endorsing mind-body dualism (Spinoza excepted), there are four main domains of discussion.

(1) Body->body: Does the causal relation obtain between purely physical events? That is, can one physical event cause another physical event?

(2) Mind->body: Can mental events (such as thoughts, perceptions, desires) cause physical events (as when your feeling of hunger leads your arm to move to the fridge)?

(3) Body->mind: In the opposite direction, can physical events (such as Josh calling you) cause mental events (such as your perception of his voice)?

(4) Mind->mind: Can mental events cause other mental events—either within one mind (one thought of yours leading to the next thought) or between two minds (for example if you could get someone to think something merely by willing that she think it)?

These are a lot of possible combinations, but the philosopher must examine them all. Different considerations arise in the different domains, and it's possible to take different positions in different domains. For our purposes, a brief survey below must suffice.

As for the "different positions" in different domains, let's introduce the main competitors.

Interactionism is the doctrine that there does exist a causal relation in the relevant domain. An interactionist regarding the mind->body domain holds that mental events truly do cause physical events.

Occasionalism is the doctrine that there does *not* exist a causal relation in the relevant domain, but rather the first event is merely the occasion upon which *God* directly causes the second event. An occasionalist regarding the mind->body domain holds that your desire for a snack (for example) does *not* cause your arm to move to the fridge. Instead your desire is the occasion on which God causes your arm to move. Though this may sound strange, we'll see shortly that it must be taken seriously.

Pre-established harmony is of course the Leibnizian doctrine that there does *not* exist a causal relation between *any* pairs of events involving any two distinct substances. Rather each substance runs its own internal program in perfect synchrony with every other. The only true causation is internal, within the substance.

That's a lot to digest at the start, so let's just begin.

Descartes

In the purely physical (body->body) domain, most scholars interpret Descartes, in fact, to be an occasionalist. Physical events don't actually cause other physical events. Instead, God causes all the motion in the physical world.

There are several reasons to interpret Descartes this way. For one thing, matter, in his mechanical philosophy, is merely extension, and thus passive and inert. It just "takes up space," and thus is incapable of moving itself or anything else. If one physical motion is followed by some other (such as in billiard balls colliding), then we should not say that the first motion caused the second. For a second reason, Descartes also worked out what he took to be the laws governing the motion of bodies. But part of this work included an explicit derivation of these laws directly from the nature of God—implying that, ultimately, God is the causal source of all the motion in the physical world.

In the mind->body domain, most scholars interpret Descartes to be an interactionist. Mental events can cause physical events, so your desires (say) truly cause your body to move. Though there are several problems with this view, the most famous is **the mind-body problem**, generated by Descartes's sharp dualism: if matter is extended and the mind is non-extended, then how could the two possibly interact? Purely physical objects (like billiard balls) could causally affect each other (at least in principle) by colliding, by banging into each other. But something non-extended, that doesn't have any spatial properties, that doesn't even exist anywhere *in* space, cannot collide with something that does exist in space. So it seemed unintelligible, almost miraculous, that a mental state could cause a bodily motion, or that a brain state could cause a mental state. While Descartes himself thought this objection could be met, many thinkers in his time and to this day disagree. That's partly why some of his contemporaries sought alternatives, either to his dualism (Spinoza and Berkeley; see chapter 9) or to his mind->body interactionism (as we'll see in a moment).

In the body->mind domain for Descartes, however, the situation is not clear. On the one hand, Descartes seems to be an interactionist, as his proof for the external world (see above) strongly suggests that physical bodies cause our mental perceptions. But on the other hand, the mechanical philosophy dictates that matter is entirely passive, and if a piece of matter cannot even cause motion in another piece of matter with which it is capable of coming in contact, then how could it cause perceptions to arise in a non-extended mind, across the mind-body divide? It isn't clear, then, how we should interpret Descartes in this domain.

Nicolas Malebranche (1638–1715)

Around the time French thinker Malebranche was ordained as a priest, in 1664, he happened upon Descartes's posthumously published *Treatise on Man* in a bookstall, a book he found so exciting that he suffered cardiac palpitations from reading it. He subsequently immersed himself in Descartes's science and philosophy, then commenced his own prolific philosophical output, soon becoming the most famous philosopher in France in his time. Two of his many important works are his *On the Search after Truth* (1674–1675), and *Dialogues on Metaphysics and Religion* (1688). Despite his prestige in his day, Malebranche's work fell into relative obscurity, undeservedly so. In the English-speaking world in particular it was only rediscovered several decades ago, and is now enjoying a renaissance.

If there is one doctrine he is most associated with today it is occasionalism, which he defended across the board, in every domain. Let us look at several of his arguments.

(1) *Occasionalism dissolves the mind-body problem.* Malebranche follows Descartes in endorsing mind-body dualism, and so inherits the mind-body problem we've been discussing. But occasionalism, in its favor, dissolves that problem. It doesn't *solve* it, for to solve it would be to explain just how mind and body engage in causal interactions. Rather, it simply doesn't

suffer from the problem because it denies that mind and body *do* engage in causal interactions. Mental states are the occasions on which God causes physical states, and vice versa: no problem. (At least not for theists, which included essentially all the major philosophers in these debates.)

(2) *The know-how argument for occasionalism*. Here Malebranche's focus is on the mind->body domain. We might summarize this argument as follows:

For a mind to cause a physical event it must know how to bring that event about.
We do not know how to bring about physical events.

Therefore, our minds do not cause physical events.

Both premises may seem strange to us, so require a bit of elaboration. One idea behind the first premise is this. Minds don't do or cause things inadvertently, or unintentionally, but by *willing* them. That's why philosophers have spent centuries discussing "free will," for it is by means of our "will" that we choose, we act, we undertake, we endeavor—we cause. A second idea is that the mind is transparent. Following Descartes's theory of the mind, Malebranche holds that since mind is essentially consciousness, it must be aware of anything actively occurring in it. Put these two ideas together and we get the first premise. The mind causes by willing, and must know what it wills. But then if the mind is to cause something like a bodily event, it must know specifically what to do to bring that event about in order to will accordingly.

NICOLAS MALEBRANCHE

The transparency of the mind is essential to the second premise as well. How do you move your arm, Malebranche asks? You will to move it, and it moves. But that is no answer. If the mind is transparent and it is moving the arm, then it must be aware specifically of what it is doing to move the arm. But moving your arm involves a long complex series of physiological events. To move your arm you (or your mind) must know which muscles to contract, which chemical processes to initiate to make those muscles contract, which neurons to fire to initiate those chemical processes. But probably you have no idea whatsoever of what your anatomy is, what muscles you have, much less which neurons you have and how to trigger them.

What all this suggests is that, strictly speaking, we have no idea *how* we move our arms, or our bodies in general. We just will them to move, and they do. But combined with the first premise of his argument this means that, strictly speaking, we ourselves do not cause our bodies to move. We will our arms to move, and God, who does have the requisite knowledge, causes them to move, just as occasionalism says.

(3) *The continuous creation argument for occasionalism*. Like most thinkers of his time and like most religious thinkers of our own time in fact, Malebranche accepted **continuous**

creation, the doctrine that God continuously creates the world. This means that for all things, all minds and bodies, God causes them to exist at every moment in which they do exist. So if you exist at a given time (like now!), what explains your existing at that time is that God wills that you exist at that time. Were God at any time to cease willing

> You find yourself in the world, without any power, immovable as a rock, stupid, so to speak, as a log of wood.
>
> **—Nicolas Malebranche**

your existence, *poof!* you would go out of existence. (Space limits prevent our looking at any arguments for this doctrine, but many are provided by Malebranche, Descartes, Aquinas, and others.)

So Malebranche next argues that, once you accept continuous creation (which most of the theists debating causation accept anyway), you should also accept occasionalism.

With respect to physical bodies, Malebranche begins,

> God [cannot] will that a body exist nowhere, nor that it does not stand in certain relations of distance to other bodies. Thus, God cannot will that this armchair exist . . . without situating it here, there, or elsewhere. (*Dialogues on Metaphysics and on Religion* VII.X, in ed. Nicholas Jolley, transl. David Scott, *Nicolas Malebranche: Dialogues on Metaphysics and on Religion* [Cambridge: Cambridge University Press, 1997], 115)

When God creates the armchair, He has to specify its location: He has to put it *somewhere*. That means that God is not only fully responsible for the existence of every physical body at every time, but also the specific locations of every physical body.

But that in turn means that God is fully responsible for the state of motion or rest of every body as well. For a body to be in motion is just for it to be in different locations at sequential times; to be at rest is to be in the same location at different times. If God is responsible for existence and location at every time, then He is responsible for all motion.

But now according to the mechanical philosophy (you'll recall), everything in the physical world may be fully explained in terms of the size, shape, and motion of all the physical bodies. If God continuously creates all bodies, then He is *Himself* fully responsible for their sizes, shapes, and motions at all times. But then there is literally nothing left over in the physical world for anything else, minds or bodies, to be causally responsible for.

In short, God causes everything in the physical world. Two physical billiard balls collide: God moves them toward the collision and causes their motion after the collision. Or you may (mentally) desire your arm to move, but God moves your physical arm. Thus occasionalism is true, at least where there are physical effects, that is the body->body and mind->body domains.

What about the body->mind domain?

While Malebranche makes this specific argument using only purely physical examples, it certainly seems to generalize. For God also continuously creates souls or minds, including yours. But now when He creates a mind, He must create it in *some* state or another, thinking something, perceiving something, and so forth. But then it follows that God is fully causally responsible for the particular states of every mind at every time. But then we shouldn't say that (for example) physically putting your hand on the stove was the cause of your mentally feeling that subsequent pain. Rather, that is only the occasion on which God creates your mind, at that time, feeling that pain. So again, God causes everything, and nothing else does anything.

Once you accept continuous creation, in short, you get occasionalism in every domain.

(4) *The necessary connection argument for occasionalism*.

Malebranche's next argument returns us to the first question we mentioned at the start of our causation discussion. Just what is the nature of the causal relation? Just what do we mean when we call one thing or event, *x*, the "cause" of another, *y*?

It is that *x* made or compelled *y* to happen; that, given that *x* occurred in those circumstances, it was impossible for *y* *not* to happen. Thus, common sense says that the striking of the match caused it to light because it was impossible for the match *not* to light, in those conditions, once it was struck. To see this, imagine for a moment that it was *not* impossible for the match *not* to light in those conditions: you could just as well have struck the match that way without its lighting. If that were so, if the match could just as well light as not light, then the fact that it *did* light would seem to be random, not something the striking *made* or caused to happen.

When events are connected in this way, when the occurrence of the first makes it impossible for the second not to occur, philosophers say that the events are **necessarily connected**. To say "*x* causes *y*," then, is to say that "there is a necessary connection between *x* and *y*": whenever *x* occurs in those conditions, it's *impossible* for *y* not to occur.

That is a plausible conception of causation, even today, and it was widely accepted in Malebranche's time. (In chapter 9 we'll discuss David Hume's attack on it.) But if that is what causation is, Malebranche next argues, occasionalism follows:

> Causation is a matter of necessary connections.
> There are no necessary connections between any pair of ordinary events, physical or
>   mental.
> There is a necessary connection between God's willing and the events He wills.
> ----------
> Therefore, God is the only true cause, of everything.

The first premise is just our conception of causation, so let's turn to the second. Think of any two events, such as your mental desire to get a snack and your subsequent bodily motion toward the fridge. We can easily conceive of circumstances in which you might have that same desire and yet that motion fails to occur: you might be paralyzed or restrained, or you might only be dreaming about the fridge, or you might only *be* a mind (per *Meditation Two*) and not even *have* a body, and so on. Most of all, if you are a theist, then it's always within *God's* power to override any desire you might have, so He could always prevent your body motion. But if it's even *possible* to have the desire without the motion then there is no *necessary* connection between them. And if not, then the desire cannot be said to cause the motion.

Similar reasoning applies to any other pair of events. Any theist would grant God the power, even if miraculous, of overriding the normally expected sequence of events. So no physical event ever *guarantees* any subsequent physical or mental event (bodily motion, or thought or perception); nor does any ordinary mental event (desire, will) ever guarantee any subsequent physical or mental event (bodily motion, additional thoughts). There are no necessary connections, and therefore no true causation, between any pairs of ordinary events.

Necessary connections are to be found only in one place, Malebranche observes:

> But when one thinks about the idea of God, i.e., of an . . . all-powerful being, one knows there is such a connection between His will and the motion of all bodies, that it is impossible to conceive that He wills a body to be moved and that this body not be moved. (*The Search after Truth* 6.2.3, in transls., eds. Thomas Lennon and Paul Olscamp, *Nicolas Malebranche: The Search after Truth* [Cambridge: Cambridge University Press, 1997], 448)

There is actually a contradiction in the idea that an infinitely powerful being (God) might will for something to happen and yet that thing doesn't happen. After all, "infinite" power is by definition power without limits, so nothing *could* override it. So if that being wills something, that thing *must* occur. But that is just to say that there *is* a necessary connection between the will of God and whatever it is that He wills. And that means that only with respect to God do we ever find genuine causality.

If causation is necessary connection, then, no ordinary things ever cause anything, and God causes everything. Occasionalism is true in every domain.

A final thought on Malebranche. While occasionalism does have its own problems, the important point is that these problems are worth responding to in the first place, as Malebranche attempts to do. For Malebranche's greatest achievement may be in simply making occasionalism a serious contender at all, by showing rather compellingly that you should accept occasionalism if you accept any one of a number of other doctrines. Obviously if you are an atheist, then occasionalism will be a non-starter for you. But if you are a theist then even today you must work out God's causal relationship to His creation, and you will have to seriously entertain the idea of continuous creation; and once you do *that* you will be practically all the way there to occasionalism. Moreover, if you (quite plausibly) think causation is a matter of necessary connection, then, again, you just may have to accept occasionalism. (In fact Malebranche's argument against necessary connections between ordinary events was extremely influential in Hume's later critique of causation, as we'll see.) Whatever you finally think about occasionalism, then, you must at least think about it seriously.

Leibniz

We conclude our survey of rationalist debates on causation by returning to Leibniz. Above we sketched his doctrine of pre-established harmony, and looked at one important argument for it, the truth argument. We also saw that Leibniz thought the doctrine had certain "advantages," which further suggested its correctness. To these we now turn.

Pre-established harmony makes two essential claims: (1) individual substances do not causally interact and (2) yet they genuinely do have *internal* causal powers, as their internal programs cause their sequence of internal states. Competing causal theories reject either of these claims. Interactionism rejects (1), by affirming that substances do causally interact, while occasionalism rejects (2), by denying that ordinary substances have any causal powers at all. Leibniz now criticizes these competitors, and shows how his own doctrine avoids those criticisms.

Mind->body interactionism (to focus on that domain) suffers from at least two problems, Leibniz argues.

The first is that it violates the laws of motion that govern the entire physical universe. These laws—which Descartes, Leibniz, and Isaac Newton among others were working out—dictate what happens in the physical world. If bodies of certain sizes and shapes are moving a certain way at one moment, the laws dictate how and where they would be moving in the next moment. But now suppose your (mental) desire for a snack causes your (physical) neurons to fire a certain way. Your brain is a physical body, so the laws of motion already dictate which way they should fire. So if your desire actually affects their motion, it must be by overriding the motion the laws dictate, thus violating them. So every instance of mind-body interaction would be literally a miracle!

The second problem is deeper. As we saw, the rationalist typically demands that the world be intelligible. To demand that, is to demand that we be able to understand precisely how and why events occur, how and why earlier events bring about or cause subsequent events. But this is precisely where mind->body and body->mind interaction fail:

> When I began to meditate about the union of [mind] and body, I felt as if I were thrown . . . into the open sea. For I could not find any way of explaining how the body makes anything happen in the soul, or *vice versa*. ("New System," 142–43)

This is of course the mind-body problem. Given the distinct nature of the mental (unextended) and physical (extended), Leibniz claims it is simply unintelligible how one could causally influence the other. So interactionism violates intelligibility.

Now occasionalism might avoid these problems. If the mind does not truly cause physical motion then it needn't violate the laws of motion, and if there is no causal interaction then there is nothing unintelligible occurring. But Leibniz thinks that occasionalism ultimately fares no better than interactionism, suffering from its own problems.

First, Leibniz suggests, occasionalism does not pay proper respect to God as the creator of the world. God's perfection implies that what He creates should have some perfection as well, and entirely powerless creatures, impotent creatures, would not reflect well on their creator. More importantly, occasionalism actually does *not* do any better with respect to intelligibility than interactionism. For to say, of every event, that God causes it is to admit, ultimately, that we do not understand how it comes about. Imagine that you hired a scientific expert to determine what caused a certain explosion, and after his or her lengthy investigation he or she informs you that "God did it." You would not be satisfied with that answer, and for good reason. A proper explanation, a proper understanding, would show how events arise from the natures of the objects involved in the events. If you show how the explosion arose as a result of the properties of the chemicals involved, then you have understood it. But that is precisely what occasionalism denies.

In contrast to both interactionism and occasionalism, Leibniz thinks, pre-established harmony shines. Substances (minds, bodies) do have genuine causal powers, *internal* causal powers, to generate their own sequence of internal states. Thus they reflect appropriately on God's perfection, and it is possible (at least in principle) to explain how or why events occur, as arising from the natures of the substances involved. But since there is no causation between substances you avoid the two problems for interactionism. There is nothing unintelligible occurring between mind and body, and minds aren't violating the laws of motion.

So, Leibniz concludes, logic itself supports pre-established harmony (by the truth argument), and the doctrine avoids important problems that its competitors face. "Surprising" as it may sound on first hearing, he noted (above), on reflection it seems "inevitable," and (as he wrote) "has very great advantages and rather considerable beauty"—precisely the sort of world (you might think) that Leibniz's highly rational God, aiming to produce the best overall possible world, would bring about.

SUMMARY

1. In the early modern philosophers we find epistemology and metaphysics closely intertwined. They are standardly divided into the schools of rationalism and empiricism, where the former stresses the role of reason in generating knowledge and the latter stresses perceptual

experience. The rationalists include René Descartes, Nicolas Malebranche, Baruch Spinoza, and G. W. Leibniz, while the empiricists include John Locke, George Berkeley, and David Hume. Immanuel Kant, concluding the period, is said to have synthesized the two schools.

2. Descartes is the "father of modern philosophy." He earns this title by rejecting the Christian Aristotelianism that dominated the medieval period, and by developing new theories of the natures of mind and of matter. He begins by seeking epistemological foundations, beliefs of which he can be absolutely certain, and aims to base all knowledge on those foundations. To discover such foundations he employs the method of radical skepticism, which discloses that he can initially be certain only of one thing, that he exists as a thinking thing. This passage is summarized by the expression "I think therefore I am," or *cogito ergo sum*.

3. From the *cogito*, Descartes derives his clear and distinct criterion for truth, then uses this criterion to prove that God exists. That God exists, and that God would not inescapably deceive us, next support his argument that the external physical world exists. But our senses often deceive us about this world, so we must only accept that which we clearly and distinctly grasp about physical bodies, namely their mathematical properties.

4. Descartes provides several arguments for his dualism, including a theological argument, some metaphysical arguments, and an empirical argument.

5. Descartes's theory of mind consists of the representational theory of mind, the claim that the mind is possessed of the four properties of indubitability, incorrigibility, transparency, and unity, and that its defining property is thought or consciousness. Descartes offers two arguments for the representational theory of mind: the dream argument, and the relativity of perception argument.

6. Descartes's theory of matter is the mechanical philosophy, consisting of at least five claims: the defining property of matter is extension, matter is the same everywhere, the world is a plenum, perceivable differences in matter are due to variations in motion, and God is responsible for the motion in nature.

7. Spinoza's famous doctrines include his pantheism and his monism. There exists only one substance, the infinite substance which is God or Nature. Mind and matter are different aspects of that one substance, different ways we can think about it. Other famous Spinoza doctrines include his necessitarianism and determinism.

8. Leibniz defends pre-established harmony, holding that all the substances in the world (or monads) are running their own internal program, with no causal interaction between them. Supporting it are the truth argument and the advantages it has over its competitors when it comes to matters of causation.

9. Rationalists are deeply interested in the nature of causation, as causation is one aspect of the intelligibility of the world. Their debate addresses the four different domains of causation: body->body, mind->body, body->mind, and mind->mind. The three main contenders are interactionism, occasionalism, and pre-established harmony.

10. Descartes endorses occasionalism in the body->body domain, probably interactionism in the mind->body domain, and it's unclear how to interpret him in the body->mind domain. Malebranche offers several arguments for occasionalism in every domain, including the know-how argument, the continuous creation argument, and the necessary connection argument. Leibniz defends pre-established harmony in every domain, both by means of the truth argument and by showing how pre-established harmony avoids problems he raises for its competitors.

KEY TERMS

clear and distinct criterion

cogito ergo sum

continuous creation

continuous creation argument for
    occasionalism

determinism

dream argument for RTM

dualism

early modern philosophy

empirical argument for dualism

empiricism

extension intuition

idea

idealism

incorrigibility

interactionism

know-how argument for occasionalism

the mechanical philosophy

metaphysical arguments for dualism

the mind-body problem

monad

monism

natural philosophy

necessary connection

necessary connection argument for
    occasionalism

necessitarianism

occasionalism

pantheism

personal immortality

plenum

pre-established harmony

radical skeptic

rationalism

relativity of perception argument

representational theory of mind (RTM)

simple unity

skeptic

substance

theological argument for dualism

transparency

truth argument for pre-established
    harmony

REVIEW QUESTIONS

1. What are the two standard schools of early modern philosophy?
2. For what reasons is Descartes considered the "father of modern philosophy"?
3. Briefly summarize Descartes's theory of mind and his theory of matter.
4. In what way(s) might Spinoza's pantheism be understood as a kind of atheism?
5. What is Leibniz's "truth argument for pre-established harmony"?
6. Briefly summarize any two of Malebranche's arguments for occasionalism.

NOTES

1. *Meditations* quotes from transl., Donald Cress, in René Descartes, *Meditations on First Philosophy*, 3rd ed. (Indianapolis/Cambridge: Hackett Publishing Company, 1993).

2. Ed., Transl., R. H. M. Elwes, *The Chief Works of Benedict De Spinoza*, (New York: Dover, 1951), Vol. II, 75–76.

3. Letter to Arnauld (April 30, 1687), in transl., eds., Roger Ariew and Daniel Garber, *G. W. Leibniz: Philosophical Essays* (Indianapolis: Hackett, 1989), 84.

4. This section is adapted from Andrew Pessin, *Uncommon Sense: The Strangest Ideas from the Smartest Philosophers* (Lanham, MD: Rowman & Littlefield, 2012), ch. 10.

5. *Discourse on Metaphysics 8*, in transls., eds. Roger Ariew and Daniel Garber, *G. W. Leibniz: Philosophical Essays* (Indianapolis, IN: Hackett Publishing Company), 41.

■ Reading

Meditations on First Philosophy

DESCARTES

From Meditations on First Philosophy *(1640); transls., John Cottingham, Robert Stoothoff, and Dugald Murdoch,* The Philosophical Writings of Descartes, Vol. 2 *(Cambridge, UK: Cambridge University Press, 1984), pp. 12–20.*

In this excerpt Descartes uses radical skepticism to seek foundational, indubitable beliefs, derives the *cogito*, and begins to sketch his dualism.

FIRST MEDITATION: WHAT CAN BE CALLED INTO DOUBT

Some years ago I was struck by the large number of falsehoods that I had accepted as true in my childhood, and by the highly doubtful nature of the whole edifice that I had subsequently based on them. I realized that it was necessary, once in the course of my life, to demolish everything completely and start again right from the foundations if I wanted to establish anything at all in the sciences that was stable and likely to last. But the task looked an enormous one, and I began to wait until I should reach a mature enough age to ensure that no subsequent time of life would be more suitable for tackling such inquiries. This led me to put the project off for so long that I would now be to blame if by pondering over it any further I wasted the time still left for carrying it out. So today I have expressly rid my mind of all worries and arranged for myself a clear stretch of free time. I am here quite alone, and at last I will devote myself sincerely and without reservation to the general demolition of my opinions.

But to accomplish this, it will not be necessary for me to show that all my opinions are false, which is something I could perhaps never manage. Reason now leads me to think that I should hold back my assent from opinions which are not completely certain and indubitable just as carefully as I do from those which are patently false. So, for the purpose of rejecting all my opinions, it will be enough if I find in each of them at least some reason for doubt. And to do this I will not need to run through them all individually, which would be an endless task. Once the foundations of a building are undermined, anything built on them collapses of its own accord; so I will go straight for the basic principles on which all my former beliefs rested.

Whatever I have up till now accepted as most true I have acquired either from the senses or through the senses. But from time to time I have found that the senses deceive, and it is prudent never to trust completely those who have deceived us even once. Yet although the senses occasionally deceive us with respect to objects which are very small or in the distance, there are many other beliefs about which doubt is quite impossible, even though they are derived from the senses—for example, that I am here, sitting by the fire, wearing a winter dressing-gown, holding this piece of paper in my hands, and so on. Again, how could it be denied that these hands or this whole body are mine? Unless perhaps I were to liken myself to madmen, whose brains are so damaged by the persistent vapours of melancholia that they firmly maintain they are king when they are paupers, or say they are dressed in purple when they are naked, or that their heads are made of earthenware, or that they are pumpkins, or made of glass. But such people are insane, and I would be thought equally mad if I took anything from them as a model for myself.

A brilliant piece of reasoning! As if I were not a man who sleeps at night, and regularly has all the same experiences while asleep as madmen do when awake—indeed sometimes even more improbable ones. How often, asleep at night, am I convinced of just such familiar events—that I am here in my dressing-gown, sitting by the fire—when in fact I am lying undressed in bed! Yet at the moment my eyes are certainly wide awake when I look at this piece of paper; I shake my head and it is not asleep; as I stretch out and feel my hand I do so deliberately, and I know what I am doing. All this would not happen with such distinctness to someone asleep. Indeed! As if I did not remember other occasions when I have been tricked by exactly similar thoughts while asleep! As I think about this more carefully, I see plainly that there are never any sure signs by means of which being awake can be distinguished from being asleep. The result is that I begin to feel dazed, and this very feeling only reinforces the notion that I may be asleep.

Suppose then that I am dreaming, and that these particulars—that my eyes are open, that I am moving my head and stretching out my hands—are not true. Perhaps, indeed, I do not even have such hands or such a body at all. Nonetheless, it must surely be admitted that the visions which come in sleep are like paintings, which must have been fashioned in the likeness of things that are real, and hence that at least these general kinds of things—eyes, head, hands, and the body as a whole—are things which are not imaginary but are real and exist. For even when painters try to create sirens and satyrs with the most extraordinary bodies, they cannot give them natures which are new in all respects; they simply jumble up the limbs of different animals. Or if perhaps they manage to think up something so new that nothing remotely similar has ever been seen before—something which is therefore completely fictitious and unreal—at least the colours used in the composition must be real. By similar reasoning, although these general kinds of things—eyes, head, hands, and so on—could be imaginary, it must at least be admitted that certain other even simpler and more universal things are real. These are as it were the real colours from which we form all the images of things, whether true or false, that occur in our thought.

This class appears to include corporeal nature in general, and its extension; the shape of extended things; the quantity, or size and number of these things; the place in which they may exist, the time through which they may endure, and so on.

So a reasonable conclusion from this might be that physics, astronomy, medicine, and all other disciplines which depend on the study of composite things, are doubtful; while arithmetic, geometry and other subjects of this kind, which deal only with the simplest and most general things, regardless of whether they really exist in nature or not, contain something certain and indubitable. For whether I am awake or asleep, two and three added together are five, and a square has no more than four sides. It seems impossible that such transparent truths should incur any suspicion of being false.

And yet firmly rooted in my mind is the long-standing opinion that there is an omnipotent God who made me the kind of creature that I am. How do I know that he has not brought it about that there is no earth, no sky, no extended thing, no shape, no size, no place, while at the same time ensuring that all these things appear to me to exist just as they do now? What is more, since I sometimes believe that others go astray in cases where they think they have the most perfect knowledge, may I not similarly go wrong every time I add two and three or count the sides of a square, or in some even simpler matter, if that is imaginable? But perhaps God would not have allowed me to be deceived in this way, since he is said to be supremely good. But if it were inconsistent with his goodness to have created me such that I am deceived all the time, it would seem equally foreign to his goodness to allow me to be deceived even occasionally; yet this last assertion cannot be made.

Perhaps there may be some who would prefer to deny the existence of so powerful a God rather than believe that everything else is uncertain. Let us not argue with them, but grant them that everything said about God is a fiction. According to their supposition, then, I have arrived at my present state by fate or chance or a continuous chain of events, or by some other means; yet since deception and error seem to be imperfections, the less powerful they make my original cause, the more likely it is that I am so imperfect as to be deceived all the time. I have no answer to these arguments, but am finally compelled to admit that there is not one of my former beliefs about which a doubt may not properly be raised; and this is not a flippant or ill-considered conclusion, but is based on powerful and well thought-out reasons. So in future I must withhold my assent from these former beliefs just as carefully as I would from obvious falsehoods, if I want to discover any certainty.

But it is not enough merely to have noticed this; I must make an effort to remember it. My habitual opinions keep coming back, and, despite my wishes, they capture my belief, which is as it were bound over to them as a result of long occupation and the law of custom. I shall never get out of the habit of confidently assenting to these opinions, so long as I suppose them to be what in fact they are, namely highly probable opinions—opinions which, despite the fact that they are in a sense doubtful, as has just been shown, it is still much more reasonable to believe than to deny. In view of this, I think it will be a good plan to turn my will in completely the opposite direction and deceive myself, by pretending for a time that these former opinions are utterly false and imaginary. I shall do this until the weight of preconceived opinion is counter-balanced and the distorting influence of habit no longer prevents my judgement from perceiving things correctly. In the meantime, I know that no danger or error will result from my plan, and that I cannot possibly go too far in my distrustful attitude. This is because the task now in hand does not involve action but merely the acquisition of knowledge.

I will suppose therefore that not God, who is supremely good and the source of truth, but rather some malicious demon of the utmost power and cunning has employed all his energies in order to deceive me. I shall think that the sky, the air, the earth, colours, shapes, sounds and all external things are merely the delusions of dreams which he has devised to ensnare my judgement. I shall consider myself as not having hands or eyes, or flesh, or blood or senses, but as falsely believing that I have all these things. I shall stubbornly and firmly persist in this meditation; and, even if it is not in my power to know any truth, I shall at least do what is in my power, that is, resolutely guard against assenting to any falsehoods, so that the deceiver, however powerful and cunning he may be, will be unable to impose on me in the slightest degree. But this is an arduous undertaking, and a kind of laziness brings me back to normal life. I am like a prisoner who is enjoying an imaginary freedom while asleep; as he begins to suspect that he is asleep, he dreads being woken up, and goes along with the pleasant illusion as long as he can. In the same way, I happily slide back into my old opinions and dread being shaken out of them, for fear that my peaceful sleep may be followed by hard labour when I wake, and that I shall have to toil not in the light, but amid the inextricable darkness of the problems I have now raised.

SECOND MEDITATION: THE NATURE OF THE HUMAN MIND, AND HOW IT IS BETTER KNOWN THAN THE BODY

So serious are the doubts into which I have been thrown as a result of yesterday's meditation that I can neither put them out of my mind nor see any way of resolving them. It feels as if I have fallen unexpectedly into a deep whirlpool which tumbles me around so that I can neither stand on the bottom nor swim up to the top. Nevertheless I will make an effort and once more attempt the same path which I started on yesterday. Anything which admits of the slightest doubt I will set aside just as if I had found it to be wholly false; and I will proceed in this way until I recognize something certain, or, if nothing else, until I at least recognize for certain that there is no certainty. Archimedes used to demand just one firm and immovable point in order to shift the entire earth; so I too can hope for great things if I manage to find just one thing, however slight, that is certain and unshakeable.

I will suppose then, that everything I see is spurious. I will believe that my memory tells me lies, and that none of the things that it reports ever happened. I have no senses. Body, shape, extension, movement and place are chimeras. So what remains true? Perhaps just the one fact that nothing is certain.

Yet apart from everything I have just listed, how do I know that there is not something else which does not allow even the slightest occasion for doubt? Is there not a God, or whatever I may call him, who puts into me the thoughts I am now having? But why do I think this, since I myself may perhaps be the author of these thoughts? In that case am not I, at least, something? But I have just said that I have no senses and no body. This is the sticking point: what follows from this? Am I not so bound up with a body and with senses that I cannot exist without them? But I have convinced myself that there is absolutely nothing in the world, no sky, no earth, no minds, no bodies. Does it now follow that I too do not exist? No: if I convinced myself of something then I certainly existed. But there is a deceiver of supreme power and cunning who is deliberately and constantly deceiving me. In that case I too undoubtedly exist, if he is deceiving me; and let him deceive me as much as he can, he will never bring it about that I am nothing so long as I think that I am something. So after considering everything very thoroughly, I must finally conclude that this proposition, *I am, I exist,* is necessarily true whenever it is put forward by me or conceived in my mind.

But I do not yet have a sufficient understanding of what this "I" is, that now necessarily exists. So I must be on my guard against carelessly taking something else to be this "I," and so making a mistake in the very item of knowledge that I maintain is the most certain and evident of all. I will therefore go back and meditate on what I originally believed myself to be, before I embarked on this present train of thought. I will then subtract anything capable of being weakened, even minimally, by the arguments now introduced, so that what is left at the end may be exactly and only what is certain and unshakeable.

What then did I formerly think I was? A man. But what is a man? Shall I say "a rational animal"? No; for then I should have to inquire what an animal is, what rationality is, and in this way one question would lead me down the slope to other harder ones, and I do not now have the time to waste on subtleties of this kind. Instead I propose to concentrate on what came into my thoughts spontaneously and quite naturally whenever I used to consider what I was. Well, the first thought to come to mind was that I had a face, hands, arms and the whole mechanical structure of limbs which can be seen in a corpse, and which I called the body. The next thought was that I was nourished, that I moved about, and that I engaged in sense-perception and thinking; and these actions I attributed to the soul. But as to the nature of this soul, either I did not think about this or else I imagined it to be something tenuous, like a wind or fire or ether, which permeated my more solid parts. As to the body, however, I had no doubts about it, but thought I knew its nature distinctly. If I had tried to describe the mental conception I had of it, I would have expressed it as follows: by a body I understand whatever has a determinable shape and a definable location and can occupy a space in such a way as to exclude any other body; it can be perceived by touch, sight, hearing, taste or smell, and can be moved in various ways, not by itself but by whatever else comes into contact with it. For, according to my judgement, the power of self-movement, like the power of sensation or of thought, was quite foreign to the nature of a body; indeed, it was a source of wonder to me that certain bodies were found to contain faculties of this kind.

But what shall I now say that I am, when I am supposing that there is some supremely powerful and, if it is permissible to say so, malicious deceiver, who is deliberately trying to trick me in every way he can? Can I now assert that I possess even the most insignificant of all the attributes which I have just said belong to the nature of a body? I scrutinize them, think about them, go over them again, but nothing suggests itself; it is tiresome and pointless to go through the list once more. But what about the attributes I assigned to the soul? Nutrition or movement? Since now I do not have a body these are mere fabrications. Sense-perception? This surely does not occur without a body, and besides, when asleep I have appeared to perceive through the senses many things which I afterwards realized I did not perceive through the senses at all. Thinking? At last I have discovered it—thought; this alone is inseparable from me. I am, I exist—that is certain. But for how long? For as long as I am thinking. For it could be that were I totally to cease from thinking, I should totally cease to exist. At present I am not admitting anything except what is necessarily true. I am, then, in the strict sense only a thing that thinks; that is, I am a mind, or intelligence, or intellect, or reason—words whose meaning I have been ignorant of until now. But for all that I am a thing which is real and which truly exists. But what kind of a thing? As I have just said—a thinking thing.

What else am I? I will use my imagination. I am not that structure of limbs which is called a human body. I am not even some thin vapour which permeates the limbs—a wind, fire, air, breath, or whatever I depict in my imagination; for these are things which I have supposed to be nothing. Let this supposition stand; for all that I am still something. And yet may it not perhaps be the case that these very things which I am supposing to be nothing, because they are unknown to me, are in reality identical with the "I" of which I am aware? I do not know, and for the moment I shall not argue the point, since I can make judgements only about things which are known to me. I know that I exist; the question is, what is this "I" that I know? If the "I" is understood strictly as we have been taking it, then it is quite certain that knowledge of it does not depend on things of whose existence I am as yet unaware; so it cannot depend on any of the things which I invent in my imagination. And this very word "invent" shows me my mistake. It would indeed be a case of fictitious invention if I used my imagination to establish that I was something or other; for imagining is simply contemplating the shape or image of a corporeal thing. Yet now I know for certain both that I exist and at the same time that all such images and, in general, everything relating to the nature of body could be mere dreams and chimeras. Once this point has been grasped, to say "I will use my imagination to get to know more distinctly what I am" would seem to be as silly as saying "I am now awake, and see some truth; but since my vision is not yet clear enough, I will deliberately fall asleep so that my dreams may provide a truer and clearer representation." I thus realize that none of the things that the imagination enables me to grasp is at all relevant to this knowledge of myself which I possess, and that the mind must therefore be most carefully diverted from such things if it is to perceive its own nature as distinctly as possible.

But what then am I? A thing that thinks. What is that? A thing that doubts, understands, affirms, denies, is willing, is unwilling, and also imagines and has sensory perceptions.

This is a considerable list, if everything on it belongs to me. But does it? Is it not one and the same "I" who is now doubting almost everything, who nonetheless understands some things, who affirms that this one thing is true, denies everything else, desires to know more, is unwilling to be deceived, imagines many things even involuntarily, and is aware of many things which apparently come from the senses? Are not all these things just as true as the fact that I exist, even if I am asleep all the time, and even if he who created me is doing all he can to deceive me? Which of all these activities is distinct from my thinking? Which of them can be said to be separate from myself? The fact that it is I who am doubting and understanding and willing is so evident that I see no way of making it any clearer. But it is also the case that the "I" who imagines is the same "I." For even if, as I have supposed, none of the objects of imagination are real, the power of imagination is something which really exists and is part of my thinking. Lastly, it is also the same "I" who has sensory perceptions, or is aware of bodily things as it were through the senses. For example, I am now seeing light, hearing a noise, feeling heat. But I am asleep, so all this is false. Yet I certainly *seem* to see, to hear, and to be warmed. This cannot be false: what is called "having a sensory perception" is strictly just this, and in this restricted sense of the term it is simply thinking.

From all this I am beginning to have a rather better understanding of what I am.

REVIEW AND DISCUSSION QUESTIONS

1. Explain how Descartes uses radical skepticism to derive his foundational belief.

2. What argument(s) for dualism are suggested by the text? Explain.

3. Which properties of the mind, as discussed in the main text, can you find presented in the excerpt?

■ Reading

"The Most Dangerous Error of the Philosophy of the Ancients"

Nicolas Malebranche

"From The Search after Truth, *Book 6: Part 2, Chapter 3, ed., transl., Thomas Lennon and Paul Olscamp (Cambridge, UK: Cambridge University Press, 1997), 448–50. Reprinted with permission.*

In this excerpt Malebranche presents the know-how argument and the necessary connection argument for occasionalism.

In order that we shall no longer be able to doubt the falseness of this detestable philosophy [that ordinary things have causal powers] . . . it is necessary . . . to prove in few words that there is only one true cause because there is only one true God; that the nature or power of each thing is nothing but the will of God; that all natural causes are not *true* causes but only *occasional* causes. . . .

It is clear that no body, large or small, has the power to move itself . . . We have only two sorts of ideas, ideas of minds and ideas of bodies; and as we should speak only of what we conceive, we should only reason according to these two kinds of ideas. Thus, since the idea we have of all bodies makes us aware that they cannot move themselves, it must be concluded that it is minds which move them. But when we examine our idea of all finite minds, we do not see any necessary connection between their will and the motion of any body whatsoever. On the contrary, we see that there is none and that there can be none. We must therefore also conclude . . . that there is absolutely no mind created that can move a body as a true or principal cause, just as it has been said that no body could move itself.

But when one thinks about the idea of God, i.e., of an infinitely perfect and consequently all-powerful being, one knows that there is such a connection between His will and the motion of all bodies, that it is impossible to conceive that He wills a body to be moved and that this body not be moved. We must therefore say that only His will can move bodies if we wish to state things as we conceive them and not as we sense them. The motor force of bodies is therefore not in the bodies that are moved, for this motor force is nothing other than the will of God. Thus, bodies have no action; and when a ball that is moved collides with and moves another, it communicates to it nothing of its own, for it does not itself have the force it communicates to it. Nevertheless, a ball is the natural cause of the motion . . . not a real and true but only an occasional cause, which determines the Author of nature to act in such and such a manner in such and such a situation. . . .

Now it appears to me quite certain that the will of minds is incapable of moving the smallest body in the world; for it is clear that there is no necessary connection between our will to move our arms, for example, and the movement of our arms. . . .

For how could we move our arms? To move them, it is necessary to have animal spirits, to send them through certain nerves toward certain muscles in order to inflate and contract them, for it is thus that the arm attached to them is moved. . . . And we see that men who don't know that they have spirits, nerves, and muscles move their arms, and even move them with more skill and ease than those who anatomy best. Therefore, men will to move their arms, and only God is able and knows how to move them. . . . [T]here is no man who knows what must be done to move one of his fingers by means of animal spirits.

■ Reading

Dialogues on Metaphysics and Religion

Nicolas Malebranche

From Dialogues on Metaphysics and Religion, *Dialogue VII (1688); from ed., Nicholas Jolley, transl., David Scott,* Malebranche: Dialogues on Metaphysics and Religion *(Cambridge, UK: Cambridge University Press, 1997), pp. 113–16.*

In this excerpt Malebranche briefly defends the doctrine of continuous creation, then uses it to support occasionalism.

But because the universe has been created from nothing, it is so dependent on the universal cause that it would necessarily relapse into nothingness, were God to cease conserving it. For God neither does nor indeed can produce a creature independent of His volitions. . . . Thus, if bodies are [to be] essentially dependent on the creator, to subsist they need to be sustained by His continual influence, by the efficacy of the same volition which created them. If God simply stops willing their existence, it will follow necessarily and from this very fact alone that they will no longer exist. . . .

Creation does not pass, because the conservation of creatures is—on God's part—simply a continuous creation, a single volition subsisting and operating continuously. Now, God can neither conceive nor consequently will that a body exist nowhere, nor that it does not stand in certain relations of distance to other bodies. Thus, God cannot will that this armchair exist, and by this volition create or conserve it, without situating it here, there, or elsewhere. It is a contradiction, therefore, for one body to be able to move another. Further, I claim, it is a contradiction for you to be able to move your armchair. Nor is this enough; it is a contradiction for all the angels and demons together to be able to move a wisp of straw. The proof of this is clear. For now power, however great it be imagined, can surpass or even equal the power of God. Now, it is a contradiction that God wills this armchair to exist, unless He wills it to exist somewhere and unless, by the efficacy of His will, He puts it there, conserves it there, creates it there. Hence, no power can convey it to where God does not convey it, nor fix nor stop it where God does not stop it, unless God accommodates the efficacy of His action to the inefficacious action of His creatures.

REVIEW AND DISCUSSION QUESTIONS

1. Briefly summarize each of the three arguments for occasionalism in these two excerpts (know-how, necessary connection, and continuous creation).

2. How might an atheist respond to these arguments, exactly?

3. How might a theist who is not inclined to accept occasionalism respond to them?

■ Reading
"New System of Nature"
G. W. Leibniz

Transls., Roger Ariew and Daniel Garber, in eds., Roger Ariew and Eric Watkins, Modern Philosophy: An Anthology of Primary Sources, *2nd Edition (Indianapolis: Hackett, 2009), pp. 273–74.*

In this excerpt Leibniz sketches his doctrine of pre-established harmony.

Therefore, since I was forced to agree that it is not possible for the soul or any other true substance to receive something from without . . . I was led, little by little, to a view that surprised me, but which seems inevitable, and which, in fact, has very great advantages and rather considerable beauty. That is, we must say that God originally created the soul (and any other real [substance]) in such a way that everything must arise for it from its own depths, through a perfect *spontaneity* relative to itself, and yet with a perfect *conformity* relative to external things. And thus, since our internal sensations . . . are merely phenomena which follow upon external beings, or better, they are true appearances and like well-ordered dreams, these internal perceptions in the soul itself must arise because of its own original constitution . . . [that] makes the perceptions or expressions of external things occur in the soul at a given time, in virtue of its own laws, as if in a world apart, and as if there existed only God and itself. . . . There will be a perfect agreement among all these substances, producing the same effect that would be noticed if they communicated through the transmission of species or qualities. . . . In addition, the organized mass, in which the point of view of the soul lies . . . is in turn ready to act by itself, following the laws of the corporeal machine, at the moment when the soul wills it to act, without disturbing the laws of the other. . . . It is this mutual relation, regulated in advance in each substance of the universe, which produces what we call their *communication*, and which alone brings about the *union of soul and body*.

■ Reading

"Clarification of the Difficulties Which Mr. Bayle Has Found in the New System of the Union of Soul and Body"

G. W. LEIBNIZ

In ed., transl., L. Loemker, G. W. Leibniz: Philosophical Papers and Letters, 2nd ed. (Dordrecht D. Reidel, 1969), 493–94.

In this excerpt Leibniz responds to some objections raised by Pierre Bayle, an occasionalist, to pre-established harmony. In doing so he identifies some of the advantages he believes his own theory has over its competitors.

Mr. Bayle continues:

I understand why a dog passes immediately from pleasure to pain if we strike him with a stick just when he is very hungry and is eating some bread.

I am not sure that we do fully understand this. No one knows better than Mr. Bayle himself that it is just here that the great difficulty lies in explaining why whatever occurs in the body makes a change in the soul, and that it is this which has forced the defenders of occasional causes to have recourse to the care which God must take to represent continually in the soul the changes which occur in its body. . . . Bayle continues:

But that his soul is constructed in such a way that he should feel pain at the moment he is struck even if no one were to strike him . . . this I cannot understand.

Nor do I recall having said this. And one can speak in this way only by a metaphysical fiction. . . . For since the nature of the soul has been made in such a way from the beginning as to represent successively the changes of matter, the situation which we assume could not arise in the natural order. God could give to each substance its own phenomena independent of those of others, but in this way he would have made as many worlds without connection, so to speak, as there are substances, almost as we say that when we dream, we are in a world apart and that we enter into the common world when we wake up. . . . Mr. Bayle says further:

Furthermore, it seems to me that this able man dislikes [occasionalism] because of a false assumption, for one cannot say that the system of occasional causes makes the action of God intervene by a miracle in the reciprocal dependence of body and soul. For since God's intervention follows only general laws, he does not therein act in an extraordinary way.

This is not the only reason why I dislike [occasionalism]. . . . But let us see whether the system of occasional causes does not in fact imply a perpetual miracle. Here it is said that it does not, because God would act only through general laws according to this system. I agree, but in my opinion that does not suffice to remove the miracles. Even if God should do this continuously, they would not cease being miracles, if we take this term, not in the popular sense of a rare and wonderful thing, but in the philosophical sense of that which exceeds the powers of created beings. It is not enough to say that God has made general laws, for besides the decree there is also necessary a natural means of carrying it out, that is, all that happens must also be explained through the nature which God gives to things. The laws of nature are not so arbitrary and so indifferent as many people imagine. . . .

REVIEW AND DISCUSSION QUESTIONS

1. Briefly summarize Leibniz's doctrine of pre-established harmony.
2. Identify two distinct objections Bayle makes to Leibniz's doctrine, and summarize Leibniz's response to each.

Epistemology and Metaphysics
The Empiricists and Kant

HE RATIONALISTS shared a deep commitment to two ideas: that the world was intelligible (capable of being understood), and that reason was the primary tool to understand it. Fair enough, now, but for many that leaves something important out of the epistemological action: our senses. For we seem to have at least *two* main avenues for coming to understand the world, reason *and* sensory experience. The rationalists tend to be dismissive toward the senses, granting them some secondary role in the generation of knowledge but also laying on the criticisms. Plato, an ancient rationalist, claimed the world of the senses was illusory, for only the Forms, grasped by the intellect, were truly real; Descartes stressed that sensory information often deceives us, and must be corrected by reason before being accepted as knowledge; and though we didn't look at this, Malebranche's strongly Christian perspective took anything grounded in the body (as the sense organs are) to be inherently sinful and something to be overcome by a well-guided rational mind.

None of the early modern philosophers would disparage *reason* the way that some disparaged the senses; after all, reason is at the heart of the whole philosophical project. But it was possible to disparage the heavy emphasis that the rationalists put on reason, at the expense of the senses. As we saw, the reason-emphasizing rationalists not only reach very different conclusions about the world, but sometimes quite strange conclusions. (Ask your friends what they think of Spinoza's pantheistic monism, Malebranche's occasionalism, and Leibniz's pre-established harmony!) And anyway, the senses clearly have *some* role to play in epistemology, even for the Christians—for why would God give you your senses if not at least partly in order to know the world?

In this chapter we turn to the other major school in early modern philosophy, the empiricists. Less satisfied with the emphasis on reason they sought, first, to understand how the mind operates, its overall structure and contents, then to work out just how the mind goes about knowing the world, and what limits there might be to that knowledge. Sensory experience, they discover, is not only essential to knowledge but also sets limits to what's knowable. As such,

> What peculiar privilege has this little agitation of the brain which we call thought, that we must make it the model of the whole universe?
>
> —**David Hume** (1711–1776),
> *Dialogues concerning Natural Religion*

given the close connection between epistemology and metaphysics, it also sets constraints on what we can say about the world. By the time we reach David Hume and his critique of rationalist causation, in fact, we will find ourselves returning to the skepticism expressed in Descartes's *Meditation One*, which triggered early modern philosophy in the first place: nothing can be known about the world at all, which is therefore utterly unintelligible. As early modern rationalism (stressing reason) eventually led to the impasse of diverse, strange theories, so too early modern empiricism (stressing sensory experience) will lead to the impasse of skepticism. The crisis engendered by this result will threaten the whole philosophical enterprise, until the great Immanuel Kant steps up to save the day.

But we get ahead of ourselves.

JOHN LOCKE (1632–1704)

Locke was born in Somerset, England. Educated at Oxford in medicine, he became the personal physician of the Earl of Shaftesbury. Shaftesbury's later attempt to prevent James II's accession to the English throne led to Shaftesbury's exile to Holland, with Locke accompanying him.

There Locke met William and Mary of Orange, and when this couple took the throne of England in 1688, Locke returned home with them. Two years later saw the publication of the two works that made him famous as a philosopher and political theorist: *An Essay Concerning Human Understanding*, and *Two Treatises of Government*. Both were enormously influential, the former on the whole history of philosophy, the latter on political history, by providing the philosophical justification not only for the English Revolution of 1688 but for the American Revolution of 1776, and by shaping the language and ideas of both the Declaration of Independence and the American Constitution. Locke was among the first to argue for various claims essential to the development of western democracies, including that (1) civil government derives its power from the consent of its members; (2) its purpose is the defense of individual liberty and property, because human beings are "all equal and independent" and possess the rights to "life, health, liberty and possessions"; (3) in government the legislative branch is more authoritative than the executive; and (4) there should be a strict separation between these two branches and between church and state.

JOHN LOCKE

Locke himself saw a close connection between his two major works. His reason for undertaking his investigation "into the original, certainty, and extent of human knowledge, together with the grounds and degrees of belief, opinion, and assent" was not merely theoretical. He lived through decades of violence all over Europe, and he hoped to determine the sources and validity of the beliefs that brought people into such conflict with one another. He thought that if he could show how people's differing ideas resulted from their different experiences, they might become more tolerant of each other and thus avoid the agony of conflict and war.

Locke's Attack on Nativism

An Essay Concerning Human Understanding opens with an attack on **nativism**, the doctrine that some ideas and beliefs are innate, that is, the mind is simply born with them. Rationalists had inclined toward nativism since Plato, arguing that some ideas and beliefs display traits that mere sensory experience can't explain. Plato, as we've seen, held that we grasp the eternal and unchanging Forms, but nothing in sensory experience is eternal and unchanging; for Descartes, our ideas of God and of mathematics refer to the infinite and involve not **contingent truths** but **necessary truths**, while nothing in experience is ever infinite or necessary; for Leibniz nothing enters the mind from outside, so the mind must be born with all the ideas and beliefs it will ever have, even if it's not initially aware of them.

If there were innate ideas or beliefs, Locke suggests, we might expect them to be possessed universally, by everyone; but in fact he argues that there are no ideas or beliefs that all human beings have, not even mathematical ones. Children and the mentally disabled, obviously, do not have such ideas or beliefs ready formed in their minds, so they cannot be born with them. To the objection that they are born with them but are unaware of them until they reach the age of reason, he replies that there cannot be any ideas in the mind of which one is not aware—reflecting his endorsement of Descartes's view that the mind is transparent, that is, it is aware of everything in it. Besides, Locke continues, if reason is necessary to discover these ideas, there is no need for them to be innate. Reason can just generate them later. Similar points apply to moral beliefs. In the age of colonial imperialism, Europeans were discovering many new and different cultures around the world. They were learning that moral beliefs varied dramatically between societies, thus weren't universal either.

Instead of being born with ideas and beliefs, Locke suggests,

> Let us then suppose the mind to be, as we say, white paper, void of all characters, without any *ideas*. How comes it to be furnished? From where does it come by that vast store which the busy and boundless fancy of man has painted on it with an almost endless variety? From where does it have all the materials of reason and knowledge? To this I answer, in one word, from *experience*; our knowledge is founded in all that. (*Essay*, II.I.2)

That all knowledge ultimately comes from sensory experience Locke now takes as his point of departure. Having said this, however, we must note that Locke's overall metaphysical system was actually not very far from the rationalist Descartes's. In particular, he adopted not only Descartes's dualism but also Descartes's overall theories of mind and of matter. Thus, he accepted the representational theory of mind (RTM), according to which the immediate object of the mind is an idea, a mental representation; and he accepted the mechanical philosophy, according to which physical matter is just extension, possessing only size, shape, and motion. Locke's contributions, then, were not revolutionary as were his predecessor's. Working within Descartes's framework, he offered a careful analysis of the contents and structure of the mind and a methodical defense of the mechanical philosophy.

The Structure and Contents of the Mind, and Substance

With no innate ideas or beliefs, the mind at birth (Locke says) is like a *tabula rasa*, Latin for a "blank tablet," on which experience then makes its marks. Experience consists of sensation and reflection, and we are incapable of having any idea that does not come from these two sources. **Ideas of sensation** come to us when some external body stimulates our sense organs (ideas of yellow, cold, bitter, hard, etc.); **ideas of reflection** arise from observing the operations of our own mind (ideas of thinking, doubting, remembering, willing, etc.). Some of these ideas are **simple ideas**, meaning they do not have any ideas as parts or components, while others are **complex ideas**, meaning that they do. The idea of a horse is complex, for example, because it is composed of ideas of its body, its legs, its color, its smell, and so on; the idea of its body is also complex, itself composed of ideas of flesh and blood and color, etc.; but eventually we reach ideas which are not composed of anything further, perhaps the idea of a pure color or smell. The mind can combine the ideas it has in new ways, to create new complex ideas it has not acquired from sensation. For example, you can combine the ideas of a horse and a horn to construct the idea of a unicorn, even if you have never seen a unicorn. But the mind cannot invent or construct any new *simple* ideas of sensation, as these must be sensed directly. Thus a blind man can have no idea of colors, and you can have no idea (say) of some simple taste if you have never experienced it.

These points about ideas in turn generate some insights about the nature of substances. Instead of thinking directly about the "things" in the world (metaphysics), what we must work with are our ideas (epistemology). Consider some of the particular substances in the world, things such as gold, house, boy, or sugar. When we analyze our *ideas* of these, we find that they are complex, that is, combinations of several, separate sensory ideas—plus something else. Our idea of a piece of gold, for example, is a combination of sensory ideas, such as its color, extension, and so on. But then we realize we need a further idea, the idea of these sensory ideas being joined or connected together in some way. This further idea supports the other ideas, and is thus distinct from them. Locke's term for this further idea is **substratum**, literally, "the level beneath": the substratum is the thing which *has* the color, extension, and so on, and is responsible for them being joined together. But when we examine the idea of the substratum itself, Locke observes, we find that we have no distinct idea of it at all. What then is it? In a famous phrase, Locke replies that it is a something, "we know not what" (XXIII.4).

I shall here insert a problem of that very ingenious and studious promoter of real knowledge, the learned and worthy Mr. Molineaux. . . . Suppose a man born blind and now adult, and taught by his touch to distinguish between a cube and a sphere . . . so as to tell, when he felt one and the other, which is the cube, which the sphere. Suppose then the cube and sphere placed on a table and the blind man be made to see. [Question:] whether by his sight, before he touched them, he could now distinguish and tell which is the globe, which the cube?

—**John Locke**, *An Essay Concerning Human Understanding* (1689), about to apply his empiricist doctrines in response to the "Molineaux Problem"

The Distinction between Primary and Secondary Qualities

Locke's careful analysis of ideas also leads him to the famous distinction between the *primary and secondary qualities* of physical bodies. This distinction is not original with him, as it is part of the mechanical philosophy; his contribution, as we mentioned, is in his methodical defense of it.[1]

"Whatever the mind perceives in itself or is the immediate object of perception, thought, or understanding," Locke begins, "that I call *idea*, and the power to produce any *idea* in our mind I call a *quality* of the subject in which that power is" (II.VIII.8).

From RTM, what we are aware of, when perceiving, are not physical bodies but mental representations, or *ideas*. This naturally raises the question of where these ideas come from, of what causes them, which dualists answer by invoking physical bodies (the mind-body problem from chapter 8 notwithstanding). So physical bodies have the causal powers to produce these mental ideas in perceivers. These powers Locke calls *qualities* in the physical body.

Locke next offers three criteria for classifying the various qualities of bodies into the two categories. A quality is a **primary quality** if (1) it is "utterly inseparable" from the body; (2) it "really does exist" in the body; and (3) our idea of it resembles what's in the body. A **secondary quality** is one to which none of these apply, but rather it *is* separable from the body, it does not *really* exist in the body, and our idea of it does *not* resemble what's in the body.

So what does all this mean?

Locke elaborates on the first criterion as follows. No matter what you do to any given physical body, there are certain qualities it will always have; similarly no matter how small a physical body is, it will always have these qualities; and you cannot even *conceive* of any bodies lacking such qualities. Take a grain of wheat, for example, and divide it into two parts, and each part will have size, shape, and motion; divide the parts again, and each part will still have a size, shape, motion, and so on. These primary qualities are thus inseparable from body, just as the mechanical philosophy says.

Of course we also have ideas corresponding to these qualities, namely our *sensations* of the sizes, shapes, and motions of bodies. But by the second and third criteria above, Locke is saying that it doesn't merely look to us this way but in fact it *really is* this way: bodies *really do* possess size, shape, and motion, independently of our sensations or ideas, and so our sensations of them *resemble* what is in the body itself. This doesn't mean our sensations are always accurate: how big something looks may be different from how big it actually is. But that it has *some* size is always true; and what size, shape, and motion are as qualities in the body resembles, in general, what size, shape, and motion look like to our senses.

In contrast, secondary qualities, such as color, sound, and flavor—though we'll focus on color—are "nothing in the objects themselves but powers to produce various sensations in us by their *primary qualities*" (II.VIII.10).

Sensation occurs when physical particles cause motions in our sensory organs and brains, which in turn cause sensory ideas to arise in our minds. Some of these are sensory ideas *of* the size, shape, and motion of the external bodies, ideas which do resemble those bodies, which really have those qualities. But other sensory ideas do *not* resemble the bodies at all, since bodies do *not* really have those qualities. These are ideas of secondary qualities. We may see yellow, but that sensation is caused by bits of matter of various sizes, shapes, and motions, but which *are not themselves yellow*. Secondary qualities are "separable" from bodies, then, in the sense that bodies can, and do, exist without them. So color as we perceive it is not really a property of a physical body, but exists only as an idea in the mind of the perceiver.

Now we need some reasons to believe this is true.

Four Arguments for the Distinction between Primary and Secondary Qualities

(1) **The science argument** comes straight from Descartes. The most successful science of Locke's day was the mechanical philosophy, which offered many compelling explanations of

phenomena by ascribing to matter *only* the mathematical properties of size, shape, and motion, the primary qualities. The mechanical philosophy admitted no color or other secondary qualities in the physical world; and if that's what your most successful science believes, then so, perhaps, should you.

(2) **The almond argument**. "Pound an almond," Locke writes,

> and the clear white *color* will be altered into a dirty one . . . What real alteration can the beating of the pestle make in any body but an alteration of the *texture* of it? (II.VIII.20)

Assuming that the almond is clear white all the way through, then Locke's argument is this: if that clear white color were really in the almond itself, all the way through, then pounding the almond wouldn't change its color. Why not? Because pounding only changes its *texture*, the arrangements of its molecules; and if all its molecules are really white, why should merely rearranging them affect the almond's overall white color?

Yet pounding does affect its color.

The best explanation seems to be that color is not really in the almond after all. Rather, some molecular arrangements cause clear white color sensations in the perceiver, and other arrangements of the same molecules cause "dirty" white sensations. Pounding affects the arrangements, and in this indirect way affects the perceived color. But then color is in the perceiver, not the body. (See the Lucretius reading in chapter 2 for a similar argument.)

(3) **The analogy argument**. The same fire which at some distance causes in us a pleasing sensation (or "idea") of warmth, Locke observes, causes close up a sensation or idea of burning pain. But everyone agrees that pain is a sensation "in us," in our minds, not a quality in the body. When you step on a nail you never say, "I'm perceiving the pain in this nail!" You say, rather, that the qualities of the nail, its solidity and sharpness, cause a sensation of pain in *you*. But now the sensory processes in the two cases are precisely analogous. In perceiving both the warmth of the fire and the pain of the burn, the size, shape, and motion of the fire particles cause physical changes in our skin, which cause sensations in us. Since everyone agrees that the resulting pain is only in the mind of the perceiver, we ought to admit that the warmth is too.

Similarly, a spoiled piece of food may look white and taste perfectly sweet, but then upon being consumed causes nausea in us. Everyone agrees that nausea is a sensation "in us," not a quality in the food, but the physical processes causing sensations of color and taste are precisely analogous to those causing nausea: the primary qualities of the body affect our sensory organs and cause sensations. So if nausea is merely a sensation in us, then so too are color and taste.

Again, secondary qualities are not genuinely properties of bodies.

(4) **Relativity of perception arguments**. We first officially met this family of arguments in chapter 8, where they served as one of Descartes's arguments for RTM. A relativity of perception argument is any argument with the following general form:

> A perceived quality varies.
> The body itself does not vary.
> ----------
> Therefore, the perceived quality is not in the body itself.

Locke's classic example is the **two hands in a bucket** case. Imagine putting one hand in the freezer for a few minutes while you put the other in a mildly heated oven. You then place both hands into a stirred bucket of room temperature water. Presumably the freezer-hand will feel a warm sensation while the oven-hand will feel a cool sensation.

This scenario now fulfills the two premises above. A perceived quality varies, here between the two hands, as one perceives warmth while the other perceives coolness. But the body itself doesn't vary: it's the same water felt by the two hands.

But then the conclusion seems to follow, that warmth and coolness are not qualities in the water itself but only in the mind of the perceiver. As Locke puts it, since warmth and coolness are opposites they can't *both* literally be in the water, for that would be a contradiction. But if warmth and coolness are caused as sensations *in the perceiver* by moving particles, then we can understand how the same water might produce these opposing sensations when perceived in different circumstances (here, by the different hands).

Once you are aware of relativity of perception phenomena, in fact, you'll find them everywhere. As we saw in chapter 8, the perceived color of an otherwise unchanging body can vary dramatically across different contexts, perceivers, animals; the quality of a sound can vary without the thing making the sound varying; how something tastes depends on who is tasting it, and in what circumstances, and so on. In each case the conclusion seems the same: colors (flavors, sounds, etc.) are secondary qualities, not genuine properties of bodies but merely sensations in the mind of the perceiver.

While the mechanical philosophy no longer has the scientific status it once had, and the almond argument is a little idiosyncratic for many, the analogy and relativity of perception arguments still do exert pulls on twenty-first-century intellects, at least when updated in various technical ways. So much so that with respect to color anyway—even when, or perhaps because, the science of color perception is so far advanced from Locke's seventeenth century—probably the majority of today's philosophers are persuaded that colors are really just in the mind.

After Locke's analysis of the nature of ideas, along with its implications for the natures of substances, bodies, and qualities, we can now state briefly what knowledge amounts to for him. In the framework of RTM, the mind cannot know the physical world directly, but only through the mediation of ideas. Knowledge, therefore, cannot extend further than one's ideas do. We obtain knowledge of the world when our ideas conform with or correspond to the reality of things in the world.

The question that now arises is this. If all we are aware of are ideas and not the things themselves, how can we know that there *is* a correspondence between our ideas and the world? What justifies us in believing that there is *any* likeness between our perceptions and the things that produce them in us—even in the case of our ideas of primary qualities—if what we know are perceptions only? To prove such a correspondence, we would need to step outside our perceptions to compare them with the things that cause them, and that we cannot do. We cannot compare our perception of a body with the body itself. We can only compare it with another perception.

Though Locke shares much with his rationalist predecessor Descartes, his empiricist stress on sensory experience, and thus on ideas, starts suggesting these troubling questions. These questions are very much on the mind of our next great empiricist.

GEORGE BERKELEY (1685–1753)

Berkeley was born in Kilkenney, Ireland, in 1685. Exposed to the works of Descartes, Malebranche, and Locke as a student at Trinity College, Dublin, he went on to receive ordination in the Anglican Church in 1709. Through his twenties, he produced some of his most important works: his

Essay Towards a New Theory of Vision (1709), concerned with explaining how we perceive the distance, magnitude, and position of bodies, his *Treatise concerning the Principles of Human Knowledge* (1710), defending the *idealism* for which he would become famous, and *Three Dialogues between Hylas and Philonus* (1713), a more popular version of the *Treatise*. In his thirties Berkeley became enthused about a plan for building a missionary college in Bermuda devoted to "the propagation of the Gospel among the American savages."[2] Berkeley sailed in 1728 for Newport, Rhode Island, to establish farms to supply the planned college. Though financial support for the project didn't materialize, Berkeley stayed several years in Newport, where he founded divinity schools both there and in Connecticut and aided the young universities of Yale and Harvard with donations of property and books. On returning to England he was named Bishop of Cloyne, and remained in southern Ireland for the next eighteen years. He died in 1753, shortly after moving to Oxford to supervise the education of one of the only three of his children (out of seven) to survive their childhoods.

GEORGE BERKELEY

Turning to his philosophy, now, Berkeley begins at Locke's starting point but (as we'll see) ends up in a very different place. He agrees that the materials of our knowledge are mental objects, ideas, both of sensation and reflection. In addition, there is some substance that has or experiences those ideas, and this is called variously *mind*, *soul*, or *spirit*. So far we have the mental component of dualism and RTM: there exist minds, and minds are aware only of ideas.

But that is all we will get, according to Berkeley. For while Locke (like Descartes before him) goes on to defend **materialism**—Berkeley's name for dualism, the doctrine that in addition to minds there exists a mind-independent physical world—Berkeley instead defends **idealism**, the doctrine that *all* that exists in the world are minds and their ideas.

Three Lines of Argument against Materialism and for Idealism

Berkeley is led to this surprising doctrine by several lines of argument.

(1) First, there are the questions we raised above. Locke claimed that some of our sensory ideas, those of the primary qualities of size, shape, and motion, resemble what actually exists in physical bodies. But how could we ever know this? We cannot compare our perceptions or ideas of bodies with the bodies themselves, so on what ground could we claim that any of our ideas resemble what's in the body? In fact, we can never even justifiably believe in the very existence of an external physical world at all—for what evidence could suggest that physical bodies cause our sensory ideas, if all we ever observe are the ideas?

True, Descartes (and also Locke) offered some argument for the existence of the physical world. Our sensory ideas arise involuntarily, they noted, which suggests that something external to us causes them. And Descartes in particular claimed that God would be inescapably deceiving us if our sensory ideas, which seem to come from external bodies, in fact did not.

But Berkeley finds these arguments wanting. The fact that our sensory ideas are involuntary merely suggests that *something* exists outside our minds, causing our perceptions, but it doesn't at all show these must be physical bodies. In fact, the cause of our perceptions could just as well be other minds and/or God Himself! Nor would those possibilities mean that God is somehow deceiving us. For we would be deceived only if our sensory ideas *seemed* to come from bodies when in truth they did not. But since all we ever experience are ideas, how could ideas "seem to" come from bodies, which are not themselves experienced? Rather, sensory ideas simply arise in our minds and don't "seem to" come from anywhere. So God wouldn't be deceiving us if there aren't any physical bodies after all.

(2) Berkeley next continues with an all-out assault on the distinction between primary and secondary qualities. This distinction is essential to materialism because the primary qualities are allegedly mind-independent, which would mean they are grounded in something outside the mind and thus physical.

He begins by reinforcing the notion that secondary qualities exist only in the mind and not in the bodies, endorsing Locke's arguments there. But he then shows that similar arguments apply to primary qualities—in which case even *they* must exist only in the mind as well!

Recall, for example, the earlier relativity of perception arguments, of which Locke's classic example was the *two hands in a bucket* case. Consider the primary quality of size. A dust mite appears very small to our eye, and its foot even smaller. But the mite's foot would appear to the mite itself as being of some moderate size, and would appear as even larger to any creatures smaller than the mite. But then the perceived quality (size) is varying between perceivers, while the alleged body itself, the mite's foot, is not varying. If the size being perceived is varying while the body itself isn't, then the size being perceived must not belong to the body itself. So the "primary quality" of size is in the mind of the perceiver after all!

Berkeley makes similar arguments about shape and motion. Whether a body's motion is fast or slow, for example, is a function of how much distance is covered over a certain time. But the perception of time is clearly subjective. A given interval may seem short to one perceiver and long to another. Thus a motion that the former perceives as swift would be perceived by the latter as slow. (One reason it's so hard to swat a fly, apparently, is that what looks like the fast motion of the swatter *to you* looks like a slow, leisurely descent *to the fly*.) But of course it's allegedly the same single, unvarying bodily motion. Perceived motion varies, but the body itself does not—therefore again, the "primary quality" of motion is in the mind, and not in the body.

There are also other reasons to reject the distinction between primary and secondary qualities. Locke holds that colors exist in the mind while shapes exist in the bodies. But color is inseparable from shape. We only perceive colors as areas in our visual field, taking up a certain space. If perceived color is in the mind (as Locke grants), then so must perceived shape be.

Thus there's no real distinction between primary and secondary qualities after all, Berkeley concludes: *all* qualities are in the mind. But then there's nothing left over to exist "out there," in the mind-independent physical world posited by the materialist.

(3) Finally, there is the **inconceivability argument** for idealism. Materialism isn't merely false, Berkeley argues, it's actually logically contradictory: there are no conceivable circumstances under which it could possibly *ever* be, have been, or become true.

For is it even logically *possible* for a mind-independent physical body to exist?

To say that something is *logically possible* (you'll recall from chapter 7's discussion of omnipotence) is to say that it may be conceived without contradiction. But now try to conceive of something existing outside of all minds, Berkeley urges. Try to conceive of some tree (for example) existing independently or outside of all minds. You can't do it, for the very act of conceiving of it ensures that it is in some mind, namely yours! To say that you are conceiving of some body existing outside all minds is to say that you have *in* your mind a body *outside* all minds, a clear contradiction. Thus there is a contradiction in the very idea of a mind-independent body, in which case mind-independent bodies are logically impossible. But then, obviously, so is materialism, which believes in such bodies.

Putting all these arguments together: What, then, are we perceiving, when we take ourselves to be perceiving physical bodies? Ideas, as Descartes and Locke said. All we perceive are ideas, and we are never justified in reasoning our way to the existence of mind-independent physical bodies.

Berkeley's arguments seem easier to dismiss than to actually refute:

When discussing how Berkeley's philosophy appeared to be self-evidently false, but impossible to refute, Dr. Johnson kicked out at a nearby stone, exclaiming "I refute it *thus*!"

—**James Boswell**, The Life of Samuel Johnson (1791)

But that all [Berkeley's] arguments, though otherwise intended, are, in reality, merely sceptical, appears from this, that they admit of no answer and produce no conviction. Their only effect is to cause that momentary amazement and irresolution and confusion, which is the result of scepticism.

—**David Hume**, An Enquiry Concerning Human Understanding (1748)

Hence all that exists are minds and their ideas, or, as Berkeley summarizes it in a phrase, *esse est percipi*: "to be is to be perceived."

Idealism, Materialism, and Common Sense

While idealism may seem to be a strange view opposed to common sense, Berkeley insists that it actually fits better with common sense than materialism. We may see this by asking three simple questions. Do we perceive bodies in the world directly? Are our minds basically capable of knowing the world? Is fire hot?

Now common sense would answer *yes* to all three. You open your eyes and directly see that tree (for example), and although we are fallible about the world our senses largely allow us to perceive it with some accuracy, and of course fire is hot. But materialism as Locke construes it would answer *no* to all three, according to Berkeley. We perceive not the tree but an idea of the tree, our minds are therefore incapable of perceiving the alleged physical world at all, and *heat* is a secondary quality in the mind, not in the fire itself. His own idealism, however, echoes the answers of common sense. If all that exists are minds and our ideas, then we directly see the tree (which is just a bundle of sensory ideas), what we see is what there is ("to be is to be perceived") so we can know the world, and heat is just one of the sensory ideas constituting the bundle of sensory ideas which is the fire.

So idealism actually fits better with common sense than materialism, once you carefully examine what common sense holds!

Some Problems for Idealism

Of course idealism, like all philosophical doctrines, must deal with a number of problems. If "to be is to be perceived," then is a dreamed tiger as real as a "real" tiger? And what is the difference between an optical illusion or a misperception and an accurate perception? (For example, when a stick placed in water looks bent, must it in fact *be* bent? If a round coin looks oval from a certain angle, must it in fact be oval?) Most famously, what happens when bodies are no longer perceived? When you leave your room does everything in the room go out of existence? When you cover a table with a tablecloth so you can no longer see it, does it go out of existence? If a tree falls in the forest and there's no one around to hear it . . . not only might it not make a sound, but if there's no one around to perceive it does the whole tree even exist?

Berkeley, among the cleverest of philosophers, has plenty to say in response to these problems, and idealism becomes an extremely sophisticated theory by the time he is done with it. Starting from Locke's empiricist epistemological premises—that the direct objects of the mind are ideas and that all knowledge must ultimately derive from sensory experience—Berkeley built a metaphysical view that was its diametrical opposite, rejecting materialism in favor of idealism. And while his arguments were primarily philosophical, there was a religious component as well. For materialism, he believed, led quickly to skepticism and atheism. The external physical world was unknowable, and if bodies could exist on their own and cause our sensory ideas then little stopped one from dispensing with God's role in our daily lives altogether. Idealism, to the contrary, both leaves the world knowable and leaves God quite busy causing many of our sensory ideas. For a philosophical theist, then, the choice (according to Berkeley) was clear.

We'll next see what happens when Berkeley's powerful arguments are adopted by an equally clever philosophical *a*theist.

On unperceived bodies, according to idealism:

[Berkeley] maintained that material objects only exist through being perceived. To the objection that, in that case, a tree, for instance, would cease to exist if no one was looking at it, he replied that God always perceives everything; if there were no God, what we take to be material objects would have a jerky life, suddenly leaping into being when we look at them; but as it is, owing to God's perceptions, trees and rocks and stones have an existence as continuous as common sense supposes. This is, in his opinion, a weighty argument for the existence of God.

—**Bertrand Russell**, *A History of Western Philosophy* (1945)

There was a young man who said, "God
Must think it exceedingly odd
That this little tree
Should continue to be
When there is no one about in the quad."

Reply:

"Dear Sir, your astonishment's odd;
I am always about in the quad,
And that's why this tree
Will continue to be
Since observed by Yours faithfully, God."

—attributed to **Ronald Knox** (1888–1957)

DAVID HUME (1711–1776)

Scottish philosopher David Hume, the last of the major early modern empiricists, entered Edinburgh University at the tender age of eleven. On finishing there, he spent several years writing his first great work, *A Treatise of Human Nature*, which was published in 1739 but fell, in his own words, "dead-born from the press," not even exciting a "murmur among the zealots." He didn't give up, however, and over the next decade rewrote the material and published it anew in 1748, as *An Enquiry concerning Human Understanding*, to much greater murmuring. The zealots were mostly concerned about Hume's apparent atheism and general skepticism, and it was enough to prevent him from obtaining any academic posts. Instead he became a librarian, and wrote a six-volume, best-selling history of England (1754–1762) that afforded him financial independence. On learning that he had intestinal cancer, he wrote a brief but beautiful autobiography, then arranged for posthumous publication of his most zealot-exciting book, *Dialogues concerning Natural Religion* (which deeply criticized religious belief, some of which we saw in chapter 7), before departing from this world in 1776.

Hume, too, starts with Locke's empiricist epistemology, but ends up at an even more extreme destination than Berkeley. What we are aware of are ideas, and knowledge must always trace back to sensory experience. So any alleged idea that cannot be traced back to experience (or constructed from experience) must be nonsense, and must be discarded. Berkeley was correct, therefore, to reject the notion of a material substance or body, since we have no direct sensory experience of such a thing, only of ideas. But Berkeley didn't go far enough, Hume argues, since he still accepted the idea of a mental substance, a mind or soul—of which, in fact, we lack sense impressions as well:

DAVID HUME

> For from what impression cou'd this idea [of self or soul] be deriv'd? . . . If any impression gives rise to the idea of self, that impression must continue invariably the same, thro' the whole course of our lives; since self is suppos'd to exist after that manner. But there is no impression constant and invariable. . . . For my part, when I enter most intimately into what I call myself, I always stumble on some particular perception or other, of heat or cold, light or shade, love or hatred, pain or pleasure. I never can catch myself at any time without a perception, and never can observe any thing but the perception. (*Treatise*, Book I.IV.VI, 252-2)[3]

When we reflect on ourselves, we are aware only of our passing sequence of ideas or mental states, not of the "self" having those ideas. But if we have no sensory awareness of the self, of the mental substance, then the very idea of a *mind* is meaningless.

Since we know nothing of an external physical world or of an internal self, we cannot, Hume concludes, know the origin of our sensory experiences. All we can know is that a series of experiences is occurring, from unknown sources.

Relations of Ideas and Matters of Fact

That being said, there is a certain kind of knowledge that we can have, although it is not, strictly speaking, "about the world." As Hume puts it, all the judgments we make (or propositions we contemplate) may be divided into **relations of ideas** and **matters of fact**. Judgments concerning the former are (as the name suggests) only about the ways our ideas are related to each other. That *wet is contrary to dry*, that *bachelors are unmarried males*, that *7+5=12*: all of these concern merely our ideas, and thus we can grasp that they are true merely by reflecting on the ideas themselves. As long as you understand English and thus have the relevant ideas, in other words, you know that *wet is contrary to dry* is true, as is *bachelors are unmarried males*. You do *not* need to make any empirical observations. You do not need to survey lots of wet things to see if any are dry, nor survey all the bachelors to confirm they are all male and unmarried. This suggests that these judgments are not really "about the world"—for if they did make some claim about how the world is, we *would* need to examine the world to see if they are true. Rather, their truth is a matter of definition, and not a matter of how the world is.

There's another way to make the same point. Judgments we make about relations of ideas have their **truth-value**—are either true or false—completely independently of what exists in the world, which suggests that they are not making any claims about the world. "Though there never were a circle or triangle in nature," Hume writes, "the truths demonstrated by Euclid would forever retain their certainty" (*Enquiry* IV.I). For this reason, too, these judgments reflect *necessary* truths. No matter how the world changes, even if all the single men get married, it remains true that bachelors are unmarried males—even if there aren't any.

Judgments concerning (or propositions expressing) matters of fact, to the contrary, *are* about more than just our ideas, but also about the world. That *Ashton Kutcher enjoys playing*

I was a man of mild dispositions, of command of temper, of an open, social, and cheerful humour, capable of attachment, but little susceptible of enmity, and of great moderation in all my passions. Even my love of literary fame, my ruling passion, never soured my temper, notwithstanding my frequent disappointments. My company was not unacceptable to the young and careless, as well as to the studious and literary; and as I took a particular pleasure in the company of modest women, I had no reason to be displeased with the reception I met with from them. In a word, though most men anywise eminent have found reason to complain of calumny, I never was touched or even attached by her baleful tooth; and though I wantonly exposed myself to the rage of both civil and religious factions, they seemed to be disarmed in my behalf of their wonted fury. My friends never had occasion to vindicate any one circumstance of my character and conduct; not but that the zealots, we may well suppose, would have been glad to invent and propagate any story to my disadvantage, but they could never find any which they thought would wear the face of probability. I cannot say there is no vanity in making this funeral oration of myself, but I hope it is not a misplaced one; and this is a matter of fact which is easily cleared and ascertained.

—**David Hume**, *Autobiography* (1776)

squash, that *the far side of the moon is dry*, that *bachelors live on average less long than married men*: merely understanding these propositions, merely having the relevant ideas, is *not* enough to know whether they are true. In fact, chances are that you understand all three of these perfectly well without knowing whether they are true. Unlike relations of ideas, these are not merely a matter of definition but *are* about the world, so to determine their truth-value you need to make empirical observations. You need (for example) to survey bachelors and married men and compare the numbers. And while they may well turn out to be true, they wouldn't be *necessary* truths, as the world can always change. Perhaps Ashton Kutcher likes squash now, but grows bored of it; perhaps the moon is dry now, but conditions change.

For Hume, knowledge concerning relations of ideas is no problem. We have it, as in our mathematics, but it is not really about the world, only about our ideas. Knowledge of the world, of matters of fact, however, *is* a problem. To see why, we enter into Hume's famous critiques of the rationalist notion of causation and of the justifiability of inductive knowledge.

> When we run over libraries, persuaded of these principles, what havoc must we make? If we take in our hand any volume—of divinity or school metaphysics, for instance—let us ask: *Does it contain any abstract reasoning concerning quantity or number?* No. *Does it contain any experimental reasoning concerning matter of fact and existence?* No. Commit it then to the flames, for it can contain nothing but sophistry and illusion.
>
> —**David Hume**, An Enquiry concerning Human Understanding (1748)

Hume's Critique of Causation[4]

"All reasonings concerning matter of fact seem to be founded on the relation of *cause and effect*," Hume writes. "By means of that relation alone we can go beyond the evidence of our memory and senses" (*Enquiry* IV.I). You believe your friend is in France because you have an e-mail from him saying as much. Your sensory experience of that e-mail leads you to that conclusion because you believe his being in France caused him to send the e-mail. You find a watch on a beach and you conclude a person had been there. Your sensory perception of the watch leads you, by inference, back to the thought that someone caused the watch to be there. And of course the rationalist uses causal reasoning to infer the existence of the physical world itself (as the cause of our sensory experiences), as well as the existence of God (as the cause of the physical world).

But if you take empiricism seriously, Hume argues, all such causal reasoning fails.

What do we mean by *causation*? As we saw in chapter 8, the sheer fact that two events might be close in time or space does not make one the cause of another. Your professor lectures and you scratch your nose. The lecturing immediately precedes and is near your scratching, but not the cause of it. Rather, it's a kind of accidental pairing. True causation, to the contrary, is a matter of **necessary connection**. To say that a given event x causes an event y is to say that x necessitates y, x compels y, it's impossible for x to occur in those circumstances without y occurring. Your professor often lectures without your scratching your nose, so it's clearly possible for her to lecture without your scratching. So her lecturing doesn't necessitate your scratching, and therefore does not cause it.

But no two distinct events, Hume now argues, are *ever* necessarily connected.

His first argument, his **conceivability argument against necessary connection**, is deeply influenced by Malebranche, who made the same points in arguing for occasionalism (as we saw in chapter 8). A necessary connection means it's impossible for the first event to occur without the second; but to say something is impossible means it involves a contradiction, since anything *not* involving a contradiction is possible at least in principle. But now, Hume insists, there is never any contradiction in conceiving of any one distinct event occurring without another.

Why not? Because every event is a distinct entity from every other event, so contemplating any one event cannot lead the mind necessarily to contemplating any other event. But that is just to say that any event can be conceived to occur without any other event; which is to say that it is always possible for any given event to occur without any other given event. But then no two events are necessarily connected, and nothing causes anything else.

So, for example, you strike a match and it lights. But it's easy to conceive of that match striking in just those same conditions, but without lighting: you just did, with no contradiction to be found! But then it is possible for the match to strike without the lighting, in which case we cannot say the striking caused the lighting.

You may be tempted to object. "But given the laws of physics and chemistry, if you strike that match in those conditions it *is* impossible for it not to light!"

But now what exactly are these *laws of nature*?

They are *matters of fact*, discoverable only through sensory experience, and not *relations of ideas* derivable by pure logical reasoning. And what sensory experience has given us is only perceptions of many similar strikings followed by similar lightings. It does not give us any necessity, and therefore doesn't allow us to say that strikings *compel* the lightings. At most, then, the laws of nature merely summarize patterns of past behavior, and therefore carry no necessity with them. And in any case, it is just as easy to conceive of the laws of nature themselves as not existing, or as being different from what they are. No contradiction there! And if you can conceive of that, then you can conceive of the match striking in those conditions without lighting, in which case, again, it's not impossible to have the first without the second. So, again, the first does not cause the second.

The same holds for all our common sense examples of causation:

> When I see, for instance, a billiard ball moving in a straight line towards another . . . may I not conceive that a hundred different events might as well follow from that cause? May not both these balls remain at absolute rest? May not the first ball return in a straight line or leap off from the second in any line or direction? (*Enquiry* IV.I)

Of course these unusual outcomes are rarely or never observed to occur, but Hume's point is just that as far as we can conceive, they *could* occur. But that is to say that no event ever guarantees any other, that no two events are ever necessarily connected—that no event is ever the cause of any other event.

Hume's second argument, the **deducibility argument against necessary connection**, is a variation of the first. Let's begin with some of Hume's examples:

> Adam [i.e., the first human being], though his rational faculties are supposed entirely perfect . . . could not have inferred from the fluidity and transparency of water that it

would suffocate him, or from the light and warmth of fire that it would consume him. . . . Present two smooth pieces of marble to a man who has no [scientific knowledge]; he will never discover that they will adhere together in such a manner as to require great force to separate them in a direct line, while they make so small a resistance to a lateral pressure . . . [N]or does any man imagine that the explosion of gunpowder or the attraction of a [magnet] could ever be discovered by [pure reasoning] . . . We fancy that were we brought, all of the sudden, into this world, we could at first have inferred that one billiard ball would communicate motion to another upon [contact] and that we did not need to have waited for the event in order to pronounce with certainty concerning it. (*Enquiry* IV.I)

We are never able to infer or deduce, by pure reasoning alone, any one event from any other. The first time you saw water you simply could not infer that it would suffocate you; the first time you saw billiard balls about to collide you could not infer what would happen next. But now why is this? Because the contemplation of any one event never compels us, necessarily, to contemplate any other event. Given that each event is distinct, we can always conceive of any one event occurring without any other; thus from any one event occurring, nothing at all follows logically about what must happen next. But that just means, again, that no two events are necessarily connected, and thus that no event ever is the cause of any other.

Hume's third and last argument, the **"no idea" argument against necessary connection**, is where his empiricism reaches its most extreme point. Just as we don't have legitimate (i.e., experience-derived) ideas of material or mental substance, we also don't have a legitimate idea of the necessary connection between events:

Shall we then assert that we are conscious of a power or energy in our own minds when, by an act or command of our will, we raise up a new idea, fix the mind to the contemplation of it, turn it on all sides, and at last dismiss it for some other idea when we think that we have surveyed it with sufficient accuracy? I believe the same arguments will prove that even this command of the will gives us no real idea of force or [power]. . . .

Volition is surely an act of the mind with which we are sufficiently acquainted. Reflect upon it. Consider it on all sides. Do you find anything in it like this creative power by which it raises from nothing a new idea . . . ? [We are] far from being conscious of this energy in the will.

—**David Hume**, *An Enquiry concerning Human Understanding* (1748)

When we look about us towards external objects . . . we are never able . . . to discover any power or necessary connection, any quality which binds the effect to the cause and renders the one an infallible consequence of the other. We only find that the one does actually in fact follow the other. The impulse of one billiard ball is attended with motion in the second. (*Enquiry* VII.I)

All events seem entirely loose and separate. One event follows another, but we never can observe any tie between them. They seem *conjoined*, but never *connected*. And as we can have no idea of anything, which never appears to our outward sense or inward sentiment, the . . . conclusion *seems* to be that we have no idea of connection or power at all and that these words are absolutely without any meaning. (*Enquiry* VII.II)

The idea of the necessary connection between events does not come from deductive reasoning, the first two arguments showed; but neither does it come from sensory experience. We never literally observe any one physical event *compelling* any other, we merely observe the second event following the first. We see the match struck, and it lights; we don't see the match making it *impossible* for the lighting not to occur. So our perceptual experience of the external world does not yield the idea of necessary connection.

Nor do we get it from our awareness of our own inner mental states and processes. As Malebranche's "know-how argument" had pointed out (chapter 8), we are aware of our desire to move our body and of our body moving, but not of our desire compelling the motion. We may similarly observe our thoughts or feelings occurring in various sequences, but we are never aware of ourselves actually controlling or compelling those sequences. They just happen.

So the idea of necessary connection does not come from reasoning, nor from sensory experience, either outer or inner. But since these are the only possible sources of ideas, the conclusion is inevitable. We don't really *have* the idea of necessary connection after all! The whole suggestion that one event could be necessarily connected to another, that there is causation in the universe, turns out to be *unintelligible nonsense.*

But wait, you might object. How could so many people have believed for so long that there are necessary connections between events and then turn out to have been so fundamentally misinformed about their own ideas?

Hume has an answer. It's that people have been mistaken about what "necessary connection" means. In fact there *is* something in perceptual experience to which we refer when we think of necessary connections. It's just not genuine necessary connections.

To see this, let's now note the reason why all of Hume's examples in the deducibility argument above stressed the first time you observe something. For the first time you observe something, you wouldn't have any inkling of a necessary connection. You'd see the striking and the lighting, the first ball colliding with the second, and merely observe the sequential events with no thought of necessary connection. But then experience accumulates. You observe *many* strikings followed by lightings. And over time you come to feel that the first event *does* compel the second, that there *is* a necessary connection between them. But of course this feeling is illusory: if necessary connection were not literally observable in the first instance, it wouldn't be observable in any subsequent instances either.

So something else must be going on:

> [T]his idea of a necessary connection among events arises from a number of similar instances which occur, of the constant conjunction of these events. . . . But there is nothing in a number of instances, different from every single instance [alone] . . . except only that after a repetition of similar instances the mind is carried by habit, upon the appearance of one event, to expect its usual attendant and to believe that it will exist. This connection, therefore, which we *feel* in the mind . . . is the sentiment or impression from which we form the idea of . . . necessary connection. (*Enquiry* VII.II)

We *think* there is a necessary connection between the striking and lighting, because after having observed many strikings-lightings we *psychologically anticipate* the lighting on the occasion of a striking. Then when the lighting occurs, we feel a sense of fulfillment, that things happened just as we anticipated they would. But we then mistake that purely *subjective* feeling of fulfilled anticipation, within our minds, for the allegedly *objective* necessary connection between the events themselves in the world. We feel that when things happen as we anticipate, they *had* to happen that way. That is why you *think* you have a genuine idea of necessary connection, because there *is* something to which you refer with that notion; except that what that is, is not genuine necessary connection "out there" in the world, but merely some subjective feelings *entirely within you.*

There are no necessary connections out there. There's just a sense of anticipation, in here.

So there is no causation in the world. The cosmological arguments using causal reasoning to prove God's existence must therefore fail (see chapter 7). The rationalist arguments using causal reasoning to prove the existence of the external physical world (Descartes, and Locke), to prove determinism (Spinoza), to prove pre-established harmony (Leibniz), must therefore fail. Berkeley's belief in the existence of mental substances, minds—gone. Without causation and causal reasoning we cannot understand how or why things happen. We can merely observe that they simply do happen. Our very effort to understand the workings of the world, the very intelligibility of the world—like material substance, minds, God—gone.

That, to many, is a rather depressing conclusion.

It gets worse.

Hume's Critique of Inductive Reasoning

Okay, fine: there is no causation, and no understanding why things happen. But does that mean we have *nothing*?

For even if there is no causation, strictly speaking, Hume admits that we still have all those past results, those past patterns of "constantly conjoined" events that triggered us to *think* there were necessary connections. We've observed plenty of strikings followed by lightings, so even if we cannot say that the strikings *cause* the lightings, isn't it at least reasonable to predict, and to believe, that the next time we strike a match in similar conditions it will be followed by a lighting? Perhaps not a guarantee, not "understanding," but something, at least, to navigate the world by, a little?

What we're proposing, in short, is that we could still use **inductive reasoning**. As we saw in chapter 4, inductive arguments do not aim to prove their conclusions with certainty or necessity, the way **deductive arguments** do, but only with some degree of probability. One common example involves generalizing from past experiences. You see a white swan, and then another, and then another, and you infer that the next swan you see will be white, or perhaps that all swans are white. No one supposes that either conclusion is necessary, for it's always possible that the next swan will break the pattern. But the more white swans in a row you have seen, it seems, the more *probable* it is that the next one will be white, or that all are white.

In fact we use inductive reasoning all the time, every day. Consider, for our example now, your trip to the kitchen this morning to make breakfast. You surely were confident that the ground would support your weight in every step that you took. (If you thought you might disappear into a sinkhole with your next step, would you have dared to move?) And what justifies you in believing that your "next" step won't be into a brand new sinkhole? Well, past results are no *guarantee*. It is always at least possible that the next step will be your last. But doesn't the ground's record of supporting your previous billion steps at least make it *reasonable to believe* that it will support your next step? Doesn't it *justify* your believing that your next step will very probably be fine?

Hume says no.

For the ground's past record would give you good (or at least *some*) reason to believe that it will support your next step only on one condition: if you may justifiably assume that the future will be like the past. (For if the future won't be like the past, you would probably want to rethink your little excursion.) But then the question becomes this. How would you justify that assumption itself, that the future will be like the past?

Let's spell this out. Imagine the following argument:

The ground supported step 1.
The ground supported step 2.
The ground supported step 3.

Therefore, the ground will support my next step.

It surely looks, to the untrained eye, that the truth of those premises at least increases the likelihood of the truth of the conclusion, as in our swan example. But as we train our eye we realize that this argument actually requires a hidden premise, namely that assumption that the future will be like the past. We'll call that assumption **the uniformity of nature**, and abbreviate it with a (U):

The ground supported step 1.
The ground supported step 2.
The ground supported step 3.
(U) The future will be like the past.

Therefore, the ground will support my next step.

To see that this additional assumption is necessary, imagine for a moment that it's false, that the future will not be like the past. Well if the ground has supported all your previous steps and the future will *not* be like the past, then that surely wouldn't increase the likelihood that the ground will support your next step! So if the original premises are to support the conclusion at all, it must be because we are assuming that (U) is true, as we indicated.

But now, how can we justify (U) itself?

Well, so far the world has been pretty consistent. In the past, the future has always been like the past with respect to things like the ground supporting our steps. So don't we have good reason to believe that, in the future, the future will continue to be like the past?

To represent this as an argument we might say:

Relative to three days ago, the future was like the past.
Relative to two days ago, the future was like the past.
Relative to yesterday, the future was like the past.

Therefore, relative to today, the future will be like the past.

That is,

Three days ago, (U) was true.
Two days ago, (U) was true.
Yesterday, (U) was true.

Therefore, today (U) will be true.

To say that three days ago the future was like the past is to say, roughly, that from the perspective of three days ago, what came afterward followed the same pattern as what came before. Insofar as the world has remained consistent, then, these premises all seem to be true.

The problem, however, is that even so, these premises cannot support the crucial conclusion, (U), that the future will *continue* to be like the past. Why not? Because just as we saw that the earlier inductive argument needed to include (U) as a hidden premise, so too *here* we must include (U) as a hidden premise:

> Three days ago, (U) was true.
> Two days ago, (U) was true.
> Yesterday, (U) was true.
> (U) The future will be like the past.
> ----------
> Therefore today (U) will be true.

Why? Because, in effect, if (U) is false and the future won't be like the past, then the fact that it was like the past, in the past, won't mean that it will be like the past, in the future! (Got that?)

Or let's put it another way. The argument in question must *assume* that past patterns—now, about the future being like the past—will continue to hold into the future. *But that is the very assumption we're trying to justify in the first place!* And you can't justify something by assuming it's true, as we saw in the fallacy of *begging the question* in chapter 5. You can only justify something by giving some other, independent reason to believe it is true.

In short, all inductive arguments assume (U), that the future will be like the past. But the only way to justify (U) is to make an inductive argument for it: (U) has always been true so far, so will probably continue to be true. But then the argument for (U) must itself assume (U), which means that we have offered no real reason to believe (U) is true.

Hume's conclusion, then, is that you actually have no good reason at all to believe that the future will be like the past. The future could just as easily be different from the past as like it. Which means that past results don't merely not guarantee future performance, *they don't give you any guide to it at all.*

So Hume's critique of causation meant that we cannot justifiably believe in matter, minds, or God, or, more generally, explain why anything happens. We only thought we could because we observed the regular patterns of events in the world (strikings followed by lightings, etc.). His critique of induction now shows that we have no good reason to believe that things will even continue to happen the regular way they have been. Nor, for that matter, that they won't continue to happen that way. We have no idea, basically, why things have happened the way they have and why they will happen the way that they will, however that is.

They just do.

The final result of Hume's strict empiricism is thus an extreme form of skepticism. If Descartes's *Meditations* began with an expression of radical skepticism, then after nearly two centuries of philosophy we seem to be back where we started.

Enter Immanuel Kant.

IMMANUEL KANT (1724–1804)

Kant was born in Königsberg, in East Prussia (today called Kaliningrad, a Russian territory squeezed between Poland and Lithuania). He lived in this small city all his life, never traveling more than a few miles from it. He entered the University of Königsberg at the age of sixteen, intending to embark on a career in theology. By twenty-two, however, both his parents had died, and Kant had to make his own way. He supported himself for years by being a private tutor, until he gained a lecturing appointment at the University. Though you wouldn't guess it from his dense writing style, he was widely admired as a speaker. He taught five hours a day, six days a week, starting at 7 a.m., but students had to arrive by 6 a.m. to obtain a seat in the room. He eventually completed his doctorate and, in 1770, at the age of forty-six, was elevated to professor, a position he held to his retirement in 1797.

Although originally pursuing theology, Kant found himself attracted to science and then to philosophy. His first published work was in cosmology, in 1755, but then for the next twenty-five years he published only occasional papers, slowly working out his own original philosophy. Then in one decade, as he approached his sixties, he published five great works: *Critique of Pure Reason* (1781), *Prolegomena to Any Future System of Metaphysics* (1783), *Foundations of the Metaphysics of Morals* (1785), *Critique of Practical Reason* (1788), and *Critique of Judgment* (1790). In the late 1790s he became senile, and died in 1804.

One point of interest is that Kant was the first of the major early modern philosophers to spend his career as a professor. As a result his writings have a different feel from the others we have been discussing. Rather than being aimed at the general educated public they are aimed at other academics, and thus are dense, difficult, and jargon-filled. You can get quite a lot out of reading the other early moderns on your own, but reading Kant takes more work, as you

KANT AND HIS CIRCLE

nearly have to learn another language to do it. With that said, we'll try in what follows to get a sense of what he is up to.

Three Ways to Frame the Discussion

(1) First, we might understand Kant's overall project as an attempt to reconcile science with religion and morality.

By the late eighteenth century the European Enlightenment was in full force, fueled partly by the great advances in physical science pioneered by Isaac Newton (1643–1727). On the Newtonian view of the world—itself advancing upon the earlier mechanical philosophy—the world was a mechanical system of physical bodies operating according to strict laws that necessitated their behavior. Moreover, there seemed to be no limits to scientific investigation. Newtonian science seemed to apply to the entire cosmos, and it was only a matter of time before it would offer natural explanations of *everything*.

This worldview, however, seemed to conflict with religion and morality. There was no room for God as a supernatural force operating within the world. At most God created the cosmos at the beginning but then let it operate on its own, a popular Enlightenment doctrine known as **deism**. Nor was there room for a non-physical mind or soul. As we saw with the mind-body problem in chapter 8, the laws of nature explained all physical motion, with nothing left over for minds to contribute. Nor, finally, was there room for our acting

> I freely admit that the remembrance of David Hume was the very thing that many years ago first interrupted my dogmatic slumber and gave a completely different direction to my researches in the field of speculative philosophy.
>
> —**Immanuel Kant**, *Prolegomena to Any Future Metaphysics* (1783)

freely, as everything was determined by the laws of nature. With no human freedom, there could be no morality, for we are only morally responsible for actions we do freely.

To avoid dismissing religion and morality as mere superstition and illusion, then, Kant sought some way not to refute the science (for it was impressive and persuasive) but to set limits to it, to leave some sort of conceptual space for belief in God, freedom, and morality.

(2) A second way to understand Kant's project is as an attempt to rescue the possibility of objective knowledge from Hume's skeptical arguments.

Objective knowledge is knowledge of how the world is in some sense independent of your individual perspective on it. You may be aware of how a situation feels to you, or of what something looks like from where you are standing, but that is subjective. Objective knowledge is a matter of how things *are*, no matter how they may appear to you or what you think about them at any given moment. In a famous passage Kant remarks that reading Hume awakened him from his "dogmatic slumber," forcing him to realize that objective knowledge was in trouble. For Hume deeply challenges the possibility of objective knowledge: all that we can know is the sequence of perceptions, feelings, thoughts, and so forth. we are having, which are all entirely subjective. It is not possible to reason our way out of our experiences to conclusions about how things are independent of them, about what exists (matter, mind, or God), about what causes what, about what will happen next.

(3) Finally, we can understand Kant's project as an attempt to "synthesize" rationalism and empiricism, to combine what was best about each while avoiding their respective difficulties.

For each, on its own, had reached a kind of dead end, as we've seen. The rationalists had great confidence in reason, but their reasonings reached profoundly different, and strange, conclusions. They created ambitious systems of thought, but these, for all their brilliance, struck those more scientifically minded as mere castles in the air, lacking solid foundation. Empiricism meanwhile had great confidence in experimental science, yet ultimately could not give an adequate account of some basic concepts underlying science itself, such as *matter*, *mind*, and *cause*. Worse, it ended up in Hume's extreme skepticism, leaving us unable to know *anything*, pretty much.

Overall, Kant observed, metaphysics in general was a mess. After twenty-two centuries philosophers were still largely addressing the same questions as Plato and Aristotle. Worse, they were incapable of reaching resolution or consensus, as we have seen in the early moderns. But while metaphysics was stagnant, and in chaos, scientific knowledge was growing by leaps and bounds, as was mathematics. Moreover both science and mathematics reflected the traits of true knowledge in a way that metaphysics did not: they were rigorous, methodical, seemed objective, and they did produce resolution and consensus. What science and mathematics showed was that genuine objective knowledge of the world *was* possible, somehow, despite Hume's critiques. In their basic methods and assumptions they must be doing something right, Kant thought, that metaphysics was doing wrong.

Perhaps the failures of both rationalism and empiricism were a clue. Perhaps each overemphasized their main epistemological method without adequate recognition of its competitor's. Clearly *both* reason and sensory experience were relevant to obtaining knowledge. "There is no doubt whatever that all our cognition begins with experience," Kant writes in the *Critique of Pure Reason*,[5] for in no other way could our faculty of knowledge get any material to work upon. But this does not mean that all our cognition arises *from* experience, for reason itself makes some contribution to the knowledge process. To paraphrase a famous passage from the *Critique*, reason without experience is empty, while experience without reason is blind. The problem, then, was to figure out precisely how to fit them together, to balance them, to synthesize them.

A First Pass through Kant's Answer

All previous philosophies—including rationalism and empiricism—had started from a common view about the relationship between mind and external bodies or objects. The mind was distinct from the object, which it tried to "know"; but the act of knowing was essentially passive. An object was merely "given" to the mind, which simply absorbed it, took it in as it was, and thus came to know it. With this starting point, it is no wonder that both rationalism and empiricism ran into difficulties. Rationalism was unable to explain how the mind's innate ideas and capacity for reasoning could generate knowledge, for why should there be any conformity between the ways of the mind and the ways of mind-independent objects? And empiricism was unable to explain how we could ever attain anything more than collections of sensory experiences lacking all necessary connections and predictive power, as Hume showed.

It was this basic assumption, underlying both schools, that Kant questioned. For if the mind is to attain genuine knowledge of objects, then the objects known cannot after all be entirely independent of the mind. The mind cannot be simply a passive spectator; it must itself contribute actively to the process of knowing the objects that confront it in experience, and thus in some sense shape them.

Or as Kant memorably puts it, knowledge is not a matter of the mind conforming to the object known, but of the object known conforming to the mind. This reversal Kant compares to the revolution in cosmology brought about by the astronomer Nicolaus Copernicus (1473–1543):

[W]hen [Copernicus] did not make good progress in the explanation of the celestial motions if he assumed that the entire celestial host revolves around the observer, [he] tried to see if he might not have greater success if he made the observer revolve and left the stars at rest. (*Critique*, Preface, 110)

Just as some of the motions the stars appeared to possess were not really due to them but to our own earthly motion, so too, Kant suggested, certain characteristics that known objects have will be due not to them but to the activity of the knowing mind. And just as the heavens never looked the same again after Copernicus's revolution, neither would metaphysics, Kant expected, after his own.

And how will metaphysics look? If we accept his revolution, he suggests, then we shall be able to prove (with the rationalists) that certain kinds of knowledge of the world are possible after all and thus reply to Hume's skepticism. But we will discover (with the empiricists) that the only world we can truly know is that given to us in sense experience. We will see that we cannot have genuine knowledge of anything lying beyond experience. In particular, we will see that we cannot and never will be able to establish three points that have been important to metaphysics: the existence of God, of freedom, and of immortality.

But although this challenges rationalism, which claims to attain such knowledge, Kant insists that we can find only meaning and value in these ideas if knowledge of them is *not* possible. And this would seem to follow from his basic empiricist premise, for if knowledge is restricted to what we can experience, then if God were knowable, He would have to be a physical thing, bound by the limitations of all physical things. Such a God would lose all meaning and value for us. Similarly with freedom and immortality—if these are to have any meaning for us, they must refer to a sort of reality lying beyond our empirical world, beyond the world as we experience it, and thus be unknowable.

And so Kant makes a remarkable assertion: "Thus I had to deny knowledge [of God, freedom, and immortality] in order to make room for faith" (*Critique*, Preface, 117). But while this suggests that Kant agrees with Hume that we cannot have some knowledge we wish we did, he will also show that we possess a good deal more knowledge about the world than Hume believed.

Kant names his overall doctrine **transcendental idealism**, but we must not confuse it with Berkeley's idealism. *Idealism* for Berkeley was the doctrine that all that exists are minds and their perceptions, and there is no external physical world. Kant explicitly rejects Berkeley's idealism. Instead, his *idealism* refers to the notion that the objects known must conform to the

> With the appearance of Kant former systems of philosophy, which had merely sniffed about the external aspect of things, assembling and classifying their characteristics, ceased to exist. Kant led investigation back to the human intellect, and inquired what the latter had to reveal. Not without reason, therefore did he compare his philosophy to the method of Copernicus. Formerly, when men conceived the world as standing still, and the sun as revolving round it, astronomical calculations failed to agree accurately. But when Copernicus made the sun stand still and the earth revolve round it, behold! Everything accorded admirably. So formerly reason, like the sun, moved round the universe of phenomena, and sought to throw light upon it. But Kant bade reason, the sun, stand still, and the universe of phenomena now turns round, and is illuminated the moment it comes within the region of the intellectual orb.
>
> —**Heinrich Heine**, *Religion and Philosophy in Germany* (1835)

mind, to the mind's "ideals." The objects may well be physical bodies, but in being knowable they must (as we'll see) conform to our knowing mind. The *transcendental* part refers to his notion that some kinds of objective knowledge are possible after all, Hume notwithstanding: we are able to transcend the purely subjective nature of our experience.

Let's now see how he gets there.

Four Kinds of Judgments

You'll recall Hume's distinction between *relations of ideas* and *matters of fact*. Hume claimed that all the judgments we make, all the propositions we reason about, fall into these two categories. The former are (when true) true by definition, thus necessary truths, and thus their truth-value may be grasped merely by reflecting on the meanings of the words involved; as such they don't say anything about the world but merely express how "ideas are related." (Examples included mathematical propositions, *bachelors are unmarried males*.) *Matters of fact*, to the contrary, are (when true) more than merely a matter of definition, they are about the facts in the world; thus they are not necessary truths (but contingent), and grasping their truth-value requires knowing the meanings of the words *plus* knowing how the facts are, and thus require sensory experience. (Examples included *Ashton Kutcher enjoys playing squash, bachelors live less long than married men.*) Hume's view that these categories exhaust the possibilities leads quickly to his skepticism: relations of ideas don't even make any claims about the world (so don't constitute knowledge of it), and matters of fact lack necessary connections and predictive powers.

But Hume, Kant now observes, has made a subtle mistake here. He didn't realize that there were actually two very different distinctions in play, which he conflated.

The first is an *epistemological* distinction, between judgments or propositions that are **knowable a priori** and those only **knowable a posteriori**. The former can be known to be true apart from, or in some sense prior to, sensory experience, in the way that mathematicians deduce their theorems and truths (such as $7+5=12$) without requiring sensory observations. Since their truth-value is in some sense independent of any particular experiences, these propositions will remain true no matter how experience varies. Thus they are universal and necessary, meaning they are true everywhere and can't possibly be or become false. In contrast are judgments or propositions knowable only *a posteriori*: these are knowable only with the help of sensory experience, such as (for example) *the grass is green*. Since sensory experience varies over place and time, these are never universal or necessary.

The second distinction is a *semantic* one, concerning linguistic meaning, between **analytic propositions** and **synthetic propositions**. Propositions are typically expressed as sentences, and sentences typically take a "subject-predicate" form: the subject is what the sentence is about, the predicate is what the sentence is saying about the subject. ("The grass" is the subject of the previous example, "is green" is the predicate.) An *analytic proposition* is one whose truth-value is determined strictly by the meanings of the words involved, and it is true when the notion expressed by the predicate is "contained in" or "part of" the notion expressed by the subject. Consider *bachelors are unmarried males*. Since being unmarried is part of the very notion or definition of being a bachelor, this proposition is analytic. In expressing it we are simply drawing out, or analyzing, the subject term of the proposition. This being so, the predicate term adds nothing to the subject term that it didn't already contain, and the proposition therefore does not provide us with any new knowledge about the world. If you understand English, then that suffices to know that the proposition is true.

In contrast, judgments or propositions such as *the house is burning* are *synthetic*. In these the predicate is *not* contained in the subject. We may analyze the subject term of such a judgment *ad infinitum* and never elicit from it the notions expressed by the predicate term. The predicate is therefore adding something to the subject that it didn't already contain. Its truth-value, then, depends on more than merely the meanings of the words but on whether the facts in the world correspond to those meanings. As such, these propositions are making claims about the world. Recall *bachelors live longer than married men*. How long they live is not part of the definition of bachelor, but adds something to the concept. Understanding English isn't enough to grasp whether it's true, so you have to go check out how things are in the world.

So we have two different distinctions, one about knowledge, one about meaning. Prior to Kant, these were treated as the same. What made a certain proposition knowable *a priori*, independent of experience, was simply that it was analytic, as knowing the meanings of the words sufficed for knowing the truth. What made a proposition knowable only *a posteriori* was that it was synthetic, as you needed experience to know whether it was true since the truth depended on more than the meanings of the words. Indeed, Hume's own discussion also treated these as the same. Hume's *relations of ideas* are merely analytic *a priori* propositions: they are universal and necessary, but they do not make any claims about the world because they concern only word meanings, how "ideas" are related, and thus can be known by pure reasoning. Hume's *matters of fact* are synthetic *a posteriori* propositions, which, while making claims about the "facts" in the world and knowable only by sensory experience, are neither universal nor necessary.

But there is Hume's error, Kant observes—for the two distinctions are *not* the same, one being epistemological, the other being semantic. And therefore you cannot simply equate analytic with *a priori*, and synthetic with *a posteriori*. In fact with two different distinctions in play there are four possible combinations.

What the table below shows is that in addition to Hume's relations of ideas and matters of fact there could in principle be two other kinds of judgment or proposition: synthetic *a priori* and analytic *a posteriori*. Kant dismissed the latter as an empty category, but realized that there could be judgments of the former category. These synthetic *a priori* judgments would be remarkably valuable—for as *a priori* they would be discoverable independently of experience yet universally and necessarily true, and as synthetic they would truly be informative about the world.

But are there such propositions? For how could it be possible for us to obtain by pure reasoning alone knowledge that is truly informative about the world, yet necessary and universal? The difficulty is that if these are synthetic propositions, the subject and the predicate are two distinct notions. But then how can they nevertheless be necessarily connected in some way, so that the proposition "S is P" is always true? This problem does not arise for analytic propositions, for here P is just contained in S. It does not arise for synthetic *a posteriori* propositions,

Could there be synthetic a priori judgments?

	a priori	a posteriori
analytic	relations of ideas	X
synthetic	?	matters of fact

By Andrew Pessin

for they do not assert any necessary connection, anything that is necessarily true. But it does arise for synthetic *a priori* propositions.

So are there any?

Synthetic A Priori Judgments

There are indeed such judgments, Kant argues, in mathematics and in science (by which he means Newtonian physics). Focusing on the former, everyone agrees that the propositions of arithmetic and geometry are knowable *a priori*, derivable by logical deduction, and necessarily and universally true: *7+5=12* and *the angles of a triangle add up to 180 degrees* are both true everywhere, and always. The question now is whether they are also synthetic.

Hume had granted that mathematics contains necessary truths, but defended empiricism by claiming that they involved only relations of ideas, and thus enjoyed their necessary truth by definition. So, for example, what makes *bachelors are unmarried males* necessarily true is that we have defined *bachelor* as *unmarried male*: we wouldn't *call* something a *bachelor* unless it were an unmarried male. There's no necessary connection between the things that are bachelors and the things that are unmarried males. These are just the same thing, known by two names, which are only linked by the conventions of English. Similar considerations apply to mathematics, Hume thinks. What makes *7+5=12* necessarily true is just that we have defined those terms such that *7+5* and *12* are names for the same thing. There are no necessary connections between two distinct entities in the world here, just a necessary link due to the way we have decided to use our words.

Kant disagrees. Arithmetic statements are not true by definition. That *7+5* comes out specifically to *12* is not merely contained in the idea of their being united in this way, but adds something to it. Thus *7+5* and *12* are not merely two names for one different thing, but two different things that *are* necessarily related. Similarly, that a straight line is the shortest path between two points is a necessary truth from geometry, but the concept of *straightness* in no way contains the concept of *shortest*, the former being a quality and the latter a quantity. Thus geometric principles are synthetic as well.

But if mathematical judgments are synthetic, then they are making genuine claims about the facts in the world. And since everyone agrees they are knowable *a priori*, we have precisely what Hume said was impossible: genuine knowledge about how distinguishable things are necessarily connected to each other. Hume thought he could relegate all necessities to relations of ideas, a product of definition, but had overlooked the possibility of synthetic *a priori* propositions, expressing necessities that *are* about the world, not just about definitions.

Not only are nearly all mathematical judgments or propositions synthetic *a priori*, Kant holds, but so also are those in Newtonian science. For him these include such principles as *in all changes in the material world the quantity of matter remains unchanged, in all communication of motion action and reaction are equal, every event has a cause, the world consists of enduring objects which exist independently of perceivers,* and so on. Again, in calling them synthetic *a priori* Kant is saying these are derivable by pure reasoning, they express necessary and universal truths, and they are truly about the world, not merely about definitions.

Finally, Kant observes, some of the propositions of metaphysics at least appear to be synthetic *a priori*, such as those about the existence and nature of God, the immaterial soul and its immortality, and human freedom. We've already seen, however, that unlike mathematics and science, metaphysics has failed to generate genuine knowledge. This then moves Kant to formulate the fundamental problem in terms of several questions. How is mathematics possible, he asks—that is, how does it succeed in generating synthetic a *priori* propositions? How is science possible (doing the same)? And in light of whatever is to be learned by answering the first two questions, is metaphysics in fact possible, given all its failures?

How Is *Mathematics Possible?*

We'll start with the short answer, focusing on geometry. Geometry generates necessary and universal truths that are derivable in advance of experience via pure reasoning, yet are genuinely truths about the world we experience. How is that possible?

Answer. Geometry is the science of space. It summarizes everything about the properties of spatial things, their sizes and shapes. But it could be guaranteed to apply to everything in our sensory experience, Kant observes, only if the mind itself contributes spatiality to experience. Put differently, if the mind, in constructing your experience, contributes spatiality to the objects experienced, then it is guaranteed in advance that everything you experience will have spatial properties. In Kant's language, it's our **faculty of sensibility**—that feature of the mind which generates sensory perceptions—that contributes the spatiality to our experiences. And if "outer experience," of the external world, is guaranteed to feature spatial objects, then geometry is guaranteed to apply to everything we experience.

(Consider an analogy. Suppose you were fitted with blue contact lenses. It would then be guaranteed that everything you see will look bluish, precisely because your organ of seeing contributes the blue.)

Similar considerations apply to "inner experience," the mind's awareness of itself, best accessed perhaps when you minimize your external senses, if you can. Pure inner awareness would not feature spatial objects, since your vision is turned off. But what it would feature is temporality. Inner experience always has a temporal nature, a sequential nature, a linearity. For Kant, arithmetic applies to temporality in the way that geometry applies to spatiality, since sequentiality is like counting. If the faculty of sensibility contributes spatiality to external experience, accounting for the guaranteed applicability of geometry to the objects experienced, then it also contributes temporality to inner experience, thus accounting for the guaranteed applicability of arithmetic to inner experience. (In turn, your awareness of the outer world itself involves awareness of your own sequence of perceptions, of your own inner awareness; so external experience also displays sequentiality.)

Kant offers various arguments for his claim that the mind's faculty of sensibility contributes spatiality and temporality to experience. One basic one is that our experience of externality is, on the level of bare sensation, nonspatial. We have sensations of this object or that object, and the sensations in question, although they differ in quality, do not, as bare sensations, differ in terms of their different spatial locations. It's as if the mind arrays the different sensations over the field of vision (put yellow patch here; put red patch there). The spatiality sensations come to possess is something that our minds give to them. (In fact twenty-first-century cognitive scientists are well aware that being able to see spatial relationships is something it takes time to learn, in babies and even in adults who were sight-deprived at birth but have their sight restored. We don't realize this because we've long ago mastered the skill.)

Similarly, we unhesitatingly believe certain things about space and time that we lack all sufficient evidence for, if we only derived our notions of those properties from experience. We find it inconceivable that space or time might be different from what we experience them to be, space being three dimensional, time being linear, continuous, irreversible.[6] We may conceive of a space with no objects in it or a temporal interval with nothing occurring during it, but we cannot conceive of the absence of space and time altogether. We also believe that space and time are universal, everywhere the same, that everything in the cosmos exists in the same great space, and undergoes the same overall flow of time.[7] None of these beliefs could be grounded in our actual sequence of sensory experiences, since these are very limited in scope. But we do believe them, and believe them firmly—a sign, Kant thinks, that we do not derive our notions of space and time *from* what we experience, but rather that we bring them with us *to* experience.

That's why we're confident that, were we to perceive a triangular object on Mars, a billion years in the future, Euclid's theorems will still apply to it. It's because our minds bring spatiality to perception, so every perception will be spatial in nature. Space and time are guaranteed features of every perceptual experience because they are due to our mind's faculty of sensibility. As such the mathematics of geometry and arithmetic are guaranteed to apply to everything we experience.

Does this mean, then, that space and everything in it is unreal? Kant's answer to this is that if by *things* you mean things as they are in themselves, then space does not define them and is not real. But if you mean things as we experience them, then it is both true of them and real enough. For space is the only way in which we, as human beings with the minds we have, can experience the world presented to us. This is perhaps not the only way it can be experienced, perhaps. Maybe other animals, life-forms, even aliens, might experience things differently. There may well be ways of viewing reality that are completely closed to us. But for human beings, space and time are the only ways in which that reality can be perceived by us.

> That all our knowledge begins with experience there can be no doubt. For how is it possible that the faculty of cognition should be awakened into exercise otherwise than by means of objects which affect our senses, and partly of them selves produce representations, partly rouse our powers of understanding into activity, to compare, to connect, or to separate these, and so to convert the raw material of our sensuous impressions into a knowledge of objects, which is called experience? In respect of time, therefore, no knowledge of ours is antecedent to experience, but begins with it. But though all our knowledge begins with experience, it by no means follows, that all arises out of experience. For, on the contrary, it is quite possible that our empirical knowledge is a compound of that which we receive through impressions, and that which the faculty of cognition supplies from itself.
>
> —**Immanuel Kant**, *Critique of Pure Reason* (1781)

This does not mean we live in a world of illusion. But it does mean that our world is a human world and that the knowledge we have of it is a human knowledge. If it is an illusion, it is a universal one. This is both unfortunate and fortunate. It is unfortunate since what we know about this reality is infected by that human viewpoint; but it is fortunate in that, although that knowledge is therefore limited, we need not doubt its certainty. And thus the very thing that enables us to know certain things is also what makes it impossible to know other things. If you must wear blue contact lenses all your life, you can know in advance and with certainty the color of any object you will ever experience—but you cannot ever know what it *really* looks like.

And this is what Kant means when he speaks of **phenomena**, or *things as they appear to us*, and **noumena**, or *things in themselves*. The world of appearances is not a world of illusion. It is the world as it must appear to creatures with minds such as our own. How the world is in itself we cannot know. But to know that much—that it must appear the way it does because of the way we are—is to know a great deal.

How Is Science Possible?

Let's turn to the second question. The overall answer will have the same general form as that to the first question, with different details. Synthetic *a priori* mathematics is possible because the mind brings spatiality and temporality to our perceptual experience. Synthetic *a priori* science, too, will be possible also because the mind brings the relevant features to experience. But what exactly are these?

First, Newtonian science, for Kant, construes the world as consisting of objects whose behavior is governed by universal laws of nature. The question now is where we actually get the notions that there are *objects* in the world, and that they are governed by *laws*? The empiricists might claim that sensory experience provides them. But, Kant argues, influenced by Hume's critique of earlier empiricists, sensory experience is actually too impoverished to provide either.

The mind initially senses the material that comes to it in certain ways (as we just saw), imposing spatiality and temporality to create a sequence of sensory experiences. But (to focus on vision) each of these sensory experiences consists, on its basic level, only of patches of colors and lights across a visual field. What we don't actually see is an *object*, something relatively enduring over time. We just get ever-changing arrays of light and color. The notion that these arrays are all of one enduring object is not itself present *within* the experience. Similarly, Hume showed that sensory experience at best provides us with *constant conjunctions*, sequences of regularly paired events. What we don't actually *see* is any genuine necessary connection or causation between events. Thus the notion that laws govern events is also not present *within* experience.

So sensory experience is too impoverished to satisfactorily describe even our ordinary perceptual experience with the world. If you walk into a room and describe what you perceive, after all, you would never say, "I perceive a sequence of ever-changing arrays of light and color." You would say, "I perceive people and tables and chairs and furniture, I perceive that man turning on the light, that woman spilling her soda," and so forth. We perceive the world as consisting of relatively enduring objects, with these objects involved in various relations with each other, including causal relations. But if that is the way we perceive the world, and sensory experience itself is too impoverished to yield *objects* and *causal relations*, then ordinary perception must involve more than mere sensory experience.

It also involves the way we understand or think.

In sensing the world, the mind's faculty of sensibility imposes sensory properties such as spatiality and temporality, but the perceptual process does not end there. For the mind's **faculty of understanding**—that feature of the mind which generates our overall perceptual experience—further organizes those sensory elements by means of what Kant calls **categories**, or **pure concepts**. Kant identifies a dozen of these, but we'll limit our discussion to two, *substance*, and *cause*.

Thus, Kant argues, the faculty of understanding processes the ever-changing flux of spatial-temporal sensations generated by the faculty of sensibility and classifies those patterns into relatively enduring objects, or *substances*. That's why you perceive the room as consisting of objects, because your understanding organizes your sensations as such.

Similarly, the faculty of understanding processes sensations and produces experiences reflecting causal relations. To say a bit more, we naturally form **hypothetical judgments** about the objects in the world in terms of "if-then," or hypothetical, relationships. Thus, we say such things as "If it rains, then the party is called off," "If you drop this glass, then it will break," and so on. These all have the same form, "If P then Q." P (you'll recall) is the *antecedent* of the hypothetical, and Q is the *consequent*. Insofar as we take P to give the reason for, or explain, Q, then we take P to describe a cause and Q to describe an effect.

Kant's point, which he defends at length, is that just as the faculty of understanding applies the category of *substance* to the flux—thus organizing the sensory flux into objects—it also applies the category of *cause* to those objects, organizing them into events that are related as cause and effect. But given that this is how the mind functions in generating perceptual experience, it follows that every perceptual experience will be *of* objects and events in causal relations. In the same way that sensory experience is guaranteed to have a spatial-temporal character (because the mind brings space and time to the experience it generates), overall perceptual experience is guaranteed to consist of objects in causal relations (because the mind brings categories to the experience it generates).

What's crucial here is that such notions as *substance* and *cause* are not elements we derive *from* experience, again, but elements that our mind, in constructing experience, brings *to* experience. That is the only way it can be guaranteed in advance that experience will contain these elements. And that is how the synthetic *a priori* propositions of science are possible: the mind contributes *substance* and *cause* to experience, thus guaranteeing that everything we experience will consist of objects governed by causal laws. Science, then, is the study of just which specific objects and laws exist. But that the world we experience must consist of objects governed by laws is due to our faculty of understanding's organizing of experience by means of the categories.

Of course what we experience, in the end, are phenomena, not noumena. But while the cost of Kant's doctrine is that we can never obtain any knowledge of noumena—we cannot say whether the world in itself consists of spatial-temporal objects and causal relations—the benefit is that we can obtain certain, *a priori* knowledge about phenomena, the world as we experience it.

Why Metaphysics Is Impossible

As anticipated, the answers to our questions about mathematics and science provide the answer to our last question. Metaphysics, as the attempt to generate certain kinds of synthetic *a priori* truths about the world, turns out to be impossible.

Kant's teaching produces in the mind of everyone who has comprehended it a fundamental change which is so great that it may be regarded as an intellectual new-birth. It alone is able really to remove the inborn realism which proceeds from the original character of the intellect . . . which has quite a peculiar, and, we might say, immediate effect upon the mind in consequence of which it undergoes a complete undeception, and forthwith looks at all things in another light. . . . [H]e who has not mastered the Kantian philosophy, whatever else he may have studied, is, as it were, in a state of innocence; that is to say, he remains in the grasp of that natural and childish realism in which we are all born, and which fits us for everything possible, with the single exception of philosophy. Such a man then stands to the man who knows the Kantian philosophy as a minor to a man of full age.

—**Arthur Schopenhauer**, *The World as Will and Representation* (1818)

Why? Because what makes mathematics possible is that the mind brings space and time to sensory experience, thus guaranteeing that geometry and arithmetic will apply to everything we experience. What makes science possible is that the mind organizes experience into objects and causal relations, thus guaranteeing that scientific inquiry will apply to everything we experience. What both answers share is that the mind brings the relevant features to the world we experience, the world of phenomena. As long as we restrict our inquiries to the world of experience, our knowledge is fine.

But that is what metaphysics traditionally fails to do. It attempts to derive necessary truths about matters such as God, the soul, immortality, freedom. But each of these, Kant argues, lies beyond possible experience. If they lie beyond possible experience, then the analyses of mathematics and science won't work for them. We cannot say that these things must be a certain way because our minds bring relevant features to our experience of them. The attempt to derive necessary truths about such matters instantly confronts the earlier problem. What guarantee could there be that the way we think about things corresponds to the way things are, in themselves? Answer: none.

Precisely because what you say about such matters never has to match up to anything in experience, anything goes. That's why philosophers have cooked up innumerable diverse theories, Kant thinks, and are never able to reach consensus—because they are reasoning about matters that go beyond possible experience. For no genuine knowledge of noumena, of things as they are in themselves, independent of our experiences of them, is ever possible.

But while this is a negative result, it also has positive advantages, thinking back to our three ways of framing the discussion. We cannot know how the world is, whether souls exist, or whether God exists, because reason only works with respect to matters of possible experience, phenomena. But, first, reason works quite *well* with phenomena: we can, contra Hume, obtain genuinely objective mathematical and scientific knowledge of the world of phenomena. And second, while we cannot in the end prove God's (noumenal) existence directly, we also cannot disprove it; and while science may rule out human freedom within the realm of phenomena, it cannot rule it out in the realm of noumena; and with that possibility of genuine noumenal human freedom comes the possibility of moral responsibility. By limiting what is knowable to that which is capable of being experienced, Kant has, as he put it, made room for faith in some of the matters that matter most.

SUMMARY

1. The early modern empiricists, represented by John Locke, George Berkeley, and David Hume, stress (against the rationalists) the role that sensory experience plays in epistemology.

2. Locke begins his *Essay* with an extended attack on nativism, arguing that we are born with our minds like a blank slate, which then fills up with ideas as we have sensory experience. He shared Descartes's dualism, representational theory of mind, and mechanical philosophy. His major contribution is his careful analysis of the contents and structure of the mind and methodical defense of the mechanical philosophy. In particular, he offers a detailed defense of the distinction between primary and secondary qualities, including four arguments for the distinction: the science argument, the almond argument, the analogy argument, and relativity of perception arguments.

3. Berkeley is most famous for *idealism*, summarized by the slogan *esse est percipi*. He provides three lines of argument for idealism and against materialism. First, materialism leads to skepticism, and its arguments for the external world fail to show that world is physical. Second, there are several reasons to reject the distinction between primary and secondary qualities. Third, the inconceivability argument claims that the very idea of a mind-independent physical

body is contradictory. Berkeley further argues that idealism fits better than materialism with common sense.

4. Hume, like Berkeley, starts with Locke's epistemological premise—that all knowledge must be traced back to experience—but ends at a far more extreme destination. We can have no ideas of any sort of substance, physical or mental, or God, or causation. He distinguishes between *relations of ideas* and *matters of fact*. The former have their truth-value by definition, and necessarily, but make no claims about the world (concerning only our ideas). The latter have their truth-value contingently, due to whether they conform with the facts, and do make claims about the world. All propositions concerning matters of fact not immediately present rely on the notion of causation.

5. Hume offers three arguments against the existence of causation in the world, or necessary connections between distinct events: the conceivability argument, the deducibility argument, and the "no idea" argument. With respect to the latter, he argues that we mistake our subjective experience of fulfilled anticipation for an objective necessary connection between events.

6. Hume also argues against the justifiability of inductive reasoning, claiming that we have to assume the reliability of inductive reasoning in order to justify it, which begs the question. Combined with his critique of causation this generates his extreme skepticism: we cannot know anything other than what we are immediately perceiving at this moment, and we're never justified in making inferences about what might come next.

7. We can frame Immanuel Kant's project in three ways: as an attempt to reconcile science with religion and morality, to rescue the possibility of objective knowledge from Hume's critique, to synthesize rationalism and empiricism.

8. Kant's transcendental idealism, his "Copernican revolution," inverts the normal assumption: knowledge involves not the mind conforming to the objects known, but the objects known conforming to the mind. In brief, the mind contributes certain features to experience, which guarantees that everything we experience will have those features.

9. Kant notes that Hume overlooked the possibility of synthetic *a priori* judgments. Overlooking these, Hume failed to recognize that mathematics and science offer genuinely objective knowledge of the world. The question is how that is possible.

10. The faculty of sensibility brings spatial and temporal properties to experience, thus guaranteeing that geometry and arithmetic will apply to every object we experience. The faculty of understanding brings categories (such as *substance* and *cause*) to experience, thus guaranteeing that scientific inquiry will apply to every object we experience. Thus Kant explains the possibility of genuine objective knowledge of phenomena, recognizing that we can have no knowledge of noumena.

11. His analysis also explains why traditional metaphysics is impossible, because it attempts to generate genuine knowledge of objects beyond the realm of possible experience (such as the soul, God, and freedom).

KEY TERMS

the almond argument

the analogy argument

analytic proposition

categories (or pure concepts)

complex ideas

conceivability argument against necessary
   connection

connection hypothetical judgments

contingent truths

deducibility argument against necessary

deductive reasoning

deism

esse est percipi

faculty of sensibility

faculty of understanding

idealism

ideas of reflection

ideas of sensation

inconceivability argument for idealism

inductive reasoning

knowable *a posteriori*

knowable *a priori*

materialism

matters of fact

nativism

necessary connection

necessary truths

"no idea" argument against necessary
   connection

noumena

objective knowledge

phenomena

primary quality

relations of ideas

relativity of perception arguments

the science argument for the distinction
      between primary/secondary qualities

secondary quality

simple ideas

substratum

synthetic proposition

tabula rasa

transcendental idealism

truth-value

two hands in a bucket

uniformity of nature

REVIEW QUESTIONS

1. What does Locke share with Descartes, and in what way(s) does he disagree with Descartes?

2. How does Locke explain the distinction between primary and secondary qualities? Briefly summarize any two of his arguments for the distinction.

3. Berkeley rejects the distinction between primary and secondary qualities. Briefly summarize any one of his arguments.

4. On what basis does Berkeley suggest that idealism fits better with common sense than materialism?

5. What is the definition or conception of causation that Hume is examining and critiquing? Summarize one of his arguments against the existence of causation in the world, so conceived.

6. Why does Hume think that inductive reasoning cannot be justified?

7. What does Kant mean by synthetic *a priori* judgments or knowledge? What are two examples of such judgments or knowledge he offers?

8. How is mathematics possible, according to Kant? How is science possible?

NOTES

1. This section is excerpted and adapted from Andrew Pessin, *Uncommon Sense: The Strangest Ideas from the Smartest Philosophers* (Lanham, MD: Rowman & Littlefield, 2012), ch. 8.

2. Ed. Alexander Campbell Fraser, *The Works of George Berkeley, D.D., Formerly Bishop of Cloyne: Philosophical works, Vol. II: 1732-33* (Oxford, UK: Clarendon Press, 1901), Preface, 5.

3. Ed. P. H. Nidditch, *David Hume: A Treatise of Human Nature* (Oxford: Clarendon Press, 1978).

4. This and the next section are excerpted and adapted from Andrew Pessin, *Uncommon Sense: The Strangest Ideas from the Smartest Philosophers* (Lanham, MD: Rowman & Littlefield, 2012), ch. 12.

5. Transl., ed., Paul Guyer and Allen Wood, *Immanuel Kant: Critique of Pure Reason* (New York: Cambridge University Press, 1998), Introduction, 137. All *Critique* quotes are from this edition.

6. Twenty-first-century science might challenge these, but remember Kant is talking about space and time as we experience them, not as they may be represented in abstract scientific theories.

7. See previous note about twenty-first-century science here!

■ Reading
"First Dialogue"

GEORGE BERKELEY

From "First Dialogue," in Three Dialogues between Hylas and Philonous *(1713), based on the Jacob Tonson edition of 1734.*

In this excerpt, Berkeley (in the character Philonous), shows how the same relativity of perception arguments that demonstrate that secondary qualities are not in bodies but rather in the perceiver, apply equally to primary qualities such as size and motion.

Hyl. I frankly own, *Philonous,* that it is in vain to stand out any longer. Colours, Sounds, Tastes, in a word, all those termed *Secondary Qualities,* have certainly no Existence without the Mind. But by this Acknowledgment I must not be supposed to derogate any thing from the Reality of Matter or external Objects, seeing it is no more than several Philosophers maintain, who nevertheless are the farthest imaginable from denying Matter. For the clearer Understanding of this, you must know sensible Qualities are by Philosophers divided into *Primary* and *Secondary.* The former are Extension, Figure, Solidity, Gravity, Motion, and Rest. And these they hold exist really in Bodies. The latter are those above enumerated; or briefly, all sensible Qualities beside the Primary, which they assert are only so many Sensations or Ideas existing no where but in the Mind. But all this, I doubt not, you are already apprised of. For my part, I have been a long time sensible there was such an Opinion current among Philosophers, but was never thoroughly convinced of its Truth till now.

Phil. You are still then of Opinion, that Extension and Figures are inherent in external unthinking Substances.

Hyl. I am.

Phil. But what if the same Arguments which are brought against Secondary Qualities, will hold proof against these also?

Hyl. Why then I shall be obliged to think, they too exist only in the Mind.

Phil. Is it your Opinion, the very Figure and Extension which you perceive by Sense, exist in the outward Object or material Substance?

Hyl. It is.

Phil. Have all other Animals as good Grounds to think the same of the Figure and Extension which they see and feel?

Hyl. Without doubt, if they have any Thought at all.

Phil. Answer me, *Hylas.* Think you the Senses were bestowed upon all Animals for their Preservation and Well-being in Life? or were they given to Men alone for this End?

Hyl. I make no question but they have the same Use in all other Animals.

Phil. If so, is it not necessary they should be enabled by them to perceive their own Limbs, and those Bodies which are capable of harming them?

Hyl. Certainly.

Phil. A Mite therefore must be supposed to see his own Foot, and Things equal or even less than it, as Bodies of some considerable Dimension; though at the same time they appear to you scarce discernible, or at best as so many visible Points.

Hyl. I cannot deny it.

Phil. And to Creatures less than the Mite they will seem yet larger.

Hyl. They will.

Phil. Insomuch that what you can hardly discern, will to another extremely minute Animal appear as some huge Mountain.

Hyl. All this I grant.

Phil. Can one and the same thing be at the same time in itself of different Dimensions?

Hyl. That were absurd to imagine.

Phil. But from what you have laid down it follows, that both the Extension by you perceived, and that perceived by the Mite itself, as likewise all those perceived by lesser Animals, are each of them the true Extension of the Mite's Foot, that is to say, by your own Principles you are led into an Absurdity.

Hyl. There seems to be some Difficulty in the Point.

Phil. Again, have you not acknowledged that no real inherent Property of any Object can be changed, without some Change in the thing itself?

Hyl. I have.

Phil. But as we approach to or recede from an Object, the visible Extension varies, being at one Distance ten or a hundred times greater than at another. Doth it not therefore follow from hence likewise, that it is not really inherent in the Object?

Hyl. I own I am at a loss what to think.

Phil. Your Judgment will soon be determined, if you will venture to think as freely concerning this Quality, as you have done concerning the rest. Was it not admitted as a good Argument, that neither Heat nor Cold was in the Water, because it seemed warm to one Hand, and cold to the other?

Hyl. It was.

Phil. Is it not the very same Reasoning to conclude, there is no Extension or Figure in an Object, because to one Eye it shall seem little, smooth, and round, when at the same time it appears to the other, great, uneven, and angular?

Hyl. The very same. But doth this latter Fact ever happen?

Phil. You may at any time make the Experiment, by looking with one Eye bare, and with the other through a Microscope.

Hyl. I know not how to maintain it, and yet I am loth to give up *Extension*, I see so many odd Consequences following upon such a Concession.

Phil. Odd, say you? After the Concessions already made, I hope you will stick at nothing for its Oddness. But on the other hand should it not seem very odd, if the general reasoning which includes all other sensible Qualities did not also include Extension? If it be allowed that no Idea nor any thing like an Idea can exist in an unperceiving Substance, then surely it follows, that no Figure or Mode of Extension, which we can either perceive or imagine, or have any Idea of, can be really inherent in Matter; not to mention the peculiar Difficulty there must be, in conceiving a material Substance, prior to and distinct from Extension, to be the *Substratum* of Extension. Be the sensible Quality what it will, Figure, or Sound, or Colour; it seems alike impossible it should subsist in that which doth not perceive it.

Hyl. I give up the Point for the present, reserving still a Right to retract my Opinion, in case I shall hereafter discover any false Step in my Progress to it.

Phil. That is a Right you cannot be denied. Figures and Extension being dispatched, we proceed next to *Motion.* Can a real Motion in any external Body be at the same time both very swift and very slow?

Hyl. It cannot.

Phil. Is not the Motion of a Body swift in a reciprocal Proportion to the time it takes up in describing any given Space? Thus a Body that describes a Mile in an Hour, moves three times faster than it would in case it described only a Mile in three Hours.

Hyl. I agree with you.

Phil. And is not Time measured by the Succession of Ideas in our Minds?

Hyl. It is.

Phil. And is it not possible Ideas should succeed one another twice as fast in your Mind, as they do in mine, or in that of some Spirit of another kind?

Hyl. I own it.

Phil. Consequently the same Body may to another seem to perform its Motion over any Space in half the time that it doth to you. And the same Reasoning will hold as to any other Proportion: That is to say, according to your Principles (since the Motions perceived are both really in the Object) it is possible one and the same Body shall be really moved the same way at once, both very swift and very slow. How is this consistent either with common Sense, or with what you just now granted?

Hyl. I have nothing to say to it.

In this excerpt Berkeley responds to what seems to be a devastating objection to idealism: the claim that we simply see things at a distance from ourselves. For if we do directly see distances in this way, then we are seeing the world of space, of extended objects, and these are just what physical bodies are supposed to be. Berkeley responds by denying that we do see distance after all. Rather, we make judgments about distance, and these, of course, may be in error.

Hyl. I profess I know not what to think, but still there are some Scruples remain with me. Is it not certain I see Things at a Distance? Do we not perceive the Stars and Moon, for Example, to be a great way off? Is not this, I say, manifest to the Senses?

Phil. Do you not in a Dream too perceive those or the like Objects?

Hyl. I do.

Phil. And have they not then the same Appearance of being distant?

Hyl. They have.

Phil. But you do not thence conclude the Apparitions in a Dream to be without the Mind?

Hyl. By no means.

Phil. You ought not therefore to conclude that sensible Objects are without the Mind, from their Appearance or Manner wherein they are perceived.

Hyl. I acknowledge it. But doth not my Sense deceive me in those Cases?

Phil. By no means. The Idea or Thing which you immediately perceive, neither Sense nor Reason inform you that it actually exists without the Mind. By Sense you only know that you are affected with such certain Sensations of Light and Colours, &c. And these you will not say are without the Mind.

Hyl. True: But beside all that, do you not think the Sight suggests something of *Outness* or *Distance*?

Phil. Upon approaching a distant Object, do the visible Size and Figure change perpetually, or do they appear the same at all Distances?

Hyl. They are in a continual Change.

Phil. Sight therefore doth not suggest or any way inform you, that the visible Object you immediately perceive, exists at a Distance, or will be perceived when you advance further onward, there being a continued Series of visible Objects succeeding each other, during the whole time of your Approach.

Hyl. It doth not; but still I know, upon seeing an Object, what Object I shall perceive after having passed over a certain Distance: No matter whether it be exactly the same or no: There is still something of Distance suggested in the Case.

Phil. Good *Hylas*, do but reflect a little upon the Point, and then tell me whether there be any more in it than this. From the Ideas you actually perceive by Sight, you have by Experience learned to collect what other Ideas you will (according to the standing Order of Nature) be affected with, after such a certain Succession of Time and Motion.

Hyl. Upon the whole, I take it to be nothing else.

Phil. Now is it not plain, that if we suppose a Man born blind was on a sudden made to see, he could at first have no Experience of what may be suggested by Sight?

Hyl. It is.

Phil. He would not then according to you have any Notion of Distance annexed to the Things he saw; but would take them for a new Set of Sensations existing only in his Mind.

Hyl. It is undeniable.

Phil. But to make it still more plain: Is not *Distance* a Line turned endwise to the Eye?

Hyl. It is.

Phil. And can a Line so situated be perceived by Sight?

Hyl. It cannot.

Phil. Doth it not therefore follow that Distance is not properly and immediately perceived by Sight?

Hyl. It should seem so.

Phil. Again, is it your Opinion that Colours are at a Distance?

Hyl. It must be acknowledged, they are only in the Mind.

Phil. But do not Colours appear to the Eye as coexisting in the same place with Extension and Figures?

Hyl. They do.

Phil. How can you then conclude from Sight, that Figures exist without, when you acknowledge Colours do not; the sensible Appearance being the very same with regard to both?

Hyl. I know not what to answer.

Phil. But allowing that Distance was truly and immediately perceived by the Mind, yet it would not thence follow it existed out of the Mind. For whatever is immediately perceived is an Idea: And can any *Idea* exist out of the Mind?

REVIEW AND DISCUSSION QUESTIONS

1. What are "relativity of perception" arguments, and how do they show that a given perceived quality is in the mind, rather than the body?

2. Which allegedly primary qualities does Berkeley apply relativity of perceptions to?

3. Why is it so important to Berkeley to deny that we see distance directly? Briefly summarize one argument he makes toward that conclusion.

Reading

"Sceptical Doubts concerning the Operations of the Understanding"

DAVID HUME

From An Enquiry concerning Human Understanding, *Section IV, Part I (1748). Text from the 1777 edition.*

> In this excerpt Hume introduces his distinction between relations of ideas and matters of fact, then presents his conceivability and deducibility arguments against necessary connections between distinct events.

All the objects of human reason or enquiry may naturally be divided into two kinds, to wit, *Relations of Ideas*, and *Matters of Fact*. Of the first kind are the sciences of Geometry, Algebra, and Arithmetic; and in short, every affirmation, which is either intuitively or demonstratively certain. *That the square of the hypothenuse is equal to the square of the two sides*, is a proposition, which expresses a relation between these figures. *That three times five is equal to the half of thirty*, expresses a relation between these numbers. Propositions of this kind are discoverable by the mere operation of thought, without dependence on what is any where existent in the universe. Though there never were a circle or triangle in nature, the truths, demonstrated by Euclid, would for ever retain their certainty and evidence.

Matters of fact, which are the second objects of human reason, are not ascertained in the same manner; nor is our evidence of their truth, however great, of a like nature with the foregoing. The contrary of every matter of fact is still possible; because it can never imply a contradiction, and is conceived by the mind with the same facility and distinctness, as if ever so conformable to reality. *That the sun will not rise to-morrow* is no less intelligible a proposition, and implies no more contradiction, than the affirmation, *that it will rise*. We should in vain, therefore, attempt to demonstrate its falsehood. Were it demonstratively false, it would imply a contradiction, and could never be distinctly conceived by the mind.

It may, therefore, be a subject worthy of curiosity, to enquire what is the nature of that evidence, which assures us of any real existence and matter of fact, beyond the present testimony of our senses, or the records of our memory. This part of philosophy, it is observable, has been little cultivated, either by the ancients or moderns; and therefore our doubts and errors, in the prosecution of so important an enquiry, may be the more excusable; while we march through such difficult paths, without any guide or direction. They may even prove useful, by exciting curiosity, and destroying that implicit faith and security, which is the bane of all reasoning and free enquiry. The discovery of defects in the common philosophy, if any such there be, will not, I presume, be a discouragement, but rather an incitement, as is usual, to attempt something more full and satisfactory, than has yet been proposed to the public.

All reasonings concerning matter of fact seem to be founded on the relation of *Cause and Effect*. By means of that relation alone we can go beyond the evidence of our memory and senses. If you were to ask a man, why he believes any matter of fact, which is absent; for instance, that his friend is in the country, or in France; he would give you a reason; and this reason would be some other fact; as a letter received from him, or the knowledge of his former resolutions and promises. A man, finding a watch or any other machine in a desert island, would conclude, that there had once been men in that island. All our reasonings concerning fact are of the same nature. And here it is constantly supposed, that there is a connexion between the present fact and that which is inferred from it. Were there nothing to bind them together, the inference would be entirely precarious. The hearing of an articulate voice and rational discourse in the dark assures us of the presence of some person: Why? Because these are the effects of the human make and fabric, and closely connected with it. If we anatomize all the other reasonings of this nature, we shall find, that they are founded on the relation of cause and effect, and that this relation is either near or remote, direct or collateral. Heat and light are collateral effects of fire, and the one effect may justly be inferred from the other.

If we would satisfy ourselves, therefore, concerning the nature of that evidence, which assures us of matters of fact, we must enquire how we arrive at the knowledge of cause and effect.

I shall venture to affirm, as a general proposition, which admits of no exception, that the knowledge of this relation is not, in any instance, attained by reasonings *a priori*; but arises entirely from experience, when we find, that any particular objects are constantly conjoined with each other. Let an object be presented to a man of ever so strong natural reason and abilities; if that object be entirely new to him, he will not be able, by the most accurate examination of its sensible qualities, to discover any of its causes or effects. Adam, though his rational faculties be supposed, at the very first, entirely perfect, could not have inferred from the fluidity, and transparency of water, that it would suffocate him, or from the light and warmth of fire, that it would consume him. No object ever discovers, by the qualities which appear to the senses, either the causes which produced it, or the effects which will arise from it; nor can our reason, unassisted by experience, ever draw any inference concerning real existence and matter of fact.

This proposition, *that causes and effects are discoverable, not by reason, but by experience,* will readily be admitted with regard to such objects, as we remember to have once been altogether unknown to us; since we must be conscious of the utter inability, which we then lay under, of foretelling, what would arise from them. Present two smooth pieces of marble to a man, who has no tincture of natural philosophy; he will never discover, that they will adhere together, in such a manner as to require great force to separate them in a direct line, while they make so small a resistance to a lateral pressure. Such events, as bear little analogy to the common course of nature, are also readily confessed to be known only by experience; nor does any man imagine that the explosion of gunpowder, or the attraction of a loadstone, could ever be discovered by arguments *a priori*. In like manner, when an effect is supposed to depend upon an intricate machinery or secret structure of parts, we make no difficulty in attributing all our knowledge of it to experience. Who will assert, that he can give the ultimate reason, why milk or bread is proper nourishment for a man, not for a lion or a tyger?

But the same truth may not appear, at first sight, to have the same evidence with regard to events, which have become familiar to us from our first appearance in the world, which bear a close analogy to the whole course of nature, and which are supposed to depend on the simple qualities of objects, without any secret structure of parts. We are apt to imagine, that we could discover these effects by the mere operation of our reason, without experience. We fancy, that were we brought, on a sudden, into this world, we could at first have inferred, that one Billiard-ball would communicate motion to another upon impulse; and that we needed not to have waited for the event, in order to pronounce with certainty concerning it. Such is the influence of custom, that, where it is strongest, it not only covers our natural ignorance, but even conceals itself, and seems not to take place, merely because it is found in the highest degree.

But to convince us, that all the laws of nature, and all the operations of bodies without exception, are known only by experience, the following reflections may, perhaps, suffice. Were any object presented to us, and were we required to pronounce concerning the effect, which will result from it, without consulting past observation; after what manner, I beseech you, must the mind proceed in this operation? It must invent or imagine some event, which it ascribes to the object as its effect; and it is plain that this invention must be entirely arbitrary. The mind can never possibly find the effect in the supposed cause, by the most accurate scrutiny and examination. For the effect is totally different from the cause, and consequently can never be discovered in it. Motion in the second Billiard-ball is a quite distinct event from motion in the first; nor is there any thing in the one to suggest the smallest hint of the other. A stone or piece of metal raised into the air, and left without any support, immediately falls: But to consider the matter *a priori*, is there any thing we discover in this situation, which can beget the idea of a downward, rather than an upward, or any other motion, in the stone or metal?

And as the first imagination or invention of a particular effect, in all natural operations, is arbitrary, where we consult not experience; so must we also esteem the supposed tye or connexion between the cause and effect, which binds them together, and renders it impossible, that any other effect could result from the operation of that cause. When I see, for instance, a Billiard-ball moving in a straight line towards another; even suppose motion in the second ball should by accident be suggested to me, as the result of their contact or impulse; may I not conceive, that a hundred different events might as well follow from that cause? May not both these balls remain at absolute rest? May not the first ball return in a straight line, or leap off from the second in any line or direction? All these suppositions are consistent and conceivable. Why then should we give the preference to one, which is no more consistent or conceivable than the rest? All our reasonings *a priori* will never be able to shew us any foundation for this preference.

In a word, then, every effect is a distinct event from its cause. It could not, therefore, be discovered in the cause, and the first invention or conception of it, *a priori*, must be entirely arbitrary. And even after it is suggested, the conjunction of it with the cause must appear equally arbitrary; since there are always many other effects, which, to reason, must seem fully as consistent and natural. In vain, therefore, should we pretend to determine any single event, or infer any cause or effect, without the assistance of observation and experience.

■ Reading
"On the Idea of Necessary Connection"
DAVID HUME

From *An Enquiry Concerning Human Understanding*, Section VII (1748). Text from the 1777 edition.

> In this excerpt Hume presents his "no idea" argument against necessary connections between distinct events. He concludes by identifying our idea of necessary connection with our subjective sense of anticipation.

PART I

There are no ideas, which occur in metaphysics, more obscure and uncertain, than those of *power, force, energy,* or *necessary connexion,* of which it is every moment necessary for us to treat in all our disquisitions. We shall, therefore, endeavour, in this section, to fix, if possible, the precise meaning of these terms, and thereby remove some part of that obscurity, which is so much complained of in this species of philosophy.

It seems a proposition, which will not admit of much dispute, that all our ideas are nothing but copies of our impressions, or, in other words, that it is impossible for us to *think* of any thing, which we have not antecedently *felt,* either by our external or internal senses. . . .

To be fully acquainted, therefore, with the idea of power or necessary connexion, let us examine its impression; and in order to find the impression with greater certainty, let us search for it in all the sources, from which it may possibly be derived.

When we look about us towards external objects, and consider the operation of causes, we are never able, in a single instance, to discover any power or necessary connexion; any quality, which binds the effect to the cause, and renders the one an infallible consequence of the other. We only find, that the one does actually, in fact, follow the other. The impulse of one billiard-ball is attended with motion in the second. This is the whole that appears to the *outward* senses. The mind feels no sentiment or *inward* impression from this succession of objects: Consequently, there is not, in any single, particular instance of cause and effect, any thing which can suggest the idea of power or necessary connexion.

From the first appearance of an object, we never can conjecture what effect will result from it. But were the power or energy of any cause discoverable by the mind, we could foresee the effect, even without experience; and might, at first, pronounce with certainty concerning it, by the mere dint of thought and reasoning. . . .

Since, therefore, external objects as they appear to the senses, give us no idea of power or necessary connexion, by their operation in particular instances, let us see, whether this idea be derived from reflection on the operations of our own minds, and be copied from any internal impression. It may be said, that we are every moment conscious of internal power; while we feel, that, by the simple command of our will, we can move the organs of our body, or direct the faculties of our mind. An act of volition produces motion in our limbs, or raises a new idea in our imagination. This influence of the will we know by consciousness. Hence we acquire the idea of power or energy; and are certain, that we ourselves and all other intelligent beings are possessed of power. This idea, then, is an idea of reflection, since it arises from reflecting on the operations of our own mind, and on the command which is exercised by will, both over the organs of the body and faculties of the soul.

We shall proceed to examine this pretension; and first with regard to the influence of volition over the organs of the body. This influence, we may observe, is a fact, which, like all other natural events, can be known only by experience, and can never be foreseen from any apparent energy or power in the cause, which connects it with the effect, and renders the one an infallible consequence of the other. The motion of our body follows upon the command of our will. Of this we are every moment conscious. But the means, by which this is effected; the energy, by which the will performs so extraordinary an operation; of this we are so far from being immediately conscious, that it must for ever escape our most diligent enquiry.

For *first*, is there any principle in all nature more mysterious than the union of soul with body; by which a supposed spiritual substance acquires such an influence over a material one, that the most refined thought is able to actuate the grossest matter? Were we empowered, by a secret wish, to remove mountains, or control the planets in their orbit; this extensive authority would not be more extraordinary, nor more beyond our comprehension. But if by conscious-ness we perceived any power or energy in the will, we must know this power; we must know its connexion with the effect; we must know the secret union of soul and body, and the nature of both these substances; by which the one is able to operate, in so many instances, upon the other.

Secondly, We are not able to move all the organs of the body with a like authority; though we cannot assign any reason besides experience, for so remarkable a difference between one and the other. Why has the will an influence over the tongue and fingers, not over the heart or liver? This question would never embarrass us, were we conscious of a power in the former case, not in the latter. We should then perceive, independent of experience, why the authority of will over the organs of the body is circumscribed within such particular limits. Being in that case fully acquainted with the power or force, by which it operates, we should also know, why its influence reaches precisely to such boundaries, and no farther. . . .

Thirdly, We learn from anatomy, that the immediate object of power in voluntary motion, is not the member itself which is moved, but certain muscles, and nerves, and animal spirits, and, perhaps, something still more minute and more unknown, through which the motion is successively propagated, ere it reach the member itself whose motion is the immediate object of volition. Can there be a more certain proof, that the power, by which this whole operation is performed, so far from being directly and fully known by an inward sentiment or con-sciousness, is, to the last degree, mysterious and unintelligible? Here the mind wills a certain event: Immediately another event, unknown to ourselves, and totally different from the one intended, is produced: This event produces another, equally unknown: Till at last, through a long succession, the desired event is produced. But if the original power were felt, it must be known: Were it known, its effect must also be known; since all power is relative to its effect. And *vice versa*, if the effect be not known, the power cannot be known nor felt. How indeed can we be conscious of a power to move our limbs, when we have no such power; but only that to move certain animal spirits, which, though they produce at last the motion of our limbs, yet operate in such a manner as is wholly beyond our comprehension?

We may, therefore, conclude from the whole, I hope, without any temerity, though with assurance; that our idea of power is not copied from any sentiment or consciousness of power within ourselves, when we give rise to animal motion, or apply our limbs to their proper use and office. . . .

Shall we then assert, that we are conscious of a power or energy in our own minds, when, by an act or command of our will, we raise up a new idea, fix the mind to the contemplation of it, turn it on all sides, and at last dismiss it for some other idea, when we think that we have surveyed it with sufficient accuracy? I believe the same arguments will prove, that even this command of the will gives us no real idea of force or energy. . . .

PART II

But to hasten to a conclusion of this argument . . . We have sought in vain for an idea of power or necessary connexion, in all the sources from which we could suppose it to be derived. It appears, that, in single instances of the operation of bodies, we never can, by our utmost scrutiny, discover any thing but one event following another; without being able to comprehend any force or power, by which the cause operates, or any connexion between it and its supposed effect. The same difficulty occurs in contemplating the operations of mind on body; where we observe the motion of the latter to follow upon the volition of the former; but are not able to observe or conceive the tye, which binds together the motion and volition, or the energy by which the mind produces this effect. The authority of the will over its own faculties and ideas is not a whit more comprehensible: So that, upon the whole, there appears not, throughout all nature, any one instance of connexion, which is conceivable by us. All events seem entirely loose and separate. One event follows another; but we never can observe any tye between them. They seem *conjoined*, but never *connected*. And as we can have no idea of any thing, which never appeared to our outward sense or inward sentiment, the necessary conclusion *seems* to be, that we have no idea of connexion or power at all, and that these words are absolutely without any meaning, when employed either in philosophical reasonings, or common life.

But there still remains one method of avoiding this conclusion, and one source which we have not yet examined. When any natural object or event is presented, it is impossible for us, by any sagacity or penetration, to discover, or even conjecture, without experience, what event will result from it, or to carry our foresight beyond that object, which is immediately present to the memory and senses. Even after one instance or experiment, where we have observed a particular event to follow upon another, we are not entitled to form a general rule, or foretel what will happen in like cases; it being justly esteemed an unpardonable temerity to judge of the whole course of nature from one single experiment, however accurate or certain. But when one particular species of event has always, in all instances, been conjoined with another, we make no longer any scruple of foretelling one upon the appearance of the other, and of employing that reasoning, which can alone assure us of any matter of fact or existence. We then call the one object, *Cause*; the other, *Effect*. We suppose, that there is some connexion between them; some power in the one, by which it infallibly produces the other, and operates with the greatest certainty and strongest necessity.

It appears, then, that this idea of a necessary connexion among events arises from a number of similar instances which occur, of the constant conjunction of these events; nor can that idea ever be suggested by any one of these instances, surveyed in all possible lights and positions. But there is nothing in a number of instances, different from every single instance, which is supposed to be exactly similar; except only, that after a repetition of similar instances, the mind is carried by habit, upon the appearance of one event, to expect its usual attendant, and to believe, that it will exist. This connexion, therefore, which we *feel* in the mind, this customary transition of the imagination from one object to its usual attendant, is the sentiment or impression, from which we form the idea of power or necessary connexion. Nothing farther is in the case. Contemplate the subject on all sides; you will never find any other origin of that idea. This is the sole difference between one instance, from which we can never receive the idea of connexion, and a number of similar instances, by which it is suggested. The first time a man saw the communication of motion by impulse, as by the shock of two billiard-balls, he could not pronounce that the one event was *connected:* but only that it was *conjoined* with the other. After he has observed several instances of this nature, he then pronounces them to be *connected.* What alteration has happened to give rise to this new idea of *connexion*? Nothing but that he now *feels* these events to be *connected* in his imagination, and can readily foretel the existence of one from the appearance of the other. When we say, therefore, that one object is connected with another, we mean only, that they have acquired a connexion in our thought, and give rise to this inference, by which they become proofs of each other's existence: A conclusion, which is somewhat extraordinary; but which seems founded on sufficient evidence.

REVIEW AND DISCUSSION QUESTIONS

1. Explain what it means when we say that two events are necessarily connected.

2. Briefly summarize Hume's conceivability and deducibility arguments, as presented in the first excerpt.

3. Hume seeks the "impression" (or sensory experience) on which our idea of necessary connection is based. Briefly summarize how his search goes, before summarizing his final conclusion.

CONTEMPORARY DIRECTIONS

Twentieth to Twenty-First Century Developments

T HERE IS A NICE STORY one can tell about the early modern period in philosophy, as we saw. Descartes set the table, the philosophers of the period divided into two neat schools, both schools reached impasses, then Kant arrived and synthesized them. That is simplified, but it's a quick way to summarize two rich centuries of philosophy.

There is no such story to tell as we skip ahead to the twentieth century and the contemporary period. There was plenty of important philosophy in the nineteenth century, much of it responding to Kant just as the early moderns were responding to Descartes. But partly due to Kant's influence and partly to social circumstance, philosophy started to become more of a professional discipline, so it became denser, more technical and jargon-filled, and therefore less easy to summarize concisely. As we make our way into the twentieth century there is an enormous growth in both the quantity and quality of philosophy: there are more universities, more philosophers, more books, more journals, and more areas of philosophical inquiry than ever before. Moreover, it becomes harder to tell just which philosophers, movements, or ideas will be the important ones. We're just too close to them to know which will stand the test of time.

So we can't tell an easy story about philosophy as we approach our own time. So we won't try. Instead we shall just provide a sample of some matters of particular interest, without trying to be either comprehensive or unified. We'll begin with a look at the famous early twentieth-century movement known as *existentialism*, and then look at some recent developments within the domains of ethics, religion, epistemology, and metaphysics.

EXISTENTIALISM

Existentialism is a loose family of movements that emphasize the existence of the individual as a free and responsible agent determining his or her own development through acts of the will, all in the face of the potential meaninglessness of life. It arose in Europe and came into its own after World War II. The events of that terrible period made many people feel that life was absurd, meaningless, that there was no grand design to it. These feelings follow, existentialists suggested, from the realization that we inhabit a world devoid of objective values, a world in which things simply are with no reason for being as they are, a world we futilely try to make sense of. The key word here is *objective*: to say the world is devoid of objective values is to say that nothing about the world itself distinguishes *good* from *bad*, or *right* from *wrong*, or suggests that anything has any point or purpose. The world itself is indifferent to value.

That the world might be devoid of objective values is actually a relatively modern idea. For the ancient Greek Plato, the eternal Form of the Good ultimately guided the structure of the cosmos. For the Western monotheistic medievals, God was the source of all value, being infinitely good, imparting His goodness to the world He created, and establishing the moral standards for behavior. For the early modern rationalists, reason guided us to objective truths about the world, including those of value, reaching a pinnacle in Leibniz's idea that God necessarily creates the best of all possible worlds.

But the early modern empiricists began putting cracks in the edifice, particularly Hume. If all knowledge must be derived from sensory experience, then it seems that sensory experience does not and cannot tell us what is "objectively" good or right. The senses tell us how things are, but objective values concern how things ought to be, and, as Hume observed, it isn't clear how to derive any *ought* statements from *is* statements. In fact all we have to work with are our own subjective desires, preferences, concerns. Any morality we come up with would be our own invention, aiming to maximize those things we want or prefer. But that is a far cry from genuine *objective* morality. Different people want or prefer different things and would thus create different moralities. Our desires and preferences reflect how we are, but genuine morality concerns how we ought to be—what we *ought* to want and prefer, not what we happen to.

In responding to these problems, some philosophers turn toward religion, some toward a kind of nihilism, and some toward a **humanism** that stresses the fundamental value of human beings. Existentialism comes in all three varieties, as we'll see. But if there is one concept that is common to all, it is that of the absurd. Existentialism is what you get when you grapple seriously with the thought that life, the universe, everything, is simply absurd.

We begin with a pair of nineteenth-century existentialists.

Søren Kierkegaard (1813–1855) and Religious Existentialism

Kierkegaard, the Danish theologian and philosopher, is considered the father of existentialism, particularly in its religious (Christian) form. In his short life of forty-two years he wrote many literary, theological, philosophical, psychological, devotional, and polemical works, some published anonymously. Bearing such dramatic titles as *Either/Or, Fear and Trembling*, and *The Sickness unto Death*, these made little impression on his fellow Danes and almost none on those outside his homeland. At the start of the twentieth century, however, his works were translated into several other languages and began to make an enormous impact. This strange thinker, who had lived and worked much of his life as a near recluse, had found his audience.

Through the long medieval history of philosophical theology, philosophers attempted to produce a coherent and extensive understanding of God, as we saw in chapter 7. Against this, Kierkegaard insists that God cannot be understood or known *at all*. God is utterly *other*, transcendent, inconceivable. God is especially not knowable by reason, nor even expressible in the many propositions of the faith. For genuine faith is not a matter of propositions. It is rather a way of being or existing, of maintaining some form of personal relationship to this utterly unknowable object, and it is entirely opposed to reason.

Faith in fact is grounded in the absurd, in the unresolvable paradox of the eternal, infinite, transcendent God becoming temporal, finite, and concrete in the person of the (Christian) savior. The only way for someone to obtain that personal relationship to the unknowable God is therefore by *suspending* the rational.

But that suspension doesn't typically happen immediately, instead proceeding through several stages. The first Kierkegaard calls the **aesthetic stage**, and this is the life most of us live most of the time. Here we are immersed in sensuous experience, in pleasure and egotism, in satisfying our own desires and preferences, all with minimal reflection.

Though some remain in this stage, others begin to find it empty and self-serving, a life avoiding responsibility, apart from community. In response we begin confronting the question of what we should do with our lives, and so we move on to the **ethical stage**. Here we embrace the social and moral norms of society, recognizing that we are bound by the same rules as everyone else and ought not pursue merely our own pleasure. Some actions, we now see, are genuinely good and others evil, and we ought to pursue only the former; and do so not merely by habit but by *choosing* to act by the universal rules.

SØREN KIERKEGAARD

Again, some remain here. Yet while this is a decent life of rational decision making and commitment, even this stage has its limitations. For our life here depends on conditions outside our control, on these social norms which we have had no personal role in constructing. And that may leave us in a state of despair.

That despair may then lead us to the **religious stage**. This may involve a *suspension* of the ethical, as illustrated by the Biblical story of God commanding Abraham to sacrifice his son Isaac. By ordinary social norms that would make Abraham a murderer, and he ought not to do it, but yet the devoted commitment to God overrides the ethical demands. By our rational norms we may be unable to understand why God commanded Abraham to sacrifice his son, and why God's command is *not* an evil one of murder. But we must make a leap of faith and simply accept it without comprehending it. We must embrace the absurd, in other words, in order to attain the religious state of mind, the religious way of being or existing.

It is quite true what philosophy says; that life must be understood backwards. But then one forgets the other principle: that it must be lived forwards. Which principle, the more one thinks it through, ends exactly with the thought that temporal life can never properly be understood precisely because I can at no instant find complete rest in which to adopt a position: backwards.

— **Søren Kierkegaard**
(1813–1855), Journals

This way of existing is one not of reason but of subjective passion, of a devotion to the unknowable God that is supremely personal and unmediated by clergy or human artifacts or anything else. It is each individual's way of being and his alone. Nor do you make this choice of faith, to live with this passion, once and for all. Rather it confronts you continually, you must renew it at every moment. Your true self, your best or proper way of being, is only realized in this very repetition.

In Kierkegaard's religious existentialism, then, we must forget logic and dogma and institutions. The proper way of being is one of relationship to God, and that relationship must be personal, immediate, and ongoing, a life of passion and not of reason. We must embrace the absurd in order to experience our existence right.

Friedrich Nietzsche (1844–1900) and Nihilistic Existentialism

One of the greatest writers in any discipline ever, Nietzsche was born near Leipzig, Germany, in 1844. At the University of Leipzig he discovered the work of the philosopher Arthur Schopenhauer (1788–1860), which captured him powerfully. In 1868 he met the famous composer Richard Wagner (1813–1883), and began a stormy, decade-long, quasi-father-son relationship with the older man. In 1869 the University of Basel appointed him Professor of Philology at the unheard age of twenty-four, beginning his stormy, decade-long relationship with academia itself, ending with his 1879 resignation due to very bad health. The remaining decade of Nietzsche's sanity was spent meandering through Europe, composing some of the greatest philosophical and literary works ever produced. On January 3, 1889, in Turin, he suddenly threw his arms around the neck of a horse being beaten and collapsed, then spent the last decade of his life insane.

FRIEDRICH NIETZSCHE

He is often called a **nihilist**, someone who rejects all meaning, value, authority, and so on. This isn't entirely wrong, but it isn't the whole picture either. What he does reject are all *traditional* forms of meaning, value, authority, including and particularly the existence of God. (He is perhaps most famous for his phrase "God is dead," appearing in several of his works.) But many people overlook the other aspect of his work, in which he tries to replace these with something else. Though his work is deeply *sui generis*—in a class of its own—he is considered an early existentialist insofar as he attacks all objective forms of value and emphasizes, in the end, that the proper way of life involves attaining a certain state of mind or attitude toward the world that lacks those objective values.

One must philosophize, Nietzsche memorably proclaims, "with a hammer." For too long (he says) we human beings have created our own idols then bowed down before them and suffered. Reason, the "real world," the soul, free will, morality, *all* are idols. And then the greatest of them all: *God.* But when you are confronted with an idol, he insists, you must *start smashing.* (There's the nihilism for you.)

Already for some time, he observes, God has slowly been dying at the hands of the philosophers. They've seen that the cruder anthropomorphic conceptions of God, as a person, a father, a judge, cannot bear scrutiny. And they have seen that the many attempts to prove God's existence are all fatally flawed. But to finally refute the God-hypothesis you must go a step further. You must examine how this belief in God originally arose and acquired its force for human beings. When you recognize where it came from, he thinks, you shall no longer be tempted by it.

Where it came from, he argues, is human weakness. From everything inferior in human beings. From the worst in, and of, us. That is the shameful origin of the God-hypothesis, in the form specifically of Christianity:

> That lambs dislike great birds of prey is not strange; only it gives no ground for *reproaching* these birds of prey for bearing off little lambs. And if the lambs say, "These birds of prey are evil; and whoever is least like a bird of prey, but rather its opposite, a lamb—would he not be good?" there is no reason to find fault with this, except that the birds of prey might view it rather ironically and say, "*We* don't dislike *them* at all; we even *love* them: nothing is more tasty than a tender lamb."[1]

> God is dead. God remains dead. And we have killed him. Yet his shadow still looms. How shall we comfort ourselves, the murderers of all murderers? What was holiest and mightiest of all that the world has yet owned has bled to death under our knives: who will wipe this blood off us? What water is there for us to clean ourselves? What festivals of atonement, what sacred games shall we have to invent? Is not the greatness of this deed too great for us? Must we ourselves not become gods simply to appear worthy of it?
>
> —**Nietzsche**, *The Gay Science* (1882)

This is Nietzsche's story of Christianity. The ancient world had their powerful, aristocratic, and strong, but also their weak and lowly and meek. All understood that it was good to be the former and bad to be the latter. But then the priests, resenting their lower status, pulled off a dramatic *inversion of values*—by teaching that the *wretched* are the good, that the poor, the impotent, the suffering, the sick, the ugly alone are blessed and loved by God, and all the rest are evil. The weak could not literally defeat the strong so they did the next best thing. They invented a worldview *in which they are the greater*.

It was brilliant, and cunning, Nietzsche grants. But they had to go further. Since no one seriously could believe that being weak is better than being strong they invented another world, an afterworld, where the lowly here would prosper and the superior would suffer. They did so to slander *this* world, this reality, this life, since they were such failures in it. This fiction was their mechanism for coping

> The very word "Christianity" is a misunderstanding—in truth, there was only one Christian, and he died on the cross.
>
> —**Nietzsche**, *The Anti-Christ* (1895)

with their failure, and they became addicted to it, as so many still are today. People believe in God and the next life because they cannot manage in this life, because they are too afraid not to.

But now, now that we recognize how the God-hypothesis got started, now that we recognize its inversion of values, its rejection of this life, we are ready to give it up. At last God shall be dead. We human beings who originally gave Him life shall also have killed Him.

(You might reflect here on whether Nietzsche's approach commits *the genetic fallacy* from chapter 5. It might, but then again this might be a case where the origins of an idea really should change the way you think about it.)

If God is dead, if the idea of God has lost its power over people, Nietzsche thinks, then we are accountable to no one but ourselves, and there is no need to seek salvation somewhere beyond us. Nor is there any longer a need to subdue our nature, or dampen our spirits, or deny our will in hope of eternal rewards in another world. That idea is false and misguided, a product of centuries' worth of Christianity's life-denying ethic.

> Today as always, [people] fall into two groups: slaves and free. . . . Whoever does not have two-thirds of his day for himself, is a slave, whatever he may be: a statesman, a businessman, an official, or a scholar.
>
> —**Nietzsche**, *Human, All Too Human* (1878)

But this life is all there is, says Nietzsche as he turns to the more positive part of his program. And so one must embrace it, and love it, and most of all *live* it. For life, the will to life, the will to power—this is the fundamental value, the only value, *our* value.

And so contra the "nihilist" label Nietzsche in fact becomes one of the most life-affirming writers you will ever read. One way he expresses the affirmative attitude he believes we should have is in his notion of **amor fati**, Latin for *love of fate*:

> My formula for greatness in a human being is *amor fati*: that one wants nothing to be different, not forward, not backward, not in all eternity. Not merely bear what is necessary, still less conceal it . . . but *love* it.[2]

No matter what your life contains, in other words, you should love it, and every moment of it. (Recall Spinoza's account of "blessedness," in chapter 8, as consisting of coming to love whatever our life is fated to be.)

This idea receives an even more dramatic characterization in this inimitable passage:

> What, if some day or night a demon were to steal after you into your loneliest loneliness and say to you: "This life as you now live it and have lived it, you will have to live once more and innumerable times more; and there will be nothing new in it, but every pain and every joy and every thought and sigh and everything unutterably small or great in your life will have to return to you, all in the same succession and sequence—even this spider and this moonlight between the trees, and even this moment and I myself. The eternal hourglass of existence is turned upside down again and again, and you with it, speck of dust!"
>
> Would you not throw yourself down and gnash your teeth and curse the demon who spoke thus? Or have you once experienced a tremendous moment when you would have answered him: "You are a god and never have I heard anything more divine." If this thought gained possession of you, it would change you as you are or perhaps crush you. The question in each and every thing, "Do you desire this once more and innumerable times more?" would lie upon your actions as the greatest weight. Or how well disposed would you have to become to yourself and to life *to crave nothing more fervently* than this ultimate eternal confirmation and seal?[3]

Here we see Nietzsche's famous doctrine of the **eternal recurrence**, the idea that everything that occurs will reoccur, in the same sequence, over and over again. Here it is offered as a kind of psychological litmus test. How would you feel, in reflecting on your life, your decisions, your actions, were you to learn that you would relive each of them over and over, an infinite number of times? Would that thought be a source of dread and depression? Or would you say *yes* to the prospect, and do so joyously—thus reflecting your profound affirmation of life?

Jean-Paul Sartre (1905–1980) and Humanistic Existentialism

Born in Paris, Sartre studied philosophy in Berlin in the early 1930s, where he came under the influence of Edmund Husserl (1859–1938), a German existentialist thinker. It was also in Berlin that Sartre wrote his novel *Nausea* (1938), which he considered his overall best work. It was in this book that he struck one of the major chords of his philosophy, that we are trapped in a world without sense or purpose. During World War II, he was active in the French Resistance movement and was captured by the Germans. While a prisoner of war, he read Martin Heidegger (1889–1976), another German existentialist. This study led to Sartre's major philosophical work, *Being and Nothingness* (1943), which was then followed by many other works, literary and philosophical. In 1964 Sartre was awarded the Nobel Prize in literature but declined it, insisting that writers should be judged only by their words and not on the basis of awards they may have received. He had a lifelong and sometimes stormy relationship with Simone de Beauvoir (1908–1986), whom he met in college and who also became a renowned playwright, novelist, and essayist.

JEAN-PAUL SARTRE

According to Sartre, it is our sad fate to be trapped in a world that makes no sense. Whether we like it or not, this fact is inescapable. The world simply is as it is. There is no explanation that we can uncover for its existence or nature. Everything could just as well have been different—again, for no conceivable reason. And because there is no reason why the world should be one way rather than some other way, there also seems to be no reason why we should live one sort of life rather than another, choose one action rather than another, or come to value one thing rather than another. Experiencing all this, seeing how empty it all really is, makes us dizzy and fills us with nausea, or what some people refer to as existentialist **angst**, or anxiety.

So what shall we do? We are free to do what we like, and anything we like. The world being arbitrary and senseless, it doesn't matter what we do, for what difference could it make? Rather than finding this prospect pleasing, we find it "dreadful." We are free to choose but can find no way to decide what to choose, as there are no guides, signs, or certainties in this absurd world into which we have been thrust.

What to do then? Well, choose we must, for not to do so is to remain forever in the "nausea of existence." We must choose and act, knowing that the choices may prove disastrous, but no other path exists to an authentic life and existence. In a world where there is no God, nothing more can be done than to firmly make one's own decisions and heroically live by them. It is up to us to fill the void of the world without God, without value, without meaning. Human beings have no particular nature or essence, and there is no special plan or goal to life. We have only being or existence, and so our *existence precedes essence* rather than the other way around (as philosophy had traditionally believed until now). We are not here to fulfill some preordained human essence but must create our own from scratch. We must make our selves, choose our own essences—with no guide whatsoever to help us. We have been thrust into this world, and it is up to us to make of it what we can.

As appealing as such humanistic reflections are, they have not found favor with everyone. Existentialists, some argue, have abandoned philosophy for literature. For philosophy has always been marked by careful, logical analysis and detailed examination of problems and issues, but what we find in the pages of such writers as Sartre is emotion and exhortation.

The existentialists . . . are, like Descartes, dissatisfied with the uncertainty of empirical knowledge but, unlike Descartes, they realize that any search for certainty is a vain one. The world is as we find it, but there is no necessity in its being as it is; it might have been different. The laws of nature are not rules of logic, and we cannot deduce what the world is like from self-evident truths.

Such an inescapable conclusion causes the existentialist to look upon human life as absurd—absurd because it is devoid of logical sense. He longs to discover some necessity in things and events, and when he finds that he cannot, because the world is not a deductive system, he feels the situation to be intolerable. It is the realization that induction does not lead to necessary truths that produces the "nausea" which plays such an important part in the philosophy of Sartre and the existentialists.

—**Frederick Vivian**, *Thinking Philosophically* (1969)

SOME DEVELOPMENTS IN ETHICS

In our discussion of ethics in chapter 6, we noted that ancient thinkers tended to emphasize practical ethics (what sorts of actions or life we should pursue and shun) and that thinkers of recent past centuries emphasized ethical theory (the underlying theoretical reasons for the proper lines of conduct). As we enter the contemporary period we find that many thinkers focus on metaethics, on the very meanings of ethical concepts such as *good*, or *right*. Their concern is less about which particular actions are good or right, in other words, but about what we *mean* when call any action *good* or *right*.

Let's begin by returning, briefly, to David Hume, mentioned above. We may credit him for the modern trend of thinking of ethics as fundamentally subjective, as a matter of how we human beings think and feel rather than an intrinsic feature of the world itself.

Take any action allow'd to be vicious [i.e. morally bad]: Wilful murder, for instance. Examine it in all lights, and see if you can find that matter of fact, or real existence, which you call *vice*... The vice entirely escapes you, as long as you consider the object. You never can find it, till you turn your reflexion into your own breast, and find a sentiment of disapprobation, which arises in you, towards this action. Here is a matter of fact; but 'tis the object of feeling, not of reason. It lies in yourself, not in the object. So that when you pronounce any action or character to be vicious, you mean nothing, but that . . . you have a feeling or sentiment of blame from the contemplation of it. Vice and virtue, therefore, may be compar'd to sounds, colours, heat and cold, which, according to modern philosophy, are not qualities in objects, but perceptions in the mind. (*A Treatise of Human Nature* III.1 [London: John Noon, 1739], 468–69)

There are at least three distinct points here worth stressing.

First, there's the epistemological point from earlier. Hume, as an empiricist, seeks to ground moral knowledge in sensory experience, and notes that when we observe various acts we consider good or bad, we can perceive various features of them but not their goodness or badness itself. You witness a murder, you see the knife, the stabbing, the blood, you hear screams—but you do not observe *badness* itself.

Second, therefore, if we seek the source of the badness of this act, it is not in the act itself. It is in our *reaction* to the act, our feelings about it. Morality is a matter not of objective facts, and therefore not of reason, but of subjective sentiment or feeling.

Third, finally, there's a semantic point, about meaning, a metaethical point. Hume is suggesting an account of what words like *good/right* and *bad/wrong* mean. To call an action *good* is, roughly, to say that you have positive feelings about it, you approve it; to call an action *bad* is to say you have negative feelings, you disapprove. Moral terms therefore refer not to objective features of the actions but to subjective feelings in the person.

We now move ahead one hundred fifty years, to the twentieth century.

A. J. Ayer (1910–1989) and Logical Positivism

British philosopher A. J. Ayer was a central figure in the twentieth-century movement known as **logical positivism** (alternatively **logical empiricism**). Inspired by Hume, these philosophers aimed to develop an empiricist analysis of modern science, which was advancing rapidly in the early decades of the twentieth century. Motivated by the Humean idea that meaningful words must trace back to sensory experience, they were vexed by the fact that science (in particular physics), while so successful in explaining and predicting events, and in developing technology, was filled with terms referring to unobservable things (like atoms, particles, forces, etc.). They were thus keenly interested in working out empiricist theories of meaning for scientific terminology. Like Hume, too, they became skeptical of much traditional philosophy, claiming it was filled with words and concepts that failed to refer to anything in experience, and thus were meaningless. As part of this skepticism they turned their sights onto traditional metaphysics, theology, and ethics, the latter of which concerns us here.

A. J. AYER

Ayer's seminal work was his book *Language, Truth and Logic* (1936), which devotes a chapter to ethics, and focuses on the metaethical problem of saying what ethical words like *good* and *bad* mean. Since empiricism strongly suggests that ethical properties are not objective (as we've seen), the theories to be explored will all be subjectivist in character.

Ayer's Critique of Metaethical Subjectivism and Metaethical Utilitarianism

The first Ayer simply calls subjectivism. **Metaethical subjectivism** is the view that when we call an action, A, *good* or *right*, what we mean is something like "I approve of A" (while to call it *wrong* means "I disapprove"). But while this appears to be Hume's view in the passage quoted above, Ayer, though much influenced by Hume's subjectivism, rejects it as a metaethical doctrine. Ethics is indeed subjective in character, Ayer agrees, but he presents two arguments against holding that "A is good" simply means "I approve of A."

The first amounts to recognizing our general fallibility, that we are capable of making errors even in our ethical judgments. Thus there is no contradiction (Ayer claims) in asserting that some actions that we approve of may not be, after all, good or right, for that is just what a mistaken moral judgment would involve. But now on subjectivism, "A is good" simply means "I approve of A," and "A is not good" means "I do not approve of A." To admit that we may have made a mistake is then to admit it's possible that "I approve of A though A is not good," which on subjectivism would become "I approve of A though I do not approve of A"—a contradiction.

Or to put this point differently, if subjectivism is right then "A is good" means "I approve of A." But surely we are infallible with respect to how we feel, with respect to what we approve and disapprove. So on subjectivism we should be infallible in our judgments about what is good. But we are fallible on everything, including morality. So subjectivism cannot accommodate our fallibility.

Ayer's second argument against subjectivism is due to his senior compatriot, G. E. Moore (1873–1958). While Ayer doesn't endorse the particulars here, he appreciates the general thrust. According to Moore, if subjectivism were true then there would be no genuine disagreements about morality. Why? Suppose that Michael and Tanya disagree about whether assisted suicide is morally permissible. Michael says that it is, while Tanya says that it isn't. On subjectivism, what Michael is saying is "I approve of assisted suicide," and what Tanya is saying is, "I do not approve of assisted suicide." But now notice this: that Michael approves and that Tanya disapproves is *not* in dispute. Both of them agree that Michael approves and that Tanya disapproves. So if they are really disagreeing about the moral status of assisted suicide, they must be doing something more than merely stating how they feel. Thus subjectivism, which translates moral claims into assertions about feelings, fails.

> No moral system can rest solely on authority.
>
> —**A. J. Ayer**, *Humanist Outlook* (1968)

Ayer next turns to a second theory, utilitarianism. As a metaethical theory, utilitarianism is roughly the claim that when we say "A is good," what we mean is that "A maximizes overall happiness." But Ayer points out that the first argument against subjectivism above also applies here. There is no contradiction, he claims, in saying that it may sometimes be wrong to perform some action that would actually produce the greatest overall happiness. (In fact we saw such cases in chapter 6, if you recall the problem of the *tyranny of the majority*, among others.) But now if "A is good" just means "A maximizes happiness," then to say "A is morally wrong although it maximizes happiness" would be equivalent to "A fails to maximize happiness although it maximizes happiness," which is a contradiction. So as long as it's even *possible* (i.e., non-contradictory) for there to be a case where maximizing happiness is wrong, then utilitarianism fails as a metaethical theory.

So what *do* moral terms mean then, according to Ayer?

Ayer's Emotivism

Ayer does not dispute the subjective character of ethics, recall; he merely disputes that ethical terms can simply be translated into subjective equivalents. The way to do this, he suggests, is surprising. He denies that ethical terms *mean anything at all.*

In fact, he observes, we use language in many different ways. Often we use it to "state facts," to make claims about the world that are then either true or false, depending on whether they correspond to the facts. But not all language works this way. You may utter a command, such as "Sit down!", but this perfectly legitimate sentence isn't expressing any facts but rather trying to get someone to do something. Or you may cheer for your favorite team, or scream happily at a concert, or utter an expletive when you stub your toe, all of which are (again) legitimate uses of language that do not express any facts. None of those utterances has a truth-value. None is even in the business of being "true" or "false," precisely because they don't express facts. What they do instead, perhaps, is express your feelings or attitudes about the thing in question. When you cheer for your team or curse when you stub your toe, everyone can tell how you feel about those events. But what you are not doing is saying or *stating* how you feel.

Something similar is now the case for ethical language, Ayer argues. Ethical statements, despite appearances, do not actually state or assert any facts. When you say "Stealing is wrong" you are not asserting *any* fact. As Hume had argued, you are not stating any objective fact about the action itself. But contra metaethical subjectivism and utilitarianism, you are also not stating any *subjective* facts about what's going on inside you. Since no facts are asserted, what you say is neither true nor false.

But if you are not asserting any subjective facts, you are *expressing* some. You are expressing your feelings about the action, much as you express your feelings when you cheer for your team and curse when you stub your toe.

This is the metaethical doctrine of **emotivism**: ethical statements state or assert no facts, but merely express feelings. As Ayer puts it,

> Thus if I say to someone, "You acted wrongly in stealing that money," I am not stating anything more than if I had simply said, "You stole that money." In adding that this action is wrong I am not making any further statement about it. I am simply evincing my moral disapproval of it. It is as if I had said, "You stole that money," in a peculiar tone of horror.... The tone ... adds nothing to the literal meaning of the sentence. It merely serves to show that the expression of it is attended by certain feelings in the speaker. (*Language, Truth and Logic* [New York: Dover Publications, 1946/1952], 107)

On emotivism, ethics is indeed fundamentally subjective in that it concerns our feelings. Ayer merely rejects the subjectivist account of meaning that the previous theories had offered.

Note, then, how emotivism avoids the problems confronting those earlier theories. Subjectivism rendered us (incorrectly) infallible in our moral judgments: if "A is good" means "I approve of A," and we are infallible about our feelings, then we would be infallible about A being good. But emotivism denies that "A is good" asserts any facts about our feelings, so our infallibility about how we are feeling is not relevant. Instead we can recognize a kind of fallibility our feelings themselves may display. They are "fallible" not in the sense of "possibly false," because feelings, not asserting anything, are not in the true/false business at all. But they may be fallible in other relevant senses. Perhaps we don't have the most appropriate feelings, or feelings like others in our community, or the feelings we wish we had, and so on. In this respect emotivism allows our moral utterances to be fallible, in those alternative senses.

The second problem concerned moral disagreement. If ethical claims were assertions of feelings, then the two disputants don't actually disagree, as each agrees that "Michael approves" and "Tanya disapproves." But on emotivism Michael and Tanya are not making assertions about their feelings, they are merely expressing them. And there is a clear sense of disagreement here, in that they simply have different feelings. No, they don't disagree on whether certain propositions are true or false, since emotivist ethics is not about truth and falseness. But they do differ in their feelings, which is all the moral disagreement one needs.

SOME DEVELOPMENTS IN PHILOSOPHY OF RELIGION

Philosophical theology was quiet for a while in the twentieth century.

There was Ayer's logical positivism, whose empiricist rejection of objective values and attack on terms that weren't grounded in experience suggested that all talk about God's existence and nature was meaningless. There were developments in other disciplines, in the history, psychology, and sociology of religion and in Biblical criticism, much of which suggested that religious beliefs and scriptures were merely human inventions filling various emotional or other needs. Religious beliefs (in this view) were a matter of fiction and myth, so why bother philosophizing about God? And then there were world events. With its terrible wars and Holocaust, the twentieth century raised serious challenges for all believers in God, and in general the century has seen a major rise in secularism and atheism in the Western world.

So for some decades philosophical theology was down. But it was never quite out, and shortly after the midpoint of the twentieth century it did something remarkable.

It got back up.

One important event was the resurrection of Anselm's famous ontological argument. As mentioned in chapter 7, many believed that Immanuel Kant (1724–1804) had decisively refuted it. But then in 1960, Norman Malcolm (1911–1990) published an article arguing that Anselm actually offered two different ontological arguments, and that Kant's critique only applied to one, leaving the other alive and well. Several years later, Alvin Plantinga (b. 1932) built on Malcolm's work to create a version of the ontological argument using advanced contemporary logic, in turn inspiring great discussion and debate. The ontological argument, dormant for centuries, was back on the table.

Nor was the ontological argument alone in its renaissance. Medieval cosmological arguments, aiming to prove God's existence based on the impossibility of an infinite regress of events going back into the past, were resurrected by William Lane Craig (b. 1949), in a 1979 book called *The Kalām Cosmological Argument*.

And teleological arguments in particular have been reinvigorated. William Paley's biological teleological argument, thought to have been refuted by Darwin's theory of evolution, is now back in the guise of **intelligent design**, an umbrella term for movements that see the world as requiring an intelligent cause. Biochemist Michael Behe (b. 1952) has especially aroused controversy in arguing that evolution cannot explain some basic features of living things, namely those displaying **irreducible complexity**. Something is irreducibly complex if it requires many components to be in place before it provides any evolutionary advantage, and so it cannot evolve by the small random steps that evolutionary theory proposes. Behe offers many examples: the lactose-utilizing system of the bacterium *E. coli*, the blood-clotting process, the bacterial flagellum, and so on. And while most scientists and philosophers are unpersuaded by his arguments, the point for now is merely that the biological teleological argument is once more being discussed.

More interestingly, the twentieth century has seen the rise of teleological arguments based in *physics*. The basic idea of the **fine-tuning argument** is that the laws of physics themselves contain many features that seem precisely fine-tuned so as to permit the existence of our specific form of life, with our consciousness, rationality, morality. Were any of a long list of features to have been different—were the force of gravity to be just a bit larger or smaller, or the charge of the electron, or the speed of light—then nothing resembling our universe could ever have formed, containing organized clumps of matter both large (stars and planets) and small (the bodies of organisms, and brains). But Darwin's theory of evolution could not explain this fine-tuning (as it could perhaps explain apparent biological order), since nobody thinks the laws of physics have evolved over time. British physicist Paul Davies (b. 1946) offers a provocative account of this argument in his book *The Mind of God* (1992), and it has inspired much fascinating debate.

> All the evidence suggests that this is not just any old universe, but one which is remarkably well adjusted to the existence of certain interesting and significant entities. . . . A long list of additional "lucky accidents" and "coincidences" has been compiled. . . . Taken together, they provide impressive evidence that life as we know it depends very sensitively on the form of the laws of physics, and on some seemingly fortuitous accidents in the actual values that nature has chosen for various particle masses, force strengths, and so on. . . . If it is the case that the existence of life requires the laws of physics and the initial conditions of the universe to be fine-tuned to high precision, and that fine-tuning does in fact obtain, then the suggestion of design seems compelling.
>
> —**Paul Davies**, *The Mind of God* (1992)

These last several examples suggest something perhaps surprising. Since at least Galileo (1564–1642) it has widely been thought that science and religion are in conflict. There is no shortage of people who think that science either refutes belief in God, or at least makes it unnecessary. But what the recent incarnations of the cosmological and teleological arguments suggest is that science itself might provide the best evidence *for* God's existence. You need to understand the biochemistry and the physics, after all, to reach an informed opinion on these contemporary arguments.

Or perhaps, in a surprising twist, we might say something stronger. Perhaps the very success of science *requires* the existence of God. For this thought we turn to preeminent contemporary philosopher Alvin Plantinga.

Alvin Plantinga (b. 1932) on Science and Theism

Perhaps no philosopher has done more than Plantinga to turn philosophy of religion into a major branch of twenty-first-century philosophy. Born in Michigan, trained at Harvard, the University of Michigan, and Yale, he taught for nineteen years at Calvin College, then twenty-eight at Notre Dame, before returning to Calvin. In his many books and articles he has contributed to many areas of philosophy, with important work in metaphysics, epistemology, and logic in addition to philosophical theology. What concerns us here, however, is his most recent work on the relationship between science and theism, as reflected in his book *Where the Conflict Really Lies: Science, Religion, and Naturalism* (New York: Oxford University Press, 2011)

As a bit of background, then, we begin by asking what we mean when we speak of the success of contemporary science. Obviously that success is partly reflected in technology. But when we push further we would probably add that it involves the ability of science to produce true beliefs or theories about the world. After all, we can develop our technology only because we understand the relevant physics and chemistry and biology. So let's grant that at least one impressive thing about contemporary science is its ability to get at the truth about how the world works.

But it's not just science that should impress us this way. For whatever ability we have to get at scientific truths must be grounded in a more fundamental ability to get at the truth. To get at true theories in physics and biology we must first be able to trust, generally, that our senses reliably inform us about the world, and that our other cognitive processes, such as reasoning and remembering, are also more or less reliable. We don't need perfect infallibility, but we do need

> There is superficial conflict but deep concord between science and theistic religion, but superficial concord and deep conflict between science and naturalism.
>
> —**Alvin Plantinga**, *Where the Conflict Really Lies: Science, Religion, and Naturalism* (2011)

something like reliability. To put it most generally, we need to have minds, consciousness, and rationality, and we need to have various mechanisms for forming beliefs of many different sorts about the world, and those mechanisms must be more or less reliable.

So now let's ask the next question. What best accounts for the existence of our minds, and for our minds' ability to reliably generate true beliefs? We'll say more about the nature of minds in the metaphysics section below. For now we shall turn to what Plantinga has to say about our ability to generate true beliefs.

His overall argument has two main parts.

The first is to argue that theism makes it reasonable for us to regard our cognitive faculties as reliable, that is, generally capable of generating true beliefs, and thus makes it reasonable for us to believe that the scientific theories we develop via our cognitive faculties may also succeed in being true.

The second explores the relationship between science and **naturalism**, the latter being, here, the doctrine that the phenomena in the world require nothing supernatural for their explanation. Many people think that science affirms naturalism, and that naturalism is in tension with theism. But Plantinga will argue that naturalism makes it *un*reasonable to believe that our cognitive faculties are reliable, and thus *un*reasonable to believe that our scientific theories are true. Despite the superficial concord between science and naturalism, then, they turn out to be in deep tension with each other. If you believe in the latter then it is unreasonable to believe in the former.

So if it's the success of science that impresses you—its ability to generate true theories—then theism shall be the more reasonable view for you to hold.

Theism and the Reliability of Our Cognitive Faculties

We can be brief with the first part of the argument. Western monotheists typically hold that God created us with our minds, and that the primary purpose of minds is for knowing the world and knowing God, to the degree possible. To fulfill that purpose, clearly, our cognitive faculties must be reliable. At the least it would be surprising were God to exist, but it turns out He gave us cognitive faculties that were largely unreliable. What would be the point of doing *that*? So if you are a theist, then it makes sense that our senses and reason and other faculties are reliable.

Naturalism and the Reliability of Our Cognitive Faculties

The more controversial work is in the second part of the argument. Why exactly does naturalism undermine the reasonableness of believing that our cognitive faculties are reliable?

According to the dominant naturalist theory, we human beings are the product of evolution by natural selection. What's key is that this process is conceived as "unguided": a series of random mutations occur, some provide advantages to the survival and reproduction of a plant or animal (mostly as a matter of luck and circumstance), these get passed on to progeny, and over time, by small steps, new species evolve from earlier species. Along the way brains develop, and then more complex brains, and these brains develop consciousness and the ability to think, and to form beliefs. And that, in an abbreviated nutshell, is us.

But this picture of ourselves, Plantinga argues, gives us no reason to think that our beliefs have much if any relationship to *truth*. Plantinga calls this **Darwin's doubt**, since even Darwin himself expressed it, namely the view that evolution gives us reason to doubt that our cognitive faculties produce, for the most part, true beliefs.

The details are many, and they would take us into a long discussion of contemporary philosophy of mind (some of which below), but the basic idea is this. For a naturalist, consciousness, mind, beliefs are all to be identified with or grounded in our physical brains. A particular belief would be a certain state of the brain, a different belief would be a different state, and so on. These brain states would have various physical and neurophysiological properties of the sort that neuroscientists study.

But insofar as a particular state is a belief it would also have another property, a *content*: it would be *about* something. In Plantinga's example, you may believe that Marcel Proust is a more subtle writer than Louis L'Amour. That belief, as a state of the brain, would have neurophysiological properties, but as a *belief* it would have a content that we express via the proposition, *Proust is a more subtle writer than Louis L'Amour*. This content is a very different sort of property than any physical property. You could look into someone's brain, either directly or via medical imaging (MRI, CT scans, etc.), and perhaps discover all of that brain state's physical properties. But you would never observe this way *what* it is the person is thinking or believing.

This difference between the physical properties and the content is key. For whether a belief is true or not depends on its content. If what you believe is in fact the case, your belief is true. But evolution doesn't care at all about the contents of beliefs. The only thing that matters is how and whether brain mechanisms contribute, via behavior, to survival and reproduction, and this they do purely in terms of their physical properties. Your brain state gets you to flee from an approaching tiger by sending electrical and chemical impulses toward your leg muscles, which then contract. The fact that the brain state may also have a content, and whether that content is true or false, plays absolutely no role in that physical process.

In a particularly colorful example from an earlier book, Plantinga writes,

> Perhaps Paul very much *likes* the idea of being eaten, but when he sees a tiger, always runs off looking for a better prospect, because he thinks it unlikely the tiger he sees will eat

him. This will get his body parts in the right place so far as survival is concerned, without involving much by way of true belief. . . . Or perhaps he thinks the tiger is a large, friendly, cuddly pussycat and wants to pet it; but he also believes that the best way to pet it is to run away from it. . . . Clearly there are any number of belief-desire systems that equally fit a given bit of behavior.[4]

The point is that the only thing that matters, from an evolutionary perspective, is that you avoid the tiger. It doesn't at all matter what you are thinking or believing when you do so. As far as naturalism is concerned, this can all be a *purely physical process*. In a similar way, certain marine bacteria are physically structured so as to automatically move toward deeper water, without forming anything like beliefs to do so. So, too, brains can autonomously track their body's blood pressure, temperature, saline content, insulin level, and many other things without any form of conscious awareness or belief. All of these are essential for survival and reproduction, and none makes reference to beliefs or their contents.

If you believe in naturalism, then, what you believe is that our brains have been selected for their various physical properties and behaviors. The contents of our beliefs, and thus whether what we believe is true or not, plays no role. Naturalism, Plantinga concludes, thus provides no grounds for believing that many or most of our beliefs are true. Any particular belief is as likely to be false as true. And if this is the case for ordinary beliefs derived from perceptions of our immediate environment, it's all the more so for our scientific beliefs, which are extremely removed from evolutionary relevance. Could it really make a difference to your survival and reproduction whether you believe that quantum theory is true or false?

So putting the two parts of the argument together: if theism is true then we have good reason to believe (as we generally do) that our belief-forming mechanisms are generally reliable. But if naturalism is true, then we have no good reason to believe that they are, nor that most of our beliefs are true, including our scientific beliefs—including the theory of evolution! If you believe that naturalism is true, then, you should believe that your beliefs are not likely to be true, including your belief in naturalism. Or as Plantinga puts it,

[Biologist Richard] Dawkins claims that the living world came to be by way of unguided evolution: "the evidence of evolution," he says, "reveals a universe without design." What he actually argues, however, is that there is a Darwinian series for contemporary life forms. As we have seen, this argument is inconclusive; but even if it were air-tight it wouldn't show, of course, that the living world, let alone the entire universe, is without design. At best it would show, given a couple of assumptions, that it is not astronomically improbable that the living world was produced by unguided evolution and hence without design. But the argument form *p is not astronomically improbable therefore p* is a bit unprepossessing.

—**Alvin Plantinga**, *Where the Conflict Really Lies: Science, Religion, and Naturalism* (2011)

The belief that both [naturalism] and evolution are true is self-refuting. It shoots itself in the foot. Therefore it can't be rationally held.[5]

To be clear, though, Plantinga is not arguing that the theory of evolution by natural selection is false. It's rather that it is not reasonable to believe both that theory and naturalism, for the belief in naturalism undermines the reasonability of believing that the theory of evolution is true.

What we can believe, however, is that the theory of evolution is compatible with non-naturalism, here, theism. We can believe that we are the products of evolution roughly as Darwin describes, in other words, as long as we also believe that the process was in some way guided by God. For if it were guided by God, as the first part of the argument showed, then we would have reason to believe that our cognitive faculties were generally reliable, and thus were in a good position to generate true beliefs, such as the theory of evolution.

Contra most people's intuitions, in short, we can make better sense of the success of science on the supposition of theism than on that of atheism.

SOME DEVELOPMENTS IN EPISTEMOLOGY

The twentieth century was very productive for epistemology. Indeed epistemological considerations were at play in almost all other areas of philosophy. Logical positivism was essentially an epistemological movement, driven by Humean empiricism, and its account of ethical concepts reflected the point that moral properties are not observable. Obviously Plantinga's argument in the philosophy of religion just above also involved epistemology, focusing on the reliability of our cognitive (i.e., epistemic) faculties. Similarly, much of the philosophy of religion in the past half-century has addressed the question of the rational justifiability of belief in God. According to a movement known as **reformed epistemology**, for example, it can be rational to believe in God even without specific evidence because belief in God is as epistemologically basic as belief in the world around us or belief in the past. (An **epistemologically basic belief** is one we are justified in holding without inferring it from other justified beliefs.) Much argument is needed to defend this claim, of course, and much argument is provided. But our point now is that general epistemological questions—in what circumstances are beliefs justified? Do all beliefs require justification on the basis of other beliefs?—are at work in other areas of philosophy. (Similar points apply to twentieth-century metaphysics, hinted at below.)

Epistemologists were especially busy formulating theories of knowledge. A **theory of knowledge** attempts to describe, roughly, what is required for us to be considered rationally justified in believing something, that is, in accepting a proposition as true. In the seventeenth century Descartes gave us **foundationalism,** the view that some beliefs (such as the *cogito*) are certain or **self-evident**, or justified in themselves, and subsequently serve as foundations on which to justify other beliefs. The twentieth century was not kind to foundationalism, challenging it with many questions. Which beliefs (if any) can serve this role? (How far could the *cogito* take you, anyway?) Must foundational beliefs be absolutely certain, or could we be fallible in holding them? If no beliefs fit the foundationalist bill, must we give up the possibility of knowledge?

As foundationalism faltered from these questions, philosophers began to develop alternative theories. According to **coherentism**, a belief may be justified insofar as it coheres with a system of beliefs. The advantage of coherentism is that it dispenses with foundations, so no single belief need be certain, we need not be infallible, and so forth. The disadvantage is that a coherentist account of knowledge steers dangerously close to justifying conspiracy theories. A *conspiracy theory* is a case where someone weaves together a complex web of beliefs that may be internally coherent but which strikes most others as, well, *crazy*. Examples include those with various accounts of the Kennedy assassination, who deny that Americans actually made it to the moon, who hold that President Bush orchestrated 9/11, and so on. Many questions are raised for, and discussed by, coherentists. What constitutes *cohering*? How many beliefs are required for something to count as a *system*? Is it possible to have two completely different systems of beliefs, each internally coherent, but opposed to each other at every point? If so, what then?

The ascent of coherentism itself coheres nicely with another epistemological trend beginning in the twentieth century. As both the existentialists and the logical positivists rejected the objectivity of ethics, so philosophers began challenging the objectivity of knowledge in general. Following the Kantian line, perception was seen not as a mode of simply observing how the world is, but as our human way of interacting with the world—which might well vary between species, cultures, and individuals. The philosophy of science thus saw the rise of the idea of **theory-laden observation**. Observations or experiments were no longer seen as neutral between competing theories, and thus able to test which of the competing theories is right. Rather, they themselves already presume the truth of a great amount of theory, so that what you observe in an experiment depends heavily on what you already believe, and thus cannot simply tell you, objectively, how the world is. The classic example was the *cloud chamber* in physics, a device that lets you track the motion of an otherwise invisible particle because the particle leaves a trail of smoke behind it. You will see this trail *as* observational evidence for the particle only if you already have a full theory of the nature of particles and the technical operations of the cloud chamber in mind. Someone who has a different theory of matter, or a different theory of the gases in the cloud chamber, will look at that same smoke trail and *not* see it as observational evidence of a particle. Each observer may well have a strong, internally coherent web of beliefs, mutually justifying each other, but one sees a particle there and one does not. Who is right?

Perhaps neither. Or both. If our beliefs and theories are not in the business of matching or describing objective reality, the world as it is in itself independent of us, then neither is right in the sense of "describing reality correctly." But if our beliefs and theories *are* in the business of cohering with each other in ways we find useful or advantageous, then both are right—for "being right" means only "fits with the data in a coherent and useful way," and both might well do that.

> On [William] James's view, "true" resembles "good" or "rational" in being a normative notion, a compliment paid to sentences that seem to be paying their way and that fit with other sentences which are doing so.
>
> —**Richard Rorty**, *Consequences of Pragmatism* (1982)

> Truth is what your contemporaries let you get away with.
>
> —**Richard Rorty**, *Philosophy and the Mirror of Nature* (1979)

American philosopher Richard Rorty (1931–2007) was particularly vociferous in defending **scientific antirealism**, the doctrine that science is not actually in that business of "describing reality correctly." Support for antirealism comes from many directions, in addition to coherentism in epistemology: Kantian views on perception as reflecting the structure of our minds, early modern views that secondary qualities (such as colors, flavors, etc.) exist only subjectively in minds and not "out there" objectively in the world, arguments (as in the previous section) that evolution selects minds for survivability and not for getting at "truth," and so on.

Not even the "success" of science described earlier means that scientific theories are *true*, in fact. In *The Structure of Scientific Revolutions* (1962), Thomas Kuhn (1922–1996) influentially argued that science adopts and rejects its theories not from purely rational considerations (such as evidence) but from various non-rational considerations, including that older scientists who dominate a field eventually die, to be replaced by younger scientists who simply hold different theories. So the fact that a certain theory takes over, or becomes widely accepted, doesn't mean that it's true. It might merely be popular, or trendy, or held by more powerful people who influence others, and so forth. In a similar vein, the classic paper "A Confutation of Convergent Realism" (*Philosophy of Science* 48, 1, 1981) by Larry Laudan (b. 1941) shows how scientific theories have been successful for centuries by all relevant measures only to be given up for later theories. So much for "success" suggesting truth! And in any case, does anyone believe that were you to time travel to the future, ten thousand years from now, scientists then would still hold the same theories in physics, chemistry, and so on that they do today? So however successful science is today, it doesn't make it very likely that our scientific theories are *true*.

(It would be interesting to reflect here on how or whether scientific antirealism affects Plantinga's argument in the previous section.)

Even reason, the vaunted tool of philosophers, comes under attack in the twentieth century. More or less since Plato, philosophers have treated reason as universally valid, the same for everyone, everywhere, and thus as an essential tool for obtaining true objective knowledge about the world. But now we already know that different individuals can look at the same facts and reach divergent opinions. Different scientists can share all the same data yet rationally infer very different theories to explain it. Some brilliant people these days think that reason conclusively refutes God's existence, while some equally brilliant *other* people think that reason conclusively affirms it. The twentieth century saw the rise of **feminist epistemology**, a movement that examines gender issues in epistemology and questions the idea that knowledge and reason work the same way in all people.

Now our discussion so far has mentioned various questions about knowledge: whether it requires foundational beliefs or mere coherence, whether perceptions are distinct from beliefs or entwined with them ("theory-laden"), whether science is in the business of describing the world or merely allows us to succeed in it, and so on. Similarly our previous two chapters explored the early moderns' views on the relative roles that reason and perceptual experience play in producing knowledge. What we have not managed to do, so far, is actually say what knowledge *is*, that is, to define it.

The Traditional Definition of Knowledge

One philosopher attempted to do so a long time ago. Plato's Forms, you'll recall from chapter 3, were about providing the essences of things: the Form of Triangle expressed what triangularity *is*, so all individual particular triangular things would share that essence. Now essences are best expressed in definitions. To understand what a bachelor is, to grasp the essence of bachelorhood, is to define it: unmarried adult human male, say.

Now definitions, ideally, or at least traditionally, provide both necessary and sufficient conditions for the thing in question. **Necessary conditions** are conditions that must be met by something if it is to fall into the category being defined; **sufficient conditions** are conditions such that, if a thing has them, that suffices for it to fall into the category. These are different concepts, though easily confused. Having a functioning car may be a sufficient condition for getting to tonight's concert, but it isn't necessary (because you could get there by other means); being male is a necessary condition for being a bachelor, but it isn't sufficient, because other conditions are also required. But, arguably, being an unmarried adult human male is both necessary *and* sufficient for being a bachelor: it's necessary because you need all four properties in order to be a bachelor, and it's sufficient because any creature which has all four is in fact a bachelor.

An ideal definition of knowledge, then, would offer necessary and sufficient conditions for something counting as knowledge. Plato, in his *Theaetetus*, undertook to offer just that. While his discussion was subtle, and while his conclusion was that his effort was *in*conclusive, the dialogue bequeathed a working definition of knowledge that remained in place until the twentieth century. In more contemporary language, Plato suggested that knowledge is constituted by three factors.

> Socrates: Now this is just where my difficulty comes in. I can't get a proper grasp of what on earth knowledge really is. Could we manage to put it into words?
>
> —**Plato** (429–347 B.C.E.), *Theaetetus*

First, there must be belief. A person counts as knowing a certain proposition only if she believes it. (If you don't even believe that the earth goes around the sun, we surely wouldn't say that you know that it does.)

Second, the belief must be true. A person's false beliefs do not count as knowledge. (You may believe that 7+5=13, but we wouldn't say you succeed in knowing it, because it's false.)

But true belief is not yet sufficient for knowledge. That means you can have some true beliefs that do not yet count as knowing. Suppose you are trying to decide if there is life on the moon. You toss a coin: heads you'll believe there is, tails you'll believe there isn't. You toss, heads, and now you believe there is life on the moon. Some years later NASA gets to the moon again and discovers life there. So you had a true belief, it turns out. But it hardly seems like knowledge. It was more like a lucky, random guess that happened to be true.

So it's not enough for knowledge to have true belief. You must have some good reason for having the belief, some good reason to believe that the relevant proposition is true. If you believed that there is life on the moon because of evidence, of studies you had made or read, *then* we might say you know or knew there was life on the moon. A fancy word for this that we've already used is *justification*. You must have adequate justification for believing the thing, for it to count as knowledge.

What counts as adequate justification, as good reasons to believe various things, is a matter of much ongoing debate, and indeed much of chapters 8 and 9 as well as the present section are addressing that. But as far as *some* justification being required to complete the definition of knowledge, that's what Plato bequeathed to us.

In short, the necessary and sufficient conditions for knowledge are belief, truth, and justification, that is, knowledge is true justified belief. That's how it's been since the time of Plato. Then came 1963.

The Gettier Problem

Philosopher Edmund Gettier (b. 1927) dropped a bomb on epistemology with a little three-page paper called "Is Justified True Belief Knowledge" (*Analysis* 23, 1963). In it he provides two cases where it seems that an individual has true justified belief in a certain proposition, yet where we would not consider that to be knowledge. In short, he challenges the 2,500-year-old idea that true justified belief is sufficient for knowledge. Here we'll briefly summarize just the first case.

Suppose, Gettier begins, that Smith and Jones have applied for a certain job, and Smith has strong evidence for believing that

(A) Jones will get the job, and Jones has ten coins in his pocket.

Perhaps the human resources person told Smith that Jones was going to get it, and perhaps Smith saw Jones empty his pocket and then put ten coins in. In these conditions we would say that Smith is justified in believing (A).

But (A) now logically entails this proposition:

(B) The man who will get the job has ten coins in his pocket.

To say (A) logically entails (B) is to say that if (A) turns out to be true, then (B) would have to be true too. And indeed, if Jones *will* get the job and has ten coins in his pocket, then the man who will get the job has ten coins in his pocket. Smith understands that (A) entails (B), and, already justified in believing (A), now comes to believe (B), and is justified in so doing. (For surely you are justified in believing what's logically entailed by things you already are justified in believing.)

But now imagine it turns out that *Smith* will get the job, not Jones; and that Smith happens to have ten coins in his pocket too, though he doesn't realize it. On this scenario (A) turns out false, while (B) turns out true. More importantly, Smith has a *true justified belief* that (B). We already mentioned he was justified in believing that (B), and now (B) turns out to be true.

But does Smith *know* that (B)? It doesn't seem so. It seems almost like a lucky accident that Smith had this true justified belief. After all, he believed (B) was true on the basis of believing that Jones has ten coins in his pocket, while what in the end makes (B) true was partly the fact that *Smith* has ten coins in *his* pocket. Something has gone wrong, but what? For even given the point just made, it remains the case that Smith has a true justified belief that doesn't amount to knowledge.

So the traditional definition of knowledge fails.

There are several points to make, the first two of which Gettier himself points out.

First, you can be justified in believing a certain proposition even if that proposition turns out to be false. This point reflects the common sense view that our knowledge rarely or never attains complete certainty (except perhaps in Descartes's *cogito*!). We're almost always fallible, so there always remains the possibility that what we believe may be false. To be justified in believing something means we have good reasons to believe it, maybe even compelling reasons to believe it, but even compelling reasons may fall short of certainty. So justified belief need not necessarily be true belief.

Second, logical reasoning itself is a source of justification. If you are justified in believing a proposition, and that proposition logically entails another proposition, and you realize this and so come to believe the other proposition, then you are justified in believing the second proposition too.

Third, we must say a little something about the fallout from the Gettier cases. Epistemologists began scrambling furiously. There were so many possible ways to begin responding, without clear consensus on what was right. Did Gettier's cases prove that true justified belief was not sufficient for knowledge? Was there some way to refute the cases and preserve the definition? Could you keep the definitions but somehow eliminate the role of luck, or false evidence, in play? Or was it necessary to add some additional condition to knowledge, to say that knowledge is true justified belief PLUS *x*? The possible candidates for *x* were nearly as numerous as the number of epistemologists responding to the problem, including such fancy-sounding things as causal conditions, defeasibility conditions, pragmatic conditions, and so forth. Along the way literally dozens of variations on Gettier's cases were generated, innumerable different thought experiments in which to test one's intuitions about what knowledge is or requires.

While no clear consensus has emerged about how to respond to Gettier, great progress was made in getting clearer on what's meant by such basic concepts as truth, justification, and belief, and in getting a sense of what else might be necessary in order for us to count as having knowledge.

Quite an impressive consequence of a modest three-page paper.

SOME DEVELOPMENTS IN METAPHYSICS

As with epistemology, it has been a great past century for metaphysics. The twentieth century began with a bang, with J. M. E. McTaggart (1866–1925) arguing in "The Unreality of Time" (*Mind* 17, 1908) that time is unreal and setting off heated discussion continuing to this day. Lest that sound too crazy, McTaggart's claim is that the passing of time is a subjective illusion, and that a proper objective account of the world would include events occurring at different temporal moments but without time actually flowing between those moments. Lest *that* sound too crazy, that is also apparently the verdict of Albert Einstein's theory of relativity, so it's in good company.

Speaking of Einstein, metaphysics has developed some intimate relationships with science over the past century. Scientific developments, particularly in physics—such as quantum theory and the two theories of relativity, special and general—raise many difficult philosophical questions about time, space, causation, matter, mind and free will, and more. Philosophers have been quite busy learning the science and working out the philosophy.

One metaphysical pursuit that has particularly blossomed in this time is reflection on the nature of mind. Long a subdivision of metaphysics, the twentieth century saw it grow into its own field, the philosophy of mind, now one of the most vibrant areas of philosophy today. And while philosophy of mind also has close connections to science—to psychology, computer science, cognitive science—we'll mostly avoid those as we survey its history over the past century.

The Attack on Descartes's Dualism

The twentieth century began with dualism largely in place, with mind conceived as non-physical and non-spatial. But (as we saw) the early decades of the century were dominated by logical positivism, with its empiricist emphasis on observability. Scientific terms, it was insisted, must be analyzed in terms of what is observable. The problem with Descartes's theory was clear: non-physical minds are not observable, or not directly at any rate. You cannot observe anyone else's mind, to be sure; and as Hume taught, we don't observe our own minds either, but are only aware of a passing sequence of mental states. But then how could scientists, or philosophers, speak meaningfully about the mind?

Answer, they can't. Instead the modern science of psychology arose not as a "science of the mind" but as a "science of behavior." **Scientific behaviorism** is the doctrine that psychologists should only study observable behaviors and its causes, spearheaded by Harvard psychologist B. F. Skinner (1904–1990). Rejecting both Descartes's dualism and the psychoanalytic psychology of Sigmund Freud (1856–1939)—both of which were very much "inner" directed— Skinner argued that science should simply study the various conditions under which various sorts of behavior might be produced, without ever referring to what goes on "inside." This was a successful scientific program, dominating psychology until well past the middle of the century. (Many mark its demise in 1959, when linguist Noam Chomsky [b. 1928] published a scathing

review of Skinner's 1957 book *Verbal Behavior.*
Chomsky critiqued Skinner's effort to explain
our use of language without reference to inner mental states, returning scholars' attention
back inside the mind.)

Philosophical (or logical) behaviorism,
relatedly, was an account of the semantics
(or meanings) of mental language. Associated
primarily with Gilbert Ryle (1900–1976), it
claimed that words apparently referring to internal mental states in fact indirectly refer only
to patterns of behavior. You might say "Fred
believes it's raining," referring to a *belief,* an internal mental state. But, Ryle argues, sentences
like these are merely shorthand references to
behavior. In this example, it merely indicates
that he is likely to carry an umbrella, wear a
raincoat, perhaps stay inside, all of which are
observable behaviors. Similar considerations
apply to other mental terms such as *desires,*
perceives, is intelligent, and so on.

B. F. SKINNER

Philosophical behaviorism had its day, but in the end did not succeed. The translations
seemed unworkable: "Fred believes . . ." just cannot be translated into sentences about
behavior in a convincing way. Moreover, our introspective awareness clearly acquaints us with
an interior life to which our mental language does seem to refer. The existence of the non-
physical mind could not just be eliminated by some fancy linguistics.

But while behaviorism faded, the inspiration—to reject Descartes's non-physical mind—
continued. The next major theory, associated with U. T. Place (1924-2000) and J. J. C. Smart
(1920-2012) was the **identity theory,** claiming that mental states are not non-physical but to be
identified with physical brain states. This idea arose in our discussion of Plantinga above: your
belief that *Proust is a more subtle writer than Louis
L'Amour* is a mental state insofar as it is a belief
with a content, but is identified with, is one and
the same thing as, some particular state of your
brain. Other mental states (such as perceptions,
thoughts, or feelings) would be identified with
other brain states, the details to be worked out by
neuroscientists. The theory seems intuitive to many, and would reconcile three plausible facts:
that we have mental states, that these have something to do with our brains, and that our brains
are purely physical entities.

Give me a child and I'll shape him into
anything.

—**B. F. Skinner** (1904–1990)

Despite these virtues, however, the identity theory soon met many objections. We know
exactly what we mean when we refer to our pain (say), we know that *feeling,* and we are surely
not referring to some brain activity when we speak of our pain. Most of us have no idea what's
going on in our brains, and lots of creatures (children, animals) are fully aware of their pain
without even knowing they have "brains." Moreover, brain states and mental states differ in
many ways, which suggests they must be different sorts of things. Your brain may be at 98.6

degrees, but it makes no sense to say your belief that it's raining is; your brain has a size and shape, but your thoughts don't have sizes and shapes, and so on. Moreover, you may be dreaming of a nice bright yellow lemon (say), but nothing in your brain is bright and yellow like that lemon. So how can we identify the dreamed lemon with anything in the brain?

These objections (you may have noticed) are mostly variations on Descartes's own arguments for dualism (see chapter 8). And while identity theorists had responses to them, there was one new objection that most philosophers found unanswerable: the **multiple-realization objection**.

Mental states are *multiply-realizable*, it was objected, meaning that the same mental state could be "realized in," or "occur in," very different physical entities. You may feel a sharp pain when you step on a nail, but so could your dog; and maybe so could primates, or birds, or fish, or aliens from Mars. But your brain and your dog's (and the fish's, etc.) are all very different, so when you feel the pain, your brain could not possibly be in the same state as the brains of all those other creatures when they feel the pain. But then you cannot identify a mental state with a brain state when the same mental state could occur in different brain states. At the least we would have no account of just why these entirely different brain states all count as *pains*. (The same points apply for other mental states, such as beliefs. You and the alien with the silicon brain may both believe it's raining today, but your brains have nothing in common.)

In light of these objections, the identity theory soon gave rise to another, more technical theory, two of whose major developers were Hilary Putnam (b. 1926) and Ned Block (b. 1942). On this theory, **functionalism**, what defines a mental state is its causal or "functional" role, namely the causal relations it bears to bodily input, other types of mental states, and behavioral outputs. What makes a given state count as *pain*, for example, is that it typically results from bodily injury, it typically causes other mental states such as the belief that one has been injured, and it typically produces outputs such as groaning or avoidance behaviors. Similarly, the *belief that it's raining* is typically caused by the presence of rain, causes other rain-related thoughts (*Will camp be cancelled today?*), and causes raincoat and umbrella behaviors. What's key is that functionalism places no constraints on what realizes or instantiates the state, on just what sort of entity fills that functional role. Any system, no matter what it's made of, can be "in pain" or "believe it's raining."

This distinction between the causal role and the entity filling that role allowed functionalism to avoid Descartes's dualism. As an analogy, we make a distinction between the role of Hamlet and the actor who may play that role on any given occasion. The role remains the same, defined by the words and stage directions in the play. The actor changes all the time. But there's nothing non-physical going on here. The play (we might say) is just physical words on a physical page. Actors are just physical bodies and brains (we may assume). But actors engaging in various causal relations (uttering words, behaving) "play roles." So, too, different physical brains and brain states can play the same causal roles. Thus two very different brains can be in pain, or believe that it's raining, without anything non-physical going on.

The advantages of functionalism are many. It reflected the good parts of behaviorism, by recognizing that mental states are partly defined by their roles in producing behavior. It handled the multiple-realizability objection that sunk the identity theory, by embracing it. In fact it played a crucial role in the early days of **artificial intelligence**, the research program that uses computers to theorize about the mind and/or attempts to program them to *have* minds. Many philosophers thought it successfully explained just what it is for us to have mental states such as beliefs, thoughts, or desires.

But it, too, met some notable objections.

John Searle (b. 1932), for example, famously denied that it successfully explains those mental states. In his paper, "Minds, Brains, and Programs" (*Behavioral and Brain Sciences* 3, 1980), Searle developed the **Chinese room thought experiment**. In brief, imagine you are in a room and notes are being passed in through a slot, containing Chinese markings. (We're assuming you can't read Chinese; if you can, choose another language.) You don't know what these mean, but you have a rulebook (in English) that says when certain squiggles come in, you should draw other squiggles on a paper (equally meaningless to you) and slide them back out. Suppose now that, unbeknownst to you, the squiggles coming in and the squiggles you send out are meaningful Chinese expressions, and the process is working so well that the Chinese speakers outside the door believe they are communicating with a native Chinese speaker.

> I will argue that in the literal sense the programmed computer understands what the car and the adding machine understand, namely, exactly nothing.
>
> —**John Searle**, "Minds, Brains, and Programs" (1980)

Now you are, in this room, arguably, functionally equivalent to a Chinese speaker: certain inputs in cause certain behavioral responses back out. But there's all the *mental* difference in the world between you and the genuine speaker. She understands Chinese, and you do not. This shows, Searle concludes, that there is more to mental states (such as *understanding*) than functionalism can capture. (The literature responding to Searle is enormous, not least because his argument, if it works, would sink the entire project of programming computers to be genuinely intelligent.)

A second major objection to functionalism is that it cannot account for an essential feature of many mental states: their subjective character, what it's like to think or feel something, what pain *feels* like, colors look like, how things taste or sound, and so on. Many thought experiments are available to explore these points, but we'll mention just two.

The first is known as the possibility of **inverted qualia**. *Qualia* is the fancy term for the subjective character of mental states, the conscious character, what they "feel" like. Now it seems conceivable that two people might have inverted qualia relative to each other. For example, you and your friend both call ripe bananas *yellow* and grass *green*, but perhaps what's going on inside you is different. When your friend looks at a ripe banana he sees green, but he has learned to call that color *yellow*; when he looks at grass he sees yellow, but he has learned to call that color *green*. If this were the case, then you and he would be functionally equivalent, as your mental states would play all the same causal roles: you look at the same objects and use the same color words. But, again, there seems to be all the difference in the world between your mental states, for they are as different as yellow is from green! But then functional role cannot explain these features of mental states.

Even more disturbingly, there is the possibility of **absent qualia**. As far as we can tell, two people could be functionally equivalent yet one of them lacks qualia or consciousness altogether! Think *zombies* from classic horror films, now discussed at length by many contemporary philosophers. (Particularly thorough treatment may be found in the 1996 book, *The Conscious Mind* by David Chalmers [b. 1966], who even maintains a website on zombies: http://consc.net/zombies.html.) Searle's Chinese room illustrates the possibility. The system composed of you and the room passes for a Chinese speaker to those on the outside, but there's no relevant "subjective awareness" experienced by you and the room. When computers imitate human behavior—when Apple's Siri interacts with you like a real person—is there any subjective awareness on the inside? Or should we say that the circuits are functionally equivalent to a person, their inputs and outputs are identical, but there's no subjective consciousness in there? If the latter, then functionalism fails. There's more to the mind than causal roles.

Consciousness and Dualism

Qualia—consciousness, subjective awareness—has turned out to be the thorn in the side of those trying to reject dualism. All that exists is physical matter, they say, and mental states must reduce to or be identified with brain states. But behaviorism fails, the identity theory fails, and so does functionalism, even if the latter does (to many) a fair job on mental states such as beliefs, thoughts, and desires. Consciousness remains what David Chalmers calls *the hard problem* in the philosophy of mind, where dualism refuses to give up.

Some recent philosophers, in fact, invoke qualia and consciousness to argue strongly *for* something like Descartes's dualism. One example is the well-known paper by Thomas Nagel (b. 1937), "What Is It Like to Be A Bat?" (*The Philosophical Review* 83, 1974). Nagel is not arguing for dualism, strictly speaking, only that we cannot conceive how **physicalism** could be true (i.e., the doctrine that all that exists is physical matter). But since it's a short step from there to believing that dualism is true, and since many philosophers invoke Nagel's argument for that conclusion, we shall follow suit.

Nagel focuses on the "subjective character of experience," or "what it's like" to be a given organism, as we mentioned. Where there is conscious experience, he observes, there is always some individual subject whose experience it is, who stands in a unique relationship to the experience, so it's not merely that there's something that it's like to smell garlic (for example), but that there's something that it's like for *you* to smell garlic. Not only might it be different for someone else to smell garlic, but you have a privileged access to your own experience. You know what you are experiencing in a way no one else does or can, both directly and with the incorrigibility Descartes identified (see chapter 8): you can never make a mistake about how things seem to you. Others, to the contrary, have no direct access to your experience and can easily be mistaken about what you are experiencing. As Nagel puts it, your subjective experience is connected with your own unique *point of view* on the world.

But that's what raises the problem for physicalism. Physical states, such as brain states, have no subjective character. Physical science aims for objectivity, for achieving truths that are independent of anyone's point of view, that state how the world is not from this or that perspective but *period*, in itself. Your brain states are *public*, in principle accessible to anyone. In fact, a physician or neuroscientist might, by medical imaging, know more about what's going on inside your brain than you. There is nothing private (in principle) about anything physical, nothing subjective, nothing unique to anyone's point of view. But then we can have no way of understanding how subjective consciousness could be identified with, reduced to, or even related to physical phenomena such as brain states. How can you generate subjectivity just by linking or combining purely objective things?

Nagel vividly illustrates this argument with his famous bat example. Science knows a great deal about how a bat's brain works physically, about how a bat navigates the world by sonar, identifies and locates its prey, swoops down and captures it, and so on. But what science cannot tell us, what we cannot even conceive, is the specific subjective character of a bat's experience, *what it's like to be a bat*. No amount of extrapolation of our own experience will suffice, since the experiences are surely of grossly different qualitative kinds. You may imagine flying around with your eyes closed, listening for insects, hanging upside down in a cave—but that is to imagine what it would be like for *you* to act *like* a bat, not what it's like for *a bat* to *be* a bat. Science might perhaps tell us the complete physical, objective story to how a bat works. But it leaves something out. It cannot tell us the subjective story, of what it's like to be a bat.

The subjective character of conscious experience suggests, then, that there's more to the world than physical science can tell us. The same point is also defended by Frank Jackson (b. 1943) in "Epiphenomenal Qualia" (1982)[6], and "What Mary Didn't Know" (1986).[7] (To call qualia **epiphenomenal** is to say that they lack causal powers, an idea we won't pursue here.) At the heart of the argument is a thought experiment:

> Mary is a brilliant scientist who is, for whatever reason, forced to investigate the world from a black and white room via a black and white television monitor. She specializes in the neurophysiology of vision and acquires, let us suppose, all the physical information there is to obtain about what goes on when we see ripe tomatoes, or the sky, and use terms like 'red', 'blue', and so on. She discovers, for example, just which wavelength combinations from the sky stimulate the retina, and exactly how this produces *via* the central nervous system the contraction of the vocal chords and expulsion of air from the lungs that results in the uttering of the sentence 'The sky is blue'. . . . What will happen when Mary is released from her black and white room . . .? Will she *learn* anything or not? It seems just obvious that she will learn something about the world and our visual experience of it. But then it is inescapable that her previous knowledge was incomplete. But she had *all* the physical information. *Ergo* there is more to have than that, and Physicalism is false. ("Epiphenomenal Qualia," 25–26)

> [B]at sonar, though clearly a form of perception, is not similar in its operation to any sense that we possess, and there is no reason to suppose that it is subjectively like anything we can experience or imagine. . . . Our own experience provides the basic materials for our imagination, whose range is therefore limited. It will not help to try to imagine that one has webbing on one's arms . . . that one has very poor vision . . . and that one spends the day hanging upside down by one's feet in an attic. In so far as I can imagine this . . . it tells me only what it would be like for *me* to behave as a bat behaves. But that is not the question. I want to know what it is like for a *bat* to be a bat. Yet if I try to imagine this, I am restricted to the resources of my own mind, and those resources are inadequate to the task.
>
> —**Thomas Nagel**, "What Is It Like to Be a Bat?" (1974)

To be clear, Mary has been brought up in the black and white environment her whole life, so she herself has never seen the colors in question. The argument contained in this passage, known as the **knowledge argument against physicalism**, may then be put like this:

Mary knows all the physical facts about human color vision before her release.
But she learns something about human color vision upon her release.

Therefore, there are non-physical facts about human color vision.

The first premise is true by hypothesis, as we reflect on the thought experiment. As for the second premise, what is it that Mary would learn upon her release? Something about qualia, about the subjective character of conscious experience: either what those colors look like, or what it's like to see those colors. These appear to be genuine facts about human color vision, after all, but facts that are not contained in all the physical facts about how brains and eyeballs and light work. But then if she learns something upon her release, the conclusion follows, that there are more facts about human color vision than are contained in the physical story.

Jackson goes on to offer another version of the argument via another example. Imagine a person, Fred, who for some reason can see a color unknown to normal human perceivers. Naturally we would want to know what it looks like, or what it's like to see it. Fred might attempt to describe it, but as the empiricists taught us long ago, if we cannot see it ourselves we would be unable to form any idea or conception of it. In fact it seems that no amount of physical knowledge about his brain or about how his visual system processes color information will provide us the answer. We might learn that he has some cells in his retina that respond to light of wavelengths that our retinal cells don't respond to. But how will that help? We still wouldn't know what it feels like to be on the receiving end of that light.

The conclusion is the same. There's more to the story of human color perception than a purely physical account can capture. And of course the examples generalize to the other senses, and perhaps even further. We couldn't know what it's like for a bat to be a bat, but perhaps we also cannot know in general what it's like for anyone else to be who they are. What would it be like to be a musical genius, like Beethoven? To be a peasant in fourteenth-century Europe? To be Aristotle? If you are the sort who doesn't, then what would it be like to like brussels sprouts? To like football, or sports in general? What it would be like to be a psychopath? To be a rich celebrity? To be cool (if you aren't), or uncool (if you are)?

Nagel's and Jackson's arguments have generated many responses, as physicalists try to resist their conclusions. What would be useful for physicalists would be a nice complete account of the brain that fully explained subjective experience. But that is currently lacking, and not yet on the horizon. That fact alone should not count against physicalism, of course, since the science is still in its infancy. But now Nagel's and Jackson's arguments are not based on the current lack of physical explanations of subjective consciousness. They are based on an examination of the very natures of physical and subjective facts in general, and provide reason to believe that physical facts are simply of the wrong general kind to explain subjective facts. They thus provide reason to believe that no physical explanation could *ever* suffice.

That cannot be entirely conclusive, naturally, because no one can confidently predict what physical science might look like in the near and distant futures. But from where we are now, they suggest, there's something about consciousness that just doesn't fit with the physical story, as we currently understand it. If you were to review chapter 8 you would discover how closely these contemporary arguments resemble the seventeenth-century arguments for dualism made by Descartes. So while his dualism is not generally in favor in the first decades of the twenty-first century, it still seems very much in the running.

SUMMARY

1. Existentialism is grounded in the sense that there are no objective values and that life is meaningless and absurd. It comes in several forms: religious, nihilistic, and humanistic, represented by Søren Kierkegaard, Friedrich Nietzsche, and Jean-Paul Sartre respectively.

2. In the past century ethics has emphasized metaethics. Influenced by Hume, logical positivists (such as A. J. Ayer) take a subjectivist approach to ethics. Ayer rejects metaethical subjectivism and metaethical utilitarianism, supporting emotivism instead: moral statements do not express any facts and thus are neither true nor false.

3. The philosophy of religion has seen the resurrection of many traditional arguments for theism, including the ontological argument, cosmological arguments, and biological teleological arguments. Added to this is the fine-tuning argument, a teleological argument based in physics.

4. Alvin Plantinga argues that the success of science actually fits better with theism than atheism. The naturalistic account of the world, on which human minds arose via undirected evolution, cannot explain why our cognitive faculties are generally capable of producing true beliefs. But then the truth of naturalism would undermine our confidence that our belief in naturalism is true. To the contrary, on theism we can be confident that our cognitive faculties are generally reliable.

5. Epistemologists have done much work exploring theories of knowledge, such as foundationalism and coherentism. The latter in particular helps promote the theory-ladenness of observation, as well as scientific antirealism. Thinkers such as Richard Rorty, Thomas Kuhn, and Larry Laudan all argue for the idea that science is not in the business of generating true descriptions of the world, but merely helps us navigate and control the world. The attack on the objectivity of reason itself is reflected in feminist epistemology.

6. While Plato's definition of knowledge as true justified belief was the norm for twenty-five centuries, Edmund Gettier's modest three-page paper challenges it.

7. In metaphysics the philosophy of mind came into its own in the past century. Much of the focus is on rejecting Descartes's dualism, attempts being made by scientific behaviorism, philosophical behaviorism, the identity theory, and functionalism. The latter is the most influential, but John Searle's Chinese room thought experiment, and the possibilities of inverted and absent qualia, suggest that subjective awareness, qualia, and consciousness cannot be captured in physical or functionalist terms.

8. Thomas Nagel and Frank Jackson provide arguments that qualia and consciousness involve facts of a very different sort from physical facts, and thus suggest dualism.

KEY TERMS

absent qualia	irreducible complexity
aesthetic stage	knowledge argument against physicalism
amor fati	logical empiricism
angst	logical positivism
artificial intelligence	metaethical subjectivism
Chinese room thought experiment	multiple-realization objection to identity
coherentism	theory
Darwin's doubt	naturalism
emotivism	necessary condition
epiphenomenal	nihilism
epistemologically basic belief	philosophical (or logical) behaviorism
eternal recurrence	physicalism
ethical stage	qualia
existentialism	reformed epistemology
feminist epistemology	religious stage
fine-tuning argument	scientific antirealism
foundationalism	scientific behaviorism
functionalism	self-evident
humanism	sufficient condition
identity theory	*sui generis*
intelligent design	theory-laden observation
inverted qualia	theory of knowledge

REVIEW QUESTIONS

1. How would you characterize existentialism in its different varieties?

2. What is Ayer's doctrine of emotivism, and how does it differ from metaethical subjectivism?

3. In what way is the fine-tuning argument safe from the Darwinian objection made earlier to Paley's biological teleological argument?

4. Is Descartes an epistemological foundationalist or coherentist?

5. What is the "Gettier Problem"?

6. Some objections to identity theory are "variations on Descartes's own arguments for dualism (see chapter 8)." Identify some and explain.

7. Summarize Jackson's argument against physicalism.

NOTES

1. *On the Genealogy of Morals*, I.13. In ed., transl. Walter Kaufmann, *Basic Writings of Nietzsche* (New York: The Modern Library, 1966/1968), 480–81.

2. *Ecce Homo*, "Why I Am So Clever," 10. In ed., transl. Walter Kaufmann, *Basic Writings of Nietzsche* (New York: The Modern Library, 1966/1968), 714.

3. *The Gay Science*, 341. In transl. Walter Kaufmann, *Friedrich Nietzsche: The Gay Science* (New York: Vintage Books, 1974), 273–74.

4. *Warrant and Proper Function* (New York: Oxford University Press), 1993, 225–26.

5. Interview in The *New York Times*, February 9, 2014.

6. Frank Jackson in "Epiphenomenal Qualia," *Philosophical Quarterly* 32 (1982): 127–36. Reprinted in *Consciousness and the Mind-Body Problem: A Reader*, Torin Alter and Robert Howell, eds., (New York: Oxford University Press, 2012), 23–30.

7. Frank Jackson, "What Mary Didn't Know," *Journal of Philosophy* 83 (1986): 291–95.

■ Reading
"A Panegyric upon Abraham"

SØREN KIERKEGAARD

"A Panegyric Upon Abraham" (1843); from Fear and Trembling, *in* Fear and Trembling and The Sickness Unto Death, *transl., Walter Lowrie (Princeton, NJ: Princeton University Press, 1941/1954), 30–37. Reprinted with permission.*

> In this excerpt the religious existentialist Kierkegaard studies the great biblical figure of Abraham and the event of his near sacrifice of his son Isaac.

If there were no eternal consciousness in a man, if at the foundation of all there lay only a wildly seething power which writhing with obscure passions produced everything that is great and everything that is insignificant, if a bottomless void never satiated lay hidden beneath all—what then would life be but despair? If such were the case, if there were no sacred bond which united mankind, if one generation arose after another like the leafage in the forest, if the one generation replaced the other like the song of birds in the forest, if the human race passed through the world as the ship goes through the sea, like the wind through the desert, a thoughtless and fruitless activity, if an eternal oblivion were always lurking hungrily for its prey and there was no power strong enough to wrest it from its maw—how empty then and comfortless life would be! But therefore it is not thus, but as God created man and woman, so too He fashioned the hero and the poet or orator. The poet cannot do what that other does, he can only admire, love and rejoice in the hero. Yet he too is happy, and not less so, for the hero is as it were his better nature, with which he is in love, rejoicing in the fact that this after all is not himself, that his love can be admiration. He is the genius of recollection, can do nothing except call to mind what has been done, do nothing but admire what has been done; he contributes nothing of his own, but is jealous of the intrusted treasure. He follows the option of his heart, but when he has found what he sought, he wanders before every man's door with his song and with his oration, that all may admire the hero as he does, be proud of the hero as he is. This is his achievement, his humble work, this is his faithful service in the house of the hero. If he thus remains true to his love, he strives day and night against the cunning of oblivion which would trick him out of his hero, then he has completed his work, then he is gathered to the hero, who has loved him just as faithfully, for the poet is as it were the hero's better nature, powerless it may be as a memory is, but also transfigured as a memory is. Hence no one shall be forgotten who was great, and though time tarries long, though a cloud's of misunderstanding takes the hero away, his lover comes nevertheless, and the longer the time that has passed, the more faithfully will he cling to him.

No, not one shall be forgotten who was great in the world. But each was great in his own way, and each in proportion to the greatness of that which he *loved*. For he who loved himself became great by himself, and he who loved other men became great by his selfless devotion, but he who loved God became greater than all. Everyone shall be remembered, but each became great in proportion to his *expectation*. One became great by expecting the possible, another by expecting the eternal, but he who expected the impossible became greater than all. Everyone shall be remembered, but each was great in proportion to the greatness of that with which he *strove*. For he who strove with the world became great by overcoming the world, and he who strove with himself became great by overcoming himself, but he who strove with God became greater than all. So there was strife in the world, man against man, one against a thousand, but he who strove with God was greater than all. So there was strife upon earth: there was one who overcame all by his power, and there was one who overcame God by his impotence. There was one who relied upon himself and gained all, there was one who secure in his strength sacrificed all, but he who believed God was greater than all. There was one who was great by reason of his power, and one who was great by reason of his wisdom, and one who was great by reason of his hope, and one who was great by reason of his love; but Abraham was greater than all, great by reason of his power whose strength is impotence, great by reason of his wisdom whose secret is foolishness, great by reason of his hope whose form is madness, great by reason of the love which is hatred of oneself.

By faith Abraham went out from the land of his fathers and became a sojourner in the land of promise. He left one thing behind, took one thing with him: he left his earthly understanding behind and took faith with him—otherwise he would not have wandered forth but would have thought this unreasonable. By faith he was a stranger in the land of promise, and there was nothing to recall what was dear to him, but by its novelty everything tempted his soul to melancholy yearning—and yet he was God's elect, in whom the Lord was well pleased! Yea, if he had been disowned, cast off from God's grace, he could have comprehended it better; but now it was like a mockery of him and of his faith. There was in the world one too who lived in banishment from the fatherland he loved [the prophet Jeremiah]. He is not forgotten, nor his Lamentations when he sorrowfully sought and found what he had lost. There is no song of Lamentations by Abraham. It is human to lament, human to weep with them that weep, but it is greater to believe, more blessed to contemplate the believer.

By faith Abraham received the promise that in his seed all races of the world would be blessed. Time passed, the possibility was there, Abraham believed; time passed, it became unreasonable, Abraham believed. There was in the world one who had an expectation, time passed, the evening drew nigh, he was not paltry enough to have forgotten his expectation, therefore he too shall not be forgotten. Then he sorrowed, and sorrow did not deceive him as life had done, it did for him all it could, in the sweetness of sorrow he possessed his delusive expectation. It is human to sorrow, human to sorrow with them that sorrow, but it is greater to believe, more blessed to contemplate the believer. There is no song of Lamentations by Abraham. He did not mournfully count the days while time passed, he did not look at Sarah with a suspicious glance, wondering whether she were growing old, he did not arrest the course of the sun, that Sarah might not grow old, and his expectation with her. He did not sing lullingly before Sarah his mournful lay. Abraham became old, Sarah became a laughing-stock in the land, and yet he was God's elect and inheritor of the promise that in his seed all the races of the world would be blessed. So were it not better if he had not been God's elect? What is it to be God's elect? It is to be denied in youth the wishes of youth, so as with great pains to get them fulfilled in old age. But Abraham believed and held fast the expectation. If Abraham had wavered, he would have given it up. If he had said to God, "Then perhaps it is not after all Thy will that it should come to pass, so I will give up the wish. It was my only wish, it was my bliss. My soul is sincere, I hide no secret malice because Thou didst deny it to me"—he would not have been forgotten, he would have saved many by his example, yet he would not be the father of faith. For it is great to give up one's wish, but it is greater to hold it fast after having given it up, it is great to grasp the eternal, but it is greater to hold fast to the temporal after having given it up.

Then came the fullness of time. If Abraham had not believed, Sarah surely would have been dead of sorrow, and Abraham, dulled by grief, would not have understood the fulfillment but would have smiled at it as at a dream of youth. But Abraham believed, therefore he was young; for he who always hopes for the best becomes old, and he who is always prepared for the worst grows old early, but he who believes preserves an eternal youth. Praise therefore to that story! For Sarah, though stricken in years, was young enough to desire the pleasure of motherhood, and Abraham, though gray-haired, was young enough to wish to be a father. In an outward respect the marvel consists in the fact that it came to pass according to their expectation, in a deeper sense the miracle of faith consists in the fact that Abraham and Sarah were young enough to wish, and that faith had preserved their wish and therewith their youth. He accepted the fulfillment of the promise, he accepted it by faith, and it came to pass according to the promise and according to his faith—for Moses smote the rock with his rod, but he did not believe.

Then there was joy in Abraham's house, when Sarah became a bride on the day of their golden wedding.

But it was not to remain thus. Still once more Abraham was to be tried. He had fought with that cunning power which invents everything, with that alert enemy which never slumbers, with that old man who outlives all things—he had fought with Time and preserved his faith. Now all the terror of the strife was concentrated in one instant. "And God tempted Abraham and said unto him, Take Isaac, thine only son, whom thou lovest, and get thee into the land of Moriah, and offer him there for a burnt offering upon the mountain which I will show thee."

So all was lost—more dreadfully than if it had never come to pass! So the Lord was only making sport of Abraham! He made miraculously the preposterous actual, and now in turn He would annihilate it. It was indeed foolishness, but Abraham did not laugh at it like Sarah when the promise was announced. All was lost! Seventy years of faithful expectation, the brief joy at the fulfillment of faith. Who then is he that plucks away the old man's staff, who is it that requires that he himself shall break it? Who is he that would make a man's gray hairs comfortless, who is it that requires that he himself shall do it? Is there no compassion for the venerable oldling, none for the innocent child? And yet Abraham was God's elect, and it was the Lord who imposed the trial. All would now be lost. The glorious memory to be preserved by the human race, the promise in Abraham's seed—this was only a whim, a fleeting thought which the Lord had had, which Abraham should now obliterate. That glorious treasure which was just as old as faith in Abraham's heart, many, many years older than Isaac, the fruit of Abraham's life, sanctified by prayers, matured in conflict—the blessing upon Abraham's lips, this fruit was now to be plucked prematurely and remain without significance. For what significance had it when Isaac was to be sacrificed? That sad and yet blissful hour when Abraham was to take leave of all that was dear to him, when yet once more he was to lift up his head, when his countenance would shine like that of the Lord, when he would concentrate his whole soul in a blessing which was potent to make Isaac blessed all his days—this time would not come! For he would indeed take leave of Isaac, but in such a way that he himself would remain behind; death would separate them, but in such a way that Isaac remained its prey. The old man would not be joyful in death as he laid his hands in blessing upon Isaac, but he would be weary of life as he laid violent hands upon Isaac. And it was God who tried him. Yea, woe, woe unto the messenger who had come before Abraham with such tidings! Who would have ventured to be the emissary of this sorrow? But it was God who tried Abraham.

Yet Abraham believed, and believed for this life. Yea, if his faith had been only for a future life, he surely would have cast everything away in order to hasten out of this world to which he did not belong. But Abraham's faith was not of this sort, if there be such a faith; for really this is not faith but the furthest possibility of faith which has a presentiment of its object at the extremest limit of the horizon, yet is separated from it by a yawning abyss within which despair carries on its game. But Abraham believed precisely for this life, that he was to grow old in the land, honored by the people, blessed in his generation, remembered forever in Isaac, his dearest thing in life, whom he embraced with a love for which it would be a poor expression to say that he loyally fulfilled the father's duty of loving the son, as indeed is evinced in the words of the summons, "the son whom thou lovest." Jacob had twelve sons, and one of them he loved; Abraham had only one, the son whom he loved.

Yet Abraham believed and did not doubt, he believed the preposterous. If Abraham had doubted—then he would have done something else, something glorious; for how could Abraham do anything but what is great and glorious! He would have marched up to Mount Moriah, he would have cleft the fire-wood, lit the pyre, drawn the knife—he would have cried out to God, "Despise not this sacrifice, it is not the best thing I possess, that I know well, for what is an old man in comparison with the child of promise; but it is the best I am able to give Thee. Let Isaac never come to know this, that he may console himself with his youth." He would have plunged the knife into his own breast. He would have been admired in the world, and his name would not have been forgotten; but it is one thing to be admired, and another to be the guiding star which saves the anguished.

But Abraham believed. He did not pray for himself, with the hope of moving the Lord—it was only when the righteous punishment was decreed upon Sodom and Gomorrha that Abraham came forward with his prayers.

We read in those holy books: "And God tempted Abraham, and said unto him, Abraham, Abraham, where art thou? And he said, Here am I." Thou to whom my speech is addressed, was such the case with thee? When afar off thou didst see the heavy dispensation of providence approaching thee, didst thou not say to the mountains, Fall on me, and to the hills, Cover me? Or if thou wast stronger, did not thy foot move slowly along the way, longing as it were for the old path? When a call was issued to thee, didst thou answer, or didst thou not answer perhaps in a low voice, whisperingly? Not so Abraham: joyfully, buoyantly, confidently, with a loud voice, he answered, "Here am I." We read further: "And Abraham rose early in the morning"—as though it were to a festival, so he hastened, and early in the morning he had come to the place spoken of, to Mount Moriah. He said nothing to Sarah, nothing to Eleazar. Indeed who could understand him? Had not the temptation by its very nature exacted of him an oath of silence? He cleft the wood, he bound Isaac, he lit the pyre, he drew the knife. My hearer, there was many a father who believed that with his son he lost everything that was dearest to him in the world, that he was deprived of every hope for the future, but yet there was none that was the child of promise in the sense that Isaac was for Abraham. There was many a father who lost his child; but then it was God, it was the unalterable, the unsearchable will of the Almighty, it was His hand took the child. Not so with Abraham. For him was reserved a harder trial, and Isaac's fate was laid along with the knife in Abraham's hand. And there he stood, the old man, with his only hope! But he did not doubt, he did not look anxiously to the right or to the left, he did not challenge heaven with his prayers. He knew that it was God the Almighty who was trying him, he knew that it was the hardest sacrifice that could be required of him; but he knew also that no sacrifice was too hard when God required it—and he drew the knife.

Who gave strength to Abraham's arm? Who held his right hand up so that it did not fall limp at his side? He who gazes at this becomes paralyzed. Who gave strength to Abraham's soul, so that his eyes did not grow dim, so that he saw neither Isaac nor the ram? He who gazes at this becomes blind.—And yet rare enough perhaps is the man who becomes paralyzed and blind, still more rare one who worthily recounts what happened. We all know it—it was only a trial.

If Abraham when he stood upon Mount Moriah had doubted, if he had gazed about him irresolutely, if when he drew the knife he had by chance discovered the ram, if God had permitted him to offer it instead of Isaac—then he would have betaken himself home, everything would have been the same, he has Sarah, he retained Isaac, and yet how changed! For his retreat would have been a flight, his salvation an accident, his reward dishonor, his future perhaps perdition. Then he would have borne witness neither to his faith nor to God's grace, but would have testified only how dreadful it is to march out to Mount Moriah. Then Abraham would not have been forgotten, nor would Mount Moriah, this mountain would then be mentioned, not like Ararat where the Ark landed, but would be spoken of as a consternation, because it was here that Abraham doubted.

Venerable Father Abraham! In marching home from Mount Moriah thou hadst no need of a panegyric which might console thee for thy loss; for thou didst gain all and didst retain Isaac. Was it not so? Never again did the Lord take him from thee, but thou didst sit at table joyfully with him in thy tent, as thou dost in the beyond to all eternity. Venerable Father Abraham! Thousands of years have run their course since those days, but thou hast need of no tardy lover to snatch the memorial of thee from the power of oblivion, for every language calls thee to remembrance—and yet thou dost reward thy lover more gloriously than does any other; hereafter thou dost make him blessed in thy bosom; here thou dost enthral his eyes and his heart by the marvel of thy deed. Venerable Father Abraham! Thou who first wast sensible of and didst first bear witness to that prodigious passion which disdains the dreadful conflict with the rage of the elements and with the powers of creation in order to strive with God; thou who first didst know that highest passion, the holy, pure and humble expression of the divine madness which the pagans admired—forgive him who would speak in praise of thee, if he does not do it fittingly. He spoke humbly, as if it were the desire of his own heart, he spoke briefly, as it becomes him to do, but he will never forget that thou hadst need of a hundred years to obtain a son of old age against expectation, that thou didst have to draw the knife before retaining Isaac; he will never forget that in a hundred and thirty years thou didst not get further than to faith.

REVIEW AND DISCUSSION QUESTIONS

1. In this excerpt is Kierkegaard praising Abraham or condemning him? Either way, for what reason does he do so?

2. Given the account of Kierkegaard's philosophy given in the main text, why do you think that this episode, of Abraham being called by God to sacrifice his son, is so important to him?

■ Reading

Nausea

J E A N - P A U L   S A R T R E

From Nausea *(1938); translated by Lloyd Alexander, from* Nausea, *©1964 by New Directions Publishing Corp., 126–35. (Librairie Gallimard 1938, Penguin Books 1963, Penguin Classics 2000.) Reprinted by permission of New Directions Publishing Corp., Penguin Books Ltd., and Editions Gallimard.*

In this famous passage the main character of Sartre's novel, Antoine Roquentin, has
an existentialist moment in contemplating a chestnut tree.

6.00 *p.m.*

I can't say I feel relieved or satisfied; just the opposite, I am crushed. Only my goal is
reached: I know what I wanted to know; I have understood all that has happened to me since
January. The Nausea has not left me and I don't believe it will leave me so soon; but I no longer
have to bear it, it is no longer an illness or a passing fit: it is I.

So I was in the park just now. The roots of the chestnut tree were sunk in the ground just
under my bench. I couldn't remember it was a root any more. The words had vanished and
with them the significance of things, their methods of use, and the feeble points of reference
which men have traced on their surface. I was sitting, stooping forward, head bowed, alone in
front of this black, knotty mass, entirely beastly, which frightened me. Then I had this vision.

It left me breathless. Never, until these last few days, had I understood the meaning of
"existence." I was like the others, like the ones walking along the seashore, all dressed in their
spring finery. I said, like them, "The ocean *is* green; that white speck up there *is* a seagull," but
I didn't feel that it existed or that the seagull was an "existing seagull"; usually existence hides
itself. It is there, around us, in us, it is *us*, you can't say two words without mentioning it, but
you can never touch it. When I believed I was thinking about it, I must believe that I was thinking nothing, my head was empty, or there was just one word in my head, the word "to be." Or
else I was thinking . . . how can I explain it? I was thinking of *belonging*, I was telling myself
that the sea belonged to the class of green objects, or that the green was a part of the quality of
the sea. Even when I looked at things, I was miles from dreaming that they existed: they looked
like scenery to me. I picked them up in my hands, they served me as tools, I foresaw their
resistance. But that all happened on the surface. If anyone had asked me what existence was,
I would have answered, in good faith, that it was nothing, simply an empty form which was
added to external things without changing anything in their nature. And then all of a sudden,
there it was, clear as day: existence had suddenly unveiled itself. It had lost the harmless look
of an abstract category: it was the very paste of things, this root was kneaded into existence. Or
rather the root, the park gates, the bench, the sparse grass, all that had vanished: the diversity of
things, their individuality, were only an appearance, a veneer. This veneer had melted, leaving
soft, monstrous masses, all in disorder—naked, in a frightful, obscene nakedness.

I kept myself from making the slightest movement, but I didn't need to move in order to
see, behind the trees, the blue columns and the lamp posts of the bandstand and the Velleda,
in the midst of a mountain of laurel. All these objects . . . how can I explain? They inconve-
nienced me; I would have liked them to exist less strongly, more dryly, in a more abstract way,

with more reserve. The chestnut tree pressed itself against my eyes. Green rust covered it half-way up; the bark, black and swollen, looked like boiled leather. The sound of the water in the Masqueret Fountain sounded in my ears, made a nest there, filled them with signs; my nostrils overflowed with a green, putrid odour. All things, gently, tenderly, were letting themselves drift into existence like those relaxed women who burst out laughing and say: "It's good to laugh," in a wet voice; they were parading, one in front of the other, exchanging abject secrets about their existence. I realized that there was no half-way house between non-existence and this flaunting abundance. If you existed, you had to *exist all the way*, as far as mouldiness, bloatedness, obscenity were concerned. In another world, circles, bars of music keep their pure and rigid lines. But existence is a deflection. Trees, night-blue pillars, the happy bubbling of a fountain, vital smells, little heat-mists floating in the cold air, a red-haired man digesting on a bench: all this somnolence, all these meals digested together, had its comic side. . . . Comic . . . no: it didn't go as far as that, nothing that exists can be comic; it was like a floating analogy, almost entirely elusive, with certain aspects of vaudeville. We were a heap of living creatures, irritated, embarrassed at ourselves, we hadn't the slightest reason to be there, none of us, each one, confused, vaguely alarmed, felt in the way in relation to the others. *In the way*: it was the only relationship I could establish between these trees, these gates, these stones. In vain I tried to *count* the chestnut trees, to *locate* them by their relationship to the Velleda, to compare their height with the height of the plane trees: each of them escaped the relationship in which I tried to enclose it, isolated itself, and overflowed. Of these relations (which I insisted on maintaining in order to delay the crumbling of the human world, measures, quantities, and directions)—I felt myself to be the arbitrator; they no longer had their teeth into things. *In the way*, the chestnut tree there, opposite me, a little to the left. *In the way*, the Velleda. . . .

And I—soft, weak, obscene, digesting, juggling with dismal thoughts—I, too, was *In the way*. Fortunately, I didn't feel it, although I realized it, but I was uncomfortable because I was afraid of feeling it (even now I am afraid—afraid that it might catch me behind my head and lift me up like a wave). I dreamed vaguely of killing myself to wipe out at least one of these superfluous lives. But even my death would have been *In the way*. *In the way*, my corpse, my blood on these stones, between these plants, at the back of this smiling garden. And the decomposed flesh would have been *In the way* in the earth which would receive my bones, at last, cleaned, stripped, peeled, proper and clean as teeth, it would have been *In the way*: I was *In the way* for eternity.

The word absurdity is coming to life under my pen; a little while ago, in the garden, I couldn't find it, but neither was I looking for it, I didn't need it: I thought without words, *on* things, *with* things. Absurdity was not an idea in my head, or the sound of a voice, only this long serpent dead at my feet, this wooden serpent. Serpent or claw or root or vulture's talon, what difference does it make. And without formulating anything clearly, I understood that I had found the key to Existence, the key to my Nauseas, to my own life. In fact, all that I could grasp beyond that returns to this fundamental absurdity. Absurdity: another word; I struggle against words; down there I touched the thing. But I wanted to fix the absolute character of this absurdity here. A movement, an event in the tiny coloured world of men is only relatively absurd: by relation to the accompanying circumstances. A madman's ravings, for example, are absurd in relation to the situation in which he finds himself, but not in relation to his delirium. But a little while ago I made an experiment with the absolute or the absurd. This root—there was nothing in relation to which it was absurd. Oh, how can I put it in words? Absurd: in relation to the stones, the tufts of yellow grass, the dry mud, the tree, the sky, the green benches.

Absurd, irreducible; nothing—not even a profound, secret upheaval of nature—could explain it. Evidently I did not know everything, I had not seen the seeds sprout, or the tree grow. But faced with this great wrinkled paw, neither ignorance nor knowledge was important: the world of explanations and reasons is not the world of existence. A circle is not absurd, it is clearly explained by the rotation of a straight segment around one of its extremities. But neither does a circle exist. This root, on the other hand, existed in such a way that I could not explain it. Knotty, inert, nameless, it fascinated me, filled my eyes, brought me back unceasingly to its own existence. In vain to repeat: "This is a root"—it didn't work any more. I saw clearly that you could not pass from its function as a root, as a breathing pump, *to that,* to this hard and compact skin of a sea lion, to this oily, callous, headstrong look. The function explained nothing: it allowed you to understand generally that it was a root, but not *that one* at all. This root, with its colour, shape, its congealed movement, was . . . below all explanation. Each of its qualities escaped it a little, flowed out of it, half solidified, almost became a thing; each one was *In the way* in the root and the whole stump now gave me the impression of unwinding itself a little, denying its existence to lose itself in a frenzied excess. I scraped my heel against this black claw: I wanted to peel off some of the bark. For no reason at all, out of defiance, to make the bare pink appear absurd on the tanned leather: to *play* with the absurdity of the world. But, when I drew my heel back, I saw that the bark was still black.

Black? I felt the word deflating, emptied of meaning with extraordinary rapidity. Black? The root *was not* black, there was no black on this piece of wood—there was . . . something else: black, like the circle, did not exist. I looked at the root: was it *more than* black or *almost* black? But I soon stopped questioning myself because I had the feeling of knowing where I was. Yes, I had already scrutinized innumerable objects, with deep uneasiness. I had already tried—vainly—to think something *about* them: and I had already felt their cold, inert qualities elude me, slip through my fingers. Adolphe's suspenders, the other evening in the "Railwaymen's Rendezvous." They *were not* purple. I saw the two inexplicable stains on the shirt. And the stone—the well-known stone, the origin of this whole business: it was not . . . I can't remember exactly just what it was that the stone refused to be. But I had not forgotten its passive resistance. And the hand of the Self-Taught Man; I held it and shook it one day in the library and then I had the feeling that it wasn't quite a hand. I had thought of a great white worm, but that wasn't it either. And the suspicious transparency of the glass of beer in the Cafe Mably. Suspicious: that's what they were, the sounds, the smells, the tastes. When they ran quickly under your nose like startled hares and you didn't pay too much attention, you might believe them to be simple and reassuring, you might believe that there was real blue in the world, real red, a real perfume of almonds or violets. But as soon as you held on to them for an instant, this feeling of comfort and security gave way to a deep uneasiness: colours, tastes, and smells were never real, never themselves and nothing but themselves. The simplest, most indefinable quality had too much content, in relation to itself, in its heart. That black against my foot, it didn't look like black, but rather the confused effort to imagine black by someone who had never seen black and who wouldn't know how to stop, who would have imagined an ambiguous being beyond colours. It *looked* like a colour, but also . . . like a bruise or a secretion, like an oozing—and something else, an odour, for example, it melted into the odour of wet earth, warm, moist wood, into a black odour that spread like varnish over this sensitive wood, in a flavour of chewed, sweet fibre. I did not simply *see* this black: sight is an abstract invention, a simplified idea, one of man's ideas. That black, amorphous, weakly presence, far surpassed sight, smell and taste. But this richness was lost in confusion and finally was no more because it was too much.

This moment was extraordinary. I was there, motionless and icy, plunged in a horrible ecstasy. But something fresh had just appeared in the very heart of this ecstasy; I understood the Nausea, I possessed it. To tell the truth, I did not formulate my discoveries to myself. But I think it would be easy for me to put them in words now. The essential thing is contingency. I mean that one cannot define existence as necessity. To exist is simply *to be there;* those who exist let themselves be encountered, but you can never deduce anything from them. I believe there are people who have understood this. Only they tried to overcome this contingency by inventing a necessary, causal being. But no necessary being can explain existence: contingency is not a delusion, a probability which can be dissipated; it is the absolute, consequently, the perfect free gift. All is free, this park, this city and myself. When you realize that, it turns your heart upside down and everything begins to float, as the other evening at the "Railwaymen's Rendezvous": here is Nausea; here there is what those bastards—the ones on the Coteau Vert and others—try to hide from themselves with their idea of their rights. But what a poor lie: no one has any rights; they are entirely free, like other men, they cannot succeed in not feeling superfluous. And in themselves, secretly, they are *superfluous,* that is to say, amorphous, vague, and sad.

How long will this fascination last? I *was* the root of the chestnut tree. Or rather I was entirely conscious of its existence. Still detached from it—since I was conscious of it—yet lost in it, nothing but it. An uneasy conscience which, notwithstanding, let itself fall with all its weight on this piece of dead wood. Time had stopped: a small black pool at my feet; it was impossible for something to come *after* that moment. I would have liked to tear myself from that atrocious joy, but I did not even imagine it would be possible; I was inside; the black stump did *not move,* it stayed there, in my eyes, as a lump of food sticks in the windpipe. I could neither accept nor refuse it. At what a cost did I raise my eyes? Did I raise them? Rather did I not obliterate myself for an instant in order to be reborn in the following instant with my head thrown back and my eyes raised upward? In fact, I was not even conscious of the transformation. But suddenly it became impossible for me to think of the existence of the root. It was wiped out, I could repeat in vain: it exists, it is still there, under the bench, against my right foot, it no longer meant anything. Existence is not something which lets itself be thought of from a distance: it must invade you suddenly, master you, weigh heavily on your heart like a great motionless beast—or else there is nothing more at all.

There was nothing more, my eyes were empty and I was spellbound by my deliverance. Then suddenly it began to move before my eyes in light, uncertain motions: the wind was shaking the top of the tree.

It did not displease me to see a movement, it was a change from these motionless beings who watched me like staring eyes. I told myself, as I followed the swinging of the branches: movements never quite exist, they are passages, intermediaries between two existences, moments of weakness, I expected to see them come out of nothingness, progressively ripen, blossom: I was finally going to surprise beings in the process of being born.

No more than three seconds, and all my hopes were swept away. I could not attribute the passage of time to these branches groping around like blind men. This idea of passage was still an invention of man. The idea was too transparent. All these paltry agitations, drew in on themselves, isolated. They overflowed the leaves and branches everywhere. They whirled about these empty hands, enveloped them with tiny whirlwinds. Of course a movement was something different from a tree. But it was still an absolute. A thing. My eyes only encountered completion. The tips of the branches rustled with existence which unceasingly renewed itself and which was never born. The existing wind rested on the tree like a great bluebottle, and the tree shuddered. But the shudder was not a nascent quality, a passing from power to action; it was a thing; a shudder-thing flowed into the tree, took possession of it, shook it and suddenly abandoned it, going further on to spin about itself. All was fullness and all was active, there was no weakness in time, all, even the least perceptible stirring, was made of existence. And all these existents which bustled about this tree came from nowhere and were going nowhere. Suddenly they existed, then suddenly they existed no longer: existence is without memory; of the vanished it retains nothing—not even a memory. Existence everywhere, infinitely, in excess, for ever and everywhere; existence—which is limited only by existence. . . .

I got up and went out. Once at the gate, I turned back. Then the garden smiled at me. I leaned against the gate and watched for a long time. The smile of the trees, of the laurel, *meant* something; that was the real secret of existence. I remembered one Sunday, not more than three weeks ago, I had already detected everywhere a sort of conspiratorial air. Was it in my intention? I felt with boredom that I had no way of understanding. No way. Yet it was there, waiting, looking at one. It was there on the trunk of the chestnut tree . . . it was *the* chestnut tree. Things—you might have called them thoughts—which stopped halfway, which were forgotten, which forgot what they wanted to think and which stayed like that, hanging about with an odd little sense which was beyond them. That little sense annoyed me: I *could not* understand it, even if I could have stayed leaning against the gate for a century; I had learned all I could know about existence. I left, I went back to the hotel and I wrote.

REVIEW AND DISCUSSION QUESTIONS

1. Summarize any two or three distinct points that Roquentin seems to be making here.

2. What existentialist themes discussed in the main text can be found in this passage?

3. In what way(s) does existentialism seem well suited for a literary treatment, rather than a straightforwardly philosophical one?

■ Reading
"A Critique of Ethics and Theology"

A. J. AYER

"Critique of Ethics and Theology" (1936); from Language, Truth and Logic, *2nd edition (New York: Dover, 1952/1946/1936), Chapter VI. Reprinted with permission.*

In this excerpt Ayer critiques metaethical subjectivism and utilitarianism, and introduces his own emotivism.

What we are interested in is the possibility of reducing the whole sphere of ethical terms to non-ethical terms. We are enquiring whether statements of ethical value can be translated into statements of empirical fact.

That they can be so translated is the contention of those ethical philosophers who are commonly called subjectivists, and of those who are known as utilitarians. For the utilitarian defines the rightness of actions, and the goodness of ends, in terms of the pleasure, or happiness, or satisfaction, to which they give rise; the subjectivist, in terms of the feelings of approval which a certain person, or group of people, has towards them. Each of these types of definition makes moral judgements into a sub-class of psychological or sociological judgements; and for this reason they are very attractive to us. For, if either was correct, it would follow that ethical assertions were not generically different from the factual assertions which are ordinarily contrasted with them. . . .

Nevertheless we shall not adopt either a subjectivist or a utilitarian analysis of ethical terms. We reject the subjectivist view, that to call an action right, or a thing good, is to say that it is generally approved of, because it is not self-contradictory to assert that some actions which are generally approved of are not right, or that some things which are generally approved of are not good. And we reject the alternative subjectivist view that a man who asserts that a certain action is right, or that a certain thing is good, is saying that he himself approves of it, on the ground, that a man who confessed that he sometimes approved of what was bad or wrong would not be contradicting himself. And a similar argument is fatal to utilitarianism. We cannot agree that to call an action right is to say that of all the actions possible in the circumstances it would cause, or be likely to cause, the greatest happiness, or the greatest balance of pleasure over pain, or the greatest balance of satisfied over unsatisfied desire, because we find that it is not self-contradictory to say that it is sometimes wrong to perform the action which would actually or probably cause the greatest happiness, or the greatest balance of pleasure over pain, or of satisfied over unsatisfied desire. And since it is not self-contradictory to say that some pleasant things are not good, or that some bad things are desired, it cannot be the case that the sentence "*x* is good" is equivalent to "*x* is pleasant," or to "*x* is desired." And to every other variant of utilitarianism with which I am acquainted the same objection can be made. . . .

We begin by admitting that the fundamental ethical concepts are unanalysable, inasmuch as there is no criterion by which one can test the validity of the judgements in which they occur. So far we are in agreement with the absolutists. But, unlike the absolutists, we are able to give an explanation of this fact about ethical concepts. We say that the reason why they are unanalysable is that they are mere pseudo-concepts. The presence of an ethical symbol in a proposition adds nothing to its factual content. Thus if I say to someone, "You acted wrongly in stealing that money," I am not stating anything more than if I had simply said, "You stole that money." In adding that this action is wrong I am not making any further statement about it. I am simply evincing my moral disapproval of it. It is as if I had said, "You stole that money," in a peculiar tone of horror, or written it with the addition of some special exclamation marks. The tone, or the exclamation marks, adds nothing to the literal meaning of the sentence. It merely serves to show that the expression of it is attended by certain feelings in the speaker.

If now I generalise my previous statement and say, "Stealing money is wrong," I produce a sentence which has no factual meaning—that is, expresses no proposition which can be either true or false. It is as if I had written "Stealing money!!"—where the shape and thickness of the exclamation marks show, by a suitable convention, that a special sort of moral disapproval is the feeling which is being expressed. It is clear that there is nothing said here which can be true or false. Another man may disagree with me about the wrongness of stealing, in the sense that he may not have the same feelings about stealing as I have, and he may quarrel with me on account of my moral sentiments. But he cannot, strictly speaking, contradict me. For in saying that a certain type of action is right or wrong, I am not making any factual statement, not even a statement about my own state of mind. I am merely expressing certain moral sentiments. And the man who is ostensibly contradicting me is merely expressing his moral sentiments. So that there is plainly no sense in asking which of us is in the right. For neither of us is asserting a genuine proposition.

What we have just been saying about the symbol "wrong" applies to all normative ethical symbols. Sometimes they occur in sentences which record ordinary empirical facts besides expressing ethical feeling about those facts: sometimes they occur in sentences which simply express ethical feeling about a certain type of action, or situation, without making any statement of fact. But in every case in which one would commonly be said to be making an ethical judgement, the function of the relevant ethical word is purely "emotive." It is used to express feeling about certain objects, but not to make any assertion about them. . . .

We can now see why it is impossible to find a criterion for determining the validity of ethical judgements. It is not because they have an "absolute" validity which is mysteriously independent of ordinary sense-experience, but because they have no objective validity whatsoever. If a sentence makes no statement at all, there is obviously no sense in asking whether what it says is true or false.

REVIEW AND DISCUSSION QUESTIONS

1. What argument does Ayer make in the text against metaethical subjectivism and utilitarianism?

2. In what way(s) does emotivism differ from those two positions?

3. According to the text, in what sense are people capable of having moral disagreements?

■ Reading
"Is Atheism Irrational?"

ALVIN PLANTINGA

Interview of Alvin Plantinga by Gary Gutting; from The Stone, *in the* New York Times, *February 9, 2014.* © 2014 *the* New York Times. *All rights reserved. Used by permission and protected by the Copyright Laws of the United States. The printing, copying, redistribution, or retransmission of this Content without express written permission is prohibited.*

> In this interview, Plantinga explores the question of whether it is rational (or rationally justifiable) to be a theist. Proofs for the existence of God, the problem of evil, whether atheism needs proof (or is a rational default position), and his argument that naturalism and evolution are in tension all play a role.

Gary Gutting: A recent survey by PhilPapers, the online philosophy index, says that 62 percent of philosophers are atheists (with another 11 percent "inclined" to the view). Do you think the philosophical literature provides critiques of theism strong enough to warrant their views? Or do you think philosophers' atheism is due to factors other than rational analysis?

Alvin Plantinga: If 62 percent of philosophers are atheists, then the proportion of atheists among philosophers is much greater than (indeed, is nearly twice as great as) the proportion of atheists among academics generally. (I take atheism to be the belief that there is no such person as the God of the theistic religions.) Do philosophers know something here that these other academics don't know? What could it be? Philosophers, as opposed to other academics, are often professionally concerned with the theistic arguments—arguments for the existence of God. My guess is that a considerable majority of philosophers, both believers and unbelievers, reject these arguments as unsound.

Still, that's not nearly sufficient for atheism. In the British newspaper *The Independent*, the scientist Richard Dawkins was recently asked the following question: "If you died and arrived at the gates of heaven, what would you say to God to justify your lifelong atheism?" His response: "I'd quote Bertrand Russell: 'Not enough evidence, God! Not enough evidence!'" But lack of evidence, if indeed evidence is lacking, is no grounds for atheism. No one thinks there is good evidence for the proposition that there are an even number of stars; but also, no one thinks the right conclusion to draw is that there are an uneven number of stars. The right conclusion would instead be agnosticism.

In the same way, the failure of the theistic arguments, if indeed they do fail, might conceivably be good grounds for agnosticism, but not for atheism. Atheism, like even-star-ism, would presumably be the sort of belief you can hold rationally only if you have strong arguments or evidence.

The failure of arguments for God would be good grounds for agnosticism, but not for atheism.

G.G.: You say atheism requires evidence to support it. Many atheists deny this, saying that all they need to do is point out the lack of any good evidence for theism. You compare atheism to the denial that there are an even number of stars, which obviously would need evidence. But atheists say (using an example from Bertrand Russell) that you should rather compare atheism to the denial that there's a teapot in orbit around the sun. Why prefer your comparison to Russell's?

A.P.: Russell's idea, I take it, is we don't really have any evidence against teapotism, but we don't need any; the absence of evidence is evidence of absence, and is enough to support a-teapotism. We don't need any positive evidence against it to be justified in a-teapotism; and perhaps the same is true of theism.

I disagree: Clearly we have a great deal of evidence against teapotism. For example, as far as we know, the only way a teapot could have gotten into orbit around the sun would be if some country with sufficiently developed space-shot capabilities had shot this pot into orbit. No country with such capabilities is sufficiently frivolous to waste its resources by trying to send a teapot into orbit. Furthermore, if some country *had* done so, it would have been all over the news; we would certainly have heard about it. But we haven't. And so on. There is plenty of evidence against teapotism. So if, à la Russell, theism is like teapotism, the atheist, to be justified, would (like the a-teapotist) have to have powerful evidence against theism.

G.G.: But isn't there also plenty of evidence against theism—above all, the amount of evil in a world allegedly made by an all-good, all-powerful God?

A.P.: The so-called "problem of evil" would presumably be the strongest (and maybe the only) evidence against theism. It does indeed have some strength; it makes sense to think that the probability of theism, given the existence of all the suffering and evil our world contains, is fairly low. But of course there are also arguments *for* theism. Indeed, there are at least a couple of dozen good theistic arguments. So the atheist would have to try to synthesize and balance the probabilities. This isn't at all easy to do, but it's pretty obvious that the result wouldn't anywhere nearly support straight-out atheism as opposed to agnosticism.

G.G.: But when you say "good theistic arguments," you don't mean arguments that are decisive—for example, good enough to convince any rational person who understands them.

A.P.: I should make clear first that I don't think arguments are needed for rational belief in God. In this regard belief in God is like belief in other minds, or belief in the past. Belief in God is grounded in experience, or in the *sensus divinitatis*, John Calvin's term for an inborn inclination to form beliefs about God in a wide variety of circumstances.

Nevertheless, I think there are a large number—maybe a couple of dozen—of pretty good theistic arguments. None is conclusive, but each, or at any rate the whole bunch taken together, is about as strong as philosophical arguments ordinarily get.

G.G.: Could you give an example of such an argument?

A.P.: One presently rather popular argument: fine-tuning. Scientists tell us that there are many properties our universe displays such that if they were even slightly different from what they are in fact, life, or at least our kind of life, would not be possible. The universe seems to be fine-tuned for life. For example, if the force of the Big Bang had been different by one part in 10 to the 60th, life of our sort would not have been possible. The same goes for the ratio of the gravitational force to the force driving the expansion of the universe: If it had been even slightly different, our kind of life would not have been possible. In fact the universe seems to be fine-tuned, not just for life, but for intelligent life. This fine-tuning is vastly more likely given theism than given atheism.

G.G.: But even if this fine-tuning argument (or some similar argument) convinces someone that God exists, doesn't it fall far short of what at least Christian theism asserts, namely the existence of an all-perfect God? Since the world isn't perfect, why would we need a perfect being to explain the world or any feature of it?

A.P.: I suppose your thinking is that it is suffering and sin that make this world less than perfect. But then your question makes sense only if the best possible worlds contain no sin or suffering. And is that true? Maybe the best worlds contain free creatures some of whom sometimes do what is wrong. Indeed, maybe the best worlds contain a scenario very like the Christian story.

Think about it: The first being of the universe, perfect in goodness, power and knowledge, creates free creatures. These free creatures turn their backs on him, rebel against him and get involved in sin and evil. Rather than treat them as some ancient potentate might—e.g., having them boiled in oil—God responds by sending his son into the world to suffer and die so that human beings might once more be in a right relationship to God. God himself undergoes the enormous suffering involved in seeing his son mocked, ridiculed, beaten and crucified. And all this for the sake of these sinful creatures.

I'd say a world in which this story is true would be a truly magnificent possible world. It would be so good that no world could be appreciably better. But then the best worlds contain sin and suffering.

G.G.: O.K., but in any case, isn't the theist on thin ice in suggesting the need for God as an explanation of the universe? There's always the possibility that we'll find a scientific account that explains what we claimed only God could explain. After all, that's what happened when Darwin developed his theory of evolution. In fact, isn't a major support for atheism the very fact that we no longer need God to explain the world?

A.P.: Some atheists seem to think that a sufficient reason for atheism is the fact (as they say) that we no longer need God to explain natural phenomena—lightning and thunder for example. We now have science.

As a justification of atheism, this is pretty lame. We no longer need the moon to explain or account for lunacy; it hardly follows that belief in the nonexistence of the moon (a-moonism?) is justified. A-moonism on this ground would be sensible only if the sole ground for belief in the existence of the moon was its explanatory power with respect to lunacy. (And even so, the justified attitude would be agnosticism with respect to the moon, not a-moonism.) The same thing goes with belief in God: Atheism on this sort of basis would be justified only if the explanatory power of theism were the only reason for belief in God. And even then, agnosticism would be the justified attitude, not atheism.

G.G.: So, what are the further grounds for believing in God, the reasons that make atheism unjustified?

A.P.: The most important ground of belief is probably not philosophical argument but religious experience. Many people of very many different cultures have thought themselves in experiential touch with a being worthy of worship. They believe that there is such a person, but not because of the explanatory prowess of such belief. Or maybe there is something like Calvin's *sensus divinitatis*. Indeed, if theism is true, then very likely there *is* something like the *sensus divinitatis*. So claiming that the only sensible ground for belief in God is the explanatory quality of such belief is substantially equivalent to assuming atheism.

G.G.: If, then, there isn't evidence to support atheism, why do you think so many philosophers—presumably highly rational people—are atheists?

A.P.: I'm not a psychologist, so I don't have any special knowledge here. Still, there are some possible explanations. Thomas Nagel, a terrific philosopher and an unusually perceptive atheist, says he simply doesn't *want* there to be any such person as God. And it isn't hard to see why. For one thing, there would be what some would think was an intolerable invasion of privacy: God would know my every thought long before I thought it. For another, my actions and even my thoughts would be a constant subject of judgment and evaluation.

Basically, these come down to the serious limitation of human autonomy posed by theism. This desire for autonomy can reach very substantial proportions, as with the German philosopher Heidegger, who, according to Richard Rorty, felt guilty for living in a universe he had not himself created. Now there's a tender conscience! But even a less monumental desire for autonomy can perhaps also motivate atheism.

G.G.: Especially among today's atheists, materialism seems to be a primary motive. They think there's nothing beyond the material entities open to scientific inquiry, so there there's no place for immaterial beings such as God.

A.P.: Well, if there are only material entities, then atheism certainly follows. But there is a really serious problem for materialism: It can't be sensibly believed, at least if, like most materialists, you also believe that humans are the product of evolution.

G.G.: Why is that?

A.P.: I can't give a complete statement of the argument here—for that see Chapter 10 of *Where the Conflict Really Lies.* But, roughly, here's why. First, if materialism is true, human beings, naturally enough, are material objects. Now what, from this point of view, would a *belief* be? My belief that Marcel Proust is more subtle that Louis L'Amour, for example? Presumably this belief would have to be a material structure in my brain, say a collection of neurons that sends electrical impulses to other such structures as well as to nerves and muscles, and receives electrical impulses from other structures.

But in addition to such neurophysiological properties, this structure, if it is a belief, would also have to have a *content*: It would have, say, to be the belief that *Proust is more subtle than L'Amour.*

G.G.: So is your suggestion that a neurophysiological structure can't be a belief? That a belief has to be somehow immaterial?

A.P.: That may be, but it's not my point here. I'm interested in the fact that beliefs cause (or at least partly cause) actions. For example, my belief that there is a beer in the fridge (together with my desire to have a beer) can cause me to heave myself out of my comfortable armchair and lumber over to the fridge.

But here's the important point: It's by virtue of its material, neurophysiological properties that a belief causes the action. It's in virtue of those electrical signals sent via efferent nerves to the relevant muscles, that the belief about the beer in the fridge causes me to go to the fridge. It is *not* by virtue of the content (*there is a beer in the fridge*) the belief has.

G.G.: Why do you say that?

A.P.: Because if this belief—this structure—had a totally different content (even, say, if it was a belief that *there is no beer in the fridge*) but had the same neurophysiological properties, it would still have caused that same action of going to the fridge. This means that the content of the belief isn't a cause of the behavior. As far as causing the behavior goes, the content of the belief doesn't matter.

G.G.: That does seem to be a hard conclusion to accept. But won't evolution get the materialist out of this difficulty? For our species to have survived, presumably many, if not most, of our beliefs must be true—otherwise, we wouldn't be functional in a dangerous world.

A.P.: Evolution will have resulted in our having beliefs that are adaptive; that is, beliefs that cause adaptive actions. But as we've seen, if materialism is true, the belief does not cause the adaptive action by way of its content: It causes that action by way of its neurophysiological properties. Hence it doesn't matter what the content of the belief is, and it doesn't matter whether that content is true or false. All that's required is that the belief have the right neurophysiological properties. If it's also true, that's fine; but if false, that's equally fine.

Evolution will select for belief-producing processes that produce beliefs with adaptive neurophysiological properties, but not for belief-producing processes that produce true beliefs. Given materialism and evolution, any particular belief is as likely to be false as true.

G.G.: So your claim is that if materialism is true, evolution doesn't lead to most of our beliefs being true.

A.P.: Right. In fact, given materialism and evolution, it follows that our belief-producing faculties are not reliable.

Here's why. If a belief is as likely to be false as to be true, we'd have to say the probability that any particular belief is true is about 50 percent. Now suppose we had a total of 100 independent beliefs (of course, we have many more). Remember that the probability that all of a group of beliefs are true is the multiplication of all their individual probabilities. Even if we set a fairly low bar for reliability—say, that at least two-thirds (67 percent) of our beliefs are true—our overall reliability, given materialism and evolution, is exceedingly low: something like .0004. So if you accept both materialism and evolution, you have good reason to believe that your belief-producing faculties are not reliable.

But to believe that is to fall into a total skepticism, which leaves you with no reason to accept any of your beliefs (including your beliefs in materialism and evolution!). The only sensible course is to give up the claim leading to this conclusion: that both materialism and evolution are true. Maybe you can hold one or the other, but not both.

So if you're an atheist simply because you accept materialism, maintaining your atheism means you have to give up your belief that evolution is true. Another way to put it: The belief that both materialism and evolution are true is self-refuting. It shoots itself in the foot. Therefore it can't rationally be held.

REVIEW AND DISCUSSION QUESTIONS

1. What point is Plantinga making when he talks about whether there are an even number of stars? In your opinion, are there any important differences between accepting "even-star-ism" and atheism?

2. What point is Plantinga making when he brings up "a-moonism"? In your opinion, are there any important differences between accepting "a-moonism" and atheism?

3. Are there any stronger grounds for atheism, in your opinion, than Plantinga acknowledges?

■ Reading
"What Mary Didn't Know"

F R A N K   J A C K S O N

From The Journal of Philosophy, *Vol. 83, No. 5 (May, 1986), pp. 291–95. Reprinted with permission.*

In this excerpt Jackson presents the knowledge argument against physicalism.

Mary is confined to a black-and-white room, is educated through black-and-white books and through lectures relayed on black-and-white television. In this way she learns everything there is to know about the physical nature of the world. She knows all the physical facts about us and our environment, in a wide sense of 'physical' which includes everything in completed physics, chemistry, and neurophysiology, and all there is to know about the causal and relational facts consequent upon all this, including of course functional roles. If physicalism is true, she knows all there is to know. For to suppose otherwise is to suppose that there is more to know than every physical fact, and that is just what physicalism denies.

Physicalism is not the noncontroversial thesis that the actual world is largely physical, but the challenging thesis that it is entirely physical. This is why physicalists must hold that complete physical knowledge is complete knowledge simpliciter. For suppose it is not complete: then our world must differ from a world, W(P), for which it is complete, and the difference must be in nonphysical facts; for our world and W(P) agree in all matters physical. Hence, physicalism would be false at our world [though contingently so, for it would be true at W(P)].

It seems, however, that Mary does not know all there is to know. For when she is let out of the black-and-white room or given a color television, she will learn what it is like to see something red, say. This is rightly described as *learning*—she will not say "ho, hum." Hence, physicalism is false. This is the knowledge argument against physicalism in one of its manifestations. This note is a reply to three objections to it mounted by Paul M. Churchland.

I. THREE CLARIFICATIONS

The knowledge argument does not rest on the dubious claim that logically you cannot imagine what sensing red is like unless you have sensed red. Powers of imagination are not to the point. The contention about Mary is not that, despite her fantastic grasp of neurophysiology and everything else physical, she *could not imagine* what it is like to sense red; it is that, as a matter of fact, she *would not know*. But if physicalism is true, she would know; and no great powers of imagination would be called for. Imagination is a faculty that those who *lack* knowledge need to fall back on.

Secondly, the intensionality of knowledge is not to the point. The argument does not rest on assuming falsely that, if S knows that *a* is F and if *a* = *b*, then S knows that *b* is F. It is concerned with the nature of Mary's total body of knowledge before she is released: is it complete, or do some facts escape it? What is to the point is that S may know that *a* is F and *know* that *a* = *b*, yet arguably not know that *b* is F, by virtue of not being sufficiently logically alert to follow the consequences through. If Mary's lack of knowledge were at all like this, there would be no threat to physicalism in it. But it is very hard to believe that her lack of knowledge could be remedied merely by her explicitly following through enough logical consequences of her vast physical knowledge. Endowing her with great logical acumen and persistence is not in itself enough to fill in the gaps in her knowledge. On being let out, she will not say "I could have worked all this out before by making some more purely logical inferences."

Thirdly, the knowledge Mary lacked which is of particular point for the knowledge argument against physicalism is *knowledge about the experiences of others*, not about her own. When she is let out, she has new experiences, color experiences she has never had before. It is not, therefore, an objection to physicalism that she learns *something* on being let out. Before she was let out, she could not have known facts about her experience of red, for there were no such facts to know. That physicalist and nonphysicalist alike can agree on. After she is let out, things change; and physicalism can happily admit that she learns this; after all, some physical things will change, for instance, her brain states and their functional roles. The trouble for physicalism is that, after Mary sees her first ripe tomato, she will realize how impoverished her conception of the mental life of *others* has been *all along*. She will realize that there was, all the time she was carrying out her laborious investigations into the neurophysiologies of others and into the functional roles of their internal states, something about these people she was quite unaware of. All along their experiences (or many of them, those got from tomatoes, the sky, . . .) had a feature conspicuous to them but until now hidden from her (in fact, not in logic). But she knew all the physical facts about them all along; hence, what she did not know until her release is not a physical fact about their experiences. But it is a fact about them. That is the trouble for physicalism.

II. CHURCHLAND'S THREE OBJECTIONS

(i) Churchland's first objection is that the knowledge argument contains a defect that "is simplicity itself" (23). The argument equivocates on the sense of 'knows about'. How so? Churchland suggests that the following is "a conveniently tightened version" of the knowledge argument:

(1) Mary knows everything there is to know about brain states and their properties.
(2) It is not the case that Mary knows everything there is to know about sensations and their properties.
Therefore, by Leibniz's law,
(3) Sensations and their properties ≠ brain states and their properties (23).

Churchland observes, plausibly enough, that the type or kind of knowledge involved in premise 1 is distinct from the kind of knowledge involved in premise 2. We might follow his lead and tag the first 'knowledge by description', and the second 'knowledge by acquaintance'; but, whatever the tags, he is right that the displayed argument involves a highly dubious use of Leibniz's law.

My reply is that the displayed argument may be convenient, but it is not accurate. It is not the knowledge argument. Take, for instance, premise 1. The whole thrust of the knowledge argument is that Mary (before her release) does *not* know everything there is to know about brain states and their properties, because she does not know about certain qualia associated with them. What is complete, according to the argument, is her knowledge of matters physical. A convenient and accurate way of displaying the argument is:

(1)' Mary (before her release) knows everything physical there is to know about other people.

(2)' Mary (before her release) does not know everything there is to know about other people (because she learns something about them on her release).

Therefore,

(3)' There are truths about other people (and herself) which escape the physicalist story.

What is immediately to the point is not the kind, manner, or type of knowledge Mary has, but *what* she knows. What she knows beforehand is ex hypothesi everything physical there is to know, but is it everything there is to know? That is the crucial question.

There is, though, a relevant challenge involving questions about kinds of knowledge. It concerns the *support* for premise 2'. The case for premise 2' is that Mary learns something on her release, she acquires knowledge, and that entails that her knowledge beforehand (*what* she knew, never mind whether by description, acquaintance, or whatever) was incomplete. The challenge, mounted by David Lewis and Laurence Nemirow, is that on her release Mary does not learn something or acquire knowledge in the relevant sense. What Mary acquires when she is released is a certain representational or imaginative ability; it is knowledge how rather than knowledge that. Hence, a physicalist can admit that Mary acquires something very significant of a knowledge kind—which can hardly be denied—without admitting that this shows that her earlier factual knowledge is defective. She knew all *that* there was to know about the experiences of others beforehand, but lacked an ability until after her release.

Now it is certainly true that Mary will acquire abilities of various kinds after her release. She will, for instance, be able to imagine what seeing red is like, be able to remember what it is like, and be able to understand why her friends regarded her as so deprived (something which, until her release, had always mystified her). But is it plausible that that is *all* she will acquire? Suppose she received a lecture on skepticism about other minds while she was incarcerated. On her release she sees a ripe tomato in normal conditions, and so has a sensation of red. Her first reaction is to say that she now knows more about the kind of experiences others have when looking at ripe tomatoes. She then remembers the lecture and starts to worry. Does she really know more about what their experiences are like, or is she indulging in a wild generalization from one case? In the end she decides she does know, and that skepticism is mistaken (even if, like so many of us, she is not sure how to demonstrate its errors). What was she to-ing and fro-ing about—her abilities? Surely not; her representational abilities were a known constant throughout. What else then was she agonizing about than whether or not she had gained factual knowledge of others? There would be nothing to agonize about if ability was *all* she acquired on her release.

I grant that I have no *proof* that Mary acquires on her release, as well as abilities, factual knowledge about the experiences of others—and not just because I have no disproof of skepticism. My claim is that the knowledge argument is a valid argument from highly plausible, though admittedly not demonstrable, premises to the conclusion that physicalism is false. And that, after all, is about as good an objection as one could expect in this area of philosophy.

REVIEW AND DISCUSSION QUESTIONS

    1. In what way(s) is Jackson's argument similar to Thomas Nagel's argument in "What Is It Like to Be a Bat?"

    2. Do you share Jackson's intuition that Mary, on her release, will learn something new? If not, why not? If so, can you defend it further?

Contemporary Moral Problems and Peter Singer

THE NEWSPAPER ARTICLE was titled "Doctor's Choice Causes Furor."[1] Its subtitle revealed why: "Life or Death for Brain-Damaged Infant?" The story managed to touch on many difficult ethical dilemmas.

The baby was born with serious birth defects and, after five agonizing days, the doctor decided the best thing to do was to let him die "mercifully."

Last Friday, after determining the infant was near death because of . . . a seriously defective brain, the doctor withdrew food from the baby.

Instead of following the standard practice of writing feeding orders the physician wrote nothing—in effect telling the staff the baby would be allowed to die.

The baby was not fed Saturday or Sunday but on Monday another physician in the hospital countermanded the orders and once more placed the infant on food.

Today the baby is still alive and apparently in no imminent danger of dying. He is taking some food by mouth but it is too early to tell whether he is growing. He has a good heart, lungs, and kidneys—the essentials of physical life.

It is not always easy to determine how near to death anyone may be. On Friday one doctor thought the baby was at death's doorstep; by Monday the baby seemed to be doing better.

The case has become a cause célèbre among the staff at the hospital. . . . Some of the nursing staff believe the decision not to feed the baby was tantamount to euthanasia. Some call it murder. Others, perhaps the majority, are in total agreement with the initial decision.

A rabbi who has learned of the case from a distraught nurse is shocked that physicians take it upon themselves to make decisions that he believes to be moral, not medical.

"The medical profession cannot presume to make moral judgments with impunity," the rabbi says. "It may be that the decision not to feed the baby was morally correct, but I don't think any physician has the right to make such a decision exclusively."

Whose decision should this be? Doctors' opinions are clearly relevant, since one must know all the medical facts, as far as they are clear. But the decision whether to feed the baby is an ethical one, and doctors don't necessarily have any more moral expertise than anyone else.

So who else should be involved? Parents? Grandparents? Other relatives? Religious institutions? Society in general? The government in particular?

> A cross-section of medical school pediatricians queried by the *Times*—at least those willing to comment on such a sensitive issue—said they would never under any circumstances fail to feed a baby.

This sounds as if they would never fail to feed an infant. Would (or should) they have the same view if the patient were a decrepit old man? Or old woman? Or poor person, supported by taxpayer-funded welfare, Medicaid? Or mentally deficient? Or member of a disadvantaged minority? Or a criminal? Should such questions be decided on the basis of the pity that is aroused? (We may feel more emotional about babies, but is that a legitimate ground for distinguishing between babies and other individuals?)

> It is not rare for doctors in a large population area . . . to be confronted with a decision such as the one this physician was forced to make. Not all of them—possibly not even the majority—would have made an identical decision. But this case and the decision reached could have occurred in many hospitals.
>
> Usually such cases involve persons with terminal diseases or head injuries—whether the machines and drugs being used to keep them alive should be withdrawn, allowing the patient to die quietly.
>
> Sometimes, as in this case, the patient is a baby born with severe impairments. Often nature takes care of things by allowing the infant to die, no matter what the doctors may try.
>
> In other cases, the defects may be such that the child will live for years, but with physical and mental defects that place him at an enormous disadvantage.
>
> What should the doctor—and the parents if they are around—do?

So far the question is whether it's worth doing something relatively minimal (feed the baby) to keep it alive. But we might also ask precisely how *much* we should invest in keeping any such baby alive. Should we do "everything possible," making use of complicated surgeries, expensive medicines, round-the-clock care? Should we fly the baby across the country to other medical centers that may have expertise? If so, who should pay for this? Or at some point do we decide it's not worth investing so much in attempting to save this particular baby? (At what point is that?) And how might our answers differ (again) as we change the patient under discussion? How much should be invested to save or prolong the life of the adult terminally ill, or severely ill, or the elderly?

These are not merely theoretical questions, but real, concrete, practical ones. People will live or die depending on how you answer them.

To return to the baby:

> The baby's doctor said Thursday that epileptic seizures which a week ago were occurring frequently have been controlled with drugs and that dosage is being diminished. He admits that he miscalculated in determining that death was imminent when he withdrew food and says he agrees that the baby should be fed.
>
> The doctor now recognizes he had "miscalculated." . . . He [also] said he cannot say with 100% certainty that the baby is mentally retarded, but tests indicate his brain is

structurally abnormal. The baby is believed to be blind. He has a double cleft palate and lip and his arms are tiny stubs.

An extremely important point, as noted above: we often must decide under conditions of uncertainty. Mistakes can be made about whether a person is likely to die shortly; it can be unclear whether the child is mentally deficient, even whether it is blind. Cases dot the literature of individuals who were removed from life-support and expected to die, who then lived a long time afterward; and of individuals in extended vegetative states who unexpectedly woke up later on. Some may use this uncertainty, and the possibility of error, to argue we have no right "to play God," and we should oppose the action taken by this physician under any circumstances. But then again, isn't it "playing God" to intervene in the first place? And shouldn't we do what it's "most reasonable" to do, even recognizing our fallibility? If we judge it highly or extremely likely that the child is mentally deficient, even if less than perfectly certain, isn't that relevant?

Then there may be other facts to consider, besides the immediate medical condition of the baby.

The infant's mother is unwed. She did not share directly in the decision not to feed her baby. However, when the baby was admitted to the hospital, she told the doctor she wouldn't care if she did not see the baby again.

"Some doctors believe that a 100% effort must be made on all babies to sustain life. To me this is reasonable, but it's a copout. It doesn't take into consideration the circumstances that surround a baby's life," the doctor said in an interview.

"The mother has had a very tough time in life. She's unwed. She has three children at home. She said, 'How can I help this baby through a tough life with all these defects laid on him?'"

"If she had showed some concern, some willingness to care for the baby, my decision would have been influenced."

The doctor's argument is stronger here and his action, perhaps, more understandable, but should his decision have been merely "influenced" had the mother shown more concern? Or should it have proven decisive in keeping the baby alive? Should the mother's rights in such a case be absolute? And if not, why not? More generally (and perhaps uncomfortably), should society have a stake in the decision here—if a child growing up in such circumstances were more likely to contribute negatively to society, or to require society's support?

> In quixotically trying to conquer death doctors all too frequently do no good for their patients' "ease" but at the same time they do harm instead by prolonging and even magnifying patients' dis-ease.
>
> —**Jack Kevorkian**, *Prescription Medicide: The Goodness of Planned Death* (1991)

The physician said he does not think of his action as **euthanasia**, a term which comes from the Greek for "easy death" and refers generally to the practice of intentionally ending a life in order to ease suffering and pain.

I had a picture of euthanasia as doing something to kill someone—an overt action. For example, giving an overdose of drugs to a terminal cancer patient who is in deep pain.

In that case the doctor is doing an action. I was doing an inaction—I was refraining from writing feeding orders. I was saying I am not going to contribute to continuing this particular problem.

On the other hand, suppose I had a baby who was not responding to treatment for hyaline membrane disease, a potentially lethal lung disorder, and who was having seizures and heart arrests. If someone told me to turn off the respirator, I would have a hard time doing that.

Is there a morally significant difference between actively doing something to make someone die versus refraining from doing something in order to allow the person to die? Between *killing* versus *letting die*? Holding someone's head under the bathtub water seems heinous to us ("murder"), but is it any morally different from passively watching someone drown in the bathtub without lifting a finger to help? You may not have directly caused the drowning here, but aren't you equally morally responsible for it?

In some cases, some feel that the "not acting" is actually morally worse than the "acting":

Of four pediatricians consulted by the *Times*, all indicated a strong aversion to withholding food from defective babies.

But one of them—a woman physician—who was the most adamant against that course of action said that she would have far less inhibition against pulling the plug on a respirator if she thought the case was hopeless—the exact opposite of the situation with the physician in this story.

So this woman believed that actively pulling the plug in certain cases is morally better than passively refraining from feeding. Is she correct? Which cases would merit one treatment, which the other? Or is there no real difference between active/passive, so all cases should be treated the same way? Again, at what point (if any) should we just "let nature take its course"? (And is the fact that this person is a woman relevant? Might men and women have different moral intuitions in cases like these, or in general? And if so, what do we do with that information?)

It is expected that the baby, whose care is being paid by the Medicaid program, soon will be moved from the hospital because he is not sick enough to stay and the cost . . . is prohibitive.

He probably will be transferred to a nursing home. What happens then will involve other difficult medical and possibly moral decisions.

Again, we may think of medical decisions as personal, but at what point should society have a say? In fact there is little any of us do that impacts ourselves alone. Your behavior impacts your family, your friends, your colleagues, your acquaintances, and plenty of strangers. If you die prematurely—from tobacco-caused cancer, from a helmet-less or seatbelt-less vehicle crash, from an accident in some "extreme sport"—the financial and emotional impact on others often is substantial. If the baby above were your baby, your decisions impact not only the child but yourself, his siblings and extended family, all the people who will be involved in his care, all the people who will have to accommodate his needs, all the people who will pay for his care. If what you do impacts others, should they have some say in what you do?

There are a lot of difficult ethical questions here. All these questions arise in just this one domain of contemporary life, health, and medicine, and even in this domain we've only sketched a small percentage of the questions.

Before birth, there are questions about the permissibility of assisted reproduction, of birth control, cloning, genetic engineering. Should parents be allowed to choose the sex of their child? To manipulate their skin color? To conceive a child in order to harvest one of its kidneys to save an older sibling? Should it ever be permissible to abort a fetus? If so, what are the allowable circumstances? Conceived via rape, incest? Severe birth defects in the fetus? Parents' resources and preferences?

After birth, there are questions such as these. What do we do with the severely brain-damaged and disabled? How much should we invest in attempting to save lives? Does that vary for children, adults, seniors? Should people have the right to end their lives, and if so, under what circumstances? How should we allocate society's resources in general? Should we mandate universal health insurance? Should we subsidize it? Should we turn people away from emergency rooms if they cannot pay? Should alcoholics have as much right to receive a liver transplant as a non-alcoholic? Should we require people to donate their organs upon death?

And the health and medicine domain is just one of so many contemporary domains with pressing ethical questions. These days there are major debates about sexuality and gender, about the permissibility of gay marriage, about discrimination against those with non-traditional gender identities. There are questions about the permissibility of the death penalty, either in principle or in practice, including the different methods used to inflict the punishment. Many of these are part of a larger domain about the relative weight of privacy and individual rights versus society's interests. Should the government be permitted to regulate guns, or drugs, or sex, or business in general? Should the government play an active role in regulating and manipulating racial matters? In an era of security threats, should the government be permitted to restrict individual liberties, freedom of movement, freedom of communication and assembly? To search your person, monitor your communications, for the "public good"?

One particularly rapidly growing domain is that known as *environmental ethics.* What obligations do we have to protect the environment, if any? What ought we to do about climate change, global warming? How are our decisions about these affected by the less-than-perfect certainty we have about our own contributions to the problem? Is it morally important to preserve species, ecosystems, just for their own sake? What if doing so harms the economic interests of various people? Or are we permitted to use the non-human planet for our own purposes? Even if the latter, what (if anything) do we owe to our children, our grandchildren, our unborn future descendants? These questions are also connected to those of global justice. Is it acceptable that some countries are rich, and others poor? Do Western citizens exploit non-Western citizens in various ways?

We live in a complicated world, with complicated questions—but questions that cannot be ignored, because they are real, concrete, and pressing. In fact you can't *avoid* answering them, because every behavioral choice, every policy decision, amounts to an answer. Your community either allows capital punishment, or doesn't; either allows gay marriage, or doesn't; either permits government regulation or intrusion, or doesn't. Since whatever you do amounts to answering the question, you may as well give the question some thought, and try to work up a good answer, a coherent answer, not to mention an answer that truly reflects your values.

So *how* should we go about answering these questions? Not merely for ourselves, but for society in general?

As we saw in chapter 6, ethical inquiry has generally taken three different directions: meta-ethics, ethical theory, and practical or applied ethics. But while an inquiry can emphasize one over the other, they are not entirely separable from each other. Metaethics informs your ethical theory: if (for example) you think of morality as objective you will prefer certain kinds of ethical theories over others. And ethical theory is essential for practical ethics as well. Without some ethical theory your approach to practical ethics risks being random, inconsistent, based on intuitions that vary from case to case. Moreover, you need some foundation in place to be able to argue, reasonably, about practical ethics. Your inquiry will not be productive if you simply say, "capital punishment is wrong, always," without being able to say *why* it is wrong, whether it's wrong in principle or merely in practice, and how your views on this issue are related to your views on (say) justice and criminal law in general. Ethical theory provides that foundation, helps you unify your views, and makes them consistent and coherent.

Our limited space precludes our exploring all the many complicated questions above. Instead we shall simply examine how one might go about addressing some practical ethics questions with an ethical theory in place, leaving the necessary longer discussions for you to develop on your own or in conversation with others. With that objective in mind we can hardly do better than to adopt a simple version of utilitarianism (despite its imperfections, from chapter 6) and see how it might play out on several important issues.

Nor can we do better than focus on a single contemporary thinker whose views are both controversial and deeply influenced by utilitarianism.

PETER SINGER (B. 1946)

Born in Melbourne, Australia, Singer studied philosophy at university but found metaphysics dry compared to ethics and political philosophy. He did a doctoral thesis at Oxford on civil disobedience just as the war in Vietnam and the American civil rights movement were at their heights, realizing that his intellectual interests were more in practical matters than theoretical. In 1972 he published his first major paper, "Famine, Affluence, and Morality," which is now assigned in ethics courses around the world, and in 1975 he published *Animal Liberation,* now a canonical book in animal rights theory. He taught for over two decades at Monash University, where he founded its Centre for Human Bioethics, then in 1999 joined Princeton University's University Center for Human Values. In 2005 he began splitting his time between Princeton and the University of Melbourne's Centre for Applied Philosophy and Public Ethics. Along the way he has published many books and articles, spoken around the globe, and won many distinctions and awards, including being named, in 2012, a Companion of the Order of Australia for his service to philosophy and bioethics. Not bad for someone described by the *New Yorker* in 1999 as "The Dangerous Philosopher" and perhaps "the most controversial philosopher alive," who even attracted death threats on his appointment to Princeton.

So what is it, exactly, that garners both awards and death threats?

It starts modestly enough, in his fundamentally utilitarian approach to ethics. Ethical principles, in Singer's view, are not absolute truths, not laws imposed from heaven, but come from ourselves, from our being conscious, reasoning beings. "We are free to choose what we are to be," he writes, "because we have no essential nature, that is, no given purpose outside ourselves. . . . [W]e simply exist, and the rest is up to us."[2] Since ethical principles, or values, are not "out there," they come from within is, and all that is valuable is what *we* value: "If there were no beings with desires or preferences of any kind, nothing would be of value and ethics would lack all content."[3] Actions themselves have no intrinsic value, but may only be evaluated in terms of their impact on the parties affected, insofar as they are capable of having interests at all—which they are insofar as they are conscious, capable of experiencing pleasure and pain, or happiness and unhappiness, and/or having preferences. Morally good actions will be those that maximize pleasure and happiness, and/or maximize the satisfaction of preferences:

> I must, if I am thinking ethically, imagine myself in the situation of all those affected by my action (with the preferences that they have). I must consider the interests of my enemies as well as my friends, and of strangers as well as family. Only if, after taking fully into account the interests and preferences of all these people, I still think the action is better than any alternative open to me, can I genuinely say that I ought to do it. At the same time I must not ignore the long-term effects of fostering family ties, of establishing and promoting reciprocal relationships, and of allowing wrongdoers to benefit from their wrong doing. (*How Are We to Live?*, 206)

PETER SINGER

That is the basic utilitarian perspective that leads to all the trouble.

"All Animals Are Equal" (1974)[4]

One afternoon in 1970 the young Peter Singer was invited to lunch, at Oxford, by a fellow graduate student. Singer heard his colleague ask whether the spaghetti sauce contained meat, and then order a meatless salad instead. He asked his colleague why he had avoided meat, and the conversation that followed, Singer says, changed his life. The essay "All Animals Are Equal," appearing the year before his book *Animal Liberation*, grew from that event.[5]

"I am urging," Singer proclaims in that essay, "that we extend to other species the basic principle of equality that most of us recognize should be extended to all members of our own species." To put that simply, we must give equal moral weight to all beings affected by our actions, including non-human animals (henceforth just "animals"). Animals, in short, are our moral equals. Those who reject extending equality to other species, which he thinks includes most human beings, ultimately (if unwittingly) endorse **speciesism**, that is, a prejudice or bias in favor of the interests of members of their own

> Lisa: "Do we have any food that wasn't brutally slaughtered?"
> Homer: "Well, I think the veal died of loneliness."
>
> **—The Simpsons** (television show)

species over the interests of members of other species. (Similarly, a racist is one who has a prejudice or bias in favor of the interests of members of his or her own race over those of others.)

The Principle of Equality

Now there are obviously many important factual differences between human beings and animals. But the **principle of equality**, Singer explains, is not the claim that different individuals or species are equal in the sense of being the same, any more than the claim that men and women are equal amounts to the claim that men and women are the same. (There are many biological and other sorts of differences between the sexes.) It is, rather, the claim that we should give *equal consideration* to the diverse interests of different individuals and species.

Indeed we must avoid basing our moral claims (such as that we should give equal consideration) on any sort of factual equalities. To see why, Singer explores how the principle of equality works against racism and sexism. Like it or not, he notes, human beings come in different shapes and sizes, with "differing moral capacities, differing intellectual abilities, differing amounts of benevolent feeling and sensitivity to the needs of others." If justifying the claim that we should treat all people with equal consideration required their in fact "being the same," then the racist or the sexist might end up being justified in *not* treating others with equal consideration. For suppose it were to turn out, empirically, that people of one race were on average more intelligent than people of another, or that people of one sex were on average more governed by emotions rather than reason. The racist would then have ready justification in the first case for privileging the more intelligent race, and the sexist (perhaps) for privileging one of the sexes. For those who are *opposed* to racism and sexism, Singer writes, it is therefore dangerous to base their cases on the unforeseeable outcome of complicated empirical questions that are still far from being settled.

Instead we should recognize that the principle of equality is a *moral* ideal, not depending on factual features such as intelligence, moral capacity, physical strength, and so on. Individuals may differ dramatically in those features without providing any justification for treating the interests of some differently from the interests of others. Morally speaking, more intelligent people matter no differently than less intelligent people, stronger no differently than weaker, one skin color no differently than another, and so on. Our moral concern for others "ought not to depend on what they are like, or what abilities they possess. . . . It is on this basis that the case against racism and the case against sexism must both ultimately rest."

The Principle of Equality and Speciesism

But now if this is how the principle of equality rejects racism and sexism, it must also reject speciesism. To see this, we must ask more carefully on what basis the principle of equality rests. On what basis, in other words, does any being have the right to equal consideration of its interests?

To answer this question Singer quotes a famous passage from utilitarian Jeremy Bentham (recall chapter 6):

> The day may come when the rest of the animal creation may acquire those rights which never could have been witholden from them but by the hand of tyranny. The French have already discovered that the blackness of the skin is no reason why a human being should be abandoned without redress to the caprice of a tormentor. It may one day come to be recognized that the number of the legs, the villosity of the skin . . . are reasons equally

insufficient for abandoning a sensitive being to the same fate. What else is it that should trace the insuperable line? Is it the faculty of reason, or perhaps the faculty of discourse? But a full-grown horse or dog is beyond comparison a more rational, as well as a more conversable animal, than an infant of a day, or a week, or even a month, old. But suppose they were otherwise, what would it avail? The question is not, Can they reason? nor, Can they *talk?* But, *Can they suffer?* (*The Principles of Morals and Legislation* Ch. 17 [1789])

The ability to suffer and to enjoy things, Singer elaborates, is a prerequisite for having any interests at all. It doesn't matter what happens to a stone, or inanimate matter, since they lack sentience. But if a being is capable of experiencing, then that experience must be taken into moral consideration. Since a mouse can suffer, for example, it has an interest in not being tormented. To mark the boundary between "those whose interests matter" and "those whose interests don't" by features like intelligence or strength is to mark it in an arbitrary way. You might as well mark it by skin color, as the racist does. But marking it between those who can experience pain and pleasure, and those who can't, is to mark it in just the right place.

If the racist violates the principle of equality by giving greater weight to the interests of his own race, then, so does the speciesist when he gives greater weight to the interests of human beings over those of animals.

How We Are Speciesists

Various human practices, Singer explains, illustrate how broadly we are speciesists. (Though he is writing in 1974, much of what he says remains true.)

First and foremost, we *eat* other species. In doing so we "regard their life and well-being as subordinate to our taste for a particular kind of dish," and thus use them purely as means to our own ends. No good case can be made for the necessity of eating animals, since there are many other sources for our nutritional needs.

Far worse is what we inflict on animals leading *up* to our eating them. Singer takes us through horrifying anecdotes about the way chickens and pigs are bred, kept, and fattened for mass slaughter, with the corporation's economic efficiency always in mind. Suffice to say that the animals' comfort is not high on the list of considerations for the companies aiming to make profits. (Whether this situation has improved in the twenty-first century all morally concerned people are obligated to find out.) "[N]one of these practices cater for anything more than our pleasures of taste," Singer writes, so meat-eating amounts to the "sacrifice of the most important interests of other beings in order to satisfy trivial interests of our own." To avoid being a speciesist, you must simply stop the practice, and stop supporting it. (True to his word, Singer has been a vegetarian for many decades.)

Morally problematic, too, is the widespread practice of experimenting on other species "in order to see if certain substances are safe for human beings, or to test some psychological theory about the effect of severe punishment on learning, or to try out various new compounds just in case something turns up." Most of these practices are of no vital medical purpose, he insists, listing various upsetting examples—including the infamous practice of cosmetics companies testing their products by blinding live rabbits. (In 1998 Singer published *Ethics into Action*, a biography of animal-rights activist Henry Spira (1927–1998), who almost single-handedly brought an end to that latter practice.) As Singer summarizes the situation, "the possible benefits to mankind [of many of these experiments] are either nonexistent or fantastically remote; while the certain losses to members of other species are very real."

(And while animal testing practices have changed significantly since 1974, the fact that they have is at least partly attributable to Singer's influence. Indeed, that many people now care about establishing guidelines for animal experimentation, and about seeking alternatives thereto, is testament to his work. See, for example, Johns Hopkins University Center for Alternatives to Animal Testing (CAAT) or the University of California Davis Center for Animal Alternatives.)

Ask the experimenters why they experiment on animals, and the answer is: "Because the animals are like us." Ask the experimenters why it is morally okay to experiment on animals, and the answer is: "Because the animals are not like us." Animal experimentation rests on a logical contradiction.

—**Charles R. Magel**

Speciesism and Racism

To show how closely speciesism resembles racism, Singer offers a thought experiment. Proponents of animal experimentation sometimes argue that these experiments may save many human lives. The question that Singer raises is this: would such a proponent perform those experiments on an orphaned human infant, if that were the only way to save those lives? If not, then his readiness to use animals is simple discrimination, for there is no relevant characteristic that human infants possess that adult mammals (say) lack. If anything, adult mammals are even more aware of what is happening to them than an infant would be. So if the proponent would do to animals what he wouldn't do to infants, and if there is no morally relevant feature that distinguishes the two, then he is showing an unjustifiable bias in favor of his own species. The racist does precisely the same thing, in favoring members of one race over those of some other.

Now some people respond here by stressing the "intrinsic dignity" or "sanctity" of human life over lives of other species. But while this idea is long enshrined in mainstream religious dogma, it's essentially an empty concept that amounts to merely *insisting* that we are more special or more deserving, without defending that insistence. To defend the claim would be to offer features or capacities that all and only humans possess, and no other creatures. The first problem (as above) is that all the possibly relevant features (such as awareness, intelligence, and so on) are shared with other species. The second problem is that, when you try to rule out other creatures—for example by demanding a certain level of intelligence or self-awareness—you will simultaneously rule out many human beings, such as those with mental deficits, severe brain damage, and infants. If the fact that a creature lacks those features means that you are justified in ignoring its interests, then you would be just as justified in eating and experimenting on the comatose human being as you would a chicken.

To insist that the human being—every human being, even those lacking the relevant features—has "intrinsic dignity" amounts, in Singer's view, to "preferring the interests of members of our own species [simply] because they are members of our own species." Change the word *species* to *race* and you can see how morally problematic that is.

In summary, then, Singer's main point is that the same ethical principle on which we base our strong sense of human equality (that we should treat all human beings equally regardless of sex, race, and so on) requires us to extend equal consideration to animals. What drives the argument overall is the simple form of utilitarianism that takes pain and pleasure, suffering and enjoyment, to be the foundation for our moral behavior. Put baldly, if your actions generate (far) more suffering than pleasure, or privilege one individual's suffering and pleasure over another's, then they are wrong. (Singer's overall utilitarianism is actually more sophisticated, holding that the right action maximizes the satisfaction of the preference of the various beings affected by the action, but that doesn't change the argument here.)

Some Responses to Singer on Animal Rights

As with many issues, Singer's work here ignites controversy both within and outside the academy. First, it's clear that despite important developments since 1974 (including that of the animal rights movement), his view remains a minority position, only marginally endorsed in the Western world at best. Meat eating continues robustly, and animal experimentation remains widespread. As Singer put it wistfully in 1999, "All you have to do is walk around the corner to McDonald's to see how successful I have been."[6]

But what about on the theoretical level? Certainly the traditional position has long been that it is permissible to use animals for our own purposes. The Bible tells us we have dominion over the earth's creatures, and great philosophers from Aquinas through Descartes and Kant were quite explicit that we could do with animals what we please. True, the great medieval Jewish thinker Maimonides (1135–1204), as well as Aquinas, held that we should avoid unnecessary cruelty to animals—but that was not because animals deserved consideration but because being cruel made us into worse human beings. Kant echoes that point, but insists that animals, lacking self-consciousness, earn no obligations from us and may be used purely for our ends.

More contemporary opponents of Singer, while agreeing that causing animals unnecessary pain is unacceptable, typically argue that animals do lack one or more properties that are essential for having full moral status. Having a soul, having the capacity to form certain kinds of social relationships, having human DNA, being capable of moral reflection, being able to reason—there are many candidates for discussion. But as you think about these suggestions, recall the arguments Singer made. Why should a physical trait such as a specific kind of DNA matter, any more than having a certain skin color, or five fingers? If we met intelligent sentient agents from another planet who didn't have our DNA, would we rule them out for moral consideration? Or if it's the capacity for reason or moral reflection, then what should we say about infants and the brain-damaged? If it's a "soul," well, that would need a lot more said about what a *soul* is supposed to be and just why it is worthy of special consideration, lest that suggestion amounts to no more than merely insisting without argument that humans are special.

And God said, "Let us make Man in Our image, after Our likeness. They shall rule over the fish of the sea, the birds of the sky, and over the animal, the whole earth, and every creeping thing that creeps upon the earth."

—*Genesis* 1:26

Every moving thing that lives shall be food for you. . . .

—*Genesis* 9:3

Many other questions remain. How confident are we in our judgments about the quantity and quality of animal suffering? A philosopher as brilliant as Descartes famously argued that animals lack consciousness altogether, being no more than complicated non-sentient machines (see Andrew Pessin, *Uncommon Sense* [2012], chapter 7). While few agree today, it is perhaps possible that animals don't feel pain in the way we do. Their overall cognitive systems are different, they seem to lack full self-consciousness; it's hard to be sure. But if their pain is of a lesser quantity or quality than we think, then that might weaken Singer's conclusions.

And if utilitarianism is driving the argument, then shouldn't we factor into the calculation that most domesticated animals wouldn't even *exist* if we didn't breed them for our purposes?

Perhaps cows and chickens don't have the most pleasurable lives, and obviously suffer at various points including their slaughter, but if, overall, their individual lives are worth having, if the balance of pleasure over pain is positive, then wouldn't it be morally preferable to breed them for slaughter than not to breed them at all? After all, mass vegetarianism would get us to grow a lot of plants, but plants, lacking sentience, are non-sentient and have no "interests." So that might *not* be the way to maximize pleasure and the satisfaction of interests.

And what about the costs of changing our behavior? To be sure, if a practice is morally wrong then we should give it up, all else being equal; but if utilitarianism is driving our thinking, then our decision must take all consequences into account. Like it or not, the global economy is dependent to some degree on our animal industries. To stop breeding animals for food, clothing, and research would put people out of work. How many, and for how long, is an empirical question to be resolved by economists and others. But before we jump to Singer's conclusions, we are obligated to do these calculations.

Finally, some philosophers simply embrace the label of speciesism. Here is Carl Cohen:[7]

> Racists . . . do grave moral wrong precisely because there is no morally relevant distinction among the races. . . . [But] between (for example) humans on the one hand and cats or rats on the other—the morally relevant differences are enormous, and almost universally appreciated. Humans engage in moral reflection; humans are morally autonomous; humans are members of moral communities. . . . Human beings do have rights; theirs is a moral status very different from that of cats or rats.
>
> I am a speciesist. Speciesism is not merely plausible; it is essential for right conduct, because those who will not make the morally relevant distinctions among species are almost certain, in consequence, to misapprehend their true obligations. . . . If biomedical investigators abandon the effective pursuit of their professional objectives because they are convinced that they may not do to animals what the service of humans requires, they will fail, objectively, to do their duty. Refusing to recognize the moral differences among species is a sure path to calamity.

Cohen goes on to argue that even if you insist on using the utilitarian calculus in determining the moral status of biomedical research in particular, you must be sure you apply it correctly. By the time you add in all the future benefits to humans of the research, it may well be that even the correct utilitarian action is to perform the research, despite the necessary animal suffering. Consider the "elimination of horrible disease, the increase of longevity, the avoidance of great pain, the saving of lives, and the improvement of the quality of lives."

There is much to think about here. In endorsing speciesism Cohen is insisting that he is *justified* in doing so, that there are real, relevant differences between humans and animals that justify (and require) giving different weight to their interests. So one question is whether the kinds of factual differences he mentions do entail the moral differences. As you think about that, again, think of Singer's replies to those sorts of suggestions, and especially what the implications would be for disabled or infant human beings who fail to display the properties Cohen mentions.

At the same time there may be more in common between the disputants than at first appears. Everyone agrees that unnecessary cruelty to animals is morally unacceptable, though not always for the same reasons. (Some because it violates the animals' rights, others because it is not beneficial for humans to be cruel.) And Singer, as a utilitarian, might agree that if the utilitarian calculus really showed the overall benefit to pleasure or "satisfaction of preferences" outweighed the harms inflicted, then that becomes the right thing to do. So there's an empirical question in play, or set of questions. Singer suggested the possible benefits to human beings are "either nonexistent or fantastically remote; while the certain losses to members of other species are very real." So we have to think long and hard about our judgments about the possible benefits, clearly. If, via painful animal experiments, you developed the cure for cancer, that would be terrific. But how certain can you be that this outcome will result? How do you weigh the possible outcomes of your experiments before you've even done them?

"Is the Sanctity of Life Ethic Terminally Ill?" (1995)[8]

If Singer's work on animal rights was controversial, we now skip ahead two decades for some *real* controversy. We'll focus on the article mentioned in the heading, which introduces some themes Singer develops at greater length in his book, *Rethinking Life and Death: The Collapse of Our Traditional Ethics* (1994).[9]

Some Background

We begin with the notion of the **sanctity of life**. We glimpsed it above, in the idea that human life possesses an intrinsic dignity (or sanctity, i.e., holiness, sacredness) that distinguishes it from animal life. The idea has long been grounded in religious thought, as we mentioned, but it also seems intuitive to many people. But intuitions aren't enough, now. We must defend it rationally, by argument. The religious context provides some, assuming, of course, that one accepts theism in general. Here are some relevant remarks from the Catholic Church's 1980 "Declaration on Euthanasia":[10]

> Human life is the basis of all goods, and is the necessary source and condition of every human activity and of all society. Most people regard life as something sacred and hold that no one may dispose of it at will, but believers see in life something greater, namely a gift of God's love, which they are called upon to preserve and make fruitful. And it is this latter consideration that gives rise to the following consequences:
>
> 1. No one can make an attempt on the life of an innocent person without opposing God's love for that person, without violating a fundamental right, and therefore without committing a crime of the utmost gravity.
>
> 2. Everyone has the duty to lead his or her life in accordance with God's plan. . . .
>
> 3. Intentionally causing one's own death, or suicide, is therefore equally as wrong as murder; such an action on the part of a person is to be considered as a rejection of God's sovereignty and loving plan.

If God is the source of human life, and if human life is the source of all good, then clearly we owe to human life in general the highest possible moral respect. Not merely would this fit poorly with animal equality (as discussed above), but it has many

> You shall not kill.
>
> —*Exodus* 20:13.

bioethical ramifications, from conception onward, to prenatal testing and the treatment of severely disabled infants, to the care of severely disabled and suffering people, to the terminally ill, to the possibility of suicide (even in order to end terrible suffering), to euthanasia.

On the latter subject the document continues:

By euthanasia is understood an action or an omission which of itself or by intention causes death, in order that all suffering may in this way be eliminated. . . . It is necessary to state firmly once more that nothing and no one can in any way permit the killing of an innocent human being, whether a fetus or an embryo, an infant or an adult, an old person, or one suffering from an incurable disease, or a person who is dying. Furthermore, no one is permitted to ask for this act of killing, either for himself or herself or for another person entrusted to his or her care, nor can he or she consent to it, either explicitly or implicitly. Nor can any authority legitimately recommend or permit such an action. For it is a question of the violation of the divine law, an offence against the dignity of the human person, a crime against life, and an attack on humanity.

The sanctity of life doctrine is quite clear. If human life is sacred then you are almost never permitted to bring about the end of any life, even if for good reasons (to alleviate suffering). But again, you need not be religious to share the overall intuitions. If, for example, you are persuaded by some of the considerations in the previous section distinguishing humans from animals, you might invoke those to support a sanctity of life approach to euthanasia and related matters.

Things now start to get more complicated when we realize we lack a clear definition, on many levels, of the key word, *life*. DNA is essential for life as we know it, but is DNA itself alive? (It's just a string of inanimate molecules.) Viruses are bits of genetic material that get themselves reproduced by host organisms. Are they alive, or just mechanical devices? Living things are composed of cells, but are the cells themselves alive, or (again) just mechanical devices, made up of inanimate molecules? Not everyone agrees whether human fertilized cells are alive; or if they are, whether they are alive as *persons* in a sense conferring moral status, or alive in some lesser sense. Then there are the medical cases, of people "kept alive" by artificial means. Does the machine help you breathe, or do your breathing for you? (The former sounds more like you are alive than the latter.) When machines take over the work of your heart during surgery, are they keeping you alive or, sort of, living *for you*? If everything biological in you stops for a moment or several, but then re-starts, were you alive during the interval? And speaking of machines, could a sufficiently programmed computer be alive?

These general philosophical questions lead us to our next bit of background, the report of the Ad Hoc Committee of the Harvard Medical School to Examine the Definition of Brain Death.[11] The report observes this:

From ancient times down to the recent past it was clear that, when the respiration and heart stopped, the brain would die in a few minutes; so the obvious criterion of no heart beat as synonymous with death was sufficiently accurate. In those times the heart was considered to be the central organ of the body; it is not surprising that its failure marked the onset of death. This is no longer valid when modern resuscitative and supportive measures are used. These improved activities can now restore "life" as judged by the ancient standards of persistent respiration and continuing heart beat. . . . In [some] situations "life" can be maintained only by means of artificial respiration and electrical stimulation of the heart beat, or in temporarily bypassing the heart, or . . . reducing with cold the body's oxygen requirement. (342)

The traditional definition of life, the report suggests, has become obsolete. But that isn't merely an academic matter, but one of major practical significance:

There are two reasons why there is need for a [new] definition. (1) Improvements in resuscitative and supportive measures have led to increased efforts to save those who are desperately injured. Sometimes these efforts have only partial success so that the result is an individual whose heart continues to beat but whose brain is irreversibly damaged. The burden is great on patients who suffer permanent loss of intellect, on their families, on the hospitals, and on those in need of hospital beds already occupied by these comatose patients. (2) Obsolete criteria for the definition of death can lead to controversy in obtaining organs for transplantation.

In essence, sustaining brain dead people—those suffering from irreversible coma, loss of intellect and consciousness—is both extremely burdensome to many and in many ways (emotionally, physically, financially) and complicates the process of transplanting their organs to those desperately in need of them, whose lives might be improved or saved by so doing. Defining these people as *dead* (despite their heartbeat or breathing) makes it morally and legally easier to stop sustaining them (what moral imperative is there to sustain a dead person?) and to harvest their organs (for if they are dead, they no longer need them).

This may seem like a semantic trick, but that wouldn't be fair. One has to define death *somehow*, so any definition is a semantic decision. What the report does is recognize, first, that our traditional definition has become outmoded due to medical advances; and further, that we have many legitimate, competing moral concerns at play in these decisions. So why not bring *everything* into consideration in our definitions of death—technology, finances, and the needs of others besides the patient, whose lives are impacted by the decisions?

> The certain prospect of death could sweeten every life with a precious and fragrant drop of levity—and now you strange apothecary souls have turned it into an ill-tasting drop of poison that makes the whole of life repulsive.
>
> —**Friedrich Nietzsche** (1844–1900)

So in our background we have two things: the traditional doctrine of the sanctity of life, and the non-traditional new definition of life itself.

Enter Peter Singer

His article, "Is the Sanctity of Life Ethic Terminally Ill," notes several events (recent as of the 1995 article) suggesting the impending collapse of the traditional sanctity of life ethic:

(1) In 1993, Britain's highest court allowed a brain dead young man to be removed from life support[.]

(2) In 1993, the Netherlands legalized the giving of lethal injections to patients who suffer unbearably without hope of improvement, and who ask to be helped to die[.]

(3) In 1994, Michigan jurors acquitted Dr. Jack Kevorkian of assisted suicide, despite his admitted help in providing equipment to a man suffering dreadfully from the nerve disorder ALS, or "Lou Gehrig's disease."

Though they differ in many details, all three are measures wherein societal approval is being granted to allowing, or assisting, the end of human lives. Thus all three are inconsistent with the sanctity of life ethic as described above.

Singer next continues with an analysis of the Harvard Committee's redefinition of death. That it was a *revolution*, Singer suggests, is clear:

> [It] meant that warm, breathing, pulsating human beings are not given further medical support. If their relatives consent (or in some countries, as long as they have not registered a refusal of consent), their hearts and other organs can be cut out of their bodies and given to strangers.

Put more dramatically, the redefinition now excluded a whole class of human beings from the moral community. If the brain dead are *dead*, then they are no longer entitled to the moral considerations of the living. Moreover, Singer adds, it was "a revolution without opposition." The redefinition had already become widely adopted even before the committee's report, accepted in many countries and many states in the United States, and in some places even without legal consultation.

And why was it so widely and easily adopted? Because it does not harm the brain dead patients, and it benefited everyone else: "the families of brain dead patients, the hospitals, the transplant surgeons, people needing transplants, people who worried that they might one day need a transplant, people who feared that they might one day be kept on a respirator after their brain had died, taxpayers, and the government." As win-win-win a situation as you could hope for, it seems, especially for the transplant industry. Brain dead people are a prime source of good transplantable organs, since once a person has—well, died more *completely*—the organs quickly degenerate. By declaring brain death to be death, more and better organs become available sooner, filling a serious need and saving many other lives.

From a utilitarian perspective the choice also seems clear. Declaring a brain dead person *dead* saves money, resources, and pain, and in facilitating transplants saves more lives. But the question Singer now asks, more philosophically, is this. Is it really necessary, and does it really make sense, to consider a brain dead person *dead*?

Surely that doesn't fit common sense or parlance. Singer cites a newspaper headline announcing "Brain Dead Woman Gives Birth, then Dies," which clearly distinguishes between being brain dead and being dead. Surveys of medical professionals showed that what brain death meant, to them, was merely that the person was "irreversibly dying"—not that the person was dead, period. In fact, Singer suggests, the

> brain death criterion of death is nothing other than a convenient fiction. It was proposed and accepted because it makes it possible for us to salvage organs that would otherwise be wasted, and to withdraw medical treatment when it is doing no good.

But while that might make it useful, even morally desirable, Singer thinks that the concept of brain-death death is simply not stable.

Problems with Brain Death as Death

First of all, the notion of brain death itself isn't so clear. Though often defined as the irreversible cessation of brain function, more recent research has shown that even when major diagnostic tests reveal that most brain function has ceased, some functions continue. Hormones that control various bodily activities, for example, continue to be regulated by the brains of most people otherwise classified as brain dead. Moreover,

> [w]hen brain dead patients are cut open in order to remove organs, their blood pressure may rise and their heartbeat quicken. These reactions mean that the brain is still carrying out some of its functions.

These reactions seem so *alive* that it is hard to think of such people as truly dead.

To avoid this outcome we could make the brain death definition stronger, by making it the cessation of literally *all* brain functions, including those hormonal ones. But there is a serious downside to doing that. To comply with that definition, doctors would have to dramatically increase the testing they do on such patients. Then after that extensive, expensive testing, some people first considered brain dead would be reclassified as brain alive, and thus would require continued and indefinite respirator support at great costs emotional and financial to all concerned. Others first considered brain dead would remain brain dead, but as a result of the delays from testing their organs would deteriorate, ruining them for transplantation. The utilitarian question, then, is this. Would strengthening the brain death definition this way do more harm than good?

On Singer's view, any such gain here is seriously outweighed by the harms. Keeping more irreversibly unconscious bodies running on expensive support systems is hardly a gain, and is outweighed by the harm to the families, hospitals, potential transplant recipients, and taxpayers. Better to stick with the weaker definition of brain death, since it makes it easier to declare death and so avoids all these additional harms. But then the weaker definition has the problem that it just doesn't seem to capture *death*, as we saw.

So there's something wrong with the whole "brain death = death" approach, so far.

A better approach, Singer thinks, is this: on the sanctity of life ethic, "all human life is of equal value," so the *quality* of a human life makes no difference to the wrongness of ending it. That in turn makes it wrong to end the life of a merely brain dead person unless we declare that person dead. But convincingly going that way requires the cessation of *all* brain function, which generates the utilitarian harms just mentioned. To avoid that outcome we must recognize that quality of life *does* matter to the decision about ending life, and thus should replace the sanctity of life ethic with the **quality of life ethic**.

Brain Death That Reflects the Quality of Life Ethic

So what does this mean?

What should matter, Singer thinks, isn't preserving life period, but preserving *quality* of life. So if you want to define brain death as death, then the first order of business is to decide just which brain functions mark the difference between a life of sufficient quality and not.

The answer, presumably, is those related to consciousness. Why? Because what most people really care about is not the body but *the person*. As Singer quotes the chair of the Harvard Committee, Henry Beecher, what's essential to being a person is "the individual's personality, his conscious life, his uniqueness, his capacity for remembering, judging, reasoning, acting, enjoying, worrying, and so on." There are many factors here, but the general gist is clear enough. If brain death is to count as death, then the criterion of brain death should be the irreversible cessation of those brain functions responsible for personhood, which amounts to the cerebral cortex, *not* the whole brain. A person would be brain dead, and therefore dead, when the *person* is gone—even if his body, and some or many brain functions, remain intact.

That's a start, Singer thinks, but unfortunately even this now weaker definition of brain death fails, for it confronts the same problem as before. If people already have trouble accepting that a warm body with a beating heart on a respirator is really dead, how much more trouble would they have accepting that the same body, breathing perfectly well on its own, is dead? The real problem, then, is not which definition of brain death to use. It's that brain death itself is not, for most people, *death*.

The Harvard Brain Death Committee admirably sought to deal with two serious problems: patients in hopeless conditions were maintained indefinitely on respirators that everyone was afraid to turn off, and organs that could save lives were being wasted by waiting for those patients' hearts to stop. They tried to solve both problems by classifying as *dead* those whose brains no longer showed the relevant activity. Since the practical consequence of that move benefited everyone (as mentioned above), there was no resistance to it. But the theoretical problem remains, that, simply, brain death is not death.

What's necessary is to start over, Singer recommends, but this time free not merely of the sanctity of life ethic but of the notion of brain death as well.

The Quality of Life Ethic without Brain Death

The court case in Britain mentioned above shows the way. Tony Bland, a seventeen-year old, was crushed in a stampede and left in a vegetative state, with no possibility of regaining consciousness. After lengthy legal proceedings including appeals, the British court ruled that

> when a patient is incapable of consenting to medical treatment, doctors are under no legal duty to continue treatment that does not benefit a patient. In addition, the judges agreed that the mere continuation of biological life is not, in the absence of any awareness or any hope of ever again becoming aware, a benefit to the patient.

What matters is only what is in the best interests of the patient; and a patient in that state perhaps cannot be said to have any interests at all. One judge quoted by Singer states, cautiously, "It is . . . perhaps permissible to say that to an individual with no cognitive capacity whatever, and no prospect of ever recovering any[,] . . . it must be a matter of complete indifference whether he lives or dies."

Thus sustaining Tony Bland's life as it was brought him no benefit, for life itself is not automatically a benefit to a person, irrespective of its quality. Contra the sanctity of life ethic, *quality* of life determines the overall value of a life.

More importantly, the legal conclusion here allowed doctors to undertake actions intended to bring about Bland's death. Though the court denied they were legalizing euthanasia—understanding by that term actively ending a life as opposed to simply refraining from supporting it—that's not particularly relevant here. What matters is that the court was permitting measures, active or not, aimed at the patient's death.

And *that* is the key advance from the Harvard Committee, Singer thinks. In order to avoid the harms and to make organs available to transplant, the Committee tried, unsuccessfully, to define such patients as already dead. But the British decision shows you don't have to do

> Make a living will. Talk about it. Death is going to happen to everybody. Write it down. Even if you write it on a piece of paper at home and have your family witness it, you need to write it down.
>
> —Michael Schiavo. His wife Terri suffered from cardiac arrest in 1990 and remained in a vegetative state until, after years of legal battles, she was finally removed from life support on March 18, 2005. After almost two weeks of being starved and dehydrated, she died on March 31, 2005.

that. In fact it allows us now to distinguish three separate questions which had been blended together:

1. When does a human being die?
2. When is it permissible for doctors intentionally to end the life of a patient?
3. When is it permissible to remove organs from a human being for transplant?

Under the sanctity of life ethic, the answer to the first question was "when the blood stops circulating," or something similar; to the second, "never"; and the third, "when the patient is dead." The brain death definition changed the answer to the first question, so that brain dead people were now dead, but in doing so it didn't have to change the answers to the other two questions. It thus didn't address those questions, while allowing more respirators to be turned off and more organs to be harvested.

The British decision doesn't directly address the first and third questions, but dramatically changes the answer to the second. Instead of "never," the answer becomes, "when the patient's continued life is of no benefit to her," such as when the person becomes irreversibly unconscious. But once we've answered the second question this way, then no reason remains to preserve the original answer to the third question. If it is permissible to end the life of a person in that state, surely it would be permissible to harvest the organs as well.

Once we have answered the second and third questions this way, the first question becomes much less relevant. In fact, disconnected from the pressing concerns of what to do with brain dead patients, it becomes quite *ir*relevant. It doesn't *matter* how we answer it. So we have no reason to go with the Harvard Committee, whose contorted definition of death was devised merely to change our answers to the second and third questions. If we change those answers independently, then we may go back to our original, traditional understanding of death, in terms of the irreversible cessation of the circulation of the blood.

The Quality of Life Ethic and Utilitarianism

Although utilitarianism isn't explicit in this essay, Singer's position is informed by it throughout. The stress on quality of life, not simply life, mirrors the utilitarian identifications of pleasure, happiness, and/or the satisfaction of preferences as fundamental values. Only a conscious being is capable of experiencing these, so consciousness is a minimum condition for a life to have any value whatsoever. We also see utilitarianism in the details, in the calculations. What are the gains and harms of expanding the brain death definition to all brain functions? What are the gains and harms of keeping brain dead patients on life support? What does the patient gain, if anything, compared to the harms suffered by others, including those deprived of life-saving organs? We can also see the continuity between this essay and the one on animal rights. Insofar as animals are conscious and capable of pleasure and pain, they are morally considerable, just as are we.

Most profoundly, we see how starkly utilitarianism contrasts with the sanctity of life ethic. Once you invoke utilitarianism you start quantifying, as we saw in chapter 6: how much pleasure and pain, happiness and unhappiness, and so on. Once you do that, different lives may no longer be of equal value. Individuals with greater cognitive capacities, with greater capacity to think and to feel, whose actions impact more other people, in more powerful ways, will count more. Individuals of lesser capacities, suffering from diseases and inflictions, disabled and disadvantaged, impoverished and powerless, will count less. It is no surprise that on this general view, a brain dead person on a respirator counts as having no value himself. Any value in keeping him alive must be due to his value to others. But by the same token, any value in letting him die will also be due to the value to others of his dying.

The question then becomes that of calculating which is the greater value.

Some Responses to Singer on the Sanctity of Life

It's one thing to argue we should be nicer to animals. But it's another to argue that we need to be less nice to human beings, which is how many people interpret Singer in this discussion.

The most profound disagreement is religious in origin. Singer's utilitarianism is explicitly *not* grounded in religious belief. He rejects theism largely because of the problem of evil, and so will not ground ethics in any divine source. But common to the Western monotheisms is the idea that God is the source of all value, and in particular the source and sovereign of all human life. From that perspective Singer's subjectivist utilitarianism, grounding all value in our happiness and preferences, looks nearly idolatrous. From that perspective, Singer's apparent ease in turning off life support looks suspiciously like "playing God."

This difference in worldview is not a mere "objection" to Singer. The disagreements are so profound that the conversation must start elsewhere (such as in debates about whether God exists). But it is worth considering whether even a theist must adopt the sanctity of life ethic that Singer is challenging. Purely philosophically, apart from official Church doctrines, does the sanctity of life clearly follow from basic monotheism? Many questions arise here. If God is the source and sovereign of human life, should we *never* intervene in matters of health and life? (Why save someone, if God wants him or her to die?) Or if we are justified in intervening, to what extent are we obligated? (How much money should be invested in saving each person? What is the cut-off point?) If the reason we should strive to save lives is that people have souls, then how can we know at precisely what moment the soul becomes affiliated with the body? (This is relevant to the moral permissibility of abortion, but also to the end of life: is it possible that a brain dead person has, in the loss of all consciousness, already lost his soul?)

Another line of resistance to Singer invokes the classic **slippery slope**. A slippery slope argument is roughly of the form "If you accept proposition P, then you'll have to accept Q; and if you accept Q, then you'll have to accept R . . . but R is so problematic or offensive or simply false that you better not accept P." The worry here is that once you start thinking like Singer in this case, you'll think like him in other cases that are more problematic.

So, what matters for Singer is "quality of life," including the capacity for sensation and reasoning, and the maximization of happiness and preference satisfaction. Individuals who lack these capacities simply do not factor into your moral calculations. So it becomes permissible to unplug brain dead people whenever unplugging them satisfies other parties. But then you could say the same thing about unborn babies, especially early in pregnancy, before conscious activity has begun—and abortions, for any reason at all, become permissible. Worse, you could say something similar about already born babies, especially if they are disabled or brain damaged, and infanticide becomes permissible. Worse still, you could say the same even of healthy babies: yes, their capacity for happiness and preferences must now be factored in, but if enough people impacted by their existence would prefer them to die, then infanticide has *really* become permissible. And not just babies, but children, adolescents, adults. Singer's line of thought appears to permit not merely suicide and assisted suicide, but even worse, non-voluntary euthanasia, as long as enough other parties would benefit from the death of the person in question. Perhaps not surprisingly, advocates for the disabled have been very vocal against Singer, arguing that his views suggest both that life with various disabilities is less worth living and that it would be permissible for society to end such lives, either before or shortly after birth, or later.

Similar remarks apply to the implications of Singer's views for sexuality. Singer writes elsewhere, "The moral case for acceptance of sexual relationships between consenting adults that do not harm others is . . . clear-cut."[12] As long as happiness is produced and preferences are satisfied, basically, anything goes: sex out of marriage, homosexuality, promiscuity, prostitution. But if happiness and preferences are all that matter, then what's to rule out incest, if the parties are willing and no harm results? And what's to limit these conclusions to adults? If no one is explicitly hurt, then what stops this line of thought from endorsing pedophilia? (This is not to claim that Singer himself endorses any of these things. But critics charge that his principles lead quickly to endorsing them.)

Other slippery slopes are of a more practical nature. Suppose Singer's utilitarianism persuades you that actions such as abortion, assisted suicide, and euthanasia are permissible, perhaps if restricted to carefully specified circumstances. The worry here is that once you permit them at all, you open the system to abuses. You permit abortion, but then people become casual about abortion. Rather than obtain them only in certain conditions (rape? incest? severe birth defects?) people soon push for them when they merely prefer not to have the baby. Or you permit euthanasia where the patient is suffering irreversibly. But then the patient's relatives start urging the euthanasia against the patient's wishes because they don't want the burden of caring for him any longer. Would people start pressuring Grandma to end her life, rather than have to provide for her? In light of these foreseeable outcomes it may be better simply not to permit the practices *at all.*

Similarly with the issue of brain death and organ transplants above. Organ transplanting is not merely a life-saving measure, it turns out, but a very profitable business for doctors and hospitals. Doctors and hospitals therefore have a strong financial stake in making organs available. But doctors and hospitals are also the ones making the declarations of death, and brain death. Anecdotes abound of hospitals being too quick to declare someone brain dead (and therefore dead) in order to quickly harvest and sell their organs.[13] But if this behavior is the inevitable result of permitting harvesting the organs of the brain dead, then perhaps it shouldn't be permitted at all?

This last situation also brings out an important epistemological point. There are limits to

> Like a real-life version of Robin Cook's medical thriller *Coma*, Teresi paints a grisly picture of organ harvesting and raises uncomfortable questions: Is the donor actually dead rather than at the point of death? Might he or she be revived given time and proper medical attention? . . . Provocative.
>
> —*Kirkus Review* of Dick Teresi's *The Undead: Organ Harvesting, the Ice-Water Test, Beating-Heart Cadavers: How Medicine Is Blurring the Line Between Life and Death* (2012)

what we can know, and to our degree of confidence in our medical assessments. How certain can we be that various conditions are irreversible? One hears of people who awaken after years of coma. How certain can we be that there is no conscious or mental activity, no experience, going on inside the "brain dead"? Some recent research suggests that as many as 40 percent of patients diagnosed as vegetative may have some degree of awareness; in some cases, even, scientists have developed techniques to communicate indirectly with the patient.[14] There are also terrifying stories about patients undergoing operations where the anaesthetics didn't work.

Instead they were conscious but paralyzed during the operation, experiencing excruciating pain while looking to the medical staff as if they were unconscious. What if, then, when doctors harvest organs of the brain dead—the patients are actually *experiencing* the procedure?

The claim isn't that this happens regularly. It's merely questioning how confident we can be that it *never* happens. And if our confidence is limited, then should that impact our judgments of how to proceed in these cases?

The Life You Can Save: How to Do Your Part to End World Poverty
(New York: Random House, 2009)

So if utilitarianism can make you nicer to animals and less nice to some human beings, it can now make you nicer to *other* human beings. (And not surprisingly, Singer will get flak for that too!)

In 2009 Singer published *The Life You Can Save*. The book sold vigorously around the world (and continues to), along the way donating its proceeds to the organization he founded to combat world poverty (www.thelifeyoucansave.org). Its impact has been both wide and deep. It has inspired thousands of ordinary people to "take the pledge" to donate 1 percent of their income to appropriate charities, and even Bill and Melinda Gates and Warren Buffett were partly inspired by it to launch the "Billionaires' Pledge," calling on billionaires to give at least half their wealth away to philanthropy. It similarly inspired Dustin Moskovitz, a Facebook cofounder and the world's youngest self-made billionaire, to cofound Good Ventures (www.goodventures.org), which works closely with a charity evaluator called GiveWell (www.givewell.org). Sometimes philosophy is abstract, and removed from the real world. But Singer's is a case where philosophy makes a real concrete difference. Here it has actually saved lives.

Perhaps it isn't surprising why. As one reviewer describes it,

> So let me start with a reason not to read [the book]: it will make you uncomfortable. It certainly made me uncomfortable. It started by asking me a simple question—would I sacrifice time and money to save a stranger's life? If so, why don't I give more of my income to charity?—and pounded away relentlessly, tearing apart every excuse I had until I was left with "I'm really selfish."
>
> I've appreciated many books for making me feel scared, or angry, or sad. Now there's one to make me feel personally guilty.[15]

You may be reminded of Socrates here, starting off with a simple question, pounding away, tearing apart your responses, making you scared, and angry, and guilty, until . . . Well, it didn't end so well for Socrates, as we saw in chapter 3. And Singer has received his share of threats from his earlier controversial work, as we mentioned. But fortunately the controversy that the present book generates isn't of the physically threatening sort.

"I have been thinking and writing for more than thirty years," Singer writes in the preface, "about how we should respond to hunger and poverty." In fact the main philosophical argument in the book may be found in its essence in one of Singer's earliest articles, from 1972: "Famine, Affluence, and Morality."[16] We shall follow the book in our discussion, but for those seeking more technical arguments, that article rewards reading.

The Shallow Pond and the Moral Monster

The starting point is the famous thought experiment known as **the shallow pond.**

> On your way to work, you pass a small pond . . . only about knee-deep. . . . [Y]ou are surprised to see a child splashing about in the pond. As you get closer, you see that it is a very young child, just a toddler, who is flailing about, unable to stay upright or walk out of the pond. . . . [T]here is no one else around. The child is unable to keep his head above the water for more than a few seconds at a time. If you don't wade in and pull him out, he seems likely to drown. Wading in is easy and safe, but you will ruin the new shoes you bought only a few days ago, and get your suit wet and muddy. By the time you hand the child over to someone responsible for him, and change your clothes, you'll be late for work. What should you do? (3)

This is what is nicely called a *no-brainer*. Obviously you should save the child. But what about your shoes, your suit? Being late to work? Only some kind of moral monster (most people think) would value those over saving the child's life.

When Singer wrote the original article he talked about how, in November of 1971, people were dying in large numbers in East Bengal from lack of food, shelter, and medicine. At the start of the book he provides some devastating statistics about the state of poverty around the world today, and its fatal consequences. For just one example, according to UNICEF "nearly 10 million children under five years old die each year from causes related to poverty." But most of these deaths are preventable, with just a little money. The World Bank in 2008 set the international poverty line at $1.25 a day. What that means is, roughly, that in many places around the world people could subsist relatively adequately on about $1.25 a day. They also noted that in 2008 about 1.4 billion people lived *below* that line. These people, especially their children, are the ones dying at terrible rates from poverty-related causes, for lack of $1.25 a day.

"Now think about your own situation," Singer writes.

> By donating a relatively small amount of money, you could save a child's life. Maybe it takes more than the amount needed to buy a pair of shoes—but we all spend money on things we don't really need, whether on drinks, meals out, clothing, movies, concerts, vacations, new cars, or house renovation. Is it possible that by choosing to spend your money on such things rather than contributing to an aid agency, you are leaving a child to die, a child you could have saved? (5)

It seems not merely *possible* but rather clearly *actual*. Think about how little you would have to sacrifice to raise a child above that poverty line, to provide her with food, clean water, and medicine to survive.

The comparison to the shallow pond case is clear. Only a moral monster would refrain from saving a child in order to spare his own suit and shoes. Only a moral monster could value those items over that of a child's life. But every time you go to the movies (for example), every time you spend $15 on admission and popcorn, that is $15 that could have been donated to an organization, that could have provided food to a starving child, clean water to a dehydrated child, medicine to a child dying of measles. Are *you* perhaps a moral monster for valuing your night out over the life of a child? (Not to mention the morning coffee, the bottled water, the shopping, the traveling, and so on—perhaps even the college degree?)

Singer starts with a simple question. Would you save the drowning child? Of course. But things quickly become complicated when we realize that, in fact, we *are* the bystander at the shallow pond.

The Basic Argument

So far we have just been pulling at intuitions, but Singer now formalizes the line of thought behind the shallow pond example into an argument:

(P1) Suffering and death from lack of food, shelter, and medical care are bad.

(P2) If it is in your power to prevent something bad from happening, without sacrificing anything nearly as important, it is wrong not to do so.

(P3) By donating to aid agencies, you can prevent suffering and death from lack of food, shelter, and medical care, without sacrificing anything nearly as important.

(C) Therefore, if you do not donate to aid agencies, you are doing something wrong.

Now ask yourself, Singer suggests, if you can deny the premises of the argument. That seems unlikely. Of course suffering and death are bad, all else being equal; and of course you should prevent bad things, if the cost of doing so is relatively small. The third premise too seems undeniable, particularly if we supplement it with the assumption that we can be reasonably confident that the aid agencies are reliable and efficient. (If we can't, then the moral obligation expands to requiring us to do some research into the aid agencies themselves—which is what organizations such as GiveWell are up to.)

So if the premises are correct, is the argument valid? Do the premises ensure the truth of the conclusion? They surely seem to, in which case the argument would be not merely valid but sound.

But then the rational person must accept its conclusion.

> Charity gives every man a title to so much out of another's plenty, as will keep him from extreme want, where he has no means to subsist otherwise.
>
> —**John Locke**, *Two Treatises of Government* (1689) Book I, par. 42.

The Implications of the Argument

Easy enough to admit the conclusion, perhaps, but then in doing so, Singer says, "our lives would be changed dramatically" (17). If you wanted to be a good person, you would forgo your next shopping trip and donate the money to an aid agency instead, thereby saving the lives of one or more children. But before you celebrated your good deed by treating yourself to a movie or a nice meal, you would realize that the money for those items should be sent to the aid agency as well. In fact you would have to cut out *all* your unnecessary spending and save lives, all the way to the point where if you were to give any more, you would be sacrificing something nearly as important as a child's life—wherever that point might be for you.

Chances are, that would be a *dramatic* change in your behavior. But that's what you'd expect, in fact, because this simple argument actually brings about a major change in our moral assumptions. For most people, being *good* is satisfied by basic behaviors such as not harming people, keeping promises, supporting one's children and elderly parents, perhaps contributing to needier members of one's local community. "Giving to strangers, especially those beyond one's community, may be good," Singer writes,

> but we don't think of it as something we *have* to do. But if the basic argument presented above is right, then what many of us consider acceptable behavior must be viewed in a new, more ominous light. When we spend our surplus on concerts or fashionable shoes,

on fine dining and good wines, or on holidays in faraway lands, we are doing something *wrong*. (18, emphasis added)

Helping distant people is no longer **supererogatory**, something that is good to do but not *obligatory*, and therefore not wrong *not* to do. Helping distant people *is* now obligatory, and when we choose not to do it, when we privilege our comforts over saving that life, we are doing something wrong. Suddenly some of our very ordinary behaviors become those of moral monsters.

Despite Singer's conflict with religion in the previous section, here his view agrees with the major Western faiths, which see helping the poor (for example) as being not voluntary but a moral obligation.

It's also worth adding here how, again, utilitarianism informs Singer's position. Utilitarianism generally gives the interests of everyone equal consideration. While that sounds agreeable enough, it actually conflicts with another powerful moral intuition (as we saw in chapter 6), that some people's interests do and should count more than others. You may owe your family members (or your friends, or neighbors, or fellow citizens, or fraternity brothers) more than you do random strangers. But if your moral obligation is to maximize happiness or preference satisfaction, then everyone counts equally. People close to you count as much as people far away. Strangers count as much as acquaintances, friends, family.

> Hence whatever certain people have in superabundance is due, by natural law, to the purpose of succoring the poor.
>
> —**Thomas Aquinas** (1225–1274), **Summa Theologica** Q66.A7

An anonymous starving child across an ocean counts as much as you. And when you do the utilitarian calculation, saving the life of that child will outweigh many of the simple pleasures to which you treat yourself. To take a night out at the movies is to ignore the dying child, so you are a moral monster.

That's the simple conclusion of the simple but compelling argument. All this takes up no more than about nineteen pages of Singer's book. The remaining 184 pages deal with objections both philosophical and practical, present the empirical facts about the nature and process of providing aid toward global poverty, and explore the practical obstacles confronting getting people to give more. In our limited space we will merely examine some of the objections and complications generated by the main argument.

Practical Obstacles

We'll start with some practical obstacles, saving the philosophical objections for the next section.

Now most people say immediately that you should save the drowning child, and if Singer's argument above is right, then most people on some level do or should believe that they ought to save the starving children. So why don't they in fact do more to do so? In the chapter "Why Don't We Give More?", Singer outlines some of the well-studied psychological factors that diminish people's willingness to give. Obviously, some or many people are simply selfish, inclined to favor their own interests over those of others. But that doesn't mean it's morally *right* to be selfish, just that selfishness is something we morally ought to overcome.

But there are other psychological factors as well. Studies show that "identifiable victims" are more likely to elicit aid than abstract or statistical victims. Put a name or a face on someone in need, and people will give more than if merely told, abstractly, about the hundreds of children dying somewhere. (That's why advertisements soliciting aid always feature a specific child, showing his or her face, asking you to save *this very child*, for that moves us more effectively than abstract statistics about world poverty.)

Studies also show that we are more likely to give locally than far away. Americans gave four times as much money to victims of Hurricane Katrina in 2005 than to those of the tsunami in Southeast Asia in 2004, despite the fact that the latter killed 200 times more people and left millions destitute and homeless. You probably feel the same way, psychologically, when you read the news. Horrible things that happen far away bother us for a few minutes, then we move on. In 2008 an earthquake in China killed 70,000 and left 5 million homeless; in 2010 an earthquake in Haiti killed perhaps 200,000 and devastated the lives of millions. You watch the news for a few days, then the stories drop from the headlines and disappear.

We are affected by the perceived futility of the situation. In one study people were more willing to help 1,500 people when told there were 3,000 people suffering than they were to help the same number of people out of 10,000 suffering. We are also affected by the diffusion of responsibility. We are much less likely to provide help if the responsibility for helping doesn't rest on us alone. We all feel the sense that we don't have to help because someone else will. (That's why in an emergency you shouldn't merely say "someone, help!" but point at a specific person and say, "You, get the police!") There's also the sense of fairness involved. Our willingness to help others can be reduced if we think we are doing more than our fair share.

But now, as with selfishness, these are all psychological factors that affect how we *in fact* behave, but they do not provide any philosophical objections to Singer's argument about how we *ought* to behave. The fact that we are less moved to give by statistics doesn't mean it's right *not* to give. Singer's argument concludes that we ought to save as many dying children as we can without causing nearly equal harm by so doing, even *if* the children are unidentified. Similarly, as we noted, the utilitarian considerations offer no grounds for discriminating on the basis of proximity. There may be practical considerations to focus your giving on people nearer rather than farther, but morally speaking you are as equally obliged to help others no matter how far away they are. The same with the perceived futility, the diffusion of responsibility, and the sense of fairness. If you can save even one life without sacrificing anything nearly as important, then you should—even if there are other lives you can't save, even if other people could help, even if others are not doing their share. After all, just because others act immorally, by failing to help, doesn't mean that you *should* act immorally. It may increase your tendency to actually be immoral, but it doesn't *justify* it.

So the practical obstacles to giving don't offer grounds to resist Singer's conclusion in the simple argument above.

Some Philosophical Responses to the Argument

The philosophical attention focuses on the second premise of the argument: "If it is in your power to prevent something bad from happening, without sacrificing anything nearly as important, it is wrong not to do so." In his book, Singer surveys and responds to many of these, but we shall focus on the objections rather than his replies, to give you an opportunity to figure out what you think.

Louis Pojman (1935–2005) usefully classifies the major ethical responses to the problems of world hunger into three categories: the "neo-Malthusian" response, the conservative (or libertarian) response, and the liberal response, the latter represented by Singer.[17] In brief, the liberal response holds that we have a moral obligation to feed the hungry either due to the right the hungry have to our aid or (in Singer's version) to utilitarian considerations about maximizing welfare. The neo-Malthusians deny such a right and suggest that utilitarian conclusions go the opposite way, *against* feeding the hungry. Conservatives, in the middle, hold that we have no obligation to aid the hungry but also no obligation not to, making the action supererogatory. Both neo-Malthusians and conservatives generate various objections to Singer's argument, while Pojman offers his own response to Singer.

The neo-Malthusian response is named for Thomas Malthus (1766–1834), who in 1798 published a book called *An Essay on the Principle of Population*. Malthus argued that population tends to increase beyond the resources necessary to sustain it, leading inevitably to population correction (i.e., massive death) from mechanisms such as war, disease, and famine. Neo-Malthusians thus look at problems such as world hunger through the lens of a population grown beyond the earth's natural capacities. This perspective is represented in the work of Garrett Hardin (1915–2003), who by his colorful metaphors gave rise to the notion of **lifeboat ethics**.

In his essay "Living on a Lifeboat" (1974),[18] Hardin suggests that the world is like a sea in which a few lifeboats (the wealthy nations) are surrounded by masses of drowning people (the global hungry). But the lifeboats are of limited capacity, with limited resources. Suppose the lifeboat can handle fifty people and is currently full, and there are one hundred people in the surrounding waters. What are those in the lifeboat morally obligated to do for those not in the lifeboat? Hardin runs through the options. They could take in all the surrounding people, which is nice but results in swamping the boat and everyone drowning. That could hardly be their moral obligation. So perhaps they could take in a few. But the lifeboat is already full to capacity, or at least near to capacity. If it is full, then they can afford to take in none as in the previous case. But if there's a little room, then taking in even a few dramatically increases the risk to those already in the boat, by pushing it to capacity. Again, it could hardly be their moral obligation to increase their own risk significantly for the sake of saving a few. (Not to mention the difficult problem of deciding which few to let in.)

What is left? Take in none. This preserves the lives of those on board, allowing them a small safety buffer (if there is a little room left). It may seem abhorrent, but in the situation described, it may be hard to see how our moral obligations could be otherwise.

Hardin goes on to offer a detailed argument that aiding the poor in general ultimately makes things worse off for everyone. Suppose a nation's people are starving because the land cannot support their needs, and well-meaning altruists step in and save them. The people then continue to procreate and soon outstrip their capacities once again, only worse, because there are more of them—and *more* well-meaning people step in again, and the process is repeated, each time getting worse as the population grows. Eventually a time will come when there are so many people overall that even the altruists' resources are threatened. In effect, by aiding the world's

> The last solution [admit no one to the lifeboat] is abhorrent to many people. It is unjust, they say. Let us grant that it is.
>
> "I feel guilty about my good luck," say some. The reply to this is simple: *Get out and yield your place to others.* Such a selfless action might satisfy the conscience of those who are addicted to guilt but it would not change the ethics of the lifeboat.
>
> —**Garrett Hardin**, "Living on a Lifeboat" (1974)

poor we are, in the long run, swamping our lifeboat, if not in our own generation then in our children's or grandchildren's.

As Hardin puts it, "To be generous with one's own possessions is one thing; to be generous with posterity's is quite another" (670). If you take the utilitarian calculations seriously, then, the right thing to do is *not* to aid the poor now, despite their suffering, so that you may maximize everyone's welfare over the long term. As a response to Singer's argument, we might understand this not as rejecting the second premise, but as an argument that saving those dying children *does* amount to sacrificing something "nearly as important," namely long term welfare for all. So you shouldn't save those children.

(Variations on Hardin's line include the charges that by aiding the world's poor, we are breeding dangerous and unhealthy dependency; and that we are undermining the possibility of real political change that would, long term, prevent such impoverishment and starvation in the first place.)

Now the *conservative response* to world hunger admits of many versions, represented by thinkers as diverse as Thomas Hobbes (1588–1679), Ayn Rand (1905–1982), and Robert Nozick (1938–2002). But the key idea they share is to reject the claim that anyone has natural or intrinsic rights that entail moral duties on the part of others to help them or promote their good. You can't hold, in other words, that the poor, or starving, or dying have any *right* to our aiding them, and therefore that we have any obligation to help them. It even follows that we have no obligation to dirty our new shoes to rescue Singer's drowning child. Of course you aren't entitled to harm others, either. But key for now is that you are not obligated to help them.

What drives this view is the claim that the only right we have is that of freedom, the right to be left alone, to possess our property in peace. As long as your property is legitimately owned, no one has any right to require you to share it in any way. Any other obligations we may incur we do so by means of contracts or agreements freely entered into. But absent some kind of explicit (or perhaps implicit) contract, no one has *any* obligations to anyone else.

Unlike the neo-Malthusian view, this view simply rejects Singer's second premise. It may be in your power to prevent something bad without sacrificing anything nearly as important, but still you are not obligated to do so, so it is *not* wrong not to do so. You aren't forbidden from helping, either, of course. You are free to help if you wish, and we may even think highly of you for helping. But part of what makes such behavior a moral ideal (perhaps) is precisely that is not obligatory. You did it not because you were obligated to but because you were just that kind of person. You are not behaving wrongly for not helping, but you may be behaving well by helping.

This point of view is also articulated by Canadian philosopher Jan Narveson (b. 1936).[19] Singer himself summarizes the view nicely:

> We are certainly responsible for evils we inflict on others, no matter where, and we owe those people compensation. . . . Nevertheless, I have seen no plausible argument that we owe something, as a matter of general duty, to those to whom we have done nothing wrong. (28)

Framed this way, the debate might well turn empirical, as it often is today in our globalized world. To what degree (for example) are wealthy nations actually responsible for the state of poverty and starvation in other nations?

Let's turn now to some objections to Singer's second premise suggested by Pojman. Perhaps the most fundamental one derives from utilitarianism's basic idea that all people should count equally. But that simply isn't how most people feel, as we mentioned, not merely psychologically but morally. Most feel that we *are* justified in weighing the interests of some over those of others, starting with ourselves, then expanding outward to family, relatives, friends, and so on. But Singer's second premise, construed strongly, may suggest that we have duties to others that require us to sacrifice a lot of our own interests. Suppose a stranger will die unless he receives a kidney, and you are nearby with healthy kidneys. A kidney is not "nearly as important" as a life. The surgery has some risks but you are likely to be fine, to live a good life afterward, and in so doing you will save a life. But it seems to many that it is too much to say you are wrong in *not* donating the kidney. You owe yourself more than you owe a complete stranger, and while the kidney may not be "nearly as important" as the life, sacrificing it isn't negligible either. Perhaps we ought to make *reasonable*

The risks are in the [kidney transplant] operation. "I had a one-in-four-thousand chance of dying," Kravinsky told me. "But my recipient [a total stranger] had a certain death facing her." To Kravinsky, this was straightforward. "I'd be valuing my life at four thousand times hers if I let consideration of mortality sway me [into not donating]. . . . But many people felt the way my wife did: she said, "No matter how infinitesimal the risk to [you and] your family, we're your family, and the recipient doesn't count."

—"The Gift" by Ian Parker, a profile of Zell Kravinsky, who donated his kidney to a complete stranger (*The New Yorker*, August 2, 2004)

sacrifices for others, and then debate whether giving up the kidney is reasonable. But being required to make "reasonable" sacrifices seems itself more reasonable than being required to sacrifice anything that isn't "nearly as important." (Remember, you needn't deny that giving up the kidney would be a good thing to do. The question is only whether we are morally obligated to do so.)

But there are problems even if you interpret Singer's second premise more weakly. Suppose you read it to obligate you to prevent anything bad as long as you needn't sacrifice anything *significant* to you in so doing. (This change lessens how important the thing needs to be before you are obligated to sacrifice it.) The problem now is that what we value, what we take to be significant, may well vary dramatically, and legitimately, from person to person. What Singer suggests are luxuries—meals, electronics, clothing, entertainment, and so on—may truly matter to some people. For some people their brand new shoes might matter a great deal, and might not be "insignificant" to them. But then the second premise no longer obligates that person to save the drowning child, for doing so *would* require sacrificing something significant. On this response, Singer's second premise may still count as true, but it would no longer support the conclusion that we, or most people, are obligated to aid the poor.

To allow this variation in values is essentially to reject the idea that people count equally. Some people simply, and legitimately, value their family's and friend's interests over others'. But if your parents' happiness (say) is more valuable to you than that of some stranger, then it may be morally permissible even from a utilitarian perspective for you to increase their happiness a little instead of increasing the stranger's happiness a lot. Suppose you have $100 to spend and must decide whether to buy a nice anniversary gift for your parents or send the money to a charity and save a distant life. Assume the gift will increase your parents' happiness two units, and the life saved will increase that person's (and others') total happiness ten units. If all people counted equally, then utilitarianism says give the money to charity. But if you value your parents (say) six times more than the stranger, then utilitarianism says you should buy the anniversary gift, for that yields 6 x 2 or 12 units of happiness as opposed to 1 x 10 or 10 units of happiness.

That may sound cavalier as an example, but it's worth thinking deeply about the point. If you are justified in choosing your own values, you are justified in your moral weightings; and if so, you will be much less easily obligated to save those far away lives. (It might be worth exploring whether utilitarianism must count everyone equally, or can accommodate these concerns; and, if so, how that affects Singer's overall argument.)

This point about the diversity of values leads to another kind of criticism, one voiced by Colin McGinn (b. 1950). McGinn has called Singer's second premise "positively bad, morally speaking," for "it encourages a way of life in which many important values are sacrificed to generalized altruism" and devalues "spending one's energies on things other than helping suffering people in distant lands. . . . Just think of how much the human race would have lost if Newton and Darwin and Leonardo and Socrates had spent their time on charitable acts!"[20]

There are at least two ways to understand McGinn's point. For one, he may be noting that we value other things besides aiding the poor and saving lives, including intellectual and artistic and philosophical pursuits, and so on. Not all values, we might put it, are strictly moral values. So while Singer may be correct to say that we have a moral obligation to aid the poor, it doesn't mean we are acting *wrongly* for not doing so. It might just mean that sometimes we are justified in not doing the morally right thing, for example when there is something else we legitimately value more.

Alternatively, McGinn may be suggesting that Singer is doing the utilitarian calculus incorrectly. The calculation of the long-term happiness of humanity must take into account *everything*, not merely the happiness generated by giving aid to the poor but also by all the other things human beings do with their time. When you add it all up historically, humanity is better off (overall happier) because certain individuals spent their time producing mathematics and science and art rather than aiding the poor. On this reading, we might say that Singer's second premise is basically acceptable, but that Singer wrongly applies it in concluding we should aid the poor—for doing that *does* amount to sacrificing something "nearly as important," long term.

So now, it's up to you to decide how to spend your time. Should you get your college degree, or quit and go work for an aid organization? Should you give up your luxuries and donate far more money to charity? What counts as a luxury, anyway? Are you a moral monster for going to the movies once in a while? How can you do the most good, over the long term? What *is* the most good, over the long term?

Good luck with your deliberations.

SUMMARY

1. In this chapter our emphasis has been on practical ethics. Many pressing questions are raised about how to behave in many different domains, including health and medicine, sexuality, capital punishment, the individual versus society, environmental ethics, and so on. Deciding how to behave involves a mix of metaethics, ethical theory, and practical ethics, and to illustrate some of the issues, we focused on the ethical theory of utilitarianism and on the work of Peter Singer.

2. In "All Animals Are Equal" (1974), Singer argues that animals, given their ability to experience pain and pleasure, should be given equal moral consideration to human beings. The

principle of equality requires this, and those who violate it are speciesists. That most people are speciesists is demonstrated by our consumption of animals for food and use of them for experimentation.

3. In response to Singer, the Bible, and many traditional religious thinkers, hold that animals exist for human ends. Even a utilitarian could agree, if the calculations suggest that overall, for the long term, our use of animals provides adequate benefits (particularly with respect to scientific and medical experiments).

4. In "Is the Sanctity of Life Ethic Terminally Ill?" (1995), Singer rejects the sanctity of life ethic and the attempt to define brain death as death. What should matter is quality of life, not merely life, and when lives lose the possibility of an appropriate degree of quality (as in the case of brain death), then we should be morally permitted to end them. The Harvard Committee attempted to justify this by defining brain death as death. But those definitions are not convincing, and ultimately unnecessary, once you adopt the quality of life ethic.

5. In response to Singer, religious thinkers adopt the traditional sanctity of life ethic, according to which all lives are of equal (sacred) value regardless of their "quality." Others worry about the slippery slope Singer leads us onto. Once you permit unplugging the brain dead because they have lost the capacity for consciousness, you may soon be permitting abortion, infanticide, and suicide both assisted and unassisted. Similar considerations allow an "anything goes" approach to sexuality, including promiscuity, pedophilia, and incest. Other slippery slopes are of a more practical nature. If you permit harvesting organs from brain dead people who are yet alive, then (for example) doctors and hospitals will have a financial incentive to declare people brain dead very quickly, with perhaps tragic consequences.

6. In *The Life You Can Save* (2009), Singer presents the shallow pond thought experiment. Just as you would be acting wrongly in ignoring the drowning child in order to save your shoes, he argues, you are acting wrongly almost all the time by spending money on things other than aiding dying children. The key principle is the second premise in his argument: "If it is in your power to prevent something bad from happening, without sacrificing anything nearly as important, it is wrong not to do so." Most would immediately agree, but then the surprising conclusions quickly follow.

7. There are many practical obstacles that keep people from giving. People are selfish, or unmoved by abstract statistics, or inclined to give only locally, or disinclined to give when it appears futile, or others aren't doing their fair share. But none of these are morally relevant. You are still acting wrongly in giving in to them, and your moral obligation is to overcome them.

8. Philosophical objections come from several directions. Neo-Malthusians, such as Garrett Hardin, adopt a lifeboat ethics, according to which we have no obligations to help the poor and, in addition, the utilitarian calculations suggest that long-term we are acting wrongly in helping the poor. Conservatives hold that the poor have no rights to our aid, so we have no obligation to them. Louis Pojman critiques Singer's second premise, suggesting that we are justified in holding that we owe ourselves and our families (etc.) far more than we owe strangers. As a result, "small sacrifices" might count heavily for us, freeing us from the obligation to help strangers. Colin McGinn argues that we are justified in valuing other things besides helping others, including the pursuits of science and art. So even if we are morally obligated to help others, we are justified sometimes in not doing what morality obliges.

KEY TERMS

euthanasia
lifeboat ethics
principle of equality
quality of life ethic
sanctity of life

the shallow pond
slippery slope
speciesism
supererogatory

REVIEW QUESTIONS

1. Identify any three ethical questions raised by the case of the baby that introduced this chapter.

2. What is speciesism, and in what way(s) is it like racism and sexism?

3. Summarize how utilitarianism is at play, either explicitly or implicitly, in all three of the Singer arguments discussed in this chapter (concerning animal equality, the sanctity of life ethic, and the obligation to save the dying children).

4. Summarize one objection raised to each of the three arguments.

NOTES

1. *Los Angeles Times*, March 17, 1972. Reprinted by permission.

2. *How Are We to Live? Ethics in an Age of Self-Interest* (Melbourne, Australia: Text Publishing, 1993), 5.

3. *How Are We to Live?*, 275.

4. *Philosophic Exchange*, vol. 1, 103–16.

5. He updated the essay in 1993, in his book *Practical Ethics*, 2nd ed. (Cambridge; New York: Cambridge University Press, 1993).

6. *The New Yorker*, September 6, 1999, 50.

7. C. Cohen, "The Case for the Use of Animals in Biomedical Research," *The New England Journal of Medicine* 315(14), October 2, 1986, pp. 865–70.

8. Singer, "Is the Sanctity of Life Ethic Terminally Ill?" *Bioethics* 9(3–4), July 1995, pp. 307–43.

9. Singer, *Rethinking Life and Death* (Melbourne, Australia: Text Publishing, 1994).

10. Reprinted in Helga Khuse and Peter Singer (eds.), *Bioethics*, 2nd ed. (Malden, MA; Oxford: Blackwell, 2006).

11. *Journal of the American Medical Association* 205: 6 (August 1968). Reprinted in *Bioethics*, 2nd ed.

12. *How Are We to Live?*, 18–19.

13. See Dick Teresi, *The Undead: Organ Harvesting, the Ice-Water Test, Beating Heart Cadavers: How Medicine Is Blurring the Line Between Life and Death* (New York: Pantheon, 2012).

14. http://mosaicscience.com/story/mind-readers (April, 2014).

15. http://blog.givewell.org/2009/03/06/review-of-the-life-you-can-save-by-peter-singer/

16. *Philosophy and Public Affairs* 1 (Spring 1972), 229–43.

17. Pojman, "World Hunger and Population," from *Life and Death*, 2nd ed., Wadsworth. Reprinted in Lewis Vaughn, *Contemporary Moral Arguments* (New York: Oxford University Press, 2010).

18. Hardin, "Living on a Lifeboat," *Bioscience* 24 (1974). Reprinted in Vaughn, *Contemporary Moral Arguments*.

19. Narveson, "'We Don't Owe Them a Thing!' A Tough-Minded but Soft-hearted View of Aid to the Faraway Needy," *Monist* 86(3), 2009.

20. Quoted in "The Gift" by Ian Parker (*New Yorker*, August 2, 2004), 54.

■ Reading
"Of Duties to Animals . . ."

IMMANUEL KANT

"Of Duties to Animals ..." (c. 1790); from Lectures on Ethics, *trans. Peter Heath, eds. Peter Heath and J. B. Schneewind (Cambridge, UK: Cambridge University Press, 1997), pp. 212–13. Reprinted with permission.*

In this excerpt Kant argues that we have only indirect duties to animals.

[Baumgarten] here goes on to speak of duties to beings that are above us and beneath us. But since all animals exist only as means, and not for their own sakes, in that they have no self-consciousness, whereas man is the end, such that I can no longer ask: Why does he exist?, as can be done with animals, it follows that we have no immediate duties to animals; our duties towards them are indirect duties to humanity. Since animals are an analogue of humanity, we observe duties to mankind when we observe them as analogues to this, and thus cultivate our duties to humanity. If a dog, for example, has served his master long and faithfully, that is an analogue of merit; hence I must reward it, and once the dog can serve no longer, must look after him to the end, for I thereby cultivate my duty to humanity, as I am called upon to do; so if the acts of animals arise out of the same [principle] from which human actions spring, and the animal actions are analogues of this, we have duties to animals, in that we thereby promote the cause of humanity. So if a man has his dog shot, because it can no longer earn a living for him, he is by no means in breach of any duty to the dog, since the latter is incapable of judgement, but he thereby damages the kindly and humane qualities in himself, which he ought to exercise in virtue of his duties to mankind. Lest he extinguish such qualities, he must already practice a similar kindliness towards animals; for a person who already displays such cruelty to animals is also no less hardened towards men. We can already know the human heart, even in regard to animals. Thus Hogarth, in his engravings, also depicts the beginnings of cruelty, where already the children are practicing it upon animals, e.g., by pulling the tail of a dog or cat; in another scene we see the progress of cruelty, where the man runs over a child; and finally the culmination of cruelty in a murder, at which point the rewards of it appear horrifying. This provides a good lesson to children. The more we devote ourselves to observing animals and their behavior, the more we love them, on seeing how greatly they care for their young; in such a context, we cannot even contemplate cruelty to a wolf.

Leibnitz put the grub he had been observing back on the tree with its leaf, lest he should be guilty of doing any harm to it. It upsets a man to destroy such a creature for no reason, and this tenderness is subsequently transferred to man. In England, no butcher, surgeon or doctor serves on the twelve-man jury, because they are already inured to death. So when anatomists take living animals to experiment on, that is certainly cruelty, though there it is employed for a good purpose; because animals are regarded as man's instruments, it is acceptable, though it is never so in sport. If a master turns out his ass or his dog, because it can no longer earn its keep, this always shows a very small mind in the master. . . . Thus our duties to animals are indirectly duties to humanity.

REVIEW AND DISCUSSION QUESTIONS

1. Briefly summarize Kant's view on what our moral obligations are toward animals.
2. In what way(s) does his view differ from Peter Singer's, as described in the main text?

■ Reading
"Abortion and Infanticide"

PETER SINGER

From Practical Ethics, *3rd Edition (Cambridge, UK: Cambridge University Press, 2011), 151–54.*
Reprinted with permission.

In this excerpt Singer examines some of the moral issues raised by aspects of childbirth.

There remains one major objection to the argument I have advanced in favour of abortion. We have already seen that the strength of the conservative position lies in the difficulty liberals have in pointing to a morally significant line of demarcation between an embryo and a newborn baby. The standard liberal position needs to be able to point to some such line, because liberals usually hold that it is permissible to kill an embryo or fetus but not a baby. I have argued that the life of a fetus (and even more plainly, of an embryo) is of no greater value than the life of a nonhuman animal at a similar level of rationality, self-awareness, capacity to feel and so on, and that because no fetus is a person, no fetus has the same claim to life as a person. Now we have to face the fact that these arguments apply to the newborn baby as much as to the fetus. A week-old baby is not a rational and self-aware being, and there are many nonhuman animals whose rationality, self-awareness, capacity to feel and so on, exceed that of a human baby a week or a month old. If, for the reasons I have given, the fetus does not have the same claim to life as a person, it appears that the newborn baby does not either. Thus, although my position on the status of fetal life may be acceptable to many, the implications of this position for the status of newborn life are at odds with the virtually unchallenged assumption that the life of a newborn baby is as sacrosanct as that of an adult. Indeed, some people seem to think that the life of a baby is more precious than that of an adult. Lurid tales of German soldiers bayoneting Belgian babies figured prominently in the wave of anti-German propaganda that accompanied Britain's entry into the First World War, and it seemed to be tacitly assumed that this was a greater atrocity than the murder of adults.

I do not regard the conflict between the position I have taken and widely accepted views about the sanctity of infant life as a ground for abandoning my position. In thinking about ethics, we should not hesitate to question ethical views that are almost universally accepted if we have reasons for thinking that they may not be as securely grounded as they appear to be. It is true that infants appeal to us because they are small and helpless, and there are no doubt very good evolutionary reasons why we should instinctively feel protective towards them. It is also true that infants cannot be combatants, and killing infants in wartime is the clearest possible case of killing civilians, which is prohibited by international convention. In general, because infants are harmless and morally incapable of committing a crime, those who kill them lack the excuses often offered for the killing of adults. None of this shows, however, that the death of an infant is as bad as the death of an (innocent) adult.

In attempting to reach a considered ethical judgment about this matter, we should put aside feelings based on the small, helpless and—sometimes—cute appearance of human infants. To think that the lives of infants are of special value because infants are small and cute is on a par with thinking that a baby seal, with its soft white fur coat and large round eyes deserves greater protection than a gorilla, who lacks these attributes. Nor can the helplessness or the innocence of the infant *Homo sapiens* be a ground for preferring it to the equally helpless and innocent fetal *Homo sapiens*, or, for that matter, to laboratory rats who are 'innocent' in exactly the same sense as the human infant, and, in view of the experimenters' power over them, almost as helpless.

If we can put aside these emotionally moving but strictly irrelevant aspects of the killing of a baby, we can see that the grounds for not killing persons do not apply to newborn infants. The indirect, classical utilitarian reason does not apply, because no one capable of understanding what is happening when a newborn baby is killed could feel threatened by a policy that gave less protection to the newborn than to adults. In this respect, Bentham was right to describe infanticide as 'of a nature not to give the slightest inquietude to the most timid imagination'. Once we are old enough to comprehend the policy, we are too old to be threatened by it.

Similarly, the preference utilitarian reason for respecting the life of a person cannot apply to a newborn baby. Newborn babies cannot see themselves as beings that might or might not have a future, and so they cannot have a desire to continue living. For the same reason, if a right to life must be based on the capacity to want to go on living, or on the ability to see oneself as a continuing mental subject, a newborn baby cannot have a right to life. Finally, a newborn baby is not an autonomous being, capable of making choices, and so to kill a newborn baby cannot violate the principle of respect for autonomy. In all this, the newborn baby is on the same footing as the fetus, and hence fewer reasons exist against killing both babies and fetuses than exist against killing those who are capable of seeing themselves as distinct entities, existing over time.

It would, of course, be difficult to say at what age children begin to see themselves as distinct entities existing over time. But a difficulty in drawing the line is not a reason for drawing it in a place that is obviously wrong, any more than the notorious difficulty in saying how much hair a man has to have lost before we can call him 'bald' is a reason for saying that someone whose pate is as smooth as a billiard ball is not bald. Granted, where rights are at risk, we should err on the side of safety. There is some plausibility in the view that, for legal purposes, because birth provides the only sharp, clear and easily understood line, the law of homicide should continue to apply from the moment of birth. Because this is an argument at the level of public policy and the law, it is quite compatible with the view that, on purely ethical grounds, the killing of a newborn infant is not comparable with the killing of an older child or adult. Alternatively, recalling Hare's distinction between the critical and intuitive levels of moral reasoning, one could hold that the ethical judgment we have reached applies only at the level of critical morality; for everyday decision making, we should act as if an infant has a right to life from the moment of birth. In the next chapter, however, we shall consider another possibility: that there should be at least some circumstances in which a full legal right to life comes into force, not at birth, but only a short time after birth—perhaps a month. This would provide the ample safety margin mentioned previously.

If these conclusions seem too shocking to take seriously, it may be worth remembering that our present absolute protection of the lives of infants is a distinctively Christian attitude rather than a universal ethical value. Infanticide has been practised in societies ranging geographically from Tahiti to Greenland and varying in culture from nomadic Australian aborigines to the sophisticated urban communities of ancient Greece or mandarin China or Japan before the late nineteenth century. In some of these societies, infanticide was not merely permitted but, in certain circumstances, deemed morally obligatory. Not to kill a deformed or sickly infant was often regarded as wrong, and infanticide was probably the first, and in several societies the only, form of population control.

We might think that we are more 'civilized' than these 'primitive' peoples, but it is not easy to feel confident that we are more civilized than the best Greek and Roman moralists, nor than the highly sophisticated civilizations of China and Japan. In ancient Greece, it was not just the Spartans who exposed their infants on hillsides: both Plato and Aristotle recommended the killing of deformed infants. Romans like Seneca, whose compassionate moral sense strikes the modern reader (or me, anyway) as superior to that of the early and mediaeval Christian writers, also thought infanticide the natural and humane solution to the problem posed by sick and deformed babies. The change in Western attitudes to infanticide since Roman times is, like the doctrine of the sanctity of human life of which it is a part, a product of Christianity. Perhaps it is now possible to think about these issues without assuming the Christian moral framework that has, for so long, prevented any fundamental reassessment.

REVIEW AND DISCUSSION QUESTION

1. What do *you* think about the many issues Singer raises in this reading?

■ Reading
"Taking Life: Humans"

PETER SINGER

From Practical Ethics, *3rd Edition (Cambridge, UK: Cambridge University Press, 2011), 158–67. Reprinted with permission.*

In this excerpt Singer examines nonvoluntary euthanasia, particularly in the controversial case of infanticide.

NONVOLUNTARY EUTHANASIA

These two definitions leave room for a third kind of euthanasia. If a human being is not capable of understanding the choice between life and death, euthanasia would be neither voluntary nor involuntary, but nonvoluntary. Those unable to give consent would include incurably ill or severely disabled infants and people who through accident, illness or old age have permanently lost the capacity to understand the issue involved, without having previously requested or rejected euthanasia in these circumstances.

In 1988 Samuel Linares, an infant, swallowed a small object that stuck in his windpipe, causing a loss of oxygen to the brain. Had such a case occurred fifty years earlier, Samuel would undoubtedly have died soon afterwards, and no decision would have had to be made. Instead, given the availability of modern medical technology, he was admitted to a Chicago hospital in a coma and placed on a respirator. Eight months later he was still comatose, still on the respirator, and the hospital was planning to move Samuel to a long-term care unit. Shortly before the move, Samuel's parents visited him in the hospital. His mother left the room, while his father produced a pistol and told the nurse to keep away. He then disconnected Samuel from the respirator and cradled the baby in his arms until he died. When he was sure Samuel was dead, he gave up his pistol and surrendered to police. He was charged with murder, but the grand jury refused to issue a homicide indictment, and he subsequently received a suspended sentence on a minor charge arising from the use of the pistol.

In Canada in 1993, Robert Latimer killed his twelve-year-old disabled daughter Tracey by placing her in the cabin of the family truck and piping exhaust fumes into it. Evidence suggested that Tracey, who had a severe form of cerebral palsy, could not walk, talk, or feed herself and had suffered considerable pain. Latimer said that his priority was 'to put her out of her pain'. He was convicted of murder and sentenced to life imprisonment with a minimum of ten years before parole. Many Canadians felt the sentence was unreasonably harsh, but several appeals failed to free Latimer. He was granted parole in 2008.

Obviously, such cases raise different issues from those raised by voluntary euthanasia. There is no desire to die on the part of the person killed. The question can be raised whether, in such cases, the death is carried out for the sake of the infant or for the sake of the family as a whole. Caring for Samuel Linares would have been a great and no doubt futile burden for the family and a drain on the state's limited medical resources; but if he was comatose, he could not have been suffering, and death could not be said to be in (or contrary to) his interests. It is therefore not euthanasia, strictly speaking, as I have defined the term. It might nevertheless be a justifiable ending of a human life.

Because cases of infanticide and nonvoluntary euthanasia are the kind of cases most nearly akin to our previous discussions of the status of animals and the human fetus, we shall consider them first.

JUSTIFYING INFANTICIDE AND NONVOLUNTARY EUTHANASIA

As we have seen, euthanasia is nonvoluntary when the subject has never had the capacity to choose to live or die. This is the situation of the severely disabled infant or the older human being who has been profoundly intellectually disabled since birth. Euthanasia or other forms of killing are also nonvoluntary when the subject is not now but once was capable of making the crucial choice and did not then express any preference relevant to her present condition.

The case of someone who has never been capable of choosing to live or die is a little more straightforward than that of a person who had, but has now lost, the capacity to make such a decision. We shall, once again, separate the two cases and take the more straightforward one first. For simplicity, I shall concentrate on infants, although everything I say about them would apply to older children or adults whose mental age is and has always been that of an infant.

Life and Death Decisions for Disabled Infants

If we were to approach the issue of life or death for a seriously disabled human infant without any prior discussion of the ethics of killing in general, we might be unable to resolve the conflict between the widely accepted obligation to protect the sanctity of human life and the goal of reducing suffering. Some say that such clashes of fundamental values can only be resolved by a 'subjective' decision, or that life and death questions must be left to God and Nature. Our previous discussions have, however, prepared the ground, and the principles established and applied in the preceding three chapters make the issue much less baffling than most take it to be.

In Chapter 4, we saw that the fact that a being is a human being, in the sense of a member of the species *Homo sapiens*, is not relevant to the wrongness of killing it; instead, characteristics like rationality, autonomy and self-awareness make a difference. Infants lack these characteristics. Killing them, therefore, cannot be equated with killing normal human beings or any other self-aware beings. The principles that govern the wrongness of killing nonhuman animals that are sentient but not rational or self-aware must apply here too. As we saw, the most plausible arguments for attributing a right to life to a being apply only if there is some awareness of oneself as a being existing over time or as a continuing mental self. Nor can respect for autonomy apply where there is no capacity for autonomy. The remaining principles identified in Chapter 4 are utilitarian. Hence, the quality of life that the infant can be expected to have is important.

This conclusion is not limited to infants who, because of irreversible intellectual disabilities, will never be rational, self-aware beings. We saw in our discussion of abortion that the potential of a fetus to become a rational, self-aware being cannot count against killing it at a stage when it lacks these characteristics—not, that is, unless we are also prepared to count the value of rational self-aware life as a reason against contraception and celibacy. No infant—disabled or not—has as strong an intrinsic claim to life as beings capable of seeing themselves as distinct entities existing over time.

The difference between killing disabled and normal infants lies, not in any supposed right to life that the latter has and the former lacks, but in other considerations about killing. Most obviously, there is the difference that often exists in the attitudes of the parents. The birth of a child is usually a happy event for the parents. They are likely to have planned for the child. The mother has carried it for nine months. From birth, a natural affection begins to bind the parents to it. So one important reason why it is normally a terrible thing to kill an infant is the effect the killing will have on its parents.

It is different when the infant is born with a serious disability. Birth abnormalities vary, of course. Some are trivial and have little effect on the child or its parents, but others turn the normally joyful event of birth into a threat to the happiness of the parents and of any other children they may have.

Parents may, with good reason, regret that a disabled child was ever born. In those circumstances, the effect that the death of the child will have on its parents can be a reason for, rather than against, killing it. Of course, this is not always the case. Some parents want even the most gravely disabled infant to live as long as possible, and their desire is then a reason against killing the infant. But what if this is not the case? In the discussion that follows, I shall assume that the parents do not want the disabled child to live. I shall also assume that the disability is so serious that—again in contrast to the situation of an unwanted but normal child today—there are no other couples keen to adopt the infant. This is a realistic assumption even in a society in which there is a long waiting list of couples wishing to adopt normal babies. It is true that from time to time, when a case of an infant who is severely disabled and is being allowed to die has been publicised, couples have come forward offering to adopt the child. Unfortunately, such offers are the product of the highly publicised dramatic life-and-death situation and do not extend to the less publicised but far more common situations in which parents feel themselves unable to look after a severely disabled child, and the child then languishes in an institution.

Consider, for instance, Tay-Sachs disease, a genetic condition that within the first year of life causes the child's muscles to atrophy. The child becomes blind, deaf, unable to swallow and eventually paralysed. The child also suffers mental deterioration and has seizures. Even with the best medical care, children with Tay-Sachs disease usually die before their fifth birthday. This seems to be a life that can reasonably be judged not to be worth living. When the life of an infant will be so miserable as not to be worth living, from the internal perspective of the being who will lead that life, both the 'prior existence' and the 'total' version of utilitarianism entail that if there are no 'extrinsic' reasons for keeping the infant alive—like the feelings of the parents—it is better that the child should be helped to die without further suffering.

A more difficult problem arises—and the convergence between the two views ends—when we consider disabilities that make the child's life prospects significantly less promising than those of a normal child, but not so bleak as to make the life one not worth living. Haemophilia may serve as an example. The haemophiliac lacks the element in normal blood that makes it clot and thus risks prolonged bleeding, especially internal bleeding, from the slightest injury. If allowed to continue, this bleeding leads to permanent crippling and eventually death. The bleeding is painful, and although improved treatments have eliminated the need for constant blood transfusions, haemophiliacs still have to spend a lot of time in hospital. They are unable to play most sports and live constantly on the edge of crisis. Nevertheless, haemophiliacs do not appear to spend their time wondering whether to end it all; most find life definitely worth living, despite the difficulties they face.

Given these facts, suppose that a newborn baby is diagnosed as a haemophiliac. The parents, daunted by the prospect of bringing up a child with this condition, are not anxious for him to live. Could euthanasia be defended here? Our first reaction may well be a firm 'no', for the infant can be expected to have a life that is well worth living, even if not quite as good as that of a normal child. The 'prior existence' version of utilitarianism supports this judgment. The infant exists. His life can be expected to contain a positive balance of happiness over misery. To kill him would deprive him of this positive balance of happiness. Therefore, it would be wrong.

On the 'total' version of utilitarianism, on the other hand, we cannot reach a decision on the basis of this information alone. The total view makes it necessary to ask whether the death of the haemophiliac infant would lead to the creation of another being who would not otherwise have existed. In other words, if the haemophiliac child is killed, will his parents have another child whom they would not have if the haemophiliac child lives? If they would, is the second child likely to have a better life than the one killed?

Often it will be possible to answer both these questions affirmatively. Like the mountaineer we considered in the previous chapter, a woman may plan to have two children. If one dies while she is of child-bearing age, she may conceive another in its place. Suppose a woman planning to have two children has one normal child, and then gives birth to a haemophiliac child. The burden of caring for that child may make it impossible for her to cope with a third child; but if the disabled child were to die, she would have another. It is also plausible to suppose that the prospects of a happy life are better for a normal child than for a haemophiliac.

If we favour the total view rather than the prior existence view, then we have to take account of the probability that when the death of a disabled infant will lead to the birth of another infant with better prospects of a happy life, the total amount of happiness will be greater if the disabled infant is killed. The loss of happy life for the first infant is outweighed by the gain of a happier life for the second. Therefore, if killing the haemophiliac infant has no adverse effect on others, it would, according to the total view, be right to kill him.

The total view treats infants as replaceable, in much the same way as it treats animals that are not self-aware as replaceable (as we saw in Chapter 5). Many will think that the replaceability argument cannot be applied to human infants. The direct killing of even the most hopelessly disabled infant is still officially regarded as murder. How then could the killing of infants with far less serious problems, like haemophilia, be accepted? Yet on further reflection, the implications of the replaceability argument do not seem quite so bizarre. For there are disabled members of our species whom we now deal with exactly as the argument suggests we should. These cases closely resemble the ones we have been discussing. There is only one difference, and that is a difference of timing—the timing of the discovery of the problem and the consequent killing of the disabled being.

Prenatal diagnosis is now routine for pregnant women. There are various medical techniques for obtaining information about the fetus during the early months of pregnancy. At one stage in the development of these techniques, it was possible to discover the sex of the fetus but not whether the fetus would suffer from haemophilia. Haemophilia is a sex-linked genetic defect from which only mates suffer—females can carry the gene and pass it on to their male offspring without themselves being affected. So a woman who knew that she carried the gene for haemophilia could, at that stage, avoid giving birth to a haemophiliac child only by finding out the sex of the fetus and aborting all males fetuses. Statistically, only half of these male children of women who carried the defective gene would have suffered from haemophilia, and so half of the fetuses being killed were normal. This practice was widespread in many countries and yet did not cause any great outcry. Now that we have techniques for identifying haemophilia before birth, we can be more selective, but the principle is the same: women are offered, and usually accept, abortions in order to avoid giving birth to children with haemophilia.

The same can be said about several other conditions that can be detected before birth. Down syndrome is one of these. Children with this condition have intellectual disabilities, and most will never be able to live independently, but their lives, like those of children, can be joyful. The risk of having a Down syndrome child increases sharply with the age of the mother, and for this reason in many countries prenatal diagnosis is offered to all pregnant women over thirty-five. The overwhelming majority of pregnant women who are told that their child will have Down syndrome end their pregnancy, and many start another pregnancy, which in most cases leads to the birth of a child without this condition.

Prenatal diagnosis, followed by abortion in selected cases, is common practice in countries with liberal abortion laws and advanced medical techniques. I think this is as it should be. As the arguments of the last chapter indicate, I believe that abortion can be justified. Note, however, that neither haemophilia nor Down syndrome is so crippling as to make life not worth living from the inner perspective of the person with the condition. To abort a fetus with one of these disabilities, intending to have another child who will not be disabled, is to treat fetuses as replaceable. If the mother has previously decided to have a certain number of children, then what she is doing, in effect, is rejecting one potential child in favour of another. She could, in defence of her actions, say: the loss of life of the aborted fetus is outweighed by the gain of a better life for the normal child that will be conceived only if the disabled one dies.

When death occurs before birth, replaceability does not conflict with generally accepted moral convictions. That a fetus is known to be disabled is widely accepted as grounds for abortion. Yet, in discussing abortion, we saw that birth does not mark a morally significant dividing line. It is not easy to defend the view that fetuses may be 'replaced' before birth but newborn infants may not be. Nor is there any other point, such as viability, that does a better job of dividing the fetus from the infant. Self-awareness, which could provide a basis for holding that it is wrong to kill one being and replace it with another, is not to be found in either the fetus or the newborn infant. Neither the fetus nor the newborn infant is an individual capable of regarding itself as a distinct entity with a life of its own to lead, and it is only for newborn infants, or for still earlier stages of human life, that replaceability should be considered to be an ethically acceptable option.

Some disability advocates object strongly to this conclusion. They say that to replace either a fetus or a newborn infant because of a disability is wrong, for it suggests to disabled people living today that their lives are less worth living than the lives of people who are not disabled. Yet that belief is the only way to make sense of actions that we all take for granted. Recall thalidomide: this drug, when taken by pregnant women, caused many children to be born without arms or legs. Once the cause of the abnormal births was discovered, the drug was taken off the market, and the company responsible had to pay compensation. If we really believed that there is no reason to think the life of a disabled person is likely to be any worse than that of a normal person, we would not have regarded the use of thalidomide by pregnant women as a tragedy. No compensation would have been sought by parents or awarded by the courts. The children would merely have been 'different'. We could even have left the drug on the market, so that women who found it a useful sleeping pill during pregnancy could continue to take it. If this sounds grotesque, that is only because we are all in no doubt at all that it is better to be born with limbs than without them. To believe this involves no disrespect at all for those who are lacking limbs; it simply recognizes the reality of the difficulties they face.

In any case, the position taken here does not imply that it would be better that no people born with severe disabilities should survive; it implies only that the parents of such infants should be able to make this decision. Nor does this imply lack of respect or equal consideration for people with disabilities who are now living their own lives in accordance with their own wishes. As we saw at the end of Chapter 2, the principle of equal consideration of interests rejects any discounting of the interests of people on grounds of disability.

Even those who reject abortion and the idea that the fetus is replaceable are likely to regard possible people as replaceable. Recall the second woman in Parfit's case of the two women, described in Chapter 5. She was told by her doctor that if she went ahead with her plan to become pregnant immediately, her child would have a disability (it could have been haemophilia); but if she waited three months, her child would not have the disability. If we think she would do wrong not to wait, it can only be because we are comparing the two possible lives and judging one to have better prospects than the other. Of course, at this stage no life has begun; but the question is, when does a life, in the morally significant sense, really begin? In Chapters 4 and 5, we saw several reasons for saying that life only gains its full moral significance when there is awareness of one's existence over time.

Regarding newborn infants as replaceable, as we now regard fetuses, would have considerable advantages over prenatal diagnosis followed by abortion. Prenatal diagnosis still cannot detect all major disabilities. Some disabilities, in fact, are not present before birth; they may be the result of extremely premature birth or of something going wrong in the birth process itself. At present, parents can choose whether to keep their disabled offspring only if the disability happens to be detected during pregnancy. There is no logical basis for restricting parents' choice to these particular disabilities. If newborn infants were not regarded as having a right to life until some time after birth, it would allow parents, in consultation with their doctors, to choose on the basis of far greater knowledge of the infant's condition than is possible before birth.

All these remarks have been concerned with the wrongness of ending the life of the infant considered in itself rather than for its effects on others. When we take effects on others into account, the picture may alter. Obviously, to go through the whole of pregnancy and labour only to give birth to a child who one decides should not live would be a difficult, perhaps heartbreaking, experience. For this reason, many women would prefer prenatal diagnosis and abortion rather than live birth with the possibility of infanticide; but if the latter is not morally worse than the former, this would seem to be a choice that the woman herself should be allowed to make.

Another factor to take into account is the possibility of adoption. When there are more couples wishing to adopt than normal children available for adoption, a childless couple may be prepared to adopt a haemophiliac. This would relieve the mother of the burden of bringing up a haemophiliac child and enable her to have another child, if she wished. Then the replaceability argument could not justify infanticide, for bringing the other child into existence would not be dependent on the death of the haemophiliac. The death of the haemophiliac would be a straightforward loss of a life of positive quality not outweighed by the creation of another being with a better life.

The issue of ending life for disabled newborn infants is not without complications, both factual and philosophical. Philosophically, the most difficult issue is whether to accept the prior existence or the total version of utilitarianism (or some other view altogether), because in the case of infants with disabilities whose lives are nevertheless worth living, the justifiability of a decision to end the infant's life will depend on which view we choose. Nevertheless, the main point remains clear, even after the various objections and complications have been considered: killing a disabled infant is not morally equivalent to killing a person. Very often it is not wrong at all.

REVIEW AND DISCUSSION QUESTION

1. What do *you* think about the many issues Singer raises in this reading?

■ Reading
"Life after God? The Ethics of Peter Singer"

PETER MAY

From ed. Tony Watkins, Playing God: Talking About Ethics in Medicine and Technology. © 2006 The *Damaris Trust. Published by Authentic Media, Milton Keynes, UK. Reprinted with permission.*

In this excerpt May provides a brief summary of, and Christian response to, Peter Singer's ethics.

Peter Singer is arguably the most famous and influential modern philosopher, offering the most radical challenge to traditional Judeo-Christian values. . . . Much of what follows is focused on his book *How Are We to Live?* (New York: Oxford University Press, 1993) with various references to other writings. [All page references are to this volume unless specified.]

HIS BROAD PERSPECTIVE

Singer is an atheist who very easily dismisses Judeo-Christian ethics as being out of date and irrelevant: 'We have no need to postulate gods who hand down commandments to us because we understand ethics as a natural phenomenon.'[1] He asks, 'What do I think of as a good life in the fullest sense of that term? This is an ultimate question' (9). The choice is ours because, in Singer's view, ethical principles are not laws written up in heaven. Nor are they absolute truths about the universe, known by intuition. The principles of ethics come from our own nature as social, reasoning beings. So he writes, 'We are free to choose what we are to be, because we have no essential nature, that is, no given purpose outside ourselves. Unlike say, an apple tree that has come into existence as a result of someone else's plan, we simply exist, and the rest is up to us' (5).

His principle reason for rejecting the Christian God is the existence of suffering in the world. In particular, he dismisses the idea that mankind is distinct from other animals by being 'made in the image of God'. Hence the 'Sanctity of Human Life' argument, which hangs on that distinction, goes out of the window. All that remains are 'Quality of Life' issues. This leads him to the utilitarian principle of 'The greatest happiness for the greatest number', which undergirds so much modern political thought. Pleasure (or, rather, 'preference satisfaction') becomes the greatest good; suffering and pain the only evils. Utilitarianism, therefore, invites an examination of the consequences of our actions, studying the effects of our choices on others. Our actions themselves have no intrinsic moral value—what matters is what happens. Our intentions count for nothing; the starting point is preference not idealistic motivation. Reducing ethical choices to a concern for personal preferences and useful consequences sounds like a simplification of life's moral dilemmas. However, the ethical process involved in arriving at such a decision can be extremely complicated. He writes:

> I must, if I am thinking ethically, imagine myself in the situation of all those affected by my action (with the preferences that they have). I must consider the interests of my enemies as well as my friends, and of strangers as well as family. Only if, after taking fully into account the interests and preferences of all these people, I still think the action is

better than any alternative open to me, can I genuinely say that I ought to do it. At the same time I must not ignore the long-term effects of fostering family ties, of establishing and promoting reciprocal relationships, and of allowing wrongdoers to benefit from their wrong doing. (206)

ABORTION AND INFANTICIDE

Suffering is, of course, more than just the experience of pain. It has to do with self-conscious awareness of suffering, involving the memory of past freedom from suffering, understanding the causes of suffering, and anticipating the future implications and possible options. An unborn child cannot suffer in this way—and, of course, cannot be said to have personal preferences, whether or not they could ever be expressed. If other people have preferences that the unborn child should not survive, and assuming the procedure can be done painlessly, there remains no moral barrier to terminating the pregnancy. So in his view:

> Those who regard the interests of women as overriding the merely potential interests of the foetus are taking their stand on a morally impregnable position. (18)

Furthermore, the situation is essentially unchanged for the newborn child, who does not understand what life is about and therefore can have no preference in the matter. If no one else has a preference that the child should live, infanticide within the first month of life can be morally justified. Here Singer introduces his ethic of *replaceability*. A child may not be wanted for various reasons, such as timing, gender or congenital disease. The decision-making process can be profoundly influenced if the death of an unwanted child subsequently allows the parents the freedom to have a wanted child who would replace it. Such ethics have not endeared him to the disabled community in general. They fear that his views support discrimination against them. Neither have they gone down well in Germany with its painful memories of the eugenics movement for genetic purity.

EUTHANASIA—VOLUNTARY AND NON-VOLUNTARY

Singer's overthrow of the 'Sanctity of Human Life Ethic', replacing it with a 'Quality of Life Ethic', comes most sharply into focus when considering voluntary euthanasia. This is most fully discussed in his book, *Rethinking Life and Death*, where he offers some new rules:[2]

Firstly, we should not see all human lives as of equal worth but recognise that some are more valuable than others. Such judgements should be made on the basis of the individual's capacity to think, relate and experience. Patients in a persistent vegetative state have none of these faculties. Without consciousness, life has no value. In cases of brain damage making it impossible for the patient to express a preference, this principle obviously opens the door to non-voluntary euthanasia.

Secondly, the taking of human life is not a moral issue in itself; the consequences of the action determine the ethical rightness of it. The preferences of the individual—if they can be expressed—are of central importance.

Thirdly, suicide is not intrinsically wrong. An individual's desire to die should be respected. Hence, it is ethical for a doctor to assist a suicide in fulfilling the patient's considered preference.

Singer distinguishes *human beings* in the biological sense from *persons*, who are rational and self conscious beings. He has no basis for seeing human beings in a different category from other animals. In general, humans have more intelligence and greater self-awareness, but some humans lack these faculties. In the newborn they are undeveloped; in the severely brain damaged they are lost; and in the dementing they are fading day by day. They are humans, but not persons. Some adult animals, however, are remarkably intelligent. They are persons, though not human.

More important for Singer is the division between sentient creatures, which can experience pleasure and suffering, and non-sentient creatures which cannot. Most—but not all—humans come in the first category, as do many animals. Hence the protection afforded to persons should be extended to such non-humans. The division between these categories is not always obvious. Some animals even seem to demonstrate a moral awareness by altruistic behaviour. He cites dolphins helping injured dolphins to breathe, wolves taking food back to the pack, chimpanzees calling others when they find ripe fruit, and gazelles putting their own lives at risk by warning of predators (102).

The focus of Singer's concern about animals is the human tendency to think in terms of species. While sexism and racism assert the superiority of one sex or race over another, *speciesism* asserts that humans are superior to other animals. Such discrimination, in Singer's view, is indefensible.[3] His philosophy not only rules out all cruelty to self-conscious, sentient beings, which includes adult mammals, but also rules out their killing. Fur coats and leather shoes cannot then be justified, and neither, in general, can eating meat.[4] If animal experimentation can ever be justified, then it must be equally justifiable to perform such experiments on severely mentally-retarded human adults, or normal infants who are not aware of what is being done to them.[5]

SEXUALITY

'The moral case for acceptance of sexual relationships between consenting adults that do not harm others is . . . clear-cut,' he writes (18–19). As long as the consequences of sexual acts fulfil the preferences of those involved and do not harm others, sexual ethics are of little or no importance. In his view, the important ethical issues in the world today are the fact that racial hatred stops people living together, that people are starving in an affluent world, that animals are bred in factory farms, and that we are damaging the ecological system of our planet. He writes:

> Once it is generally understood that ethics has no necessary connection with the sexually-obsessed morality of conservative Christianity, a humane and positive ethic could be the basis for a renewal of our social, political and ecological life. (18–19)

In a review article entitled *Heavy Petting*,[6] Singer asks what is wrong with human sexual activity with animals. The argument that bestiality is unnatural because it cannot lead to procreation is not good enough, he says, because many widely practised sexual activities, which are seen to be natural, cannot lead to procreation either. Isn't bestiality cruel and harmful? Not necessarily. Can animals meaningfully give consent to sex? Well, sometimes they initiate it, as for instance a dog rubbing its genitals against a human leg. If the animal shows a preference and there are no harmful consequences, there appear to be no grounds in Singer's ethical framework to object.

PART IV Contemporary Directions

Singer castigates Christians for their attitude to world poverty.[7] He sees a major discrepancy between their passion for the sanctity of life argument as it relates to the embryo, the unwanted infant and the terminally ill, and their failure to take seriously—in his view—Christ's teaching about possessions and the needs of the poor. He sees Christians being concerned for those who express no desire to live while ignoring the lives of countless people who long to hang on to life. Christ's teaching to the rich young ruler is certainly stark, and the wealth of Western Christians is disturbingly great.

CRITIQUE OF SINGER ON CHRISTIANITY

Singer finds it easy not to take Christianity seriously, He writes:

> Once we admit that Darwin was right when he argued that human ethics evolved from the social instincts that we inherited from our non-human ancestors, we can put aside the hypothesis of a divine origin for ethics. (*Ethics*, p. 6)

He has not written a substantial critique of Christianity, but his general antipathy is clear. He does not understand the dynamics of the gospel of grace, and so has a 'salvation by works' understanding of Christian theology, where ethical behaviour is driven by self-interest in rewards (212–13) and fear of punishments (20ff.). He is left with 'a man of straw' to knock down—or rather, marginalise.

As we have seen, central to his concerns is speciesism and the Judeo-Christian view that mankind is made uniquely in the image of God. He emphasises the Bible's view that humanity has been given dominion over the animals. This he always describes in terms of dominating rule, never as responsible, caring stewardship. Christians, however, do not believe that animals are their possession, to do with as they think fit. Singer emphasises *Genesis* 1:28 which speaks of 'rule' but ignores *Genesis* 2 which introduces the ideas of a 'duty of care' and also companionship. In fact, there are many references in the Bible to the well-being of animals, which Singer chooses to ignore. These passages qualify and describe how 'dominion' over the animals is to be expressed.[8]

In the New Testament, Jesus pointed to God's provision for the birds, but in saying that people are more valuable than they are, he is clearly not saying that they are without value before God (*Matthew* 6:26). Singer clearly does not like the way that Jesus cast out demons and sent them into a herd of pigs (*Matthew* 8:28-34), but he ignores the significance of Christ challenging the legalism of the Pharisees by asking, 'If one of you has a son or an ox that falls into a well on the Sabbath day, will you not immediately pull him out?' (*Luke* 14:5). Graham Cole comments that juxtaposing a child at risk and an ox at risk indicates the expanse of Christ's circle of compassion.[9] Cole also notes that in his letters, Paul describes God's ultimate purposes for the whole of creation[10] which Singer fails to consider. In other words, Singer's treatment of Scripture is misleading and unbalanced, if not unethical. He selects proof texts to support his argument, without trying to see them in their wider context.

CRITIQUE OF SINGER'S UTILITARIANISM

There are several well-documented difficulties with utilitarian philosophy.[11]

1. Consequences

The intellectual challenge of chess is to think through the consequences of a move and predict the knock-on effects. A move you think is brilliant may prove a short cut to being caught in checkmate. The game must be played slowly. The difficulty is that we cannot cope with too many possible alternatives, which is why most of us play chess badly! Only God can see the future; the rest of us have to settle for shrewd guesses. One amusing story about Singer is that he fed a vegetarian diet to his cat—with the result that the cat became very skilled at catching mice! According to Craig and Moreland, the consequences by which the action is to be judged have, 'an uncertainty that paralyses moral decision-making.' Furthermore, it 'brings to centre stage a tentativeness about duty that is not conducive to the development of conviction and character'.[12]

Consider the consequences of sexual activity. Commonly regarded as harmless pleasure, it is far from easy to predict the implications of a given sexual encounter, either emotionally, physically or socially. The consequences of an unwanted pregnancy should be obvious enough, but are frequently overlooked. Many, presumably to their great surprise, have found themselves quickly addicted to a new sexual partner or a new sexual behaviour that becomes very destructive to them and their families. Sexually transmitted diseases—often leading to infertility or cervical cancer—occur commonly and may be incurable, but they rarely seem to be anticipated. The single greatest cause of pain and suffering in the world today is due to the devastation brought by the sexual transmission of HIV, which does not even feature in Singer's list of 'the crucial moral questions of our day' (18–19). How could he overlook it? We do not know how the virus crossed from monkeys to humans—it could even have occurred through bestiality; whatever happened, the consequences could not have been imagined. Less surprising is his failure to even begrudgingly acknowledge that the only practice that could resolve the HIV epidemic (and do so largely within a generation) is the biblical ideal of one sexual partner for life. How can he think that sexual ethics are irrelevant?

2. Happiness

Each attempt to explain the principle of utilitarianism presents its own difficulties. The best known description is that it seeks 'the greatest happiness for the greatest number'. Two issues immediately arise that may well be in conflict.

Imagine that I have £1,000,000 to give away. If I was concerned for the greatest happiness, I might decide to give it all to one person and make him very happy indeed. However, if I was concerned for the greatest number, I might give £1 to each of a million people. Many would not even consider thanking me! Yet one might think that giving away money would be among the simpler moral decisions.

But there is a second, more fundamental problem. What exactly is happiness? And if I knew, how might I obtain it and then hold on to it? Those who experience the most intense happiness find they cannot maintain it. It inevitably fades. Similarly, those who experience the deepest tragedies seem, in the passage of time, to recover and once more find things to smile about. It is an extraordinary feature of life that some of the poorest people are among the most contented, while some of the wealthiest are among the most wretched. This is true of individuals, but it is also true of societies: 'Ghana, Mexico, Sweden, the United Kingdom and the United States all share similar life satisfaction scores despite per capita income varying ten-fold between the richest and the poorest country'.[13] If happiness is so poorly correlated to wealth, the same study, among others, shows that it *is* strongly correlated to the traditional family unit.

The divorce rate in Britain has quadrupled since 1970, and currently 40,000 children a year are prescribed anti-depressants. Therefore, one might suppose that the morality of actions that undermine the family unit, cannot be advocated on utilitarian grounds—again underlining the central importance of sexual ethics for human well-being.

3. Reductionism

Preference consequentialism seems a flat earth way of doing ethics. The whole process is reduced to a two-dimensional view of life: our actions are evaluated only in terms of preferences and consequences (whether or not they are actually predictable or measurable). There is no recognition of ultimate goodness, no acknowledgement of the importance of motive and intent, no significance attached to the agonies of conscience or the depths of moral revulsion, no sense of overall meaning and purpose, no exploration of the nature of self-denying love rather than 'preference satisfaction', no realisation of the need for forgiveness, no understanding of the fallibility of human moral character and no basis for considering justice. Nor does Singer allow the subtle influences of our relationships in moral decision making, even though his own rationality proved an insufficient guide in dealing with his mother's death from Alzheimer's disease.[14] His tough talk about euthanasia evaporated in the face of the personal reality. Morality is evaluated only on our preferences and the consequences of our actions, but most of us realize that there is rather more going on here as we make our choices.

4. The Yuk Factor[15]

In his letter to the Romans, Paul teaches that certain truths about right behaviour are instinctive. We don't need to be taught them, but if we suppress such intuitive awareness, it will affect our rational grasp of ethical judgements (*Romans* 1:18-32). In Paul's phrase, we will become 'futile in our thinking.'

Several aspects of Singer's teaching cause deep intuitive revulsion—not just in Christians, but in people who make many different assumptions about the nature of truth and ethics. Singer claims the taboos are falling one by one[16] (late abortion, infanticide in the first month of life, non-voluntary euthanasia and bestiality are four such categories, which he clearly advocates). However, there are some taboos he seems reluctant to discuss. Given his grounds for justifying sexual activities between consenting adults, how can he raise adequate objections to promiscuity or, indeed, prostitution? And what about incest, if there are no harmful consequences and both parties desire it? As there is no internationally agreed age at which children become adults, he is also left without strong grounds for condemning paedophilia. Why is he so quiet about that explosive subject? Is it not another major, modern, ethical issue? What has he got to say about it? Chuck Colson has written:

> Every rationale that Singer employs to justify (sexual) activities with animals can be applied to relations with children. Actually, the case is stronger since the "physical similarities" Singer identifies are greater in the case of children. (*A Beast of a Theory*, www.boundless.org)

5. Is it Liveable?

Gordon Preece maintains that preference utilitarianism is actually unliveable: Singer's demanding universal utilitarianism is much more opposed to individual pleasure and almost infinitely guilt-inducing compared to Christianity.[17] The problems of the entire world are set before us. And it is not just the greatest happiness for the greatest number of humans which must direct our moral choices, but of all sentient mammals. The task is overwhelming.

Of course, the demands of world poverty distress us all. Historically, however, it has never been like this. In apostolic times, for instance, a church community might learn from a traveller about a distant fellowship experiencing hard times, and collect some money to help them. In general, they remained entirely ignorant of the human condition worldwide. For the most part, people lived in small, self-contained communities within which they learned to carry one another's burdens (*Galations* 6:2). In such communities, the New Testament asserts our primary responsibility for our immediate family (1 *Timothy* 5:8), but then to care for widows and orphans (*James* 1:27), to show hospitality to strangers (*Hebrews* 13:2) and, as opportunity arises, to do good to everyone (*Galations* 6:9–10). But in all this, the family is central. As the fundamental building block of society, it is without rival. Certainly states should provide welfare, but who would prefer institutionalized care? Any philosophy or political policy which damages or undermines the integrity of the family unit, as Singer does in dismissing the importance of sexual ethics, undermines the central structure of care in the community throughout the world. (I think immediately of my patients: a man struck blind in his 30s from Multiple Sclerosis, cared for by his wife and 10 yr old daughter; a single mother helped by her grand-parents to care for her teenage daughter with Cystic Fibrosis; the mutual care a 90 year old couple give to each other, supported by their children; an awkward old man living alone in a caravan, scooped up and taken home by his caring nephew.) Singer's quest for a renewal of our social and political life, disconnected from traditional sexual ethics, is a pipe-dream (19).

Today, however, the tragedies of the world find their way onto the screens in our living rooms. We are not absolved responsibility for how we respond (1 *John* 3:17-18), but the New Testament is realistic saying that we should 'not grow weary of doing good . . . as we have opportunity' (*Galations* 6:9–10). We are not to lay up treasures on earth but in heaven (*Matthew* 6:20), and hard choices face each of us. For all that Christians say in criticizing our consumerist society, we still drive expensive cars, make our homes very comfortable and fly around the world for pleasure with seemingly little concern. So we should take note of Singer's serious challenge for Christians to behave Christianly.[18]

Yet utilitarianism gives us no respite. If we were to take Singer at face value, our lives would be minimalist. We could hardly waste money buying books of any sort; education would be basic and presumably prevent the sort of expensive researches which might lead to significant benefits for the world's poor. We could forget about the arts and entertainment—luxuries no one should afford. In order to remain sane with such pressing demands, Singer apparently gives away 20% of his income. This is impressive, and certainly puts many Christians to shame.[19] But given the needs of the world, the figure is quite arbitrary. If you have a large income, far more than enough to supply your basic needs, why not make it 50%? However, on consequentialist thinking, any such self-inflicted poverty/misery is endured to bring the greatest amount of happiness to the greatest number. Is it defeating the primary objective of happiness to advocate miserly restraint? So we return to some very basic questions. Perhaps we should not give away more than we are happy to give, so that we don't add to the pot of suffering. We are told, 'God loves a cheerful giver' (2 Corinthians 9:7).

At the end of the day, we can understand the idea of acting morally towards the people we meet. It is quite possible, if more difficult, to act morally to those we do not know. Acting morally to everyone in the world is quite beyond us, but acting morally and equally to every sentient mammal robs morality of any real meaning. The best we can do is respond as and when we have the opportunity. Christians have grounds for believing that God is ultimately responsible for his world, but has put us in caring and supportive family units so that we might be agents of his mercy and compassion.

THE POINT OF VIEW OF THE UNIVERSE

Jesus took as the central plank of his ethical teaching, the Old Testament commandment, 'You should love your neighbour as yourself' (*Lev.* 19:18, *Luke* 10:25–28). Not surprisingly, he was then asked the crucial question, 'Who is my neighbour?' In answering it, Jesus told one of the world's greatest stories: 'A certain man went down from Jerusalem to Jericho . . .' (*Luke* 10:30–35). The despised foreigner from Samaria is cast as the rescuer, going out of his way to help the injured man at significant personal inconvenience, risk and cost—he is the true neighbour. Singer sees the commandment, with Christ's explanation as to who our neighbour is, as a universal ethic. It is also expressed as Christ's 'golden rule' that you should, 'Do to others what you would have them do to you' (*Matthew* 7:12). Singer claims it lifts us from our subjective, personal point of view to a wider, objective perspective, encouraging equal consideration of interests, ultimately even what he calls 'the point of view of the universe' (272). In supporting this idea, he appeals to 'all the major ethical traditions', naming Rabbinic Judaism, Hinduism and the teaching of Confucius, whom he claims 'appear to have reached the same position independently of each other.' He does not mention the Koran, which has no similar statement, nor any other religion.

What he fails to notice is that Christ alone puts the golden rule in the positive form. The other three all say in effect that you should *not* do to others what you would *not* want them to do to you.[20] The Rabbinic version says, "Do not do to your neighbour what is hateful to you; this is the whole law, all the rest is commentary", which seems a far cry from the tone and intention of the Old Testament commandment. Confucius justified his saying with self-interest: "What you do not wish upon yourself, extend not to others. Then there will be no resentment against you, either in the family or in the state." This, it seems, is the wisdom of the world. It is a recipe for detachment. It concerns what you shouldn't do, not what you should do. It presumably, in Christ's story of the Good Samaritan, enabled the priest and the Levite to pass by on the other side. What Christ taught was quite unique. We cannot pass by. We are under obligation to treat others as we would wish to be treated.

In the modern world of instant communications about the most awful disasters, Christ's golden rule may seem overwhelming. However, acknowledging our failings before a merciful God, finding his forgiveness, realising that he understands our limitations, opening ourselves up to his good purposes, realizing, as Jesus taught, that 'each day has enough trouble of its own' (*Luke* 10:30–35), and also that this is God's world and not ours, the Christian is not overwhelmed—either by guilt or the size of the task. We are called to do good according to the opportunity we have, knowing that 'to him whom much is given, much is required' (*Luke* 12:48). So Christ's way is quite possible, but Singer's is crushing.

CONCLUSION

In dismissing Christianity, Singer recognises that he has been unable to find a higher ethic than Christ's, but is less than persuaded that he has found a compelling alternative as a basis for such ethical thinking. He writes:

Ethical truths are not written into the fabric of the universe. . . . If there were no beings with desires or preferences of any kind, nothing would be of value and ethics would lack all content. (275)

However, there are not only the subjective values of each individual. He writes:

The possibility of being led, by reasoning,[21] to the point of view of the universe [i.e. , Christ's golden rule] provides as much 'objectivity' as there can be . . . it is as close to an objective basis for ethics as there is to find. (275)

Again he concedes:

It would be nice to be able to reach a stronger conclusion than this about the basis for ethics. (277)

Unfortunately, he does not explore the objective, rational evidence that an ultimate moral being exists, who has uniquely revealed his own character as the basis for our ethics. The existence of God, for instance, can be argued on the basis of the very existence of moral values. As philosopher William Lane Craig expresses it:[22]

- If God does not exist, objective moral values do not exist.
- However, evil exists.
- Therefore objective moral values exist—namely, some things are evil.
- Therefore God exists.

By creating humans in his image, God not only gives us an inherent foundation for our moral values, he also equips us with the intelligence we need to make moral and rational choices. Had Singer acknowledged the uniqueness of Christ's golden rule, seeing it as 'the point of view of the universe' just might have been a clue to the unique authority of Christ the Teacher! Without such an understanding, Singer is left floundering when he writes about the meaning and significance of human life:

The possibility of taking the point of view of the universe overcomes the problem of finding meaning in our lives (274).

He concludes:

Most important of all, you will know that you have not lived and died for nothing, because you will have become part of the great tradition of those who have responded to the amount of pain and suffering in the universe by trying to make the world a better place. (280)

As the violins fade, we might well ask, 'Is that enough to live by?'

REVIEW AND DISCUSSION QUESTION

1. In what specific ways does the Christian worldview (as outlined by May) conflict with Singer's—either in general, or with respect to specific moral issues?

1. Peter Singer, *Ethics* (Oxford; New York: Oxford University Press, 1994) p. 5.

2. Peter Singer, *Rethinking Life and Death* (Melbourne, Australia: Text Publishing, 1994), pp. 190–98.

3. Peter Singer, *Animal Liberation*, 2nd ed. (London: J. Cape, 1990), p. 243.

4. He allows that the Inuit, for example, may be able to justify eating animals, as they have no other option. Singer, *Practical Ethics* (New York; Cambridge: Cambridge University Press, 1993), p. 59ff.

5. Singer, *Practical Ethics*, p. 59ff.

6. Peter Singer, "Heavy Petting," *Nerve.com*, 2001 (www.utilitarian.net/singer/by/2001----.htm, accessed on August 12, 2014).

7. Peter Singer, "Christians, Riches and Camels," *Free Inquiry* 22 (Summer, 2002).

8. For instance, there are laws for the well-being of animals (e.g., *Deut.* 25:4). The wisdom literature teaches that 'A righteous man cares for the needs of his animal' (*Prov.* 12:10). Singer also fails to notice God's compassion expressed in the story of Jonah: 'Nineveh has more than 120,000 people living in spiritual darkness, not to mention all the animals. Shouldn't I feel sorry for such a great city?' (*Jon.* 4:11).

9. Graham Cole, "Singer on Christianity: Characterized or Caricatured?", in Gordon Preece (ed.), *Rethinking Peter Singer* (Downers Grove, IL: InterVarsity, 2002), p. 102.

10. See, for example, *Romans* 8:19–25; *Colossians* 1:15–23.

11. For example, David John Atkinson, David Field, Arthur F. Holmes, and Oliver O'Donovan, *New Dictionary of Christian Ethics and Pastoral Theology* (Downers Grove, IL: InterVarsity, 1995), under *Consequentialism*.

12. J. P. Moreland and William Lane Craig, *Philosophical Foundations for a Christian Worldview* (Downers Grove, IL: InterVarsity, 2003), p. 438.

13. E. Crooks and S. Briscoe, "How to be Happy," *Financial Times*, December 27, 2003, as reported by Dean Giustini, *British Medical Journal*, December 24, 2005.

14. Apparently, when Singer's mother was suffering from advanced Alzheimer's disease, he paid for her nursing care himself but did not advise euthanasia. He defended this by saying that his sister's preferences had been an important factor. See Stuart Jeffries, "Moral Maze," *The Observer*, July 23, 2005 (http://books.guardian.co.uk/review/story/0,12084,1533705,00.html, accessed on August 12, 2014).

15. Gordon Preece, *Rethinking Peter Singer*, p. 26.

16. Singer, *Heavy Petting*.

17. Preece, *Rethinking Peter Singer*, p. 25.

18. Peter Singer, *Christians, Riches and Camels*.

19. Recent evidence has shown that Christians are not as mean as Singer implies. A survey of 1,200 evangelical Christians shows that they give away nine times as much as the average householder in the UK, donating, on average, 12% of their net income annually (reported by Ruth Gledhill, *The Times*, January 4, 2006).

20. Hindu, *Mahabharata XXIII:5571*, Rabbi Hillel, *Talmud Shabbat 3*, Confucius *Analects 12:2*.

21. Singer wrongly asserts that others got there by reasoning. Jesus said he taught what the Father gave him to say (John 12;49), and Christians, too, understand it by revelation through the Spirit-inspired gospel accounts of Jesus's life and teaching. No one, it seems, got there by reason alone.

22. William Lane Craig, *God?* (Oxford; New York: Oxford University Press, 2004), p. 126.

A

absent qualia thought experiment on the possibility that a creature might be behaviorably indistinguishable from you yet lacking all qualia (e.g., "zombie").

abusive *ad hominem* unsound argument which attempts to prove a conclusion false by attacking its advocate personally.

accent fallacy arising from ambiguity or confusion in emphasis.

aesthetic stage in Kierkegaard, that way of life in which we are immersed in sensuous experience, in pleasure and egotism, in satisfying our own desires and preferences, with minimal reflection.

affirming the consequent an invalid form of argument, where the premises are *if P, then Q,* and *Q,* and the conclusion is *P.*

almond argument for the distinction between primary/secondary qualities, based on the premise that an almond changes color when pounded.

amor fati "love of fate" (Latin).

amphiboly fallacies that result from faulty or careless sentence structure.

analogy argument for the distinction between primary/secondary qualities, based on the analogy between perceiving pain and perceiving warmth, color, etc.

analytic proposition one whose truth-value is determined by the meanings of the words alone, on the basis of whether the predicate is contained in its subject.

angst existentialist anxiety, an English word borrowed from the original Danish, Dutch, and German.

antecedent the first statement in a conditional statement (i.e., *P,* in *if P, then Q*).

anthropomorphism the assignment of human characteristics to nonhuman beings.

apeiron the "boundless" (Greek); according to Anaximander, the fundamental element, a kind of neutral, indeterminate stuff, unlimited in amount.

apologia the Greek term for a defendant's speech at a trial.

a posteriori "after" experience (Latin).

a priori "before" experience (Latin).

argument reasoning in which one or more statements (the premises) are offered as logical support for some other statement (the conclusion).

artificial intelligence the research program that uses computers to theorize about the mind and/or attempts to program them to have minds.

atheism the doctrine that God does not exist.

atomism the theory, propounded by Leucippus and developed by Democritus, that the world is ultimately made of indivisible, indestructible "atoms" (literally, "uncuttables").

B

begging the question the fallacy of simply repeating a conclusion rather than providing proof for it. Alternatively, the fallacy of simply assuming the very claim that needs to be proved.

best possible world theodicy a greater goods theodicy, in which the existence of evils are justified as their being necessary for producing the best possible world overall.

bifurcation the fallacy of presuming that a certain distinction is exhaustive when other alternatives are possible. Also known as the "either/or fallacy" or "black or white" fallacy.

C

categorical imperative in Kant, a strictly unconditional (hence moral) imperative that commands us to act purely from duty, independent of our interests or ends.

categorical proposition a simple, declarative sentence such as *The table is brown*.

categories (or pure concepts) in Kant, the concepts by means of which the faculty of understanding processes the sensory output of the faculty of sensibility.

Chinese room thought experiment in Searle, invoking a room that functionally mirrors a Chinese conversation without truly understanding Chinese.

circumstantial *ad hominem* unsound argument which attempts to prove a conclusion false by suggesting that the conclusion merely serves the advocate's own interests.

clear and distinct criterion Descartes's criterion of truth: if it would be contradictory to deny the truth of a certain proposition, then the proposition was certainly true.

cogito ergo sum "I think therefore I am" (in Latin).

coherentism a theory of knowledge on which a belief may be justified insofar as it coheres with a system of beliefs. No belief need be foundational.

compatibilism the doctrine that our acting freely is compatible with our actions being causally predetermined.

complex ideas ideas that have (other) ideas as parts or components.

conceivability argument against necessary connection Hume's argument based on the premise that you may always conceive of any event occurring without any other, without contradiction.

conclusion in an argument, the statement being supported by the premises.

conditional statement a statement of the form *if P, then Q*.

consequent the second statement in a conditional statement (i.e., Q, in *if P, then Q*).

contingent truth a statement is a contingent truth if and only if it is true, but it is logically possible that it be or become false. (Compare *necessary truth*.)

continuous creation the doctrine that God continuously creates the world.

continuous creation argument for occasionalism Malebranche's argument, showing how continuous creation entails occasionalism.

cosmological arguments claim that various features of the cosmos (such as motion, causation, the contingency of events, etc.) demonstrate God's existence.

creation *ex nihilo* creation out of nothing.

D

Darwin's doubt the view that evolution gives us reason to doubt that our cognitive faculties produce, for the most part, true beliefs.

deducibility argument against necessary connection Hume's argument based on the premise that you can never deduce a second event occurring based only on the idea or concept of a first event.

deductive argument (or reasoning) an argument (or reasoning) in which the conclusion is presented as following from the premises with certainty or necessity.

deism doctrine that God created the cosmos at the beginning but then lets it operate on its own.

denying the antecedent an invalid form of argument, where the premises are *if P, then Q*, and *Not-P*, and the conclusion is *Not-Q*.

design arguments alternative name for teleological arguments.

determinism the doctrine that everything that occurs in the world is necessarily caused to occur by earlier events, and thus pre-determined.

disjunctive syllogism a valid argument form where the premises are *either P or Q (or both)* and *Not-P*, and the conclusion is *Q*.

dream argument for RTM Descartes's argument based on the indistinguishability between dreaming and waking experience.

dualism the doctrine that mind and matter are two fundamentally different kinds of things or substances, and that both exist.

E

early modern philosophy is constituted by the work in roughly the seventeenth and eighteenth centuries, from Descartes through Kant.

elements the fundamental building blocks of the world; in ancient traditions, these would be earth, air, fire, and water.

emotivism the metaethical doctrine that ethical statements state or assert no facts, but merely express feelings.

empirical argument for dualism Descartes's argument that language and reasoning could not be satisfactorily explained in purely physical terms.

empiricism from the Greek *empeiria*, for experience; that school of early modern philosophy that emphasizes the role of sensory experience in epistemology.

epiphenomenal lacking causal powers.

epistemologically basic belief one we are justified in holding without inferring it from other justified beliefs.

epistemology theory or study of knowledge (from the Greek), or the area of philosophy concerned with the nature and sources of knowledge.

equivocation fallacy occurring when a word shifts its meaning during the course of an argument.

esse est percipi "to be is to be perceived" (Latin).

eternal timeless

eternal recurrence in Nietzsche, the idea that everything that occurs will reoccur, in the same sequence, over and over again.

ethical hedonism the doctrine that pleasure and happiness are the morally appropriate goal of our actions.

ethical stage in Kierkegaard, that way of life in which we embrace the social and moral norms of society, recognizing that we are bound by the same rules as everyone else and ought not pursue merely our own pleasure.

ethical theory addresses the underlying theoretical reasons for distinguishing proper and improper lines of conduct.

ethics the area of philosophy concerned with how we should order our lives, what goals we should seek, which actions are good or right and which are bad or wrong.

euthanasia "easy death" (from Greek), refers generally to the practice of intentionally ending a life in order to ease suffering and pain.

ex nihilo Latin, for "out of nothing."

existentialism a loose family of movements that emphasize the existence of the individual as a free and responsible agent determining her own development through acts of the will, all in the face of the potential meaninglessness of life.

extension the property of taking up space.

F

faculty of sensibility in Kant, that feature of the mind which generates sensory perceptions.

faculty of understanding, in Kant, that feature of the mind which generates our overall perceptual experience by processing the sensory output of the faculty of sensibility, using categories.

fallacies arguments that may appear to be sound but for various reasons are not.

fallacies of ambiguity unsound arguments that result from ambiguity in the meanings of words. These include amphiboly, accent, and equivocation.

fallacies of presumption unsound arguments which deceive due to their similarity to valid argument forms. These include sweeping generalization, hasty generalization, bifurcation, begging the question, false analogy, and false cause.

fallacies of relevance unsound arguments which deceive due to the emotional appeal of the language. These include genetic fallacy, abusive *ad hominem*, circumstantial *ad hominem*, *tu quoque*, and poisoning the well.

false (or imperfect) analogy a fallacy of presumption in which two cases are made to appear more similar than they really are.

false cause a fallacy of presumption in which two events are made to appear causally connected in a way they are not.

feminist epistemology a movement that examines gender issues in epistemology, and questions the idea that knowledge and reason work the same way in all people.

fine-tuning argument for theism a teleological argument based on the premise that the laws of physics themselves contain many features that seem precisely fine-tuned so as to permit the existence of our specific form of life, with our consciousness, rationality, morality.

First Mover in Aquinas, a being that can initiate motion on its own without itself being moved by a preceding being.

foreknowledge knowledge of the future.

Forms according to Plato, there exist universals which are non-physical, eternal, uncreated, unchanging, and unperceivable.

foundationalism a theory of knowledge according to which some beliefs are certain or self-evident and subsequently serve as foundations on which to justify other beliefs.

functionalism the theory that what defines a mental state is its causal or functional role, namely the causal relations it bears to bodily input, other types of mental states, and behavioral outputs.

G

genetic fallacy unsound argument that attempts to prove a conclusion false by condemning its source.

golden mean Aristotle's conception of moral virtue as a mean between the vice of excess and the vice of deficiency.

good will according to Kant, the only thing that is good without qualification. A good will is one that aims to do its duty.

greater goods theodicy the idea that what justifies God in producing or permitting evils is that His doing so is a necessary means for bringing about some even greater good.

H

hasty generalization the often fallacious use of some isolated or exceptional case as a basis for a general conclusion.

hedonic calculus the method or process of calculating how much pleasure or happiness a particular action might produce.

humanism a philosophical attitude that stresses the fundamental value of human beings.

hypothetical imperative in Kant, an obligation you have if (and only if) you have certain goals or ends.

hypothetical judgments propositions of the form *if P, then Q.*

hypothetical syllogism a valid deductive argument form, where the premises are *if P, then Q* and *if Q, then R*, and the conclusion is *if P, then R.*

I

idea ideas are mental objects, existing only in the mind, serving according to the representational theory of mind (RTM), for example, as representations of physical objects.

idealism the doctrine that all that exists is mental in nature (such as minds and their ideas).

ideas of reflection come to us from observing the operations of our own mind (ideas of thinking, doubting, remembering, willing, etc.).

ideas of sensation come to us when some external body stimulates our sense organs (ideas of yellow, cold, bitter, hard, etc.).

identity theory doctrine that mental states are not non-physical but to be identified with physical brain states.

immutable God's attribute of being incapable of changing.

impassible God's attribute of being incapable of feeling pain or emotion.

impeccable God's attribute of being incapable of sin.

inconceivability argument for idealism Berkeley's argument that the notion of a mind-independent body involves a contradiction, and thus is logically impossible.

incorporeal God's attribute of being non-physical.

incorrigibility the property of the mind (according to Descartes) such that it can never make a mistake concerning what is going on inside it.

inductive argument (or reasoning) an argument (or reasoning) in which the conclusion is presented as following from the premises with merely a high degree of probability.

infinite regress a circumstance where for something to be the case, something else must be the case; and for that other thing to be the case, a third thing must be the case; and so on, without limit. An infinite regress of motion would occur if it were necessary that for any body to be moving, some other moving body must put it in motion.

innate an idea or belief or knowledge is innate if a person is born with it.

intellectual virtues according to Aristotle, those qualities tied to our intelligence that deal with our ability to discover and recognize truths.

intelligent design an umbrella term for movements that see the world as requiring an intelligent cause, and not merely as the product of undirected evolution.

interactionism the doctrine that there does exist a causal relation in the relevant domain.

intuition a cognitive faculty capable of producing intellectual understanding (or "visions") of such clarity that one has no doubt regarding the truth of what is apprehended.

invalid argument an argument where the conclusion does not logically follow from the premises; where the premises may all be true and yet the conclusion false.

inverted qualia thought experiment based on the possibility that one person's qualia may be inverted relative to another (for example, with respect to colors).

irreducible complexity something is irreducibly complex if it requires many components to be in place before it provides any evolutionary advantage, and so it cannot evolve by the small random steps that evolutionary theory proposes.

K

knowable *a posteriori* a proposition is knowable *a posteriori* if its truth-value can be determined only on the basis of experience.

knowable *a priori* a proposition is knowable *a priori* if its truth-value can be determined in some sense apart from or prior to experience.

know-how argument for occasionalism Malebranche's argument, based on the premise that we don't know how we move our bodies.

knowledge argument against physicalism from Jackson, the argument based on the thought experiment of Mary the neuroscientist brought up in a black-and-white environment.

L

Law of Non-Contradiction it is never the case that a statement and its negation are both simultaneously true. More informally, you may never legitimately contradict yourself.

lifeboat ethics Garrett Hardin's approach that looks at the problems of global hunger via the metaphor of a lifeboat limited in resources.

logical behaviorism see *philosophical behaviorism*.

logical empiricism twentieth-century movement aiming to develop an empiricist analysis of modern science. Also known as logical positivism.

logical positivism twentieth-century movement aiming to develop an empiricist analysis of modern science. Also known as logical empiricism.

logically possible to say something is logically possible is to say that it does not involve any contradictions.

M

major premise in one standard argument form, the statement of a general principle.

materialism Berkeley's name for dualism.

matters of fact in Hume, these are judgments or propositions concerning more than merely how our ideas are related to each other, but how things are in the world.

maxim Kant's term for the rule one follows in acting.

mechanical philosophy the doctrine that the defining property of matter is extension and that, therefore, the only real properties that matter has are properties such as size, shape, and motion.

metaethical subjectivism the view that when we call an action, A, *good* or *right*, what we mean is something like "I approve of A" (while to call it *wrong* means "I disapprove").

metaethics addresses the very meanings of ethical concepts such as good and evil, right and wrong.

metaphysical arguments for dualism Descartes's arguments based on the different properties possessed by minds and bodies, such as thought versus extension.

metaphysics the area of philosophy concerned with the fundamental nature of the world, with what sorts of things exist and what their nature is.

Milesian school the earliest pre-Socratic philosophers: Thales, Anaximander, and Anaximenes, centered in Miletus. Seeking a unitary source of being, they attempted to identify the fundamental stuff out of which all else was made.

mind-body problem the problem of how mind and matter can causally interact, given their distinct natures according to Descartes's dualism.

minor premise in one standard argument form, the statement of an individual case that is to fall under the major premise.

modus ponens a valid deductive argument form, where the two premises are *if P, then Q,* and *P,* and the conclusion is *Q.*

modus tollens a valid deductive argument form, where the two premises are *if P, then Q,* and *Not-Q,* and the conclusion is *Not-P.*

monad derived from the Greek for "unit," monads are the basic substances in Leibniz's system. He conceives them as non-physical minds, endlessly diverse, centers of energy, each with the capacity of reflecting the universe as a whole.

monism the doctrine that the world consists of only one kind of substance or thing.

monotheism the doctrine that one single God exists.

moral arguments for theism claim that the existence of objective morality is possible only if God exists.

moral evils the terrible things that human beings inflict upon each other, such as stealing, assaulting, murdering.

moral virtues according to Aristotle, those qualities that deal with our ability to check our appetites and passions so that we will behave properly.

multiple-realization objection to identity theory since mental states are multiply realizable in very different physical entities, they cannot be identified with any one of them.

N

nativism the doctrine that at least some of our ideas or beliefs or knowledge is or are innate.

natural evils the terrible things that nature inflicts without the direct involvement of human beings, such as earthquakes, floods, epidemics.

natural philosopher a philosopher who seeks to understand how nature works, typically in only natural (rather than supernatural) terms; today we would say *scientist*.

natural philosophy in the early modern period, the philosophy of nature; or what we today would call *science*.

natural theology the study of nature as a guide to the existence and attributes of God.

naturalism the approach that attempts to explain events in the world not in terms of anything supernatural but in terms of laws of nature.

necessary condition one that must be met by something if it is to fall into the category being defined.

necessary connection a necessary connection obtains between two events (or they are necessarily connected) if it's the case that, given that the first event occurs, it's impossible for the second event not to occur.

necessary connection argument for occasionalism Malebranche's argument based on the claim that no two ordinary events are ever necessarily connected.

necessary truth a statement is necessarily true if and only if it is true, and there is no logical possibility of its being or becoming false. (Compare *contingent truth*.)

necessitarianism the doctrine that God both exists and has His nature necessarily.

nihilism the rejection of all meaning, value, authority.

"no idea" argument against necessary connection Hume's argument based on the premise that nothing in experience itself generates our idea of necessary connection, in which case we don't really have such an idea.

normative concerning norms or ideals, for example how things should or ought to be (as opposed to how in fact things are).

noumena in Kant, things as they are in themselves.

nous brain or mind (Greek).

O

objective knowledge knowledge of how the world is in some sense independent of your individual perspective on it.

occasionalism the doctrine that there does not exist a causal relation in the relevant domain, but rather the first event is merely the occasion upon which God directly causes the second event.

omnipotent God's attribute of being all-powerful.

omnipresent God's attribute of being everywhere.

omniscient God's attribute of being all-knowing.

ontological arguments claim that the very concept or definition of God entails God's existence.

ought implies can a shorthand expression for the view that one cannot say that someone "ought" to do a particular action unless that action is actually possible for him or her.

pantheism the doctrine that everything in some sense is or is part of God.

paradox a situation where we have good reason to believe two opposing or contradictory things.

particulars in contrast to universals, these are individual, "non-repeatable" things: this red thing, that red thing.

Pascal's wager the name given to Pascal's prudential argument for theism.

peripatetic philosophy a general name for Aristotle's system of philosophy, due to his habit of teaching while strolling around.

personal immortality the doctrine that the mind or soul can survive the death of the body.

phenomena in Kant, things as they appear to us.

philosophical (or logical) behaviorism an account of the semantics (or meanings) of mental language, claiming that words apparently referring to internal mental states in fact indirectly refer only to patterns of behavior.

philosophical theology philosophical attempts to clarify the nature, and investigate the existence, of God.

philosophy love of wisdom (from the Greek), or the rational attempt to gain an overall understanding of ourselves and of the world we live in.

physicalism the doctrine that all that exists is physical matter.

plenum "fullness," from Latin. According to the mechanical philosophy, the cosmos is a plenum, entirely full, with no voids, vacuums, or empty spots.

poisoning the well unsound argument in which an attempt is made to place the opponent in a weakened position from which he or she is unable to reply.

polytheism the doctrine that many gods exist.

practical (or applied) ethics addresses the practical problem of what sorts of actions (or life) we should pursue.

pre-established harmony Leibniz's doctrine that there is no genuine causation between substances. Rather, each substance runs through its sequence of internal states in perfectly synchronized harmony with all other substances.

pre-Socratics the ancient Greek thinkers who lived and taught before the time of Socrates.

premise in an argument, a statement offered in support of the conclusion.

primary quality a primary quality (according to Locke) is "utterly inseparable" from a body, "really exists" in a body, and our idea of it resembles what's in the body. These include size, shape, and motion.

principle of equality the doctrine that we should give equal consideration to the diverse interests of different individuals and/or species.

principle of universality Kant's fundamental moral principle that one should act only in a manner that he or she could will that all others act.

principle of utility Bentham's moral principle that only the morally correct action is that which promotes the greatest pleasure or happiness for the greatest number of people.

problem of evil name for the general view that the existence of evil in the world challenges the existence of God.

prudential arguments claim not directly that God exists, but that it is rational (in the sense of prudent) to believe in God's existence.

psyche soul or mind (Greek).

psychological hedonism the doctrine that what in fact motivates our behavior is our desire for pleasure and happiness.

pure concepts (or categories) in Kant, the concepts by means of which the faculty of understanding processes the sensory output of the faculty of sensibility.

Q

qualia the subjective character of mental states, the conscious character, what they "feel" like.

quality of life ethic in contrast to the sanctity of life ethic, Singer's view that what matters isn't merely preserving life, period, but preserving the quality of life.

R

radical skeptic one who challenges the possibility of obtaining *any* knowledge.

rationalism comes from the Latin *ratio*, for reason; that school of early modern philosophy that emphasizes the role of reason in epistemology.

reformed epistemology a movement within philosophy of religion, holding that it can be rational to believe in God even without specific evidence because belief in God is an epistemologically basic belief.

relations of ideas in Hume, these are judgments or propositions concerning only the ways our ideas are related to each other, and not about the world.

relativity of perception argument a kind of argument proving that a certain perceived quality really exists in the mind, not in the physical world; based on the phenomenon that perceptions can vary while the physical object does not. These are often used in support of the distinction between primary and secondary qualities.

religious stage in Kierkegaard, that way of life in which we suspend the ethical, and make a leap of faith, embracing the absurd in embracing God.

representational theory of mind (RTM) the doctrine that the immediate object of sensation or intellect, that is, what the mind is aware of when it is perceiving or thinking, is an *idea*.

right (n.) a right is something that cannot be violated no matter what the consequences of violating it would be.

S

sanctity of life the doctrine that human life possesses an intrinsic dignity (or sanctity, i.e., holiness, sacredness) that distinguishes it from animal life.

science argument for the distinction between primary/secondary qualities, based on the premise that the successful mechanical philosophy distinguishes those qualities.

scientific antirealism the doctrine that science is not in the business of "describing reality correctly," but serves some other function (such as helping us make use of the world).

scientific behaviorism the doctrine that psychologists should only study observable behaviors and its causes.

secondary quality a secondary quality (according to Locke) is one that is separable from a body, does not really exist in the body, and our idea of it does not resemble what's in the body. These include color, small, flavor, and sound.

self-evident a self-evident belief is one that is justified in itself, that one immediately grasps as true upon understanding it.

the shallow pond Singer's thought experiment probing the moral implications of the decision whether to save a child drowning in a shallow pond.

simple the attribute of not being composed of any parts.

simple ideas ideas that do not have any ideas as parts or components.

simple unity the property of the mind (according to Descartes) such that it cannot be divided into distinct parts or components.

skeptic one who challenges the possibility of obtaining certain kinds of knowledge.

slippery slope a slippery slope argument is roughly of the form, "If you accept proposition P, then you'll have to accept Q; and if you accept Q, then you'll have to accept R . . . but R is so problematic or offensive or simply false that you better not accept P."

Sophists meaning "experts" or "wise ones" (from the Greek), a group of ancient Greek teachers who, in exchange for fees, offered instruction in rhetoric, discourse, and politics. The name came to connote those who reason fallaciously, with the intent to deceive.

soul-making theodicy a greater goods theodicy, in which the existence of evils are justified as part of a process of refining or perfecting our character or souls.

sound argument a valid argument with all true premises.

speciesism a prejudice or bias in favor of the interests of members of one's own species over the interests of members of other species.

substance something capable of existing independently from other things.

substratum "the level beneath" (Latin). Distinct from the properties of a substance, the substratum of the substance is the thing which *has* those properties and binds them together.

sufficient condition one such that, if a thing has them, that suffices for it to fall into the category in question.

sui generis "of its own kind" (Latin), meaning one of a kind, in a class of its own, unique.

supererogatory good to do but not *obligatory*, and therefore not wrong *not* to do.

supernaturalism the approach that is comfortable invoking supernatural events (such as intervention of God or gods) in explaining events in the world.

sweeping generalization the often fallacious assumption that what is true under certain conditions is true under all conditions.

syllogism an argument composed of categorical propositions.

synthetic proposition one whose truth-value is determined by more than the meanings of the words alone, on the basis of whether the predicate accurately adds something to the subject.

T

tabula rasa "blank tablet" (from Latin), Locke's phrase to describe the mind at birth.

teleological (or design) arguments claim that the order or beauty or apparent "design" in the cosmos require the existence of an orderer or designer, that is, God.

theism the doctrine that God exists.

theodicy "God" and "justice" (from the Greek), used generally for any attempt to defend the goodness of God given all the evils in the world.

theological argument for dualism Descartes's argument based on the notion of personal immortality.

theory-laden observation the idea that observations or experiments are not neutral between competing theories, but already presume the truth of a great amount of theory.

theory of knowledge a theory of knowledge attempts to describe, roughly, what is required for us to be rationally justified in accepting a proposition as true.

transcendental idealism Kant's doctrine that the objects known must conform to the mind, to the mind's "ideals," but can do so in a way that transcends subjective experience, and thus permits objective knowledge.

transparency the property of the mind (according to Descartes) such that it is fully aware of everything actively occurring in it.

truth a true statement is one which accords with the facts.

truth argument for pre-established harmony Leibniz's argument based on the nature of truth, that the predicate of a true statement is contained in the subject.

truth-value ordinary declarative propositions are typically taken to have two possible values with respect to truth: "true" or "false."

tu quoque "you, also" (in Latin), roughly, "look who's talking": an unsound argument in which the person advocating a position is charged with acting in a manner that contradicts the position taken.

two hands in a bucket thought experiment from Locke, demonstrating relativity of perception, in which you put one hand in an oven and the other in a freezer, then immerse them in a bucket of water.

tyranny of the majority the concern that, in a democracy, the majority may be empowered to mistreat the minority.

U

uniformity of nature the doctrine that the future will be like the past.

universal something is a universal insofar as it is or can be "repeatable," that is, occur in many different particular things. (For example, Redness, as there can be many distinct red things.)

utilitarianism the ethical theory, propounded by Bentham and Mill, that the morally correct action is that which promotes the greatest pleasure or happiness of the greatest number of people. Later versions claim that the correct action is that which maximizes the "satisfaction of preferences," that is, satisfies the preferences of the greatest number of people.

V

valid argument an argument where the conclusion logically follows from the premises; where, if all the premises are (or were) true, the conclusion must (or would have to) be true.

CHAPTER 1

EXCERPT from Andrew Pessin, *The 60-Second Philosopher* (Oxford, UK: Oneworld Publications, 2009), ch. 1. Reprinted with permission.

CHAPTER 2

THALES OF MILETUS (640?–546 B.C.). Greek philosopher and scientist. Antique Greek sculpture. © The Granger Collection, New York.

DEMOCRITUS (c460–c370 B.C.). Greek philosopher. Hellenistic bronze bust. © The Granger Collection, New York.

EXCERPT from F. M. Cornford, *Before and After Socrates* (Cambridge, UK: Cambridge University Press, 1932/1950), 5–27. Reprinted with the permission of Cambridge University Press.

CHAPTER 3

SOCRATES (470?–399 B.C.). Greek philosopher. © The Granger Collection, New York.

PLATO (c427–c347 B.C.). Greek philosopher. Line engraving, French, 1584. © The Granger Collection, New York.

THE DEATH OF SOCRATES (470?–399 B.C.). Greek philosopher. The death of Socrates. Wood engraving, German, 19th century. © The Granger Collection, New York.

EXCERPT from Passages from Euthyphro, Crito, and Phaedo are from transl., Hugh Tredennick, *Plato: The Last Days of Socrates* (Harmondsworth: Penguin, 1954). Reprinted with permission.

DISCUSSION OF PLATO'S FORMS adapted from Andrew Pessin, *Uncommon Sense: The Strangest Ideas from the Smartest Philosophers* (Lanham, MD: Rowman & Littlefield, 2012), ch. 1. Used by permission.

CHAPTER 4

ARISTOTLE (384–322 B.C.). Greek philosopher. Roman marble bust. © The Granger Collection, New York.

CHAPTER 8

RENE DESCARTES (1596–1650). French mathematician and philosopher. Oil on canvas, c.1649, by Frans Hals. © The Granger Collection, New York.

DESCARTES CARTOON p. 220. From *Action Philosophers!* by Fred Van Lente and Ryan Dunlavey (Evil Twin Comics, 2009). Used by permission.

"CARTESIAN THEATER" CARTOON p. 224. By Jolyon Troscianko. Used by permission.

BARUCH SPINOZA (1632–1677). Dutch philosopher. © The Granger Collection, New York.

GOTTFRIED VON LEIBNIZ (1646–1716). Full name: Baron Gottfried Wilhelm von Leibniz. German philosopher and mathematician. Line engraving, French, 19th century. © The Granger Collection, New York.

NICOLAS DE MALEBRANCHE (1638–1715). French philosopher. Steel engraving, French, 19th century. © The Granger Collection, New York.

DISCUSSION of Leibniz's truth argument adapted from Andrew Pessin, *Uncommon Sense: The Strangest Ideas from the Smartest Philosophers* (Lanham, MD: Rowman & Littlefield, 2012), ch. 10. Used by permission.

EXCERPT from Descartes, *Meditations on First Philosophy*, Meditations I, II. Transls., John Cottingham, Robert Stoothoff, and Dugald Murdoch, *The Philosophical Writings of Descartes*, Vol. II (Cambridge, UK: Cambridge University Press, 1984), pp. 12–20. Reprinted with the permission of Cambridge University Press.

EXCERPT from Nicolas Malebranche, *The Search after Truth*, Book 6, Part 2, ch. 3, ed., transl. Thomas Lennon and Paul Olscamp (Cambridge, UK: Cambridge University Press, 1997), 448–50. Reprinted with the permission of Thomas Lennon.

CHAPTER 9

JOHN LOCKE (1632–1704). English philosopher. Oil on canvas after Sir Godfrey Kneller, 1704. © The Granger Collection, New York.

GEORGE BERKELEY (1685–1753). Irish philosopher. Painting by an unknown artist. © The Granger Collection, New York.

DAVID HUME (1711–1776). Scottish historian and philosopher. Line engraving after the painting, 1766, by Allan Ramsay. © The Granger Collection, New York.

KANT AND HIS CIRCLE. Reproduction of a painting, 1893, by E. Doerstling. © The Granger Collection, New York.

DISCUSSION of Locke on primary/secondary qualities adapted from Andrew Pessin, *Uncommon Sense: The Strangest Ideas from the Smartest Philosophers* (Lanham, MD: Rowman & Littlefield, 2012), ch. 8. Used by permission.

DISCUSSION of Hume's critique of causation and induction adapted from Andrew Pessin, *Uncommon Sense: The Strangest Ideas from the Smartest Philosophers* (Lanham, MD: Rowman & Littlefield, 2012), ch. 12. Used by permission.

CHAPTER 10

SØREN KIERKEGAARD (1813–1855). Danish philosopher. Drawing by N. C. Kierkegaard. © The Granger Collection, New York.

CHAPTER 11

Andrew Pessin is professor of philosophy at Connecticut College. He is the author of numerous books including *Uncommon Sense* (2012), which was named a *CHOICE* Outstanding Title for the year. He may be found on the web at www.andrewpessin.com.

S. Morris Engel is professor emeritus at York University. Previously, he taught at the University of Southern California for twenty-five years.

Lightning Source UK Ltd.
Milton Keynes UK
UKHW032154201218
334255UK00012B/302/P